The Skywalker Symphonies

The Oxford Music / Media Series

Daniel Goldmark, Series Editor

Tuning In: American Narrative Television Music
Ron Rodman

Special Sound: The Creation and Legacy of the BBC Radiophonic Workshop
Louis Niebur

Seeing through Music: Gender and Modernism in Classic Hollywood Film Scores
Peter Franklin

An Eye for Music: Popular Music and the Audiovisual Surreal
John Richardson

Playing Along: Digital Games, YouTube, and Virtual Performance
Kiri Miller

Sounding the Gallery: Video and the Rise of Art-Music
Holly Rogers

Composing for the Red Screen: Prokofiev and Soviet Film
Kevin Bartig

Saying It with Songs: Popular Music and the Coming of Sound to Hollywood Cinema
Katherine Spring

We'll Meet Again: Musical Design in the Films of Stanley Kubrick
Kate McQuiston

Occult Aesthetics: Synchronization in Sound Film
K. J. Donnelly

Sound Play: Video Games and the Musical Imagination
William Cheng

Sounding American: Hollywood, Opera, and Jazz
Jennifer Fleeger

Mismatched Women: The Siren's Song through the Machine
Jennifer Fleeger

*Robert Altman's Soundtracks: Film, Music, and Sound from M*A*S*H to A Prairie Home Companion*
Gayle Sherwood Magee

Back to the Fifties: Nostalgia, Hollywood Film, and Popular Music of the Seventies and Eighties
Michael D. Dwyer

The Early Film Music of Dmitry Shostakovich
Joan Titus

Making Music in Selznick's Hollywood
Nathan Platte

Hearing Haneke: The Sound Tracks of a Radical Auteur
Elsie Walker

Unlimited Replays: Video Games and Classical Music
William Gibbons

Hollywood Harmony: Musical Wonder and the Sound of Cinema
Frank Lehman

French Musical Culture and the Coming of Sound Cinema
Hannah Lewis

Theories of the Soundtrack
James Buhler

Through the Looking Glass: John Cage and Avant-Garde Film
Richard H. Brown

Sound Design Is the New Score: Theory, Aesthetics, and Erotics of the Integrated Soundtrack
Danijela Kulezic-Wilson

Rock Star/Movie Star: Power and Performance in Cinematic Rock Stardom
Landon Palmer

The Presence of the Past: Temporal Experience and the New Hollywood Soundtrack
Daniel Bishop

Metafilm Music in Jean-Luc Godard's Cinema
Michael Baumgartner

Acoustic Profiles: A Sound Ecology of the Cinema
Randolph Jordan

Four Ways of Hearing Video Game Music
Michiel Kamp

Defining Cinema: Rouben Mamoulian and Hollywood Film Style, 1929–1957
Michael Slowik

Mobilizing Music in Wartime British Film
Heather Wiebe

Audiovisual Alterity: Representing Ourselves and Others in Music Videos
Michael L. Austin

Dmitry Shostakovich and Music for Stalinist Cinema (1936–1953)
Joan Titus

Korngold in America: Music, Myth, and Hollywood
Ben Winters

The Skywalker Symphonies: John Williams and the Music of Star Wars
Frank Lehman

The Skywalker Symphonies

John Williams and the Music of Star Wars

FRANK LEHMAN

OXFORD
UNIVERSITY PRESS

OXFORD
UNIVERSITY PRESS

Oxford University Press is a department of the University of Oxford.
It furthers the University's objective of excellence in research, scholarship,
and education by publishing worldwide. Oxford is a registered trade mark of
Oxford University Press in the UK and in certain other countries.

Published in the United States of America by Oxford University Press
198 Madison Avenue, New York, NY 10016, United States of America.

CIP data is on file at the Library of Congress

ISBN 9780197797129 (pbk.)
ISBN 9780197798485 (hbk.)

DOI: 10.1093/9780197797150.001.0001

Paperback printed by Marquis Book Printing, Canada
Hardback printed by Lightning Source, Inc., United States of America

The manufacturer's authorized representative in the EU for product safety is
Oxford University Press España S.A. of El Parque Empresarial San Fernando de Henares,
Avenida de Castilla, 2 – 28830 Madrid (www.oup.es/en or product.safety@oup.com).
OUP España S.A. also acts as importer into Spain of products made by the manufacturer.

FSC www.fsc.org MIX Paper | Supporting responsible forestry FSC® C103567

Contents

Acknowledgments

I can't identify a clear starting point for this book—it feels like I've been writing it in one form or another since I was a preteen. Musical realizations I had in sixth grade mingle here with cutting-edge analytical techniques I learned about just last year. This poses a problem for acknowledgments: do I thank everyone who's supported my musical curiosity for thirty-five years? The record store clerk who sold me my first *Star Wars* CD in 1996? My homeroom teacher who signed off on a Williams-centric senior project? My grandfather Karl, who endured many afternoons of me feebly fumbling at the "Rebel Fanfare" on the family piano?

I'll spare the reader my full life history and limit these acknowledgments to those people who supported *The Skywalker Symphonies* from 2022 onward—once the book had a name, a publisher, and a delivery date. Oxford University Press has been a dream partner. I'm deeply grateful to my editors Norm Hirschy and Daniel Goldmark for their unwavering support. I also owe much to the manuscript's anonymous reviewers for commentary that was trenchant, encouraging, and more extensive than a Wookieepedia edit history. My thanks also extend to Egle Zigaite and Theodore Reiner at OUP; Patterson Lamb, who copyedited the manuscript; and Narayanan Srinivasan and the production team at Newgen KnowledgeWorks. As any reader will discover, this is a book born of an encyclopedic impulse. I was therefore lucky to have an indexer as enthusiastic and capable as Erin K. Maher to sift and sort through it all so beautifully.

It is hard to imagine a more supportive place in which to pursue this kind of project than Tufts University. To keep this from becoming a roll call of every single faculty and staff member of the Music Department, I will give special mention to just a few. Rich Jankowsky and Kwasi Ampene were department chairs during the writing of this book and in a very concrete way made the conditions for its completion possible. The department and university Curricula Committees deserve my thanks too, for approving a course proposal on "The Music of John Williams and Star Wars," as does Jeffrey Rawitsch for ensuring it ran successfully in our Distler Performance Hall. I am deeply grateful to the Faculty Research Awards Committee, including

Bonnie Donohue and Ina Baghdiantz-McCabe, for granting me a Senior Semester Leave award to work on this project during the Spring of 2024, and to Dean Heather Nathans for topping that off with another semester, creating a true sabbatical during the 2023–24 academic year. Finally, I'm grateful to my dear friend and colleague Will Cheng for his advocacy in securing that support.

Throughout the writing of *The Skywalker Symphonies*, I had the privilege of exchanging ideas with many brilliant scholars: Emilio Audissino, Claire Arthur, James Buhler, Zachary Cairns, Grace Edgar, Ben Graf, Tim Greiving, Marie-Claire Gould, Erik Heine, Chloé Huvet, Dan Obluda, Matt Lawson, Brooke McCorkle Okazaki, Laura McTavish, Tristan Paré-Morin, Conor Power, Tom Schneller, and Brent Yorgason. Dominic Sewell and Mark Richards deserve a Wookiee-sized thank you for reading over some sample chapters and offering very high-level feedback.

Special thanks to my students and advisees who at some point were involved in one Williams project or another: George Behrakis, Julia Cavallaro, Claudia Dorian, Iverson Eliopoulos, Claudia Holen, Kasey Lynch, Max Luo, Abby Sommers, and Matthew Winkler—each of you inspired me in ways you may not have realized. One person in particular deserves a big tip of the lightsaber: Samantha Tripp. More than one colleague has referred to you as my padawan, but you are very much a John Williams scholar-knight in your own right.

I have been fortunate to share elements of this work across various venues and media platforms. Quite a few NPR stations—KCRW, KERA, UPR, WBUR, and WGBH—somehow allowed me to rave on air about such things as Vader-progressions and leitmotivic foreshadowing. I previewed core arguments of *The Skywalker Symphonies* in articles in *The Washington Post* and *The New York Times*. Much of this material was also workshopped in lectures, conference talks, and guest classes; to those departments and programs that invited me to test drive these ideas, I am grateful. I already feel privileged to live near the Boston Symphony Orchestra, but to be offered invitations to explore their archives, to give talks at the Tanglewood Learning Institute, and to meet and speak with the maestro himself on several occasions?—these were career highpoints.

Miscellaneous but heartfelt thanks go to Brett Abarbanel, Lorena Alessandrini, J. Russel Allyn, Maurizio Caschetto, Christie Carew, James Clarke, Sarah Donovan, Jonathan Ellis, Khouloud Gargouri, Rob Hudson, David Lane, Jonathan Lee, Stephen Rumph, Bruce Russell, Chrysanthe Tan, and Elyse Willis. I would also be remiss without mentioning the JWfan.com community, an unbelievable fount of knowledge and holdover from before the dark times, when the internet was a genuinely wonderful place to dwell.

Last, nothing written here is imaginable without the support and inspiration of my family. To my wife Kasi, for her unending insight and feedback, and for her expertise as a Celticist, on which I relied heavily for Chapter 7. To my parents Diana and William, for instilling in me an all-consuming passion for symphonic music. To my brother John, whose own interest in *Star Wars* actually predated mine; you may not remember, but I certainly do, the bus rides back from summer camp, the two of us humming "The Parade of the Ewoks" together like the cool kids we were. Speaking of fuzzballs: to Dora, Raina, and Hector, for their companionship. And, finally, to Margie, my luminous being. Yoda enjoins us to "do or do not." I do this for her.

Abbreviations and Examples

Films

Abbreviation	Film
ANH	Episode IV: *A New Hope* (1977, dir. Lucas)
ESB	Episode V: *The Empire Strikes Back* (1980, dir. Kershner)
ROTJ	Episode VI: *Return of the Jedi* (1983, dir. Marquand)
TPM	Episode I: *The Phantom Menace* (1999, dir. Lucas)
AOTC	Episode II: *Attack of the Clones* (2002, dir. Lucas)
ROTS	Episode III: *Revenge of the Sith* (2005, dir. Lucas)
TFA	Episode VII: *The Force Awakens* (2015, dir. Abrams)
TLJ	Episode VIII: *The Last Jedi* (2017, dir. Johnson)
TROS	Episode IX: *The Rise of Skywalker* (2019, dir. Abrams)

Harmony

Symbol	Meaning
C_4, $B\flat_5$, $G\sharp_3$, etc.	note and octave
$\hat{1}$, $\hat{2}$, $\hat{3}$, etc.	scale step within a key
$\sharp\hat{4}$, $\flat\hat{5}$, $\natural\hat{6}$, etc.	altered scale step
I, ii^{o}, iii^{7}, etc.	roman numeral function
iv^{6}, V^{6-5}_{4-3}, vi^{4}_{2}, etc.	figured bass
$iv^{\flat 3}$, V^{+}, $\flat$VI, etc.	altered roman numeral
I/C, V/V, etc.	applied chord
C, Cm	major, minor triad
$C^{7(sus4)}$, $C^{9/6}$, $C^{7(\sharp 9 \flat 13)}$, etc.	chordal alterations, extensions
C/E, C/$\hat{5}$, etc.	slash chord, pedal chords [top chord/bass note]
$C \mid E$, $Cm7 \mid E/G\#$, etc.	polychord [top chord $\mid$ bottom chord]
[C]	weak or implied chord
→	directed chord progression
⇝	complex, fuzzy, or non-tonal progression
↔	looping progression
. . .	elided or un-summarized progression
m2, M3, P4, d5, A6, etc	interval (minor, major, perfect, diminished, augmented)

Form

Symbol	Meaning
m., mm.	measure, measures
1m2, 3m4, etc.	cue = (film reel number) m (musical cue number)
L.M.	leitmotif
M.T.	main theme
S.T.	secondary theme
B.T.	bridge theme
phr.	phrase
ant., cons.	antecedent, consequent
pres., cont.	presentation, continuation
frag.	fragment
trans.	transition

Cadences

PAC	perfect authentic cadence (e.g., V→I)
IAC	imperfect authentic cadence (e.g., V^6→I)
HC	half cadence (e.g., ii^6→V)
DC	deceptive cadence (e.g., V→vi)
PC	plagal cadence (e.g., IV→I)
CC	chromatic cadence (e.g., ♭vi→I)

Instrumentation

Abbreviation	Instrument
picc	piccolo
fl	flute
ob	oboe
e. hn	English horn
cl	clarinet
bsn	bassoon
f. hn	French horn
tpt	trumpet
tbn	trombone
tba	tuba

timp	timpani
hp	harp
pno	piano
cel	celesta
syn	synthesizer
vn	violin
va	viola
vc	cello
cb	contrabass
wws	woodwinds
brs	brass
perc	percussion
strs	strings
chor	chorus

Themes

Abbreviation	**Leitmotif**
B.o.t.H.	Battle of the Heroes
D.o.t.F.	Duel of the Fates
K.o.R.	Knights of Ren
L.i.E.	Luke in Exile
P.o.t.S.	Psalm of the Sith
R.F.	Rebel Fanfare
S.A.	Sith Artifacts
T.A.	T.I.E. Fighter Attack
T.R.	Throne Room

Examples

All instances of music notation in *The Skywalker Symphonies* are my personal transcriptions, engraved and annotated with Adobe Acrobat Pro and Sibelius Ultimate. They are rendered in accordance with the dictates of Fair Use in the United States Copyright Act, Section 107, and are included solely for analytical and educational purposes. All musical excerpts are partial, substantially reduced, and transformative in content, containing essential layers of analysis, annotation, and interpretation. While I have checked the examples against all available sources, transcription errors or notational discrepancies—enharmonics, beamings, meters, etc.—may remain, reflecting my own hearing. Any errata will be posted on the Companion Website.

About the Companion Website

www.oup.com/skywalkersymphonies

A companion website complements *The Skywalker Symphonies*. This site includes links to audio clips of the primary musical examples discussed in this book. Additionally, supplementary audio examples, updates, and corrections will be posted to this page. Readers are encouraged to peruse these recordings, as relevant themes, scenes, and pieces come up. A discography is included in the bibliography for important *Star Wars* albums.

Introduction

The Spark

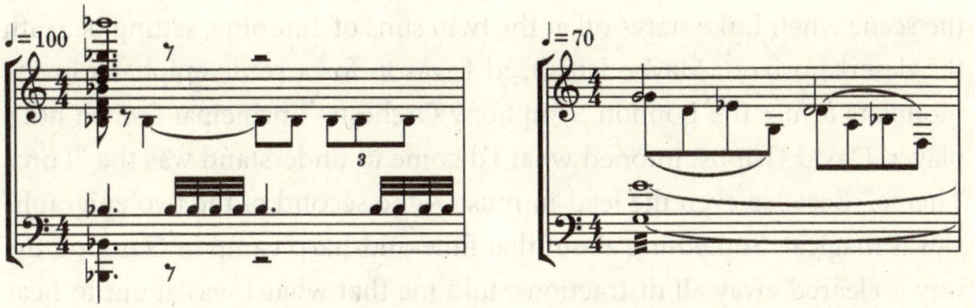

Binary Beginnings

Music lovers can often recall a spark—a moment of peak emotional intensity that ignited their lifelong passion for an artist, genre, or tradition. Usually, one spark will suffice, but in my case, there were two.[1] The first came in the form of a tape cassette called *Kid Stuff: An Afternoon at the Movies*, which I scored, appropriately enough, when I was eight. The album featured a composer named John Williams, conducting an ensemble named the Boston Pops. They played evocatively titled tracks like "Adventures on Earth" and "The Forest Battle," drawn from movies I had never seen. One number in particular captured my imagination like nothing else, right from its first, blazing chord: "STAR WARS Main Theme."

The opening peal of B♭, the first of the two epigraphs above, set some chord in me vibrating, and decades later, it hasn't stopped. The music following that initial fanfare was just so *eventful*. I didn't know the specifics, but I could tell this "Main Theme" contained conflicts and twists, moments of romance and moments of triumph. The more I listened, the more I felt like its protagonist. The music was *familiar* somehow, and not just emotionally. Even before *Kid Stuff*, I had an early and rather obsessive love of Classical music: my favorites were Dvořák's *New World* Symphony, Holst's *The Planets*, and Stravinsky's

Rite of Spring. The new pieces by John Williams spoke to me in a similar way, though part of me knew—or thought I knew—that they were not supposed to go in the same category as those other, older works.

My second spark struck a few years later, while watching *Star Wars: A New Hope* for the first time, at home with my family. (Born a year too late to have seen *Return of the Jedi* in theaters, I, like many millennials, encountered the Skywalker Saga first through home video.) It was a marvelous feeling, finally associating that mighty "Main Title" with the cinematic text from which it actually hailed. But the real transformative experience took place during the scene when Luke stares off at the twin suns of Tatooine, setting beneath the desert horizon. Maybe I realized I was in for a sonic epiphany in the moments *before* the London Symphony Orchestra's principal French horn player, David Cripps, intoned what I'd come to understand was the "Force Theme." Because even the lead-in music—the second of the two epigraphs —was magical. Something about that flute-and-harp vamp in G minor, the way it cleared away all distractions, told me that what I was about to hear concerned something bigger than one moisture farmer's story. And bigger than straightforward, discreet film scoring. It sure wasn't background music to me. The way the "Force Theme" captured my attention did not take me out of the movie: far from it, I felt even more invested in the plot, more immersed in this incredible new filmworld. By the time the movie was over, that theme was, through some mysterious force, a part of who I was, a part of how I understood the world. That same evening, I remember keeping the melody alive in my memory by singing it to myself.[2] I remember trying to reconstruct it on my little Radio Shack-brand keyboard. I remember replaying it in my mind's ear when going to sleep, over and over.

The remarkable power of John Williams's music, its ability to stimulate the mind and stir the heart, made both these formative events possible. But they involved two distinct and perhaps contradictory modes of appreciating music: a "pure" kind of listening to a composition by itself, and a mediated kind where the composition is a component part of a larger audiovisual whole. With the *Kid Stuff* album, I attended to the tracks in the same way I would Dvořák or Stravinsky: with full attention, carried along on the sort of abstract journey that instrumental music is uniquely capable of taking us. It was, broadly speaking, a *symphonic* way of hearing. With the *Star Wars* VHS, my focus was more spread out. I was simultaneously taking in visual spectacle and scenery, perceiving not only the orchestra but sound effects and dialogue, all the while letting these parallel informational streams guide my feelings and shape my understanding of the exciting plot. This way of hearing—where music is part of a complex amalgam of audio and image and storytelling—could be called *cinematic* listening.[3]

This is a sensible, intuitive scheme. It also happens to be far too neat. After all, wasn't I enacting a kind of cinematic narrative in my mind's-theater while playing that cassette tape? I may have been engrossed like I would have been with a symphony, but my delight was hardly detached or coolly intellectual! And conversely, wasn't I hyper aware of the score while watching *A New Hope*? Was Williams not taking me on a sophisticated and sustained musical journey too, just like Dvořák's Ninth or the *Rite of Spring* had?

Those early musical encounters with *Star Wars* led to a lifelong fascination, not just with the scores John Williams wrote for the series but the nature of experiencing—and re-experiencing—film music. In the years since, I have learned much more about the theory and craft of both movie scoring and Western art music. I learned other things too, like the aesthetic hierarchy in which textless "absolute" music sits at the top, while music that was commercial, programmatic, or in any way functional languished many rungs below. I learned that music in properly behaved mainstream cinema was supposed to occlude its presence, to be subliminally felt but consciously unheard. As an undergraduate, I learned that the great works of the Western canon revealed their secrets through rigorous formal analysis. As a PhD student, I learned rigorous formal analysis was actually *formalism*—and that formalism, along with its associates organicism and structural hearing, was a suspect enterprise, born of an impulse to exclude some styles and impose control over others.

I now see those lessons in a different light. Something about the immiscibility of symphonic listening and cinematic listening rubbed me the wrong way. So too did the presumption that careful formal analysis was necessarily an imposition on, or worse, a violation of, music's ineffable mystique. I have written *The Skywalker Symphonies: John Williams and the Music of Star Wars* with the hope of transcending such simplistic binaries. This book is many things, and most of its pages are not directly concerned with such heady matters; if it has a genre, it is music analysis, not music philosophy. But *The Skywalker Symphonies* does represent my attempt to bridge listening modes, to return, in a way, to a more childlike mindset, before all those outside aesthetic and cultural values took root. I truly believe a synthesis is possible, a *cine-symphonic* form of listening. That *Star Wars* happens to be the ideal score with which to make a case is not just convenient, it's inevitable. More than any other work in the orchestral repertoire from the past century—perhaps ever—John Williams's music for this series has opened our ears to the possibilities of symphonic storytelling.

✺✺✺

Williams's nine Skywalker Saga scores encompass over twenty hours of music, conceived across a forty-year span of continuous artistic growth and change. Together, they constitute the densest and likely most impactful body of music in cinema history. From the brassy blast that inaugurated the original film in 1977 to the pensive arpeggios that close the last cue in 2019, *Star Wars* is defined by its music like no other franchise. For millions, perhaps billions of listeners, *Star Wars* ranks among the world's best-known orchestral music. And happily, ubiquity coincides with quality. Though not without their shortcomings, Williams's scores are undoubtedly high-water marks in film composition, marvels of craft and bottomlessly fascinating texts, both intrinsically and as artifacts within their broader societal contexts. They are not just remarkable as movie soundtracks; they represent a major achievement in the history of late twentieth- and early twenty-first-century music.

One might assume that the musicological literature would reflect the massive canonical and cultural impact crater left by Williams's music. But while film music historians—and increasingly, just plain *music* historians—recognize the importance of these scores, surprisingly little scholarly attention has ever been paid to the music of *Star Wars*. The reasons for this neglect are several: the inaccessibility of written scores, the relatively recent birth of film musicology, the presumption that media of mass commercial appeal (especially among children and adolescents) are unworthy of study, and a long-standing bias against film scores in certain musical circles. Luckily, these impediments and prejudices are rapidly receding.[4] Recent work from John Williams scholars like Chloé Huvet and Emilio Audissino has done much to fill the *Star Wars* vacuum in academic venues like peer-reviewed journals, monographs, and conferences. There also exists no shortage of high-quality, often amazingly intensive and insightful analysis of the scores from less institutionally formalized locations: fan magazines, blogs, forums, YouTube channels, and so on.[5] But what is conspicuously absent—and what this book aims to provide—is a *synthetic* perspective on the totality of Williams's work from Episode I to Episode IX.

The Skywalker Symphonies: John Williams's Music for Star Wars is the culmination of a lifelong interest in film music, Williams's colossal legacy in particular. Ever since I got my hands on that *Kid Stuff* tape, I have been thinking about the saga in symphonic terms, rehearing and replaying, making musical connections and connecting with other people musically. Much of my personal musical identity, my sonic imagination, was shaped by this series, and I doubt I am alone in this respect. I taught myself to play the piano largely by figuring out its themes by ear; at one point as a teenager, I could render the better part of the final act of *The Empire Strikes Back* from memory—not well, granted, but with enthusiasm. My dabblings in screen scoring in college served as a way for me to inhabit the mind of a film composer, to gain insight into the craft that listening alone could not. My subsequent specialization in music theory widened that understanding even further and lent it a sophisticated descriptive vocabulary. I did not intend to carve out a niche in film music analysis—for a few years, I labored under the delusion that I would be a Wagner specialist! But the opening was there. It was clear that deep study was possible, and I saw glimmers that others were interested, too. In high school, I had discovered James Buhler's essay, "Star Wars, Music, and Myth," while browsing the aisles of the Newton Public Library. It was a different kind of spark moment for me. Seeing the "Force Theme" treated with the same critical and analytic seriousness as writing on Dvořák and Stravinsky from books on nearby shelves was profoundly affirming—and, the deeper I got into academia, profoundly motivating.

I was lucky that a new trilogy was announced just as I was establishing myself as a professional music researcher. A surge in interest surrounding *The Force Awakens* in 2015, coupled with my own desire to do more public-facing scholarship, spurred me to a number of *Star Wars*–based projects. The biggest was a "Complete Catalogue of the Musical Themes of Star Wars." At first a Microsoft Excel spreadsheet that could fit on one page, this document went through iteration after iteration, eventually growing into an eighty-page online encyclopedia of sorts. (For the curious, this compendium has a permanent home at www.franklehman.com/starwars.)

Other research appeared in more traditionally academic venues, yes, but also in a not-inconsiderable amount in Twitter threads, newspaper articles, and podcasts. Lots of podcasts. *The Skywalker Symphonies* represents a synthesis of work for these twin audiences: the music-loving public and denizens of the ivory tower. That Williams's music is so direct, so powerful, and so well known makes *Star Wars* a fabulous nexus with which to bring music analysis to the masses, and music of mass appeal to academic analysts.

Aims and Scope

To write a book on a musical corpus as wide and dense as *Star Wars* is necessarily an exercise in reduction. And, to an extent, exclusion. Many remarkable themes, cues, and concert pieces will go unexamined in these pages. And while I have attempted to devote equal ink to all nine scores, readers will detect a slight disproportion of focus on Episodes III, V, and VIII. Williams's contribution to the final installment, *The Rise of Skywalker*, receives the least attention. This is no judgment of the score—indeed, I consider Episode IX the strongest of the Sequels, musically at least—but rather a function of the incomplete representation of the score in both the film and currently available album.

This obligatory reduction of scope also extends to analytical methods and critical angles. Music sounded within the narrative world—*source* or *diegetic* music—gets short shrift here, despite the iconicity of the "Cantina Band" and other such in-universe numbers.[6] The interaction of Williams's score with other elements of *Star Wars*' auditory ecosystem is similarly bracketed; this includes not just dialogue and sound effects, but matters of process (mixing, editing, mastering) and technology (hardware and software, sound systems, venue acoustics).[7] The musical politics of the series, especially as they relate to the representation of gender and race/species, are often problematic and always fascinating; they are not, however, this book's focus, though I will spotlight research from others that gives cultural issues the attention they deserve.[8] Williams's style *beyond* the franchise in question also exceeds the book's purview, even though fully understanding the one necessitates a thorough grounding in the other.[9]

As for the ever-increasing amount of *Star Wars* music written by different composers—alas, one has to draw a line somewhere. The list is already very long: Michael Abels, Stephen Barton, Clint Bajakian, Peter Bernstein, Nicholas Britell, Jon Everist, Michael Giacchino, Mick Giacchino, Mark Griskey, Ludwig Göransson, Gordy Haab, Jesse Harlin, Natalie Holt, Chris Huelsbeck, Keiji Inai, Kazuma Jinnouchi, Frank Klepacki, Kevin Kiner, Michael Kramer, Peter McConnell, Joel McNeely, John Powell, Wilbert Roget II, David G. Russell, William Ross, Ryan Shore, Jeremy Soule. More names will surely be added in the years to come. While acknowledging that the future of *Star Wars* will be sung in new voices, here we will concentrate exclusively on the man who made it resonate to begin with.[10]

What *The Skywalker Symphonies* does revolve around is a binary system of core themes: the twin suns of **storytelling** and **symphonism.** By storytelling, I mean something weightier than a one-to-one mirroring of plot and orchestral accompaniment. Music in *Star Wars* is the *primary* driver of narrative, a radical dependency on the score virtually unique in mainstream Hollywood. To justify this bold claim, I will be recruiting a diverse set of tools: thematic analysis, topic theory, linguistics, narratology, theory of myth, and music psychology, to name a few. It is with these frameworks that we will explore Williams's compositional technique, from the tiniest minutiae of motivic construction to the grandest score-sweeping arcs. Whatever the scope, the musical choices made by Williams are storytelling devices, ways of influencing tension, interpretation, and memory. And while I often will argue for a mode of appreciation that centers music, I will always try to resist the temptation of dry formalism. Stressing storytelling function throughout ensures that we do not lapse into analysis-for-analysis'-sake. That prioritization comes in especially handy in those places where I emphasize forms of storycraft either *internal* to the series (much of Chapter 7) or outside it (Chapter 8). This angle on immanent narration acts as a crucial link to epic storytelling à la Wagner, an artistic convergence far deeper than the typical, perfunctory ascription of leitmotif to the series.

The other organizing theme of this book is the idea of treating the scores symphonically. Of course, the *Star Wars* soundtracks are *not* literally symphonies. But it is a productive analogy, one that has been made (and sometimes unmade) by many commentators, not least of whom is George Lucas himself.[11] My approach to symphonism here will be guided, and where necessary nuanced, by four interrelated propositions.

1. **The idiom of *Star Wars* is to a large extent based on, and in constant conversation with, the symphonic literature.** It is vital to view the *Star Wars* scores not just as products of film music history but as a self-conscious participant in a centuries-long tradition of symphonic music. The first two chapters dive into these connections, tracing how the distinctive *Star Wars*ian sound draws from the orchestral repertoire: symphonies, program and incidental works, ballets, operas—and yes, other film music. The debt to composers like Wagner and Ravel is examined with specificity and sensitivity to the pragmatics of film composition—not as a way of denying Williams's originality,

but as a recognition of the creative and storytelling potential of referentiality.

2. ***Star Wars* is symphonic in scope and construction.** The central analytical position of this book is that the individual Skywalker Saga soundtracks can be analyzed symphonically. The easiest comparison in this respect is Williams's usage of leitmotif, a technique conceived in the nineteenth century as a way of importing Beethovenian symphonic processes and aesthetics into the realm of dramatic (characteristically but not exclusively operatic) music. Accordingly, attention will be lavished on leitmotif throughout this book. But symphonic construction goes much further. I will also consider the following:
   - Unification through motivic development and transformation, not just recurrence
   - Presence of long-term, goal-directed musical architecture
   - Operation of a rich, constantly changing network of intra- and intertextual meanings
   - Projection of a Mahlerian "score-as-a-world" sensibility, through stylistic eclecticism, soundtrack-unifying colorations, and mythopoetic aspirations
   - Sophisticated thematic, harmonic, and tonal planning, with clear references to certain formal hallmarks like rotational organization, fugato, teleological genesis, scherzo, developing variation, and so on
   - Listening practices that these scores cultivate, especially when detached from their visual contexts and heard as pure music
3. **The nine *Star Wars* scores are akin to a single-composer symphony cycle:** A provocative but revealing way of understanding Williams's contribution is to approach the scores in the way we often do for composers of major symphony cycles—the number nine is of no small significance here! With this symphony-cycle framework, we can pose some intriguing issues, including the significance of a decades-spanning artistic development, the nature of stylistic periodization (e.g., a "late style"), the notion of summing up a career musically, and the promises and perils of canon formation. This study is unique in treating the Skywalker Saga in a musically synthetic way, dwelling as much on the recent, practically unstudied Episodes I–III and VII–IX as on the canonized Episodes IV–VI.
4. **The textual issues native to the symphony as a genre are active in *Star Wars*:** This study never loses sight of *Star Wars* music as a dependent

> and contingent text. Ever apparent is the tension between univocal, unified artistic autonomy and the messier reality of film composition, particularly since the advent of digital editing. Scholars of classical music, symphonies especially, have long had to figure out how to reconcile these issues. Their methodologies provide models for dealing with the complexities of the film-score-as-text: overlapping editions, cuts and insertions, (in)audibility, missed opportunities and critical disagreements, so-called "finale problems," and the biggest issue of all, authorial intent.

These four claims regarding symphonism, shone through the lens of storytelling, converge in this book's central thesis:

The music of Star Wars is equally—and at times more—compelling when it is the focus of one's attention as it is when heard as a subordinated part of a larger filmic whole.

This is a radical departure from mainline film musicology—not to mention the fundamental tenets of film scoring!—which holds that musical structure is inseparable from the larger text it serves. To treat the score otherwise would be to violate its raison d'être. Do not worry; I am not arguing we discard the movies! They are and will remain the first and last step of all varieties of *Star-Wars*ian aesthetic engagement. And I am under no illusions that these soundtracks are well-behaved pieces of absolute music. I highlight at every turn that Williams's contribution to the franchise is subject to contingencies considerably more thoroughgoing (and often frustrating!) than most other works, film or concert. Nevertheless, as will be shown throughout this book, these nine scores operate in a sense on their own, special plane.

Williams's music tells stories with a richness and complexity that can easily be appreciated on its own—and not only through separable paratexts like concert arrangements. In fact, in some cases, music does a *superior* job of conveying narrative arcs and central themes compared to the screenplay. Williams can seem to understand underlying character dynamics and mythic meanings more deeply than the films themselves do. The integrity of his cinematic symphonism, maintained across all nine films, ensures that even with all their inconsistencies, the abandoned motivic threads, and the editorial vagaries, the Skywalker scores still hold together uncannily well as a unit. Again, this is not an argument for treating Williams's *Star Wars* scores as absolute music: his compositions are intrinsically programmatic, to be understood in terms of a network of extramusical symbols, relationships, and plot archetypes. Rather, I claim the Skywalker "symphonies" constitute an internally coherent mythological text.

Approach

While these big-picture themes will echo across this book, the average page of *The Skywalker Symphonies* will be taken up with close musical analysis. There are amazing things to be discovered in these scores, from the smallest quirk of chord voicing to the grandest multi-film thematic metamorphosis. To identify and characterize these compositional feats requires the precision afforded by music notation and the versatile toolkits of music theory. Accordingly, each chapter is stuffed with examples, diagrams, and tables, often heavily annotated. I have also provided a leitmotif catalog as an appendix, so that every major recurring theme in the series can be easily referenced as you make your way through this book. Readers without training in music theory may find these figures forbidding, if not downright inscrutable. But they are profoundly important—indeed necessary—if we mean to study this landmark symphonic cycle with the seriousness it deserves.

The first two and final three chapters are comparatively light on jargon—a soft takeoff and landing for the theory averse. But those central chapters shouldn't scare you off. Frankly, the reputation of music theory for difficulty is vastly exaggerated. Williams's music is direct in its meaning and power, and analysis of it should be able to communicate the mechanisms of that meaning and power without layers of obscurantist terminology or abstraction. To the best of my ability, then, I have endeavored to convey my analytical claims vividly, through prose that, without shirking theoretical precision, is at times conversational, poetic, or playful. The written accounts are meant to work in concert with the various figures and diagrams that populate this book; these too are constructed in such a way that (I hope) balances comprehensiveness and accessibility. Ultimately, no analysis, however elegant, means much if it does not pass the hearability test. To that end, I provide links to online clips of all notated musical moments discussed, available by consulting the book's Companion Website. A high school–level familiarity with music theory will be sufficient to understand almost everything in this book, and in cases where especially idiosyncratic or obscure tools are employed, I will take care to signpost and define them. Even when dense and complicated, these analyses are always offered in the spirit of sharing exciting knowledge rather than mystifying it behind a repulsor field of technicality. I truly believe this book is for everyone who loves *Star Wars*, film music, symphonic music, or all three—not just trained musicians and academics.

Two modes of analysis will be used so frequently in *The Skywalker Symphonies* that they deserve a little explication. First are score excerpts, typically between eight and sixteen measures. All are heavily reduced. The loss of information, especially with respect to Williams's deft orchestration, pains me, but simplification is indispensable when the goal is to make points clearly. From here on, I will refer to leitmotifs using capital letters—not "The Force Theme" but FORCE—both in examples and text. Leitmotif designations comprise just one of the layers of data included in the score excerpts. Depending on the passage and the point being made, these layers could specify aspects of formal design, instrumentation, on-screen action, and harmony. Especially harmony.

The dimension of music designated by "harmony" is enormous, encompassing everything from scales to chord symbols, Roman numerals, cadences, chromatic transformations, atonal voice-leading, and on and on. John Williams is unrivalled in Hollywood as a harmonist, and in his hands tonality itself becomes a powerful storytelling device. Cadences—the stereotypical patterns with which musical phrases telegraph and deliver closure—are particularly important dramatic and symbolic events in *Star Wars*, for reasons that will become apparent as we progress. The cadential nomenclature in *The Skywalker Symphonies* is based on William Caplin's system for Classical-era music, but with expansions and modifications made for the looser and more varied idiom of film music, which includes phenomena such as plagal half cadences and chromatic deceptive cadences.[12]

If these concepts light up your musical brain, you are in for a treat. If not, take heart: harmonic information is included so that the analyses are as precise as possible, and nothing is conveyed in prose or diagrams that is not plainly audible in the music itself.

Figure I.1 gives an idea of what to expect, depicting the first half of that memory-searing Binary Sunset interlude. In most cases, the score-as-heard in film is the ultimate source of these examples, as opposed to the score-on-the-page or on-the-album. The notation is produced through a combination of by-ear transcription—necessary in many cases, especially for the Sequels—and consultation with the scattered print sources that are currently available. The whole piece of film music this comes from—a *cue* in industry terms—is not shown, just the first nineteen measures. During this time, three important themes occur, designated by their shorthand labels in boxed text: LUKE's leitmotif (which doubles as the series' main theme), the aforementioned FORCE theme, and a speck of the REBEL FANFARE. When themes divide into multiple parts like an antecedent and consequent, the formal subunits are specified to the right of the melody's label; in later diagrams, partial or cropped portions of a theme are indicated with a note about which measures of the theme in its complete form they represent. An ellipsis denotes that a theme continues beyond what is included in the example.

The most important aspects of harmony in "Binary Sunset" are specified in Figure I.1 by chord symbols and three flagged points of tonal articulation. All of these are involved in orienting the ear around the key of G minor. The first occurs in measure 7, home to an open-ended *half cadence*, or HC. This cadence effects closure for the cue's first module, which revolves around LUKE's theme, while building anticipation of the next, FORCE-based paragraph. The operative harmony here, D♭ major atop G, is a token of a notable *Star Wars*ian sonority—the "Planets" chord—that we will get to know better in later chapters.

Equally characteristic is the *plagal half cadence* at measure 13, marking the midpoint of the theme. This bit of musical punctuation is powered by C major, the major subdominant (IV) triad, a distinctly cinematic chord, especially compared to the dominant (V) expected from Classical tonality. Indeed, that C major triad, along with the E♭ major that arrives two measures later, is *so* striking in this context that one might mistakenly view the FORCE as nothing but a delivery mechanism for two magnificent chords. Chapter 2's breakdown of the theme's melodic structure shows this not to be the case.

Last of the cadential milestones is the *perfect authentic cadence*, or PAC, beginning at measure 17, complete with a cadential six-four at its front, a drawn-out dominant in its core, and an unambiguous tonic at its end. This pattern is, in principle, the strongest possible concluding scheme in Western music, though interestingly, Williams dilutes this one's effect by a progressive winnowing of texture and a pointed indecision of mode.

While these chords and cadences are of decisive importance to "Binary Sunset's" expressive profile, other excerpts may hinge on different parameters—harmonic function, scalar content, pitch-class sets, scale-degrees—and the book's examples will be annotated with them accordingly.

Instrumentation is also indicated in Figure I.1, but only partially, for the most important or ear-catching aspects of orchestration. Articulation and dynamic markings are omitted for simplification's sake, though a smattering of countermelodies and bass lines is depicted with small noteheads. Additional salient details may be conveyed with in-score annotations—here, for example, a remark about the way LUKE's cadence presages a significant DIES IRAE motif to come. Because these transcriptions can quickly become crowded, I generally do not include indications of what is happening on screen, either visually or in terms of dialogue and sound effects. This is, of course, a glaring omission given the functional nature of this music, and one

Figure I.1 Music for the "Binary Sunset" sequence (ANH, 3m2)

done out of a simple need for clarity. Audiovisual and narrative information will not be forsaken though! Besides in-text descriptions, supported in all cases by timestamps, I employ another, more narrative-friendly mode of analysis throughout: the form chart.

A form chart is a concise representation of musical design in tandem with the scene it accompanies. These charts offer a way of apprehending the whole of a cue or piece—something not always easy with music in general, and especially tricky with the changeable style of underscore Williams developed for the series. The exact information provided depends on whatever structural or storytelling feature is being discussed, but in all cases, they are constructed as tiered timelines. Each row captures an important category of musical and dramatic organization:

- **Timestamps** and/or **Measure Numbers** are placed at the top.
- **Formal Sections** occupy the first row. In most cues, these will be a simple numerical indication of modules—discrete chunks of underscore with a defining theme, texture, key, or similar. In more complex cases, sections may be subdivided or given more explanatory labels like A-section, Main Theme, Exposition, etc.
- **Thematic Design** is conveyed in the second row. Leitmotifs and other noteworthy themes and motifs are indicated in capital letters. Other types of material, such as vamps, stingers, and athematic passages, are depicted in plain lowercase text.
- **Harmonic Design** is described in the third row. In *Star Wars*' modulatory and chromatic tonal idiom, there is often ambiguity between what is a key versus what is a chord; this ambiguity is preserved in these diagrams. Important cadences are notated, along with the pertinent chord progression when relevant.
- **Orchestration**, a vitally important aspect of musical storytelling, is specified in the fourth row. The lead instrumental voice is specified; admittedly, this usually only gives a partial sense of the passage's overall texture and timbre.
- **Filmic Action** (dialogue, effects, shots, cuts, etc.) is summarized in the fifth row.
- **Volume and Density**, in the form of a waveform, conveys the dynamic trajectory of a cue.

A model of this style of analytical representation is given in Figure I.2, again using the "Binary Sunset" sequence.

25:11 25:30 26:09 26:31 26:45 27:21

1	2		3		4	5
Luke	vamp	**Force**	**R.F.**	stinger→ athematic	**Luke**	**Force**
B♭ **HC** ♭VII→V	Gm	**HC** i→IV **PAC** V→i	(C)…A/C♯→ C/E→F♯m/A		C♯/$\hat{5}$ **HC** ♭VII→V	C♯m **HC** IV→V **PAC** V→i C / C♯m^{6}_{9}
strs, fl → cl (solo)	fl, hp → f. hn (solo) → strs		fl→vc/cb→vln/vla		cl (solo)	fl, f. hn (solos) → strs, hp
Luke leaves dinner, Beru & Owen talk	Luke outside, wordlessly stares off at twin suns setting over horizon		Luke in garage, 3PO reactivated, reveals R2 escaped		Luke leaves for outside, scans for R2	Luke unable to find R2, goes back inside. Cut to next day, Owen inside, calling for Luke

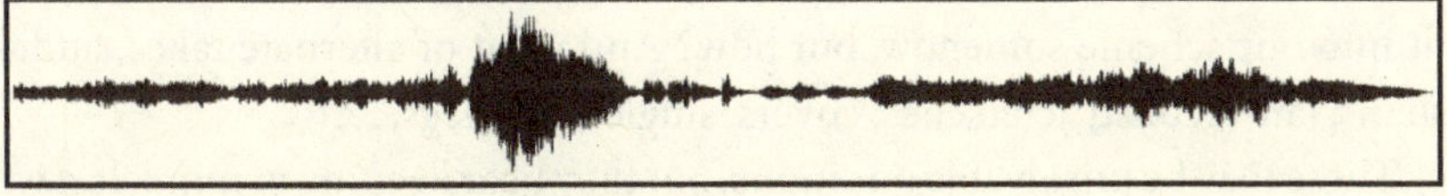

Figure I.2 Form of the "Binary Sunset" sequence

Sources

In *The Last Jedi*, we behold ancient volumes of lore, hidden away in a secret library on an unfindable world: "the sacred Jedi texts," Luke tells us. Is there a musical equivalent of these foundational, inviolable objects when it comes to the Skywalker soundtracks? Not at all. Time and again, we encounter a decided *lack* of textual definitiveness and stability. Musicologists have had to grapple with similar issues in a variety of other genres, particularly the symphonic and operatic repertoire—think of the question of cuts and extracts in Rachmaninoff's Second Symphony, or the confounding number of revisions of Verdi's *Don Carlo*. What exactly constitutes a musical "work" is already a thorny issue with pieces whose boundaries are far better defined than the average movie soundtrack; with *Star Wars*, the concept is tested to its breaking point.

Perhaps the truest glimpse into the composer's intentions would be afforded by John Williams's original pencil sketches—though at present they are as inaccessible as those tomes gathering dust in the first Jedi temple. Is the true text the conductor's score, then? Even if a thousand little ad hoc changes are made on the scoring stage and mixing board? Maybe we feel uncomfortable assigning univocal authorship to one figure when so many creative talents—orchestrators, contractors, performers, engineers, music editors—are involved in realizing and shaping a symphonic film score. Acknowledging that the film soundtrack is an intrinsically collaborative object, perhaps then it may be treated as a stable reference textual point. Yet the more one knows about these scores, the more one notices moments where the music is obscured, cut, spliced, or edited beyond any semblance of what was originally written. What ought we do when there are multiple versions of a given cue, each with something important to contribute to musical storytelling? Even entire films have differing editions. Must one choose between being a "Yub Nub" advocate (*Return of the Jedi* '83) or a "Victory Celebration" (*Return of the Jedi* '97) partisan? To what extent do we factor in extra-diegetic selections, such as the End Credits, into our analysis? Or paratexts—concert suites, radio shows, piano folios, and so on. Certainly, the soundtrack album, for many listeners the most salient musical artifact after the film itself, must fit into our scheme somehow, but how? And what of alternate takes, audio stems, fan-reconstructed cues, covers, singles, bootlegs, . . .?

These may be unsolvable questions, but they bear keeping in mind, lest we fall into the trap of assuming *Star Wars* music is one, fixed thing. As far as authorship goes, it is important not to dismiss the contributions of orchestrators and editors, but at the same time, there is no point in downplaying Williams's role, which is genuinely singular—ultimately, every last note is his.[13] The stance I aim to take for the rest of this book will be one of dogged inclusivity when it comes to what "counts" as the text. I consider ripe for consideration essentially *anything* composed for these nine films—even alternates and unused cues. But extreme care and explicit justification will be given to any music not immediately audible in the latest and most commonly consumed version of the film-as-such. In practice, this means referring to official soundtrack albums and those versions of the movies available streaming on Disney+ as of 2025. All timestamps derive from one of those two sources unless otherwise stated. All this said, the book's later chapters do reopen the issue of textual stability in their exploration of alternative *music-first* modes of listening and study.

Organization

This book's nine chapters do not cover the installments in the Skywalker Saga one by one, but rather focus on broader issues of aesthetics, design, and reception. You can very much make your way through *The Skywalker Symphonies* in a nonlinear fashion, skipping from chapter to chapter or even section to section, especially if you are looking to explore a particular leitmotif, piece, or score. However, the chapters do roughly divide into "trilogies," and there is an analytical red thread to follow for those who progress sequentially. The first trio of chapters sets the essential foundation for the study of Williams's music in this franchise and establishes frameworks that are applied in subsequent chapters. The next three are all about how Williams develops and transforms his themes. The final chapters revolve around different kinds of storytelling and the question of how—and what—we hear through film music. The book's structure is thus cumulative, and the ordering of topics is intentional, moving from neutral description to critical interpretation and, by the conclusion, bold speculation.

Chapter 1, "The *Star Wars* Style" lays out the series' soundworld and situates John Williams's contribution within its historical context. We begin by scrutinizing the claim that *Star Wars* revived a defunct symphonic tradition in Hollywood, a commonplace in both informal and scholarly appraisals of the 1977 score, and one that deserves some historiographical pressuring. At stake is not just the place of Williams's scores within an evolving musical canon but the very idea of the "symphonic," a term laden with centuries' worth of meanings and values. Many thinkers have weighed in on the nature of symphonism, and it is a useful exercise to identify and assess which of the many senses of the word apply to *Star Wars*. Two frameworks prove particularly illuminating: the Sibelius-versus-Mahler dichotomy between formal tightness and eclectic expansiveness; and the musicologist Peter Franklin's notion of late-Romantic imaginative hearing, which provides an excellent model for cinesymphonic listening. Besides "the symphonic," the other major category needed for parsing Williams's music is "the operatic." More specifically, it is the style developed by Richard Wagner in his huge music dramas, with their mythic subjects, networks of leitmotifs, and thick skeins of musical prose. Both sides of the *Star Wars*ian coin—symphonic and space-operatic—are illustrated with an analytical vignette of "Luke's Farewell" from *Empire*. The chapter concludes with a high-level overview of Williams's nine scores as (partially) unified cycles, individually distinctive but shaped by evolving creative concerns and epochal changes in film production practice.

A perennial issue in the discourse surrounding *Star Wars* is the music's purported indebtedness to other works. Chapter 2, "Rhymes and References," approaches the nature of influence from two angles: external inspirations, as from Wagner, Stravinsky, and Korngold; and strictly internal ones, which include literal thematic recurrences but also subtler echoes and processes. Along the way, I'll dispel some facile misconceptions about compositional similarity and offer a musical rehabilitation of George Lucas's unfairly maligned concept of the "rhyme."

No book on *Star Wars* would be complete without an investigation of leitmotif—or, as the composer prefers, "melodic identification." Williams's leitmotivic scoring can be amazingly refined at times, brazenly unsubtle at others. Until recently, critical assessments of the thematic process in *Star Wars* have been frustratingly superficial, rarely engaging with the music itself in a sustained or rigorous way. Chapter 3, "The Language of Leitmotif," aims to supply a more exacting treatment of the subject. Doing so involves applying the music/language analogy farther than most prior studies; though never one-to-one equivalents to thematic practices, many concepts from linguistics and the philosophy of language prove helpful in parsing the leitmotivic grammar of this series. Central among them is the idea of the melodic prototype, which anchors the analytical model used throughout the book. Much of the chapter is taxonomic in character, born of a desire for definitional precision and utility. But *Star Wars* is a creative work, often messy, rarely perfectly planned or even especially consistent. A major goal of this chapter is therefore to recognize the full variety of modes of thematic expression in the saga—and, as importantly, that which is *not* thematic, a huge and almost entirely unexamined territory. Tying it all together is a close reading of "Revisiting Snoke" from *The Last Jedi*, a cue as representative of leitmotivic musical prose as it gets.

Where Chapters 1 through 3 establish the basic materials of John Williams's language in the Skywalker scores, the next three show why "symphonic" is an apt term to describe their treatment. We begin with Chapter 4, "Transformations," a survey of the many ways musical matter changes and evolves as a means of sonic storytelling. Or, as the case may be, how musical matter is left static or unelaborated. Two themes with fascinating "phylogenetic" branches are spotlit: LUKE, the franchise's ever-present main anthem; and the THRONE ROOM, an apparent (but not actual) one-cue-wonder. From these leitmotifs, I work up to a general theory of thematic transformation in *Star Wars*, a model that accounts for developmental scope, continuity of thematic arc, and degree of alteration, from the merest of inflections to the most radical of macro-transformations.

One of the transformational strategies introduced in the context of LUKE's theme is important enough to warrant its own chapter. Chapter 5, "Seeds," explores the technique of motivic seeding, in which some isolated aspect of an important theme is extracted and allowed to spread across the score. Four case studies examine the different ways Williams sows and reaps his motivic harvests: a sprout of JAWA music in Episode IV; an intervallic germ from HAN AND LEIA in Episode V; the yet-unblossomed buds of VADER in Episode I; and REBEL cells embedded in Episode VII. Together, these analyses show how symphonic integration in *Star Wars* does not always have to be systematic or goal-driven—motivic free play, suggestive and unpredictable, is just as powerful a unifying device.

For those thematic transformations that *do* aim for a goal, Chapter 6, "Arcs," offers the deepest of dives into Williams's leitmotivic practice. These are long-range musical tales, the ones that stay on target, dramatically speaking, capable of structuring a film's form and propelling its narrative. After introducing Williams's backward-working method of thematic decomposition, one such arc from each trilogy is highlighted. The procedure of *developing variation* is shown in operation in Episode VI with respect to YODA's leitmotif. *Deferred consummation*, a technique of strategically withholding musical closure, has as its woeful exemplar the love theme from Episode II. And the idea of *teleological genesis*, usually assumed to operate only in the most vaunted pieces in the Classical repertoire, can be seen governing great stretches of the Episode VIII score as it barrels toward a stunning set piece based on the DESPERATION theme.

Chapter 7, "Epic Storytelling," shifts focus onto the way music does more than unify, but actively *tells* the story of the series. We begin by examining Williams's own conception of his role as storyteller, and how his scoring often fulfills the definition of epic narration, exhibiting distanciation, ritual formality, cyclicality, and self-reference. After a tour of sequences in which on-screen characters recount past events, I introduce ideas from the field of musical narratology that prove invaluable in explaining more complex instances of musical mythmaking. Three case studies follow: the twisty translational reticulations of "Duel of the Fates," the amiable travesty of "Threepio's Bedtime Story," and the beguiling deceptions of "Palpatine's Big Pitch."

Up to this point, *The Skywalker Symphonies* has dealt solely with music as it occurs within the *Star Wars* films themselves. But an entire sonic universe exists outside the formal bounds of the movies, much of it of profound significance to the cine-symphonic experience of the saga. Chapter 8, "Star Wars as Concert," tackles musical *paratexts*: all the forms and artifacts of listening that exist outside the two-hour frames of diegetic action. Sections on credits sequences, live performances, and soundtrack albums cover the many guises in which the saga's music exists once the movie is over. Musical form—how Williams shapes time when he has the listener's undivided attention—is of critical importance, as are issues of satisfying closure and thematic encapsulation. The unlikely heroes of Episode VI's final battle garner a case study with the concert arrangement of "The Forest

Battle." This leads to a brief meditation on the psychological affordances of *relistening*, putting all these paratexts in perspective and constructing a bridge to the final chapter.

Chapter 9, "The Battle Symphony of Hoth," is where I make my most direct and radical pitch for the music-centric appreciation of *Star Wars*. Williams's score for *The Empire Strikes Back* is a singularly rich and rewarding musical text, motivically integrated and emotionally resonant in ways that subsequent entries may occasionally match but never exceed. Of its many standout sequences, the extended military clash between Rebels and Empire is an exceptionally tantalizing subject for concerted—or better, concert-like—listening. The representation of warfare in the series is itself a worthy topic, and one to which due attention is devoted here. Also relevant are historical listening practices for so-called Battle Symphonies; though one need not appeal to the canon of Western art music to legitimize movie scores, it does not hurt our case here that Beethoven himself furnishes a fine precedent for this "Battle Symphony" of Hoth. The second half of the chapter digs into this fifteen-minute span of dazzling musical invention, stressing aspects of its tight motivic integration but also its patently cinematic surprises and reversals. This set piece may not be a symphony in the pedant's sense, but on a formal and emotional level, it satisfies as well as any work literally bearing that label.

A short postlude, "Endless Endings," follows. Here I muse on the nature of musical finality in the franchise—its obsession with concluding and re-concluding, and how every ending is really a new beginning. Two appendices follow. The first is a concise leitmotivic catalog for the series; you are encouraged to consult this while reading, and in tandem with the audio clips of an incipit (the first few notes) for each theme included on the book webpage. The second is a list of all the *Star Wars*-based concert arrangements Williams prepared and, for almost all, conducted himself.

Now, let's take our first steps into a wider world of the Skywalker symphonic saga. May the Force—and the FORCE theme—be with you!

1

The *Star Wars* Style

While writing the Star Wars script, I listened to music for inspiration and would actually arrange the script loosely into various "symphonies." I visualized the scenes in terms of symphonic music—large, grand, theatrical adventure scores.

—George Lucas

Nine is quite enough.

—John Williams

The Symphonic Score Strikes Back?

What does it mean to treat *Star Wars* as a symphonic experience? The quotes above offer a useful point of departure.[1] As George Lucas tells it, his sci-fi fable of Jedi Knights and Sith Lords was shaped by symphonic thinking from its inception. It was not that Lucas had simply played some orchestral warhorses in the background to get his screenwriterly juices flowing when he was first concocting the film in the mid-1970s. The very formal structure and expressive universe of the Skywalker Saga was conceived through the medium of the symphonic repertoire. And for a brief time, the soundtrack for his new film literally *was* the symphonic repertoire.

An early cut of the first movie—then just *Star Wars*—was accompanied purely by classical music, a "temp track" constructed by Lucas along with sound designer Ben Burtt and editor Paul Hirsch. Temp-tracking was and remains a ubiquitous practice in Hollywood, wherein the rough cut of a film is supplied with preexisting music, often sourced from other movie soundtracks, that fits a given scene's mood and tempo. This placeholder music is presented to the composer as a source of inspiration (or emulation) once he or she is brought on board. The temp track for this proto-*Star Wars* consisted of those pieces that stimulated Lucas's imagination: extracts from

Bruckner, Dvořák, Holst, Stravinsky, and so on. Thankfully for film history, Lucas's friend Steven Spielberg recommended John Williams as someone who could provide his movie with *original* music, a score that was conversant with, but not duplicative of, that "large, grand, theatrical" idiom from which Lucas drew his inspiration.[2] And so, after two months of writing in early 1977, the first Skywalker Symphony was composed. It would be the most externally referential of all nine scores, a soundtrack in which Lucas's models from the symphonic repertoire were rarely far from earshot. And, at the same time, every last note—and crucially, every stroke of musical storytelling, grand or fine—was pure John Williams.

It is with an awareness of Lucas's initial symphonic spark, and the genuinely unprecedented cycle of scores it engendered, that we should interpret Williams's quip following the 2019 release of *The Rise of Skywalker*, that "nine is enough." Anyone familiar with the history of Western music understands the magic—or curse—of this number. Beethoven wrote nine symphonies. So did Dvořák and Vaughan Williams. And, depending on how one counts, Schubert, Bruckner, Glazunov, and Arnold. Mahler tried to cheat the curse through crafty titling, only for it to catch up with him in the end, with an unfinished Tenth left behind on his desk. To reach nine symphonies is to summit a Beethovenian mountain; to exceed it is to tempt fate itself. "Any comparison with Beethoven would be sacrilegious," the then eighty-seven-year-old composer explained in an interview, "but I like the idea of completing a cycle at number nine. It will keep me quiet for a while."[3]

Never one to aggrandize his accomplishments, Williams has routinely downplayed parallels drawn between his *Star Wars* scores and works of the Classical canon—increasingly so, as comparisons with both Beethoven and (considerably more to Williams's distaste) Wagner became more irresistible with each addition to his Skywalker cycle. In the run-up to *The Empire Strikes Back*, the composer described his contribution as being, in terms of length if nothing more, "the equivalent of several Lisztian tone poems." But when his interviewer Alan Arnold added "or a couple of symphonies," Williams quickly resisted the suggestion: "Yes, except that it's not really a fair comparison, because this kind of incidental music is quicker to write than an organic piece like a symphony."[4] This expression of symphonic disavowal, and others like it, runs like a leitmotif across the composer's nearly fifty-year record of testimony on the series, and it bears taking seriously, especially Williams's calculated use of the term "organic." At the same time, a potentially fruitful means of understanding his music should not be foreclosed because of the composer's penchant for self-effacement. So long as we resist facile analogies between the arts of film and concert composition, we will find there are some very real, very deep symphonic processes in *Star Wars*.

Williams's symphonic disavowal must be understood in the context of an oft-repeated contention—not one put forward by the composer, but rather critics, journalists, and pop cultural historians: with his music for *Jaws* in 1975 and, more dramatically, *Star Wars* two years later, **John Williams revived the symphonic film score.** Variations swap the word "revive" with "resurrect," "reintroduce," "resuscitate," or "resurgence." Rarely, the assertion is qualified by a hedge like "is credited with reviving"; more often, it is intensified by the modifier "single-handedly."[5] These claims were not just retroactive judgments made with chronological and critical distance; they were part of the contemporary discourse from the start. One variation was expressed by Steven Spielberg upon the release of *Jaws*: "The soundtrack is a stunning symphonic achievement and a great leap ahead in the revitalization of film music as a foreground component for the total motion picture experience."[6]

The story is nothing if not a tidy one. American cinema in the 1970s was in a state of orchestral withdrawal. Filmmakers, surfeited on the gushing late-Romantic extravagance of Classical Hollywood (roughly 1929 through 1960), had in the '60s turned to alternative models for scoring their pictures. Music became more sparse, more experimental, more *idiosyncratic* in its deployment. Soundtracks shifted away from through-composed underscore, which was now heard as tired and indulgent, and toward fresher resources, namely, popular idioms (rock, folk, jazz, electronics, etc.) and compilations of preexisting songs or pieces. Alfred Newman, Max Steiner, and Miklós Rózsa were out; Isaac Hayes, Simon and Garfunkel, and Ligeti were in.

And then, the story goes, another paradigm shift rocked the scoring world, thanks to the twin scores for *Jaws* in 1975 and *Star Wars* two years later. Their enormous popularity, difficult to overstate in both commercial and critical terms, heralded a return of the musically repressed. The Romantic splendor of Hollywood's Golden Age was a phoenix reborn, blazing all the brighter after its prolonged absence.[7] Huge orchestras, tuneful leitmotivic underscore, unabashed emotionality—it was suddenly all back in fashion.

This account of decline and revival, with its Williams-authored inflection point, is an anchoring narrative in the telling of movie music history. It is also an oversimplification. Lush orchestral scoring was still being practiced throughout the '60s and '70s, notably by Rózsa, Alex North, and Williams himself—though rarely with the level of nostalgic referentiality that came with *Star Wars.*[8] One particularly important figure is Jerry Goldsmith, whose omission from the revivalist historiography is egregious considering his work on sumptuously symphonic mid-1970s scores such as *Ransom*, *The Wind and the Lion*, *Logan's Run*, *The Omen*, and *Islands in the Stream.*[9] Nor is it correct to claim that *Star Wars* swept away pop and experimental scores. If anything, they became more standardized after 1977, more commercially ascendant in the years after Lucas's blockbuster. Pop music retained its relevancy through the chart-topping singles and soundtracks of the 1980s and '90s. Musical experimentalism took more time to reassert itself in mainstream film, but its impact on post-Millennial soundtracks, with their proliferation of electronic sounds and timbralist techniques, is undeniable.

The sea change that swept in Williams's big scores of the 1970s is thus, to use a term of inescapable relevance in discussing *Star Wars*, a myth: a reductive attribution of world-historical change to a single, heroic figure. Figures like Spielberg and Lucas obviously had a hand in constructing this narrative, but Williams himself put little stock in this simplistic view of his music. In 1980, he tempered critic Richard Dyer's acclamation that he restored cinematic symphonism, offering instead that he doubted "what I have been doing for the last two or three years will last—nothing ever does; already in some studios, they are calling for more pop music."[10] This is half true: the '80s saw the solidification of pop music and synth-heavy soundtracks in mainstream film. But Williams hardly stopped producing sweeping and highly acclaimed orchestral scores after *Return of the Jedi.* And the success of *Star Wars* helped open space for several successive generations of younger composers like Alan Silvestri, Howard Shore, and John Powell to write their own symphonic barnburners. Without *Star Wars*, there is no *Back to the Future*, no *Lord of the Rings*, no *How to Train Your Dragon*, to name a handful of franchises with impeccably crafted leitmotivic scores.

Another version of the myth of resurrection was offered to Williams in 1997—plenty of time after the original to reflect on its impact—that *Star Wars* "changed the shape of film music [after Hollywood] had really abandoned the idea of the big full orchestral idea."

> Well, I don't know if it's fair to say the *Star Wars* films brought back symphonic scores per se. We've been using symphony orchestras since even before sound. Anyone interested in film knows that music seems to be an indispensable ingredient for filmmakers. . . . I think if the use of symphony

> orchestras went out of fad in the '50s and '60s for some reason it was just that: it was out of fad. Someone would have brought it back. It's too useful and too successful not to have it back.[11]

The composer's response is telling, and not only in his genuine, if calculated, modesty but also in the way he pressures the premise of the question. Asked about the "big orchestral" score, Williams rewords the subject to be about "symphonic" scores—a subtle but significant reframing. He goes on to cast his role as that of a facilitator of a basically inevitable historical change, given the crucial usefulness of the resource of the orchestra and the cyclical tendency of fads to come and go. Williams simply happened to be in the right place at the right time.[12]

The composer's carefully phrased disavowals notwithstanding, the account of symphonic revival is a persistent myth for a reason, as it contains several kernels of truth. The novelty of *Star Wars*' score was real, if not entirely singular. Its popularity was massive, but not universal. Its role in ushering in what John Williams scholar Emilio Audissino calls the "neoclassical" scoring idiom was powerful, but not all-encompassing.[13] Yet if those claims require provisos, there is one idea that can be stated with basically no reservation: *Star Wars* marked a watershed in the experience of film music *as* music. Williams's Skywalker Saga scores supercharged a nascent movement toward the celebration of film music on its own terms, without need of apology or adjustment to make it palatable to listeners. Starting with that first installment in 1977, the Skywalker soundtracks turned into objects of intense and lasting appreciation, both within the bounds of the filmic form and outside it. Among other things, the commercial and aesthetic triumph of *Star Wars* led to Williams's epochal appointment as conductor of the Boston Pops in 1980, an institution that over the next decades would become a nexus of the legitimization of film music, where, in Audissino's words, "the 'iron curtain' that isolates film music from art/absolute music" was decisively cracked.[14] *Star Wars*, more than any score before or since, taught the world not just to hear, but to *listen*, to film music.

Over the course of this chapter, we will endeavor to establish the groundwork for studying the Skywalker Saga *as* a musical experience. This will include examining the cycle's twin roots in nineteenth-century instrumental and operatic styles, its stylistic evolution across all nine films, and the integrity of each individual score as a compelling—if never perfectly unified—standalone musical text. First, however, it is worth exploring more deeply the meaning behind this term "symphonic" so often invoked by creators and critics alike. As already suggested, a rich and complex conceptual field surrounds the word and its relatives ("symphonism," "symphonist," and of course "symphony" itself), one which Williams and his commentators invariably, if sometimes implicitly and selectively, tap into. And it is a conceptual field that could stand to grow.

Star Wars Symphonism

Consider the following scenarios:

> *Having zoned out during a live performance of the* "Star Wars—Main Theme," *you are surprised to find yourself experiencing full-body chills when the contrabasses come in during Leia's theme.*
>
> *You're working out and listening to music. When you feel the need for a boost of adrenaline, you pull up the track "General Grievous" from* Revenge of the Sith *soundtrack and imagine yourself chasing down a rogue cyborg. Your heart rate shoots up.*
>
> *It's the last night of a Star Wars movie marathon. As Rey visits Tatooine in the final scene, your ears tingle with vague recognition. Listening closer to the harp and celesta figure playing in the background, you suspect the score is referencing and synthesizing motives from all three trilogies, though you can't place exactly how.*

Experiences like these are not how we assume music for cinema is normally heard—passively, distractedly, with attention focused squarely on a movie's dialogue or action.[15] Nor do these scenarios accord with customary ideas of appreciating *symphonic* works, as objects to be concentrated on fully, approached with a mindset that is somehow both totally rapt and coolly detached. Yet such encounters with film music are neither aberrant nor the mark of unsophisticated listening. Finding yourself profoundly moved, or motivated, or fascinated by the score for *Star Wars*—or any other screen music for that matter—is a way of participating with and understanding the world *through* music that deserves celebration and study. If traditional theories of cinematic listening see these scenarios as violations of screen scoring's prime directive to be "unheard," then they have missed whole universes of ways that lovers of music routinely engage with film scores, within and without their parent texts. And if traditional notions of symphonic listening fail to account for such profound forms of engagement, then we need a more expansive vision of symphonism.

Let us start with the two directors most closely associated with John Williams in his role as avatar of Hollywood symphonism. At the beginning of his career, Steven Spielberg found something enchanting in Williams's facility with an otherwise bygone musical idiom. After hearing the broad-brushed scores for Mark Rydell's *The Reivers* (1969) and *The Cowboys* (1972), Spielberg became determined to meet this "modern relic from a lost era of film symphonies," a man whom he felt was the right composer for his first feature film, *The Sugarland Express* (1974).[16] An early fruit of this collaboration would be the first of Williams's now famous "film symphonies," *Jaws* in 1975. The score is, in fairness, more than just its sharp-toothed theme. But what a theme! Williams's award-winning work on *Jaws* deserves its accolades, but the soundtrack's greatest distinction is the part it played in initiating a new economic model for American film production and distribution.

Spielberg's experience on *Jaws* led him to recommend Williams to George Lucas. Once again, the composer's knack for symphonism was hailed, now from Lucas: "[Spielberg] raved about Johnny, a wonderful jazz composer who also had an amazingly thorough understanding of symphonic music. Many film composers can write small orchestral pieces or various kinds of indigenous scores, but there are few with the talent to create the full-on, old fashioned movie score for a large orchestra that I envisioned."[17] If anything, Lucas's cinematic atavism was deeper than Spielberg's. The director frequently likened *Star Wars* to a silent film, insofar as it communicated to the audience primarily through visuals and music. (This framing is convenient when one considers Lucas's talents as a writer of spoken dialogue.) For Lucas, symphonism meant that "the music carries the story"—and more than only on an emotional level. By bestowing sonic and thematic continuity across cuts and scenes, music becomes the film's *structure*.[18]

Relevant though they are, Lucas's and Spielberg's conceptions only scratch the surface of what it means to call something "symphonic." The concept is so expansive that pithy definitions, such as the one offered in the *Grove Music Encyclopedia* entry on the subject, are necessarily inadequate. Per *Grove*,

Stylistic	Full orchestra, nineteenth-century size or larger
	Dense, blended late-Romantic-style orchestration
	Difficult but idiomatic and non-soloistic instrumental writing
	Conversant with/allusive to late-Romantic (esp. Germanic) repertoire
	Conversant with/allusive to Classical Hollywood repertoire
	Standardized plan of four contrasting but interdependent movements
	Sonata form as determinant of form of outer movements
Thematic	Simplicity and developmental amenability of thematic materials
	Strong formal contrast between themes
	Strong expressive/topical contrast between themes
	Motivically and topically diverse but organically unified materials
	Interweaving and interacting of themes
	Calculated, cyclic, rotational recurrence of thematic materials
	Continuous, goal-directed development
Aesthetic	Monumental in scope, duration, complexity
	Dynamic, impelled by contrasts and binaries
	In dialogue with past—possibly to point of artistic conservatism
	High prestige relative to other musical genres
	Democratic and populistic, communally accessible
	Structural autonomy; excludes reference to all external matters
	Intertextual; interpreted in terms of composer's cycle, larger tradition, etc.
Experiential	Irresistible; addresses listener in rhetorically strong way
	Embracing; encompasses wide range of human experience, events, memory
	Moving; emotionally direct, explicit, even manipulative
	Intellectual; demands cool, rational aesthetic contemplation
	Immersive; provides feeling of absorption, inhabitation, timelessness
	Spiritual; provides feeling of sublimity, exultation
	Imaginative; creates opening for personal imagery, association, narrative

Figure 1.1 Various meanings of "symphonic"

"the adjective 'symphonic' applied to a work implies that it is extended and thoroughly developed."[19] Figure 1.1 gathers a set of symphonic qualities extrapolated from the truly voluminous literature on the subject.

The twenty-eight traits in Figure 1.1 are distilled from a handful of the most important theorists of symphonism from the past one hundred years, in particular the Russian musician and critic Boris Asaf'yev, the German philosopher and social theorist Theodor Adorno, and the British musicologists Peter Franklin and David Fanning.[20] Those traits are sorted into four categories: (1) *stylistic*, encompassing the broadest of generic and idiomatic expectations; (2) *thematic*, pertaining to the character of melodic and motivic materials; (3) *aesthetic*, which involves the music's social and philosophical aspirations; and (4) *experiential*, the actual subjective, phenomenal encounter with the music. The point of reference here is the symphonic repertoire from Haydn and (especially) Beethoven onward; the implicit association with Austro-German music culture after Haydn is unavoidable. Deplore it as reductive and ahistorical if you will, but few today, on hearing "symphonic," think first of an eighteenth-century symphonist like Johann Stamitz—let alone an eighteenth-century *Italian* like Giovanni Battista Sammartini—however influential they were. That said, most of the enumerated qualities are not wedded to the actual form of the Classical symphony. Many have been ascribed to other genres, including opera, ballet, and even rock and pop music. Nor should the categories be taken as rigid or exclusive. Some are flatly contradictory, like the opposing aesthetic pulls of structural autonomy and intertextuality. Such paradoxes befit a musical genre driven by contrasts and binaries.

Not all the qualities in Figure 1.1 apply in obvious ways to the music of *Star Wars*, if they do at all. It would require some very willful mishearing to interpret any cue as conforming to sonata form, even in the most unconventional or vestigial manner. That said, it is at times possible to discern the spirit, if not the letter, of those traditional formal expectations in Williams's music. Throughout the Skywalker Saga, one hears contrasts between themes considerably more sharply drawn than in most other film scores—and not just along the accustomed modal or affective polarities, but a host of other axes: diatonically functional versus pantriadic, grammatical versus discursive, tight-knit versus lyrical, developmental versus immobile, and more. Similarly, the closely regulated tonal games of the Classical symphony are mostly irrelevant to this series; there will be no mention of essential expositional closure or medial caesuras in these pages. But the idea of tonal *drama*—of structural dissonance, harmonic memory, modulation as adventure, tonal stability as an expressive device—is very much at play. These formal qualities are important to *Star Wars*' underscore, and they become decisive in Williams's set pieces and concert arrangements, a topic tackled in Chapter 8.

Before we delve into the aesthetic aspirations and experiential postures that attend symphonic writing and listening, it is important to highlight one of the more fraught qualities in Figure 1.1: the symphony's prestige. The point of this book is not to assert a symphonic status for *Star Wars* because it would boost or rescue the scores from some non-prestigious musical ghetto. Nor is it an attempt to forcibly jam them into a different musical genre than they already occupy. Such projects ought to prompt strenuous objections from anyone aware of the valuative agendas embedded within symphonism—and canon formation for that matter. But none of this should stop us from exploring how Williams's scores are symphonic, or perhaps better, how they exist within a discursive frame of symphonism. Many listeners and critics already treat the *Star Wars* soundtracks in this way. And the act of granting, even in a highly qualified way, a symphonic imprimatur to the Skywalker Saga is a signal with wider implications. It suggests that *a lot* more screen music should be admitted to this category, not left on the margins of Western music history as an intrinsically lesser expression of musical thought, just because it does not play by an old or orthodox genre's rules. Idealistically, the discussion to follow will be read as a plea for inclusion and a broadening of perspective, not an underhanded way of smuggling Beethovenian values into a kids' movie series.

Symphonic Orchestration

Form may be of perpetual fascination to music theorists, but when most commentators describe a film score as "symphonic," they probably have something more immediate in mind: the first trait in Figure 1.1, the sound of a large orchestra. This instrumental assemblage enjoyed its heyday during the Studio Era of Hollywood, at which time it served as the default resource for composers with as otherwise diverse aesthetics as Max Steiner, Miklós Rózsa, and Franz Waxman. "Symphonic" in the orchestrational sense implies a contrast not just with smaller ensembles, but alternative performance forces, specifically electronic ones. By the time of *Star Wars* '77, the groundbreaking electronic score for *Forbidden Planet* was over twenty years old; unearthly timbres from non-acoustic sources were easier to produce than ever, and as a matter of expressive content, eminently legible—if still deeply strange—for audiences to hear in sci-fi movies. But the electronic path was never one Lucas and Williams entertained. They agreed at the outset on the fittingness of an "acoustic and natural" score, one arrayed in familiar if then-passé orchestral garb. The sound of the symphony orchestra alone, irrespective of any particular idiom, would orient the viewers emotionally and serve as a pre-acclimatized counterweight to the alienating weirdness of "creatures unknown, places unseen, and noises unheard of."[21] Synthesized sounds do peek into a corner or two of Episodes V and VI, and even constitute timbral focal points in a handful of cues in the Prequels, but they are always treated as sonic adjuncts or special effects.[22] A *Star Wars* score always has an acoustic heart.

The four chambers of this orchestrational organ are the string, wind, brass, and percussion sections. And they are big, muscular chambers. By any standard, *Star Wars* '77 employed a large orchestra: eighty-six players from the London Symphony Orchestra, a number that would swell with subsequent installments, particularly as human voices became a significant component of the series' timbral palette.[23] However, "symphonic" does not just entail the performance ensemble by itself, but a certain manner of orchestrating for it. An indisputable trademark of the Skywalker cycle is Williams's brass writing, which occupies the forefront of many of the series' most arresting musical moments, starting with the two excerpts cited on this book's first page. Woodwinds provide constant color and commentary, the percussion, especially timpani, heft and urgency. The orchestra's auxiliary forces—harp, celesta, piano, chorus—may add subtle atmosphere or be a powerful, scene-defining timbre, depending on the cue. But, ultimately—and in proper Romantic fashion—the string section is the driving pump of *Star Wars*' dramatic underscore, powering most of the moment-to-moment musical mythmaking.

Williams does not choose colors from his timbral palette arbitrarily; instruments and instrumental combinations are vital storytelling devices in this series. Daniel Godsil, in his study of the soundworld of *A New Hope*, argues that Williams's orchestration "takes on a narrative function of its own. . . . [I]t elaborates and amplifies aspects of the film equally as well as melodic craft."[24] Though historically treated as a secondary parameter by music theorists, timbre is very much a *primary* one in *Star Wars*, and we will do well to keep this in mind lest we start fixating on the more easily systematized and analyzed elements of harmony or motive.

One way that the orchestral soundworld of this series tells its stories is by channeling meanings and associations from prior symphonic and symphony-adjacent genres. The lushness and density of detail of a late-Romantic paragon like Strauss or Rachmaninoff (and Hollywood successors like Korngold and Newman) are characteristic of *Star Wars* at its most iconic. Less often do we hear a Mahlerian chamber-like refinement or Stravinskian brittleness, though passages of comparatively exposed instrumentation do play a limited role, especially early in the franchise. In later entries, motoric textures and arpeggiated figurations in the manner of the minimalists Steve Reich, Philip Glass, and John Adams work their way into the orchestra. And across all nine films, Williams's timbral palette borrows hues from Holst, Vaughan Williams, Walton, Prokofiev, Shostakovich, and Ravel. In particular, the latter's *Daphnis et Chloé*—possibly the most symphonic piece in the ballet repertoire—furnishes precedents for many of the series' signature orchestrational routines: its high wind curlicues, lumbering bass ostinati, alluring dreamy choral washes, and rapid trumpet triadic planes.[25] Importantly, though difficult to articulate in precise terms, Williams's *harmonic* sensibility in *Star Wars* is itself often a function of his orchestration, a point to which we will return in the final chapter.

Symphonic Aspiration

The late Romantic orchestra, with its timbral inexhaustibility and symbolic freight, is a *sine qua non* of the *Star Wars* soundscape. But for some commentators, there is more to the series' symphonic status than its choice of ensemble. Symphonic signification is paramount; Susan McClary notes that "the skill with which John Williams . . . manipulates the semiotic codes of the late nineteenth-century symphony in *E.T.* or *Star Wars* is breathtaking."[26] So is formal construction. Mervyn Cooke characterizes the whole of Williams's imprint on cinema as a "new symphonism," an adoption not just of the instrumental forces of the Golden Age composers, but the "structural principles" of their craft.[27] Those principles include enriched tonality, leitmotif, precise synchronization, emotional directness, and wall-to-wall scoring (or something close to it). Above all, there is a grandeur of conception to the new symphonism; Williams's music for *Star Wars*, like the output of Newman and Steiner, is *expansive* in scope. It takes sizable durations to make its point. It is unified in its intent but eclectic in its stylistic roots. Its materials are diverse, and all bear the potential—taken or not—for thorough thematic development. The aspirations of symphonic music are as great as the artform can sustain, its dimensions grand to the point of unmappability.[28]

And yet, for some symphonic aspirants, it is not enough just to be cosmic: the work must also be *dialectical*, animated by deep and dynamic conflicts.[29] A symphonic piece is imagined as a sonic playground—or battlefield—where various dichotomies and binaries are set in contest, many of which exceed simple technical content like key schemes or differentiated tempi and veer into the philosophical. Among such "grand dualisms" that are ripe for symphonic working-out that David Fanning cites are "good/evil, life/death, light/dark, movement/stasis, mental/physical, old/new."[30] Fanning may be echoing other theorists of symphonism like Theodor Adorno here, but the dichotomous, metaphysically charged terminology might as well have come from Yoda.

There is also a grand *meta*-dualism in the discourse of symphonism, a dichotomy that proves essential in understanding Williams's contribution to the *Star Wars* franchise. Succinctly, it is the contrast between tight self-sufficiency on one hand, and unbounded eclecticism and universality on the other. Nowhere is the dialectic articulated more clearly than in a famous exchange in 1907 between Gustav Mahler and Jean Sibelius, then preeminent symphonists of Austria and Finland, respectively. Both happen to be composers with a purported imprint on the Skywalker scores.[31] As Sibelius's biographer Karl Ekman recounts the Finnish master saying:

> When our [Mahler's and my] conversation touched on the symphony, I said that I admired its style and severity of form, and the profound logic that created an inner connection between all the motifs. This was my experience in the course of my creative work. Mahler's opinion was just the opposite. "No!" he said, "The symphony must be like the world. It must be all-embracing."[32]

There is a whiff of overstatement in this anecdote, on the part of both composers (and probably Ekman too). Sibelius's own symphonies, tightly argued though they are, are also expansive worlds unto themselves, and few now would argue that Mahler's essays in the genre are not marvels of motivic rigor sustained over the most gargantuan of canvases. But this meta-dualism is nevertheless quite vividly active, in their works—and in *Star Wars*.

On one hand, the nine Skywalker soundtracks have as strong a claim to Sibelian organic integration as any film series in history. Each is knitted together by a profoundly connected and carefully developed weave of themes and motifs. This organic homogeneity also extends to technical procedures beyond motivicism; the *Star Wars* scores are full of recurrent and arguably unity-bestowing quirks of voice-leading, harmonization, chord spacing, associative orchestration, and much else. Nor does the ambition for self-consistency stop at the level of the single score. Installment after installment, Williams aimed to "use the earlier material" and to "develop new material that would coexist with it and hopefully feel like a part of the fabric [of the larger series]."[33] In fact, some of that new material is *so* in keeping with other, earlier *Star Wars* music that it can be difficult to determine what is a distinct new theme, an intentional variant on an old one, or a happy but unplanned motivic convergence.

Williams has at times imagined the Saga in biological terms, as a growing organism: "It does feel for me, writing the music for *Star Wars*, that it's one entity, that it's one body, and that I'm adding parts to it every time, and that there is a continuity there in musical terms that is, as far as I know in film *unique*."[34] Of course, not everyone agrees that Williams's music attains the level of motivic systematicity or formal inevitability worthy of Sibelius (nor do all commentators on Sibelius for that matter!). And it is true that there are moments of thematic underdevelopment and spans of less-than-"severe" formal argumentation throughout the franchise. Certainly, the most extreme version of symphonic organicism—a vision like Adorno's of radical motivic integration, constant development, and impregnable self-sufficiency—is unlikely to be found in the pages of *Star Wars*.[35] But the compositional logic and sometimes breathtaking integration of these scores tends to shine through upon close analysis, and a qualified type of Sibelian organicism is something that will be vigorously, if not dogmatically, argued for as we proceed.

Where Sibelius is focused on a single argument, Mahler squeezes the totality of human experience into four panoramic movements: the summits of joy and hammer blows of tragedy, the thrills of love and the pits of regret, the lightest of comedy and bitterest of satire. If the case for Sibelian organicism in *Star Wars* is plausible if in need of qualification, the universalizing aesthetics of Mahler are everywhere plainly in evidence. Williams's Skywalker symphonies are as eclectic in idiom, as overflowing in ideas and references as any large-scale compositions from the past hundred years. Though there are few passages that sound directly like anything Mahler wrote, the epithet "Mahlerian" might well be more apt for the Skywalker Saga than any other composer-based proper adjective. The expansiveness of spirit and omnivory of style is clear from the first dozen bars of *A New Hope*, which stitch together a half-dozen musical styles at least—more on this in the next chapter.

If anything, this stylistic heterogeneity *grows* with the next few installments, peaking in the Prequel Trilogy before receding in the leaner, less externally referential Sequels.

Symphonic Imagination

The Skywalker scores really are musical worlds, containing more than could ever be captured by a neat, unified organicist account. And like any world, they invite exploration, immersion, inhabitation. Though Adorno's maximalist stance toward motivic autonomy will not get us far in understanding Williams's music, his ideas about the *experience* of a symphonic work will. For Adorno, "symphonic" entailed a feeling of absorption and timelessness. The listening subjects find themselves *inside* the piece, invited into "a symphonic space . . . not only as something before one, but something around one, a medium in which one lives."[36] This immersiveness is enabled as much by the work's internal cohesion as by its rhetorical posture—"Attend to me! Give yourself over to me!" For those in the right mindset, a symphonic piece of music can seem to arrest, even obliterate the flow of time. Indeed, to the detached, contemplative listener, the totality of the symphonic artwork can be perceived as if in one transcendental instant.

Alas, nothing disrupts the "symphonic contraction of time" for Adorno quite as egregiously as music with an episodic organization—or worse, a story-driven basis. But let us not count *Star Wars* out just yet; after all, Adorno vaunted Mahler above all contemporary symphonists, and Mahler's symphonic imagination is nothing if not episodic, extramusically dense, and narratively charged. To hear the Skywalker Saga symphonically cannot mean ignoring that narrative content and treating it as absolute music, be it tautly controlled like Sibelius or an overflowing crucible like Mahler. *Star Wars* symphonism is inseparable from storytelling.

Peter Franklin, a scholar of both Classical Hollywood film music and late-Romanticism, provides a way forward. Franklin takes seriously the idea that music of the cinematic Golden Age exists in the same tradition as Beethoven and Mahler, and that films and film scores are "able to construct what we might legitimately call a symphonic experience," even if only a "refracted and fragmented echo" of that tradition.[37] He grants that the idiom readily adapted certain symphonic structures and technical resources—"recurring material and thematic or motivic signifiers," even if their capacity for long-range coherence is likely degraded by the exigencies of cinematic form. Franklin also sees a strong affinity in film music's textual scope and philosophical ambitions, as scores "may span lifetimes and seek to encompass and dramatically 'explain' large and potentially chaotic tracts," even if their aspirations are debased when put in service of populist escapist entertainment.[38] But Franklin's most profound insight concerns not style or aesthetics, but the symphonic experience itself.

The essential context here is the symphony as it was written after Richard Wagner. In the hands of late-Romantic composers like Tchaikovsky, Chausson, Strauss, and Zemlinsky, the genre became a site of wild contest between opposing aesthetic imperatives left unresolved in Wagner's wake. Composers now needed to negotiate between autonomy and programmaticism, formal convention and expressive need, unending melody and dramatic discontinuity, moral edification and hedonic enjoyment, liberatory musical truth content and emotional manipulation—the stakes of these dichotomies were heady indeed. Yet despite all these internal contradictions, Franklin argues the post-Wagnerian symphony actually ended up providing its audience with a new form of control over their experience, a "creative, subjective *agency*" to seek out musical pleasure.

And the pleasures the post-Wagnerian symphony offered its listeners were many. You could delight in tracking a cyclically recurring motif; quiver in anticipation of the climax of some indulgently beautiful or erotically charged theme; thrill to the sensation of having your body vibrated by a sixteen-piece brass complement playing fortissimo. Of particular relevance to the cinematic repertoire a few decades to come, the late-Romantic symphony invited its audiences to indulge in an imaginative fantasy of narrative construction, crafting a story from its succession of musical incidents, perhaps with the listeners imagining themselves as a protagonist. (Of course, programmatic symphonies have a deeper lineage than the post-Wagnerians. One subgenre of note, the "Battle Symphony," will be explored in the final chapter.) No, these are certainly not the kinds of pleasure that symphonic purists value. But whether idealists like Adorno wished it or not, the pursuit of musical euphoria is how most audiences accessed this enthralling repertoire. And the majority of other musical styles too, if we are honest.

Franklin's next step is to ascribe this late-symphonic listening practice to Classical Hollywood movie music, both as underscore and in standalone media like albums and concerts. Listening to the soundtrack of Erich

Wolfgang Korngold's *Anthony Adverse*, for instance, may foster a debased form of narrativized hearing that would make Adorno shudder, but not one that comes at the expense of aesthetic unity. Korngold's score offers "a cumulatively cogent structure of action, anticipation, and reminiscence" that is quintessentially symphonic. Its narrative-sculpting, pleasure-eliciting affordances are not a hindrance but a defining feature.[39]

Being deeply versed in the repertoire of post-Wagnerian symphonies is no requisite for this kind of imaginative hearing, though it enriches the experience immensely. Nor does one need physical media to cultivate it: when the music is known well enough, a person's private storehouse of memory is sufficient. Franklin's most persuasive case for the innate symphonism of Classic-style film scoring is an anecdote, not involving the Golden Age scores from Steiner or Korngold, which he otherwise focuses on, but *Star Wars*. He recounts witnessing a boy on a train in 2002 who, in an imaginative reverie, quietly sang to himself Skywalker-Saga themes while playing with a toy light saber. The young fan was using his knowledge of the leitmotivic material of the series "to accompany or even structure something seen in his mind's eye, a sort of virtual movie" that was *intrinsically* musical.[40] Even at seven years old, assuredly unaware of patterns of reception of pieces from a hundred years prior, this boy "was visualizing a musical narrative in a way that could have been equally appropriate to a symphony" written in that post-Wagnerian idiom. Not exactly the dispassionate Adornian connoisseur, but to Franklin, this boy's activity was no less historically valid, no less legitimately symphonic.

At risk of summarizing the unsummarizable, here is an overview of the ground we have just covered. Symphonism refers to many things, some contradictory. It is an orchestral sound, lush and romantic. It is an aspiration for, if never full attainment of, unity of motivic and formal structure. It is an expansiveness, a world-encompassing eclecticism. And it is a distinct way of experiencing musical time, one that is immersive and imaginative. To hear something symphonically is to plumb its compositional intricacies and arguments to the last note, but it is also a willingness to give oneself over to the many forms of sheer pleasure—especially the pleasure of *story*—that the music affords. Applied to music written for the movies, this attitude admits all the illustrative, associative, and affective potencies of film. Not just symphonic listening, then, but *cine*-symphonic listening. To listen to *Star Wars* cine-symphonically is to approach its score with the same curiosity, the same emotional openness and attentiveness—though it need not be dispassionate or uninterrupted—that one would when attending an orchestra concert. Or, perhaps, the opera...

Space Opera

The theories of symphonism encountered in the previous section are largely the brainchildren of twentieth-century thinkers like Asaf'yev and Adorno. However, the terms of this discussion were set during the 1800s. After Beethoven, all Western classical composers had to grapple with the legacy he left behind. A vigorous discourse emerged concerning symphonic autonomy, rigor, and pretension, and by mid-century, one figure stood at the center of every debate on the subject: Richard Wagner. To properly situate *Star Wars* musically, we must grapple with him.

Not a symphonist of note himself, but a composer of opera, Wagner nevertheless went to great lengths to place himself as the true recipient of the Beethovenian gauntlet. For his legion of partisans, he was not just successful; he eclipsed the achievement of his model. In Beethoven's Ninth Symphony, which famously exceeded the bounds of instrumental form with its texted and in places patently operatic choral finale, Wagner found his lodestone. He envisioned his operas as the ideal outlet for those poetic and dramatic energies released by the Ninth. Wagner proceeded to shatter the formulaic containers that had governed opera for generations, most notably the distinction between aria (lyrical, periodic, music-centered) and recitative (declamatory, aperiodic, text-centered). With that binary collapsed, opera could finally take on the vitality of thematic development, continuity of musical thought, and autonomy of the work-concept that, for Wagner, amounted to the Beethovenian ideal. The style that results in *Tristan und Isolde* and *Götterdämmerung* is singularly fascinating in the history of music, not just for the spellbinding appeal of the music itself but also for the way it manages to project so many "pro-symphonic" features while simultaneously sounding so revolutionarily anti-symphonic.

It is difficult to overstate the shockwaves in European musical culture left by Wagner's operas, especially the so-called "Music Dramas" that commenced with the composition of *Das Rheingold* in 1854 and ended with *Parsifal* in 1882. One of history's great victims of logorrhea, Wagner also produced a tremendous corpus of written tracts and screeds, some of them quite influential. His polemics contain, among other things, the coinage of the term "absolute music" (which he meant disparagingly) and no shortage of over-articulated, self-aggrandizing, often nakedly bigoted theorizations of his musical practices.[41] It comes as either a relief or an unshakable source of anxiety for generations of Wagner-lovers that his music is, despite all the noise, as utterly captivating as it is.

Accounts are plentiful of Wagner's anticipation of cinematic aesthetics—not just musical but, as befits the originator of *Gesamtkunstwerk*, everything worthy of the adjective "filmic." We have already seen one manifestation of the Wagnerian ripple-effect: the narrativizing turn taken in late Romantic music, which offers historical precedent for treating *Star Wars* as an inherently musical experience. Where the various meanings of "symphonic" in the previous section were rather abstract, the conceptual cluster surrounding "Wagnerian" is full of directly applicable and concrete compositional routines with which to inspect this series. To call the *Star Wars* films "Space Operas" is thus not just to locate them in the same melodramatic sci-fi genre as books like *John Carter of Mars* or serials like *Flash Gordon*: it is to recognize an essential and constantly apparent musical lineage from Wagner.[42]

So overwhelming is the richness of Wagnerian opera, and so numerous the points of contact with *Star Wars*, that we must be careful to be concise and precise here, lest this book become more about Wagner than Williams. As Figure 1.1 did for symphonism, Figure 1.2 breaks down the "Wagnerian" conceptual cluster. Entire libraries can be packed with books explaining Wagner's aesthetic principles and techniques, which were neither internally consistent nor constant across his career, and no small amount of ink has been spilled exploring their assumption into film and film music.[43] Still, Figure 1.2 gives us a place to start. Two categories help differentiate between formal techniques (thematic construction, formal organization, etc.) and aesthetic and dramatic matters (subject, iconography, temporality). Even more than with the "symphonic," these are but the shakiest of divisions. Wagnerian style is its substance, and the medium its message.

Every single trait listed in Figure 1.2 could be attributed to *Star Wars*. As the most immediately evident of Wagner's fingerprints on the music of the series, ***leitmotif*** deserves its spot at the top of the table. Notwithstanding loose precedents in Weber, Spohr, and Marschner, the leitmotif concept is a true Wagnerian innovation. Earlier applications of thematic recurrence in dramatic music tended to involve poignant melodies recalled only rarely and with little alteration (so-called "reminiscence motifs") or single melodic subjects that persisted across a work (the Berliozian *idée fixe*). Leitmotifs, by

Formal	**Leitmotif**: distinct, recurrent, symbolic, variation-prone motifs
	Thematic Transformation: variation, mutation, evolution, etc. of motifs
	Associativity: non-melodic parameters given a signifying role
	Tonality: pervasive linear and pantriadic chromaticism, wandering tonality
	Musical Prose: non-periodic & non-repetitive units, 'poetic musical periods'
	Continuity: unending melody, artful transition, blurring of aria/recitative
	Extractability: performance of preludes, set pieces, and 'bleeding chunks'
	Timbre: massive, texturally complex, blended, foregrounded orchestra
Aesthetic	**Gesamtkunstwerk**: total artwork, unifying all fine-arts disciplines
	Myth: legendary or fantastical subject matter and iconography
	Phantasmagoria: experience is immersive, hypnotic, overwhelming
	Commentative: orchestral underscore as chorus, revealer of the psyche
	Reflexivity: constant self-reference, esp. by internal narrative, monologue
	Temporality: layered time-frames, suggestion of past/present/future tense
	Legacy : (self-)location in Beethovenian symphonic lineage
	Message: strong if allegoricized philosophical/ethical/political outlook

Figure 1.2 Various meanings of "Wagnerian"

contrast, are the very atoms out of which the epic architectures of Wagner's mature operas are built, integral and infinitely recombinable.

Definitions vary, but for the purposes of this study, a leitmotif has four basic properties: it is (1) melodically distinctive, (2) laden with symbolism, (3) prone to variation, and (4) noticeably recurring.[44] These pliable particles of musical matter were Wagner's solution to the problem of musical coherence in the absence of the prefabricated musical forms of traditional opera that he discarded. Carl Dahlhaus observes that the symphonic quality of Wagner's music largely inheres in its reliance on leitmotif, which "can be viewed as a method intended to 'sublate' the symphony into the music drama. . . . Unlike reminiscence motives, which were restricted to turning points in the plot, the leitmotivs in a music drama form a dense web spread over the whole of the orchestral setting, determining its structure at any given moment."[45] Leitmotif provided a means of musical storytelling often far more vivid and compelling than the words sung by Wagner's dramatis personae. And its adaptation—*not adoption*—in the Skywalker Saga is a defining musical characteristic as well as the most tangible technique that Williams revived from the Classical Hollywood scoring practice.

The leitmotifs of *Star Wars* account for many of its most well-known sonic emblems: the FORCE theme, VADER's march, DUEL OF THE FATES. But the category also encompasses some recurring ideas—GLOOM, for instance, or the MAP motif—that are so understated as to go unnoticed by all but the most attentive listeners. These elusive leitmotifs are likely less iconic than many *non-recurrent* themes, such as Episode V's "The Asteroid Field." Determining how to label, categorize, and relate these melodic identifications is a huge project, made challenging not so much by the sheer volume of music involved, but by those textual contingencies mentioned at the end of this book's Introduction. While sorting out all these distinctions and designations can seem like an adventure in esoterica, the question that underlies the study of leitmotif is of deep significance to both filmgoers and music appreciators: how do these little musical atoms end up being such potent storytellers?

Williams's use of the leitmotif technique can be impressively systematic and inventive. Few composers in the history of film boast such a natural skill for musical characterization, and fewer still were granted such a vast canvas on which to ply their thematic imagination. Yet the leitmotivic approach Williams employs in *Star Wars* is at other times frustratingly—or, depending on one's perspective, *frustratedly*—inconsistent. Leitmotif is the first, and for many only, point of music-analytical contact with these scores. Little surprise, then, that the most pointed critiques of Williams's contribution to the Skywalker Saga revolve around his treatment of leitmotif. Nor is it startling that these grumbles invariably echo the same ones leveled against Wagner a century before him.

We will defer an extended exploration of these critical fault lines for the time being, but the crux of the matter is not too hard to articulate. It is the issue of rigidity: that is, how firmly or flexibly leitmotifs maintain their symbolic content and/or their formal structure. Adorno, who inveighed against the technique both in Wagner and film music, voiced the basic complaint memorably in his monograph *In Search of Wagner*, accusing leitmotifs of being little more than "miniature pictures" whose "supposed psychological variations involve only a change of lighting."[46] Fifty years later in his groundbreaking essay "Star Wars, Music, and Myth," James Buhler claimed, with some Adornian hyperbole, that "nothing actually happens musically in any of these scores."[47]

Adorno and Buhler are formidable music analysts, and their claims deserve careful consideration, which will arrive in subsequent chapters. At this stage, it suffices to note that while rigidity of meaning and form can be a feature of (some) leitmotivic material in the Skywalker Saga, its fixity in such cases is usually a deliberate storytelling choice. The fact that VADER's theme (a.k.a. "The Imperial March") appears so often in *The Empire Strikes Back*, and so rarely with any development, may grate on the ears of someone who dislikes the theme, but it is no artistic shortcoming. The leitmotif's rigidity is itself symbolic, a signal of the oppressive, inescapable might of Vader and his Empire. It is also not the norm. Careful analysis of the Skywalker scores reveals that leitmotifs are very much prone to transformation of both symbolic/semantic and formal/syntactic content. Case in point: starting in the next movie and continuing through the rest of the saga, the VADER motif grows, develops, and transforms in exciting ways. Thematic rigidity is a moving target.

Within the present discussion of the stylistic bases of *Star Wars*, it will serve to focus on one aspect of the Wagnerian style: ***musical prose***. A somewhat fuzzy practice whose formulation owes as much to Schoenberg and Dahlhaus as it does Wagner himself, musical prose is more of an ideal than a set of compositional instructions.[48] In contrast with the repetitiveness and restraints of poetry, musical prose is continuously new and unconstrained, free of "padding or empty repetition" as Schoenberg sees it.[49] Its spans are not four-square phrases but irregular units that are impelled forward by elided cadences, sequences, pedals, and harmonic special effects. Dense and developmental, but also capricious and nonhierarchical, Wagnerian musical prose epitomizes the simultaneously pro-symphonic and anti-symphonic impulses in the post-Beethovenian music dramas. This discursive idiom proved the ideal, probably inevitable, vessel for the continuously unspooling motivic commentary that threads together the incidents of a *Rheingold* or a *Tristan*. It is also the model for much of Williams's leitmotivic underscore, especially for scenes heavy in dialogue and steeped in mythic subtext. Williams's approach to musical prose changes in a few ways across his entries in the Skywalker Saga, as we will see. Nevertheless, certain features remain consistent across all nine installments. These include tonal mutability, non-periodicity of phrases, and the careful allocation of thematically articulated versus thematically unmarked material.

One last hallmark of the Wagnerian style—and the symphonic idioms it drew from and later influenced—carries over into the Skywalker Saga:

musical tense. Again by analogy with written language, orchestral underscore is capable of more than just describing the present; it can evoke the past and provide glimpses of the future.[50] Musical prose is wonderfully effective in generating the feeling of mythic temporality so important to *Star Wars.* It can both describe and surprise, foreshadow or remember, sometimes selectively, often fallibly. And while purely metaphorical—music is not actually a language and does not really have grammatical tense—Williams's brand of musical prose nevertheless carefully teaches us to listen in such suggestively metaphorical terms. While training Luke in *The Empire Strikes Back*, Yoda tells him, "Through the Force, things you will see. Other places. The future. The past. Old friends long gone." Substitute "hear" for "see" and "Wagnerian scoring" for "the Force," and the Jedi Master could have been describing Williams's music. And on the topic of scoring Luke and Yoda, it is well past time to put these abstract categories to use and examine some actual *Star Wars* music.

Luke's Farewell

To establish the basic soundworld of this saga, we can turn to one representative scene. Luke's departure from Dagobah in *The Empire Strikes Back* features three melodically well-identified characters (Luke, Yoda, and Obi-Wan), a narrative turning point (Luke's decision to cut short his training to save his friends), and heaps of pregnant dialogue regarding fate, the Force, and such. Besides containing some beautiful leitmotivic statements and vibrant orchestrations, this sequence exemplifies Williams's brand of film-musical prose—that synthesis of operatic and symphonic impulses which is so unique and unusual among commonly heard musical genres.

At two and a half minutes, "Luke's Farewell" is the length of a short song or instrumental miniature. But it differs in almost every other way from styles more accustomed to a "music-first" mode of listening. The sequence, which is the second half of a larger, four-minute-long cue ("Lando's Palace"), is built from seven successive spans of distinct but connected melodic and expressive content. These units of musical form below the level of cue will be called *modules* from this point forward. An additional "zeroth" module serves to segue from the previous scene on Bespin, after C-3PO is blasted by hidden stormtroopers. Within "Luke's Farewell," Williams showcases four leitmotifs—LUKE, FORCE, VADER, and YODA—that we will get to know well over the course of this book. The cue traverses eight keys, first hovering around G♯ minor and ending via a winding but intentional path in G♮ minor. Though highly mobile, tonality is a meticulously controlled parameter in Williams's underscore and a significant factor in generating a symphonic "long line." As his orchestrator for the Original Trilogy Herb Spencer noted, "He sees [scenes and films] with continuity. He doesn't see them as 30-second things, but he sees the whole damn thing, because the key structures are so well managed."[51]

With respect to thematic and pitch design, "Luke's Farewell" thus represents a kind of median *Star Wars* cue. It is neither as static as some purely atmospheric spans nor as changeable as the average action set piece. But while sitting between extremes of immobility and dynamism, the Wagnerian prose-based scoring illustrated here nevertheless tends to be the *least* conventional in form, hardest to square with the expectations of what a proper "piece" of music—symphonic, vocal, or otherwise—ought to do. In that way, sequences like "Luke's Farewell" are among the sharpest tools with which to test the limits of cine-symphonic listening.

Figure 1.3 summarizes the basic form of "Luke's Farewell" in terms of thematic material, tonality, and the main instrumental carrier of melody. The reader is encouraged to listen to the cue several times while following along with this diagram. Consider the music both in its filmically intended form, as underscore for a specific audiovisual scenario, and in the less orthodox "symphonic" mode. When inspecting the cue in conjunction with image and dialogue, ask yourself why certain leitmotifs seem to occur when they do, and how the overall emotional arc of the scene is guided by their succession and interaction. When listening to "Luke's Farewell" on its own, think about whether those two and a half minutes make sense as a single, sustained

1:22:48 1:22:55 1:23:14 1:23:29 1:23:38 1:23:59 1:24:35 1:24:49 1:25:25

[0]	1	2	3	4	5	6	7
--	LUKE	FORCE	VADER	--	YODA	LUKE	FORCE
Em / G♯m	E/G♯→D/F♯	Fm	Gm	B♭sus^2_4	G	B	Gm HC i→IV PAC V→I
f. hn	cl, e. hn	fl, ob, bsn	b. cl, bsn	f. hn	fl, ob	f. hn	fl, ob → wws → vc
Bespin: 3PO attacked	*Dagobah*: Luke packs	Obi-Wan appears	Warnings about the Dark Side	Luke vows to return	Yoda makes final plea	Luke's resolve is clear	Final farewells, Luke takes off, "…no, there is another…."

Figure 1.3 Form of "Luke's Farewell" (ESB, 8m3)

musical thought. For both modes, pay special attention to the cue's emotional arc and especially the way in which it concludes.

Much can be said about these forty-two measures of music, and in subsequent chapters we will devote more sustained analysis to cues of its type. At present, it will suffice to list a few representative aspects.

- **Cadences**: Firm phrase-ending punctuation is either absent or evaded. Even themes that complete their main ideas land on unresolved sonorities—e.g., YODA ending on an A^9/G chord in module 5. The exception is for the end of cues, as with the Perfect Authentic Cadence (PAC) that closes the FORCE in module 7.
- **Full Themes**: The one complete thematic statement (FORCE in module 7) is reserved for the *ending*, where it serves a formal bookend on multiple levels, closing out the leitmotif itself, the cue 8m3, and ultimately, the film's whole second act.
- **Key Changes**: Chromatic modulation, both within and between themes, is a pervasive and strong expressive device—e.g., the shift from B to Gm between modules 6 & 7.
- **Phrase Lengths**: Melodic phrases and modules are irregular in duration, with changes of meter as well as free expansion and fragmentation of thematic ideas.
- **Signification**: Leitmotifs are deployed at varying degrees of literality, from on-the-nose to semantically oblique. In general, the lengthier the leitmotivic statement, the less likely it is to be subordinated to immediate audiovisual events.
- **Temporality**: The music can be responsive and quick to change to the dramatic present, but it also conveys at various junctures a sense of deep history and vague foreshadowing.
- **Thematic Interactions**: The impression of a conversation happening between musical ideas runs through the whole cue, both in explicit ways—e.g., VADER-tinged-with-YODA disrupting the FORCE in module 3—and as a more indefinable push-and-pull of identification and memory.
- **Tonal Centers**: A sense of a stable tonic is never a given, but always provisional, something to be posited, undermined, or (as with the tension between G minor and major) only gradually clarified.

- **Transitions**: Thematic phrases and modules are conjoined by simple but elegant bridging procedures, including pedals, sequences, common-tones, and interstitial passages.
- **Unmarked Materials**: Spans of less thematically distinct material still may derive from established motifs, especially as a means of subtly preparing them—e.g., the horn solo in module 4, which is a refraction of Yoda's theme.

Other aspects of this cue embodying Wagnerian principles require more extended analysis than the present discussion demands. However, two facets are worth drawing attention to. First, the importance of fluid bridging passages between leitmotivic thoughts cannot be overstated: not without reason did Wagner refer to the "most delicate and profound art, the art of transition."[52] Without disregarding the role of the inverse—musical disjunction and discreteness have a role to play in *Star Wars*, too—prosy passages like "Luke's Farewell" demonstrate how thoroughly Williams internalized the lessons of late-Romantic transitional alchemy.

Figure 1.4 presents the hinges between a few leitmotivic modules where Williams's transitional artistry is on display. Here and elsewhere in this book, the excerpts are highly simplified. Even in an unfussy sequence like "Luke's Farewell," Williams's textures and harmonies are too complex to represent in their entirety. The notation of these passages is reduced to the barest essentials, whatever is relevant for whatever analytical point is being made. In this case, that means only the main melodic line, plus chord symbols and indicators of active leitmotifs.

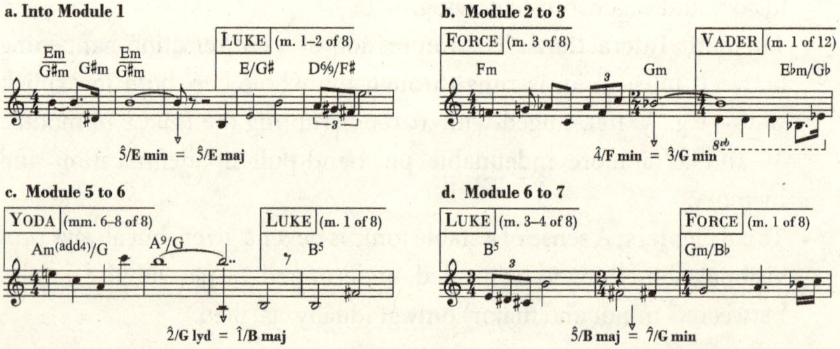

Figure 1.4 Examples of transitions between modules in "Luke's Farewell"

The transitional deftness of these passages depends on the coordination of two compositional techniques: the irresolution of the first module and the smoothness of connection with the second. Often, smoothness is produced through a common tone—a pitch shared by both modules' border chords—which functions as a melodic stitch. For instance, the ninth of A^9/G^5 on which YODA's theme is left dangling (contextually $\hat{3}$ of G major) is, as if by magic, transmuted into the tonic of B major for the statement of the LUKE theme that follows. Such devices are not individually complicated, nor do they get drawn out into the endless flux of motivic becoming and chromatic convolution of, say, *Tristan und Isolde*. But their aggregate result is a supple fabric, at once spontaneous and somehow inevitable in its design.

The other component of "Luke's Farewell" worth foregrounding is the aforementioned *tensed* quality of mythic scoring. This is music that is attuned to its own past and future, and frequently seeks to direct its listener's mind to one or the other. It is no accident, for example, that the statement of the FORCE theme at the cue's end is its most complete since the saga's first mythic turning point, "Binary Sunset," in Episode IV, and lies in the same G-minor key, too. Meanwhile, the melodic transformations hinted at with YODA's theme here anticipate—and add profound significance for knowing listeners—the REVELATIONS motif introduced in *Return of the Jedi*—a musical journey we will trace in Chapter 6.[53]

The Three Trilogies

So far, we have treated the music of *Star Wars* as one big entity whose creation happened to span forty years. This is a simplification that helps establish the basic symphonic and space-operatic qualities of the series, but a more discerning view is now called for. No cycle of nine film scores composed across four decades, for five directors, and within a constantly shifting terrain of filmmaking practices, could help but change with the times. It is a splendid thing that the Skywalker Saga has such a dependable musical through-line. But part of treating these scores seriously as artworks is recognizing their distinctive and time-bound qualities.

That the *Star Wars* films fit into neat ternary schemes makes certain distinctions easy to draw. Each individual movie has three musically differentiated acts. Each trilogy in turn comprises three generically and tonally distinct installments. The overall ennealogy divides into sub-cycles of three movies with shared themes and scoring idioms, both within their respective trilogies and across them; the middle installments (Episodes II, V, and VIII), for example, tend to most mirror each other musically. Thinking of the Skywalker scores in this way inevitably suggests comparison with the output of major symphonists. Composers like Beethoven and Mahler see their oeuvres subdivided into early/middle/late phases even by historians fully aware of the reductiveness of such periodizations. We need not go so far as to posit a "late-period" for John Williams or any other biographical generalization to see the value in assessing these scores from a bird's-eye view.

Starting at the grossest level, there are the three trilogies. When his involvement with the Original Trilogy (1977–1983) began, Williams was already a well-established composer, with almost two decades of experience scoring feature films. Although a few of his previous projects were rich in themes and broad in scope (*The Cowboys*, *The Towering Inferno*, *Jaws*), nothing quite anticipated the extravagance of *Star Wars*. Though Lucas's designs were always grander than a single film, the first entry in 1977 was understood by Williams to be a standalone piece of entertainment; as a result, its score is tighter and more self-contained as a musical text than any of the remaining installments. A happy upshot is that when *The Empire Strikes Back* was green-lit, it gave Williams an opportunity to reconfigure the sound of the franchise *mid*-trilogy. Relative to its predecessor, Episode V is emotionally deeper, less derivative, more experimental, and everywhere more assured on a compositional level. *Return of the Jedi*, by contrast, marks a consolidation and refinement of, rather than essential innovation upon, the Saga's style, and for many years, Episode VI stood as the franchise's definitive statement.

Williams would later refer to his *Star Wars*ian idiom as consisting of "a similarity in harmonic modalities, a similarity in stylistic intervallic choices for melodies and so on, similarities in orchestral textural presentations and the like."[54] Often, it is those harmonic choices that are most undeniably Star-Warsian, a few of which are listed in Figure 1.5, all drawn from strictly non-thematic underscore. Every single one of these devices is already present in the first cue of the series, "Imperial Attack." With hindsight, it is clear that the *Star Wars*ian sound was largely in place in *A New Hope*, but slightly inchoate and externally referential. Those consistent similarities Williams mentions required both the expansions of palette ushered in by the score for *Empire* and the codifications—perhaps reifications—effected by *Jedi*.

Once the symphonic floodgates reopened in 1977, Hollywood could not get enough of the John Williams orchestral touch. In the gap between

Harmonic Device	First Instance
Cadential effects achieved without standard V→I motions	0:02:02
Intensificatory chromatic sequences	0:06:53
Non-diatonic 7-note scales (esp. from harm minor/major)	0:06:03
Non-functional triadic progressions within/between themes	0:02:06
"Planets" chords (e.g. D♭sus♯4/C5) at climaxes	0:02:08
Planing of melody in thirds or full triads	0:03:17
Quartal polyphony	0:00:28
Rapid and near constant shifts of key, scale, sonority	0:02:54
Special motivic weight for Cm→A♭m type progressions	0:04:35
Symmetrical scales (esp. hex, octatonic), derived sonorities	0:01:54
Triads with added ♭6, ♭2, or ♯7ths adjacent to chord tones	0:07:01
Wrong-note bass notes, bass lines	0:02:37

Figure 1.5 Characteristic harmonic devices used within first ten minutes of A New Hope

Episodes IV and VI, he penned an additional four scores that today form the core of the American cine-symphonic repertoire: *Close Encounters of the Third Kind*, *Superman*, *Raiders of the Lost Ark*, and *E.T.: The Extra-Terrestrial.* Between Episode VI in 1983 and Episode I in 1999, Williams went from being a famous film composer to a famous composer, full stop. This position was facilitated by his continuing contributions to massively popular and influential films—*JFK*, *Home Alone*, *Jurassic Park*, *Schindler's List.* But Williams's household-name status also resulted from his high-profile tenure as conductor of the Boston Pops, plus a more general prominence in the public ear through works for civic events like the Olympic Games. However, even in the early eighties, Hollywood was moving away from Williams's neoclassicism and toward a more modern, less melodic, less *symphonic* style, in all the senses described earlier in this chapter.[55] This tendency is audible in the otherwise dissimilar but distinctly non-Williamsian aesthetics of Thomas Newman and Hans Zimmer. According to musicologist Nicholas Reyland, scores from these composers (e.g., *American Beauty*, *Batman Begins*) typify the "corporate classicist" and "metaphysical" styles, respectively, a new pair of approaches to dramatic scoring that by the mid-2000s would become dominant paradigms.[56]

The Prequel Trilogy (1999–2005) falls toward the end of the transition away from the neoclassical style. While still overwhelmingly operating within the *Star Wars*ian mode established by the Originals, these three films do exhibit influences from newer Millennial scoring practices. Indeed, the difference of compositional sensibility between *Return of the Jedi* and *The Phantom Menace* is the largest stylistic break in the whole series' evolution. However, those divergences are mitigated by Williams's efforts at maintaining continuity. "The challenge for me," he noted, "was to write music that was as effective as the first trilogy, but also that would be wedded to the tapestry of the earlier films, so that it would sound like a natural outgrowth."[57]

When Williams began working on *The Phantom Menace*, fellow titans of the neoclassical Hollywood style Jerry Goldsmith and Elmer Bernstein were still scoring pictures. By the premiere of *Revenge of the Sith*, those colleagues had passed, and the new model of minimalistic, electronics-infused scoring was ascendant. Unlike in the years leading up to Episode IV, plenty of big, celebrated orchestral scores were still being written during this era—the *Harry Potter* movie franchise commenced around the same time as the Prequels, as did Howard Shore's *echt*-Wagnerian contribution to the *Lord of the Rings* trilogy. But the Romantic orchestra was now an *optional* sound, particularly for the types of genre films where symphonism had been a default.

It is in this ambivalent context that the Sequel Trilogy (2015–2019) takes place. Especially in the first and third installments, these films are hyper-focused on recalling, rather than reviving or reimagining, the idiom of the Original—though generally *not* Prequel—trilogy. In any other franchise, such sonic reversion would have sounded hopelessly out of date. Here, thanks to the continuity of composer—and the audible passion with which he approached each new entry—the scores for Episodes VII through IX still sound as inevitable as anything else from the second decade of the twenty-first century. Nevertheless, the Sequels, for all their musical marvels, are exercises in a kind of double nostalgia: an attempt to return to a sound that was in its first guise *already* retrospective and nostalgic. A fraught bargain, perhaps, trading freshness of style for familiarity. But the reward was arguably worth it: timelessness.

Figure 1.6 gives a synoptic view of the three trilogies as musical sub-cycles within the larger Skywalker symphonic saga. The traits examined are not the only axes available for comparison; rather, they are the parameters for which the starkest differences are apparent. We will not delve into each category here, though some—timbral palette in particular—could easily support a dedicated study in themselves. There is, however, one historical factor at play that influences many of these axes, especially the categories of action writing, number of cues, and rewrites: digital film editing. The impacts on musical structure precipitated by the shift from analog to digital editing in the 1990s were great. Digital editing changed both the process and aesthetic of Hollywood film scoring. Audio and visual tracks were easier to cut than ever before, in a way that tested the ability of traditionalist composers to catch all the intricacies of action and sculpt longer-range musical arguments. Compounding the challenge was the ever-later locking of the final cut during postproduction; a digitally edited film is never finished, always revisable, always rearrangeable.

When a film's dialogue, effects, and editing are still being worked out in the final weeks before release, it is almost unavoidable that the musical score will suffer changes that the composer could not anticipate. Incredibly, in the case of at least one Skywalker Saga film—Episode IX—there were *fundamental* story beats that were still being subjected to eleventh hour rewrites in the lead-up to the premiere. As a result, *The Rise of Skywalker* has the unfortunate distinction of being one of the worst handlings of one of Williams's best scores in the series.[58] In fact, the music that accompanies scenes of such likely tinkerings is among the finest wrought and affecting in the Sequel Trilogy, particularly once the gang gets to Exegol.[59] This illustrates a theme that we will see frequently as we explore the series: Williams's instincts for dramatic compensation, which ironically grant some of the most dubious scenes and sequences in *Star Wars* the most impressive music.

Chloé Huvet has chronicled many of the ways Williams's idiom evolved—or was editorially contorted so as to evolve—in light of these sea changes in film production. Though her focus lies on Episodes I–III, Huvet's insights apply equally to the if-anything *more* textually unstable Sequels.

> The treatment of the musical score in the Prequel Trilogy is part of a vast aesthetic project that is both correlated with and exacerbated by technological developments, affecting all areas of cinematographic creation. The reevaluation of the status of the film-object [as subject to near infinite alterations and reassemblies] can now be fully realized thanks to digital tools, which in turn influences the way the score is envisaged and used, not

Trait	Originals	Prequels	Sequels
New leitmotifs (LMs)	2–5 major LMs introduced per film	1–2 major LMs introduced per film	0–6 major LMs introduced per film
Recurring LMs	Major LMs well-developed, deployed in and across films	Major LMs well-developed in single films, negligibly across multiple films; OT themes used sparingly, excepting the FORCE.	Major LMs well-developed in and across films; OT themes used extensively; PT themes abandoned
Nonrecurring LMs	1–2 LMs "forgotten" from previous installment per film	1–2 LMs "forgotten" from previous installment per film	3-4 LMS "forgotten" from previous installment
Timbral palette	Romantic orchestra, frequent but brief splashes of exotic color	Romantic orchestra with film-specific, dense timbral palette with greater emphasis on voice, synth, unique percussion	Romantic orchestra with fewer splashes of novel color; leaner sound overall; no synth, percussion less varied
Action writing	Mix of long-breathed cue-specific melodies, ostinati, and LMs; consistently large musical, melody-driven paragraphs.	Focused on small units, rhythmic patterns, ostinati, and gestures; generally moderate to lengthy but easily divisible paragraphs	Mix of ostinati and LMs, with few cue specific action themes; generally short to moderate length paragraphs
Affect	Bright, optimistic; uncomplicatedly Romantic ethos	Progressively darker; brooding, overall tragic ethos	Bright, optimistic; undercurrent of subtle melancholy; overall reflective, nostalgic ethos
Consistency within trilogy	Stylistic and philosophical consonance between scores	Stylistic dissonance but philosophical consistency between episodes	Stylistic consonance but philosophical inconsistency between episodes
Average no. of distinct cues/film	47	58	108
Rewrites, editorial manipulation	Some tracking, some micro-editing, rare revisions; score in film sounds largely as-written.	Pervasive tracking, much micro-editing, some revisions.	Pervasive tracking, much micro-editing, extensive revisions.

Figure 1.6 Overview of the three trilogies

only by the music editor but also and in the first place by the composer himself.[60]

The impacts Huvet describes are especially evident in the action sequences and climactic battles of Episodes I and II.[61] For several such scenes, music editor Kenneth Wannberg almost became a secondary composer: not in writing notes to page, of course—that has always only ever been Williams—but in the radically active role he played in cutting, splicing, reordering, and generally making fit chunks of already recorded music to the final edit.[62]

At worst, the new nonlinear editorial regime described by Huvet led to confused mishmashes of incoherently cut and spliced cues, the most confounding being the "Battle of Geonosis" in Episode II and the "Speeder Chase" in Episode IX. At best, these challenges prompted from Williams some of his most structurally and timbrally innovative set pieces, cues based less on extended themes than flexible ostinati and transplantable motivic cells. The pinnacle in this respect is the not just athematic but *amelodic* "Chase Through Coruscant," a lengthy action set piece from Episode II. Yet it would be wrong to characterize this cue as all surface, no depth. Even when Williams writes in the modern cuttable idiom, his music ends up having ample long-range interest and integrity, such that it often makes for satisfying listening as a standalone "piece." We will contend with issues of digital manipulation and textual integrity throughout this book. There is, however, a danger of overstating how chaotic and editorially constructed Williams's *Star Wars* scores are after 1999, or of treating a few musical muddles like the "Battle of Geonosis" and "Speeder Chase" as baselines, rather than extreme—if symptomatic—cases. But it is no exaggeration to say that the scoring landscape of the new Millennium was of a different planet than in 1977. It is a testament to Williams's craft and professionalism that his post-Original Trilogy scores work as well as they do, both in their films and outside them.

While digital editing practices had their strongest impact on Williams's action and suspense writing, his approach to dramatic underscore—especially musical prose—also changed in some significant ways across the Skywalker Saga, and not as a simple function of the ever-growing extent of his leitmotivic glossary. The small size of that lexicon in *Star Wars* 1977 largely foreclosed the possibility for thematic saturation and free play à la Wagner. However, even with his then-modest inventory of leitmotifs, Williams was able to produce a score with operatic dimensions, through smart variations within and transitions between themes—as, for example, in the sowing of motivic seedlings from "The Little People" (to be dissected in Chapter 5) and spans of epic narration in "The Force" (to be studied in Chapter 7). With an expanded catalog and a more sophisticated approach to variation, Williams comes closer to the Wagnerian milieu in the next two entries, especially in scenes involving Yoda, as we have already seen in "Luke's Farewell."

✺✺✺

As we begin to probe deeper into the *Star Wars* soundscape, our attention will start falling on the basic units of musical thought in the series—themes, passages, cues, and eventually concert arrangements. And yet, the core argument of this book is the integrity of Williams's scores as something akin to a symphony. It therefore makes little sense to go immediately from talk of whole trilogies to fine details of thematic structure without first dwelling on the nature of the most obviously emblematic textual level, the individual soundtrack itself.

Earlier in this chapter, when I stated that "the Skywalker scores really are musical worlds" in the Mahlerian vein, I was not speaking metaphorically. First of all, Williams's music is a critical component in the *worldbuilding* of each individual film and the franchise overall. Daniel White, in his study of two children of *Star Wars*, the *Harry Potter* and *Lord of the Rings* series, stresses the dual nature of musical world building. To create a musical world for a fantasy series [which *Star Wars* also is] entails both "music's role in building the world in which the film takes place, and the ways that music draws us into the world as film viewers."[63] The task is no different in the Skywalker scores. They too construct a coherent and strongly individuated fantastic space, and they too provide an essential mechanism—perhaps *the* essential mechanism—for immersing filmgoers therein. But in this book, I wish to take an even stronger stance. Each soundtrack is a coherent and often strongly individuated artistic statement *on its own terms*, with satisfying internal arcs and deftly constructed beginning-middle-end structures. We can inhabit these musical worlds on their own, so to speak. And we risk underrating their uniqueness by prioritizing only their interconnectivity.

The exceptional qualities of each of the nine scores will be stressed *ad libitum* over the course of this book, especially in Chapter 6 on thematic arcs and Chapter 9 on the score-as-concert. Each entry, of course, introduces new themes, but these are not their sole, or even main, agents of differentiation. To help us start thinking about non-thematic aspects of symphonic individuation, it is helpful to borrow another concept from nineteenth-century opera. This time, the idea comes not from the heady airs of Wagnerian music drama but the marginally more modest realm of Italian opera: *tinta*. The term *tinta* ("tint") comes from the reception of the operas of Giuseppe Verdi—not a repertoire commonly associated with *Star Wars*—and refers to a non-melodic but recurrent and distinctive musical flavor, concern, or ambiance. Richard Taruskin, summarizing the critical literature on Verdi, enumerates a host of qualities that either in isolation or combination could comprise a *tinta*: recurring timbres, instrumental combinations, harmonic special effects, melodic turns, and characteristic rhythms.[64] Such colorations were for Verdi not inert formal devices, put in place just to lend a big musical production some degree of coherence. Rather, a *tinta* arrives with already established expressive connotations, or alternatively establishes them internally, through association and reinforcement. Strictly speaking, such tinctures are not *leit*-anything, in that they do not guide the listener through a narrative or musical argument. But they can be the stuff of musical storytelling nonetheless.

Figure 1.7 offers a sample of such tints from each *Star Wars* score, conspicuous daubs of color that, when heard, will help listeners know "this is definitely *Attack of the Clones*" or "this could only have come from *The Empire Strikes Back*." The chart strives to account for several different modes of tinta

Ep.	Distinguishing Tint	Example
IV	Exposed, chamber-like writing for woodwinds	"The Inner City" [51:41]
V	High chromatic figures played in dissonant intervals	"The Magic Tree" [1:02:43]
VI	Eerie portamentos (str. harmonics, timp., ARP synth, etc.)	"More Ewoks Appear" [1:09:30]
I	Frequent near but inexact references to VADER leitmotif	"Gone Fishin" [18:20]
II	Unique timbres (taiko drs, elec. guitar, harpsichord, etc.)	"Zam's Chase" [15:26]
III	Omnipresent MISERY TRICHORD pattern (e.g. E♭-D-C)	"News of the Attack" [1:27:26]
VII	Piercing high brass notes during action sequences	"The First Escape" [23:57]
VIII	Iterated plagal motions (e.g. Am→Em→Bm→F♯m…)	"Resistance Force" [7:40]
IX	DEFIANT UPSURGE figure of mixed 3^{rds} & 2^{nds}	"Meddling & Poe's Crush" [54:45]

Figure 1.7 Characteristic tints in each individual score

tabulation: orchestrational, tonal, topical. These qualities must not be understood as exhaustive or totalizing; how could a single chart encompass all that makes any score unique? But, as we move forward, it is well worth holding such non-thematic markers in mind, especially as our attention moves in the next few chapters to matters more leitmotivic.

2
Rhymes and References

Music That Everybody Knows?

Spend any time reading commentary on the *Star Wars* scores, and a few words are bound to come up: famous, iconic, influential, recognizable, well-known. Often these terms will be amplified with a bold modifier, "the most."[1] It is difficult to contest that the Skywalker Saga possesses some of the more widely familiar music written in the past hundred years—certainly music of the orchestral variety. Sheer cultural longevity and ubiquity have made some strains of John Williams's *Star Wars* scores simply difficult *not* to know.

Perhaps the superlatives are warranted. But how can one possibly assess a claim as sweeping as the one made in 1992 by the record producer Robert Townson? "John Williams's music for *The Star Wars Trilogy* is easily the most important symphonic work of the latter half of this century and is, quite possibly, the most widely heard orchestral music ever!"[2] The "most important" ascription is essentially unverifiable. But "most widely heard" could be in principle substantiated through a number of quantifiable criteria: film grosses, album sales, Billboard rankings, awards, and all manner of ancillary media (commercials, radio, television, games).[3] By any one of these metrics, the music of *Star Wars* is distinguished; in aggregate, it sits on a rarefied plane indeed.[4]

Buried especially deep in the world's auditory memory is the brassy melody with which each Saga film commences. Film musicologists Matt Lawson and Lawrence MacDonald dub LUKE's leitmotif "arguably one of the most famous film music themes in the history of the medium."[5] Such a claim is not without some empirical support. A psychological study on melodic recognition from 2020 found the theme to be the most "nameable" among movie and television melodies included in its corpus of 107 famous tunes.[6] Impact in the traditional spaces of concert music is harder to quantify. But if sheer frequency of performance by orchestras is a yardstick, *Star Wars* is again in a class of its own. Between 1977 and 1978 alone, the "*Star Wars* Symphonic Suite" garnered 400 performances.[7] Its inescapability will be especially apparent to concertgoers in the Boston area: as of the time of writing, the "Main Title" from Episode IV has been played on 155 occasions in the state of Massachusetts by one of the various constitutions of the Boston Symphony (the BSO, Pops, and Esplanade orchestras). That is 39 performances more than the BSO has programmed *The Planets*, and just 33 shy of *The Rite of Spring*'s 188, to name two pieces of special relevance to the Skywalker soundscape. The composer himself conducted the theme on 61 occasions with the Boston band, and more if we include encores.[8]

Data points like these need to be wielded cautiously. Record producers and concert promoters may be forgiven some hyperbole. But music historians, trained to resist totalizing claims, rarely indulge in outright superlatives in accounting for *Star Wars*' impact, even if there can be no questioning its significance in the post-1970s Hollywood scoring landscape.[9] The issue is not so much a lack of documentary evidence—that is easy enough to gather, clearly—but the intrinsic ill-definedness of concepts like iconicity and influence, and the biases (often Americentric) underlying them. This hesitance toward sweeping pronouncements is shared by the composer himself. When asked about the proposition that "everyone in the world knows" his music, Williams responded that "it feels a little bit abstract. It's wonderful when I am told that, but it's hard to fathom what that really means."[10] Ultimately, it matters little to this book if Williams's *Star Wars* music is, or ever was, the *most* anything. We will leave the facticity of historical superlatives to future scholars to prove; the story of this franchise's compositional imprint is still being written, after all. But we should linger on the subject of recognition, that idea that any component of this symphonic tapestry is well- or widely-known. For the notion of "knowing" a piece of music is subtle, and its unpacking of great use to understanding what makes these Skywalker symphonies tick.

If you are reading this book, you have presumably heard music for this series before. Maybe you can sing one or two tunes without prompting—Luke's theme most likely. Or your expertise might be rather more encyclopedic, no detail too obscure, no cut too deep. (On some matters, like unrecorded alternate cues, one suspects soundtrack aficionados know things the composer himself has likely long forgotten!) Regardless of the depth of your knowledge base, two things are certain. First: you intuitively understand what the music is telling you. And second: you have never heard *Star Wars* in a vacuum.

It is impossible to listen to *Star Wars* as utterly pure musical structure—it has always been first music *for* a film, its characters, scenes, emotions, and all. This kind of textual mediation, strictly internal to the movie and its systems of signs and story, can be, if not removed, then temporarily bracketed in a music-centered hearing. Indeed, a case for such bracketing is made near the end of this book. But one cannot simply bracket the *external* resonances of the Skywalker scores, all those things we know already from other movies and compositions, stories and scenarios. A great filter stands between the series and our ears, through which that originary experience of Williams's music is forever occluded: the filter of referentiality.

The music of *Star Wars* is in this sense not just well known; it is well *knowing*. When audiences in 1977 heard the splendiferous sounds of the "Main Title," they understood it as a throwback, a reactivated recollection of a Golden Age scoring practice and the residual emotions and significations it still bore. Williams, in a characteristically fanciful formulation, speaks of a deep collective repository of meaning latent in the series, "some memory of Buck Rogers or King Arthur or something earlier in the cultural salts of our brains, memories of lives lived in the past, I don't know."[11] Campbellian transhistorical memory or not, this affective filtration system shaped filmgoer responses in the 1970s. And its effectiveness would not have depended on whether audiences were able to consciously articulate the score's stylistic and topical referents. Yet, for those "original" listeners with a substantial acquaintance with symphonic repertoire, the field of recognition would have been wide, a huge network of sensed connections—some overt, many sublimated, most deliberate—to composers and idioms past.

Nine films later, today's listeners find themselves at a wider temporal remove from those Classical (and Classic Hollywood) styles that Williams initially tapped back in 1977. But the filter did not fade in the interim. If anything, the intertextual scrim has become more opaque, the difference being that it now refracts music primarily through *its own* weave of internal references and memories. Decades of accumulated associations, reinforced through countless replayings and rehearings, have made these scores self-mediating. At a certain indefinable point, the music of *Star Wars* became partially—maybe predominantly—about itself.[12]

Contrary to Yoda, who enjoins Luke to "unlearn what you have learned," it is not possible to entirely lift this filter. Surely not for the most over-learned icons like the "Main Title" or "Imperial March," nor for the general symphonic idiom either, which reflects back at us with two centuries' worth of connotative varnish. And while subliminal apprehension of the series' referentiality suffices for most filmgoers, those highly attuned to music are bound to engage with the Skywalker scores' "aboutness" in a more intentional and potentially critical fashion. In a process that echoes and intensifies the attitude Peter Franklin describes with respect to post-Wagnerian symphonies, *cine*-symphonic listening takes the autonomous "music first" mode and the mediated "music-plus-everything-else" mode and shoves them right together. Amazingly, little tension arises. The supposed immiscibility of these attitudes is largely a musicologist's problem, not a listener's one.

Unless the listener is hung up on questions of derivativeness, that is. To those for whom music appreciation is a game of "spot the influence," it can be as though *all* they are hearing is the filter, not the actual music playing through it. Some critiques of referentiality are well motivated, driven by a concern with the messages a film score conveys when it relies on readily established, often ideologically loaded signs and tropes. These critiques can also be covers for pure elitism, borne of a contempt for—or incomprehension of—the aesthetics of popular art.[13] Suffice it to say, there is room open for a more systematic and sympathetic understanding of Williams's referentiality. What is it, exactly, that *Star Wars* music knows?

In the previous chapter, we explored how *Star Wars* is indebted to various idioms that could be housed under the umbrella of symphonism, itself broadly conceived to encompass matters of both musical form and reception. However, we have not yet established what Williams actually thinks about *specific* references; that is, deliberate nods to individual composers, pieces, or themes. Nor have we articulated how these more concrete references operate as storytelling devices. The rest of this chapter will tackle the how and why Williams's music reaches outside of itself, and, as the series progressed, also *within* itself. We will lay some groundwork for navigating and interpreting the constellation of influences that light up these scores, including those second-order, reflexive references—what George Lucas calls "rhymes"—that came to dominate as the series matured. Along the way, we will dispel some persistent misconceptions and witness how reference is an evolving, dynamic current within the *Star Wars* symphonic sky.

To start, we must once again steer into the biggest, most perilous gravitational well in music history: Wagner.

Wagner's Shadow

Chapter 1 laid out the many ways *Star Wars* can be heard in Wagnerian terms. It omitted one crucial line of evidence, however: John Williams's own testimony. While artists are not always reliable sources when it comes to their own influences, in this case the composer's words are worth taking seriously, though with recognition that this particular musical genealogy is more fraught than most. Few figures provoke such anxiety of influence as Richard Wagner. Wagner's megalomania, his detestable politics, and the almost hypnotic effect he had on whole schools of subsequent composers are as much a part of his legacy as his music itself. Little surprise, then, that Williams—whose favorite composer is the amiable craftsman Haydn—has consistently downplayed the suggestion that any of his output refers to the dark magus of Bayreuth.[14]

Regarding the leitmotif, the most concrete Wagnerian fingerprint in *Star Wars*, musicologists have tended to stress a *cinematic* provenance. Julie Hubbert, for example, finds that Williams's technique "suggests more specifically [than Wagner] the scoring techniques of Max Steiner," the most prolific and powerful composer in Hollywood for decades.[15] Hubbert's assessment accords with that of Williams himself:

> In my coming to this leitmotivic idea, or the idea of associating themes with characters, I was really looking back to a couple of earlier periods—not only in opera but also in cinema—and using a technique that's really very good for that one-time audience. Because the audience hears subliminally or unconsciously a theme associated with a character or place, and it helps make the two-hour experience of the film a more unified, interrelated thing.[16]

Williams justifies his employment of leitmotif on the basis of the attentional limitations of mainstream film. Musical coherence cannot rely on the undivided concentration of the filmgoer, nor the luxury of repeated viewings. (Though rare is the fan of *Star Wars* who has seen/heard it only once!) In the contest between auditory and visual stimulation, Williams finds music an attentional underdog: "The more stunning [films] become visually, the more deaf we become."[17] It thus falls to repetition to counteract the memory-erasing tendency of film, which the composer views as fighting *against* the audience being "engaged aurally." Williams describes leitmotif as the technique that "admits repetition, so that you can hear a theme eight or ten times and you will accept it. In a symphonic work perhaps you would want it developed or you'd want it varied in some way."[18]

These are thoroughly pragmatic justifications for the adaptation of the leitmotif technique, as distant from the high-minded aesthetic pretensions of Wagner as can be. Williams's privileging of mnemonic expediency over thematic development is useful to keep in mind as we dig deeper into these scores. However, we should not take his (excessively self-effacing) remarks uncritically. As outlined in the previous chapter, and to be demonstrated in short order, Williams is no proponent of rote repetition, and his developmental craft is as sharp as Wagner's when the films call for it. Perhaps it would be unreasonable to expect Williams to suggest otherwise, but to consciously center music in your experience of *Star Wars* is not only possible; it is an aesthetic stance worth cultivating.[19]

Williams does not usually use the term "leitmotif" when describing these repeatable, unconsciously apprehended, unity-granting musical materials. Instead, he consistently speaks of "melodic identifications." This terminological evasion makes him *more* like Wagner than less. The composer of *The Ring* never himself referred to his "leitmotifs" as such, describing them, among other things, as "melodic moments" and "plastic moments of feeling."[20] With these locutions, Wagner elevates two features—emotional ("feeling") and temporal ("moments")—over any labeling or leading function. Williams's talk of "melodic identifications" suggests a similar double aspect. One can take "identifying" in the lexical sense, as a thing named and recalled, with leitmotif providing "an aural set of beacons or reference points" in Williams's words.[21] But also nestled in the term is identification in the emotional and psychological sense, as with some *person* related to and empathized with.

As they do for Wagner, most of the several dozen leitmotifs in *Star Wars* perform both roles. They provide a set of signposts for listeners to follow (consciously or not) as they make their way through these complex narratives, and they also create a conduit for emotional understanding, empathy, even self-location. Hearing REY's theme, for instance, may signal the character's presence on or off-screen, thus marking her role as an important narrative agent. It may also elicit a sympathetic bodily response, making us vicariously feel her dexterity and athleticism during the theme's more characteristic presentations. But most important is the glimpse that REY's leitmotif affords into her subtle and changing characterization, the way it allows us to see the galaxy from her lonely and stoical perspective.[22] The theme is an invitation to inhabit her story.

Williams never discounts *tout court* the influence of the late- and post-Romantic orchestral repertoire on his Skywalker scores. "It was not music that might describe terra incognita," he said of the series' idiom, "but music that would put us in touch with very familiar and remembered emotions, which for me as a musician translated into the use of a nineteenth-century operatic idiom, if you like, Wagner and this sort of thing."[23] Psychologists refer to *processing fluency* as the increased cognitive ease (and often pleasure) that comes from repeated stimuli. Recurring themes serve this function by giving listeners something clear and constantly reinforced to hold onto, a convenient handle—or, to use a metaphor historically closely tied to the leitmotif concept, a red thread. Here again, a crucial justification is audience identification, music being a force of emotional legibility to counter the alienation otherwise intrinsic to this strange new filmworld. That this legibility happens to revolve around Central European orchestral music from the nineteenth century is, of course, utterly historically contingent, the product of a musical "universalism" presumed—and in effect manufactured—by Classical Hollywood and emphatically re-endorsed by *Star Wars*.

When pressed about Wagner specifically, rather than a putatively universal pan-symphonic style, Williams is liable to shift discussion to other artists whom he admires, in particular, latter-day Soviet and British composers.[24] In one feature from 2011, he surprised his interviewer by claiming "I've actually heard very little of [Wagner's] music, and I'm not a particular fan of his for a lot of reasons."[25] Williams went on to cite Shostakovich, Prokofiev, and Stravinsky as figures with a greater impact, both on his personal aesthetic and—it is not at all hard to show—on the measure-to-measure sound of the Skywalker Saga. His most extended comment regarding Wagner comes in a feature with music critic and historian Alex Ross, after having completed all nine scores:

> Well, I saw the "Ring" at the Hamburg Opera, years ago, and found it somewhat inaccessible, mostly because I didn't know German. I don't really know the Wagner operas at all. If Mr. Hanslick were alive, I think I'd be sitting on the side of Brahms in the debate [between music absolutists and programmatic followers of the "New German School"]. People say they hear Wagner in "Star Wars," and I can only think, It's not because I put it there. Now, of course, I know that Wagner had a great influence on Korngold and all the early Hollywood composers. Wagner lives with us

here—you can't escape it. I have been in the big river swimming with all of them.[26]

Williams's mention of Korngold—a bridge between Wagnerian opera and Classical Hollywood if ever there were one—is strategic. His own adaptation of the leitmotif technique, and so many other Wagnerian attributes listed in the previous chapter, is *mediated* through his much deeper familiarity with and personal affection for the sound of not-so-distant film scoring practices.[27]

Is the Wagner linkage immaterial, then? Of course not—the Skywalker Saga is profoundly Wagnerian in aesthetic and construction in ways we have only just begun to broach. But, for a cycle of nine scores positively bursting with intertextual references, sometimes at the level of close paraphrase, the absence of any *direct* nods to Wagner is conspicuous. The one exception, admittedly a big one, is the FORCE theme.[28] By far the most prevalent leitmotif in the series, and its principal vessel for musico-mythic import, the FORCE would be worth unpacking even if it bore no intertextual resonances. But this very well-known melody positively vibrates with Wagnerian energy—specifically the sort given off by the theme for the *Ring*'s eventual protagonist, SIEGFRIED. A prototypical Chosen One, Wagner's Siegfried is equipped with a storied sword, a divine lineage, and a destiny to redeem the world. His leitmotif, like the FORCE, is associated with solo French horn. And like his analogue Luke Skywalker, who is linked to both FORCE and LUKE motifs, the Teutonic hero's melodic identification is split between his noble theme and a contrastingly perky tune (SIEGFRIED's HORN CALL) with connotations of adventure and activity.

Figure 2.1 depicts some of the formal and harmonic linkages between the FORCE and SIEGFRIED. The diagram transcribes no particular iteration of either theme, both of which are highly variable in practice. Rather, what is shown are prototypes, idealizations that share the same key and meter. We will expand upon this idea of prototypicality more in Chapter 3.

Williams's theme is lengthier than Wagner's, more "grammatical" in theorist Mark Richards's terminology.[29] In full statements, the FORCE is a period: a melody with symmetrical antecedent and consequent phrases, ending on a weak and strong cadence, respectively.[30] The SIEGFRIED anthem, like most of Wagner's leitmotifs, is pithy, one short basic idea followed by an equally brief contrasting one—all antecedent and no consequent.[31] But while their phrase structures are incommensurate, aspects of linear behavior

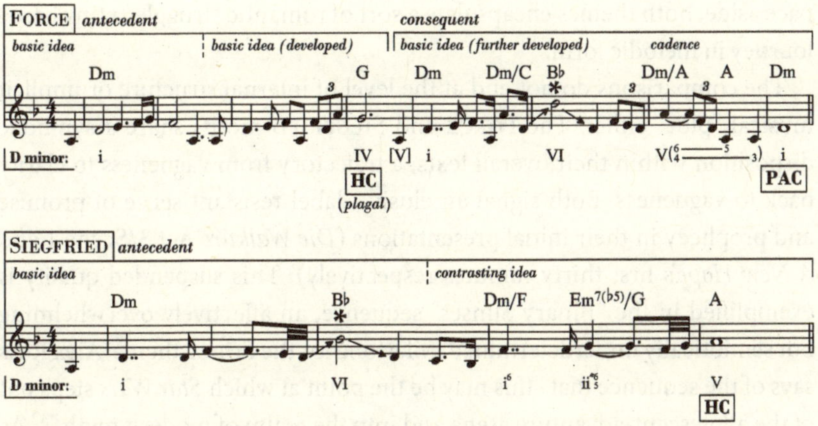

Figure 2.1 Structural comparison of Force and Siegfried leitmotifs

and harmonic focus comprise more than incidental similarity. Consider their respective melodic high points, indicated with an asterisk in Figure 2.1. Though the two leitmotifs reach different scale steps (D_5 in the Force, A_4 in Siegfried), these apex pitches are lent emphasis in an identical fashion. Both are sustained for two beats; both are approached and departed from the tonic pitch, producing the themes' biggest leaps; and both are supported by the poignant submediant triad (here B♭ major, or VI/Dm).

Less tangible but maybe more important is the *expressive* function of the Force and Siegfried leitmotifs. Serious and tinged with melancholy, these are the foremost emblems of heroic gravitas in their respective sagas. This symbolic and affective content is encoded deeply into their underlying melodic profiles. Both begin by straining upward, only to fall back briefly. The initial drop makes their second attempts at ascension all the more gratifying. Having reached their summits (in both cases trumpeted by the charged submediant chord), the melodies are content to recede. The nature of this recession constitutes the starkest difference between the themes. The Force slopes downward, sunsetting onto the tonic degree D_4 that had served as the springboard for all previous subphrases. Siegfried, the more impetuous of the two, closes with half-cadential potential rather than authentic closure, landing on the fifth degree A_4, an octave higher than the A_3 with which the melody began. That Siegfried happens to accomplish its heroic feat with haste, and the Force over a more arduous melodic path, does not obscure the essential expressive isography, however. Differences of destination and pace aside, both themes encapsulate a sort of romantic struggle, a tiny hero's journey in melodic form.

The comparisons do not end at the level of internal structure or implicit musical "plot" either. The FORCE and SIEGFRIED motifs share a symbolic disposition within their overall texts, a trajectory from vagueness to clarity back to vagueness. Both signal an elusive, label-resistant sense of promise and prophecy in their initial presentations (*Die Walküre* Act 3/Scene 1 and *A New Hope*'s first thirty minutes respectively). This suspended quality is exemplified in the "Binary Sunset" sequence, an affectively overwhelming but semiotically underdetermined milestone for the FORCE theme. Alex Ross says of the sequence that "this may be the point at which *Star Wars* steps out of the adolescent-adventure arena and into the realm of modern myth."[32] As their respective sagas progress, both Williams's and Wagner's motifs go on to latch onto their eponymous signifieds, sometimes to the point of crude literalism (e.g., the horn solo in *Siegfried* Act 2, Scene 2; many moments in *The Last Jedi*). But despite this constant pressure to rigidly represent their semantic targets, these are also the themes *most* prone to reverting to a state of floating, undifferentiated mythic import. This is the phenomenon of semantic drift and will receive due attention in Chapter 3.[33]

The similarities between the FORCE and SIEGFRIED themes are clear and important.[34] But are they intentional? Absent direct testimony or indirect evidence such as those specific pieces used for a temp track, one cannot assert that Williams was purposefully modeling the leitmotif on Wagner's. Perhaps instead it was Anton Bruckner, in one of his more Wagner-affectionate moods, who furnished a template for the FORCE leitmotif. Official accounts of the making of *Star Wars* do mention that a symphony of Bruckner's was part of the film's temp track, though not the one that has the most obvious SIEGFRIED-isms—namely, his Third and Eighth symphonies, not the Ninth as claimed.[35] Or, if not Bruckner, some other, more recent composer, thrice-removed from the composer of the *Ring*?—there certainly is no shortage of them in film music history! Maybe the shape of the FORCE was simply in Williams's ear at the time of composing *A New Hope*. His leitmotif for KABAKOV in *Black Sunday*, written a few months before *Star Wars*, sounds like a dry run for the FORCE and is for a movie no one would ever describe as operatic, much less Wagnerian.[36] Decades later, when Williams conceded that "Wagner lives with us here," he was effectively covering every possibility: intentional allusion, unconscious influence, happenstantial similarity, concerted avoidance. Even for connections as vivid and significant as that between these two leitmotifs, referentiality is never so simple as "X led to Y."

Constellations of Influence

Models and Misconceptions

Star Wars' claim to "symphonism" hinges on a conversancy with the orchestral repertoire. Part of the pleasure of listening to Williams's music is reflecting upon and responding to its manifold influences—not just because recognition can be its own reward, but because stylistic eclecticism and referentiality are fundamental to the series' DNA, musical and otherwise. The Skywalker scores *want* listeners to pick up on those external inspirations. And yet, as the foregoing examination of Wagner and Williams shows, influence is a difficult thing to quantify, especially in texts as omnivorous as these.

Sloppy analysis leads to sloppy critique. This is a regrettably common state of affairs in discussions concerning originality in film music, especially those that treat comparisons between works as the endpoint, rather than initiator, of investigation. We will not waste time re-litigating debates concerning the aesthetic worthiness of openly referential art here. Nor will we fret too much about whether a specific referential passage constitutes paraphrase, plagiarism, pastiche, paean, or passing semblance. These are matters best left to the judgment of the individual listener, and we will rely on neutral language like "channels," "echoes with," or especially "modeled on." What it means to be "modeled on" in *Star Wars* is a complex question, however, no matter the theme, cue, or score. To that end, the next two sections offer a more balanced framework of how influence works in these scores—a model of musical modeling.

To start, we need to dispel some misconceptions. The following five patterns of thought are all easy to slip into, even for the most thoughtful listeners.

1. ***Conflating topics with allusions to specific pieces.*** Widely employed musical figures with strong associations (topics) like the fanfare, the pastorale, or the hunt occur on every page and every time scale of the Skywalker scores. Many sound like similar passages in a hundred other

pieces, and it is often safer to attribute influence to the more abstract topical category than one preexisting work or another.

Example: Assuming that the wordless female chorus used for underwater scenes in Episode I [13:23, 19:19] descends directly from Holst's "Neptune" from *The Planets*, when it is more accurate to view both as instances of a more generalized *sirens* topic with an enduring pedigree. Among the exemplars Williams would most likely have known are Debussy ("Sirènes" from the *Nocturnes*), Ravel (*Daphnis et Chloé*), and Vaughan Williams (*Scott of the Antarctic/Sinfonia Antartica*). The structural characteristics of the *sirens* topos—intense chromaticism, quiet dynamics, curling melodic lines with abundant "sigh" figures—are all present in Williams's undersea cues. So are the affective and extramusical associations: the oceanic, the nocturnal, the mysterious, the feminine, the alluring.[37]

2. ***Underestimating happy accidents.*** With almost twenty hours of music written for the Skywalker Saga, it is inevitable that there will be some sound-alikes that arise from chance, rather than deliberate emulation. If these coincidences still feel contrived, it is because the referential ethos of *Star Wars* encourages making and drawing meaning from such connections.

   Example: A throwaway motif in Episode III [2:01:52, 2:02:10] bears an uncanny resemblance to the first theme of the Adagio from Bruckner's Fifth Symphony.[38] However, imitation with intent is less plausible here than accidental convergence. After the Original Trilogy, Williams rarely cites any Classical pieces so directly. In this cue he stops before the most characteristic part of the Bruckner theme: its descending melodic sevenths. Moreover, several similar figures appear sporadically through the *Revenge* score [cf. 3:16, 29:13, and much of the "Lament" from 1:21:07–1:24:54]. This suggests a more generic interval pattern, rather than a quote from Bruckner, was on Williams's mind.
3. ***Making connections with works from well-known repertoire without searching for closer kindred in less famous pieces.*** Familiarity bias and limited knowledge of the repertoire is a dangerous combination when gauging musical similarity and difference. Whenever a connection seems self-evident, it is worth digging to find other works that may be less widely known to general audiences but are of personal closeness to the composer. Of special relevance is other film music, including Williams's *own* output.

Example: Noting a coincidental similarity of the first five notes of "The March of the Resistance" with the scherzo motif from Mahler's iconic Ninth Symphony, while being oblivious to its more profound and form-determinative debt to Walton's "Spitfire Prelude and Fugue," itself adapted from his score for *The First of the Few*. Moreover, Williams's spin on this fugal march-style was developed across several of his late-1970s scores, not just *Star Wars* (cf. *Black Sunday, Close Encounters*, and *1941*).[39]

4. ***Overlooking influence at the level of long-range process in favor of surface-based melodic similarities.*** Many of the most interesting instances of referentiality occur across long timespans, such as on the level of musical form, harmonic idiom, or tonal design. Though not as quick to identify or describe, these wider-reaching references tend to be more profound than what can be gleaned from a single measure.

   Example: Fixating on an obvious but fleeting paraphrase of Sibelius in Episode V (cf. "City in the Clouds" [1:18:50] with the opening of the Violin Concerto) while failing to acknowledge the more deeply integrated impact of Bartók's orchestrational and harmonic language in that score (cf. the hexatonicism in "The Imperial Probe," timpani glissandi in "The Magic Tree," dissonant string counterpoint in "Losing a Hand," etc.).

5. ***Treating influence as a linear chain instead of a complex network.*** Musical referentiality in *Star Wars* is never as simple as piece-x is based on piece-y. Rather than seeing influence as a unitary arrow between individual works, it is better to imagine a field of many nodes. Some connections are weighted more or less strongly, some overlap, all interconnected somehow, like a twisty root system or a constellation. Importantly, this constellation model assists discussion of "soundalikes" whose connection to the theme/cue/piece in question is unprovable but audible and potentially enriching.

   Example: Attributions of a single inspiration for "The Imperial March" invariably miss how complex and multi-nodal its constellation of influence is. It is not *just* modeled on Shostakovich, nor just Prokofiev, nor Holst, nor Chopin, and so on.[40]

Keeping these misconceptions at bay does not mean one cannot draw intertextual associations. Exactly the opposite: it facilitates a more nuanced, more *textually supportable* form of listening for influence.

A Cluster of "Luke-Alikes"

The *Star Wars* "Main Title" is a good test subject with which to confront and resist these five misconceptions. Measure-for-measure, the music that opens each Saga film may be the series' most teeming with intertextual resonances. This is no accident: Williams is deliberately setting a referential tone, cueing the listener early that what follows will be a heroic throwback and a generic mishmash. But before entertaining any specific models in preexisting pieces, it is important to identify the more generalized topics that undergird the cue. Despite their centrality to much recent theorization of musical meaning, topics have proven vexingly difficult to define consistently. They are more than just stock figures but less than the arcane tangle of traits and conditions music semioticians sometimes treat them as. Janet Bourne offers a common-sense description: "Topics are conventional musical signs with clear significations understood by most hearers due to being part of a musical referential code based on use and exposure."[41] Topics are built out of simple but distinctive internal features like melodic contour or texture, and in their simplicity and markedness provide composers an efficient way to build larger spans of music with a readily understood associative grammar.[42]

The LUKE Skywalker theme as presented in the opening titles embodies two topics and may well be their most famous modern-day exemplar: the *fanfare* and the *march*. A third, less obvious signifier—but an apt one given the "Space Western" label often attached to the series—is the *Western* topic. Figure 2.2 renders the theme with annotations for those structural details that contribute to these topical references.

The fanfaric quality—and that topic's connotations of heroism and heraldry—is conveyed foremost by the fortissimo trumpet writing, and secondarily by details of intervallic and harmonic construction. Past the "Main Title," the Skywalker Saga overflows with fanfares of all shapes and styles—chromatic ones, atonal ones, comic ones, tragic ones—and the same can be said of marches, a topic similarly established right at the onset. As with the fanfare, the march genre is expressed first through orchestration here, with the snare and timpani providing rhythmic propulsion and the rest of the orchestra reinforcing that martial tread with sharp-edged chords. Though never so consistent as the march or fanfare, the Western topic does leave a tell-tale mark at the phrase's end. The "Cowboy Cadence," a formula based on approaching the half-cadential dominant chord with the subtonic, has been virtually *de rigueur* for film Westerns since the 1950s.[43] The Western flavor

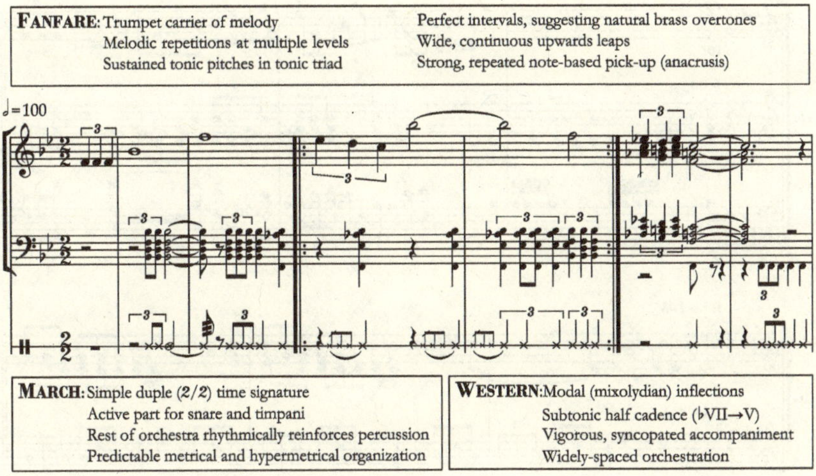

Figure 2.2 Style topics in LUKE leitmotif

imparted by that cadence, along with a few other topical traits, adds a taste of that film genre's swaggering, adventurous ethos. Indeed, a few minutes into the score, the subtonic half cadence will be detached from the LUKE theme and rendered into an autonomous leitmotif, the plucky REBEL FANFARE.

The way the fanfare topic feeds into the "Main Title" is worth dwelling on, because LUKE's anthem is preceded by two other modules: the three-measure introductory passage that leads into the big theme, and the nineteen-measure "Twentieth Century Fox Fanfare" by Alfred Newman before that. Besides retention of the B♭-major key, the link between Newman and Williams's themes is not especially strong. But the mini fanfare that comes on the heels of the Fox Logo theme boasts a library of references all its own. The quartal polyphony heard after the initiating blast of B♭ is shown in Figure 2.3, along with two sound-alikes. For Wagner-lovers, this passage is an easy trap for the third misconception—hastily misattributing influence to something famous. Someone familiar with *Tristan und Isolde* might quickly equate Williams's brass writing with the dreamy off-stage hunting horns from that opera's Act 2 Prelude (Figure 2.3b). In fairness, that passage shares with *Star Wars*' opening an analogous imitative texture and an identical harmonic function, both projecting an F dominant-eleventh chord in B♭. But as with the FORCE theme, there exist other precedents, and this time, one need not look just to a dyed-in-the-wool Wagnerian like Bruckner to find a precursor or two.[44]

Figure 2.3 "Main Title" fanfare and comparisons. **a.** Williams, "Main Title" mm. 1–3; **b.** Wagner, *Tristan und Isolde* Act 2/Scene 1 mm. 15–17; **c.** Rózsa, *Ivanhoe* "Overture" mm. 1–6

According to editor Paul Hirsch, Miklós Rózsa's score for the 1952 historical epic *Ivanhoe* was used as temp music for the *Star Wars* opening crawl.[45] And the first few bars of *Ivanhoe*'s "Prelude" (Figure 2.3c) are indeed a more palpable precedent than anything from *Tristan*. In addition to those features shared with Wagner's opera, we also have the quartal orientation, the mixolydian shadings, and crucially the *formal* function of a call-to-attention that prepares the big main tune within a film Main Title. Some of these Rózsaisms persist past the opening fanfare too—not at the level of melody, which is rather spikier than anything in Williams's title, but texture and harmony. *Ivanhoe*'s bellowing voice echoes in the way LUKE's trumpet line is accompanied by syncopated chords below and a sustained tremolo above, as it does with those parallel chords that enrich the aforementioned "Cowboy Cadence." Once heard, the linkages with Rózsa's score ought to decisively shape how one hears the start of *Star Wars*. But while Act II of *Tristan* may not be household knowledge, critics of Williams's referentiality are more likely to know that music than an obscure film soundtrack predating *A New Hope* by twenty-five years.[46] This is why claims of influence must be made in provisional terms, with humility in view of the bottomlessness of the repertoire.[47]

A lack of melodic definition—that is, hummability—to the quartal intro in the "Main Titles" has allowed it to evade notice by most critics. Not so with the Luke theme. Because innumerable other pieces exhibit the same fanfare, march, and Western topics, it is up to the melody to individuate this particular theme. And here is where we begin to face difficulty, as it happens that there are many pieces that share melodic similarities with the Luke leitmotif, particularly the first two measures of its A- and B-sections. Figure 2.4 offers another view of the theme, now crowning a nebula of comparable passages from a range of generic and expressive sources. These are all simplified and transposed to B♭ for ease of comparison.

Are any of these pieces the one true "source" of Williams's theme? No, but some might shine more brightly in its constellation than others. According to Paul Hirsch, an early cut of *A New Hope* included music by Bruckner. Hirsch cites his Ninth and final work as the model for the movie's main heroic theme. However, the lack of any Luke-esque material in Bruckner's Ninth suggests a case of temp track misremembering—not the only case one finds in the literature surrounding the first *Star Wars* film.[48] Bruckner's Fourth symphony—specifically the first movement's fifth-filled main subject—is a far more credible forerunner of Luke. Almost certainly more coincidental but still worth acknowledging are passages from Brahms, Korngold, Puccini, Suk, and Young.[49] And not to be overlooked is the allusivity of the lyrical B-section, which ushers in a whole new suite of references, including some striking Luke-alikes from Tchaikovsky and Saint-Saëns. Looming largest here though is the music of Williams's beloved William Walton. The excerpt from *Crown Imperial* included in Figure 2.4 is but a representative, and could be substituted by any number of Walton's dozen such processionals.[50] The intent of depicting so wide a cluster of sound-alikes for the Luke theme is not to imply Williams modeled his melody on any one of them in particular—and certainly not all of them![51] Rather, my aim is to put into perspective the intertextual plenitude of the piece, and so many others by extension—and to again encourage a more humble stance for would-be seekers of intertextual silver bullets.

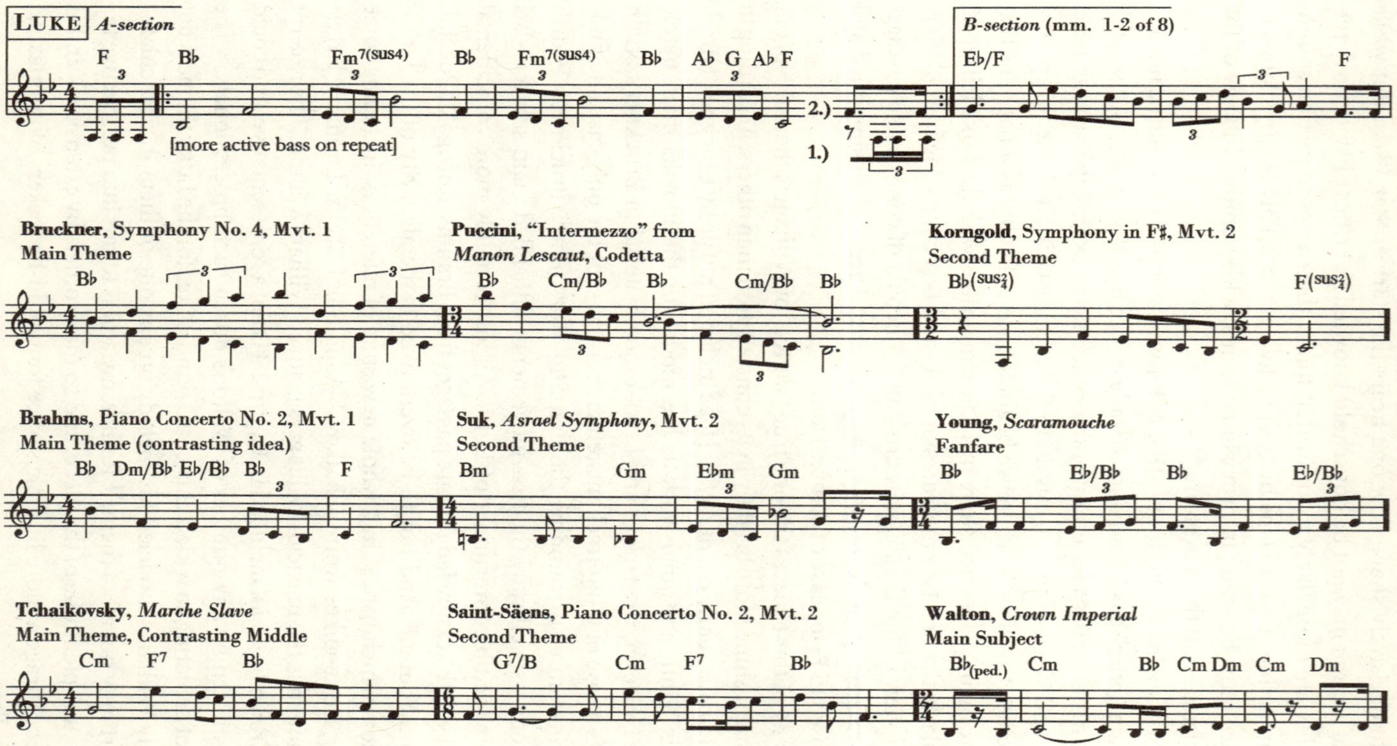

Figure 2.4 A gallery of LUKE-alikes.

Despite a plausible Bruckner connection and inspecific but undeniable indulgence in Waltoniana, the most common claim by far regarding the provenance of *Star Wars*'s "Main Title" theme involves Erich Wolfgang Korngold. Not—it should be said—the horn theme from the Scherzo of Korngold's Symphony in F♯, a snippet of which was included in Figure 2.4.[52] That is a wonderful and oft-*Star Wars*ian work, but it was not so well known in 1977. Rather, many commentators have likened the LUKE theme to the Main Title for the 1942 small-town melodrama (not knightly adventure!) *Kings Row*. Its melody is given in Figure 2.5, again transposed into B♭.[53]

We need not downplay the semblance here: Williams openly acknowledged a stylistic affinity with Korngold in *Star Wars*, and striving for this affinity was in accordance with Lucas's stated desire to replicate the swooshing, swooning sound that the Old-World composer had charted in films like *Captain Blood*, *The Adventures of Robin Hood*, and *The Sea Hawk*. Korngold's dashing idiom is itself one part Strauss (cf. *Ein Heldenleben*), one part Mahler (cf. Symphony 2, Mvt. 5), and one part his own precocious and inimitable style. Williams took Lucas's wish for "the Korngold kind of feel" to heart in *A New Hope* and never tired of channeling that soundworld.[54] Cues throughout the series brandish the Korngoldian banner proudly: "The Swashbucklers" in Episode IV, "You're Under Arrest" in Episode I, "The Speeder Chase" in Episode IX, to name a few. To paraphrase the motto of another Williams-scored franchise: if adventure music has a name, it must be Korngold.[55]

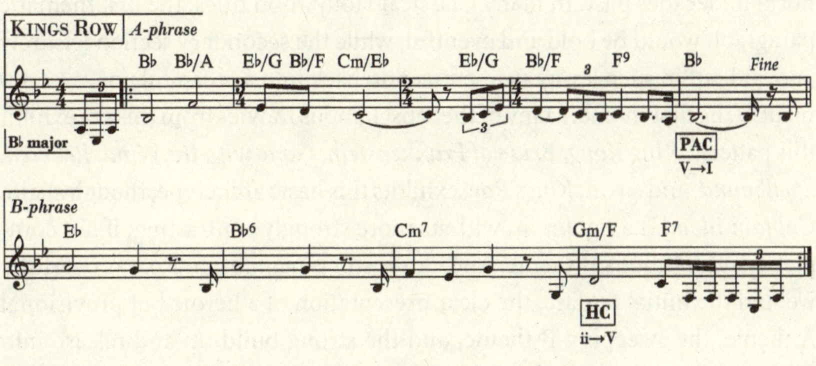

Figure 2.5 Korngold, *Kings Row* Main Title, Main Theme

The near identity of melodic structure for the first five notes of the *Kings Row* and *Star Wars* themes is always attention-grabbing to those first hearing them side by side. The likeness fades quickly, however, with the LUKE theme diverging from its 1942 cousin the moment the trumpet makes its leap from C_4 to $B\flat_4$ instead of $B\flat_3$, and from that point the two melodies venture off into quite different territories.[56] A deeper Korngoldian match in terms of thematic sub-structure might be the main subject from *Captain Blood*, which has a similar antecedent/consequent design to the LUKE A-theme, unlike the tiny ternary form (ABA) that undergirds *Kings Row*'s theme.[57]

In dissecting thematic sub-structure, we should not lose sight of *super*-structure. Recall misconception #4: the tendency to ignore matters of larger-scale form. The shape of the whole "Main Title" is itself a matter of dense referentiality. Williams's piece is based on an easy-to-follow pattern:

Stage 1: Peremptory fanfare.
Stage 2: Main idea with a heroic character, brassy and leaping, squarely on the tonic.
Stage 3: Contrastingly lyrical idea, string-based and stepwise, on closely related key.
Stage 4: Elaborated return to main idea.
Stage 5: Dissolve or transition into nondiegetic underscore.

This formal schema does not refer so much to a particular score as it does the idea of grand classic cinema itself. Though defunct at the time of *Star Wars*' premiere, a mini-overture over the opening credits had been an iron-clad norm in decades past. In many Classical Hollywood titles, the first thematic paragraph would be bold and eventful, while the secondary section leisurely and laid out in such a way as to crescendo back into a recapitulatory restatement of the first theme. Many of the most famous movies from this era exhibit this pattern: *King Kong*, *Bride of Frankenstein*, *Gone with the Wind*, *Rebecca*, *Spellbound*, and so on. *Kings Row* exhibits this basic archetype, though again, *Captain Blood* is a tighter fit, with its more strongly contrasting, if not completely autonomous B-theme. And closer still is *Ivanhoe*. In Rózsa's overture, we find the initial fanfare, the clear presentation of a heroic but provisional A-theme, the sweeping B-theme, and the strong build-up and release into a truncated, more assured recap of that A-theme. Closest of all may be that same composer's title for the biblical epic *King of Kings*. While in no specific spot as analogous as *Kings Row* or *Ivanhoe*, the overture's overall form, melodic sensibility, and harmonic milieu are closely aligned with Williams's own opening cue, like an alternative version of *A New Hope* set in Bethlehem instead of Tatooine.

We have reached a point where the number of topics, models, and allusions uncovered in the *Star Wars* "Main Title" exceeds the number of measures in LUKE's actual theme. And all this influence-hunting has been done without ever broaching other themes *by* Williams himself that host comparable form and content (e.g., *Raiders of the Lost Ark*, *Superman*, *Amazing Stories*). No listener could ever be expected to keep track of so much data, nor any composer expected to consciously intend them. Alex Ross, finding both *Kings Row* and Bruckner's 4th LUKE-alikes to be plausible, says "the theme can't have been stolen from two places simultaneously."[58] Ross's remark is ironic: his conclusion is that Williams is *not* a "mere pasticheur." It is not that the theme was "stolen" from any one place (or two), but rather it is an irreducible *synthesis* of many. The purpose of our exercise in thematic archaeology is not to pick out a single, guiding referential star but to demonstrate the sheer expansiveness of the constellation. The eclecticism of the opening of *Star Wars* is part of its effect, an encapsulation of *everything* in properly Mahlerian universalizing fashion. Though a useful one-time exercise, nowhere else in this book will we perform such a deep dive into one theme's intertextual lineage. (However, we are far from done unpacking this particular leitmotif!) In general, whenever external influence is mentioned later in this book, its inherently plural character will be emphasized. No music, *Star Wars* or otherwise, is *sui generis*, and discovering one connection always leads to scores more. This includes instances when Williams starts channeling *himself*.

The Rite Stuff

One of the difficulties in charting *Star Wars*' constellation of influences is that, as the series marched on, Williams decreasingly looked outward, to works by other composers, for inspiration. This is not surprising; to an extent, he simply "found" the franchise's idiom—that *Star Wars*ian dialect described in Chapter 1. Instead of reinventing the wheel with each new installment, Williams would thus refine and consolidate its sound. For sure, he added new elements, like the male chorus in *Jedi*, and shifted some others, like the turn toward frenetic ostinati in action cues in Episode I. But never would Williams truly upend the essential stylistic coordinates he set back in 1977.

The result is a consistency of approach that is both aesthetically well-motivated and commercially savvy. After Episode IV, the filmmakers relied progressively less on pieces from the symphonic repertoire in constructing their temp tracks, and Williams was correspondingly less likely to indulge in quotations of Classical composers. The music for the Ewoks in Episode VI, much of which is an affectionate Prokofiev homage, contains the series' last real instances of direct paraphrase. The Prequels are still thick with symphonic references, but shades of Wagner, Shostakovich, and Holst are now sublimated into that reified Star-Warsian soundworld.[59] Very little post-Episode I sounds like it could have been composed by anyone other than Williams. In those rare spots in the Prequels where cues are stylistically set-apart enough to suggest a temp track, the models are more plausibly from recent and then-trendy *film* music like *Gladiator*, *Crouching Tiger, Hidden Dragon*, and the *Lord of the Rings* trilogy.[60] Even these inter-cinematic influences are basically gone by the Sequels, at which point Williams is writing in a basically self-enclosed idiom.

A microcosm for this inter-to-intratextual trajectory can be heard in the way an initially marked and externally referential motif is absorbed into the *Star Wars*ian milieu. Early in *A New Hope*, in the cue "Imperial Attack," we hear a series of dissonant and irregularly accented orchestral stabs, a musical correlate to the sight of rebel prisoners being marched by a squad of stormtroopers. Figure 2.6 depicts the inaugural statement of this Imperial Ostinato, an idea that, over nine movies, goes from precise allusion to inexact replica to floating signifier. The ostinato's constituent sonorities are formed by the juxtaposition of a midrange minor-type chord ($B\flat^{\sharp 4}$) with a lower pitch with which that chord clashes sharply. Though recurrent and often affiliated with a proper leitmotif—the Imperial Motif—this Ostinato is decidedly not an instance of melodic identification. The figure's associative potency stems rather from its arresting rhythmic and especially harmonic character—and its vivid intertextual content.

There are several stars in the Imperial Ostinato constellation of influence, including pieces by Gustav Holst and Williams himself.[61] But one source glows brighter than the rest: *The Rite of Spring*. Igor Stravinsky's 1913 ballet was an acknowledged constituent of the temp track that Hirsch, Chew, and Lucas compiled for the initial cut of Episode IV.[62] And indeed, elements

Figure 2.6 A set of dissonant ostinati in *A New Hope* and *The Rite of Spring*. **a.** Williams "Imperial Attack" (ANH, 1m3, 5:31); **b.** Stravinsky, *The Rite of Spring*, "The Augurs of Spring" (Rehearsal Number 13)

of that riotous work are sprinkled throughout the score, many instances nearly as undisguised as the IMPERIAL OSTINATO.[63] The particular passage from "Imperial Attack" is ostensibly modeled on the "Augurs" polychord (E♭^{7}|F♭) and is depicted in Figure 2.6b.[64] An unprecedentedly harsh sonority for its time, the seven-note harmony's pounding repetitions initiate the ballet's second tableau, "The Augurs of Spring: Dances of the Young Girls."

While not an outright quotation—Williams's music centers on a different species of chord and has an alternative means of achieving its haphazard accents—the IMPERIAL OSTINATO in *A New Hope* nevertheless wears its Stravinskian influence on its sleeve. The alien, death-devoted behavior of the *Rite*'s ritualistic dancers maps with little resistance onto George Lucas's galactic fascists. But Williams's music is not fixed, not in form nor in meaning. The ostinato continues working its way into the saga's underscore after Episode IV, and with each guise, it loses some of its initial allusiveness. The first element to fade is the affiliation of the *pesante* pattern with the IMPERIAL MOTIF. Abandoned after *A New Hope*, the somewhat feeble theme was replaced with the more ear-catching "Imperial March" in Episode V. No longer containers for a recurring theme, the post-Episode IV Augur-esque chords now tend to provide a backdrop for other, more one-off motifs.[65] The rhythmic and harmonic particulars fall away too. Following *A New Hope*, the ostinato essentially becomes a generalized, though still auditorily arresting topos: metronomically repeated chord against a dissonant bass with irregular accents.

This shift of referentiality is not solely a matter of intrinsic compositional change. Contemporary audiences, increasingly familiar with *Star Wars* rather than primitivist ballet, will invariably start hearing Rite-like passages as Williams-esque rather than Stravinskian. Thus, when IMPERIAL OSTINATO-suggestive chords start appearing in *Revenge of the Sith*, the leitmotivic and intertextual associations from *A New Hope* have *both* been attenuated. A thumping sonority such as the Bm|D$\sharp^5$ in "Grievous and the Droids" (Figure 2.7) has only the flimsiest of links with the original scene in Episode IV: now it is Anakin and Palpatine who are the prisoners, escorted along by the Prequels' robotic analogues for stormtroopers. But the module does not really demand any deep narrative or thematic justification in the first place; it is functionally straightforward and hardly marked for attention compared to its ancestor in "Imperial Attack." The scene in *Revenge* simply called for a bit of tense interstitial material, something that would sound of a piece with the thrashing, major second–emphasizing sound of the rest of the cue. During these two measures, Williams simply opts to channel one topical puff from the nebulous *Star Wars*ian sound he had established over six movies. The idea of "repeated chord/dissonant bass/irregular accents," introduced via Stravinsky in Episode IV and recalled sporadically thereafter, just happened to harmonize with the overall cue's violent, mechanical demeanor. When scoring "Grievous and the Droids" Williams determined that a few bangs of a Bm|D$\sharp^5$ sonority struck the right chord, so to speak.

Just because a musical symbol sheds its original associations does not mean it is unable to sustain development. A few minutes before "Grievous and the Droids," Williams based an entire cue, 1m4 "They're Coming Around," on an Augurs-like texture. A component of the larger Battle of Coruscant set piece, this ninety-second-long chunk of action music follows Anakin and Obi-Wan in their starfighters as they attempt to evade enemy homing missiles and buzz droids. Figure 2.8 shows a few measures of what much of the cue sounds like. The cue's chordal thuds, which alternate with shorter spans of non-motivic material, bear a likeness to the basic

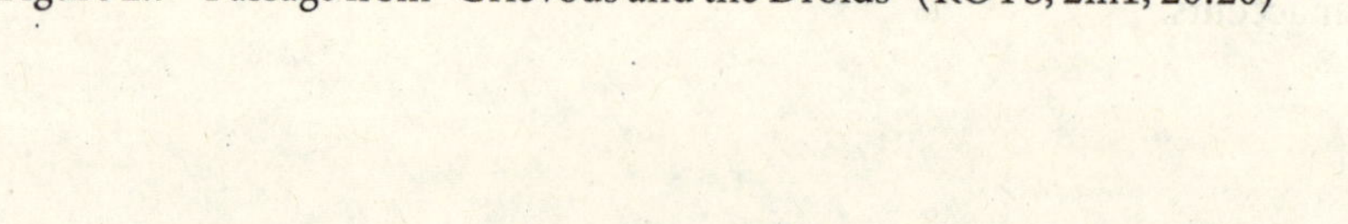

Figure 2.7 Passage from "Grievous and the Droids" (ROTS, 2m1, 20:20)

Figure 2.8 Passage from "They're Coming Around" (ROTS, 1m4, 4:38)

material from the Stravinsky, but the fitfulness of the *Rite*'s accent pattern is now swapped with an invariant rhythmic loop—123456, 123456, and so on. The coarse polychords from the original are also exchanged, at least at first, with more euphonious suspended and added-note chords. But what "They're Coming Around" lacks in close surface semblance it makes up for in sustainedness.

Williams's cue traverses through seven different chords, each one beginning a new module, represented in schematic form in Figure 2.9. Across "They're Coming Around," a parade of these chord-defined modules joins up to create a tiny musical plot. It begins with the descent from a C-based to B♭-based sonority in module 2. This is followed in the next three modules by further slumps down to A, G♯, and a cue low point of F, after which the music alters course, recovering B♭ and C in the final two modules. As this bass-progression spins its tale of sinking trouble and hopeful reversal, the harmonic content of each stage tells a similar story. After B♭$^{sus^2_4}$, each station in the chain is more saddled with strident intervals than the last, culminating in squirmingly dissonant D♭^{ma7}|F^{+}. Following that crisis chord, the last two harmonies work to restore consonance, in a sense cadencing on the C-octaves that close the sequence.[66] Importantly, nowhere are the repeated chords placed at the aural foreground; a succession of call-and-response figures from various brass choirs remains throughout the focus of melodic attention. "They're Coming Around" stands as a strong example of *integration* rather than citation—not of a theme or leitmotif, as we are accustomed to thinking of such usage patterns in film, but rather of a reference itself. Or, more precisely, a reference-turned-topos.

Perhaps the *Star Wars* score that is most *about* other *Star Wars* scores, *The Rise of Skywalker* is full of overlapping references and self-reflexive syntheses of music from the series as a whole. It thus comes as no surprise that the Imperial Ostinato should rear its spiky head once more here, its referentiality now positioned somewhere between use and mention. (The use/mention distinction will be thoroughly examined in Chapter 3.) In "The

4:38 | 5:00 | 5:13 | 5:36 | 5:45 | 6:07 | 6:14 | 6:20

1.	2.	3.	4.	5.	6.	7.
C(sus$^4_2$)	B♭(sus$^4_2$)	F♯(♯4)/A	Am/G♯	D♭maj7(♭6)/F	B♭m7(add4)	C (no chord)

Four missiles launched at heroes	Anakin dispatches two missiles	Obi-Wan still can't shake two missiles	Buzz droids attack both Ani and O-W	Droids shut down O-W's controls	Ani's ship through fire, O-W's freezes	Ani arrives to save day, onto next phase

Figure 2.9 Form of "They're Coming Around" (ROTS, 1m4, 4:38–6:20)

Figure 2.10 Passage from "Battle of the Resistance" (TROS, 7m12(a), 1:42:06)

Battle of The Resistance," the Ostinato is just one of a panoply of rapid-fire references. Second-for-second, this is the most motivically dense of all action cues from the series, with that Stravinskian pattern sharing the stage with Luke, Resistance, Friendship, Poe, Kylo, Tension, and Force themes, plus a chugging hook redolent of Episode VII's "Scherzo for X-Wings," a few cascades of Ravelian *Daphnis* chords, and an Vader-esque brass lick or two. In this almost overstuffed context, the callback to the Imperial Ostinato shown in Figure 2.10 can only be heard as just one clipping within a larger, citationally extravagant collage. But, because the chord-pattern is straining to be heard *explicitly* as a reference—not unmarked underscore like in "Grievous and the Droids"—one could plausibly hear it as alluding to Stravinsky and 1970s-era Williams. Such are the curious affordances of riotously referential music.

That the "Battle of the Resistance" bonanza sounds not just coherent but *inevitable* is a testament to Williams's ability to make genuine pieces out of diverse and extramusically motivated references—to select, tie together, and neatly package.[67] If "They're Coming Around" shows how citations can become integral to a cue through change and development, "The Battle of the Resistance" demonstrates that a cue's feeling of integration can emerge not despite, but by virtue of, Williams's occasional tendency toward jam-packed citationality.

Pre- and Refigurations

A constant state of referentiality, such as defines *Star Wars* '77, accords with the Mahlerian aesthetic of all-encompassing eclecticism. But intertextual saturation can also easily hamper expectations of symphonic self-sufficiency. Conversely, a turn inward, away from outside allusions and toward established *Star Wars* musical tropes and topics, ensures a more consistent and autonomous sound. But that can end up being a more delimited, less imaginative sound. Williams's work on the series can be read as a long-running attempt to balance these competing symphonic impulses. The tension is most pronounced in the Sequel scores. While not without their innovations, Episodes VII through IX move away from the intertextual lushness of the Original films as well as the timbral and rhythmic experimentations of the Prequels; the result is a trilogy that loses the variety and unpredictability of past entries, while maintaining a sound that is unwaveringly *Star Wars*ian.

Counterintuitively, a heightened tendency toward self-reference can produce some truly elegant and legitimately *novel* moments of musical storytelling. For the Prequels, Lucas constructed certain scenes to parallel ones in the chronologically later Original trilogy. Tellingly, he conceived of these connections in terms of a sensorial mixed metaphor, as a way to "see the echo of where it is all heading." The auditory conceit is reinforced in what he said next, his well-known and unfairly mocked dictum: "It's like poetry . . . *they rhyme*."[68] Lucas made this specific remark in reference to a *visual* plot point—Anakin blowing up an enemy battle station in Episode I, much as Luke would in Episode IV. But the principle of poetic pre/resemblance is strongly applicable to music too. In fact, Lucas later reformulated his notion of the rhyme in explicitly symphonic terms:

> The *Star Wars* saga is like a symphony, which has recurring themes. You have one theme orchestrated in a particular way and place, which then comes back orchestrated as a minor theme somewhere else. There are these little threads running through things that are constantly turning events on their head. You see two people confronting the same things with different ends. It's a rhythm. . . . It has the epic quality of following one person from the time he's nine years old to the time he dies. It's Anakin's story, but obviously there are many other characters in that story—his children, his best friend—and their stories carry through. So this isn't just a tune—it's a symphony.[69]

With its paradoxical blend of semiotic density and intrinsic suggestiveness, music is often enlisted as the series' most dependable rhyming agent. The ability to echo with itself is a significant ingredient in that all-important *tensed* quality to which Williams's musical prose aspires. Even more grandiosely, a comparison could be drawn with theological typology: the notion that events in earlier religious texts represent, prefigure, or add meaningful context for subsequent, strictly disconnected ones. The difference in *Star Wars*, of course, being that one can sometimes (although not always!) presume active creative intent, rather than divine providence, behind any such felicitous echoes.[70]

The music Williams wrote for the scene Lucas had in mind with his famous "rhyme" comment has little in common with its narratival double in *A New Hope*. Anakin's act of heroic detonation in Episode I [2:02:22] involves a rousing contrapuntal overlay of the FORCE and DUEL OF THE FATES themes. Luke's equivalent accomplishment in Episode IV [1:56:56] is accompanied by a suspenseful string of what Williams called his "Planets chords," leading to a pair of chromatic cadences (D♭$^{\sharp 4}$/G→C, F♯|A→D♭) and concluding with a REBEL FANFARE–based afterglow.[71] But elsewhere in Episode I, a sense that the future is directing the past is pervasive. In Chapter 5, we will explore a subtle method by which this effect is achieved—the score's seeding of the mature "Imperial March"/VADER theme in otherwise non-leitmotivic passages. One does not need to sound out the athematic corners of the soundtrack to discover such pre-echoes, however. The theme Williams composed for ANAKIN and showcased throughout the film is the most sustained instance of musical typology in the series. "I really sort of wrote that theme backwards," the composer attested. "It's really Darth Vader's theme taken apart and reconstructed . . . transformed into a very sweet and lyrical youthful kind of tune." Though he phrases it in more modest terms than Lucas, Williams too cast the result in literary terms, as a "sort of a poetic conceit or a trick." But, he adds, "it's a fun trick."[72]

The trick of deconstruction in ANAKIN involves several of VADER's most salient characteristics—rhythm, contour, harmony—all of which will be detailed at length in Chapter 5. At least one aspect, however, is a *negative* trait: the theme's modality. Though generally harmonized as though it were in a major key, Williams's proto-Vader melody pointedly *avoids* the positively-valenced major mediant ($\sharp\hat{3}$) scale-step, a remarkable fact given the otherwise highly chromatic disposition of the tune. It is a theme that could go either way, modally speaking. Different presentations of the ANAKIN leitmotif in Episode I play up or down these Imperial-allusive parameters, and the precise degree of poetic parallelism varies dramatically between statements. Whether we hear a vague "off-rhyme" or eerily exact premonition depends on dramatic context—including the theme's extradiegetic presentations, a fact to which we shall return in Chapter 8.[73]

Figure 2.11 depicts an iteration of ANAKIN's leitmotif from *The Phantom Menace* whose anticipation of his future theme is particularly clear. Heard while Qui-Gon and Anakin have a one-on-one chat about the Jedi Council's refusal to admit the boy into their organization, Williams is afforded an unusual chance to give a full statement of the theme, both antecedent and consequent phrases. Note the insinuated but never-exactly duplicated rhythmic and melodic contours of VADER's theme, and the chromatic leaps and strong-beat dissonances that tease a rather more unbalanced melodic identification than this. As expected, the mediant pitch (here C♯) is studiously avoided in the melody. Although the tone of the dialogue is hopeful, the leitmotif's darker aspects are starting to come to the fore, particularly with the final cadence, now supported by an Fm to A motion—a sunny spin on VADER's signature ♭vi to i progression. The conversation then moves on to the regrettable notion of symbiotic, force-infusing midichlorians, but Williams's music has told us something more important: destiny, not some ad hoc biology, has already ordained young Anakin's future, personal and musical.

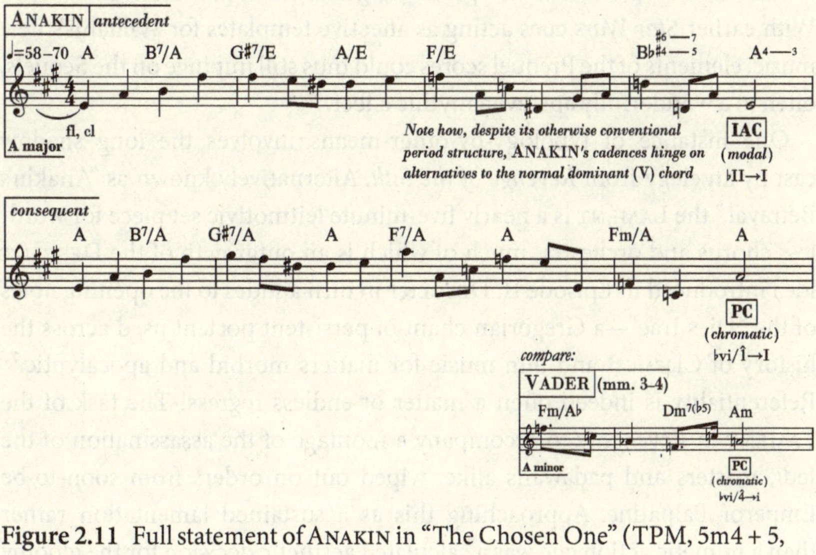

Figure 2.11 Full statement of ANAKIN in "The Chosen One" (TPM, 5m4 + 5, 1:35:20)

Poetic though it is in this instance, musical predestination in the manner of ANAKIN's theme is not uniformly applied across the Skywalker Saga. Other themes that could have been de- and re-constructed receive no such adumbrations in the Prequels. Neither LUKE, nor LEIA, nor the siblings' joint leitmotif LUKE AND LEIA, is foreshadowed in the same systematic manner as their dark father's theme, for example. Nor is there any guarantee that past leitmotifs are allowed to echo in chronologically *subsequent* entries in the series.

Death and Transfiguration

Each of the *Star Wars* trilogies invites critique along various axes, but a problem unique to Episodes VII through IX concerns their hesitancy to engage with the Prequel trilogy—a hesitancy that extends to musical references as much as visual or narratival ones.[74] Whether born of a desire to produce something new, or a wish to banish any negative aftertaste lingering after the mixed reception of Episodes I through III, the musical result was a near-total avoidance of allusion to leitmotivic materials introduced in those three movies, even where they might make good thematic sense.[75] But when an explicit referential door is shut, sometimes a more allusive window is opened. With all three of the Sequels—and *The Last Jedi* especially—large stretches of film were temp-tracked with preexisting music from the series as a whole. With earlier *Star Wars* cues acting as affective templates for Williams's new music, elements of the Prequel scores could thus still impinge on the Sequels, often to a wonderfully apt, even mythic effect.[76]

One instance of typology-by-other-means involves the long shadow cast by an elegy from *Revenge of the Sith*. Alternatively known as "Anakin's Betrayal," the LAMENT is a nearly five-minute leitmotivic set piece for wordless chorus and orchestra, much of which is an outgrowth of the DESCENT idea introduced in Episode II. DESCENT in turn alludes to the opening notes of the "Dies Irae"—a Gregorian chant of persistent portent used across the history of Classical and film music for matters morbid and apocalyptic.[77] Referentiality is indeed often a matter of endless regress! The task of the LAMENT in *Revenge* is to accompany a montage of the assassination of the Jedi, masters and padawans alike, wiped out on orders from soon-to-be Emperor Palpatine. Approaching this as a sustained lamentation rather than a mimetic action cue was a calculated aesthetic decision for the gloomy film. "*Revenge of the Sith* certainly is the darkest one of all of them," Williams noted. "Does that mean it is the darkest music? You can be looking at something that's quite horrific, but the music can be giving you a sense of compassion, rather than simply just underlining what's very dark and difficult about it."[78]

Later in the same film, the darkly compassionate music is recalled as Anakin confronts and chokes Padmé and boasts to Obi-Wan about his newfound powers. A requiem for the extermination of the Jedi Order and the soul of one man, LAMENT is a highlight of *Revenge*'s soundtrack. Its mixture of voices and instrumental timbres was symbolically loaded in Lucas's mind: "The chorus represents the personal fall of Anakin; the orchestration represents democracy's descent into dictatorship."[79] The Prequel trilogy's overriding tragic binary—the personal and the political—is here conjoined in musical (dis)harmony.

Despite the LAMENT's raw emotional power, its strains are never heard in a literal fashion following the 2005 film. However, "Anakin's Betrayal" does provide an unmistakable template for two key moments in the Sequels. The first echo comes at the conclusion of Episode VIII. After Luke's line "I will not be the last Jedi," the camera cuts to Rey, using a hitherto unseen force prowess to rescue the remnants of the beleaguered Resistance. As she levitates a heap of boulders blocking their escape, a slow and sad choral passage begins to unfurl, culminating in a rare perfect cadence, as the scene moves from a shot of Rey and Finn embracing to a pair of close-ups on Luke and Kylo Ren. Echoing in the ears of knowledgeable listeners will be the final thirty seconds of the "Anakin's Betrayal." Those bars accompany the sight of the Jedi Temple aflame—a once-welcoming sanctuary from which a concerned Senator Bail Organa learns he is now barred. The cadential progression from Episode VIII, along with its rhyme with Episode III's tearful centerpiece, is shown in Figure 2.12.

Nothing in Rey's musical feat is a direct copy of the *Revenge* cue. If anything, the association with LAMENT is dulled in the final version of the cue: while the wordless chorus is prominent through the passage's first four measures, in the ultimate film mix those voices are dialed down during the concluding bars. Yet if the two passages are disaffiliated on a timbral basis, harmonically they form an indelible link. Both spans build to an emphatic perfect authentic cadence in the key of E minor, almost liturgical in manner. And they do so with a cadential dominant chord that conspicuously enfolds both tonic (E_4) and leading-tone ($D\sharp_4$) pitches. Even were the rest of the

Figure 2.12 Rhyme of "Anakin's Betrayal" in *The Last Jedi*. **a.** "Lament" (ROTS, 5m3, 1:24:30); **b.** "Finale Part 1" (TLJ, 9m85, 2:16:50)

segment in a totally different affective universe than the Episode III cue, the identity of this cadence firmly associates the scene of Rey's apotheosis—a figurative rebirth of the Jedi—with the moment of its historical death. What else could this be called but musical poetry?

A Choir of Ghosts

A second rhyme occurs at the end of *The Rise of Skywalker*, in a cue so abundant in thematic content that Williams drolly entitled it "Name That Tune." More on the nose than the echo from *The Last Jedi*, this reference to the LAMENT occurs when the literal voices of Jedi past—including several slain during Order 66—reach out to Rey from the netherworld of the Force. Just as they fell to Palpatine's treachery in the Prequels, now they inspire Rey to rise as the collective avatar of "all the Jedi." Figure 2.13 renders this passage, again along with its prefiguration in Episode III.

An oasis of quiet during the hectic battle over Exegol, the chorale in "Name That Tune" recollects an earlier module from LAMENT than the one

Figure 2.13 Rhyme of "Anakin's Betrayal" in *The Rise of Skywalker*. **a.** "Lament" (ROTS, 5m3, 1:23:28); **b.** "Name That Tune" (TROS, 7m44, 1:57:14)

heard in *The Last Jedi*. As before, the presence of wordless chorus primes the comparison, but the deeper linkage is again a detail of pitch design. The highly marked and otherwise franchise-unique touch is the identically voiced E minor to F major progression, with a grief-stricken ♯4–3 suspension drawn over that F-chord.[80] This figure is introduced early and developed throughout "Anakin's Betrayal," contributing to various suspension chains that redouble the scene's pathos. (As if Anakin steeling himself to murder younglings in cold blood required more pathos!) In "Name That Tune," the ♯4–3 motion is more of a fleeting shadow, a twinge of leitmotivic *déjà vu* that gives way to an unusual harmonization of REY's theme over a half-diminished seventh chord. However hazy, that reactivated memory serves an important, perhaps even *Saga-defining* symphonic goal. It is the musical spark that sets in motion a leitmotivic chain reaction. With soft sorrow, the score summons Rey, urging her forward, first tentatively, then with absolute resolve, to a statement of her theme in a full suit of orchestral armor. That act of leitmotivic revivification in turn seems to activate the next module: a final clash between the FORCE and EMPEROR leitmotifs, the latter finally being disintegrated for good.[81] And so sonic strands of all three trilogies are drawn together in this powerful cue.

The level of forethought given to these multifarious influences, allusions, and callbacks is hard to gauge. If it were a matter of emulating a temp track of Williams's previous music chosen *for* him, the interpretations offered above may amount to happy convergences more than compositional masterplans. At the same time, the composer has dropped more esoteric Easter eggs for less poignant sequences. Somewhere between fortuitous and inevitable, such rhymes are prevalent and potent, binding *Star Wars*' musical galaxy together in ways even the composer might not have fully envisioned, but that sensitive listeners surely grasp. Conscious of it or not, when we hear *Star Wars,* we hear much more than a single standalone score: our listening is shaped by echoes of Stravinsky and Korngold, Holst and Walton, early Williams and late Williams. Idioms past and associations ingrained reverberate constantly across the series, modulating and transforming along the way, but never wholly dampening.

There is another category of referential music in the Skywalker Saga that is not just salient for all listeners, not just dense with echoic meaning, but also undeniably and in all cases intentional: leitmotif. What are these moments of "melodic identification" that furnish the lexicon of Williams's musical prose? And how ought we approach the leitmotivic technique in a way that is at once systematic and true to its highly mutable usage? *Star Wars* teaches us a language of leitmotif; Chapter 3 offers a guide to its grammar.

3

The Language of Leitmotif

Use and Mention

One of the best ways to understand something is to observe it in an unexpected place, outside its native habitat. Recall Yoda's apothegm invoked in the previous chapter: "you must unlearn what you have learned." When it comes to music, decontextualization is the surest pathway to enlightenment. The displacement of accustomed sounds forces us to hear with fresh ears, not a trivial task when it comes to the over-familiar music of the Skywalker Saga. And few concepts are as over-familiar, as saddled with established modes of listening, as leitmotif. Thankfully, there are many instances where these recurring melodic ideas are displaced into strange contexts over the course of the series, a few of which genuinely challenge the interpretive status quo of *Star Wars*' music. We will take up such in-text oddities in later chapters. Here, we turn to a theme that finds itself even farther from home.

John Williams composed the music for *E.T.: The Extra-Terrestrial* between 1981 and 1982, two years after his work on *The Empire Strikes Back*. Set in present-day California, *E.T.*'s world is essentially our own, right down to the time-appropriate sets of *Star Wars* merchandise in the young protagonist Elliot's bedroom. There is a deep affection in director Steven Spielberg's shots of various Kenner-brand action figures, and some narrative weight to boot; the toys serve as important a bonding agent for Elliot and E.T. as the movie's other famous branded product, Reese's Pieces. So, later in the movie when E.T. spies a child dressed as Yoda for Halloween, the impression is again of endearing verisimilitude, another touch of pop-cultural realism in this postcard of 1980s suburbia.

Williams seizes the opportunity provided by this meeting of alien species with an affectionate reference of his own, underscoring the encounter with an allusion to Yoda's theme, set in the middle of the larger cue "Halloween." The module is depicted in Figure 3.1.

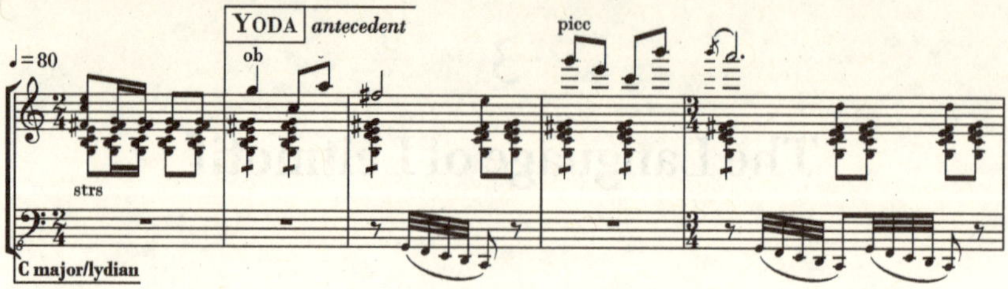

Figure 3.1 Yoda's thematic cameo in *E.T.*'s "Halloween" (7m1, 1:03:42)

A solo oboe offers the first four notes of the Jedi Master's theme, and piccolo the next five an octave higher. Besides a dainty grace note added to the last pitch, this is an unaltered presentation of the melody's antecedent phrase. For most filmgoers, the reference will pass by unnoticed, with no detriment to appreciating the scene. Jonathan Godsall, discussing sly self-quotations in film music, writes that musical "Easter eggs" are by definition inessential, a source of surplus enjoyment to be relished by "the few and not the many; to recognize them is to uncover 'a joke or bonus,' but nothing more."[1] Accordingly, the presentation of YODA in *E.T.*'s "Halloween" is not stylistically marked with respect to the rest of the cue, but it is not exactly hidden either. Like all good in-jokes, the reference is fashioned to be catchable but non-disruptive, such that those not in the know are not befuddled or irritated. Williams bends the theme to suit the tone and texture of the cue, making the normally songful melody a little more jaunty than usual. Not that YODA's material requires much finessing to fit into *E.T.*'s larger idiom: the leitmotif shares with the score an emphasis on solo woodwinds and a tendency to luxuriate in baths of lydian harmony. Thus, the extra-*Extra-Terrestrial* motif is easily and inconspicuously integrated. But to the right listener—the kind already familiar with the Episode V soundtrack and with an ear for Williams's motivic games—this four-measure quotation will be unmissable.

In fact, *E.T.*'s "Halloween" involves a double recognition, one on-screen, one off. First, there is the purely diegetic realization for the wayward alien himself, whose cries of "Home! Home!" entail a canon-muddying identification of the "galaxy far, far away" with our own Milky Way. Simultaneously, on the level of the film audience, listeners will enjoy a real "aha!" feeling, the sort that comes from grasping a cleverly presented detail or inside joke. As is often the case with both musical humor and musical allusivity, recognition is founded on the perception of *incongruity*. YODA's leitmotif is misplaced, stripped of its gravitas, perhaps even made to pose a challenge to the integrity of Williams's musical world-building.[2] This incongruity, however, is what makes the cue from *E.T.* an apt place to begin building a critical understanding of leitmotif as it normally works in *Star Wars*. Because for as long as the leitmotif technique has existed, it has been subject to strategic dislocation, be it by Debussy and Fauré or by disco and funk artists.[3] Affectionate or malicious, against-the-grain usages have a way of illuminating aspects of leitmotivic composition that the engrossing, even hypnotic force of musical prose can otherwise leave us insensible to.

What makes leitmotif such a versatile musical storytelling technique is the fact that it appears capable of meaning. Whole treatises have been written examining what grants these little melodies the ability to host semantic content, and nearly as much ink has been spilled critically examining their aesthetic and ideological implications.[4] In a lightly perverse way, E.T.'s "Halloween" provides a musical disquisition on an important issue of musical semantics: *use versus mention*. A concept from the philosophy of language, the use/mention distinction is not difficult to grasp.[5] Take the following pair of true statements:

a. Leitmotif is an important component of the musical storytelling of *Star Wars*.
b. "Leitmotif" is an anglicization of a German compound word (*das Leitmotiv*) whose first known usage was by A. W. Ambros in 1860.[6]

While the first sentence *uses* the word "leitmotif" to tell us something about a film score, the second *mentions* the word *as* a word. A used word is utilitarian, getting some point across about the outside world. A mentioned one draws attention to its status as a signifier, as some kind of utterance or element of a linguistic discourse; it points to itself.

Pedants might deplore how the distinction is ignored or flouted in philosophical treatises, but use-versus-mention is generally understood intuitively and deployed properly by everyday speakers of a language.[7] But can it be translated to music theory? Is there a sense in which the two melodic cells spelled below might be different?

a. G_4-C_4-A_4-$F\sharp_4$
b. "G_4-C_4-A_4-$F\sharp_4$"

Before we progress, a massive disclaimer is called for: music is not a language, and leitmotifs are not words. Despite having suggestively word-like qualities, short recurring themes à la Wagner possess neither the semantic nor syntactical properties required by any respectable theory of language. We are not employing the use/mention distinction as a component of a rigorous theory of leitmotivic semiosis, but as an informal comparison—albeit an important one, too rarely acknowledged by musicologists.[8]

When Williams conjures the first few notes of YODA's theme in *E.T.*, it is not because the motif is the result of some internal musical argument or in service of some essential dramatic function. Rather, he is taking "melodic identification" in a maximally literal way. The music in "Halloween" indexes its little green target directly, in a different manner of narrational address than the rest of the *E.T.* soundtrack. Because of its textual displacement, the musical citation does not just announce "this is Yoda," but "this is Yoda's *theme*." Williams's cue points to the leitmotif *as* a leitmotif, as an element of a particular *Star Wars*/John Williams/1980s-film discourse, to be apprehended on an exclusively non-narratival level.[9]

Neither use nor mention paradigm in music is intrinsically worthier than the other.[10] This is a provocative opinion, one that flies in the face of much of the reception of the leitmotif technique, especially in its filmic incarnations. Critics of leitmotif assail its tendency for coarse or disruptive signposting—toward using melodies as "calling cards," as Debussy disparaged them.[11] For some critics, the very thought of musical mention is cast as antithetical to real symphonic development.[12] Much of the most corrosive bile in Theodor Adorno and Hanns Eisler's 1947 polemic, *Composing for Films*, is directed at an alleged debasement of the leitmotif technique in American film. Classical Hollywood, they bemoan, treats the leitmotif as "the most elementary means of [musical] elucidation, the thread by which the musically inexperienced find their way about," an "ineffective and uneconomical" device that serves as naught but a "musical lackey, who announces his master with an important air even though the eminent personage is already clearly recognizable to everyone."[13] It is not difficult to imagine how they would have judged the score for *Star Wars*. An unapologetic elitism often lies behind Adorno and Eisler's rhetoric.[14] However, their basic complaint—leitmotif can be literal and lazy—is hard to deny, at least on its face.[15] Indeed, even the technique's defenders often accept this use-weighted value system when they argue that, properly applied and interpreted, leitmotif is *resistant* to signposting. Leitmotifs on this view are at their most dramatically effective when they escape their semantic targets, floating into a haze of pure suggestion and ineffable feeling.[16]

There are valid elements to critiques of leitmotivic mention, in film generally and the Skywalker Saga specifically. Williams can be too obvious with his melodic identifications, especially in the Original Trilogy. He can miss ripe opportunities for thematic development, especially in the Prequels. He can cycle through motifs in a perfunctory way, as if merely checking off musical boxes, especially in the Sequels. However, to dismiss mention completely as a compositional value also means dismissing it as a *listening* value, and in doing so, it denigrates any listeners who happen to practice it. That is a position this book categorically rejects.[17] There are delights and complexities inherent in mention, in identification for its own sake, but these are rarely acknowledged by musicologists. Philosopher Paul Saka inventories a host of "uses" for mention: "attributing exact words and thoughts to others; for distancing oneself from a given word choice (as in scare quotes); for indicating titles; for expressing irony," and for "explaining truth . . . meaning . . . external negation, and indirect discourse."[18] These functions bear fascinating and suggestive analogs with leitmotif, and we will revisit quite a few—particularly distanciation, irony, and negation—in Chapter 7.

To Saka's list, we might add the pleasing pang of recognition—and recognition's wistful cousin, nostalgia—that mention facilitates. A certain stripe of filmgoer loves Easter eggs, regardless of their tendency to breach cinematic/musical immersion. With its immense body of lore and its passionate fanbase, the *Star Wars* franchise is a naturally enticing site for the mention-paradigm, both for composers and listeners. It is remarkable then that only a few instances of leitmotifs behaving in an *entirely* citational way can be found inside the Skywalker saga—"Threepio's Bedtime Story" is the rule-proving exception, analysis of which will also be deferred to Chapter 7. Most thematic statements, even the most on-the-nose ones, exist somewhere between use and mention.

The appearance of Yoda in *E.T.* is instructive as a case of thematic mention pushed to its limit, a *reductio ad obvium* of the "leit" aspect of leitmotif. Yet while its initial presentation is, as a matter of abstract musical structure, strictly unmotivated, Yoda's theme is not treated as a completely extratextual intruder. We already noted that the tune is presented in a way that harmonizes with the childlike, Prokofievian milieu of the "Halloween" cue. More significantly, the leitmotif leaves an imprint past its preliminary mention, in music that exemplifies the use paradigm. The material that follows Yoda's antecedent phrase is depicted in Figure 3.2. Williams shifts to a more discursive, mobile musical idiom, with horn and then flutes

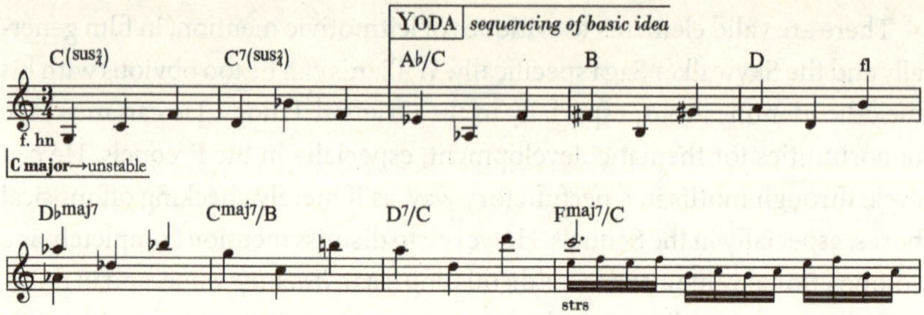

Figure 3.2 Sequential expansion of YODA in *E.T.*'s "Halloween" (7m1, 1:03:52)

modulating quickly across major keys in an upward-bending melodic arch. This forms the first link in a chain of intensificatory sequences, the terminus of which is an exultant statement of the film's FLYING theme, heard as E.T. and Elliot take their iconic ride over the moon.

On first listen, these eight measures probably sound athematic. Certainly, there are no melodic "calling cards" being handed out during the span. But while it does not brandish its motivic origin so undisguisedly as the five measures that precede it, the material in Figure 3.2 also springs from YODA's melodic fount. Starting with the A♭/C chord, the horn line's winding shape is entirely drawn from the first three notes of that theme: down a fifth, up a sixth. The aural impression is one of exuberance and buoyant energy, a thematic particle spilling out of its phrasal bounds, unable to contain itself. Here, motivic mention actually *precipitates* use.

Though atypical in placement, YODA's needle-drop in *E.T.* is illustrative of Williams's leitmotivic craft in general, in the way it freely transits between mention and use. *Star Wars* leitmotifs, even when broached first in a citational way, tend toward developmental processes like fragmentation, sequencing, and reharmonization, all seen here in microcosmic form. As we have seen, those procedures are emblematic of musical prose, in which continuously varied and transforming motives constitute—and in a sense motivate—the entire musical fabric.

If we have begun this chapter on leitmotif with an esoteric topic—use versus mention is the definition of a semantic distinction!—it is for a good reason. So much of how the Skywalker Saga tells its stories revolves around what and how these little musical particles mean. The intent of this chapter is not to summarize the vast literature on leitmotif, much less to offer a radical new theory on its nature or behavior. Rather, I intend to inspect the technique as it arises in *Star Wars* from a number of angles, always with the twin frameworks of symphonism and storytelling in mind. Following the model of this section, we will help ourselves to a number of concepts from linguistics and the philosophy of language: semantic drift, prototypicality, syntax and grammar, hypotaxis and parataxis. Again, these terms have precise meanings in the study of language, and are employed here as vivid analogies, never one-to-one mappings from language to music.

First, we will consider some big definitional issues. What gets to count as motivic, what do thematic labels accomplish, and how ought we categorize these materials? This leads to a question of motivic fluidity or fixity, and the next section will thus reflect on critiques of leitmotif in *Star Wars* that involve the relative rigidity of its themes. With a deeper appreciation of thematic identification and signification, we then turn to thematic structure itself; I will introduce a simple model that shows how different musical parameters conjoin to produce thematic meaning—or diverge and dissociate. The following two sections devote attention to some of the categories *excluded* from the leitmotivic umbrella, investigating all manner of athematic materials. Far from a digression, these sections on non-leitmotivic music are indispensable to understanding how musical prose works in this series. From there, we will be prepared to consider the issue of form, a subject of no small ambivalence when it comes to film music. The chapter concludes with a case study from *The Last Jedi* that synthesizes these topics and ties them back to the book's overriding theme of cine-symphonic listening.

Mapping the Musical Galaxy

Chapter 1 introduced a four-part definition of leitmotif: a musical idea that is distinctive, symbolic, varied, and recurrent. These criteria provide a systematic basis for mapping the *Star Wars* scores. Appendix 1 at the end of this book lists fifty-nine ideas that fulfill those conditions. As a bonus, the themes Williams contributed to the film *Solo* and TV show *Obi-Wan Kenobi* are also included. Each leitmotif garners a label, a timestamp for its first occurrence, and a reduction of its first few measures, normally enough for identification purposes. Readers are encouraged to flip back and forth to this guide while reading—or better, listening.

In presenting Williams's themes in catalogic form, we are taking part in a long-standing tradition, one in which leitmotivic works are supplemented with some sort of "map," a tool to help navigate their long and winding ways. No sooner would a new opera by Wagner premiere than a cottage industry of pamphlets, annotated scores, and guidebooks would appear that aimed to aid listeners in orienting themselves within the intricate thematic cartographies of these works. Collectively, these *Thematische Leitfäden* (thematic guiding threads) became an inseparable feature of the reception and interpretation of Wagner's mature music dramas. As exemplified by the highly successful (if only ever tacitly Wagner-approved) guides by Hans von Wolzogen that furnished each motif with a name and an account of its signification, the *Leitfäden* opened up works like the Ring Cycle to appreciative amateurs. Christian Thorau notes that a guidebook's provision of neat labels and clear meanings gave members of a mass operatic audience "a language by which [they] could join an exclusive discourse."[19] A curious mixture of approachability and technicality, these books served to democratize musical experience, but in doing so created a division of leitmotivic insiders and outsiders. There is nothing wrong with connoisseurship, of course—who would argue that having a segment of one's audience that is *more* passionate than the rest is anything but a boon. But the tendency to equate encyclopedic knowledge of an artwork with the possession of the "correct" means of accessing that artwork is as powerful as it is unjustifiable. To indulge the cartographic impulse in service of aesthetic engagement is worth celebrating, but one must take care that passion does not curdle into gatekeeping.

The social dynamics of thematic cataloging are not the only ramifications map-minded listeners should pay heed to. Musical guides also risk closing the interpretive frontier of a complex piece, fixing locales with names and leaving no musical corner *terra incognita.* One could imagine an extreme version of the Easter egg hunter of the previous section, head buried in their catalog, forcibly converting every motivic use they hear into a mention. Given that thematic labels are often gross simplifications of complex semantic networks, the pedant's approach to leitmotivic hearing might even be an act of, if not textual violence, then not exactly collaborating with a text on its own terms. Blinkered label-hunting is a nightmare scenario for absolute music purists and believers in musical ineffability. And it is not the kind of cine-symphonic stance advocated here either—not, however, because fine-grained motivic recognition is an intrinsically unworthy way of accessing the score, but because *Star Wars* is so much *more* than a string of melodic references and identifications.

A good thematic guide opens a text up to new levels of appreciation by new audiences. Speaking of Wagner, Carl Dahlhaus and John Deathridge argue that leitmotivic labeling is necessary, but its utility is only temporary:

> The identification and labeling of leitmotifs, like a bridge that one destroys on reaching the other shore, thus fulfills an exclusively heuristic function: the "clues" utter a first, not last word on the musico-dramatic processes and serve merely as a means of entry into the dense system of relationships.[20]

Attuning oneself to that dense system is a worthwhile goal, because the relational qualities between leitmotifs—not their mere existence—are a large part of what makes the Skywalker scores rewarding to hear symphonically. Yet we will do so here without destroying the bridge, if for no other reason than constructing that heuristic tool is rewarding and revealing in its own right. A leitmotif guide is itself a product of analytical deliberation, though that deliberation is occluded from its reader. What thematic material gets included or excluded? What musical features are deemed essential or secondary? What labels and annotations and cross-references are added? These are questions of interpretation, not scientific data collection, and ultimately indicate the motivic mapmaker's cultural values and priorities.

In compiling a catalog of *Star Wars* themes, I have generally erred toward inclusion. The JAWA theme, for instance, is hardly a textbook specimen of a leitmotif. It is varied little and is constrained to just three consecutive cues in a single film. But the JAWA tune is ear-catching and memorable and described by the composer himself as "a theme."[21] Nothing is lost by giving it a place at—or rather on—the thematic table. The risks of over-inclusion are tempered in any case by creating a category of *principal leitmotif*. Many fewer entries—just twenty-two—satisfy the stricter stipulations for this type of theme: (a) not just recurrence but abundance, and (b) not just variation but transformation.[22] Most films introduce just a couple of these saga-spanning ideas, and unsurprisingly, they originate more in the inaugural entries in each saga than their final installments. While principal leitmotifs may steer whole trilogies, less robustly cultivated themes like DROIDS (Ep. V only), EWOKS (Ep. VI only), and ROSE (Ep. VIII only) can still be highly salient and host thematic arcs of their own, albeit over a more limited scale.

Different listeners will have different criteria for salience, and even something as objective-seeming as a motivic proper name can be surpassingly contingent or subjective. Like the snippets of music notation that accompany them, the labels given for leitmotifs throughout this book are reductions, too: condensations of patterns of usage and denotation that are never perfectly straightforward, even in cases where the composer himself is the source of a theme's name. Even the series' seemingly most iconic leitmotifs—Luke, Vader, and the Force—have been described and utilized in a less-than-univalent way by Williams over the series' lifetime. As in any taxonomic system, the most carefully drawn borders have a way of dissolving. In fact, Williams's own conception of "melodic identification" would lead some of his own materials to slip through the cracks. Consider an idea that is heard in "The Map Scene" from *The Force Awakens*. This is the scene in which Han explains to Rey and Finn how Luke went missing while searching for the first Jedi Temple. The bulk of this cue is atmospheric and unobtrusive, revolving around two minor triads separated by a chromatic interval: first a tritone [Dm↔A♭m], then a minor second [C♯m↔Dm]. The relevant material is shown in reduced form in Figure 3.3. (Not depicted is the less repetitive violin descant.) Williams sets these chords in a soft pulsation, orchestrated so that their boundaries overlap and blur.

The wash of sound in "The Map Scene" is plenty evocative, its shifting, tonally estranged triads suggestive of unknown regions of tonal and galactic space. It is also about as far from melodic as one can get. And yet these chromatic oscillations are without question leitmotivic by our criteria. The pattern is *distinct*, possessing a consistent harmonic progression that is always voiced in the same way and treated as a standalone thought, not an accompaniment or adjunct to another theme. The chordal vacillation is *recurrent*, appearing on six occasions in Episode VII, ten if one counts unused

Figure 3.3 "The Map Scene" from The Force Awakens (TFA, 4m31, 52:41)

cues. It is also *varied*, albeit marginally. Its basic musical idea is subject to, if not anything resembling vigorous symphonic development, then at least a set of subtle modifications of texture and figuration. And it is *symbolic*, albeit less a hyper-explicit "calling card," more a diffusely glowing beacon. First presented as a musical mystery box to the audience—the tritonal juxtaposition is initially heard as Poe is handed a data drive of unknown contents—the oscillatory pattern gradually acquires a semiotic target, with each repetition focusing its association with the holographic map to Luke's whereabouts.[23] For all these reasons, and in spite of its decidedly non-melodic character, the material represented in Figure 3.3 thus deserves a label: the MAP leitmotif.[24]

For all the risks of simplification and reification, putting a label to a thing is invaluable for the purposes of identification "in the wild," especially for a nondescript morsel like this MAP motif. Having a proper name does *not* mean, however, that a leitmotif is symbolically fixed. Quite the opposite: a leitmotif's moniker should always be understood as at least a little provisional. This is mandatory for motifs as amorphous in profile and understated in treatment as the MAP. A "blink and you'll miss it" moment in *The Last Jedi* demonstrates why a naive model of leitmotif, where meaning and label are immutably one-to-one, is bound to impoverish rather than enrich hearing. The same pulsation of tritonal triads that plays sporadically in *The Force Awakens* arises in one clear instance in *The Last Jedi*. At the beginning of "Rey Awakens," a cue heard at the end of Rey's first lesson, the Dm↔A♭m oscillation reappears [51:17]. Again, the motif is presented in nebulous orchestral hues. But this token of the MAP motif does not take place during a discussion of a holographic navigational chart—that MacGuffin has already served its purpose and is not spoken of after Episode VII.[25]

Rather than literally invoking that physical object, Williams's revival of the MAP motif in "Rey Awakens" sheds light on character psychology. The progression lasts just three seconds, filling the time as Luke considers his response to Rey's realization that he has "closed [himself] off from the Force." Thus, while the MAP motif does not call to mind the star map itself, it does clarify something subtle, of deeper narratival significance than a mere plot device. Luke did not go looking for the first Jedi Temple like Han suggested, for some unspecified grand purpose; he simply did not want to be found. His exile amounted to a deliberate self-severing, both geographic and spiritual, from the world. All this meaning is suggested with a throwaway moment involving one of the series' most understated themes.

Leitmotivic Drift

The "Lesson One" scene in *The Last Jedi* is itself a useful tutorial on the value and limitations of names. If having a label such as "MAP motif" helps us pick out symbolically clear instances of its designated musical idea, it can also draw our attention to those times where meaning is not so nailed down. As with the use/mention distinction, the study of language provides a handy conceptual correlate for a purely musical phenomenon: semantic drift, or the idea that a word's meaning can change over time.[26] *Leitmotivic drift*, then, is the tendency for recurring themes to shed old denotations and absorb new ones over the course of a long musical work. The alteration of meaning is one of two basic ways in which recurring themes evolve, the other being the alteration of a leitmotif's structure over time. We will tackle the subject of changing structure in future sections; here, we dwell on meaning.

Semantic drift is a propensity to which all leitmotifs are prone, and one of particular relevance in pieces that aspire to a mythic condition. As James Buhler notes, drift is a Wagnerian aesthetic: "a certain inconsistency of leitmotivic deployment serves as a trace of self-conscious mythologization because such moments belie another logic at work besides the obvious signifying one—a musicomythic logic."[27] One may quibble with the extent that Wagner's own themes are fluid—they run the gamut from pure, vacant musical material to the most rigid of designators—but what matters is the artistic ideal, what Buhler calls a "semiosis in flux." This is a kind of primal state full of unspoken connections and vague significances, a musical universe before a rational mind (or thematic cataloger!) arrived to put everything in its proper place.

Just as leitmotifs in *Star Wars* slide between the poles of use and mention, there is a wide and freely traversed spectrum between semantic rigidity and drift in the Skywalker Saga. Flexibility in this regard fits Williams's overlapping justifications for the leitmotif technique: it is at once an on-demand mnemonic aid and a global score unifier; an easily graspable handle for listeners to parse a strange text and a constant conveyor of unplaceable mythic feeling. On a cue-to-cue basis, most leitmotivic occurrences in the Skywalker scores are more semantically consistent than not, closer in spirit to the lexical precision of themes in Wagner's *Das Rheingold* than the shifting significatory waters of *Tristan*. Buhler observes that leitmotifs for villainous characters and institutions are especially stable with respect to their referents, while good guy themes are more variable.[28] He interprets this discrepancy as a matter of ideology. Philosophically, the Light Side reflects the natural state of the universe, unbound by restrictive rules and prescriptive meanings. Themes associated with it, like LUKE and the REBEL FANFARE, correspondingly aspire to that untamed originary condition; they move around symbolically, adapt to new meanings at times, jettison them at others. The Dark Side, meanwhile, represents an inflexible and technologically perverted state—recall Obi-Wan's (supremely unself-aware) line "only a Sith deals in absolutes." Accordingly, themes affiliated with the forces of evil like "The Imperial March" and Kylo Ren's various mottos cling jealously to their labels, brandishing them as sonic emblems of power and control.

Buhler's conception of leitmotivic drift in political terms is a useful lens for interpreting the Original Trilogy. Its explanatory value decreases with the rest of the Saga, released after Buhler's essay. The Prequels are overall less leitmotivically articulated, while the light/dark and fluid/rigid binaries are blurrier in the Sequels. And while Buhler is careful to keep his ideological gloss separate from any claims of musical worth, his linkage of semantic fluidity with goodness and inflexibility (and by extension, motivic mention) with evil could be read as a tacit endorsement of those critiques voiced by leitmotif skeptics like Debussy and Adorno. Regardless of Williams's—or Buhler's—intent, the same old "calling card" complaint rears its head again here, but now with extra moral force. Musical mention is an inherent flaw: at best a compositional embarrassment; at worst, because it offers false clarity in a gray world, an actual ethical failure.

In truth, leitmotivic drift, just as much as rigidity, is an artistically neutral choice, applicable in valid and dramatically impactful ways, as well as lazy or inconsistent ones. In fact, there are two types of semantic fluctuation in *Star Wars* music, and their careful differentiation will lead us to a richer understanding of leitmotivic semiosis, one less marred by residual Debussyian/Adornian antipathy toward the technique. (The irony in subcategorizing a phenomenon defined by its refusal of taxonomy is not lost on the author.) First, there is the case of contextual drift, involving specific thematic statements that do not appear to follow from their accrued denotations. Second is a more intrinsic sort of driftiness, where certain themes almost by nature seem to resist unitary meaning.

Contextual Drift

A precedent for contextual drift is set quite definitively in *A New Hope* during Obi-Wan Kenobi's noble end. After the Jedi Master surrenders to Darth

Vader's killing blow [1:32:30], it is LEIA's theme we hear surging across the soundtrack, easily the most melodramatic iteration of that melody in the score. For the leitmotivic literalist, this rendition amounts to a thematic non sequitur; Luke is the focal character during the scene, not the Senator from Alderaan. But Williams has never been one to let lexical exactitude get in the way of hitting a powerful *emotional* beat: "I felt [Leia's leitmotif] had the most sweeping melody of all the themes in the score," and that its "wildly romantic" quality alone commended it to a scene of intense, operatic feeling.[29]

Similarly label-defying leitmotivic moments occur in subsequent entries. Episode II hosts several such suggestive realignments. The DROID ARMY theme sounds [47:34] during the reveal of the Clone Troopers—their in-universe adversaries! Similarly, a fragment of ANAKIN AND PADMÉ's love theme can be heard [2:14:19] sandwiched between heavy statements of "The Imperial March," as the full extent of the Grand Army of the Republic is shown at the end of the film. A chromatically warped version of SHMI's motif is intoned by solo trumpet as Chancellor Palpatine flatters his unwitting acolyte Anakin [26:12]. Later, the EMPEROR's own leitmotif is heard [1:25:30] as Anakin confesses to murdering the Tuskens. And, most incongruously, YODA's theme sounds [1:39:30] as Anakin and Padmé fight their way across a droid assembly line.

Listeners disturbed by the prospect of musical "continuity errors" can usually devise some justification or another for apparent inconsistencies like these. In the case of the Kamino reveal, perhaps Williams is trying to slyly communicate that the Droid and Clone armies *are* the same; after all, both militaries ultimately serve Palpatine. The appearance of ANAKIN AND PADMÉ amidst VADER's march neatly encapsulates the interpenetration of the personal and political so key to the Prequel Trilogy's meta-narrative. SHMI's rendition might be a clue that Palpatine somehow foresees how Anakin's rage upon his mother's death will prove a turning point in his fall to the Dark Side. Or it could just be an accident—sometimes Williams's music just sounds like, well, itself. The last two instances are the result of artificially tracked material from other cues, assembled by music editor Kenneth Wannberg. As such, any explanation by way of semantic drift might seem superfluous, as the composer's real musical intent is missing. However, for average listeners without such meta-textual knowledge, the EMPEROR and YODA's themes in those strange places are "canon," as it were, and amenable to rationalizations just as creative and personally meaningful as cases of more premeditated compositional planning.

Planned or not, leitmotifs sounding in strange places can be both sources of befuddlement and ripe opportunities for interpretive ingenuity.[30] But before one twists oneself up in hermeneutic knots, it is best to remember that *all* recurring themes are moving targets, especially in a score built from such an eclectic set of references, idioms, and techniques. The foundational axiom of the series' "musomythic logic" is that above all, the score must make *emotional* sense. Without vigilant reinforcement of their designations (admittedly often the case in *Star Wars*, as with villain themes), leitmotifs do tend to drift, even if they never quite revert to pure, unmarked neutral matter. A theme without a name still hosts affectively loaded topics and external references, after all.

As the most meta-*Star Wars*ian score of the nine, *The Rise of Skywalker* exemplifies this prioritization of emotional congruence over semantic correspondence in several prominent places. Music for the explosion of the Death Star from Episode IV [1:56:57] is alluded to at the (comparatively unclimactic) end of IX's "Falcon Flight" [9:56]. Luke's levitation of a submerged X-Wing late in the film [1:34:17] replays note for note the cue for Yoda's similar feat from *Empire* . To a thematic literalist, these callbacks are unearned and unneeded. But one cannot dispute that their insertion is affectively well-calibrated, and within the context of larger cues of predominantly new material, structurally well-prepared and integrated.

The sharpest example of the tension between leitmotivic semantics and sentiment occurs during the celebration that follows the Battle of Exegol at the end of *Rise*. Williams envisioned the accompanying cue, tellingly entitled "Bows," as an opportunity for a mini-suite of Light Side themes from the Original and Sequel trilogies. In itself, this is not unprecedented: the final film in the Prequel trilogy, *Revenge of the Sith*, bore a similarly summational cascade of leitmotifs for its long and dialogue-free concluding sequence, chaining together the FUNERAL, VADER, FORCE, LEIA, and LUKE motifs. But Episode IX's "Bows," a formal synopsis of which is given in Figure 3.4, takes that suite-building impulse several steps further. We hear in succession full statements of the following: LUKE, FORCE, POE, YODA, REY, LUKE AND LEIA, and FRIENDSHIP, plus a rousing but athematic introduction and a transitional module that suggests the REBEL FANFARE. The version that appears in the final film excises all of Poe Dameron's material and the first half of Yoda's (his sprightly B-theme), though these segments are preserved in the soundtrack album's penultimate track, "Reunion." As far as denotation goes, the inclusion of the principal Sequel themes is logical enough. So too is LUKE,

2:06:32 2:06:46 2:06:58 2:07:26 ------ cut ----- 2:07:30 2:08:10 2:08:27 2:09:12 2:09:44

1	2	3	4	5	6		7	8	9
Intro	LUKE	FORCE	trans. (R.F. ?)	POE	YODA		REY	LUKE & LEIA	FRIENDSHIP
					B-sect.	A-sect.			
B♭→D	D	Dm→	B♭	C→	→V/C	C	Am→B♭m	F	B♭
f. hn	f. hn, wws	f. hn, strs	wws	strs	wws	vn	wws, str	wws, strs	strs

Figure 3.4 Form of "Bows" (TROS, 9m3)

insofar as it doubles as the series' Main Theme, and the FORCE for much the same reason. But two stand out as being puzzlingly out of place. Neither Yoda nor the Skywalker twins are present on screen, nor particularly on the minds of the victors shown during their respective modules. Is Williams then "misleading" the audience here, as one widely viewed video essay contends?[31]

It is important to consider the various functions a finale cue serves within a mythical film score. On a utilitarian level, the recapitulation of themes from disparate parts of the story is meant to tie musical loose ends together and lend to the whole an impression of synthesis and finality. Yet there are less semantically driven goals too. The quasi-symphonic showcasing of themes, in a context where the constraints of dialogue and action underscoring are lifted, places greater weight on their intrinsic affective content, and might even nudge those musical materials away from the realm of absolute meaning and into a realm of mythical vagueness.[32] On a semantic level, the occurrence of YODA and LUKE AND LEIA in "Bows" may well be completely unmotivated—or rather un-leitmotivated. Indeed, the more one attempts to grapple with their implications given what is happening on screen, the more absurd their placement will seem. However, as a matter of sentiment and myth construction, the inclusion of those two motifs makes perfect sense. The affects conveyed by both themes—warmth, cheer, grace—map impeccably onto the scene; if one did not know their labels, one would assume the sequence was scored with consummate emotional sensitivity. Moreover, their selection operates on a meta-textual level, as a final farewell to two melodies that the composer is especially fond of but had little opportunity to revisit in the Sequels. (A more apt critique of this sequence would thus focus on the reliance on unmerited nostalgia rather than unfounded signification.) Always, Williams chooses what melody goes where on the basis of affective *and* narrative logic; but if one needs to take precedence, it is usually the former. Semantic meaning may drift away, but emotional meaning is never disregarded.

Intrinsic Drift

While any individual leitmotif may find itself in a semantically unexpected setting, certain thematic families are prone to a more intrinsic form of semiotic flux. This propensity to drift sets in early in *A New Hope*, and, as Buhler observed, is primarily a trait of themes associated with the good guys. Motifs for Luke, the Rebels, and especially the Force are all flexibly treated in that score, both with respect to their melodic/harmonic structure and underlying meaning. What has now become reified as "The Force Theme™" is surprisingly hard to pin down in *A New Hope*. At the time, Williams called it "Ben Kenobi's theme," and in its noble, melancholic tone the melody does seem suited to the wizened knight nicely.[33] But could it not also be heard just as strongly as a theme for Luke? Certainly, listeners are not wrong to sense an important linkage being forged between the melody and the character during the iconic "Binary Sunset," a connection reinforced later during "A Home Destroyed" and "The Last Battle," among other cues. Mythical underdetermination might well be the point here: as Buhler notes, the "Sunset" scene that spotlights this motif takes place before the eponymous "mystical energy-field" is explicitly invoked in the screenplay, much less demonstrated.

Despite the composer's "Ben Kenobi" label—an appellation already forgotten by *Empire*—Williams never insisted that it would serve as a Debussyian calling card. Rather, he had something more global and multivalent in mind: "I think of Ben Kenobi's theme as reflecting both him and, also, the Jedi Knights and the Old Republic that he remembers," as well as "the Force, the spiritual-philosophical belief of the Jedi."[34] It is better then, to interpret the tune as signifying the ineffable workings of destiny itself, a musical stamp of undifferentiated mythic significance, capable of inflecting any event with profundity. A basic truth of leitmotivic scoring is that the emptier the signifier, the more it can contain.

Though the biggest moment of semantic drift for Leia's theme—Kenobi's death—is of a contextual rather than intrinsic type, her theme is also bigger than her character, more mythically encompassing. Unlike themes for many other members of the *Star Wars* dramatis personae, the Leia motif is not at all a character sketch. If it were intended as such, Williams rather missed the mark by writing such a gentle, retiring, alluring melody, when Leia Organa as portrayed by Carrie Fisher is brusque, decisive, and sarcastic. Rather than a character's calling card, the LEIA melody is foremost a *relational* leitmotif. And this quality stems from its original conception, not as a melodic sketch of the bold and brash Princess-Senator, but as a love theme!

In the decades following *A New Hope,* Williams confessed that he composed LEIA's leitmotif for what he understood as a nascent amorous affair between Luke and Leia, before he discovered (and perhaps Lucas decided) that the characters were long-lost siblings.[35] Admittedly, it does not *function* as a traditional love theme in Episode IV—there are no kisses to score, no confessions of ardor to musically eroticize. But the melody's genesis as a romantic and relational theme is still palpable. Williams gives this away when he describes LEIA's motif as "a fairy tale type princess melody." The leitmotif is a projection, a representation of the adolescent image Luke has of Leia before meeting her.[36] (Literally a projection, when Luke stares captivated at her hologram!) And its embodiment of a kind of imaginary, indeed unreal state makes the theme a great stand-in for an even more generalized semantic/affective state: Romance with a capital R. This is most apparent in its usage in extra-diegetic settings like Episode IV's end credits and the "Princess Leia's Theme" concert arrangement, which we will inspect closely in Chapter 8. In those contexts, the melody signifies the ineffable romance of adventure, the nostalgia for a fantastic space and time, achingly longed for but forever closed off to modern listeners.

Prototypes and Parameters

"Always in motion, is the future." Yoda's line about the unpredictability of impending events applies to leitmotifs, too. As we have seen, their symbolic targets have a way of moving around, sometimes dissolving, sometimes expanding past their initial boundaries. But what about their structural, rather than semantic, boundaries? The ability to adapt, vary, even deconstruct melodies according to dramatic need is one of the great boons of the leitmotif technique and an explicit part of Williams's rationale for adopting the leitmotivic approach. The degree to which themes in *Star Wars* are treated as mutable entities is a complicated topic, one we will spend two full chapters examining. But before we dive into matters of motivic development and transformation, it is worth pausing to ask what makes up a "pre-developed" or "un-transformed" theme in the first place.

Figure 3.5 Two "morphs" of the Droids motif (ESB, 1m2 and 5m1, 6:47 and 42:34)

Following music theorist Matthew Bribitzer-Stull, we will treat leitmotifs as having *prototypes*. Another concept with roots in the study of language, a prototype is an "idealized mental construct that may or may not appear on the actual surface of the music," but nevertheless serves as a starting point and benchmark for all musical manipulations to come.[37] The Droids leitmotif from *Empire* illustrates the need for this idea of prototypicality. There is no concert arrangement, no purely self-standing rendition of this theme. Even the first two measures—its all-important hook—comprise two related but nonequivalent options, both shown in Figure 3.5. Naturally, the inaugural statement of the theme is salient, though even it has an unusual and never-quite duplicated phrase structure.[38] Yet despite the motif's fuzziness, listeners will likely extract an abstract representation across its ten-odd iterations in Episode V. What they glean is a thematic prototype, a model of the Droids motif that hosts its essential features (basic melodic profile, harmonic orientation, distinguishing contours and rhythmic patterns, etc.) while leaving available for alteration its more variable ones (meter, note repetitions, presence of a pickup, tempo, key, instrumentation, and so forth).

The prototype model is more than just a reflection of how we hear musical themes; it yields an analytical method for assessing thematic transformation and relatedness. Musicologist Stan Link observes that "the leitmotif's flexibility also lies in the fact that *any* musical parameter might become its identifying feature."[39] A prototype is a musical composite, and, as such, can be broken down into its constituent parameters: normal orchestration, normal harmonization, normal contour, and so on. These qualities may change within individual statements of a theme, and tracking their number and extent can provide a tidy if simplistic gauge of motivic relatedness—a quality that, short of the composer's explicit testimony, is often hard to determine without some kind of yardstick. Understanding a theme as a confluence of independent musical parameters can make it easier to see what changes over time and what stays the same. Of special relevance to *Star Wars*, the prototype model shows how certain parameters can be abstracted away

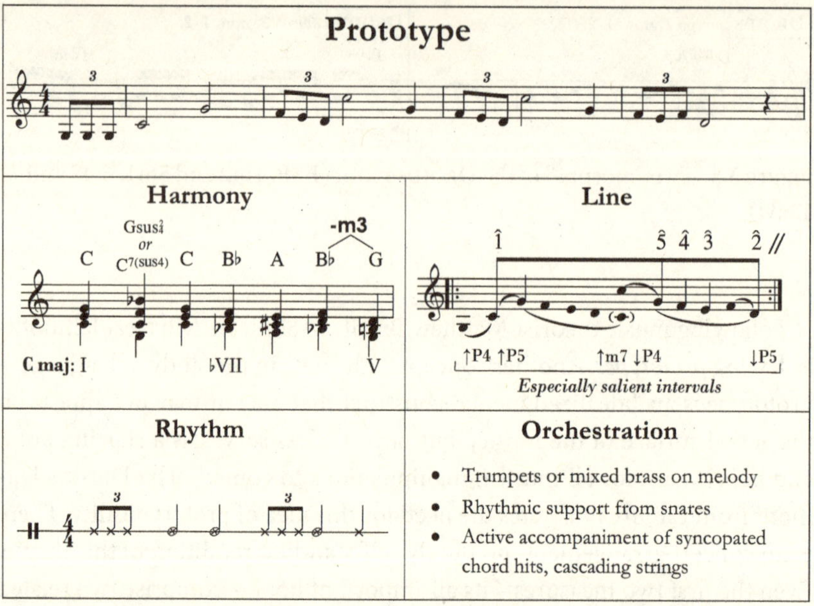

Figure 3.6 LUKE theme prototype and parameters

from their parent leitmotifs, becoming autonomous pseudo-motives in their own right. This is especially true of the harmonic progression parameter, as we will see.

Figure 3.6 demonstrates the prototype/parameter model with the LUKE theme. At the top of the chart lies the thematic prototype, a single melodic line of four measures, as plain and neutral in this guise as it is texturally flashy and elaborated in the majority of its actual statements. The notation is not drawn from any specific iteration or arrangement but rather represents a melodic Platonic ideal.

Underneath the prototype in this diagram are structural parameters judged significant to the theme's identity across its many iterations. There is LUKE's characteristic (but not mandatory) trumpet-led orchestration; its iconic (but highly variable) rhythmic mixture of long duplets and fast triplets; and its wide-leaping (but frequently inflected, inverted, or just plain truncated) linear frame. The theme's harmonic basis is particularly complex. Figure 3.6 notes the chords undergirding the melody, the functional progression from I to V that those chords effect, and the blocky voice-leading that animates and elaborates that progression. One ear-catching harmonic detail—the move from B♭ to G—occurs at the phrase-ending half cadence.

This is an intrinsically chromatic transformation, as no two major chords related by a minor third interval can belong to the same diatonic key.[40]

One thing this analytical model does not directly tell us is how much any individual musical parameter contributes to a theme's semantic content. Presenting and analyzing a leitmotif in this way is a formal exercise, though it can help us be more precise when taking the next step, of relating compositional choices to expressive ones. Isolating the line parameter, for instance, draws our attention to certain intervallic properties of LUKE that have a strong potential to "mean." We see clearly the abundance of upward perfect intervals, ideal for conveying the heroic fanfare topic, and an aspect present in a handful of affiliated leitmotifs (THRONE ROOM, LUKE AND LEIA, ANAKIN, HEROICS). We see the importance of octave displacement, with the C_5 midway through a substitution for an expected C_4 at the base of the theme's G_4-F_4-E_4-D_4 scale segment. This displacement is one aspect that strongly differentiates the theme from Korngold's *Kings Row*; the procedure is actually more redolent of Wagner, who was known to enliven descending scalar melodies by inserting a late-stage leap of a seventh.[41] In LUKE, we hear the incomplete descent from scale degree to $\hat{2}$ at the theme's end, but never all the way down to $\hat{1}$. When combined with the subtonic half-cadence—itself highly topical, as discussed in the previous chapter—the inherent incompleteness gives the theme its sense of open-endedness and unwritten promise.

It is possible to take such structure-to-sense mappings too far. Not every microscopic detail of construction is pregnant with significance, and we lose something by treating a theme as a sum of a million different parts rather than a gestalt based on their coordination and reinforcement. Ultimately, whatever expressive content a theme's various parameters contain is latent, an indefinite source of musical potential, clarified but never completely pinned down in specific filmic renditions. It is up to an involved, invested listener to imbue music's structural features with meaning.

Extra-Leitmotivic Material

Even with the holistic approach to thematicism offered in the previous sections, large and seldom-studied swathes of the Skywalker scores still remain unaccounted for. Our focus thus far on themes might give an inaccurate impression that all music in *Star Wars* either consists of freshly introduced ideas that will reappear later, or allusions to material already established. In reality, total leitmotivic saturation has never been Williams's aim, and there are many long tracts of dramatic underscore—including much that qualifies as musical prose—built from strictly non-recurrent ideas. This extra-leitmotivic music is overlooked and under-theorized but certainly not unfelt. To overcome the deep-seated analytical bias toward leitmotif, it will take more than simply acknowledging that material not based on the leitmotif principle is common and important. New, more fine-grained categories are needed to reflect the variety of forms and functions such music takes.

We begin with the matter of incidence: where does music based on something other than leitmotivic recall tend to occur? The proportion of thematic-to-athematic material can differ radically from scene to scene, but there are patterns of usage from which we can draw some tentative generalizations. Dialogue-free sequences of epic import reliably house the most prominent and extended spans of melodic identification. The Force theme-showcasing "Binary Sunset" from *A New Hope* [25:31] is archetypical, as are its rhymes in *Attack of the Clones* [1:14:22] and *The Last Jedi* [2:19:24]. The mere presence or absence of dialogue is not determinative of leitmotivic writing, however. Mood-setting cues often rely on thematically unmarked underscore, even when they do not compete with character speech—for example, a sequence tasked with evoking a location (say, the deserts of Tatooine), representing a culture (say, the stately polity of Naboo), or inducing a steady, low-arousal emotion (say, suspense for the infiltration of an enemy base). Scene transitions are similarly unlikely to garner leitmotifs, though the Death Star motif in Episode IV stands as a bold counterexample, being used as an editorial bridge five times.[42] Highly talkative scenes, meanwhile, are often the *most* thematically saturated, especially if the characters are navigating a complex relationship, or arriving at an important realization or decision. Such conversations are arguably where *Star Wars* is at its most space-operatic, and where the Wagnerian musical prose style is, appropriately, most at home. In this respect, "Luke's Farewell," already treated in Chapter 1, is representative.

The most predictably non-melodic sequences are those based on sustained negative emotions—fear, disgust, confusion—exemplars of which include the atonal atmospherics in "The Magic Tree" [1:03:42] from Episode V and its cunning rhyme in Episode VIII, the "Mirror Scene" [1:14:13].[43] Action sequences are the most variable when it comes to the inclusion of recurring themes. Synchronization is an important consideration in this respect: fitting the predetermined shape of a leitmotif into a highly choreographed and fast-changing fight scene requires a degree of compositional finesse that these films sometimes do not reward. But the real deciding factor for Williams is the level of dramatic stakes. Climactic battles and duels with mythic import often revolve around broad statements of themes; sometimes they occur in opposed pairs (e.g., LUKE VS. VADER, REY VS. EMPEROR) that do figurative battle in the orchestra as their semantic targets clash on screen.[44] Meanwhile, less mission-critical set pieces tend to lean on non-leitmotivic material, interspersed with brief, comparatively inorganic bursts of recall for moments of heroic success.[45] The REBEL FANFARE seems built for such on-the-spot injections of affect; its appearance at the end of Episode III's buzzing but otherwise non-leitmotivic "Get 'Em R2" [6:59] is characteristic. Arriving after stressful and melodically unpredictable action music, thematically distinct modules can behave like little rewards for harried listeners.

Complicating generalizations about thematic usage is the fact that there is considerable variance within the trilogies themselves. Figure 3.7 displays quantitative information on leitmotivic incidence and abundance in the Skywalker scores.[46] The final entries in each trilogy (Episodes VI, III, and IX) are the most leitmotivically populous—unsurprisingly, as they have the deepest trilogy-specific glossaries to draw from. This pattern is replicated at the level of the saga, with its final third, the Sequel Trilogy, hosting the most unique recurring themes. Meanwhile, in the Prequels, thematic activity dips markedly. Episodes I and II are both less leitmotivically dense than

Film	Distinct LMS	LM instances composed	LM time/ total runtime	LMs as % of runtime
IV	9	107	22/117 min	23%
V	11	180	48/119 min	40%
VI	16	179	41/127 min	32%
I	15	95	29/126 min	23%
II	16	68	30/132 min	23%
III	20	100	35/134 min	26%
VII	16	167	33/124 min	27%
VIII	24	266	46/142 min	32%
IX	25	214	47/131 min	33%

Figure 3.7 Leitmotivic census of the Skywalker Saga

their predecessors, with the former also having a series low of thirty musical minutes dedicated to recurring themes—roughly 22.5% of its total runtime. At the other end, Episode IX bears the highest number of distinct leitmotifs invoked (30), while Episode VIII boasts the series-highest total instances of leitmotivic usage (266) across its phenomenally busy score.[47] But the true champion when it comes to *percentage* of film time occupied by recurring themes is Episode V: leitmotifs take up a full forty-eight minutes, 40% of the whole movie. This thematic density is an important contributor to *Empire*'s exceptionally "symphonic" quality.

These raw numbers tell a somewhat misleadingly objective story—different tallying systems will result in different theme totals and percentages.[48] They certainly tell an *incomplete* story, giving us no understanding of actual thematic or athematic salience. Though fewer in number, the renditions of recurring themes arguably pack a more powerful punch in *Attack of the Clones* than they do in the leitmotivically crowded *Last Jedi*. But even if this accounting exercise somehow missed half of all Williams's recurring themes and motifs, it leaves behind many hours of music based on something other than one of a catalog of sixty-odd recurring themes. What remains is a vast terrain of non- and pseudo-motivic material. If leitmotifs represent the most visible part of the *Star Wars* musical iceberg, beneath is a titanic mass of non-leitmotivic matter that keeps the whole mythic edifice afloat. And it is far from undifferentiated.

All Things Athematic

A full mapping of all the non-leitmotivic materials in *Star Wars* is impossible. But a loose classification system, illustrated with vivid examples, can at least make this musical territory a little less *incognito*. Recall the four criteria for leitmotivic status: distinctiveness, recurrence, symbolism, and variability. With respect to athematicism, variability is essentially moot, but intersections of the other three yield some helpful categories.

Unmarked Underscore

To start, there is unmarked underscore, music that is neither repeated, nor symbolically pregnant, nor sharply articulated as a melody. "Unmarked" means that such music is not meant to be retained in memory, *not* that it is inexpressive. Scoring in this vein runs the gamut from affective neutrality to some of the most explosive gestures in the series. Almost every cue has at least a few measures of music like this: space-filling vamps, skittering bursts of passage work, nail-biting pitch plateaus, and so on—not what audience members will be whistling after leaving the theater, but functionally crucial and sometimes fascinating music in its own right.

One easily overlooked form of unmarked underscore is the low, skulking string writing Williams often utilizes for dialogue-driven scenes with a severe or menacing mood. Instances of this lugubrious style can be found across the Saga: Han's improvised conversation with Imperial security in Episode IV [1:15:16]; Chancellor Palpatine's tense conversation with the Jedi Council in Episode II [4:25]; and Admiral Hux's order to obliterate the Resistance in Episode VII [2:25]. The sparse accompaniment in such sequences suggests a distended form of operatic recitative and imparts a similarly meandering, edgy affect. The skulking strings endow their scenes with a dangerous energy, hinting at foes lurking beneath the surface and threats just biding their time.[49] A paradigmatic occurrence of this topic, depicted in Figure 3.8, comes from Palpatine's temptation of Anakin in *Revenge of the Sith*—not coincidentally a scene that takes place in the Galaxy Opera House. The contours of this subterranean string line seem as if they are methodically testing tonal weaknesses—weaknesses which, of course, they eventually find and exploit, when the Chancellor arrives at "The Legend of Darth Plagueis, The Wise." But that is a tale for another chapter...

Mimetic Scoring

Where unmarked underscore prolongs a low-intensity mood, mimetic scoring is all about catching action, quickly and precisely. Also known as "Mickey Mousing," this category encompasses musical gestures whose shape and placement is determined by their pantomimic or tactile quality.[50] Although extreme mimetic scoring in the style of a Warner Brothers cartoon

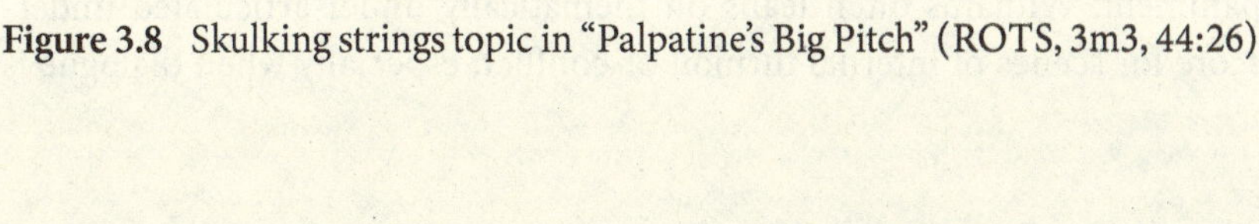

Figure 3.8 Skulking strings topic in "Palpatine's Big Pitch" (ROTS, 3m3, 44:26)

is not the norm in *Star Wars*, the series does host plenty of tactically deployed stingers, punches, wails, and pratfalls. As befits a technique with roots in animation, mimetic scoring suits scenes that are fast-paced, full of physical spectacle, and comedic in tone. When the ground battle in Episode VI begins to turn in the Ewoks' favor [1:47:10], the music becomes more cartoonishly synchronized. This correlation between mimetic scoring and humor weakens as the series goes on, however. The fierce melee between Obi-Wan and General Grievous in Episode III [1:06:12] features numerous conspicuous and exacting stingers. Here, the orchestra acts almost like an announcer at a boxing match, calling out whenever a character lands a nasty wallop.

This highly responsive idiom proves well suited to the oft-athematic action sequences of the Prequels. Yet if anything, Williams opts for *more* extravagant Mickey Mousing in the dense action cues of the Sequels—and to even more serious effect. Clashes involving Rey and Kylo Ren, either against one another or in a team-up, are particularly amenable to hyper-synchronized, almost brutalist scoring. That Williams is able to juggle familiar themes amid a torrent of split-second mimetic gestures is as virtuosic as it is atypical for film music written in the 2010s. Figure 3.9 offers a reduction of one such passage: a module from *The Last Jedi*'s "Fighting Together" in which Kylo Ren and a Praetorian Guard trade blows and parries to immaculately timed orchestral *pows*! and *whoomphs*! The harmonic language and rhythmic violence recall Stravinsky—or more accurately, the sort of once-marked Stravinsky allusion that, in the forty years between Episodes IV and VIII had become fully absorbed into the *Star Wars*ian sound. Unlike in earlier action set pieces, where a theme or even just ostinato might have defined a given cue, in "A New Alliance" and cues like it, those more conventional motivic materials are but visitors. The real structuring agents, the bricks that hold the cue together and give it shape and memorability, *are* the stingers.

Psychological Scoring

If mimetic scoring matches exterior action, psychological scoring captures what is subjective, tacit, and affectual. While the leitmotif technique has obvious and frequently exploited utility for painting a character's psyche, some mindsets are better expressed through a melodically inchoate sort of accompaniment. Williams often leans on thematically under-articulated underscore for scenes of internal turmoil or conflict, especially when dialogue is

Figure 3.9 Pinpoint-accurate mimetic scoring in "Fighting Together" (TLJ, 7m65, 1:47:00)

1:19:42 1:19:52 1:20:03 1:20:15 1:20:27 1:20:38 1:20:49

1 (end of 4m6)	2	3	4	5 (start of 4m7)	6
…fragment of **SHMI**	numbed, airy 4-note motif	turbid minor chords, rising chromatically	crescendo & timbral expansion on baleful 16th-note figure	surging scalar shards, jutting horn motif	cries, clusters, thuds, plunging pitch pyramids
f. hn (solo)	vln (mut)	low wws, brs	wws to near-tutti	strs, f. hn	brs (mut)→ strs→wws, pno
E nat. min	E5-D5-B4-C4	Fm→Em→Gm →A♭m→B♭m…	E nat. min	E doub. harm. min (mainly)	E doub. harm. min, Emma7/B
Shmi strains to say goodbye to Anakin	Death-rattle, slumps dead in her son's arms	Ani reacts in shock and disbelief	Ani closes her eyes; stunned, then grief curdling into anger	Anger into rage; cut to camp ext., lightsaber ignites	Ani slays 2 raiders sets sights on rest, wipe to Coruscant

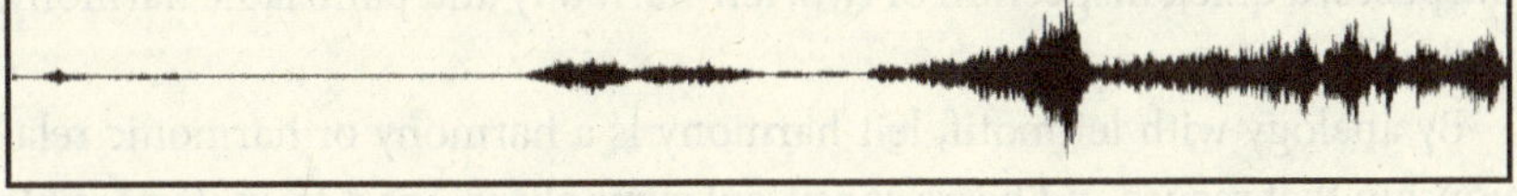

Figure 3.10 Form of Anakin's tortured interiority in "Rescuing Mother/ Exacting Revenge" (AOTC, 4m6/4m7)

elliptical or absent. Sometimes, leitmotifs, like words, simply fail to express the most extreme emotions.

A vivid example of psychological scoring occurs in *Attack of the Clones* during Anakin's discovery of his dying mother and ensuing killing spree. As Shmi Skywalker dies in her son's arms, unable to even complete the sentence "I love you," Anakin passes through a gamut of dark emotions: numbness, disbelief, anger, and finally genocidal violence. Figure 3.10 summarizes the affective rollercoaster traversed by this span of music, each module expressing a new shade of Anakin's deteriorating mental state. Although allusions to SHMI and eventually VADER's themes do frame the sequence, the heart of "Rescuing Mother/Exacting Revenge" is unnervingly non-thematic. The absence of leitmotif does not entail absence of affect: indeed, this is one of the most emotionally wrenching portions of the score. Without a familiar melody to attach to, Williams's bubbling, thrashing underscore conveys grief boiling into inarticulate rage.

Leit-Harmony

Among the musical elements that make Anakin's turn in Episode II so visceral are the ways harmony is deployed. From the pallid diatonicism of SHMI's theme, to the disorienting chromatic climb from F to B♭ minor, to the double-harmonic-minor razor blades Williams sends lacerating through the orchestra, tonality and pitch design are the scene's secret—and perhaps keenest—weapon. Associative use of harmony is rife across the whole of *Star Wars*, sometimes to the point of cliché. Unlike orchestration and texture, harmony has the advantage of an extremely well-developed theoretical language, and musicologists have comprehensive systems with which to describe all manner of constructions and relationships—sonorities, contours, scales, chord progressions, modulations, and so on. (Perhaps surprisingly, key is *not* a notably meaningful parameter, with a few exceptions.)[51] Each subcategory could easily fill a study in its own right; for our current purposes, a quick inspection of two, leit-harmony and pantriadic harmony, will suffice.

By analogy with leitmotif, leit-harmony is a harmony or harmonic relationship that recurs and bears consistent symbolism, apart from its possible presence in any specific melodic theme. Sometimes, specific chords have this property. The four-note sonority built from a minor third, perfect fourth, and minor third (e.g., E-G-C-E♭) is an example of a distinctively *Star Wars*ian chord. It occurs often in conjunction with big, bulky threats, of both mechanical and monstrous varieties, and does so with sufficient regularity that it warrants a label: the "BRUTE" tetrachord.[52] But more a characteristic type of leit-harmony involves not chords per se but motions *between* them.

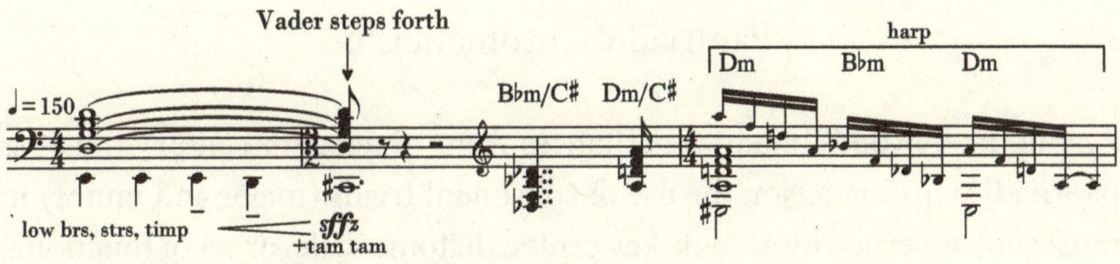

Figure 3.11 Vader's reveal in "Imperial Attack" (ANH, 1m3, 4:32)

There are many recurrent progressions in *Star Wars* with a degree of semantic consistency, but none is more determinedly maintained than the pairing of minor triads a major third apart, as in Gm↔E♭m. This relationship, which can (but does not always) express a i↔♭vi progression, has served as an almost obligatory signifier of the Dark Side since Darth Vader first set foot on the Tantive IV in *A New Hope*. His big musical reveal in that scene, represented in Figure 3.11, is heralded by a B♭m/C♯→Dm/C♯ motion in brass and reinforced, albeit at the threshold of audibility, by harp in the next measure. This bombastically arresting passage associates the chromatic move with the helmeted arch-baddie an entire film before that progression would be codified within his more iconic leitmotif. In fact, the "Vader" motion, as Erik Heine dubs it, is symbolically and formally more expansive than just "The Imperial March."[53] But, especially after *Empire*, the shadow it casts invariably bears the Dark Lord's silhouette.

Take the Gm↔E♭m motion that occurs at the climax of Jedi Steps in *The Force Awakens*. There, its apparent disaffiliation from Vader's leitmotif supercharges the already strong feeling of dire import that attends Luke's long-awaited reappearance. Or consider its role in Episode III. The progression's tendrils stretch deep into the score for *Revenge of the Sith*, becoming a harmonic free agent of sorts. It sustains stretches of ominous underscore, as in Obi-Wan's warning about the Chancellor's autocratic cling to power [F♯m→Dm$^{(\flat 6)}$, 39:47]. It congeals into polychordal masses as in Anakin's assault on the Separatists [Fm$^{(\sharp 4)}$|Am, 1:33:20]. And it even inflects otherwise gentle and decidedly non-villainous cues in Episode III, as with the lullaby-like texture when it is revealed that Padmé is carrying twins [B♭m↔F♯m, 2:04:44]. To the extent that a chord pairing can sonically stand in for an entire film franchise, the i↔♭vi motion is as indelibly *Star Wars* as the ignition of a lightsaber or growl of a Wookiee.

Pantriadic Chromaticism

Among Hollywood's many inheritances from nineteenth-century music is pantriadic chromaticism: the use of consonant triads (major and minor) in music not governed by a single key center, diatonic scale, or set of functional patterns. Pantriadic chromaticism is a harmonic style tailor-made for unusual and heightened states: feelings of awe, estrangement, frisson, uncanniness, and such. While most of Williams's themes are referable to a single tonal center, even those based on peculiar triadic juxtapositions (Emperor, Jabba), much of his athematic underscore is prone to a more wandering sort of "triadic atonality," in which the point of tonal focus is either constantly moving or blurred to the point of irresolvability. In a previous book, I explored the role of pantriadicism in film music in detail, including a close analysis of a cue from *Return of the Jedi*.[54] Here, a single flavorful example will have to stand in for this complex and fascinating compositional style as it is used in the Skywalker Saga.

The cue "The Chosen One" from *The Phantom Menace* is tasked with accompanying three successive conversations (Qui-Gon and the Jedi Council, Qui-Gon and Obi-Wan, Qui-Gon and Anakin), each of which deals with matters of prophecy, destiny, and the nature of the Force—subjects ripe for a triadically atonal treatment. One stretch of dialogue during the first phase is lent a lengthy pantriadic paragraph, shown in Figure 3.12a . Besides

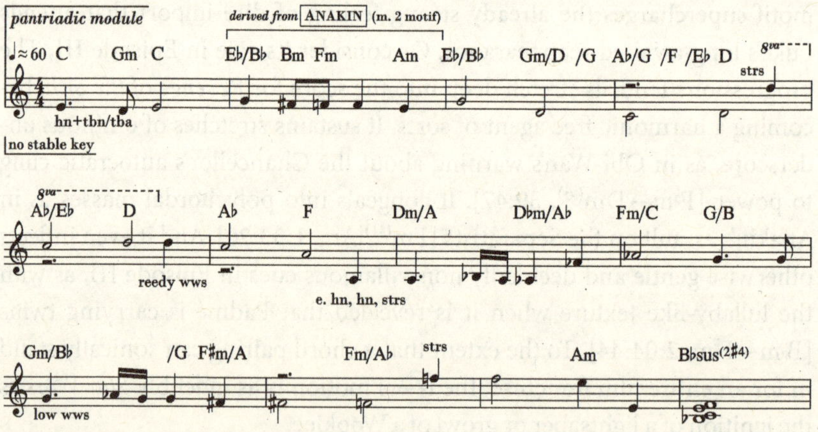

Figure 3.12a Pantriadic chromaticism in "The Chosen One" (TPM, 5m4 + 5, 1:33:44)

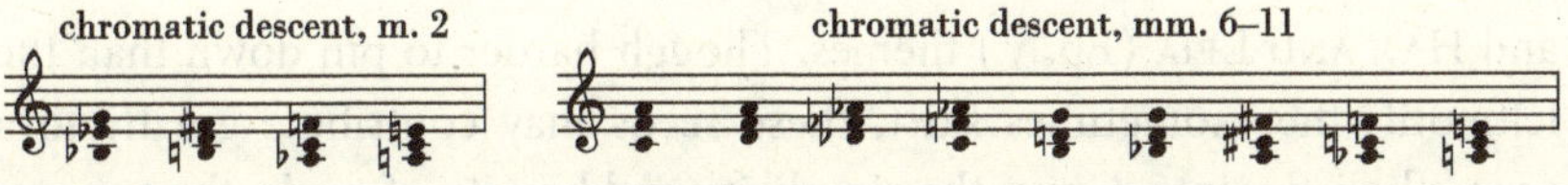

Figure 3.12b Chromatic descents enabling pantriadic progressions in "The Chosen One"

one fleeting cell in the second measure lightly evocative of ANAKIN's theme, nothing in the passage refers to preexisting melodic material. The progression is basically homophonic, voiced through a chorale-like texture and a melody almost entirely free of non-chord tones; the effect is to focus the ear squarely on the absolute quality of motion between triads. Those motions are varied and unpredictable enough to impart a pantriadic quality right at the start. After the initial C↔Gm oscillation, a taste of a C-mixolydian scale that never comes, Williams lets spill a succession of chromatic-third and tritone-related chords. The selection of these chords is not based on their projection of a key or scale but on the mystical strangeness they produce as a gestalt. Their particular qualities are unpredictable but not arbitrary.

Figure 3.12b provides a reduction of two spans, showing how much of the bizarre but tightly voice-led chord progression is powered by the melodic line's tendency to descend chromatically. This process is set up early in measure 2 with a droop from G_4 to E_4, and starting in measure 6 it expands that intervallic fill, now from A_4 to E_4, over a much longer duration—and with a few octave displacements to prevent monotony. To say this passage modulates constantly is to misunderstand modulation: there is no key to change here. A better and more filmically appropriate name for the procedure would be tonal coruscation.[55]

Melodic Seeds

While associative devices are, by definition, not tuneful, they are not solely the province of non-melodic parameters like orchestration and harmony. Take the melodic seed: a simple, pre-rhythmic pitch pattern that can fit—and grow—within multiple tonal and thematic contexts. More abstract than leitmotifs, these seeds are indeterminate in shape and need not signify at all, though many are derived from established melodic identifications. In subsequent chapters, we will closely investigate several such seeds, including ones bearing genetic markers of VADER (Ep. I), REBEL FANFARE (Ep. VII), and Han and Leia (Ep. V) themes. Though harder to pin down than the leitmotifs they sometimes skirt, these seeds may contribute greatly to a score's holistic tinta. Given the simplicity and brevity of seeds, the temptation is to hear them *everywhere.* Cine-symphonic listening means balancing the impulse to connect all dots with an acknowledgment that Williams, like any composer, has his melodic mannerisms. With musical canvases so huge, certain resemblances are simply bound to occur; how meaningful they are is up to the listener.

Revenge of the Sith is notable for the number of specifically *trichordal* (three-note) seeds that occur across its runtime. These include an incomplete neighbor figure (e.g., F-G-E), a modal lower neighbor (e.g., D-C-D), and, most consequential, a descending minor trichord (e.g., F-E-D). Closely related to the "Dies Irae" figure (e.g., F-E-F-D), this Misery Trichord appears constantly in the score, both on the musical surface and worked into more elaborate textures, a few of which are shown in Figure 3.13. An early guise, at the end of the heroes' happy landing on Coruscant, emphasizes the seed through three-fold repetition, though its cheery, lydian orientation is uncharacteristic of the score as a whole. In most subsequent instances, the descending trichord has gloomier aspect, following a $\hat{3}$-$\hat{2}$-$\hat{1}$ line in minor and often chaining multiple iterations through sequences or imitative procedures. The affective debt to the ages-old *pianto* (sigh) topic—the association of a descending minor second with grief—is clear in such passages. The Misery Trichord's quasi-canonic treatment in "News of the Attack" is typical, accompanying a scene in which Anakin, fresh off a killing spree, assures a tearful Padmé that soon all will be well. The pitch-pattern also suffuses the Lament in both of its big, tearful statements during the Order 66 sequence and Anakin's rageful rant on Mustafar. And it, along with the lower neighbor seed, is embedded into the Battle of the Heroes motif that is introduced immediately after. Despite being heard for the first time only when Anakin and Obi-Wan lock lightsabers, this new theme sounds almost inevitable: the reason for this is the systematicity with which those melodic seeds were planted earlier in the score.

Topics

Topics, musical conventions that blend a standardized set of structural parameters with a strong extramusical connotation, have already been

Figure 3.13 Instances of the MISERY TRICHORD in *Revenge of the Sith*. a. "Another Happy Landing" (2m3, 23:56); b. "News of the Attack" (5m5, 1:27:56); c. "Lament" (5m3, 1:21:32); d. "Boys Continue" (6m4, 1:55:54)

shown to be pervasive across the *Star Wars* scores. Often, they amount to references to compositional conventions that Williams taps into from a preexisting tradition, such as the fanfare, the pastorale, and the chorale. They may also be assembled *internally* in the Skywalker scores. The "trumpet cascade," for example, consists of fast scales or scale fragments, played by high brass and moving between triads in tight parallel motion. Vivid examples of the trumpet cascade topos may be found during the Battle of Endor, Coruscant, and Exegol in Episodes VI, III, and IX, respectively. There are precedents—although not *topical* ones—in the symphonic literature for this kind of brass writing; as noted in the previous chapters, Ravel's *Daphnis and Chloé* is a clear point of reference. But it is only after several films' worth of these figures that the pattern becomes an intra-Skywalker Saga style topic, unambiguous enough in denotation to be incorporated in many franchise scores by composers other than John Williams.[56]

Appearing a few scenes before Anakin and Obi-Wan's duel in Episode III is another impressive set piece, "It Can't Be." The second half of the cue, which underscores Kenobi's disclosure to Padmé of her beloved's fall, is an elegant synthesis of the Misery Trichord (e.g., F-E-D) and the lower neighbor seed (D-C-D). As in the Battle of the Heroes theme, those two seeds are stitched into a five-pitch It Can't Be cell. That motivic kernel goes on to generate a cue-spanning form: a passacaglia with fifteen statements of the basic pitch pattern, each more terrible than the last. Figure 3.14a offers a formal overview of this remarkable set piece, with additional rows to indicate the apex pitch and relative dynamic of any iteration presented alongside aspects of tonal and timbral design. Figure 3.14b produces a reduction of its first and penultimate iterations. After the fifteenth statement, when the scene cuts to Mustafar, the passacaglia theme is still present but is now liquidated into a more free-flowing coda for full brass.

In its evocation of the archaic form of the passacaglia, "It Can't Be" is dense with topics, even for *Star Wars*. All are rich with historical and affective

m. 34–40	41	43	45	47	49	51	53	55	57	59	61	63	64	66	68	70–77...
...A ending (athematic)	**B: Passacaglia** (fifteen-fold repetition of It Can't Be cell)															**C: Coda ...** (spun out from It Can't Be)
	1	**2**	**3**	**4**	**5**	**6**	**7**	**8**	**9**	**10**	**11**	**12**	**13**	**14**	**15**	
...	D_4	D_5	F_3	$B\flat_3$	A_3	A_3	D_4	F_4	G_5	$B\flat_5$	F_5	C_6	E_6	A_6	A_6	$B\flat_5$ ...
...→E♭m/C	Gm		Dm								Am			Dm		Dm...
...→*mp*	*mp*								<	*mf*		<	*f*	<	*ff*	*fff*
...wws, strs	cl, f. hn		bsn, tbn		low wws, f. hn				+ tbn		f. hn, vc		+ tbn		+tpt	full brass...

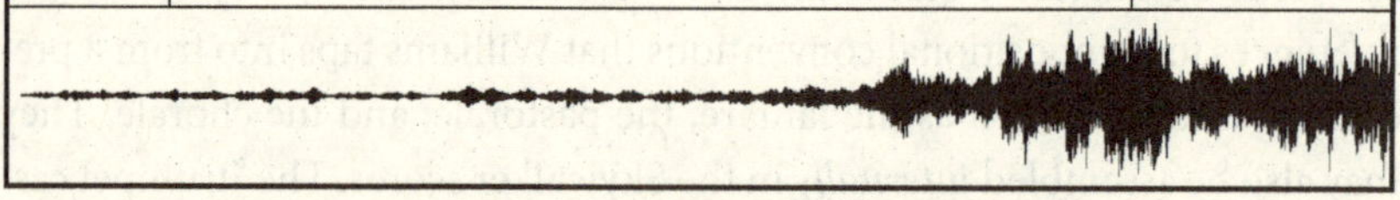

Figure 3.14a Form of "It Can't Be" (ROTS, 6m1, 1:39:02–1:41:25)

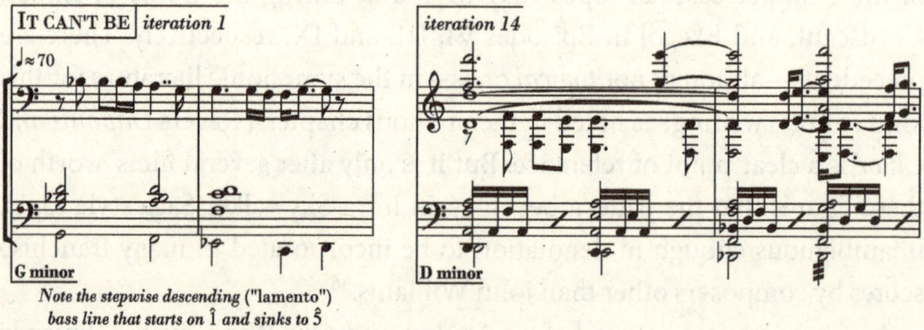

Figure 3.14b First and fourteenth iterations of It Can't Be cell (ROTS, 6m1, 1:39:02 and 1:40:37)

resonances: the *lament bass* (a steady slide down the scale from $\hat{1}$ to $\hat{5}$); the *pianto* (a sighing melodic fall, here iterated within a suspension chain); the *dirge* (a slow, repetitive, mournful procession); and the *loss* progression (an oscillation of major-third related triads, like Dm↔B♭).[57] To this is added a more modern *cumulative form* topos, wherein the incremental swelling of orchestration, volume, and tessitura leads to a grand and cathartic crescendo profile. This topical density gives "It Can't Be" an emotional punch far mightier than conveyed in its otherwise stilted scene—yet another example of Williams's honed compensatory instincts.

Incidental Motifs

The athematic materials cataloged so far can sometimes be difficult to disentangle from leitmotifs themselves—after all, themes have their characteristic timbres, progressions, extramusical tropes, and such. But there is also music in the series that operates independently of established melodic identifications, much of which fits under the umbrella of the "incidental motif." Unlike associative devices, which have clear semantic content but no definitive melodic form, incidental motifs are comparatively empty signifiers that nevertheless possess clearly etched melodic profiles. While potentially recurrent, they rarely can be said to develop. Over one hundred of these incidental motifs populate the pages of the Skywalker scores. They are the catchy ostinati that occur across multiple cues, the distinctive riffs that never coalesce into proper themes, the fragmented bits of a set piece that somehow find themselves repurposed in later scenes.

Incidental motifs are heard from one end of the Saga to the other and range widely in terms of recurrence and (non)development. The corkscrewing piccolo line that follows immediately on the heels of *A New Hope*'s opening crawl qualifies; for a long time restricted to that one iconic cue, the module was later restated verbatim and in the same place in *The Last Jedi*. Incidental motifs may sometimes be the product of tracking. In *The Rise of Skywalker*, there is a mixed-meter ostinato that sounds while various characters navigate their way to Exegol. The repetition of the hell-storming figure is an artifact of music editing: the cue it presumably was initially confined to, "Rey Travels to Palpatine" [1:38:47] was partially repurposed for Kylo Ren's similar journey earlier in the film [2:48], to good effect. Most characteristic, however, are incidental motifs that are repeated according to Williams's own devices and do so within a single film.

Figure 3.15 Incidental brass motif in "Moving Things Along" (ROTS, 5m6, 1:33:44)

Figure 3.15 depicts an emblematic tangle of brass counterpoint from *Revenge of the Sith*. This passage is deliberately written into two cues and is certainly ear-catching in profile, but it is essentially detached from the leitmotivic fabric of the overall score. This polyphonic outburst sounds first when Mace Windu goes in for a fatal strike against Palpatine [1:14:42], second when Yoda and Obi-Wan cut through a battalion of clones [1:33:44]. Were it not for the near-exact repetition, this motif would simply count as another *Star Wars*ian trope—imitative brass battle music—heard on many occasions since the Battle of Yavin in *A New Hope*. However, with its near-exact recurrence in Episode III, this specific canon stitches together an already tightly knitted score that much tauter.[58]

Set Piece Themes

Where incidental motifs have recurrence but not much symbolic heft, set piece themes are highly *significant* melodies that occupy just a single span of film time. These "one-cue wonders" owe their storytelling power precisely to their unprecedented nature. Certain set piece themes define individual cues to such an extent that their host cue can indeed start sounding more like a *piece* proper. Among the many notable examples in the Original Trilogy, "The Asteroid Field" cue from *The Empire Strikes Back* is surely the most thoroughly realized. Revolving around two long-breathed and contrasting melodies of great distinction, the set piece is enormously memorable, and on first listen seems *sui generis*, bearing no obvious connection with other elements of Episode V's thematic glossary. (As Chapter 5 will demonstrate, "The Asteroid Field" does boast some deep, if subtle, ties with major leitmotifs introduced in that installment.)

One-cue wonders are less common in the Sequels, where most set pieces either revolve around leitmotifs or various unmarked or associative particles; a rare exception is the rousing melody for Finn and Jannah that appears in the middle of the Battle of Exegol. The Prequels, by contrast, abound with one-off melodies, particularly Episode I. One such ephemeral theme is the COURTYARD CORTEGE: a stately march in the manner of Tchaikovsky, played as Nabooian captives are escorted to a palace courtyard. The melody, shown in Figure 3.16, keeps pace with the prisoners for twelve measures, completing both its antecedent and consequent phrases, and then disappears forever. A truly motivated listener might contrive a linkage with the more imposing and properly leitmotivic DROID MARCH heard elsewhere in the film; in one of its guises, the former also features a staggered descent from $\hat{4}$ to $\hat{2}$ in its second measure. Drawing hazy similarities like this is always possible—Williams is a self-consistent and economical composer. But forcing the COURTYARD CORTEGE into the leitmotivic lexicon deprives the melody of what makes it and so many other passages in *The Phantom Menace* special: its exceptionality.

Around once per trilogy, Williams constructs a one-off set piece that shoulders the weight of an event of galaxy-shaking import. This is a singular "scene or a moment," as Lucas describes it, "in which the music connects so strongly with the visual that it sends shivers up my spine."[59] When Anakin goes up in flames in *Revenge of the Sith* [1:59:46,], we hear an intense threnody for strings. Like the traumatic event it complements, the

Figure 3.16 "Courtyard Cortege" incidental theme (TPM, 2m2, 22:10)

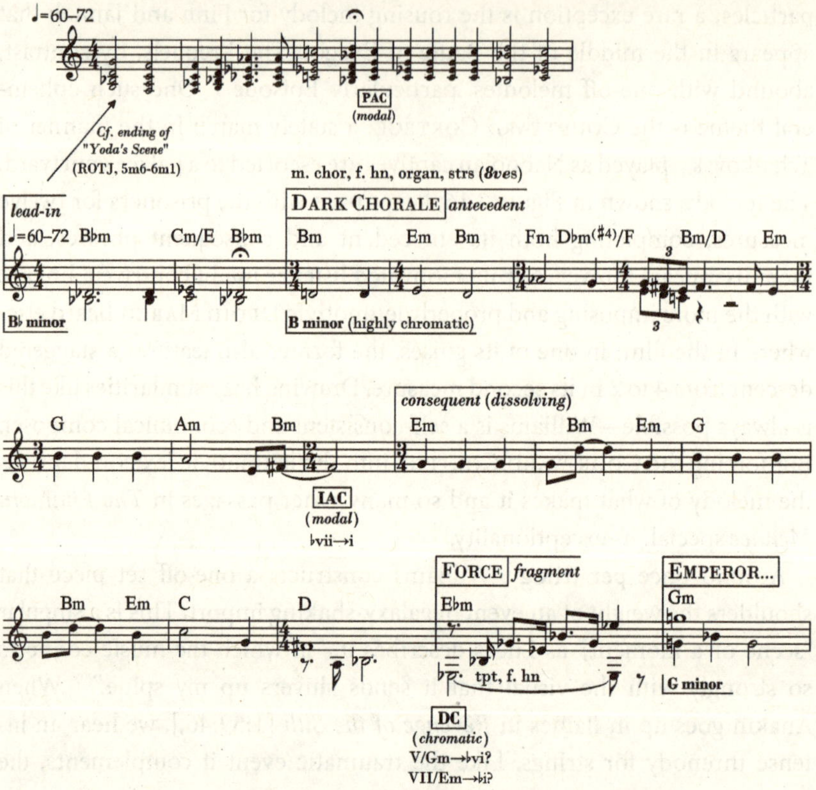

Figure 3.17 Dark Chorale one-cue wonder (ROTJ, 12m3, 1:52:40)

"Immolation Scene" seems to express an agony beyond linguistic (and, by loose analogy, leitmotivic) representation. Rather different in affect is the concluding paragraph of "The Last Jedi" [2:17:51,] from the eponymous film, wherein Kylo Ren realizes the "Luke" he has been fighting was a Force projection. Williams's music, a series of rising arpeggios in strings and held "aahs" in chorus, characterizes both the enormity of Luke's final feat and the shock of Kylo's realization—the best-handled twist in *Star Wars* since "I am your father."

The crown jewel of one-cue wonders, and a piece one cannot help but feel grateful Williams was never asked to revisit, is what could be called the Dark Chorale from *Return of the Jedi*, presented in Figure 3.17. Very much a case of playing emotion rather than on-screen action, this broad and homophonic theme accompanies Luke's enraged attack on Vader. Saturated with markers of religious music—antique modal cadences, unfathomable pantriadic shifts, wordless chorus, thick organ-like orchestration—the DARK CHORALE resembles little of what has come before, making Luke's flirtation with the Dark Side a moment of singular intensity in the entire Skywalker Saga.[60] Only one, comparatively understated passage anticipates this music: the chorale that marks Yoda's death earlier in Episode VI [45:00]. And only one other cue, almost certainly accidental, rhymes with it later on: the religioso paragraph in Episode I [46:46] when Anakin's mother describes his selflessness and "special powers." Anything more than light foreshadowing or corroboration would ruin the effect, however, which is that of a musical bolt from the blue—a thematic disjunction that introduces a whole new level of epic narrational potency. (This idea will be revisited in Chapter 7.) In a franchise that strives for a modern mythic experience, the DARK CHORALE may be the closest *Star Wars* comes to the musically sublime.[61]

Theme and Form

Thematic or not, the elements of the Skywalker scores we have examined so far have been largely in isolation—as discrete occurrences, or in the case of leitmotivic prototypes, pure idealizations. Too often, this is where film music analysis stops. If we really wish to understand *Star Wars* as a vessel for symphonic storytelling, we need to account for how distinct compositional devices arise and interact within larger contexts. To once again press the linguistic analogy that has served us throughout this chapter: it is not enough to know what individual words are to understand a language; one also needs to appreciate how they are modified, combined, and organized into larger thoughts. In linguistics, these are matters of grammar, syntax, and rhetoric. In music, the closest correlate is the concept of *form*.

Star Wars lends itself straightforwardly to formal analysis on one level: thematic phrase structure, or the way melodies are built. Thanks to the work of music theorist Mark Richards, we have a comprehensive and rigorous understanding of how movie themes are constructed.[62] Richards's typology of thematic archetypes goes well beyond the standard periods and sentences of Classical formal theory, introducing new categories like composites and clauses that better reflect the multifarious ways screen composers organize musical time.[63] One of Richards's most helpful tools is his tripartite categorization of melodic structures. He distinguishes among these archetypes:

- **Grammatical themes**, wherein a melody, generally eight measures or some multiple thereof, is built from smaller motifs, and divides into clear beginning and ending halves.
- **Discursive themes**, wherein a melody is lengthy, accumulative, and cannot be easily split into symmetrical parts.
- **Motto themes**, wherein a melody is brief and incapable of being broken down into subsidiary motifs.

Among leitmotifs we have already closely examined, the FORCE is a textbook grammatical theme, the LAMENT discursive, and the MAP a motto. Overall, grammatical themes predominate the Original Trilogy, while mottos play a larger role in the Sequels and Prequels. Themes of the discursive kind are the rarest, confined to JAWAS, JABBA, SHMI, PASTORALE, and SNOKE.

With its profusion of melodic identifications, the Skywalker saga offers unmatched potential for comparative study of thematic form. In addition to his analytical case studies of individual leitmotifs, Richards has done just that, investigating *Star Wars* from a holistic perspective, as a unified thematic corpus.[64] Richards's approach involves examining patterns of formal construction for motifs associated with either good or evil across the franchise. In a manner that corroborates James Buhler's Manichean treatment of *Star Wars* thematicism but surpasses it in detail and comprehensiveness, Richards's work blends analysis with interpretation to great effect. His study reveals some deep patterns of thematic planning and development, showing for instance a correlation between how grammatical a villain's theme is and how central and exposed their villainy within any given film. In Episode IV, the Empire is a mostly impersonal threat and Vader largely a cipher: accordingly, Williams supplies them with a single short, non-grammatical motto theme, the IMPERIALS motif. But in Episode V, when Vader takes center stage, we have the extended, more conventionally tuneful VADER/"Imperial March" theme. Particularly as we begin examining thematic transformation in coming chapters, Richards's final conclusion bears remembering: "Williams's ability to compose highly fitting leitmotifs is not limited to the content of the individual themes themselves but, at least in his *Star Wars* scores, includes consistently grouping them together by type of thematic structure, displaying a highly nuanced and appropriately tailored approach to theme writing that has always been an essential part of the *Star Wars* saga."[65]

The benefit of studies like Richards's is that they show that formal analysis need not be a dry exercise in structuralist bean counting, but an avenue for precise and fruitful interpretation—that is to say, musical hermeneutics. But the domain of applicability of theme-structural theory is not unbounded; as soon as one lifts above the level of individual melody and considers thematic behavior within *cues*, form becomes much more difficult to systematize à la Richards or Buhler. This is a potentially major impediment, because the cue, *not the theme*, is the emblematic span of symphonic storytelling in *Star Wars*.

It is difficult to imagine a typology of cue forms in *Star Wars* in the same way we categorize themes. There is no such definite, replicable thing as "the form" in *Star Wars*' nondiegetic score—the series is too broad and the dramatic tasks of each cue too unique. This is a condition inherent in film music, and a major reason that movie scores can be simultaneously so invigorating and so confounding to listen to independently. For sure, Williams is a sure-handed musical architect, a craftsman of cues that stand on their own, like self-sufficient pieces. And there are examples aplenty in Skywalker scores of well-proportioned, easily extractable musical structures. But for every "piece" like the passacaglia in *Revenge of the Sith*, there are sequences assembled according to a more ad hoc, less traditionally satisfying formal logic.[66]

Talk of formal containers like scherzo, fugue, or rondo in film underscore can only be considered in the loosest sense, if the comparison is with the tightly constructed and stylistically regulated categories of Classical music. A weakening suffix is always implicit: scherzo-esque, fugal, rondo-like, and so on. The one category in this respect that *does* apply to *Star Wars* quite consistently is, as we have already seen, Wagnerian musical prose. Rather than being based in any prefabricated formal molds, however, musical prose is defined by drama-dictated *irregularities*. And the formal implications of those irregularities run deeper than the existence or absence of such containers: the prosodic style that Williams adopts affects the very way one musical thought flows to the next.

Most classical music (and much besides) is built around balanced and interdependent sections, subsections, and supersections, all neatly nested and differentiated. This impression of formal hierarchy is the product of various types of musical dependency: structural cadences, recursive metrical patterns, clear key/chord distinctions, and exposition/recapitulation schemes. Through these dependency relations, music can suggest different degrees of musical importance and necessity—an enormously useful thing in trying to describe an individual piece's form. Carl Dahlhaus calls this hierarchical mode of musical organization *hypotaxis*, another useful concept drawn from linguistics.[67] He contrasts it to the Wagnerian leitmotif-based, prosodic approach. Musical prose is for Dahlhaus a form of *parataxis*, in which "passages of melody are loosely juxtaposed" without being hierarchically distinguished from one another. Rather than progression and dependency, parataxis is based on succession and contrast. Because so much of its material (both leitmotivic and athematic) is built from short particles arranged into modules, and because its formal imperatives are essentially external (poetic, dramatic, editorial) rather than internal (tonal/formal hierarchy), Dahlhaus would likely describe most *Star Wars* underscore as paratactic, too. According to this distinction, Williams's music would thereby stray even further away from the kind of musical organization described by standard theories of musical form.

More than the other linguistic analogies raised in this chapter, the hypo/parataxis framework should be applied with care. This is not just because music generally lacks the grammatical functions that motivate the hypotaxis/parataxis distinction in language, but because film music specifically and *Star Wars* music especially moves between such opposed modes of organization for dramatic effect. Yet Dahlhaus's dichotomy does help steer us in a productive direction—not away from form per se, but away from *formalism*: the fixation on traditional high-level dependency relations, motivic unity, and global structure over musical expression and local impact. Form in this series is unconstrained, associative, and difficult to confine to preexisting containers.[68] This does not rule out long-range musical arguments; Williams exerts amazing control over the overall formal shape of many cues. But appreciation of large-scale organization needs to factor in the tendency on the musical surface toward a kind of leitmotivic stream of consciousness. And, remembering the issue of mythic temporality from Chapter 1, that stream may just as easily turn to the past (memory, history, nostalgia) or future (premonition, anticipation, foreshadowing) as dwell in the immediate dramatic present.

A universal formal theory of *Star Wars* music is therefore impractical, but that does not mean the subject cannot be approached systematically. When examining a cue, it is always worth asking to what degree Williams's musical materials—primarily leitmotifs, but everything else in the athematic iceberg, too—*generate form*. This involves considering some occasionally subtle issues:

- **Duration**: How much of a full musical idea (leitmotif, incidental theme, etc.) is heard?
- **Expression**: How do ideas create and sustain tension and emotion?
- **Integration**: How do statements of an idea fall along the use/mention distinction?
- **Interaction**: How do ideas combine and impact each other? Is the result purely paratactic?
- **Succession**: How do different ideas succeed or transition into one another?
- **Temporality**: How do ideas help construct a scene's overall formal and emotional rhythm?

Teasing out these questions is like putting yourself in the mind of the composer. The more cues you examine in this way, the more you realize that, far from being a nullified concept, musical form is extremely important in the Skywalker Saga. Not as a set of predictable containers but as a fluid process, one steered both by the musical material itself and by on-screen action, effects, edits, and—crucially—character psychology.

Snoke Signals

We have covered a great deal of ground in this chapter. From examining motifs in terms of their meaning and structure, to charting the vast territory of non-thematic material, to mulling big questions of form, we now have a sturdy basis for understanding how Williams plies his thematic craft within the typical musical prose style of *Star Wars* underscore. As a way of putting all these concepts to work, this last section offers an analytical vignette of an entire cue: "Revisiting Snoke" from *The Last Jedi*. While not as iconic as the "Binary Sunset" or meticulously assembled as "It Can't Be," the sixty-five measures that constitute this cue are effective inside the film and make for a great test case for cine-symphonic listening outside of it. If you can appreciate "Revisiting Snoke" both as adept dramatic underscoring and a compelling piece of music in its own right, then it is a small step to hearing *Star Wars* overall as a symphonic experience.

The sequence's form is represented in Figure 3.18. In addition to labels for the various motifs in the cue, the *kind* of thematic material—thematic, incidental, and subcategories thereof—is specified. The scene finds Kylo Ren,

First Paragraph

16:23	16:33	17:05	17:16	17:37	17:42
1	**2**	**3**	**4**	**5**	**6**
Sink incidental motif	**Snoke** leitmotif (discursive)	Jitters incidental motif	**Kylo B** + Jitters leitmotif (motto) + incid. motif	-- skulking strings	**Vader** leitmotif (motto)
--	Dm	Em	Gm	(E♭m)	Am
low brs	low chor	va	f. hn	low strs	brs (mut)
"Where's Han?"	Cut to KR entering Snoke's chamber. Hux leaves, Snoke.	"How's your wound?...	"When I found you…	"your blood-line….	"…a new Vader."

Second Paragraph

17:51	18:07	18:14	18:20	18:30	18:42	18:46
7	**8**	**9**	**10**	**11**	**12**	**13**
Jitters incidental motif	**Kylo C** leitmotif (motto)	**Kylo A** leitmotif (motto)	-- skulking strings	Grasp + Jitters incid. motif	-- mimetic (stingers)	-- skulking strings
(Am)	Am	Am	→ Fm	Gm	(atonal)	Em
vla	cb. cl, cb	f. hn (mut)	low strs	f. hn (mut)	tutti	low instrs.
"…I was mistaken."	Removes helmet	C.U. KR's face, Snoke berates	"...Too much Skywalker...	…And look at you!..."	ZAP!	"Skywalker lives….

Third Paragraph

19:00	19:05	19:16	19:32	19:44	19:50 19:57
14	**15**	**16**	**17**	**18**	**19**
Snoke leitmotif (discursive)	**Snoke** + **Kylo C** leitmotif (motto)	**Kylo B** + **Kylo C** leitmotif (motto→ grammatical)	**Kylo A** leitmotif (grammatical)	**Kylo A** (frags) leitmotif /mimetic	**Kylo B**, Sink (var) leitmotif (motto)
Em	C♯m	C♯m	C♯m	C♯m	→Bm…
low chor	+ low strs	+brs (mut)→ (open)	f. hn	mixed brs, strs	f. hn
"I thought you'd be the one...	…Alas, you're no Vader…"	...in a mask." Cut to KR in elevator, considering mask	SMASH!	More helmet smashing, KR leaves elevator	KR storms off, cut to Luke/Rey

Figure 3.18 Form of "Revisiting Snoke" (TLJ, 1m9)

fresh from committing patricide in the previous film, now summoned before his master, the enigmatic Supreme Leader Snoke. Ren is reprimanded for his weakness and subjected to a spurt of electroshock therapy when he evinces a spark of defiance. The not-quite-Sith exits the room seething and humiliated. In the privacy of an elevator, he erupts in a rage, smashes his helmet—"that ridiculous thing," per Snoke's mockery—and leaves the frame in a vengeful huff.

The scene serves three main functions, neatly mapping onto the various "tenses"—past, present, and future—that epic musical prose can intimate.

1. Refamiliarize the audience with the villains of the Sequel Trilogy and hint at the continued relevance of villains thought long-gone.
2. Portray through action the volatile dynamic between Snoke and Kylo Ren.
3. Prefigure and motivate Kylo's character arc for the rest of the movie.

Williams's music does much to construct this triple-tensed framework. On a basic level, the cue offers a recap for the relevant baddie themes. (The reader may turn to the book's first appendix for their own refresher.) The first forty seconds are based on the SNOKE leitmotif. A discursive theme in Richards's sense, the Supreme Leader's melodic identification is protracted and meandering, based on an unknown Sanskrit text set slow and low, as if a medieval plainchant were passed through several blur filters. The leitmotivic rogues' gallery also includes the iconic VADER motif—a paradigmatic grammatical theme in its full presentations but here treated as a concise motto. But the most thematic attention in "Revisiting Snoke" is lent to Kylo Ren. Like his dyadic counterpart Rey, Ren's musical characterization is complex, composed of three independent leitmotifs, all mottos: KYLO A, B, and C. Each represents a facet of his unbalanced persona—bravado, hesitancy, and menace, respectively.[69]

Both SNOKE and VADER themes are infused with the feeling of ancient history here. The former is more texture than melody, a distant echo of the presumed-vanquished Emperor Palpatine's low choral associative timbre (to be further explored in Chapter 7). The latter is figuratively buried underneath the sonic gravel of a low sizzle cymbal. Very much a case of mention over use, Darth Vader's leitmotif insists upon itself here as a musical totem, to a degree that would doubtlessly repel a superficially Debussyian or Adornian listener. But the insistency is the point. Kylo Ren struggles mightily to live up to his storied ancestor, obsessing over extrinsic symbols and needless signifiers of Lord Vader, to the point that he communes with the melted remains of his grandfather's helm and models his own completely needless mask on that of his deceased role model. The citation of VADER is thus a twist

Figure 3.19 Incidental motifs in "Revisiting Snoke"

of the knife for Kylo, a musical "ridiculous thing" whose very blatancy on the soundtrack is a form of cruel psychological insight.

Besides hitting these three leitmotivic bases, "Revisiting Snoke" works in a small collage of additional non-leitmotivic material, much of which recurs in subsequent scenes in the Supreme Leader's chamber. For the majority of "Revisiting Snoke," these motivic constituents are not sonically foregrounded, instead brooding and murmuring at a low volume beneath the tense dialogue. Figure 3.19 isolates the most notable of them. One such idea is the angsty figure [Jitters] for midrange strings, an idea that pops up all over *The Last Jedi* as an incidental motif. Two four-note cells are also prominent. One, a rising gesture [Grasp] that occurs midway through "Revisiting Snoke" is a musical scold, adding bile to Snoke's bullying of his disciple. The other cell, a drooping figure [Sink], kicks off the whole cue and, with an accelerated variant, slams it shut. Jutting chromatic tetrachords like this Sink motif are not uncommon in the series, often used to bridge scenes. At first a direct reference to the four-note motto from Holst's "Uranus" [G_3-$E\flat_3$-A_3-B_2], by the Sequel Trilogy such figures are, like the *Rite of Spring* chords discussed earlier, a purely intra-*Star Wars* trope. Here, the motif functions as a musical pre-lap, a melodic analogy to Luke's line "Where's Han?," which its first three pitches catch. Its answer is swiftly forthcoming, in the form of the deep D drone that attends the cut to Solo's masked murderer.

These themes and motivic particles dovetail and overlap seamlessly against the backdrop of the Supreme Leader's basically immobile choral drone. The organizational principle in this cue is thus almost entirely paratactic; except for the final module, all of its ideas succeed one another without a sense of hierarchy or phrasal embedding within the theme. When not abutting each other directly, the modules in "Revisiting Snoke" tend to be built up or quitted by meandering lines from the low strings—channeling the aforementioned skulking topic, solemn and spooky. While purely interstitial, even these stringy modules bear motivic connections with the ideas that come before or after them. The pizzicato figure in contrabasses after the Vader theme, for example, offers a deadened echo of his leitmotif [C_2-A_1-F_1, C_2-A_1-F_1]. A few bars later, the bass/cello shadow

Figure 3.20 Stinger spasm in (TLJ,1m9, 18:42)

cast after the first statement of KYLO's main motto in A minor [E_3-$D\sharp_3$-A_2-C_2] is an embellished and partially inverted augmentation of Ren's motto in F [B_2-C_3-A_2-$A\flat_2$-F_2-$A\flat_2$].

Despite being structured around a half-dozen points of synchronization, there are only two really conspicuous audio-visual accents in this cue. The first is the reveal of Adam Driver's scarred face, coinciding neatly with his aggressive theme. The second is a spate of mimetic scoring (Figure 3.20, ▶), where one stinger matches the Supreme Leader's lightning flash and another bursts forth in response to his guards' activated weapons. Harmonically, these stingers are neatly differentiated: the electric surge garners a thick cluster chord of eight pitches while the flashed staff triggers a more widely spaced polychord, with a C♯-G tritone perched above a characteristically Williams-esque G♯m♭6/D♯ chord.

Besides those two flare-ups, "Revisiting Snoke" eschews direct Mickey Mousing in favor of a slower, more psychically responsive stream of musical commentary. The most prominent thematic particles are basically quadratic (built from units of 2 or 4 bars), but the modules they occupy are variable in duration and metrical uniformity: there are thirty-six meter changes for a cue of only sixty-five measures—an extreme proportion for most other genres, but not film music. There is no cadential telegraphing here, nor any larger-scale periodicities until the climactic statement of Ren's material that commences as he is dismissed from Snoke's chamber.

Several more aspects of this cue conspire to throw off the listener's formal compass.

- The slowly mutating timbral palette, a kaleidoscope of the orchestra's coldest colors.
- The absence of any metronomic pulse, especially in the proximity of SNOKE's theme, which prevents entraining to any sort of tactus or regular metrical grid.

- The instability of key, which changes ten times, once every twenty-one seconds on average.
- At the same time, the marked *stability* of keys within their modules, being prolonged by sustained chords and pedals rather than intra-key progressions, functional or otherwise.

Collectively, these qualities give "Revisiting Snoke" a spontaneous and supple sound, almost like it is an emanation from the Supreme Leader's sickly chamber itself. This is music that holds the listener in suspense, able to turn at the slightest shift in action, open-ended in outcome, though with little promise that any of those outcomes are good for the parties concerned. It is not the disordered collage of disconnected ideas that an uncharitable critic of leitmotif might decry. Nor is it exactly a study in motivic causality either, where musical Event A inexorably leads to Event B. As noted before, Dahlhaus's concept of parataxis, hierarchically flat but associatively deep, is especially apt for such dark musical prosody.

Given the idiosyncratic and unpredictable trajectory of this cue, it is reasonable to ask how, if at all, it works as a coherent musical argument. To listen to "Revisiting Snoke" attentively while viewing *The Last Jedi* is to marvel at the real-time shading of character psychology Williams achieves for these pseudo-Sith ciphers. But what about the cue on its own? Can it be heard as *just* music?

To an extent, "Revisiting Snoke" works as a pure mood piece, its dusky hues and malignant motives to be savored in themselves. This is not unlike what a post-Wagnerian listener might do for ominous tone-paintings that open, say, Acts 2 of *Lohengrin, Siegfried*, or *Götterdämmerung*—all extended and formally unconventional explorations of villain themes and topics. Played in an unlit room, with a powerful subwoofer to really make the Supreme Leader's choral drone vibrate your body, "Revisiting Snoke" would be a great way to tap into your own Dark Side. But as a piece, the cue is about more than ambiance. It is a mistake to assume musical prose necessitates the rejection of long-range form. If anything, formal thinking—the "tectonic" mindset—is *more important*, since the composer cannot rely on ready-made packages to control the flow of tension, memory, and anticipation. Arguably, the construction of and manipulation of listener anticipation is what elevates "Revisiting Snoke" and many cues like it onto a more symphonic plane. A piece can get away with all sorts of violations of musical logic if it ends with a well-telegraphed bang.

"Revisiting Snoke" can be read as a push toward a big musical breakthrough. For much of its duration, the cue is formally fickle, but there are goal-directed processes that grow more emphatic and inexorable as the cue barrels to its conclusion. At first Kylo Ren's various themes are clipped, as though denied breathing room. Swamped out by the domineering Snoke-drone, his motifs strain for thematic definition, only to be shot down by the double stingers at the cue's midpoint. Yet once Ren is left to his own in the elevator, the score takes on a more determined character. Not simple underscore, Williams is now offering audiences a glimpse into this man's interiority, and it is a psychic powder keg. An extended crescendo, rising in tessitura, volume, and orchestrational density, sets in module 15, and for the first time the score is based on quadratic phrase units. The passage reaches its boiling point as Ren destroys his helmet, with the score exploding with a fortissimo blast of the Vader-wannabe's motto, both its question and answer phrases. And, in a splendid bit of orchestral analogy, bits of thematic detritus are left behind in the cue's chaotic final bars as Ren storms off.

Full statements of leitmotifs are invariably salient in *Star Wars*—not just for their heightened expressive or narrative power but also their impact on musical time itself, the way they tend to warp and concentrate all the soundtrack's energies around themselves. From a storytelling perspective, it is important that Kylo Ren's most violent motif sounds as he smashes the outward manifestation of his bravado. *The Last Jedi* sees Ren grow out of the need for a mask, becoming at once more relatably human as a character and much more of a profound threat. The crescendo at the end of "Revisiting Snoke" focalizes Williams's score, providing a payoff to the rogues' gallery of villain motifs exhibited over the previous two minutes. Importantly, the music for Ren's fit has been heard before—not in the form of underscore but as an extra-diegetic presentation of the villain's thematic complex in Episode VII's "End Credits."[70] Though in this specific way unoriginal, Williams's assimilation of this preexisting music is nevertheless smooth and apt. The direct recall from the prior installment adds an additional layer of memory and anticipation for those who remember how the credits went. They'll *know*, just from the music, that Kylo is about to blow.

What should a cine-symphonic listener make of this leitmotivic cyclone? The incident is certainly operatic. These are big, melodramatic emotions, expressed in shockingly direct terms, with the added Wagnerian trait that such intensity is conveyed purely through the orchestra and as part of an ongoing weave of leitmotivic prose. Whether Kylo Ren's musical fulminations are *symphonic* is less straightforward. Certainly, there is a satisfying end-weightedness to the sequence. But like so much *Star Wars* underscore, "Revisiting Snoke" is defiantly *non*-unified, at least by traditional standards. Over its short duration, the cue phases continually between use and mention, semantic fixity and drift, rigorous motivicism and athematic digression, formal happenstance and orderly hierarchy. Yet even if its respective parts are at times contradictory, they still sum to something greater. Recall Peter Franklin's expanded vision of symphonism, "a cumulatively cogent structure of action, anticipation, and reminiscence."[71] If one can impute to Williams's cue that feeling of cumulative cogency, it will be because of the rich web of associations it invokes, and the way it draws them together into a single throbbing thread at the sequence's conclusion. Symphonic or not, this portrait of Kylo Ren is compelling as music, no modifier needed.

4
Transformations

Redecorating the Throne Room

At the end of *A New Hope*, a theme is introduced that seems to be a quintessential "one-cue wonder." As Leia confers a clutch of medals on the heroes of the Battle of Yavin, the THRONE ROOM commences its steady tread, striking a tone of formalized pageantry in line with the well-ordered pomp on screen. This melody, whose first phrase is shown in Figure 4.1, is an award in its own right. At twenty-four measures, it is Episode IV's lengthiest tune, classically proportioned in a small ternary (ABA') form, offering the comforts of tonal stability and structural balance after two hours of musical stress and strain.

Regal in style and unabashed in referentiality, the THRONE ROOM is an acknowledged homage to Williams's beloved British nationalist school. The theme is replete with an Elgarian walking bass and Waltonian enriched diatonic chords; the only thing missing is the word "Nobilmente" in the score. A chart summarizing the formal and tonal shape of the cue is provided in Figure 4.2, with the bottom rows noting topics and purported models from Lucas's original temp track.[1] Rare for *Star Wars*, the cue is entirely hypotactic in the sense described in Chapter 3: its form, though simple, is organized hierarchically, exhibiting multiple levels of musical stability, significance, and structural weight. Like the lyrical trio of a processional by Elgar or Walton, the THRONE ROOM draws expressive potency via the contrast with its more militaristic surrounds—namely, the extended rendition of the FORCE theme, now decked out in martial regalia, an apotheosis of that critical theme. But the THRONE ROOM also contrasts with its iconic neighbor in terms of its apparent self-containedness. Heard in this cue, the stately theme would seem an unlikely candidate for repetition, much less radical transfiguration.

As mentioned in Chapter 1, musicologist James Buhler sees in the Original Trilogy a perpetual reversion to musical stasis: "Nothing actually happens in these scores."[2] Thematic transformation, he argues, is not merely absent in the *Star Wars* musical universe; it is antithetical to it. Variation internal

Figure 4.1 The THRONE ROOM theme, first phrase

1:58:26 1:58:44 1:59:02 1:59:16 1:59:23 1:59:39 1:59:56 2:00:13

1a.	**2.**		**1b.**	**3.**		
Fanfare	**FORCE**		Fanfare	**THRONE ROOM**		
--	period **A** *antecedent*	**A'** *consequent*	--	small ternary **A** *exposition*	**B** *contr. middle*	**A'** *recap*
C →V/F	Fm →V/Fm	Fm	F→V/D♭	D♭→V/D♭	V/D♭→	D♭
f. hn, tbn	tpt	tpt, tbn	tpt, tbn	wws, strs	f. hn; strs	tutti
fanfare modeled on **Mendelssohn** "Wedding March"	military march modeled on **Dvořák**, Symphony 9/Mvt. IV		fanfare ibid.	stately processional modeled on **Elgar/Walton**, "Pomp and Circumstance" "Orb and Scepter," "Crown Imperial," etc.		

Figure 4.2 Form and topical/referential structure of "The Throne Room" (ANH, 12m2)

to a theme he grants, as well as superficial variation across cues.[3] But not true development, which runs contrary to the twin aesthetic ideologies of the series: earnest nostalgia and Manichean morality. Buhler holds up this THRONE ROOM theme as a model for Williams's anti-symphonic treatment of his leitmotifs, either incapable of evolving or never asked to. Absent is the sense of dynamism, of struggle and contrast and overcoming, that is essential for (a certain conception of) symphonic thought.[4] The lack of effort expended to attain the THRONE ROOM music—and, as importantly, the ostensible lack of follow-through afterward—leads Buhler to conclude that the theme "turns out to be inconsequential."[5] This secondhand "Hope and Glory" music "ultimately carries no structural weight. Nothing remains of it to alter the thematic process, to give the theme a meaningful history." A frozen object, unearned and unremembered.

These are powerful and trenchant criticisms, but Buhler's categorical dismissal of thematic transformation is much too hasty. Actual instances of thematic transformation are left unsearched for—not by Buhler specifically, but in the world of film music criticism and analysis overall. There is a tendency among even the best interpreters of the artform to concentrate on themes in an idealized, standalone state at the expense of investigating the way they behave in typical film underscore.[6] Sustained and systematic examination of the *actual score* is called for. We can start by giving the Throne Room another audience.

Whether or not *A New Hope*'s final theme can fairly be characterized as undeveloped depends on the span in which we are willing to track the melody's activity. It is true that the idea shown in Figure 4.1 is *not* the end-product of a score-spanning process nor a convergence of some previously only-hinted-at array of motivic particles. The melody seems to arrive out of the blue, already confidently ensconced in its small ternary form, as though it already existed. This is the crux of Buhler's critique of the Throne Room: the movie never properly *earned* such a majestic theme. One could imagine some alternative version of the score where Williams's motif struggled and grew along with the unfolding narrative, suffering setbacks but eventually achieving triumphant annunciation. Would this suffice to lend it "structural weight," to furnish it "a meaningful history"?

In point of fact, the head of the Throne Room *is* subtly previewed in an earlier cue, albeit at an odd time: the scene in which Threepio's arm is discovered after the Tusken attack. The short passage is depicted in Figure 4.3.[7] This is not the stuff of a grand thematic arc: the Throne Room's melodic forerunner is easily missable and, for most of the rest of the film, uncorroborated. Few but the most perceptive listeners will recollect this lost-arm motif when the Throne Room proper appears ninety minutes later. But this is beside the point; the premise that thematic "structural weight" depends on concerted and conspicuous foreshadowing is not one we must accept. There is something valid in serving the audience something new and easily

Figure 4.3 Preview of Throne Room in "Obi-Wan Kenobi" (ANH, 4m2, 32:04)

gratifying at the end of their cinematic meal, a simple dessert after a heavy main course.[8] Obscurely previewed or not, that is how the THRONE ROOM functions in *A New Hope*, as a sweet thematic confection.[9]

The THRONE ROOM does go dormant in *The Empire Strikes Back*, though it would be untrue to say it leaves no repercussions whatsoever. The melody itself is not revisited, and perhaps this is a missed opportunity: one could imagine a newly darkened take on the anthem, fragmented and harried, just as unsure as our heroes whose celebration at the end of *A New Hope* proved premature.[10] But in Episode V, Williams does retain and in fact redoubles his channeling of Elgar and especially Walton, and in a more motivically systematic way. THRONE ROOM-esque particles wend their way through many cues, both incidental—Luke's pep talk before the Battle of Hoth, to be revisited in Chapter 8 and properly leitmotivic, as in the vintage slice of Waltoniana that is the CLOUD CITY march.

Stylistic afterimages aside, the THRONE ROOM melody does indeed seem to exist on a different symbolic plane than the routinely varied and developed principal leitmotifs of the Original Trilogy, a one-and-done "piece" of music rather than an integral constituent of a motivic fabric. Once we get to *Return of the Jedi*, however, something does indeed "happen" to THRONE ROOM, the recognition of which must necessarily change our evaluation of this anthem's putative lack of structural substance—and with it, all other blanket claims concerning these scores' lack of motivic integration, dynamism, or transformative potential.

Midway through Episode VI, the Rebel Armada is preparing to leap into hyperspace for a final assault on the second Death Star. For this sequence, Williams launches into a "preparing-for-battle" musical topos, heard previously in comparable cues in Episodes IV [1:45:07] and V [23:57]. After an initial volley of trumpet planing, the cue settles into an ostensibly new theme which underscores Admiral Ackbar's instructions to the fleet and Lando's reassurances to his crew. This seventeen-measure passage, a PREPARING TO JUMP theme, is reproduced in Figure 4.4.

An unharmonized string line, urged on by snare tattoos, unspools over the course of this paragraph, doing so not in grammatical four-bar units but in a more zigzagging fashion, militant and edgy. The PREPARING TO JUMP theme's phrase rhythm is compulsively unpredictable—the metrical grouping is an impossible-to-entrain 5 + 3 + 4 + 4.5—and parsing it is further complicated by surface syncopations and free repetitions of internal motifs. A tendency toward chromatic reorientation also sets in almost immediately, with the

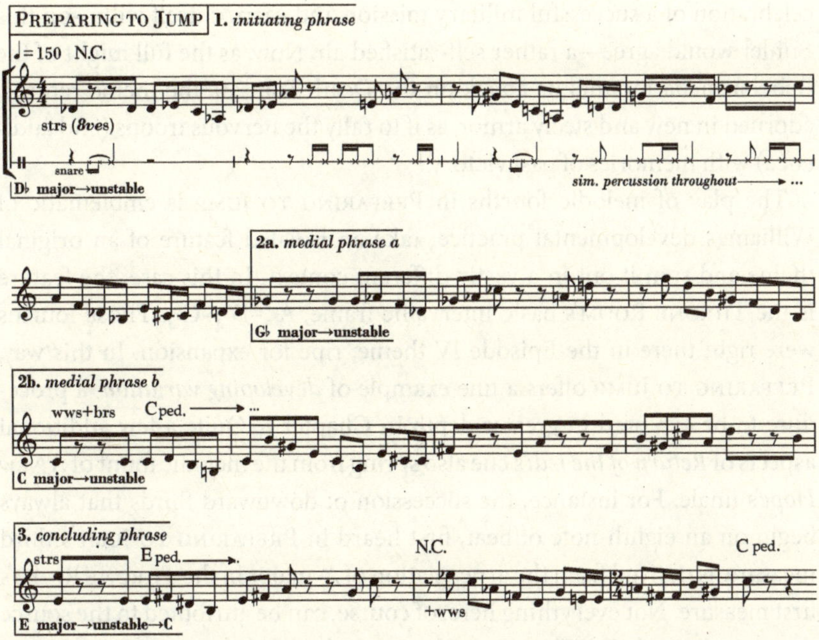

Figure 4.4 PREPARING TO JUMP theme in "The Fleet Enters Hyperspace" (ROTJ, 9m5, 1:27:08)

disruption of the five-flat harmonic field of the first measure with sharp-side pitches of uncertain function starting in bar two. While in no way a tone-row, the passage does convey the *sound* of the chromatic aggregate, a certain serialist impatience to blow through all twelve pitch-classes as quickly as possible.

These formal features—martial monophony, unpredictable phrase rhythm, doggedly anti-diatonic pitch design—conspire to conceal what is otherwise a patent derivation of this cue from the THRONE ROOM theme. Articulation and tempo aside, the opening motifs are identical, down to the key of D♭ major. The second measure's three-note gesture differs from its source by only one pitch, with $A\flat_4$ arriving on the heels of $E\flat_4$ rather than the $G\flat_4$ of the original. That small alteration in PREPARING TO JUMP, from minor third to perfect fourth, is significant, though: it is echoed with an ascending $E\natural_4$–$A\natural_4$ at the end of measure 3 and corroborated through the stacked fourths that pervade the paragraph from that point forward. There is a nice dramatic symmetry to all of this. When we first heard THRONE ROOM, it was a celebration of a successful military mission and carried itself with—on this Buhler would agree—a rather self-satisfied air. Now, as the full might of the Rebel armada mounts its attack on the Death Star 2.0, the theme returns, adorned in new and steely armor, as if to rally the nervous troops (and audience) with memories of past victory.[11]

The play of melodic fourths in PREPARING TO JUMP is emblematic of Williams's developmental practice: take an isolated feature of an original theme and spin it out in a vastly different context. In this case, the feature is the THRONE ROOM's basic intervallic frame, $A\flat_3$–$D\flat_4$–$G\flat_4$. Those fourths were right there in the Episode IV theme, ripe for expansion. In this way, PREPARING TO JUMP offers a fine example of *developing variation*, a procedure to be explored in greater depth in Chapter 6. Quite a few additional aspects of *Return of the Jedi*'s cue also spring from the melodic fount of *A New Hope*'s finale. For instance, the succession of downward thirds that always begin on an eighth-note offbeat, first heard in PREPARING TO JUMP's third measure, is derived from the arpeggiation of A♭ major in the THRONE ROOM's first measure. Not everything here, of course, can be attributed to the source theme in Episode IV. The sixteenth-sixteenth-eighth-note pickup (cf. mm. 3–4, 5–6) seems to have no melodic precedent in the THRONE ROOM, though it does factor into the INTO THE TRAP motif a few minutes later. Conversely, there are plenty of details in the original theme that are not replicated in any way in PREPARING TO JUMP. Developing variation is always at least a little selective.

In Williams's hands, these kinds of long-range manipulations are hard to confine to discrete spans of underscore; their musical ramifications tend to exceed any initial narrative justification. The transformed version of the THRONE ROOM showcased in "The Fleet Enters Hyperspace" itself provides the raw material for several passages in its vicinity (Figure 4.5). For example, a trombone motif that asserts itself at the onset of the sequence (4.5a) has little in common musically with the Episode IV theme. But it is manifestly an intervallic derivative—or more appropriately, a prefiguration—of the stacked fourths from PREPARING TO JUMP. And just as musical elements can be worked backward, they can ramify into the future. Take the next cue, "Heroic Ewok": the little horn fanfare (4.5b) that sounds before a gallant Ewok distracts the Empire's troops bears little rhythmic or intervallic resemblance to the prior cue. But as the fourths start piling up, a connection, even if only unconsciously apprehended by most listeners, is forged.

Figure 4.5 Derivatives from THRONE ROOM/PREPARING TO JUMP. **a.** "The Fleet Enters Hyperspace" (ROTJ, 9m5, 1:26:59); **b.** "The Heroic Ewok" (ROTJ, 9m6/10m1, 1:28:45)

A few scenes after PREPARING TO JUMP premieres, the Battle of Endor is under way. Williams begins the set piece with some of the most chaotic action music yet heard in the series. Nevertheless, the cues that make up the initial chunk of combat maintain taut motivic continuity with "The Fleet Enters Hyperspace." As is frequently the case in Williams's action writing, motifs that appear in one module have a way of serving up ingredients for the next, and so on, in a process we will come to call *melodic concatenation*.[12] As the melee ensues, Williams cycles through a number of particles like those shown in Figure 4.6—spurts of musical urgency drawn from the fourth-stacks and plunging chromatic arpeggios of PREPARING TO JUMP. Though some of the motives are more cryptic than others, tracking these derivatives is not an idle game of "spot the intervallic similarity": there is real dramatic weight, emotion, and tension communicated with such details. These agitated figures serve as a musical binding agent, making unified and intelligible what was, at the time, the longest and most complex battle sequence in the series. (It does not hurt that the striding intervals and dotted rhythms of the PREPARING TO JUMP derivatives integrate handsomely with both EWOK and VADER leitmotifs, which themselves start to duke it out in short order.)

This fracas on Endor is a long way from the majestic THRONE ROOM. It is unlikely that Williams expected any listener to consciously link these tense motives back to his Edwardian pastiche from two films ago. Such moments are generally not the stuff of mythic import, not marked for attention in the same way as big set pieces or iconic leitmotifs. But neither are materials such as in Figures 4.5 and 4.6 *generic*, mere grist for the action cue mill. Even such throwaway musical cells have a story to tell—in this case, a kind of panicked

Figure 4.6 Sample of additional derivatives of Preparing to Jump from the Battle of Endor. **a.** "Rebel Forces Captured" (ROTJ, 10m3, 1:36:40); **b.** "First Ewok Battle" (ROTJ,10m5/11m1, 1:37:55); **c.** "First Ewok Battle" (ROTJ,10m5/11m1, 1:38:28); **d.** "First Ewok Battle" (ROTJ,10m5/11m1, 1:38:55)

explosion into scattered bits of the formerly tightly wound Preparing to Jump module. And initiating this motivic cascade, a masterfully executed reimagining of a theme only on the fringes of most viewers' memory.[13]

✺✺✺

It should be clear that the Throne Room garners rigorous and inventive development, albeit not within the film in which it is introduced. The miniature musical saga of the Throne Room involves several devices—reorchestration, fragmentation, sequencing, diminution—that belong to a wider repertory of tools Williams uses to bind the Skywalker Saga together. We have seen, in one small context, how such techniques emerge spontaneously, sometimes almost invisibly, within the flow of nondiegetic underscore, here according to the principle of developing variation. Collectively, these techniques contribute to a musical fabric densely threaded with thematic transformations—the antithesis of Buhler's characterization of *Star Wars* as musically weightless and inconsequential.

This chapter is about thematic transformation. Defined simply, thematic transformation is the art of taking an established musical idea and altering its structure or exploding its components to the point that something new is born.[14] The principle is closely affiliated with the concept of thematic development, which differs not at the level of local compositional technique but in its presumption, or lack thereof, of a musical goal. Thematic transformation rewards a listener with a keen ear and a good memory. That "something new" at the end of a thematic journey may trigger the recollection of an old referent, or it may resummon an old feeling. But any past meanings and emotions will be cast in a new light. With thematic transformation, it is as though the score has an agency of its own, embarks on its own little story.[15] Clearly, thematic transformation has great potential for creating symbolic and affective meaning in film music, especially in a franchise with such a deep internal sense of memory.

Lest we completely bypass Buhler's critique, it should be stated: thematic transformation is *not* an ever-present aspect of Williams's writing for the Saga, and there are many moments that are motivically disconnected, uncorroborated, or attained without struggle—like the THRONE ROOM melody itself in *A New Hope*, there and elsewhere to perfectly fine and justifiable dramatic effect. But thematic transformation is active far more often than critics and analysts have tended to recognize in the Skywalker scores, and its importance to the artistic success of *Star Wars* is difficult to overstate.

The opportunity for growth, change, and interaction among themes was one of the main points Williams used to convince Lucas he was right to employ newly composed leitmotivic underscore, as opposed to preexisting classical music in the manner of *2001: A Space Odyssey*. According to the composer:

> [One can] take themes and reshape them and put them in a major key, minor key, fast, slow, up, down, inverted, attenuated and crushed, and all the permutations that you can put a scene and a musical conception through, that you wouldn't be able to tastefully do if you had taken a Beethoven symphony and scored with that.[16]

Williams here extols the sensitivity that a professionally rendered score can lend a film, and he reacts against the Kubrickian practice of laying precomposed tracks over a scene and expecting it to work as well as custom-tailored composition. He acknowledges that bending musical material at the whim of cinematic need may be tasteless according to Beethovenian expectations of structural autonomy and utmost rigor of musical development. Yet in his invocation of variation, permutation, and taste, Williams also alludes to a deeper—and, in its own way, patently symphonic—principle that animates his own film music. Comprising over twenty hours' worth of music that spans sixty-seven years of galactic history (and nearly fifty years of personal creative investment), the nine Skywalker scores stand as one of the longest experiments in the development of a set of musical ideas by a single major composer—not just in the realm of film scoring, but music, period. As the rest of this chapter and the next will make clear: thematic transformation is at the heart of the *Star Wars* musico-mythical soundscape.

Scope

To begin to grasp the sheer variety of transformational techniques that pervade the Skywalker Saga, it will be helpful to establish some categories. Admittedly, no single book could encapsulate every way in which Williams shapes and reshapes his material in *Star Wars*. Nor could it enumerate the profusion of devices—"all the permutations" in the composer's words—through which music may be understood to transform or develop.[17] But the task can be made manageable by drawing a series of distinctions pertaining to the *scope*, *continuity*, and *degree* of thematic change. Over the next three sections, each will be explored in turn, with the matter of degree garnering more space, as it entails developing a typology of both micro- and macro-transformations.

The first thing to bear in mind when examining how a musical idea is manipulated in *Star Wars* is the question of scope: over what duration does this theme's story take place? Thematic "work" happens over a range of spans in the series, from spasms of developmental activity lasting just a few measures to thematic arcs that reach across whole trilogies. This continuum of transformational time scales is depicted in Figure 4.7, along with

← *Shorter Range* *Longer Range* →

Passage	Cue	Set piece	Act	Film	Trilogy	Saga
Ep. IV (6m6, mm. 1–25)	II (4m1)	III (6m4–6m9)	VI (act 1)	VIII (entirety)	VII–IX	I–IX
That's No Moon	Jango Fight	Battle of the Heroes	Jabba	Rose	Rey	Force

Figure 4.7 Continuum of thematic transformations

Figure 4.8 THAT'S NO MOON! (ANH, 7m1, 1:04:26)

1:04:26 1:04:32 1:04:37 1:04:42 1:04:56 1:05:05 1:05:14 1:05:24

Initial Statement	**Extended Restatement**	**Pedal, Augmented**	**Increased Counterpoint**	**Intensified, Diminuted**	**Quasi-Period Structure** (antecedent)	(consequent)
B♭m	B♭m…⇝	E♭aug…⇝	…⇝…	…⇝V/B♭	B♭m ⇝ V/B	B♮m⇝V$^4_2$/C
f. hn, tbn	f. hn, tbn	tbn	f. hn, tbn	tpt	f. hn, vln	f. hn, vln
"That's no moon..."	"It's too big to be a space station…"	"I have a very bad feeling about this…"	"Lock in the auxiliary power."	"Why are we still moving towards it!?"	"They're not going to get me…"	"…there are alternatives to fighting."

Figure 4.9 Form of passage involving THAT'S NO MOON! motif (ANH, 7m1)

representative segments and the themes—some incidental, some leitmotifs—developed within them.

At the shorter end of the spectrum, there are music-developmental arcs like the one that appears in *A New Hope* when Luke and company stumble upon the Death Star. Figure 4.8 renders the idea that initiates the cue—for lack of a better label, the THAT'S NO MOON motif. This little shudder of musical distress has a lifespan of just twenty-five measures, a little over half of the forty-seven-measure cue. But within that tight frame, Williams squeezes in some serious motivic work for THAT'S NO MOON. He constructs the passage as a sustained crescendo, rising in volume and tessitura as the heroes realize their predicament, with everything leading up to a blazing statement of the REBEL FANFARE once the Millennium Falcon succumbs to the Death Star's tractor beam.

The form of the cue, up until the REBEL FANFARE lights up at 1:05:24, is shown in Figure 4.9. THAT'S NO MOON's initial utterance (mm. 1–2) is inchoate: just a pair of m3-related melodic pitches, harmonized in chromatic thirds. The germ buds into an extended restatement (mm. 3–5), and from there is subjected to several time-tested developmental—and in this context, dread-producing—procedures. Between modules 2 and 5, we hear augmentation over a dissonant pedal; outer-voice counterpoint based on imitative inversion; and mounting tonal and rhythmic energy, drawing to something of a half-cadential midpoint. At the climax of the paragraph, THAT'S NO MOON is clarified into an 8-measure period of sorts, loosely orbiting B♭ major, with a richer if still highly dissonant harmonization. The orchestra then discharges onto a module dominated by the REBEL FANFARE, in this setting on B♭ major but "in" C. And with that, THAT'S NO MOON is heard no more.[18]

More characteristic of Williams's writing are motifs that persist across a whole cue, not just a module or two, but which do not recur thereafter. The throbbing JANGO FIGHT figure that kicks off a major action set piece in *Attack of the Clones* [1:00:54] is typical. Williams has tremendous fun with the idea, contracting, expanding, and eventually dissolving it as Jango Fett and Obi-Wan trade blows in the Kaminoan rain. But all that activity is restricted to the one isolated action sequence.[19] This delimited form of development is typical of set piece themes across all nine films—especially the leitmotif-light action cues of the Prequels—and contrasts sharply with the denser musical-prose style Williams applies to dialogue underscoring.

The storytelling potential of cumulative thematic transformation at the cue level is on display during the Battle of Yavin in Episode IV with respect to LUKE's theme. Within the sequence's climactic final two minutes, Williams presents four variants of the leitmotif (Figure 4.10), each calibrated in dissonance—both tonal and rhythmic—to reflect the shifting tides of battle. None are in a straightforward major key, each being modified in some way to inflect or contradict the theme's usual tonal brightness. When Luke becomes the sole remaining trench-runner, we hear the series' second-ever modal twist on his leitmotif (4.10a). Melodically, the theme is in G minor, but it contends with multiple sheets of harmonic ambivalence: a stammering succession of wrong-note bass figures, primarily $F\sharp_2 \rightarrow E_2$, and some whirling string passagework—itself independently motivic—with elements of D harmonic major and E octatonic. The next LUKE rendition (4.10b) underscores Obi-Wan's acousmatic pep talk and injects a needed surge of musical optimism. Kenobi's line is set by the FORCE theme in F minor, but is suspended over an inverted D♭ma7 chord, suggesting a lydian reappraisal of the motif. Williams enacts the same ploy in modal reverse for LUKE: his melody is in B♭ major but lies above a bass of G, implying a steely aeolian cast.

The following leg of Luke's leitmotivic gauntlet (4.10c) is markedly more anxious. His melody is presented by harsh winds and muted trumpets, further bristled with chromatic displacements and an ambivalent harmonization. The key is basically D major, but the tonic is roiled by a fluctuation of $D^{\sharp5}$/A and $E\flat^{\flat5}$/B♭ chords. A few measures later, in the moments before the

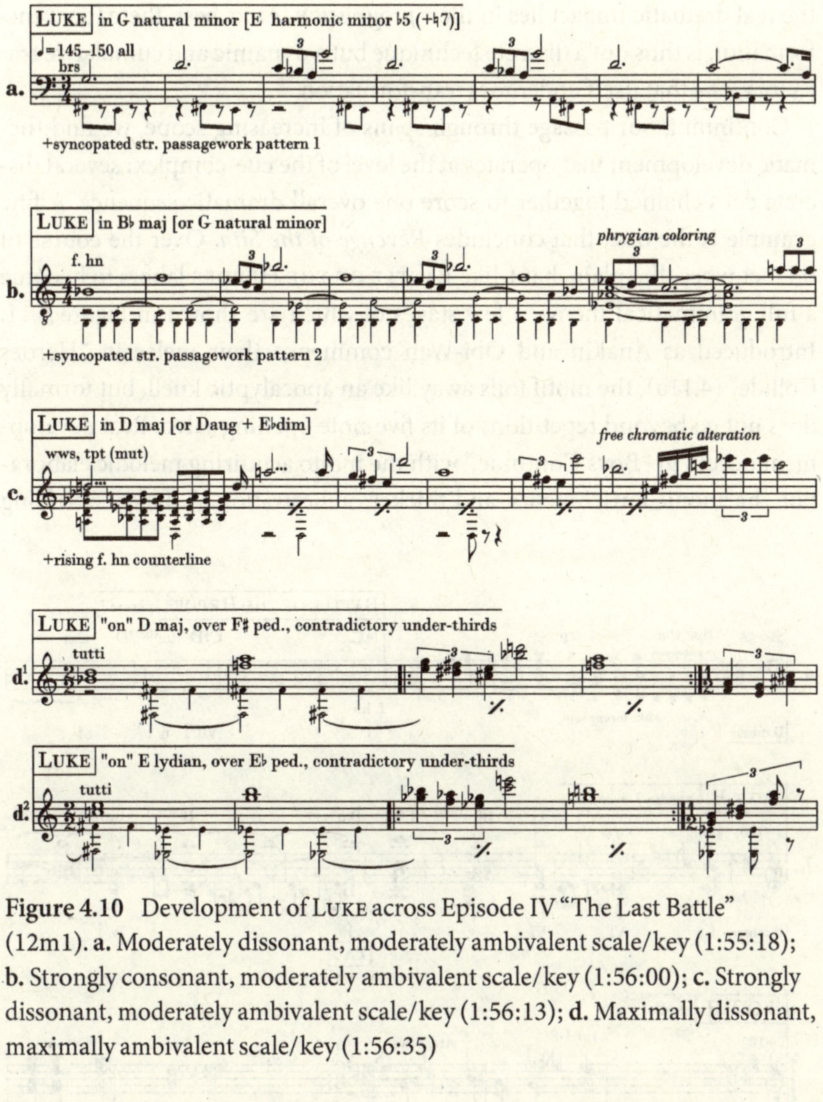

Figure 4.10 Development of LUKE across Episode IV "The Last Battle" (12m1). **a.** Moderately dissonant, moderately ambivalent scale/key (1:55:18); **b.** Strongly consonant, moderately ambivalent scale/key (1:56:00); **c.** Strongly dissonant, moderately ambivalent scale/key (1:56:13); **d.** Maximally dissonant, maximally ambivalent scale/key (1:56:35)

Death Star laser fires (4.10d), Williams subjects the leitmotif to its harshest ordeal. Scalar incongruities and wrong-note bass notes from previous iterations converge, while a parallel stream of chromatic thirds now tails the melody relentlessly. These harmonic pressures obliterate any sense of tonal security inherent to the theme, and refuse to offer relief, even when Han Solo swoops in to save his friend's skin during the second pass through the battered tune. Although each of these variants of LUKE is expressive on its own, the real dramatic impact lies in their *progression*. At its best, thematic transformation is thus not a discrete technique but a dynamic and cumulative trajectory, one that itself undergoes transformation.

Continuing our passage through spans of increasing scope, we find thematic development that operates at the level of the cue-complex: several discrete cues chained together to score one overall dramatic sequence. A fine example is the duel that concludes *Revenge of the Sith*. Over the course of this set piece, the plainchant-like BATTLE OF THE HEROES labors to become a full grammatical theme, a few stages of which are shown in Figure 4.11. Introduced as Anakin and Obi-Wan commence their melee in "Heroes Collide" (4.11a), the motif tolls away like an apocalyptic knell, but formally does not go beyond repetitions of its five-note opening salvo. Real development occurs in "Boys Continue," with the motto acquiring melodic elaboration, harmonic enrichments, and thicker orchestration. A darkly satisfying

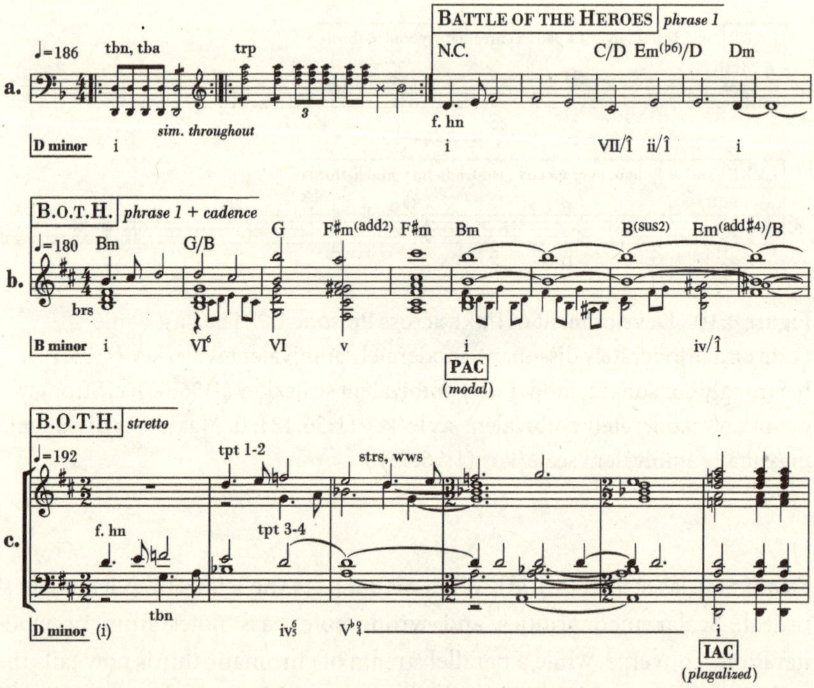

Figure 4.11 Development of BATTLE OF THE HEROES across Episode III final duel. **a.** Initial statement in "Heroes Collide" (6m4, 1:47:56); **b.** Modal cadence in "Boys Continue" (6m7, 1:54:54); **c.** Climactic stretto in "Revenge of the Sith" (6m9, 1:59:25)

highlight is the modal cadence (4.11b) that prepares the movie's most iconic image: Anakin and Obi-Wan's sabers locked, backlit by an exploding pyroclasm.

It is not until the final cue of the duel, simply titled "Revenge of the Sith," that Battle of the Heroes attains a proper melodic period. Now the theme is proclaimed by a full choir, as if there were any doubt the clash was in its endgame. Following a further flurry of fiery variants, the theme reaches its climax with a brassy stretto in five parts (4.11c). Each successive canonic entry vies to capture the melodic high ground. The separate lines coil into one of the more poetically overdetermined cadences in the series, a hubristic $A^{\flat 9(\text{omit}3)}$ dominant ("You underestimate my power!") crashing into an unyielding D-minor tonic ("Don't try it."). Like many of the most intense phrase conclusions in the series, this one mixes the hallmarks of an authentic cadence (the A-to-D bass progression) and a plagal one (the $Gm^{\text{add}\flat 6}$ above it). The former supplies functional heft, the latter spiritual gravitas and a splash of dissonance. Here and elsewhere, I call this *Star Wars*ian procedure a *plagalized* cadence.[20]

What makes the evolutionary trajectory of this theme in Episode III noteworthy is how self-contained it is. By all rights, Battle of the Heroes is the film's marquee new theme; it dominates the movie's most pivotal sequence, is freighted with enormous symbolic import, recurs in the end credits, and garners the score's sole concert arrangement. And while elements are certainly prefigured by the Misery Trichord and other motivic cells, for a leitmotif, Battle of the Heroes does not need to do much leading. The infernal theme impinges directly on no other part of *Revenge of the Sith*'s score outside the cue-complex of 9m4–9m9.

Prevalent though intermediate-range transformations like this may be in *Star Wars*, their very concision forestalls contribution to the deepest mythical undercurrents of the series' symphonic storytelling. When we imagine thematic transformation, whether in Classical music or screen music, it is usually not something that is over quickly. "Thematische Arbeit" (thematic work) in the vein attributed to Beethoven and his successors treats development as something that is *always* happening, not restricted to a particularly dynamic section of a sonata or volatile scene in an opera. Listening to music from many nineteenth-century composers—and for all their differences, Brahms and Wagner are equally characteristic here—one has the impression that thematic change is in a way a permanent state, taking place on *every* timescale of a piece. A sense of becoming, of motivic working-out, is apparent at the level of the theme just as much as it is across the whole movement or act. Or, in the case of increasingly popular cyclical forms, across whole multi-movement symphonies, concerti, operas, and, in the *Ring*, opera cycles.

It is therefore thematic transformation at the level of the *whole film score* that is most likely to impress listeners with Brahmsian/Wagnerian expectations. (Whether those expectations are warranted, or *ipso facto* worth being impressed by, is another matter entirely; recall our pressuring of the Adornian mindset earlier.) This whole-score approach is indeed the model Williams himself prefers—at least when it comes to major leitmotifs, which tend to leave their imprint over most of a movie's runtime, a topic to which we will return in Chapters 5 and 6. Exceptions, where the development of a principal theme is circumscribed, tend to be plot-driven and pragmatic. Jabba the Hutt appears only in the first third of *Return of the Jedi* and thus there is no need to sustain the JABBA theme past his dramatic relevance, or, in his case, death. Though even the grave might be enough to foreclose all thematic work. Characters have a way of coming back to life in this series, after all, and the benefit of tracking and foreshadowing ensures that few important themes are ever truly gone. (Jabba's corpulent leitmotif recurs in Episode I, reimagined as a fanfare, and Episode IV's Special Edition, in purely tracked form.) More interesting, perhaps, is the way Williams tends to extend additional development for his marquee themes through extra-diegetic vessels like suites and concert arrangements—in Jabba's case, a grotesque *Konzertstück* for virtuoso tubist.

Although written for a secondary character, ROSE's theme in *The Last Jedi* may be the purest example of a score-spanning developmental arc. Her leitmotif features in one, and only one, movie, and is subjected to a substantial amount of thematic work within it. The theme is introduced a quarter of the way through Episode VIII [38:38] and from there garners twenty-one iterations, interacting with many of the series' other big themes (FORCE, RESISTANCE MARCH, REBEL FANFARE) along the way. (We'll see these interactions more closely in Chapter 6.) Hers is very much the "theme" of the movie, affectively shouldering its core message of righteous non-aggression, "saving what we love—that's how we win." Accordingly, renditions of ROSE range in quality from awkward and shy [39:37] to exultant [1:08:14], with many emotional shades between. Confirming her thematic centrality to the score, ROSE's theme is also lent a hefty expansion and further development in the score's End Credits cue, where she is even treated to a B-theme—unheard in the film proper. Regrettably, the character is sidelined in *The*

Rise of Skywalker, as is her leitmotif. But, like Jabba and other musically memorable personages, her imprint is left on a concert arrangement, "The Rebellion Is Reborn," a bi-thematic piece in which Rose mingles with material associated with the aged and disillusioned Luke Skywalker; in the arrangement, as in the score to Episode VIII as a whole, her positivity ultimately wins the day.

Continuity

For a motif-minded film composer, the level of continuity given to a musical thought or process is of special importance. As with scope, there is a large spectrum of transformational continuity in the Skywalker Saga. On one pole, motivic germs may go underground for many cues before blossoming, sometimes acts or entire films later. Such is the case for Kylo Ren's primary theme, whose most impactful transformation occurs two scores after its introduction in *The Force Awakens*. On the other pole, there are instances of uninterrupted motivic development, without intervening material, digressions, or silence—a rare state indeed, though some chapters of the Saga, mostly in *Empire Strikes Back*, come close.

Between these extremes lies a great middle ground where most leitmotivic development happens: in moderately sized pockets across multiple disconnected cues. This discreteness is a function of the way Williams organizes leitmotivic prose more generally: themes are typically presented one at a time in *Star Wars* rather than in overlapping contrapuntal layers or unbroken sequential strands, as might be found in, say, Wagner. Long-range musical argumentation, of course, does take place, as we have seen. But dramatic exigency ultimately rules the day: the listener must always be ready to shift their aural attention on a dime, in directions dictated by editorial structure and narrative incident more than intrinsic musical necessity.

The gladiatorial sequence in *Attack of the Clones* offers an emblematic case of this tension between intermittence and continuity in thematic development. As written, the "Entrance of the Monsters" comprises a veritable theme and variations set on a memorable one-scene wonder, the Arena March. The rather discursive thematic subject, shown in Figure 4.12, is treated to nine statements, during which Williams constructs a quasi-fugal exposition and development, in the martial manner of his idols Dmitri

Figure 4.12 ARENA MARCH subject from "Entrance of the Monsters" (AOTC, 6m2, cut)

Shostakovich (Symphony 11, Mvt. 2), William Walton ("Spitfire Prelude and Fugue"), and Alex North (*Spartacus*, "Main Title"). The closest analogue in Williams's output to this long-barreled theme is the "Belly of the Steel Beast" from *Indiana Jones and the Last Crusade*, the subject of which is also an abrasive march, also developed in a discursive, pseudo-Baroque idiom. Within the *Star Wars* franchise, the DROID MARCH introduced in Episode I provides a loose precedent. Less periodic, more contrapuntally motivated than that theme for the Trade Federation's army, the ARENA MARCH assumes the role of "non-Imperial March" theme for baddies in Episode II. Its sharper edges emblematic of the score's shift away from easy (read: straightforward, optimistic, immature) idioms and thematic structures, reinforcing the observations of theorist Mark Richards with respect to melodic form and characterization as detailed in the previous chapter.

As Williams composed it, the ARENA MARCH's development within "Entrance of the Monsters" is continuous. The cue is uninterrupted by references to any competing melodies, and only lightly leavened with a few interstitial, thematically-unmarked passages. Even the most highly contrastive section—a polyphonic episode for three brass voices midway through—is traceable back to the source theme, with its intervallic and rhythmic components derived from the cue's thematic subject.[21] As such, the four-minute-long piece represents the most sustained stream of motivic work in *Attack of the Clones*, and despite not involving a genuine leitmotif, is an exemplar of continuous, hair-raisingly tense thematic transformation.

Or rather, "Entrance of the Monsters" *would* have been an exemplar of sustained and concentrated transformation, had most of the cue not been eliminated from the final cut of Episode II, only to later be spliced into a pair of unrelated scenes involving the Clone Troopers in Episode III [48:00, 1:19:13]. As it stands, only the *final*, most cumulative statement of the ARENA MARCH is played in the movie it was originally written for [1:48:33]. The filmgoer will thus hear the end product of a theme and variation set, without the initial theme . . . or its variations.

What effect, besides a possible bruising of the composer's ego, does an excision of this extremity have on the score-in-context? In truth, the scene works quite well without Williams's contribution. Every other action sequence in Episode II is blanketed with music, and the orchestra's absence here gives the whole soundtrack some needed breathing room. Affectively speaking, the ARENA MARCH was always an odd fit in *Attack of the Clones* in the first place. The use of a fugal military march for a scene whose combatants are not soldiers but unarmed hostages and giant space monsters is a little suspect. On a topical level, at least, the ARENA MARCH suits the regimented Clone Troopers, led in rhythmic lockstep by freshly dubbed Darth Vader, of Episode III, better than it ever did the savage beasts of Episode II.

Extreme though it may be, the disruption of a well-devised musical argument in "Entrance of the Monsters" is less an exception to the rule than many casual listeners might realize. Editorial circumstances unforeseeable by the composer beset all nine films, to a radical degree in *Attack of the Clones* and all three sequel-trilogy entries.[22] Numerous factors are arrayed against music-transformational continuity, but most boil down to the mutability of the film's final cut as afforded by digital editing (and sometimes as required by indecisive filmmakers). Sequences involving heavy visual effects or multiple intercut locations are especially prone to manipulation after the score has been recorded, and it is here that musical splicing, cutting, tracking, and micro-editing are most profuse. The vagaries of editing can enforce a compositionally unintended—and, in some cases, anathematic—type of intermittency on thematic development.[23] But not even the most conscientiously edited movie would lend itself to an utterly continuous, coherent flow of orchestral thought. The natural state of film scoring guarantees that thematic work takes place at irregular intervals—not in one unbroken sweep of musical thought as in Beethoven or Brahms (or Wagner, for that matter) but more in the manner of a motto theme in a cyclical symphony. That is, gradually, sporadically, and theatrically, with plenty of contrasting episodes and diversions along the way. Indeed, it is hard to imagine the mythic play of memory and allusion in Williams's scores working properly were there *not* gaps—musical negative spaces that bring those moments of truly transformative thematic development into epic relief.

Degree

Micro-Transformations

The last and, for our purposes, most important distinction when it comes to thematic transformation regards degree: how profoundly Williams alters his materials, what constitutes a *micro-* and *macro-transformation* respectively. The former involves relatively simple devices—familiar procedures like mode shift, ornamentation, and reorchestration. Never mind that a critic like Adorno would dismiss these as "changes of lighting," tricks born of a variational rather than developmental impetus. Micro-transformations can be awesomely effective as a means of musical storytelling. And they are everywhere in *Star Wars*.

A complete account of micro-transformations in the Skywalker Saga is of course impossible, but we can nevertheless aim for systematicity. Figure 4.13 enumerates twelve micro-transformational techniques found in the series, offering a brief definition and a single vivid example. Helpfully, the ubiquitous and easily recognizable Luke leitmotif can furnish a clean illustration of each category. However, even with this—the first melody most people will think of from *Star Wars*—few instances fit so tidily into neat categories as suggested in the provided table. Themes are dynamic things, and the categories used to sort them have a way of overlapping and dissolving. Transformational edge cases sometimes seem to outnumber clear-cut exemplars. Thankfully, the prototype/parameter model introduced in Chapter 3 makes assessing thematic difference something we can describe methodically. In the case of Figure 4.13, the micro-transformations of Luke hold fixed the majority of those previously specified thematic parameters (contour, harmony, orchestration, rhythm, line) while modifying a select few.

Consider a segment from Episode I's "Darth and Qui-Gon" (Figure 4.14), a cue that illustrates the *fragmentation* category. A two-measure outburst of

MICRO-TRANSFORMATIONS			
Type	**Description**	**Example (LUKE)**	**Transformation(s)**
Augmentation/ Diminution	Rhythmic values extended/reduced	V: "The Magic Tree" [1:03:10]	Basic idea slowed & stretched over dissonant bass
Compression	Phrasal form shortened	VIII: "Old Friends" [34:11]	Theme's middle bars excised
Extension	Form lengthened or supplemented	IV: "Swashbucklers" [1:28:22]	Little parenthetical measures inserted between phrases
Fragmentation	Disassembled into component ideas	I: "Darth & Qui Gon" [1:17:15]	Rhythmic shard, outside normal melodic context
Imitation	Ideas echoed in other lines, layers	V: "Carbon Freeze" [1:34:20]	Basic ideas stated and quickly repeated by diff. instruments
Mode Change	Underlying scale altered	V: "Yoda Raises the Ship" [1:10:15]	Conversion from major to natural minor mode
Ornamentation	Elaborations to melodic line	III: "A New Hope" [2:12:50]	Tonally and polyphonically elaborated
Reharmonization	Chord progression altered	IV: "More Little People" [17:13]	Unique 'Western'-style progression $[IV^7 \leftrightarrow I^6_5 \rightarrow IV^7 \rightarrow V^7/V \rightarrow V\ldots]$
Remetering	Rhythmic/metric structure altered	IX: "More Action" [1:41:21]	Statement in compound meter, slightly syncopated.
Reorchestration	Instrumentation/ texture altered	VI: "Bedtime Stories" [1:15:58]	Presented by recorder and harp
Sequencing	Repetition at distinct pitch levels	IX: "Dunkirk" [1:55:12]	Mid-phrase repetition and shift of pitch center
Truncation	Small segment of first phrase	V: "Luke's Escape" [9:48]	Opening measure sufficient to evoke whole leitmotif

Figure 4.13 Micro-transformations

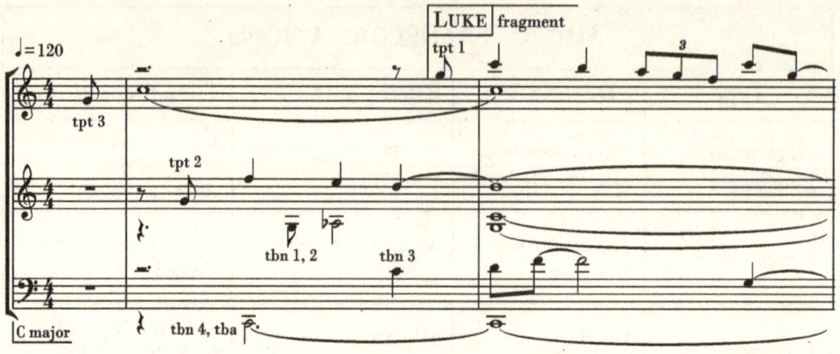

Figure 4.14 Luke fragment in "Darth and Qui-Gon" (TPM, 4m6, 1:17:15)

brassy polyphony amid an action set piece showcasing Qui-Gon's seldom-heard motif, the last notes of this passage present five parameters of the Luke theme in no uncertain terms. Readily audible is the leitmotif's characteristic contour (descending third, leaping seventh), orchestration (brass, led by trumpets), and rhythm (triplet-duplet pattern). Together, these elements unambiguously point to this being a reference to Luke's theme, and with it, all the connotations of bravery, battle, and bombast.

Of course, this little stretto would not be enlisted as an exemplar of fragmentation if *all* elements of its thematic source were present. The linear substructure of Luke is completely missing, arriving as the first trumpet part does, at the end of an otherwise wholly new set of melodic ideas. Furthermore, against the contrapuntally active and slightly dissonant texture, Luke's paradigmatic *chord progression* is also absent. Some of the sonority is there: note the way the imitative pileup forms a $C^{5(\text{sus}2,4)}$ chord, not too far from the quartally disposed sonorities of the prototype. But the little triplet burst—the most immediately recognizable component of the parent theme—is attached to a different part of the governing scale entirely: $\hat{1}$-$\hat{7}$-$\hat{6}$, rather than $\hat{4}$-$\hat{3}$-$\hat{2}$. The net effect is of a motivic reference that, while unmistakable when listening closely, is sufficiently altered to suggest a theme not-quite-ready for the spotlight yet. Such a tease is dramatically apt and in keeping with the provisional, before-the-beginning nature of *The Phantom Menace*'s storytelling.

The fragmented spin on the Luke theme in "Darth and Qui-Gon" suggests one pathway by which micro-transformations can lead to more macrocosmic ones. A thematic prototype, decomposed in the way represented schematically back in Chapter 3, encourages us to hear how motivic parameters can detach from their themes and become available for other sorts of freer developmental processes. One such process is *motivic seeding*, which is so prevalent in *Star Wars* that the next chapter will be dedicated to it entirely. Motivic seeding is the practice of extracting a parameter of a theme—a chord, an interval, a contour, etc.—and allowing that aspect to ramify throughout a cue, without necessarily building toward a musical goal. Seeding may be either retrospective or prospective. If retrospective, it involves a theme that has already been established and relies for its dramatic impact on the audience's ability to hold a prototype in their ear. If prospective, the seeded theme has yet to sprout fully; it is destined to take form only after a host of hints and false starts. Both rely on the listener's ability to synthesize and affiliate, likely only at an unconscious level, scattered and discontinuous motivic particles.

The prospective form of seeding is not uncommon, as we will see in the next chapter with respect to the Anakin and Padmé theme. But as a transformational strategy, and a demonstration of the prototype/parameter model, the retrospective mode is more illustrative. Take "The Complete Map" from *The Force Awakens*. At the end of Episode VII, as Rey, Chewie, and R2 are preparing to leave the Resistance base, Williams sandwiches a fascinating musical paragraph between two lengthy statements of the Leia and Rey themes. Between those traditional melodies is a span of less overtly thematic underscore, building to a pregnant pedal-point on C_2, full of expectancy for the next, yet-unimagined stage in our heroes' grand adventure.

Figure 4.15 provides a melodic reduction of this paragraph, with annotations for those aspects that allude to or develop out of (or into) established leitmotifs. Aspects of the Leia, Rebel Fanfare, and Pathos themes are present to varying levels of audibility. The eighth-sixteenth-sixteenth-note motifs in the second and eighth measure of the excerpt are spun out from the analogous figure that occurs throughout Leia's theme. The first six measures of her leitmotif were stated immediately before this paragraph; the effect then is of a masked, noncontiguous completion and then development of her long-breathed melody. Even more ear-catching is the downward cascade of major triads in measures 10–11. This is a kind of exuberant run-on sentence based on the Rebel Fanfare, whose own motivic seeding throughout Episode VII we will inspect in Chapter 5. But most interesting

Figure 4.15 Thematic seeds and fragments in "The Complete Map" (TFA, 8m73, 2:03:28)

from a thematic-transformational perspective is the way Williams plants germs of, and then reaps, LUKE's theme.

Four aspects of the LUKE theme, each based on a different parameter or collection of parameters of its prototype, can be discerned within this eventful patch of music.

1. The C_4-F_4-C_5 upsweep that initiates the paragraph, evoking the widely spaced linear ascent LUKE, without its characteristic rhythm or orchestration. The descending continuation, minus an octave displacement, is partially present in the following lydian-flavored descent. It also suggests, probably accidentally, the far rarer LUKE AND LEIA theme.

2. The emphasis, from the seventh measure onward, is on the C7(sus4) sonority—a characteristic chord of the Luke theme, ever since it was first revealed on the heels of those quartal fanfares in Episode IV's main title.
3. The bass line from measures 7 through 9, though not an exact replica of the Luke triplet in terms of rhythm or pitch content, stands as a very clear proxy for it in terms of contour and linear behavior.
4. The horn melody starting in measure 12 initially sounds thematically unmarked—a faint allusion to the film's Pathos theme, which shares its $\hat{5}$-$\flat\hat{6}$-$\hat{2}$ pattern—but quickly morphs into an explicit iteration of the Luke triplet figure *plus* its minor seventh leap from $\hat{2}$ to $\hat{1}$. This leads to an imitative response in the trumpets, and a swell that crests, surprisingly from a tonal perspective, with a C7$^{(sus4)}$ to Dm motion. Thence we head, via a plagal half cadence, to the A minor of Rey's theme.

The components of this iconic leitmotif thereby begin to coalesce during the "Farewell and the Trip" passage. The process begins gradually, with the faintest of adumbrations, but culminates in an obvious (if still only fragmentary) statement in the horns, artfully preparing the listener for the incoming Luke-based End Credits. Admittedly, the scope of motivic seeding is limited in "Farewell and the Trip" to one extended scene. In *Star Wars*, this type of motivic work operates more paradigmatically at the level of the *whole* score. In Williams's words, he will often "extract elements from ['that completed thing'] and present them in a somewhat fragmented way" throughout the score.[24] With a prototype-and-parameter approach to thematic analysis, the nature of those elements, and the role they play in providing a distinctive "tint" to a cue or score, becomes explicit.

Macro-Transformations

Motivic seeding may involve the smallest units of musical discourse, but the manner in which it tends to play out is anything but small-scale. Some of the alterations to the Luke theme in "Farewell and the Trip" are too substantial, involve the manipulation or elimination of too many parameters, to fit our definition of micro-transformation. We have entered the realm of *macro-transformation*. A macro-transformation can be defined straightforwardly as the result of multiple small-scale adjustments. Compared to micro-transformative devices, its alterations of individual thematic parameters are more profound, more numerous, and more systematically applied.

Williams, ever self-effacing, has pushed back at claims of extreme or totalizing motivic integration. Asked whether the Original Trilogy was like Wagner's Ring, and how his work was "so interwoven when you originally were scoring one film," Williams confessed to having no great designs in mind.

> I think if the score has an architectural unity, it's the result of a happy accident. I approached each film as a separate entity. The first one completely out of the blue, but the second one of course connected to the first one; we referred back to characters and extended them and referred back to themes and extended and developed those. I suppose it was a natural but unconscious metamorphosis of musical themes that created something that may seem to have more architectural and conscious interrelatedness than I actually intended to put there. If it's there, to the degree that it is there, it's a kind of happy accident if you like. That may sound deprecating—I don't mean it quite that way—but the functional aspect and the craft aspect of doing the job of these three films has to be credited with producing a lot of this unity in the musical content the listeners perceive.[25]

Williams's statement is worth keeping in mind as an analytic reality check, a reminder to temper our impulse to draw overly fine or implausible connections. But we should not take the claim at face value: his disavowal of "architectural unity" is hedged—and likely triggered by an unwanted comparison with Wagner, whom we have seen Williams is loath to admit influence from. In any case, the proof of whether the Skywalker scores are sites of advanced transformational techniques is in the scores themselves.

Though numerous examples of thematic metamorphoses can be found starting in Episode V—the next few chapters will cover several in depth—perhaps the clearest illustration of a macro-transformation arrives in the last chapter of the Saga, with respect to KYLO REN's primary theme. The motif undergoes something of a tonal redemption arc, the basic trajectory of which is shown in Figure 4.16. Two versions are shown, both heard early in *The Rise of Skywalker*, the first while Ren is slaughtering his enemies, the second when communing with Darth Vader. Hints at the leitmotif's capacity for evolution are sprinkled in earlier settings too—the "Lesson Two" scene in *The Last Jedi* contains a neat instance [1:01:40], as does concert arrangement of the PATHOS theme, "Adagio" [3:24]. These and other such manipulations

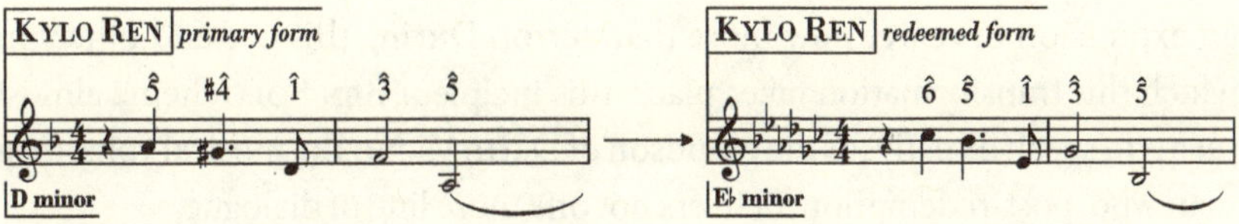

Figure 4.16 Forms of KYLO REN primary leitmotif in Episode IX. a. Typical form (1m10 [tracked], 2:00); b. Redeemed form - preliminary (1m20, 11:35)

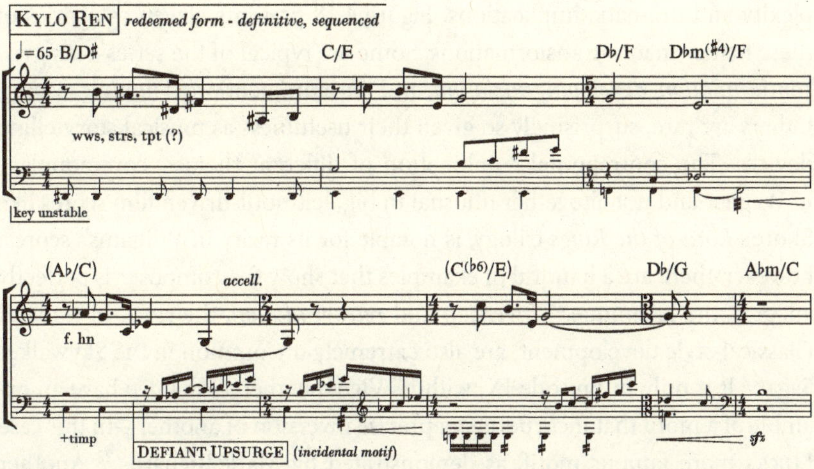

Figure 4.17 Definitive transfiguration of KYLO REN's primary leitmotif, (TROS, "Parents," 7m21, 1:48:50)

of Kylo's theme are unsystematically deployed, however, and most can be chalked up to Williams's normal developmental process rather than a goal-oriented telegraphing of his eventual turn to the light side.

It is only once Ren renounces the Dark Side two-thirds of the way through *Rise of Skywalker* that his theme undergoes its definitive and permanent change. Figure 4.17 displays the longest statement of KYLO REN in its transfigured guise. As the character—now back to Ben Solo—arrives on Exegol to save Rey, we hear several changes to his musical identification: its mode is inverted, its orchestration de-brutalized, and its erstwhile immobile harmonization thoroughly reimagined. No longer pinned to a stable minor key, the leitmotif now urges upward through continual chromatic modulations. Ren's once monstrous theme is not completely benign—it still has some sharp edges, especially with the timpani pounding away during the fourth statement. But it is a musical idea clearly hard at work to better itself. The primal $\hat{5}\rightarrow\sharp\hat{4}$ roar of the original becomes a tritone-free $\flat\hat{6}\rightarrow\hat{5}$ motion over an inverted major chord, an expression of regret now more than terror. During this cue and others in which this transformation takes place, this incipient BEN SOLO theme almost seems to speak directly for the grandson of Darth Vader: the musical voice for a man who, post-redemption, delivers not one more line of dialogue.

Far more than the sum of their micro-transformative parts, changes like the one undergone by KYLO REN's theme qualify as what Bribitzer-Stull calls "thematic evolutions," metamorphoses profound both in terms of structural complexity and dramatic implications. Figure 4.18 presents eleven categories of these heftier macro-transformations. Some are typical of the series—*deferred consummation, developing variation*, and the aforementioned *motivic seeding*. Others are rare, surprisingly so given their usefulness as musical storytelling devices. The contrapuntal combination of different themes, commonplace in Wagner and not altogether unusual in big, leitmotif-driven film scores like Shore's *Lord of the Rings* trilogy, is notable for its rarity in Williams's scores; however, there are a handful of examples that show the composer is perfectly adept at the technique.[26] *Inversion* and *retrogradation*, the stock-in-trade of Classical-style development, are also extremely uncommon in the Skywalker Saga.[27] It is only in Episode IX, with its VICTORY theme, that we have an example of a motif that incorporates a precise inversion of another—in this case LUKE's more famous motif, as demonstrated by Mark Richards.[28] Another inversional-pair candidate, the REY and KYLO REN themes, is suggestive on its face, though tempting to overinterpret; any minor melody whose basic idea includes an arpeggiated minor triad is bound to bear some incidental resemblance to other themes structured similarly.[29]

Two categories in Figure 4.18 warrant special explanation. *Teleological genesis* may well be the most all-encompassing type of thematic transformation. Formulated by James Hepokoski in a study of Sibelius's Fifth Symphony, teleological genesis captures the way the Finnish composer's music seems to evolve "towards the revelation of a higher or fuller condition."[30] Starting with the most unassuming motivic kernels—a few intervals, a scale fragment—a Sibelian theme will undergo repetition, modification, and a buildup of expressive tension, culminating in a "decisive climax or final goal (telos)." Teleological genesis doesn't just generate a climactic theme; it generates a form. It is a way of structuring a whole piece of music around thematic adumbration, adaptation, and eventual apotheosis. Tom Schneller was the first to apply the concept to the analysis of film music. Not inconsequentially, he finds the procedure in the music of John Williams, locating a thoroughgoing teleological trajectory in the score for *Close Encounters of the Third Kind*, and

Macro-Transformations			
Type	**Description**	**Example**	**Description**
Counterpoint (Single Theme)	Contrapuntal imitation of theme against itself	Luke VII: "Scherzo for X-Wings" [1:54:40]	Trumpets, trombones, and horns engage in stretto (fast overlap of transformed fragments of theme)
Counterpoint (Multi Theme)	Contrapuntal combination of many themes	Duel of the Fates + Force I: "Blowups" [2:03:04]	D.o.t.F. ostinato woven throughout climactic statement of Force
Deferred Consummation	Full structure and rhetorical closure denied until thematic apotheosis.	Anakin and Padmé II: throughout	Cadential closure frustrated until final measures of score
De/Reconstruction	Disassembly into musical parts and/or rebuilding in (new) context	Anakin I: throughout	Anakin childhood theme built from subtle melodic and harmonic features of mature Vader
Developing Variation	Constantly and freely changing variants of single motivic cell	Force VII: "Torn Apart" [1:49:50]	Theme stated, truncated, spun out & sequenced in several stages
Embedding	Inclusion of part of one theme into the melody or texture of another	Luke + Leia → Luke and Leia VI: "Leia Breaks the News" [2:03:39]	Characteristic rhythm and contour of Luke , harmonic content of Leia synthesized in Luke and Leia
Melodic Concatenation	Chaining of new motifs, each based on previous and growing into next	Vader, Rebel Logistics, etc… V: Battle of Hoth throughout	Closing idea of *a* spins into *b*, *b* provides opening idea for *c*, *c* becomes medial idea for *d*…
Motivic Seeding	Extracting parameters from theme, integrating into athematic material	Han and Leia. V: Throughout	Decoupling of interval (diminished 3rd between $\flat\hat{2}$ & $\sharp\hat{7}$) and insertion into other (non)leitmotivic contexts
Retrogradation/ Inversion	Reversing and/or intervallically flipping theme	Kylo Ren + Rey Sequels: Throughout	$\hat{5}$-$\sharp\hat{4}$-$\hat{1}$ beginning former, $\hat{1}$-$\hat{4}$-$\hat{5}$ ending latter; $\hat{1}$-$\flat\hat{3}$-$\hat{5}$ ending former, beginning latter
Teleological Genesis	Gradual building towards full-fledged theme, out of unmarked initial motifs	Desperation VII: "Holdo's Resolve" [1:51:00]	Incremental evolution out of Tension motif, towards big theme for big scene
Zero Alteration	Theme remains rigid, despite potential for, or history of, change	Vader V: Throughout	Many statements, most unaltered, assert theme's domination over soundtrack

Figure 4.18 Macro-transformations

evidence of a Sibelian mindset throughout the composer's career.[31] Schneller left the possibility of teleological genesis in Skywalker Saga open; I take this to be a standing invitation, one that will be heeded in Chapter 6.

The second category of special note is *zero alteration*. I define this as a distinct *lack* of variation or adaptation of a theme where one might expect it based on inherent evolutionary potential, or even a proven history of change in other circumstances. The insistence on "The Imperial March" in *The Empire Strikes Back*—forty-four statements total, many minimally varied—shows this "null transformation" paradigm working to great effect, conveying the implacable authority of Darth Vader in a way no subtle evolutionary path would have. The fixity of the FORCE theme for most of the duration of *The Last Jedi* is a less successful example, one we will also consider in Chapter 6.

Clearly, the blanket claim that "themes simply remain the same" in this series is false. But to determine just how rigorous Williams's approach to thematic transformation is would require sustained analytical investigation—more than can be achieved with a smattering of short excerpts. Accordingly, the next two chapters are devoted to tracking dramatically significant instances of thematic development spread across the canvas of entire soundtracks. Chapter 5 focuses on a single category of macro-transformation: *motivic seeding*. The examples examined—motivic offshoots of the JAWA, HAN AND LEIA, VADER, and REBEL FANFARE themes—are dissimilar in terms of scope, continuity, and transformational extremity. Nevertheless, they collectively give a clear sense of how, and to what dramatic effect, Williams sows his seeds across the musical fields of this series. Chapter 6 places a spotlight on the three most sophisticated transformational stratagems, techniques vaunted in figures like Brahms, Wagner, and Sibelius: *developing variation*, *deferred consummation*, and *teleological genesis*. We will see that those categories are in fact eminently, if selectively, applicable to Williams's music for the Skywalker Saga. These transformational techniques do more than unify their respective soundtracks; they tell real and impactful *stories*. Far from carrying "no structural weight," the thematic changes we are about to explore can be the *most* important things that happen in a score—the load-bearing pillars of epic musical architecture. Across both these chapters, attending to thematic metamorphosis will lead us to a more fulfilling mode of cine-symphonic listening.

5
Seeds

Out of the Sewer, into the Spaceport

Fans have been known to grouse about the changes George Lucas wrought upon the Original Trilogy for his "Special Edition" re-releases of 1997. But while many complaints are valid—Han, irrefutably, shoots first—not every alteration was detrimental, and this includes musical ones. To be sure, some changes are horrendous. There is, for instance, *The Empire Strikes Back*'s penultimate set piece "Losing a Hand," among Williams's most knife-twistingly effective essays in the art of ratcheting of tension. In the Episode V Special Edition, the cue's inexorable flow from crisis to climax is marred by a pair of clumsily tracked statements of VADER's theme. And the less said about the abominable "Jedi Rocks" from *Return of the Jedi*, the better.

Yet for every such invidious change, there is an equal number whose impact on Williams's symphonic storytelling is either neutral or beneficial. The extension of the Emperor's hologram sequence by twelve seconds in the *Empire*'s Special Edition prompted the looping of four measures of underscore, a modification basically undetectable thanks to the atmospheric and amorphous nature of the original cue. The splicing of JABBA's theme into a reinstated scene in *A New Hope* featuring the gangster is both logical from a leitmotivic perspective and apt in purely affective terms. And though it lacks the charm of its precursor "Yub Nub," the new "Victory Celebration" used at the conclusion of *Jedi* is more suitable in its dusky minor mode to the gravity of the occasion—and is neatly tied to certain harmonic patterns that would appear in the soon-to-be-composed Prequel scores.[1]

One particularly salutary alteration takes place in the Special Edition of *A New Hope*: the restoration of a previously cut cue in a fresh and fitting context, moving it from a scene in a sewer to a scene in a spaceport. In the original theatrical version of Episode IV, the arrival at Mos Eisley is underscored with a short passage within the larger cue "A Hive of Villainy." The five-measure module, shown in Figure 5.1, features a staccato figure for horns, bouncing above an active counterline on piano and a

Figure 5.1 Original music for entry into Mos Eisley in "Hive of Villainy" (ANH, 5m1, 42:26)

hocket of sorts with tuned drums. The horn part's tonal basis is obscured by its jagged contour and insistent chromaticism. Nevertheless, the counterpoint that melodic forms with the piano traces out a series of triadic downshifts: Cm→Bm→B♭m in the first measure, a semitonally transposed replica in the second, and a fragmented and accelerated version in the third. Suitably evocative music for a budgetarily constrained traversal of a lawless township, the module nevertheless does little to grab the ear in the moment and has few motivic relations with the rest of the score. It is a daub of local color, emphasis on local.

For Episode IV's Special Edition, Lucas quadrupled the duration of this tour through Mos Eisley. Within the additional twenty-seven seconds of runtime, the city's formerly depopulated streets are made to bustle through then-cutting-edge CGI, now providing new and more dynamically constructed shots of the spaceport, teeming with digitally rendered ships, droids, and creatures. With the scene thus extended, the short module from "Hive of Villainy" was rendered insufficient, both affectively and in terms of simple length. The original module was replaced with twelve bars from a sequence originally intended for much later in the movie, from "The Water Snake." A spell of slimy monster music written for the creature that lurks within the Death Star's sewage system, the cue was entirely unused in the 1977 cut. In fairness, this excision was not one of the great injustices done to Williams's score. The spectacle of Luke being pulled under the water by an unseen snakelike creature (a dianoga, per the lore) was already amply tense, made even more so with music held in abeyance. Williams's graphically gross underscore could only detract from the eerie silence left in the wake of Han and Leia's unanswered cries for their squid-snatched friend.

A representative four measures from "The Water Snake" that were repurposed for the Special Edition are provided in Figure 5.2. As it depicts an ugly situation in both the 1977 and '97 cuts—an "incredible" smelling trash compactor, a wretched hive of a spaceport—it is only right this be labeled the SCUM motif. However, this repellent music only shares one meaningful similarity with the original "Hive of Villainy": it too has as its basis a succession of chromatically related minor chords, now on the musical surface, undergirding a more traditionally flowing, if hardly lyrical, melodic line. But expressively, this tracked music offers something quite unlike its predecessor; the slithering SCUM theme imparts a feeling of dread and disgust thicker than anything the initial, basically unobtrusive cue offered. Nor is emotional recalibration the only significant upshot of this instance of musical retrofitting. By finding a new home for the forgotten sewer monster melody, the Episode IV Special Edition reinforces a form of *motivic seeding* decidedly less pronounced in the original cut of the film.

As defined in the previous chapter, motivic seeding is the practice of extracting a parameter of a theme and spreading it across the score. Perhaps the scattering of such kernels is done to some grand purpose, the harvesting of a theme in full bloom at a late hour, for example. But just as often, the aim of motivic seeding is simply to lend the soundtrack an element of consistency—a *tinta*, in other words. That the series' first score is sown with a few such seeds is already noteworthy. Despite having a smaller lexicon of leitmotifs than subsequent entries, *A New Hope* is nevertheless an eminently tight score. Indeed, Episode IV is in some ways more economical and consistent in its hues than its successors, due to Williams's assumption that it was

Figure 5.2 SCUM from "The Water Snake" as new music for entry into Mos Eisley (ANH, 8m3, 42:52 [tracked])

Figure 5.3 STRANGE motif in "The Little People" (ANH, 2m2, 14:33)

to be a one-off soundtrack, a musical statement that had to stand on its own merits and not rely on sequels to pay off thematic germs laid beforehand. The seeding that takes place in *A New Hope* generally involves materials other than major themes, such as incidental motifs, recurrent harmonies, and other topics of a generally smaller scope than the score's half-dozen true leitmotifs.[2] And few creatures in *Star Wars* are of smaller scope, physically or thematically, than the Jawas. Yet their music furnishes a disproportionate number of those unity-granting kernels, including the passage restored in the revised jaunt through Mos Eisley.

Figure 5.3 shows four measures of the passage from the cue "The Little People" that proves so rich with motivic seeds. As with much of *A New Hope*'s underscore, the segment is a showcase for exposed woodwinds—first a trio of bassoons, then oboes and clarinet. These reedy choirs carry a gangly and chromatic melody, enriched, in the typical *Star Wars*ian manner, by triadic planing. Without commitment to a leitmotif status, the idea deserves a provisional name: the STRANGE motif. The appellation is meant to capture how this melody acts as a repository of musical parameters associated with the idea of "the alien" in Episode IV. In this instance, it depicts a Sandcrawler, a hulking transport stuffed with misfit droids and other bits of sci-fi detritus. The section of "The Little People" in which the STRANGE melody occurs is the last in a chain of five modules that trace Artoo's forced incorporation into the Jawas' scavenged inventory. As with the sections that precede it, the STRANGE module is in most ways a standalone thought, differentiated from its neighbors by four-square phrase divisions and stark orchestrational shifts. That said, aspects of its texture and rhythmic profile—parallel minor triads and a dotted rising figure in its second half—affiliate the incidental motif with two preceding, more plausibly *leitmotivic* ideas associated with the Jawas; both are included for reference in Appendix 1.[3]

The Strange and Scum motifs are juxtaposed in Figure 5.4, texturally simplified and transposed to D for ease of comparison. Clearly, these are musical siblings, with the same rhythmic shape and octatonic basis. Similarity becomes precise equivalence in the second measure, when both follow exactly the same interval pattern (shown in terms of semitonal motions up or down in the diagram). Insofar as they are not identical twins, their divergences could be called phenotypic rather than genotypic, different expressions of the same underlying musical genes. The motifs' contours are in opposite directions in the first measure, but both are founded on a more basic gesture: a dissonant leap that returns after a beat to the starting note. Similarly, their melodies span different degrees within their respective scales, but this is a function of which triadic degree they happen to start on, $\hat{3}$ or $\hat{5}$. Everything else, including the inversions of those parallel harmonies marching in lockstep underneath the tunes, simply follows from the initial, somewhat arbitrary melodic condition.

The Scum motif is an obvious relative of the Strange idea, its similarity concealed only by an accident of music editing in the original cut of *A New Hope*. But it is not the only patch of score that seems seeded with material from "The Little People." Two of a surprisingly sizable number of such passages are depicted in Figure 5.5, one indirect but indisputable once pointed out, the other abstract and speculative.[4] The ponderous set piece theme from "The Walls Converge" sequence is shown in two different guises in Figure 5.5a. Only the brass-defined core of the motif is depicted; the various countermelodies and elaborations of the theme, while characterful, mask the underlying *Ur*-motif. The basic structure of the theme is almost a perfect rhythmic reduction of the Strange motif: first, a twice-repeated

Figure 5.4 Comparison of Strange and Scum motifs

plummet from a minor tonic to chromatic pole; then a stepwise climb filling out a minor third, supported by parallel voice-led chords, variously minor and augmented triads in the cue. The climactic version (Figure 5.5a), heard as the heroes are inches away from pulverization, inverts the direction of movement between triadic poles and lifts the fourth pitch in the pattern (E_4) to a higher point than the second (C_4)—precisely as the Scum motif did relative to the Strange one.[5] This late-stage shift in contour makes sense not just as an intensification but as a way of associating the cue and its "all hope is lost" affect with its predecessor. Taking place immediately after Luke is freed by the sewage creature, the motivic continuity between "The Walls Converge" and "The Water Snake" is fitting—ingenious even, when appreciated through a soundtrack album that places the cues in succession—though the unifying effect is necessarily lost in both '77 and '97 cuts of the film.

Another, subtler sprout from the Strange seed is a progression within "The Sandman Attacks" (Figure 5.5b) heard right after the Krayt dragon roar that conveniently frightens off the Tusken Raiders. Despite following the sound of a fantastical beast, this harmonic loop is not monster music at all; instead, the hushed and enigmatic progression serves as a way of rolling out the musical red carpet for Obi-Wan Kenobi and his leitmotivic attendant, the Force theme. The wide-leaping contour of the Strange motif's opening measure is detectable. Here it is produced by a pair of diatonically related block chords (D minor and G minor) which overlap in a polychordal haze. The chromatic downshift is still present, though in relation to the off-beat second chord, Gm (or perhaps Gm^9), which slips directly to F♯m by step rather than leap. Any simple triadic accounting is made additionally ambiguous by the presence of the melodic non-chord tone $\text{A}♮_5$ on the third beat, plus a lingering chromatic cluster in high strings and keyboards.

Obi-Wan's introductory progression is like a mad motivic experiment, distilling and recombining elements of the Strange theme's harmonic

Figure 5.5 Further seeding sites in *A New Hope*. **a1.** "The Walls Converge" (8m4, 1:23:06); **a2.** "The Walls Converge" (8m4, 1:24:14); **b.** "The Sand Man Attacks" (3m4/4m1, 29:39)

DNA. The mutation is obscure, to be sure—few listeners are liable to hear the vamp deriving from the JAWA music, at least not without prompting. But this connection is emblematic of the variable forms of compositional unity with which Williams imbues the *Star Wars* scores. There are sophisticated relations aplenty between motifs, but they are not uniformly applied. There are deep structural affinities between musical ideas, but their symbolic associations are loose and suggestive rather than rigid and denotative. And there are elegant instances of thematic variation and transfiguration to be found in practically every cue, but they sometimes lie beneath the threshold of audience perception—if they can be heard at all, which, in the case of the STRANGE/SCUM connection was impossible until Lucas decided to bring back some discarded scoring for the 1997 Special Edition.

The way that Williams draws together disparate strands of Episode IV's score without relying on explicit leitmotivic mention is characteristic of his at turns rigorous and ad hoc approach to large-scale musical integration. This chapter is a meditation on what integration means for a set of scores that, for all their genuinely symphonic qualities, can be disjointed in form and inconsistent in development. Motivic seeding is therefore an apt focus. Its modus operandi is not goal-driven or systematic thematic evolution, but the extraction of a discrete parameter from an established theme, set loose for motivic free play.

The three sections to come adopt the model laid out by this introduction, inspecting a case of motivic seeding within a single, self-contained score. These case studies differ, however, in focusing on true leitmotifs rather than the incidental ideas in *A New Hope* that peek out, dianoga-like, from beneath the musical surface. We will first examine an intervallic seed from HAN AND LEIA's love theme that contributes to the feeling of high drama across the *Empire Strikes Back*. Then, we will monitor the activity of "The Imperial March" in *The Phantom Menace*, never presented in its definitive form as VADER's leitmotif, but lurking nonetheless as a hidden source of evil. The contrastively bright colors of the REBEL FANFARE will be the focus of our final case study, with a treatment of that motif's seeding throughout *The Force Awakens*, in ways that span the whole semiotic spectrum, from barely noticeable use to flashing neon mention. For all three analyses, we will rely on the prototype/parameter model introduced in Chapter 3, as these instances of motivic seed-spreading all depend on the ability to decompose a well-known theme into its constituent aspects—and crucially to *hear* those decomposed aspects in terms of a referential theme still reverberating in your aural memory.

Seeds of Romance in *The Empire Strikes Back*

During the carbon freezing sequence in *The Empire Strikes Back*, Leia exclaims "I love you," to which Han, moments away from involuntary refrigeration, famously replies "I know." The film's director, Irvin Kershner, noted that to this point verbal professions of affection had been avoided in favor of snippy, even downright insulting banter—to call someone a "stuck-up, half-witted, scruffy-looking nerf herder" is an odd way to describe one's immortal beloved. The score, of course, knows better. Kershner claims that "the music *is* the dialogue. . . . It tells us what [Leia and Han] are feeling, because actually the two people are in open conflict. But the music says, 'Ahh, what you're seeing is maybe conflict, but that's a game, because actually I think they're falling in love."[6] Williams does not play nearly as coy as the screenwriter. He lays the HAN AND LEIA love theme thick, giving it twenty-two renditions across the movie, many lasting eight measures or longer, with luscious orchestrations and heaving harmonies. Admittedly, some early presentations are tentative, including the halting variant that accompanies that "nerf herder" line. And one statement, which we will examine in Chapter 6, is almost comically cut short. But overall, the leitmotif itself is never conveyed in a way that is genuinely conflicted, or snide, or insincere.

There is indeed a game-like quality to Williams's treatment of *Empire*'s love theme, lightly analogous to the flirtatious circumlocutions that mark the couple's dialogue. But this sense of play does not always come across during actual moments of romance, or even scenes involving Han or Leia. It is a game of motivic seeding, and it involves but a single parameter—a shard of intervallic content—and occurs with relative infrequency in the score. Scarcity, however, does not entail insignificance: the HAN AND LEIA seed occurs during *Empire*'s most musically arresting and dramatically heart-rending moments.

Figure 5.6 breaks down the love theme's first phrase according to the prototype/parameter model introduced in Chapter 3. There is a great deal of grist for development embedded within the leitmotif, with its tartly mixed mode—a consistent signifier in Williams's output of romance and

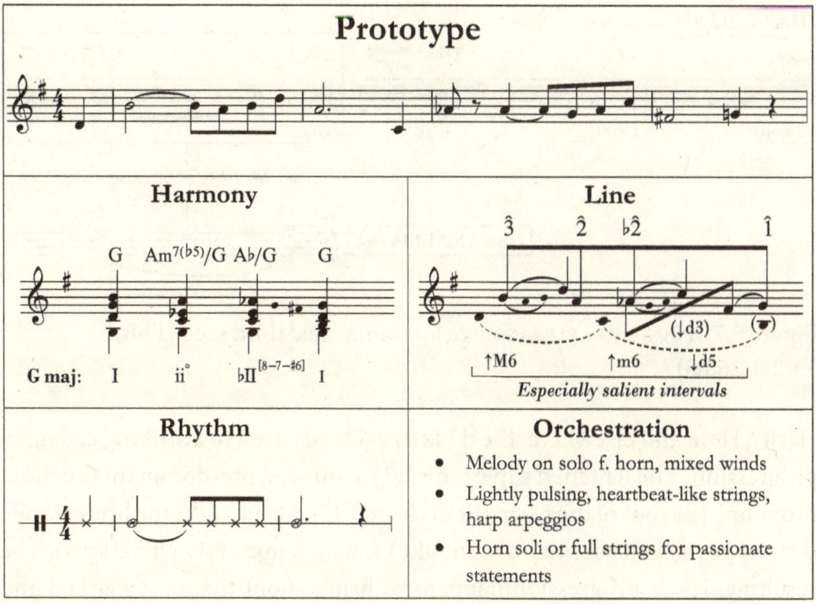

Figure 5.6 HAN AND LEIA theme prototype and parameters

femininity—and its suggestion of multiple intertwined voice-leading streams.[7] Frequently perched over a pedal bass, the leaping melody is supported by a downshifting chord progression that mimics the tune's B_4-A_4-$A\flat_4$-G_4 trajectory. The seeded element is an elaboration upon this more structural melodic descent: the melodic interval of a *diminished third* (d3) that arises between $A\flat_4$ and $F\sharp_4$. This pitch pair occurs indirectly, between the third and fourth measure, but exerts a huge influence on the way the phrase ends. The structural function of this chromatic interval is represented by the diagonal beam in the Line parameter and the descending trichord within the span of ♭II in the Harmony parameter.[8]

For a less abstract occurrence of this intervallic kernel, Figure 5.7 offers an instance of the HAN AND LEIA theme in situ, during the cue "Vader Shows Up." Sung by the cellos and accompanied by simple sustained chords, this is one of the more sedate renditions of the melody, heard during a private scene between the lovers on Bespin. The local tonality is C♯ major, enharmonically equivalent to the D♭ of the first kiss aboard the Millennium Falcon in an earlier cue. Characteristically, the diminished third interval is the result of a semitonal neighbor figure around the tonic, $\flat\hat{2}$ to $\sharp\hat{7}$ to $\hat{1}$.[9] The pattern-producing pitches of $D_3 \rightarrow C\sharp_3 \rightarrow B\sharp_2$ are set off in this diagram with a box for

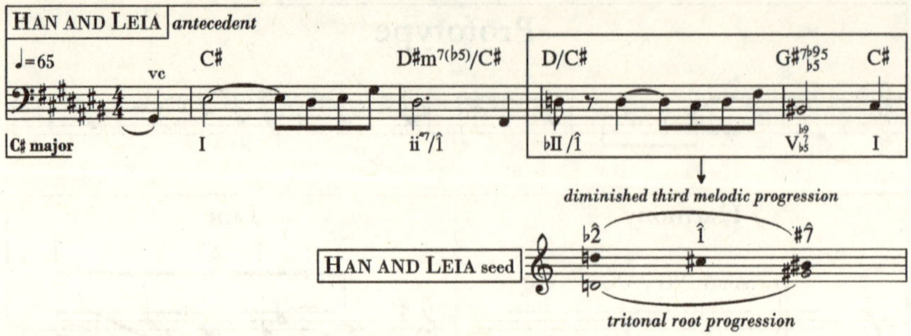

Figure 5.7 Han and Leia as source for diminished third seed (ESB, 9m2, 1:26:08)

clarity. Here and elsewhere, the d3 interval lends itself to a striking cadential progression. The flattened supertonic ($\flat\hat{2}$) assumes a pre-dominant function, providing the root of the Neapolitan chord (♭II). Meanwhile, the leading tone ($\sharp\hat{7}$) supports the cadential dominant (V^7, with some zesty alterations). The resulting ♭II→V progression happens to bring about the most marked and distant relationship between triads—motion by tritone—available within Common Practice tonality.

The Neapolitan chord has long been treated as a harmonic special effect, something best reserved for matters of utmost import and emotional force. Though not strictly a negatively valenced tonal routine, ♭II→V did become freighted with associations of pathos and tragedy starting in the mid-seventeenth century.[10] A certain direness of affect lingers into the Romantic era and thence into the Hollywood harmonic idiom. Its impact owes to that striking diminished third between $\flat\hat{2}$ and $\sharp\hat{7}$. That interval provides in turn a melodic bridge able to span the tritonal gulf opened between the theme's cadential chords.[11]

Though D and B♯ pitches are tethered in "Vader Shows Up" to unambiguous ♭II and V chords, the scale degrees assumed by these notes are of less consequence than one might think. *Star Wars*ian musical prose, with its often-fluctuating tonal idioms, sometimes places greater weight on the *absolute* nature of progressions—their inherent, isolated quality—than their functional or hierarchical implications.[12] Insofar as the diminished-third span is a unifying element of the *Empire* score, what matters are its harmonic affordances: that little chromatic gap supports the root of one triad, the fifth another, and the mediating tone a half-step away from both.

One need not look to underscore to find the diminished third *idée fixe* at work: the B-section of Han and Leia's leitmotif also sports the gesture, in an

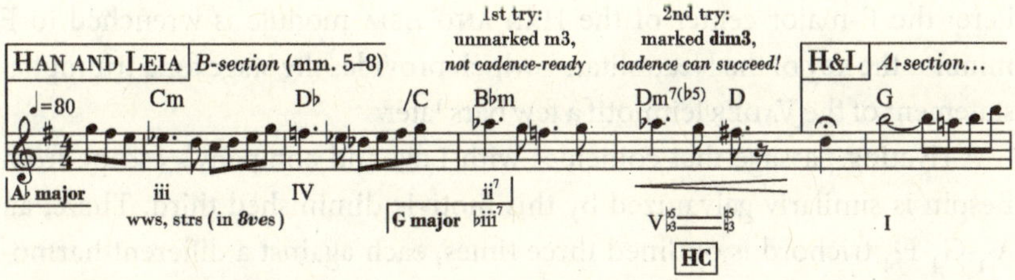

Figure 5.8 HAN AND LEIA B-section at end of *Empire* (ESB, 12m3, 2:01:32)

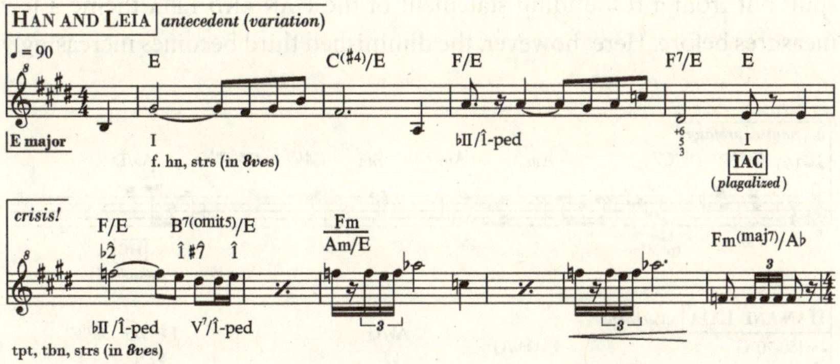

Figure 5.9 HAN AND LEIA in harmonic crisis in "Carbon Freeze" (ESB, 9m6/10m1, 1:36:01)

example of motivic development and integration taking place within, rather than exterior to, a theme's melodic structure itself. Granted, the relevant portion of that B-section is only heard twice in Episode V, during the lead-up to the couple's first kiss, and right before the End Credits roll. The latter is shown in Figure 5.8. Notice how two tries are needed to get the ultimate descent to the leading tone (F♯) right: a first try, close but not exactly on target, based on a descending minor third; and a cadentially successful second pass, based on the all-important diminished third. A moment of musical exclamation extreme even for *Star Wars*, this may be the single most dramatically underlined cadence in the series—until, that is, an exactly rhyming moment at the end of *Attack of the Clones*, to be inspected in Chapter 6.[13]

The capacity for pathos innate in the d3-interval is also wrung for all its worth during the aforementioned "Carbon Freeze" sequence, the climax of which is rendered in Figure 5.9. As Han is lowered into the chamber, the love theme seems to get trapped in a confined space too, its antecedent phrase followed by a ferocious five-measure extension spun out of the diminished third $F\natural_5 \rightarrow D\sharp_5$. Not only melody but tonality itself suffers complete defeat here: the E-major center of the HAN AND LEIA module is wrenched to F minor—the key of the Neapolitan—which provides the stage for a triumphal statement of the VADER leitmotif a few bars later.

A riveting passage that coincides with Leia and company's escape from Bespin is similarly galvanized by this motivic diminished third. There, an $A\flat_4$-G_4-$F\sharp_4$ trichord is outlined three times, each against a different harmonization within the overall key of G major. As in "Carbon Freeze," the paragraph that concludes "Through the Window," offered in Figure 5.10, is spun out from a resounding statement of the HAN AND LEIA theme a few measures before. Here, however, the diminished third becomes increasingly

Figure 5.10 Colossal cadential progression in "Through The Window" (ESB, 11m1, 1:48:49)

decoupled from its leitmotivic source, launching an extended cadential progression, twenty-one measures in duration, that merges elements of Han and Leia with the Rebel Fanfare. In one of the score's most astonishing tonal sleights, Williams shifts the target key midway from G major to C major, that latter key being confirmed at cue's end with a structural accent of tremendous finality. The analysis given in Figure 5.10 offers an interpretation of the modulation using the standard tools of diatonic theory: Roman numerals and pivot chords. The chromatic slash-chords beginning at m. 11 lead to some innately chromatic relationships that play a role in the progressive destabilization of G major, though with motivated ears, those B♭ and B slash-chords could be heard to conform to G or C tonics, if vaguely. But any explanation that rationalizes this cadential progression as "well-behaved" after all, also necessarily misses the passage's essential affect, which is one of heroic defiance.

The excerpts from "Carbon Freeze" and "Through the Window" occur in dramatic contexts involving the fates of Han Solo and Princess Leia. Additionally, in both cues the diminished third is first heard within the melodic bounds of the twosome's leitmotif, before it sprouts forth as an independent outgrowth. However, not all instances of the d3-seed in *Empire* are straightforwardly coupled with the semantic content or phrasal framework of the Han and Leia thematic wellspring. Though often coinciding with scenes involving the movie's romantic pair, the intervallic seed's expressive meaning is more tied up with Romance with a capital "R," that feeling of larger-than-life import and intensity encoded in the rare and historically pregnant Neapolitan swerve.

The conclusion of "Losing a Hand" presents a good example of how the melodic diminished third and harmonic tritone can arise independently of the scaffolding of Han and Leia. Like "Through the Window," this cue's climax revolves around an iterated melodic d3. Here, the charged interval is part of a new Defeat theme, the final block of which is depicted in Figure 5.11.[14] "Losing a Hand" finds the dismembered Luke hanging on to a weather vane for dear life, and Williams's convulsively modulating music offers him precious little support. The d3 seed within Defeat is especially ambiguous in its tonal implications, fastened as it is not to the accustomed tritone shift, but a weird distortion thereof. The F/A↔D♯m/F♯ motion serves as an *even more* nonfunctional transformation of the already alienated F↔B-type loop, barely assimilable into the tenuously established A minor tonic. Then the ground drops out from underneath the flailing motif, and

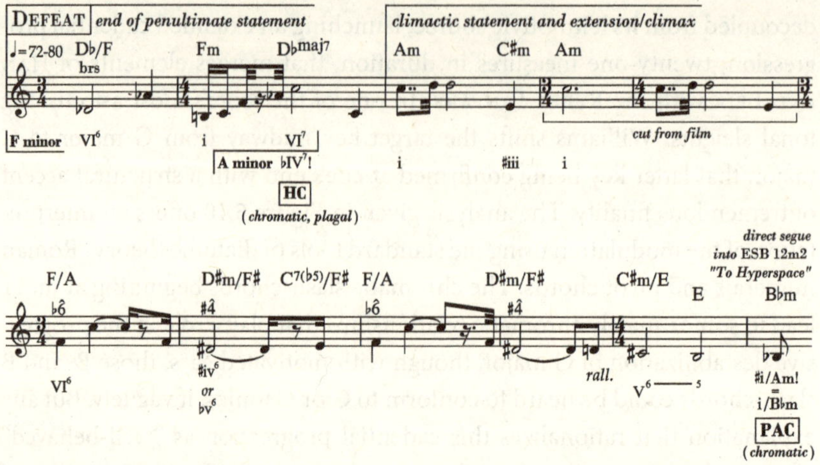

Figure 5.11 Catastrophe narrowly averted in "Losing A Hand" (ESB, 11m2/12m1, 1:55:08)

everything collapses down onto B♭ minor. Thankfully, the Millennium Falcon arrives just in time to stop Luke from plummeting to his demise.

The progression in "Losing a Hand" represents the point of deepest tension in *Empire*'s score. However, the most spectacular deployment of the diminished third comes almost an hour earlier, in the celebrated action set piece, "The Asteroid Field." An analysis that does this cue justice would require a chapter unto itself. But within the delimited subject of motivic seeding in Episode V, an inspection of the bold Asteroid Field B-theme is certainly warranted here, and the equally notable A-theme in the next section. Figure 5.12 displays the melody in question, a proper grammatical theme with a nicely balanced antecedent/consequent melodic structure—and decidedly *unbalanced* tonal structure, as we will see. The bustling orchestration that supports the trumpet-carried tune is decisive in creating its cyclonic affect and is itself not lacking in motivic connectivity with the rest of the score. Those swirling timbral layers are not based on the intervallic ingredients of Han and Leia's theme, however, and are therefore left undepicted in the diagram.

The Asteroid Field B-theme appears twice during the action sequence. On both occasions, Williams uses it to accompany shots of the Millennium Falcon weaving between ship-killing boulders, while the pursuing TIE Fighters spin, collide, and explode in a dance of interplanetary destruction. Although strictly non-leitmotivic, this B-theme resonates with a handful

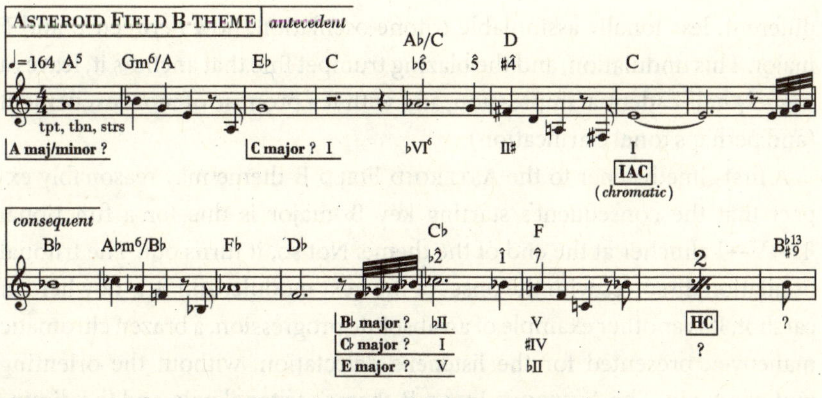

Figure 5.12 ASTEROID FIELD B-theme (ESB, 4m3, 39:01)

of other recurrent materials from the saga. The E♭→C and F♭→D♭ chord motions in mm. 3–4 and 11–12 recall the minor third-driven triadic shifts of the REBEL FANFARE. Moreover, if one considers the eighth-note pick-up that leads into these two progressions, the characteristic bacchiac (short-long-long) rhythmic shape of that motif is also present. But the strongest echo is with the *Empire*-endemic HAN AND LEIA seed, by virtue of the B-theme's tritonal vaults and the twisting diminished thirds that facilitate them melodically.

Though balanced in phrase structure, the ASTEROID FIELD B-theme is stricken with a kind of tonal vertigo. That sense of disorientation is caused by a gauntlet of ambiguous triadic relationships, which the otherwise conventional melody must successfully navigate. Unusually, the pantriadic harmony is here intrinsic to a grammatical theme, not a passing coloration or a byproduct of roving underscore. Not that the listener would know this in the first two measures. The antecedent phrase opens traditionally enough, with an ostensible A-major tonic, a key whose perceived stability is bolstered by the half-cadential end of the previous module. This A-centricity proves short-lived, however. After a series of downward chromatic shunts, the tune settles on a C-major triad. C is then secured as a local key via a tonicization of sorts through ♭VI (A♭ major) and II♯ (D major). These auxiliary chords form a tritonal but non-Neapolitan progression of their own. The consequent phrase begins similarly, though transposed up by a semitone relative to its predecessor, starting on B♭. The phrase then heads once again to a chord one minor third higher—here D♭, analogous to the previous phrase's C major. However, instead of reinforcing D♭ as a tonic, Williams undercuts it with a different, less tonally assimilable tritone oscillation, now between B and F major. This undulation, and the blazing trumpet line that anchors it, leaves a vaguely half-cadential impression, and with it a promise of more excitement (and perhaps tonal clarification).

A first-time listener to the ASTEROID FIELD B-theme may reasonably expect that the consequent's starting key B♭ major is due for a functional ♭II→V→I clincher at the end of the theme. Not so, it turns out. The tritonal oscillation dissolves with the onset of the next module, and B♭ is nowhere in earshot. It is another example of an absolute progression, a brazen chromatic maneuver, presented for the listener's delectation, without the orienting pull of a tonic. The ASTEROID FIELD B-theme's tritonal pair, and the diminished third $C♭_5$—$B♭_4$—A_4 figure it supports, are heard at the end of the B-theme, seemingly on their own, strange terms. But, as shown, those terms had already been set—by a hearty motivic seed, dispatched from the distant leitmotivic home of the HAN AND LEIA theme.

Seeds of Evil in *The Phantom Menace*

The telltale third of HAN AND LEIA's leitmotif is not the only score-spanning seed to be found whirling around "The Asteroid Field." An A-theme also runs through the scherzo, a sharp-silhouetted Prokofievian toccata with the chromatic zip of a bebop standard. Neither the stringy melody nor its throbbing accompaniment suggests anything particularly "march-like," but as Figure 5.13 shows, the ASTEROID FIELD A-theme shares more than a few intervallic and rhythmic structures with VADER's newly introduced anthem. The resemblance is far from exact, and no listener would confuse the one as a variant of the other. But the linkage is easy to hear in the context of the film. The chase sequence occurs not long after the VADER leitmotif-dominated Battle of Hoth—more on this in Chapter 9—and the A-theme comes on the heels of a sizable paragraph based on "The Imperial March" [36:46–37:57], unalloyed.

After LUKE's theme, Darth Vader's leitmotif, whose signification is split between the Sith Lord and the Empire he represents, is the series' most recognizable musical icon. It is also one of its most heavily developed. Throughout the series, "The Imperial March" is subject to de- and reconstructions, seedings and reapings, periods of stubborn immobility and periods of exuberant change. The most interesting place to examine

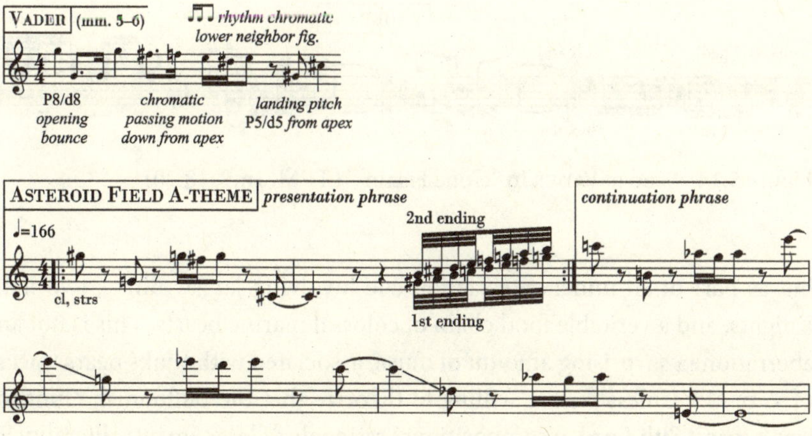

Figure 5.13 ASTEROID FIELD A-theme (ESB, 4m3, 38:02)

VADER's leitmotivic activity is the Prequel Trilogy, where its handling demonstrates a real—if not always airtight—symphonic logic. Musically speaking, the Prequels are a protracted journey to get to the mature version of this ultimate villain anthem. Particularly after Anakin's slaughter of the Tusken Raiders midway through *Attack of the Clones*, "The Imperial March" makes its presence felt with escalating aggression. However, in *The Phantom Menace*, Williams allowed himself but one *explicit* iteration of the melody, very near the end of the film, in the cue "After the Victory." Following a statement of YODA's leitmotif (also a thematic singleton in Episode I), the score slumps ominously, with low reeds uttering VADER's basic idea when the Jedi Master confesses he senses "grave danger in [Anakin's] training."[15] The brief quote is a splendid example of earned, mythically resonant motivic mention.

While Yoda's warning may occasion the sole unequivocal preview of "The Imperial March," the score to Episode I is positively blanketed with *concealed* seeds of that famous theme. When connected to ANAKIN's leitmotif—a multi-layered deconstruction of "The Imperial March" described in Chapter 2—*The Phantom Menace*'s references to VADER's theme are of clear dramatic pertinence. Yet for every instance of innocent Ani's theme that hints at his eventual turn, there are just as many germs that, in their momentary filmic context, are completely unrelated to the rise of Darth Vader.

Take, for example, the trumpet line portrayed in Figure 5.14. This threatening flourish does not arise during some premonition of Anakin's downfall,

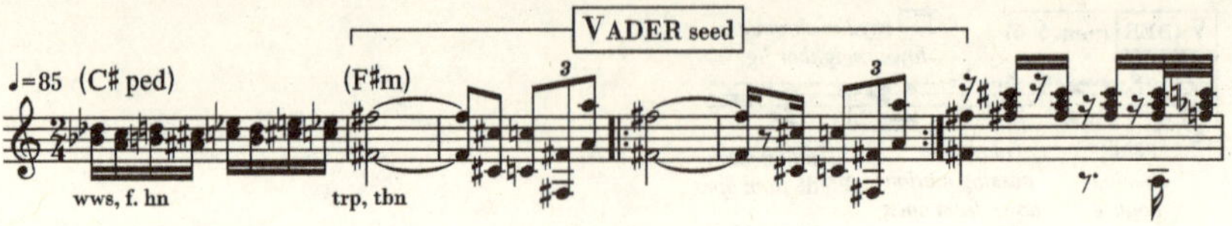

Figure 5.14 Seed of VADER in "Gone Fishin'" (TPM, 1m9, 18:20)

but as part of an underwater action cue involving Jar Jar Binks, two Jedi Knights, and a veritable food chain of colossal marine beasts. This is not an aberration: a surprising amount of music associated with Binks bears traces of VADER![16] Unless we are willing to theorize that the buffoonish Gungan was a secret Sith Lord, a compositional rationale of less semantic literality is called for.

Bits and pieces of "The Imperial March" are sprinkled like this throughout *The Phantom Menace*, collectively comprising a score-defining *tinta*. Of course, no soundtrack lasting two and a half hours can be boiled down to just one distinctive aspect, and Episode I is the most kaleidoscopic in tone and topic of the whole series. Nevertheless, the impression that the score is populated by musical shadows of VADER accounts for one of the most dramatically apt tintings in this multi-hued soundtrack, even—maybe especially—when attached to unexpected targets like Jar Jar (or, even less plausibly, Watto). Darth Vader does not yet exist at this chronological point in the saga, being felt at best as a dark potential, dimly perceived by the film's characters. But something is clearly rotten in the state of the Galactic Republic, and series-literate viewers know what awaits little orphan Ani. It thus stands to reason that the leitmotif's evil parameters should float around freely, collectively portending a nebulous ill, all while retaining plausible deniability.

Figure 5.15 shows VADER's theme as a prototype and its decomposed parameters. As with LUKE and HAN AND LEIA, the category of harmony is complex enough to warrant several additional layers of explanation. Functionally, the theme is based on that leitharmonic i↔♭vi motion. In terms of triadic transformation, that progression consists of a chromatic major-third loop (or an **LP/PL** shift, to use neo-Riemannian parlance). And with respect to voice-leading, the theme is powered by the smooth semitonal displacement of outer voices by contrary motion (G_4→$A♭_4$, C_4→B_3/$C♭_3$), while the inner voice ($E♭_4$) stays put.

Does each and every one of the VADER seeds planted with intent by Williams consciously augur the coming evil theme? Probably not. To an

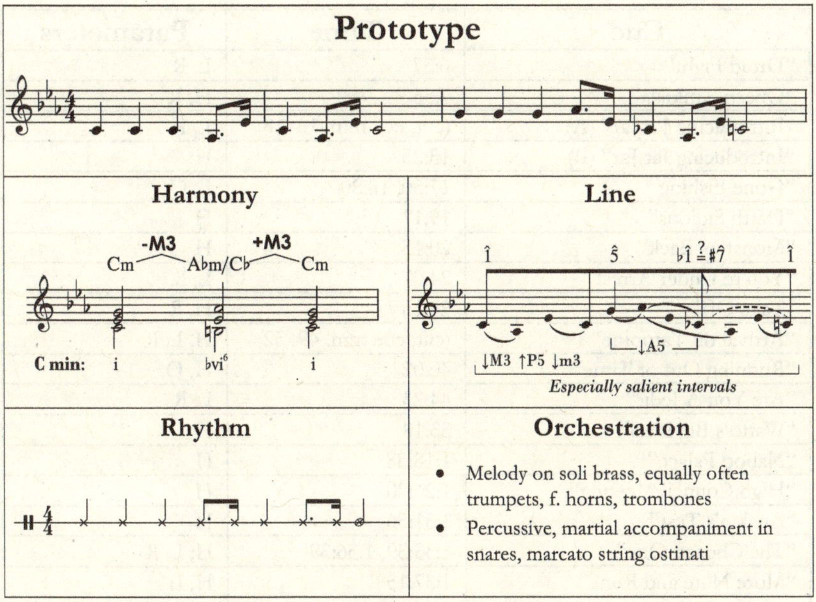

Figure 5.15 VADER theme prototype and parameters

extent, the sound of "The Imperial March" is simply part of the generalized *Star Wars* idiom—as evidenced by the fact that embryonic versions turn up in *A New Hope*, before the actual theme was conceived.[17] But thinking in terms of the prototype/parameter model can help make precise *what* about this musical moment or that stems from a source theme. Even if one is uncomfortable with outright claims of motivic derivation (and anyone properly suspicious of organicism should be at least a little uncomfortable), the prototype/parameter model can give a methodical account of why a musical idea might, if not derive from, then *echo* a more familiar source.

And echo "The Imperial March" does throughout the *Phantom Menace*, as Figure 5.16 makes clear. The chart indicates for each allusion which of the four basic parameters are present: (H)armony, (L)ine, (O)rchestration, (R)hythm. The list is not intended to be exhaustive. Because every statement of ANAKIN's theme embeds a reference to its preordained leitmotivic destination, its twenty iterations are left off in favor of less directly pertinent nods and deconstructions. Similarly excluded are the Imperial-allusive chord progressions that pervade DUEL OF THE FATES, apart from two moments. First is the i→♭vi motion that kicks off the set piece in "The Fight Begins"; this Em/G→Cm/G shift occurs before DUEL OF THE FATES has had a chance

Cue	Time	Parameters
"Droid Fight"	6:57	L, R
"Queen Amidala"	7:56	H, R
"Introducing Jar Jar" (A)	(cut, cue mm. 16–18)	L, R
"Introducing Jar Jar" (B)	13:25	H
"Gone Fishing"	17:50, 18:20	L, O
"Darth Sidious"	19:17	H
"Monsters Back"	20:15	H
"You're Under Arrest"	24:07	L, R
"Take Off"	26:15	H, R
"Arrival on Tatooine"	(cut, cue mm. 49–52)	H, L, R
"Running Out of Time"	40:02	H, O
"Are You A Jedi?"	44:23	L, R
"Watto's Big Deal"	53:18	H
"Naboo Palace"	1:18:38	H
"High Council Meeting"	1:26:20	H
"Anakin's Test"	1:31:56	H
"The Chosen One"	1:33:39, 1:36:39	H; L, R
"More Nute and Rune"	1:37:15	H, L
"Moving Forward"	1:37:23	H, R
"Lazer Fight"	(cut, cue mm. 25–34)	L, R
"The Fight Begins"	1:50:27	H
"The Droid Battle"	See **Fig. 5.18**	L, O, R
"Up The Wire"	(cut, cue mm. 7–29)	L, H, O, R
"Blowups"	2:02:45	H, R
"After The Victory"	2:06:32	H, L, O, R (literal)
"Qui Gon's Funeral"	2:08:17	H
"End Credit" [D.O.T.F. bass line]	2:11:50	H, L, O, R

Figure 5.16 Seeds and statements of "The Imperial March" in *The Phantom Menace*

to establish itself as leitmotivic and is thus more likely to be heard through the filter of an already familiar theme. Second is the bass line during a specific span of the DUEL OF THE FATES concert arrangement. During measures 66–69 of the piece, the low brass directly quotes the Imperial melody while various FATES-based ostinati and chorales blare on top.

Even without factoring in ANAKIN and FATES themes—the marquee leitmotifs of Episode I—the extent to which the tendrils of "The Imperial March" spread through this score is remarkable. Three illustrative moments from dissimilar contexts are depicted in Figure 5.17. The first (5.17a) is a spurt of urgent music from the film's first act that accompanies the heroes, striding into an enemy droid-controlled hangar bay. The VADER-seed here

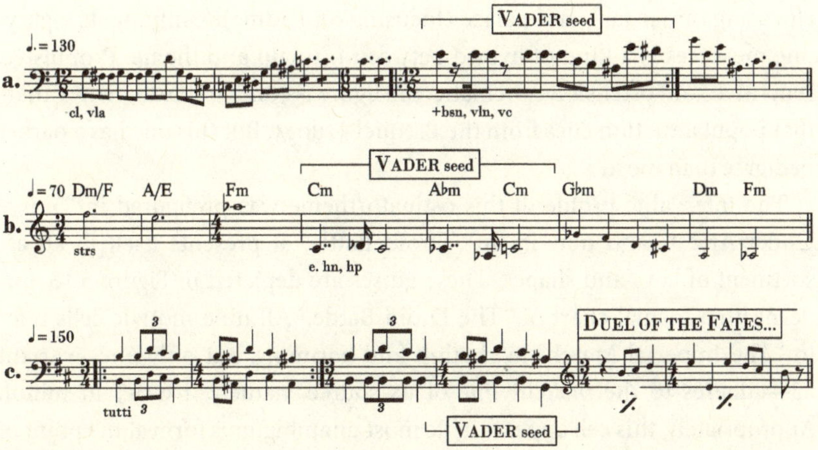

Figure 5.17 Seeds of Vader in *The Phantom Menace*. **a.** "You're Under Arrest" (TPM, 2m3, 24:07); **b.** "Watto's Deal" (TPM, 3m3, 53:18); **c.** "Blowups" (TPM, 6m10, 2:02:45)

takes a motivic form—a repeated pitch followed by a descent to ♯4̂ and leap by diminished seventh to ♭3̂—that will assume great importance later on, as we will see. The second example (5.17b) is a disreputable-sounding English horn melody (marked "conspiratorially" in the conductor's score) heard when Watto rolls a die to determine his slave Anakin's fate. The theme has the leitharmonic i↔♭vi of Vader, as well as elements of its contour. However, any thought of Imperial promise is superseded a few bars later when Watto loses his bet, and the tune is reworked into a grotesque complaint for three bassoons. The final example (5.17c) occurs at the climax of *The Phantom Menace*, when Anakin destroys an enemy battle station from the inside. The reference revolves around a distinctive ostinato figure in 7/4 time (notated as 3/4 + 4/4), which, right before propping up the main Duel of the Fates melody, alters its bassline to reproduce that of "The Imperial March." As with many nice details of Williams's writing, this one is nigh-inaudible in the film's mix, but unmistakable when heard on its own.

The standout among these Vader-siphoning incidents is the "Droid Battle." A rip-roaring scherzo in fast compound time, the cue is striking for its self-containedness. The cue falls in a neat ABA form, with the central section dedicated to a brief variation of the main Duel of the Fates melody. During its two-minute runtime, it accompanies three intercut arenas of combat during the Battle of Naboo: space (focusing on Anakin), ground (focusing on Jar Jar), and palace (focusing on Padmé). Unifying its eighty-one measures is a kind of hybrid between ostinato and theme. Propulsive, repetitive, and ostensibly athematic, the figure is comparable to many others that populate action cues from the Prequel Trilogy. But this one has a darker pedigree than most.

The intervallic profile of this ostinato/theme was prefigured in "You're Under Arrest" and now in the "Droid Battle," it presents itself in an assortment of keys and shapes. These guises are depicted in Figure 5.18, underneath a formal chart of "The Droid Battle." All nine motivic cells refer to "The Imperial March" in rhythm and harmony, but only one—variant a3—adheres to the *melodic line* of its source, namely, $\hat{1}$-$\hat{6}$-$\hat{3}$-$\hat{1}$ in minor. Appropriately, this cell appears in its most unambiguous form at the point of highest tension in the cue. There, it is emphasized by arriving on a structural downbeat and underlined by a half-cadence at the end of an intensificatory passage (variant b3). The musical punctuation lent to this most VADER-esque cell is not corroborated by any visual accent, however. This non-alignment is in all probability a product of *The Phantom Menace*'s anarchic editing during the Naboo Battle rather than a miscalculation of synchronization on Williams's part. (More on this editorial farrago in Chapter 7.) But, even in an editorially degraded state, the "Droid Battle" makes for one of the most well-proportioned, piece-like action cues from the Prequels. Remarkably, it achieves this autonomy of local form while contributing to a macro-transformational arc, one in which the presence (and promise) of Darth Vader is felt long before his actual melodic calling card is ever outright stated.

Seeds of Rebellion in *The Force Awakens*

Given the undisguised investment in returning the *Star Wars* franchise to its roots, it should come as little surprise that the first entry in the Sequel Trilogy, *The Force Awakens*, is bursting with musical reminders of what audiences loved most about the Skywalker Saga. One such token is the REBEL FANFARE. Omnipresent in the Original Trilogy, the REBEL FANFARE is the first in-narrative leitmotif heard in *A New Hope* [2:06] and turns up whenever an injection of brassy heroism is called for. As pointed out in Chapter 2, the FANFARE is derived from the fourth measure of LUKE's theme, a structural quirk that factors into its ease of interfacing with that and related leitmotifs. Apart from one rousing rendition in *Revenge of the Sith*,

1:53:03 1:53:09 1:53:13 1:53:42 1:53:59 1:54:39 1:54:58 1:55:04

Intro	Theme (VADER-esque ostinato)							Counter-Theme (DUEL OF THE FATES)		Theme (VADER-esque ostinato)						Climax
–	a1	a2	b1	a3	c1	a4	b2	d1	d2	a1'	a5	a6	a7	a2'/b3	a3'	–
(Gm)⇝	Cm	Gm	⇝	Fm	D	Em	⇝	Gm→E♭m/G Em→Am/C	Bm→Fm→ D♭/G=V/C	Cm	Dm	Fm	Cm	Gm⇝	Fm	D♭/G→Cm
Space Battle		Land Battle						Space Battle						Palace Battle		

Figure 5.18 Form and materials of "Droid Battle" (TPM, 6m5, 1:53:03–1:54:04)

the motif is absent from Episodes I–III, logically so, given the Rebellion did not yet exist. Strictly speaking, the theme is superfluous in the Sequels too, as the Rebel Alliance won back in Episode VI, and has been succeeded on an institutional level by The Resistance, which has its own, altogether sterner theme.

Yet return it does, plucky as ever, in Episode VII, and its presence is textually justified in two ways. First, the FANFARE shifts in denotation, attaching less to the idea of Rebellion and more rigidly to a specific emblem of the Rebels—the Millennium Falcon, for which the theme almost becomes a *de facto* leitmotif. Second, when not signaling the Falcon, the FANFARE is treated as a free-floating particle more than it ever was in the Originals. Figure 5.19 indicates the FANFARE's various appearances, seeds and statements alike, across *The Force Awakens.* The ubiquity of the motif—it appears in some guise over twenty times—does not necessarily unify the score in the systematic sense a motivic organicist might crave, but it does lend Episode VII's soundtrack a distinctive affective quality: a fresh and optimistic feeling, meant to hearken back to the playful mood of the Original Trilogy.

Cue	Time	Parameters
"The First Escape"	21:26	O, T
"Follow Me"	31:39	H, L, O, R, T
"The Falcon Still Flies!"	See **Fig. 5.24**	H, L, O, R, T
"Old Falcon to the Rescue"	49:07	H, L, O, R, T
"The Green Planet"	54:35	H, T
"Good Guys Shooting"	1:15:39, 1:15:44, 1:16:03	(H), O, T
"Finn and Po, Reunited"	1:21:28	H, L, T
"R2 in Hibernation"	1:22:12	T
"Preparing for the Mission"	1:33:56, (unused, mm. 38–40)	O, T
"Ice Landing"	1:35:49, 1:36:01	H, L, O, R, T
"The Bombing Run"	1:39:51, 1:40:03, 1:40:18	H, O, T
"Father and Son"	(unused, mm. 68–71)	H, O, T
"Blowing up the Oscillator"	1:54:32	H, O, T
"Flying Home"	1:59:44	H, O, T
'Finishing the Map"	2:00:09	H, T
"Completing the Map"	2:03:51	H, L, R, T
"End Credits" (Part 3/4)	2:15:58	L, O, T
"End Credits" (Part 4/4)	2:16:55	H, L, O, R, T

Figure 5.19 Seeds and statements of the REBEL FANFARE in *The Force Awakens*

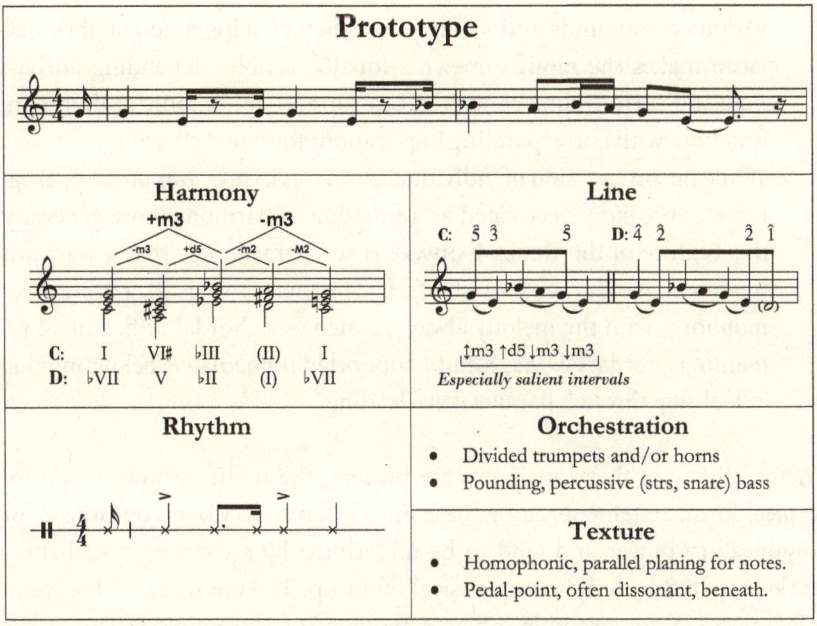

Figure 5.20 REBEL FANFARE prototype and parameters

Figure 5.20 shows a thematic prototype and its parameters. Even more than with VADER's theme in Episode I, the bright hues of the REBEL FANFARE—here detached, there integrated, always easily audible—make for a score-spanning *tinta.*

Each one of the leitmotif's parameters is the subject of transformational play:

- The motif's zippy Linear structure consists of a repeated downward minor-third interval, sometimes extended with a minor third above the initial note as well, leading to a lightly octatonic scalar orientation.
- The FANFARE's Rhythmic profile is similarly distinctive: an attention-seizing bacchiac (short-long-long) profile, with the first note treated as an upbeat figure, in much the same manner as the so-called motif d'évocation from Dukas's *The Sorcerer's Apprentice* to which Williams's theme is sometimes justifiably compared.[18]
- In terms of Orchestration, the theme adheres to the topical expectations of its namesake—high brass, piercing and heraldic.
- Harmonically, the FANFARE is also strongly individuated: all triads are major, and all related by a chromatic interval—the minor third and

various compounds and subdivisions thereof. This inherent chromaticism makes the motif somewhat tonally flexible: depending on bass note and surrounding context, it can support either tonic or dominant function, with corresponding implications for linear structure.

- While the progression of individual parts was in previous prototype/parameter breakdowns treated as a function of harmony more generally, the Texture of the REBEL FANFARE is so characteristic that it warrants treatment as a parameter unto itself. The theme's basic idea is pure homophony, with the melody always treated as a chordal fifth, and all remaining chordal degrees $\hat{3}$ and $\hat{1}$ supported immediately below, moving in lockstep through parallel voice leading.

When all five of these attributes are present, the motif assumes its prototypical form. Statements along these lines in Episode VII are optimized for significatory power and tend to be underlined by a dazzling visual spectacle prepared by a dramatic musical build-up. The big reveal of the motif (Figure 5.21), for example, offers a moment of leitmotivic clarity at the end of a somewhat thematically ill-defined action cue, "Follow Me." The FANFARE sounds at exactly the moment the Millennium Falcon is unveiled visually ("The garbage'll do!"), returning to the big screen for the first time since 1983.

Despite a smattering of unequivocal statements like the one in which Rey and Finn first lay eyes on the Falcon, most instances of the REBEL FANFARE in *The Force Awakens* are seedlings in which one or more of the leitmotif's distinguishing components are heavily altered. The two passages in Figure 5.22 provide a sense of these more typical infusions of rebel verve in Episode VII. The lush pantriadic progression in "The Green Planet" (5.22a) evokes the harmonic and textural parameters of the FANFARE, while its melody flows into and out of REY's theme. The second passage from "Good Guys

Figure 5.21 Iconic REBEL FANFARE in "Follow Me" (TFA, 2m18c, 31:39)

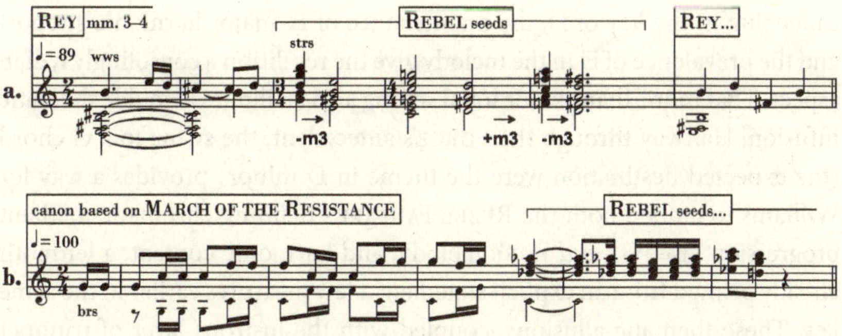

Figure 5.22 REBEL seeds interacting with other leitmotifs in *Force Awakens*. a. Pantriadic harmony growing out of by REY in "The Green Planet" (4m32, 54:32); b. Canonic appendix to RESISTANCE in "Good Guys Shooting" (5m47, 1:15:33)

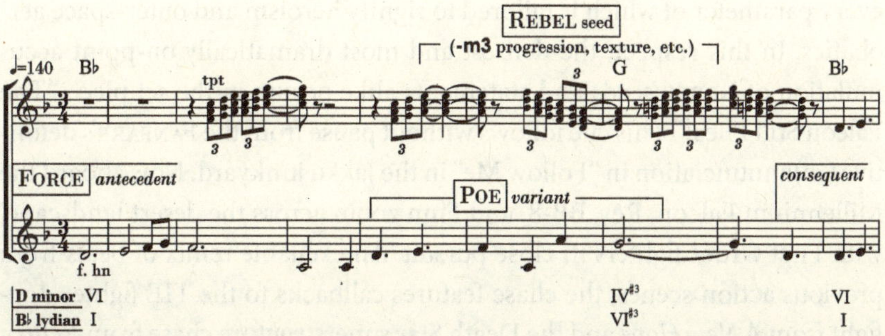

Figure 5.23 REBEL FANFARE and POE infused into FORCE in "Flying Home" (TFA, 7m68, 1:59:44)

Shooting" (5.22b) is even more abstracted, coming amid a development of the RESISTANCE march and drawing its melodic contour, rhythms, and contrapuntal disposition from that new theme, even as its voice-leading and orchestration recall its rebellious sister motif.

The summit when it comes to infusing different themes with rebellious parameters comes in "Flying Home," heard as the surviving heroes escape from the imploding Starkiller Base (Figure 5.23). The cue, and the scene it accompanies, rhymes with the destruction of the Death Star in Episode IV; where that scene was matched by a major tritone pair (C→F♯) followed by a victorious statement of the REBEL FANFARE in augmentation, *The Force Awakens* analog is more thematically synthetic. For the sight of Starkiller Base going nova, Williams offers an eighteen-measure module on an unusually long-breathed statement of the FORCE theme. Though ultimately cadencing in the key of D, the maintenance of B♭-major harmonic support and the prevalence of E♮ in the melody give the rendition a consolingly lydian aspect. That more-than-major tonal setting also facilitates a double thematic infusion. Halfway through the FORCE's antecedent, the swing to a G chord (the expected destination were the theme in D minor) provides a way for Williams to embed both the REBEL FANFARE's defining chromatic mediant progression (B♭→G) *and* POE's melodic and harmonic content, a leitmotif already primed from an explicit statement a few measures earlier in the same key. These thematic allusions, coupled with the lustrous layer of trumpet planing above the tune, make this iteration of the FORCE one of the more ingenious and gratifying of the Sequel trilogy.

Though the REBEL seeds described thus far are tied to other leitmotifs, they are nevertheless vivid conjurations of the musical *ethos* of the fanfare, every parameter of which is tailored to signify heroism and outer-space aerobatics. In this respect, the densest and most dramatically on-point accumulation of REBEL seeds and statements alike occurs in the set piece "The Falcon Still Flies!" This cue follows without pause from the FANFARE's definitive (re)annunciation in "Follow Me" in the Jakku junkyard. Now aboard the Millennium Falcon, Rey, BB-8, and Finn zoom across the desert landscape, with First Order fighters in close pursuit. An excitable remix of beats from previous action scenes, the chase features callbacks to the TIE fighter dogfight from *A New Hope* and the Death Star superstructure chase from *Return of the Jedi*. Williams's cue is based on an alteration of three types of music: a new chase leitmotif (FINN/PURSUIT) with an unusual-for-*Star Wars* 3/4 + 5/8 metrical orientation; a handful of athematic modules, mostly mimetic or interstitial in function; and the aforementioned transformations of the REBEL FANFARE. Of these elements, the last is the most salient for the cue's overall formal organization and expressive impact. By putting the FANFARE in the filmgoer's ear so insistently at the sequence's start, Williams ensures that even radical transformations are heard in relation to, and as outgrowths of, the original model.

Figure 5.24 gathers together these REBEL-derived particles in "The Falcon Still Flies"—listed not in order of appearance but in relative clarity of structure and signification. The cue is formally capricious and nonhierarchically structured, with seemingly little memory of what came before or where it is headed—paratactic in the extreme. The film version is also quite different from the cue the composer originally wrote. Yet despite being one of the most heavily micro-edited spans in the film, almost all of Williams's motivic

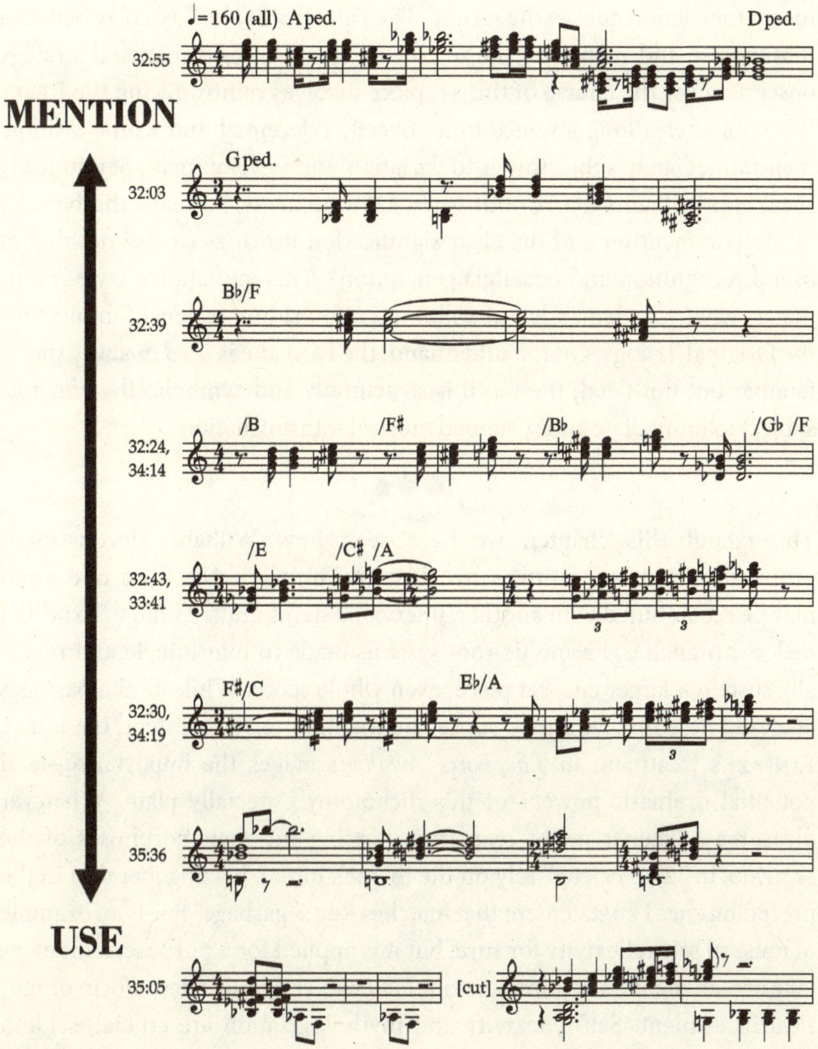

Figure 5.24 Rebel seeds in "The Falcon Still Flies" (TFA, 3m20) from mention to use

manipulations of the Rebel Fanfare remain intact, and several are reinforced by inelegant but effective looping or duplication. The sole excised cell, shown at the bottom of the figure, would have occurred near the conclusion of the climax originally written and stands the most distant cousin to the cue's nexus motif, a modally and directionally inverted spin on the familiar theme. Otherwise, what is shown is what is heard. To an extent greater than most other action cues in the series, "The Falcon Still Flies" is a play between motivic use and mention. The micro- to macro-transformational strategy observed over the course of this set piece involves reintroducing the REBEL FANFARE after a long absence in an overtly referential and iconic fashion, then immediately subjecting it to variation and development. Semiotically speaking, Williams has it both ways. On one hand, he reaps the benefits of motivic mention and the clear signification it brings (to say nothing of brand recognition and nostalgia generation). This quotational style is ultimately what was demanded of a film intent on riding residual fondness for the Original Trilogy. On the other hand, the FANFARE is *used* in a way that is familiar but not fixed; the motif is structurally and symbolically dynamic, subject to immediate and sustained musical transformation.

Throughout this chapter, we have seen how Williams deconstructs, propagates, and reconstitutes his themes. Timbral DNA from one motif may be recombined with another, intervallic stems grafted onto unexpected melodic branches, harmonic root systems made to intermingle and mutually sustain a larger cue, set piece, even whole score. While all the passages analyzed here involve a play of use and mention to some extent, the REBEL FANFARE's treatment in *The Force Awakens* makes the importance—and potential dramatic power—of this dichotomy especially plain. Whatever pleasures a listener might reap from hearing the metamorphoses of the FANFARE in "The Falcon" rely on the theme's initial, blazing mention in the preceding cue. The statement that matches Rey's "garbage" line is an example of musical self-reflexivity for sure, but it is applied for a purpose, a momentary breach of cinematic immersion that enables a longer-term form of musical investment. Self-reflexivity and mythologization are crucial, seldom discussed subjects in the universe of *Star Wars* music and will receive their due in Chapter 7. But before turning there, we shall take a journey into three of the transformational stories in this franchise *most* weighted toward use on the use-to-mention spectrum—not freely scattered motivic seeds, but fully blossoming and goal-driven thematic arcs.

6
Arcs

A Process of Building

Helmets, lightsabers, droids, planet-vaporizing technological terrors—objects that are broken apart in the Skywalker Saga tend to be reforged. This is true of leitmotifs as well. Take the first scene of *Return of the Jedi*, a miniature tale of visual and musical reconstitution. The first image after the opening crawl is another Death Star, bigger than the one destroyed in Episode IV, though not fully constructed. Mirroring the beginning of *A New Hope*, a Star Destroyer glides into the frame, though this time no space battle rocks the soundtrack. The ship quietly dispatches two TIE Fighters to escort an important-looking shuttle, occupant unknown. The pilots request clearance and are granted access to the impregnable battle station, and a carefully choreographed docking procedure ensues. The overseeing lieutenant tells an underling what the filmgoing audience has already inferred: "Inform the commander that Lord Vader's shuttle has arrived." A retinue of troops gathers in formation as a nervous Commander Jerjerrod hurries to greet his distinguished guest. The shuttle's entry platform slowly descends, and the Dark Lord makes his entrance.

Williams's cue for this sequence, "Approaching the Death Star," traverses a *thematic arc*—a coherent, incremental process of musical change that mirrors—or better, contributes to—a dramatic trajectory or plot thread. Time-honored narrative archetypes such as the tragic fall and the romantic quest all have corollaries in thematic transformation.[1] In the case of "Approaching the Death Star," the arc is one of reconstruction: scattered hints and fragments of a broken theme are gathered, tentatively powered up, and then firmly reattached, resulting in a tune the audience will know well: "The Imperial March." Though short in scope, the reconstruction involves every one of the VADER leitmotif's parameters as discussed in Chapter 5, especially its harmonic fingerprints. Figure 6.1 summarizes the structure of the entire cue. While the supple and uninterrupted flow of ideas in "Approaching the Death Star" immediately reestablishes the musical prose style of the series' underscore, it does not entail formal undifferentiation: as Figure 6.1 makes clear, the cue falls into four distinct stages that closely track the shuttle's progress. Each phase is capped off by a statement of VADER's theme, and each of those statements attains greater cadential weight and parametric completion.

Stage 1: Gathering thematic parameters [film 1:54; OST 1:26]	
Action	Pan down to moon of Endor, Death Star II in orbit. Shuttle makes approach.
Initial materials	Disassociated **VADER** A-theme particles, later B-theme. Parameters reintro'd individually harmony [1:54], contour [2:28], rhythm [2:47], orchestration [2:50].
Lead-in to culmination	None in film version; very understated resolution from F♯ to B-min in score version.
Culmination	Relatively weak, one-measure statement of **VADER** basic idea in horns, without harmonization or supporting texture.

Stage 2: Exploration of antecedent phrase [film 2:56, OST 2:52]	
Action	Docking permissions obtained, shuttle enters hangar, troops and functionaries stand ready.
Initial materials	Further ideas from **VADER** antecedent phrase, but discontinuous and stretched over multiple keys, separated by interjections of the B-theme.
Lead-in to culmination	Strongly telegraphed but non-functional cadence, resolving B♭m/D♭ to D♮ minor.
Culmination	Strong but short statement of **VADER** basic melodic idea with tutti orchestra, liquidated immediately into less thematically well-defined Stage 3 material.

Stage 3: Teasing, but withholding, full theme [film 3:25; OST 3:25]	
Action	Commander approaches, Vader descends.
Initial materials	Not directly based on **VADER**. Shifting tonal centers derived from i↔♭vi relationship, fast lower neighbor figure derived from m. 6 of theme.
Lead-in to culmination	Moderately telegraphed but functional V→i cadence, resolving D to G-minor.
Culmination	Moderately strong statement of first measure of **VADER** in low brass, quick shift in orchestration to winds, continues seamlessly into Stage 4.

Stage 4: Attainment of definitive theme [film 3:56–5:00; OST 3:56–5:09]	
Action	Vader upbraids Commander, warns of Emperor's imminent arrival, strides off. Wipe to Tatooine.
Initial materials	Entirely based on **VADER**. At first discontinuous, modulatory, shifting orchestral colors but overall a complete cycle through A-theme ant., cons. phrases.
Lead-in to culmination	Lengthy dominant prolongation and swelling, highly telegraphed V+♭vi→i cadence, synthesizing functional and chromatic elements of prior stages.
Culmination	Strong statement of **VADER** with all parameters; closes with a strong plagal cadence *within* theme's phrasal boundaries. Ends with fade-out on G-min.

Figure 6.1 Reconstituting VADER in "Approaching the Death Star" (ROTJ, 1m1, 1:54)

The first stage of *Jedi*'s introductory cue may make no overt reference to Vader's theme, but it does suggest, dimly, its constituent parts. Flowing organically from the Main Title's final bars, already thick with hexatonic sonorities, the archvillain's *leit*-harmonic hallmarks are the earliest parameters to materialize. We hear disembodied ♭vi↔i progressions, hexatonic scales, half-diminished sevenths, and slash-chords of the type Cm/B and Cm/D♭. But these pitch configurations emerge hazily, with no stable tonal center or regular phrase pattern to anchor them. Before long, more thematic parameters begin coalescing, including the head motif's basic intervallic contour [the trombone figure at 2:28] and its rhythmic ostinato [the timpani line at 2:25, reiterated in horns/marimba/strings at 2:47]. When a well-defined melodic snippet does appear, it is not from Vader's iconic A-theme but the bridge section of "The Imperial March"—a nervous figure scarcely heard in *Empire* but primed for intensive development in *Jedi*.[2] A not-inconsiderable span of fourteen measures, cut from the film but audible on the soundtrack, pushes closer and closer to the canonical theme, now with linear and orchestrational parameters slotting into place. But while audiences miss out on these extra seconds of motivic fabrication, the passage's excision poses no impediment to the cue's basic thematic arc toward Imperial-actualization, abridged but very much intact.

This first phase ends by disclosing the first measure of Vader's leitmotif in B minor, though without strong cadential underlining. The succeeding section spins through disconnected, tonally alienated portions of his antecedent phrase. Further motivic jitters interpose themselves in the theme's cracks; these too are derived from the bridge section, and serve to postpone the inevitable by a few measures at a time. By the phase's conclusion, a strong cadence—the first overwhelming audiovisual punctuation mark in the cue, and one built on the leit-harmonic ♭vi→i progression—tells us what we knew was coming. The swelling B♭m/D chord discharges onto a *tutti* statement of Vader's theme in its full dark raiment, though, at only two measures, it remains an incomplete musical thought.

The Dark Lord's theme has announced its arrival, but there is work left to be done. The next phase ventures through some sinister harmonic realms—Dm to E♭m, Bm to B♭m—embedding yet more ♭vi↔i relationships on both the musical surface and middleground. Another telegraphed cadence, here of a more functional V→i type, leads to a low and loud rendition of Vader, now at home in its quasi-associative key of G minor, as Jerjerrod and the Dark Lord begin a tense exchange. With that punctuation comes the final stage of the cue, a substantial module that works through the whole antecedent-consequent structure of the leitmotif, albeit with a few tonal twists and turns. A big bombshell is dropped—Emperor Palpatine himself is expected. With that news, Williams sets up another dominant, now in the shape of an E♭-minor triad propped against a D♮ bass. This chord blends the malign associativity of Vader's harmonic progression with the inexorable tug of a functional dominant of G minor, and Williams does not withhold resolution any longer. The Sith Master strides off, and his anthem follows, closing the sequence with a complete pass through the theme's main phrase, every bit as nasty as we remember from Episode V.

This chapter is about the musical architecture of the Skywalker Saga, how thematic development can span whole scenes, acts, and films. The preceding discussion of "Approaching the Death Star" offered a window into Williams's integrative mindset. We hear in VADER's reassembly how the transformational techniques covered previously, both micro and macro, are capable of more than on-the-spot daubs of expressive intensity or intermittent development: they can be active agents in a dynamic form of storytelling. A single thematic variant might correspond to a solitary story beat; a score-structuring succession of variants, a real story. And when multiple thematic arcs overlap and interact, one has the makings of a musical mythos.

The purpose of this chapter is to chart the large-scale symphonic development of themes, both as a unifying device and an engine for narrative change in *Star Wars*. That said, we will not overlook the sometimes not-so-symphonic caprices of blockbuster film scoring. Because, in that respect, "Approaching the Death Star" is also demonstrative—recall the excision of fourteen measures of heavy-duty leitmotivic work from the film's final cut. Practical matters broached earlier like intermittency, editorial interference, mention-versus-use all factor into the three macro-transformational analyses to come. But cinematic exigencies need not be pitted in a 100% adversarial relationship against musical integrity. "Approaching the Death Star" works well in its filmic context as a leitmotivic "suit up" for Vader, missing measures or no.

In a revealing exchange with Tavis Smiley on the eve of the release of *The Force Awakens*, Williams offered one way in which the infelicities of modern production— where simple sequential scoring of scenes is frequently unfeasible—could actually work to a score's benefit.

> If I could [I would] write the finale first, and then extract things from the finale, so that what you hear in the finale that's mature is suggested in the first three reels. The theme that becomes *more* of a theme. Four notes in the first reel, six notes in the third reel, twelve notes . . . and finally we get to the finale and you've got all twenty-four notes, and you say "I know what that is!" So, it's a process of building.[3]

The treatment of VADER's motif in "Approaching the Death Star" illustrates in microcosm Williams's notion of "a theme that becomes *more* of a theme." His "process of building" is a compelling procedure for epic musical storytelling, as it treats leitmotifs almost as characters, possessed of a kind of agency or innate will to change. Yet Williams's conversation with Smiley was not just about a high-minded, utopian film-scoring process. He went on to note the reshoot-heavy, rewrite-necessitating nature of post-production on *The Force Awakens*.

> So we did the first two or three reels, but because of this process [of re-shoots and re-edits] I had to go back and rework some of it as we went through. But I have to tell you that I'm one of the writers that you'll meet that really does not mind rewrites. . . . Hemingway said that the art of writing is the art of rewriting. You make your prose, you look at it next week, you can improve it every time you look at it, if you give it a little objectivity from getting away from it. So it took us longer to score the film . . . but I really think in the end, it gave me an opportunity to rework some things and maybe do a better job.[4]

Given Williams's preference for working backward and knowing in advance where things are headed, it may be counterintuitive that the hectic regime of modern filmmaking would be *more*, not less, conducive to symphonic writing. The anarchic production schedule of Episode VII did leave the composer beleaguered, and the next two installments even more so. Yet with *The Force Awakens*, we can hear the benefits of an extended scoring timeframe—namely, in the care and purpose with which REY's material is laid out across the movie's staggering ninety-five distinct cues.[5] Nor are these thematic arc-benefiting alterations present only in *Star Wars* movies made after the advent of digital editing. Even a cue as iconic as "Binary Sunset" from Episode IV was a late change, a FORCE-theme-based replacement for the strictly non-leitmotivic (and jarringly menacing) original take. That alternate "Binary Sunset" is now forgotten, while its replacement is among the most formally critical and mythically ramifying pieces in the series. The fact that rewrites sometimes enable Williams to "maybe do a better job" is a huge understatement.

Throughout *The Skywalker Symphonies*, we have seen how Williams grapples with the twin dilemmas of symphonic scoring. One is the tension between Mahlerian expansiveness and Sibelian refinement. The other, not unrelated, is the opposition of musical autonomy and all the countless varieties of cinematic exigency. Understanding thematic arcs in this series means taking those two axes and discovering what lies at their intersection. The analyses to come prove that this crossing of contradictions is creatively productive. Many thematic "mytharcs" of narrative significance and compositional sophistication are indeed at play in the Skywalker Saga. The very unpredictability of filmic form for series as complex as *Star Wars*—the hectic production schedules and editorial tangles, the inevitable inconsistencies of logic (or performance, writing, effects, etc.)—is in fact part of what makes symphonic storytelling possible.

The three thematic arcs we are about to examine involve macro-transformations broached in Chapter 4. The compositional techniques included in this category occupy a celebrated place in the aesthetics of Romantic and Modernist music. One needs only think of the analytical ink spilled over the form-generative intervallic cells of Brahms's Fourth Symphony, or the long-postponed resolution of the opening chord in Wagner's *Tristan und Isolde*, or the radiant metamorphosis of the Swan hymn in Sibelius's Fifth Symphony.[6] Those works exemplify the procedures of *developing variation*, *deferred consummation*, and *teleological genesis*, respectively. The presence of these techniques in Hollywood is presumed to be rare—deplorably so, if one might read between the lines of recurrent critiques of the artform, both academic and popular.[7] To "evolve" a theme necessitates both a broad canvas and a certain degree of pre-compositional design. Moreover, the macro-transformations tend to be dialectical in character, involving an interactivity of different musical materials and a sort of striving for thematic apotheosis or synthesis. A decidedly *symphonic* logic.

Developing Variation in *Return of the Jedi*

Our inspection of the rebirth of VADER's theme in "Approaching the Death Star" at the start of this chapter and "The Fleet Enters Hyperspace" in Chapter 4 gave a good sense of the motivic exuberance of *Return of the Jedi*. Indeed, all of the thematic-transformational procedures already enumerated may be located somewhere on the soundtrack for Episode VI. Williams's developmental sensibility, already honed in *The Empire Strikes Back*, is at its sharpest in this score. For the first time in the series, his symphonic underscoring approaches the level of Wagner, if not in total leitmotivic saturation—there are still important athematic set pieces—then in the structural mutability and symbolic density of Wagnerian musical prose. Throughout *Jedi*, themes new and old appear, change, and interact with one another in unexpected and mythically suggestive ways.

Those two motivic principles—mutability and density—provide fertile ground for a technique called *developing variation*. The term, coined by Arnold Schoenberg, is associated with the tightly argued instrumental music of Brahms, which often revolves around just a few tiny motivic germs. Developing variation entails a basic musical shape or unit that provides the source, in the composer's words, for "all the thematic formulations" of a piece.[8] In Schoenberg's motivic germ theory, that basic shape could be anything: an interval succession, a melodic contour, a harmonic progression. Constant change, "endless reshaping," of that unit is paramount, never simple repetition.[9] The initial alterations of the Schoenbergian source motif may be subtle, even imperceptible—a displaced pitch here, a metrical realignment there. But the process is *accumulative*, and the sum of those tiny developments is often music that sounds strikingly unlike its point of origin. (Melodic concatenation is a related but less goal-driven macrotransformational technique; it is discussed in Chapter 9.)

The notion of developing variation has not entered into the discourse of film music criticism or analysis. Little surprise, as the concept was formulated with an implicit anti-program music bias: Schoenberg meant to draw a contrast between the rigorous Brahmsian model of development and the allegedly looser, more superficial manipulation of material found in the proto-cinematic Wagner.[10] But while the term's originator would have been aghast, developing variation is a perfectly apt category in many cinematic contexts. And its aptness applies to multiple textual levels, both inside a theme and across freer passages based on its motivic ingredients.

On the intra-thematic level, the technique emerges within what Mark Richards categorizes as "developing forms." These are themes in which a melody's successive subphrases are based on evolutions of some initial germ.[11] Developing forms are driven by the free transformation of their Schoenbergian basic units, more than adherence to a predictable and symmetrical antecedent/consequent structure. Good examples in *Star Wars* include motifs for the RESISTANCE, LUKE IN EXILE, and, significantly, YODA. However, the real measure of developing variation is what takes place *outside* the bounds of a definitive thematic structure—when the basic unit suffuses transitions, digressions, sequences, contrapuntal strata, even other themes—everything.

Revelatory Developments

With apologies to Schoenberg, very few pieces—Classical or otherwise—fulfill, or even attempt, his dream of total organic unity. A sprawling and textually subordinated work like a *Star Wars* score is an unlikely place to discover a secret Brahmsian vision of motivic all-interconnectedness. Nevertheless, in *Return of the Jedi*, there are several passages in which Schoenberg's procedure is genuinely in evidence, if in an intermittent and subtle way.[12] With one thematic arc in particular, Brahms-style developing variation meets Wagnerian leitmotivic genesis: the evolution of the YODA theme into a new REVELATION motif. The way this transformation unfolds exemplifies the tension between Williams's variational mindset and the shortened attentional horizon inherent in the filmic medium.

Most of this thematic arc occurs within a single six-minute-long cue entitled "Yoda's Scene." This tableau sees the Jedi Master reunited with Luke, with whom he shares some cryptic advice and then dies. Naturally, Williams's cue revolves around YODA, along with some references to LUKE and the FORCE. Figure 6.2 provides an overview of the Jedi Master's theme in terms of its prototype and individual parameters. For clarity, the prototype is further annotated with some relevant formal information.

As noted, YODA's leitmotif exemplifies what Richards calls a "developing theme." Its eight-measure form grows from a two-bar introductory cell [a1], which is answered by three elaborated variants [a2, a3, a4], each more active and expansive than the last. Williams, aware of the melody's deceptive nuance, considers it among his favorites:

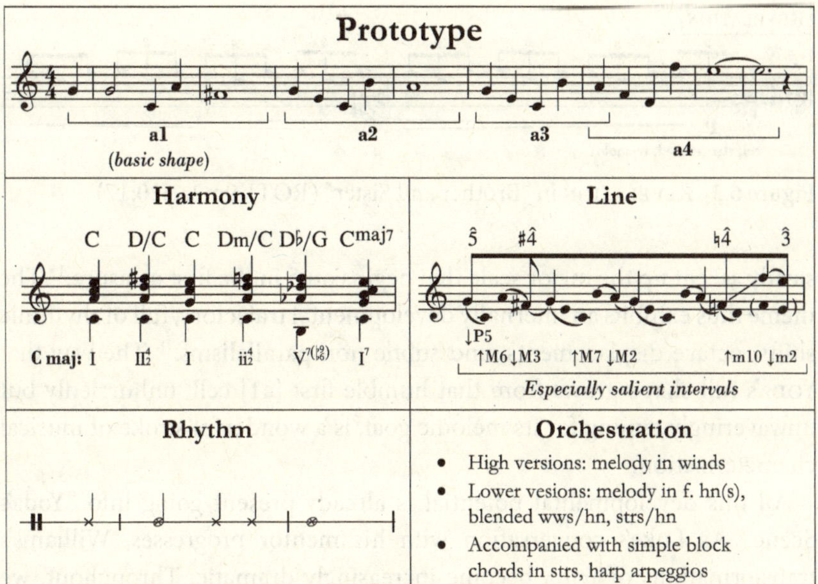

Figure 6.2 YODA prototype and parameters

> When you think about it in philosophical terms, I think that Yoda suggested to me a very ancient gentleman, very wise [and] could be portrayed musically in a very direct and very lyrical way, simple tuneful way. Yoda's theme is a very simple little tune, with consonant intervals—do and mi and so. And it moves around in a very sort of *youthful* way almost. And Yoda is 700 or 800 years old, we're told. His character's speech suggested to me the innocence of real wisdom. True wisdom that Yoda seemed to always offer was reduced to essentials, *true* simplicity.[13]

This idea of wise simplicity is a constant in the way the composer thinks of the YODA theme. In a later interview, Williams stressed that the "simplicity of the tune—combined with the logic of its intervals—seems to carry some gravitas with it. It's a combination that's hard to produce if it's too eagerly sought after."[14]

A prominent basic shape in this simple but decidedly not simplistic theme is the descending gesture at the end of each subphrase: 6̂–♯4̂, 7̂–6̂, 4̂–3̂. Each of these falling figures is preceded by a leap of increasing size (M6, M7, m10). The L(ine) parameter in Figure 6.2 highlights this intervallic gesture. The dyadic pattern overlaps, but does not align one-for-one, with a

Figure 6.3 REVELATION in "Brother and Sister" (ROTJ, 9m2, 1:20:17)

steady ascent up the major scale that begins on $\hat{5}$ in the first measure.[15] The theme thus exhibits an internally developmental trajectory, full of rhythmic shifts, octave displacements, and subtle non-parallelisms.[16] The way that YODA's full shape grows from that humble first [a1] cell, unhurriedly but unwaveringly aiming for its melodic goal, is a wonderful stroke of musical characterization.

All this developmental potential is already present going into "Yoda's Scene." As Luke's conversation with his mentor progresses, Williams's transformations of YODA become increasingly dramatic. Throughout, we can hear the process of semantic drift in real time. With each change, the leitmotif's semantic target grows a little less stable, pointing away from the Jedi Master and toward something else, some important, hidden information. This secret turns out to be the existence of a second Skywalker sibling.[17] The musical idea around which these transformations coalesce is displayed in its definitive shape in Figure 6.3. Unique to Episode VI, this REVELATION motif never quite leaps to the musical foreground as the more canonic themes do. But in its understated way, it has just as big an impact to make.

How does Williams get from leitmotivic point A to point B? To borrow a biological metaphor for leitmotivic semiosis from Matthew Bribitzer-Stull: if YODA's theme is the genetic ancestor of REVELATION, then we should be able to locate intermediate species that facilitate the one's evolution into the other. The chain of transformations pictured in Figure 6.4 gives a "genomic" account of the relationship of these two themes, showing how one motif leads to the other—or, alternatively, how one motif might be reverse-engineered to reveal its precursor. Rendered this way, it becomes clear REVELATION adopts the intervallic frame and triad-arpeggiating contour of YODA's third and fourth measures while replacing the lydian II chord supporting $\hat{7}$-$\hat{6}$ dyad with a semitonal neighbor above the fifth, $\hat{5}$-$\flat\hat{6}$. This transformation is further underlined through the acceleration of tempo, compression of ambit, and reiteration of its basic shape.[18]

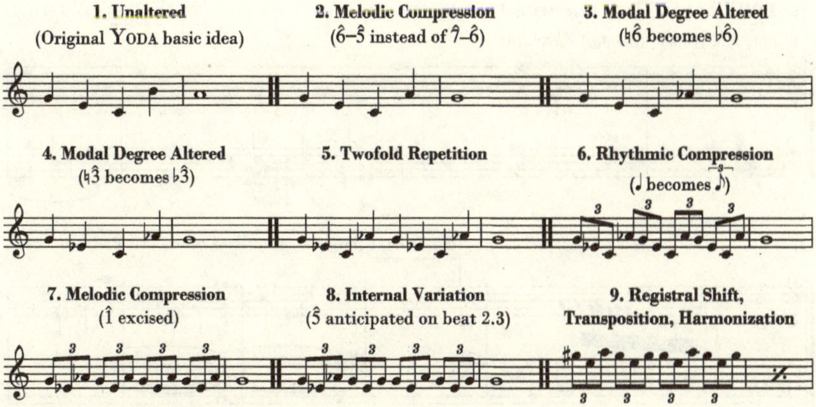

Figure 6.4 Mutational pathway from YODA to REVELATION

This mutational chain has to it a certain formalistic appeal, idealizing the process of developing variation into a series of discrete changes. (If those individual steps occur in the order presented, we might cite the YODA-to-REVELATION arc as an example of melodic concatenation in addition to developing variation.) There can be little argument that the motif represented in the ninth stage of Figure 6.4 is *derived* from that in Stage 1. But is a mutational pathway the best way of describing this "theme that becomes more of a theme"? Not necessarily. This discretized chain misrepresents Williams's process as it takes place in the actual cue, suggesting an overly straight path, when the real connection between YODA and REVELATION is drawn out progressively, dynamically, and not entirely linearly.

The excerpts in Figure 6.5a through 6.5e chart this motif's genesis over the duration of "Yoda's Scene." For concision's sake, only those modules involving the YODA/REVELATION motivic pathway are rendered, though as always, transitional material and contrasting leitmotifs are present and play an essential role in the cue's musical argument. Unlike other examples, I omit indications of instrumentation for the sake of legibility of the already dense notation, though it should be stressed that Williams orchestrates this cue with great delicacy.

Figure 6.5a depicts the scene's opening musical paragraph. It begins with a tracked rendition of YODA's theme from *Empire* (module 1), the tonal indeterminacy of which enables it to segue smoothly into the newly written music for the cue, starting with a straightforward iteration of the theme in D major (module 2a). Williams immediately begins composing out YODA's basic

Figure 6.5a "Yoda's Scene" mm. 1–16 (ESB 5m3 and ROTJ 5m1/6m1, 39:42)

shape (module 2b), now supporting a restless Cm^{ma7} chord. The following statement also features chromatic perturbances. Yet at this stage, changes to the melodic line are still heard as a novel configuration of an established theme rather than an inkling of something truly new. This threshold will be crossed in due course.

If the melodic profile of REVELATION becomes sharper over the course of the cue, it is not due to simple repetition; more impactful is the way the motif is placed in increasing affective and structural *contrast* with its oft-referenced parent theme. The next span of YODA/REVELATION music is shown in Figure 6.5b. Of particular note is module 6, whose shadowy affect matches a turn in the discussion toward Luke's dark parentage. Listeners who have intuited the parameters of Vader's theme will have no trouble identifying its source. A whiff of villainous harmony (note the Cm^{ma7}/E♭ pincushion), intervallic compression (note the downward melodic M3, rather than P5), and shade of militaristic rhythm (note the timpani triplet) associate the passage not with its primary motivic ancestor of YODA but with *VADER*. Far from being a coincidence, this variant marks the first time the character comes up in conversation between Luke and his expiring master. Moreover, it marks one of only a few places in the whole Saga in which the Sith Lord's theme directly interacts with that of the Jedi Master.[19] This is not the only time we will see that an entry of a new theme into the *Star Wars* canon involves meaningful contact with other, more established motifs.

When Yoda warns of Palpatine's might, the more clearly focalized REVELATION motif is compressed into its characteristic triplet pace, as shown in module 8 in Figure 6.5c. What had been a languid quarter-note gait, owing to the pacific nature of Yoda's theme, now assumes the more nervous rhythm

Figure 6.5b "Yoda Scene" mm. 23–35 (ROTJ, 5m1/6m1 40:55)

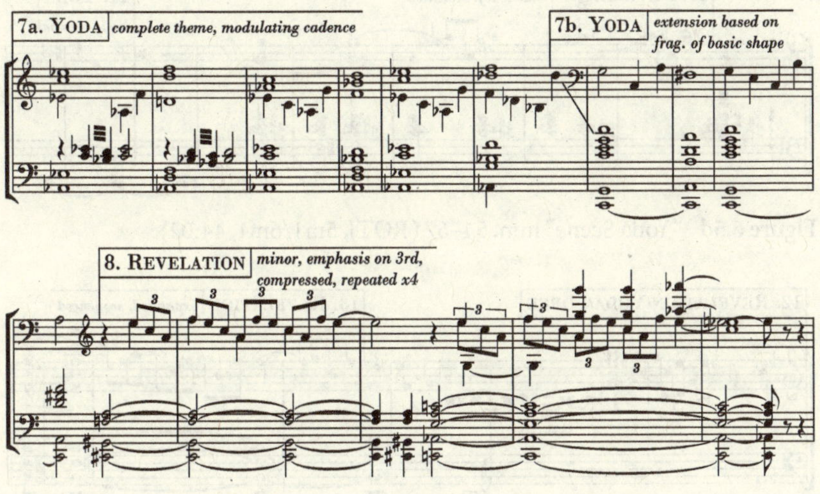

Figure 6.5c "Yoda Scene" mm. 54–67 (ROTJ, 5m1/6m1, 42:47)

it will retain for most subsequent statements. This tendency for the Emperor to pollute other leitmotifs will be revisited in the next chapter.

As if to complete the thematic trifecta, the Force theme also leaves a mark on Revelation at the emotional climax of the cue, when Luke is at his most agitated (Figure 6.5d). Serving first as an upper-registral countermelody in module 9, the triplet figure persists after the Force leaves the musical foreground. That perseverance focuses our musical attention on this "new" idea that, in actuality, has been blooming steadily for the past five minutes.

By the time Luke's master becomes one with the Force (Fig. 6.5e), a new theme has been born. Revelation is heard definitively in module 13, at the very conclusion of the cue, now fully detached from its originary source, standing motivically on its own. The motif evolved before our ears through a process of developing variation, a steady but also windingly ad hoc arc, its exact course dictated less by the idealized chain of Figure 6.4 and more

Figure 6.5d "Yoda Scene" mm. 54–67 (ROTJ, 5m1/6m1, 44:02)

Figure 6.5e "Yoda Scene" mm. 93–99 (ROTJ, 5m1/6m1, 45:27)

by immediate dramatic context. And, crucially, the theme gained semiotic resonance by its strategically staged sympathetic vibrations with three of the saga's musical cornerstones, Yoda, Vader, and the Force themes. Leitmotivic identity, far more than is generally recognized, is a function of *relational* position just as much as intrinsic make-up.

Brother and Sister

If the principle of developing variation can bring motivic beings into the world, it can just as easily fold them back into a nondescript, thematically unmarked state. This is ultimately what happens to the newly birthed Revelation. The idea recurs prominently in only one more cue in Episode VI, albeit an important one: "Brother and Sister," wherein Luke confides with Leia the fact of their secret siblinghood. Even more than "Yoda's Scene," "Brother and Sister" is a marvel of mythic underscoring, delicate in construction and emotionally complex in a way Williams rarely was afforded an opportunity in the series.[20] With its stilted dialogue, the scene was also a fine target for the composer's compensatory instincts. Notably, the success of the cue depends on the *recession* of Revelation, that it becomes musical connective tissue rather than a focal point.

Figure 6.6 displays the reemergence of Revelation, roughly a minute into "Brother and Sister." The reversion to thematic indistinction is accomplished

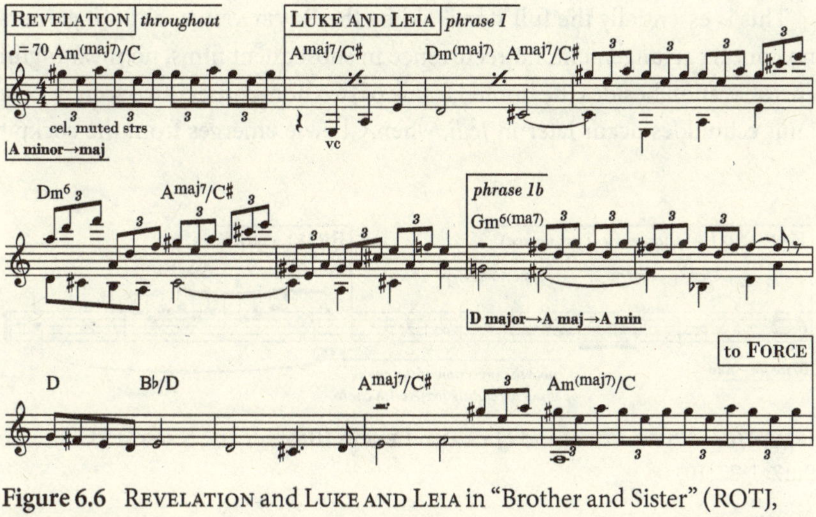

Figure 6.6 Revelation and Luke and Leia in "Brother and Sister" (ROTJ, 9m2, 1:20:17)

quickly, in a kind of mirroring of the manner by which the motif came into its own in the earlier cue. The theme is uttered first in clear outline after Luke drops his filial shocker, "my *sister* has it." Two bars later, those magic triplets fade to the background, giving way to a contrastively songful melody introduced in low strings: Luke and Leia.

As this theme unspools—Luke and Leia is the longest-breathed melody in the whole saga—Williams embroiders the cellos with strands of the Revelation motif. That motif's status as a standalone entity is subsumed by its new, more conventionally tuneful sibling. At turns, the softened strains of Revelation pause to give space to Luke and Leia's supple line. Elsewhere, the motif adjusts its pitches to fit the theme's harmonic implications. And a gradual shift of modality for Revelation facilitates a neat tonal symmetry: at the end of the passage in Figure 6.6, we hear A^{ma7}/C♯ tensing into Am^{ma7}/C♮, reversing the module's introductory progression.

A sense of both structural and semiotic assimilation is further achieved when Revelation occurs within statements of the Force and Han and Leia leitmotifs a few measures later, again as a countermelody rather than foreground idea. The scene concludes with the uncomprehending Han embracing Leia, attended by an ambivalent musical tag depicted in Figure 6.7. The revelatory triplets are heard here one last time, suitably bookending the scene. At this point, the motif is not acting in an accompanimental capacity to another theme. Nor is it really an autonomous musical thought either. Rather, it is a kind of arpeggiated afterimage, formerly the product of a concerted process of motivic solidification, now drifting out of focus.

This is essentially the full story told by the Revelation motif. It garners no concert arrangement, no recurrence in subsequent films, no meaningful corroboration besides the limited frame of two non-consecutive scenes. One faint echo does occur later in *Jedi*, when Chewie emerges from the cockpit

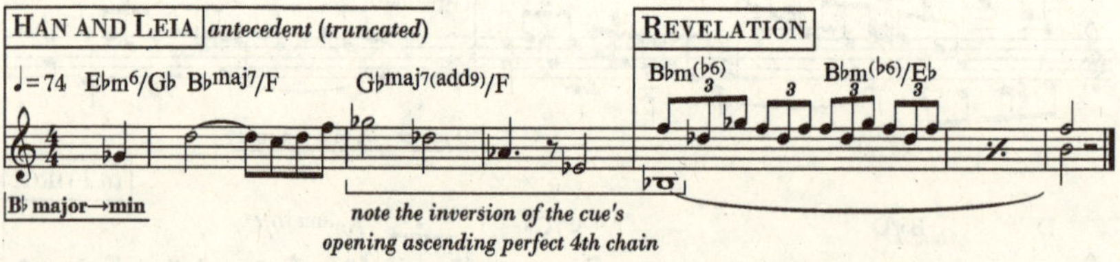

Figure 6.7 Revelation and Han and Leia in "Brother and Sister" (ROTJ, 9m2, 1:22:10)

of a commandeered Chicken Walker [1:48:32]—technically a revelation for Han, though not much of one for the audience. Nevertheless, the sprightly flute and oboe melody fails to resemble the motif in question closely enough on a structural level, nor does it connect with it profoundly enough on a mythical level, to count as real follow-through. And yet, during "Yoda's Scene" and "Brother and Sister," REVELATION does provide an instance of organic, economical motivic "work," even if its developmental horizon does not extend beyond those two cues.

As far as thematic arcs go, YODA-into-REVELATION is diminutive but powerful. It is also more developmentally complex within its small span than what some themes undergo across entire films. Not every leitmotif demands—nor warrants—Brahmsian developmental variation, and emotional impact is often greater when a musical idea is sparing or sporadic in incidence. The vanishingly infrequent LUKE AND LEIA is poignant for just that reason. Williams's motivic technique may be nonlinear, suggestive, unfulfilled. But, as the next case study will reveal, that frustration can itself be deeply expressive, even form-generative.

Deferred Consummation in *Attack of the Clones*

Effective thematic arcs depend on delayed gratification. In the Skywalker Saga, Williams rarely gives away the definitive shape of a leitmotif early, reserving its complete form for moments of climax and summation. A few rule-proving exceptions notwithstanding, themes are first presented in understated orchestral colors and indecisive harmonies.[21] The most essential aspects of melodic shape and signification will generally be clear in those early iterations, though past the initial hook, there can be considerable fluctuation of style and substance. Ambiguity is almost always banished, however, and by a film's end, the theme will have been presented with utmost definition.

Williams's compositional method lends itself to an end-weighted, cumulative style of scoring, especially in the treatment of a score's most important ideas. Emilio Audissino calls this technique "gradual disclosure of the main theme" and notes its operation in several of the composer's most iconic scores, including *Jaws* and *E.T.*[22] It is one of the few aspects of Williams's creative practice that the composer himself has consistently spoken on. In 1998, he offered the following rationale for his "process of building":

> What I have tried to do, in many films that I've done, is to try to pretty much work the ending out, so that I know where the musical material is going to land and develop, and then decompose it and take it apart, so to speak, so that individual strands of a more mature thing can be exposed singly, and then collect together in the end of the film.[23]

The *Star Wars* films include many examples of musical "strands" that Williams endeavors to "collect together." The epitome of thematic accumulation is teleological genesis, in which leitmotivic attainment involves the careful assembly of something big out of initially ill-defined particles. But there are also less *directed* forms of thematic arc-building that are supported by Williams's tendency to work backward. One method, already introduced, is motivic seeding: extracting characteristics from a finished theme and allowing them to ramify and impinge on the rest of the score without building toward some particular goal. In the composer's own words, he will "extract elements from ['that completed thing'] and present them in a somewhat fragmented way."[24] Motivic seeding becomes easier the more source material there is to draw from. We have seen in Chapter 5 how it contributes to an assortment of cues in Episodes I, V, and VII that pull from, without ever outright stating, the VADER, HAN AND LEIA, and REBEL FANFARE, respectively. But sowing aspects of a musical thought throughout a score need not involve leitmotifs per se—incidental or even purely athematic material can also be deconstructed and dispersed, as we saw with various modal-intervallic cells (e.g., the MISERY TRICHORD in *Revenge of the Sith*).

Teleological genesis and motivic seeding are core tools for Williams's (de)compositional process. However, while not necessarily rare, their workings can be understated and easily missed on first hearing. A more audibly obvious and quite common procedure is *deferred consummation*. As suggested by the name, the anticipation is everything. A theme will be established early in a film's runtime, but each time it is heard, Williams will systematically deny it two things:

- **Rhetorical** finality, in the shape of a full, foregrounded orchestral presentation.
- **Structural** finality, in the shape of melodic completion and cadential closure.

These qualities are reserved for a moment of thematic apotheosis, the place the "material is going to land," which Williams withholds for as long as the story can permit. Rhetorical finality ensures the most dramatic sonic impact possible. Structural finality establishes the thematic parameters (harmonic, linear, rhythmic) that listeners expect from well-formed, satisfying melodies. Williams applies this delaying tactic so consistently in his symphonic scores that deferred consummation itself becomes a kind of background expectation. Filmgoers know his themes tend not to reveal their full selves all at once. Even when leitmotifs are relatively substantial in their inaugural iterations, they come loaded with an implicit promise of something even bigger.

The themes that follow a path of deferred consummation are diverse in style and dramatic purpose: YODA, HAN AND LEIA, EMPEROR, EWOKS, ANAKIN AND PADMÉ, DESCENT, ROSE, and VICTORY.[25] The storytelling benefits of this approach are correspondingly varied and flexible. Deferral can set up a score-spanning leitmotivic arc, sustaining a line of musical tension that discharges to tremendous effect when the definitive rendition is finally achieved. The promise of eventual attainment is one way of effecting a future-tensed quality within mythic musical prose. Conveniently, thematic deferral is easier to consciously track than many transformational procedures, as listeners grow familiar with a theme long before its full realization. And deferred consummation proves useful for other forms of thematic work, too. Creating a sense of formal incompletion often means enlisting other transformational techniques—fragmentation, sequence, truncation—and with them a dynamic, responsive style of dramatic underscoring.

More than any other parameter, the *cadence* is the engine of thematic completion. Conversely, cadential suppression is the key to thematic denial. Williams draws on a wide range of devices to stymie closure at these crucial moments of punctuation: deceptive resolution of the dominant, dissonant disruption of the tonic, elision of a concluding measure with the onset of another less stable phrase, and so on. We have already seen ample evidence of this art of transition in Williams's underscore. Note, for instance, the cadentially closed prototype of YODA's theme in Figure 6.2 and compare it with the remarkable variety of phrasal elisions, disruptions, and suppressions the tail end of the leitmotif undergoes in "Yoda's Scene" from Episode VI. Such "contra-cadential" tendencies, as theorist and psychologist David Huron calls them, ultimately stem from—who else?—Wagner.[26] Deferral is *the* crucial ingredient in the Wagnerian "endless melody." This musical flow-state is a quality that the Skywalker Series achieves in its best sequences—those spans of mythic time where one feels as if the score is being magically urged on, full of dramatic momentum and import, never cordoning itself off in predictable eight- or sixteen-measure periods.

Star-Crossed Cadences

The most assiduously executed plan of deferred consummation belongs to the love theme from *Attack of the Clones*, ANAKIN AND PADMÉ. In an unusually overt stroke of intertextuality, Williams lent this leitmotif a Shakespearean *double entendre* of a title: "Across the Stars." The allusion to Romeo and Juliet and the famous "star-crossed lovers" is fitting for these interstellar paramours. Despite their mutual romantic attraction, Senator Padmé Amidala and her Jedi apprentice bodyguard Anakin Skywalker are barred from amorous fulfillment by a variety of philosophical and social prohibitions. The pair's leitmotif follows suit, chasing closure while finding true release evasive.

Though capable of musical intimacy and understatement, ANAKIN AND PADMÉ in its natural state is sweeping, even universalizing, in its implications. Per Williams:

> This time-honored tension [of portraying forbidden relationships in art] presents the challenge of expressing love's exultation while simultaneously suggesting the grief and tragedy that separation would eventually bring. Likewise, the title "Across the Stars" suggests the timelessness of love-eternal while dropping the hint that our lovers' knot might be ill-fated and "star-crossed."[27]

"Across the Stars" was not meant to sound like just a tragic love theme, but *the* tragic love theme. Perversely, reaching those mythic heights through music may have been made easier due to how *unconvincing* the film's romance is on every other level. With little chemistry to be seen on screen, Williams's task could only be compensatory—a situation in which film music with symphonic aspirations thrives. The unrequitable love music in *Attack of the Clones* is thus a function of the movie's bogglingly stilted script and performances. But it also strives valiantly, and for the most part successfully, to transcend those shortcomings.[28]

ANAKIN AND PADMÉ's *appassionato* air draws from competing musical codes to realize its dramatic mandate. The theme at once embodies the highly mannered quality of the central romance while also stirring up undercurrents of desire wherever possible. With respect to the former quality, "Across the Stars" partakes of a kind of Renaissance-style formality in its compound meter, antique modality, and harp-and-harpsichord-heavy instrumentation.

In places, the theme sounds closer in idiom to the composer's music for *Jane Eyre* and perhaps Nino Rota's theme from *Romeo and Juliet* than it does previous music for the Skywalker Saga.[29] At the same time, ANAKIN AND PADMÉ can convey a turgid, Late-Romantic style eroticism, contra-cadential in the extreme, inclined to huge, heart-on-sleeve musical gestures—bigger indeed than practically anything else yet heard in the series. It's not sexy music, really, but it can certainly swoon when called for.[30]

Fruitless pining in Williams's underscore is not confined to *Attack of the Clones*. After all, repetition is everything in *Star Wars*. The middle chapter of each trilogy features a scene of frustrated erotic tension, accompanied by a principal leitmotif whose conclusion is cruelly impeded; those for Episodes V and VIII are depicted in Figure 6.8.[31] In *Empire*, it is Threepio who bursts in on the romantic pair. Williams takes the HAN AND LEIA theme (Figure 6.8a), which had been mounting in ardor for a minute, and thrusts it during its climactic consequent phrase onto a $\flat II^7/\hat{1}$ chord. That pre-cadential sonority is left hanging, any hope for fulfillment negated by a sheepish clarinet dyad and motivic non-sequitur in pizzicato strings, mimicking the droid's obnoxious intrusion.

In *The Last Jedi*, a rather less traditional—and in some ways more erotically charged—coupling between Rey and Kylo Ren occurs via clandestine telepathic connection. Their liaison is annihilated when Luke, like a disapproving father, barges in. Figure 6.8b captures that moment. His disruption grinds to a halt an otherwise reconciliatory statement of the FORCE theme, at both phrase-structural juncture similar to that as *Empire* and on a comparably pressurized sonority of $\flat II^{\sharp4}$. But the follow-up is crueler than those pizzicato plucks: a terminal $D^{sus\sharp4}$ chord finds itself crushed within a stridently

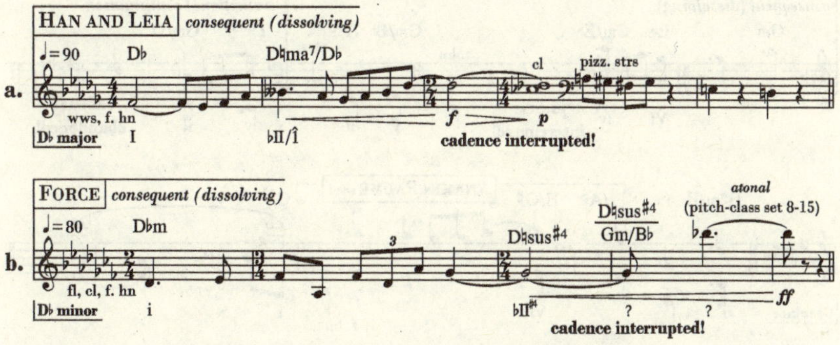

Figure 6.8 *Cadentius Interruptus*. **a.** Han and Leia in "Solo and the Princess" (ESB, 5m4, 51:52); **b.** Rey and Ren in "You're Not Alone" (TLJ, 5m46, 1:17:32)

nonfunctional pitch pyramid $[B\flat_1\text{-}G_2\text{-}D_3\text{-}F\sharp_3\text{-}A\flat_3\text{-}D\sharp_4\text{-}E_4\text{-}C\sharp_5]$. Cadentially speaking, nothing perfect, nor authentic, is to be heard here.

Leitmotive's Labour's Lost

Both instances of *cadentius interruptus* are a little on the nose for Williams, albeit in a manner befitting a device as theatrical as a broken-off kiss. The rhyme in *Attack of the Clones*, depicted in Figure 6.9, manages to be at once more melodically clever and more emotionally heavy-handed, almost to the point of parody. (The scene, with its infamously awkward sand-based wooing, is a testament to George Lucas's ability to write unspeakably wooden dialogue.) As Anakin slowly draws in for a kiss, solo oboe initiates the first phrase of Anakin and Padmé in G minor, accompanied by harp and harpsichord, as if by a sci-fi troubadour. The onset of the theme's consequent phrase matches a cut to a different angle on the couple, Padmé now reciprocating to the luscious sounds of the full string section. The passion does not last long, though—one and a half measures, to be exact—before the senator pulls away, along with the music, entirely, for a good two seconds. "No. I shouldn't have done that," she demurs, and her escort dully responds, "I'm sorry."

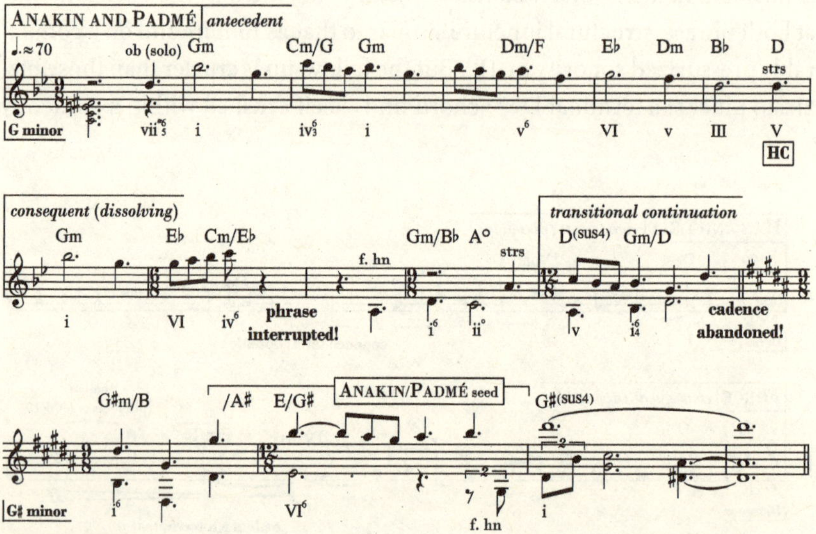

Figure 6.9 *Cadentius Interruptus* of Anakin and Padmé in "The First Kiss" (AOTC, 3m3, 45:10)

Williams's deflationary strategy for this "First Kiss" is comparable to the ploys in Episodes V and VIII, going from loud and cadence-directed to quiet and tonally unmoored. Peculiar to this instance of musical irresolution is the fact that Anakin and Padmé's theme is not entirely arrested by the ill-timed caesura. In the measures that follow the pause, the leitmotif continues, with heavy modification of the remainder of its dissolving consequent phrase. Normally, the melody concludes with an imperfect, tonic-aimed cadence that harmonizes a melodic $\hat{2}$–$\hat{5}$–$\hat{4}$–$\hat{5}$ with either i^6–♭II–i or i^6–$ii^{ø7}$–I. Williams opts for the latter here, offering a dejected, displaced horn fragment in measures 37–38. Moments later, the strings restate a shard of the theme's head motif atop a cadential six-four chord, Gm/D. Perhaps tonal resolution is not out of the question?

This, alas, is another feint, and that string plume floats off, drifting from G minor to an inverted G♯-minor triad. Then, with an impeccable voice-exchange, the theme contorts toward E major in first inversion, thereby phasing into a thoroughly alienated 4-sharp harmonic field for the cue's conclusion. The artfulness of this post-denial passage, the way the Anakin and Padmé theme does not fully grind to a stop but continues on, transformed and destabilized, almost seems like an apology of sorts for the shamelessness of the musical pull-out at the climax of the theme. It is also emblematic of the surprising degree of nuance in the *Attack of the Clones* score, coexisting with—and arguably necessitated by—shortcomings in writing and performance.

The denial strategy evident in "First Kiss" is writ large over the entire *Attack of the Clones* soundtrack. More than any other *Star Wars* score, Episode II's leitmotivic storytelling revolves around a single musical thought. The other newly introduced themes do nothing to draw attention away from the love theme. Indeed, they seem devised to focalize it even more intensely.

- The Pastorale and Gloom motifs are expressive adjuncts to Anakin and Padmé. The latter, an angsty, appoggiatura-laden thing, is even absorbed within the "Across the Stars" concert arrangement as its large-scale B-theme.
- The Descent motif, prior to *Revenge of the Sith* at least, is essentially just the Dies Irae, which is already embedded within Anakin and Padmé's second measure, and spins out further of it in the cue "Fireside Chat."

- The Mystery motif, with its minor arpeggios and side-slipping modulations, is more textural and harmonic than a melody per se.
- The marginally more tuneful Conspiracy is so understated in its deployment that one could easily miss its presence. Furthermore, its melodic basis ($\hat{3}$-$\hat{4}$-$\hat{3}$-$\hat{2}$-$\hat{3}$-$\hat{1}$ in minor) is derived from the love theme's A-phrase, down to the characteristic triplet.

With all its leitmotivic energy thus pointing to Anakin and Padmé, the *Attack of the Clones* score boasts a level of motivic integration that is both consistently applied and powerfully goal-directed. And naturally, that goal is a complete utterance of the grand new theme. But in the spirit of romantic yearning, that musical telos does not arrive until the last possible moment, when the credits start to roll. Deferred consummation is elevated to a soundtrack-defining ethos. All statements, allusions, and transformations of the love theme that take place before the end are unfulfilled, rendered inconclusive through a variety of musical means. In this specific respect, the Episode II score is the most Wagnerian in the whole Skywalker saga.

Figure 6.10 documents every time Anakin and Padmé is teased but withheld. Three main strategies of deferral are at play, all of which are structural rather than rhetorical, involving the core melodic identity of the theme rather than its outward garb. (Though needless to say, Williams reinforces their dissatisfying effect through orchestration, dynamics, and articulation.) *Fragmentation*, already detailed in Chapter 4 as a widespread microtransformational procedure throughout the series, is straightforward: only the incipit or some other small segment of the theme is heard and, often as not, subsequently spun out in a sequence. More refined is *motivic seeding*. The version of this technique active in Episode II is specifically used to the effect of adumbration, involving athematic passages that inconspicuously prefigure melodic aspects of the "Across the Stars." Finally, with *cadence-cancelling*, the theme proper is started only to conclude without a satisfying element of tonal resolution, generally by pulling back from an anticipated authentic cadence. This may take several forms, from ending on a dissonant final chord ("Meadow Picnic") or unstable bass note ("Lunch and the Younglings"), to the more involved failure staged in "First Kiss," with its thrice-denied cadences, first by silence, then by eschewal of functional dominant, then by tonal modulation and melodic dissolution. Importantly, the ability to cancel a cadence requires that an expectation for cadential resolution is built up beforehand; this is possible thanks to the fact that Anakin

Cue	Time	Strategy
"Thwarted Attempt"	6:53	Seeding
"Meeting of Anakin & Padmé"	7:16	Seeding
	8:05	Seeding
"Palpatine's Plotting"	27:20	Seeding (tracked from 1:11:40)
	29:08	Cadence Cancelling
"Departure"	29:59	Seeding
	31:16	Seeding
"Lunch and the Younglings"	35:41	Cadence Cancelling
	36:32	Seeding
	38:21	Cadence Cancelling
"First Kiss"	45:10	Cadence Cancelling, Fragmentation
"Meadow Picnic"	49:27	Cadence Cancelling
"Fireside Chat"	54:00	Cadence Cancelling
	54:31	Fragmentation
[Pensive Anakin scene]	59:23	Seeding (tracked from 1:27:39)
"Jango's Escape"	1:03:15	Seeding
"Return to Tatooine"	1:11:40	Seeding
"Carrying Mother Home"	1:23:19	Fragmentation
"Anakin Changes"	1:24:12	Fragmentation/Sequencing
"Smee's [sic] Funeral"	1:27:39	Seeding
[Conveyor belt sequence] (tracked from various cues)	1:36:51	Fragmentation
	1:38:14	Cadence Cancelling/Sequencing
	1:38:28	Fragmentation
"Love Pledge"	1:42:58	Cadence Cancelling
"Entrance of the Monsters"	1:49:06	Fragmentation
"Padmé Falls"	2:03:35	Cadence Cancelling/Sequencing
	(cut)	Fragmentation
"Dooku vs. Obi-Wan"	2:05:55	Fragmentation/Sequencing
"Finale"	2:14:19	Seeding
	2:14:48	Telos

Figure 6.10 Instances and denial strategies for ANAKIN AND PADMÉ in *Attack of the Clones*

AND PADMÉ is such a resolutely grammatical theme in the first place, and conveys that four-square lyricism—and its lack—in often big, multi-part musical paragraphs. It is, in other words, a hopelessly hypotactic theme trying to find its way in a paratactic world of underscore.

Sensibly, the seeding technique occurs most often in the first act of the film. Figure 6.11 presents a handful of early adumbrations, highlighting in each ANAKIN AND PADMÉ's unmistakable motivic fingerprint: a minor-third filling triplet, followed by a descending duplet placed a small interval

Figure 6.11 Seedings of ANAKIN AND PADMÉ in four early cues from Episode II. **a.** "Thwarted Attempt" (1m3, 6:53); **b.** "Meeting of Anakin and Padmé" (1m4, 8:05); **c.** "Departure" (2m3, 29:59); **d.** "Lunch and the Younglings" (2m6, 36:32)

higher. These four segments serve dissimilar formal functions (initiating, medial, concluding) and span a range of tonal idioms (pantriadic, modal, functionally diatonic), while all help prefigure the melodic essentials of the love theme. The chronological first instance (6.11a) is a cue-closing flourish, matching a wipe from one location on Coruscant to another. The second (6.11b) constitutes a set piece theme, situated right in the middle of a cue; the love-theme fingerprint is heard after some comical music for Jar Jar and immediately before the film's (sole!) new statement of ANAKIN's theme. The third span (6.11c) is the beginning of a cue that depicts the lovers' departure. And the fourth (6.11d) consists of a slyly concealed variant on the antecedent phrase of the love theme, veiled by an atypical planing texture and a few rhythmic displacements.

Of these adumbrations, the third owes some of its motivic saliency to coming closely on the heels of the first *literal* statement of the ANAKIN AND PADMÉ theme one scene prior. Shown in reduction in Figure 6.12, this rendition is characteristic in the way it offers the first four bars of the leitmotif in near-definitive form. The only unusual feature is a pair of augmented sixth chords, subsequently purged from the theme's harmonic vocabulary in favor

Figure 6.12 First explicit statement of Anakin and Padmé in "Palpatine's Plotting" (AOTC, 2m2, 28:57)

of straight diatonicism in later statements. More typical is the manner in which the theme simply wanders off in its sixth measure. Williams forgoes what will eventually become its consequent phrase and instead lets the oboe twirl around the motivic triplet figure before closing (but not cadencing!) in the key of the minor dominant, rather than tonic. In retrospect, this lack of closure was foreshadowed a few measures earlier, with the four-bar progression that precedes the oboe's annunciation of the Anakin and Padmé theme. The passage comprises a span of *Tristan*-esque chromatic angst that basically forecloses any chance this tragic love theme will have an affectively auspicious start after its initial utterance. (Another nice detail: immediately before that $D^{7(\sharp 5)}$ chord comes one of the more camouflaged uses of "The Imperial March" in the entire saga.)

Anakin and Padmé's theme persists in this inhibited state for the remainder of the film, carefully developed but never quite actualized. Some variants are joyful and idyllic, yet still dissolve into uncertainty, like the sunny statement in "Meadow Picnic." Others are tentative ("Yoda and the Younglings"), restless ("Entrance of the Monsters," "Dooku versus Obi-Wan"), or downright agonized ("Padmé Falls"). One statement, played

1:42:50	1:43:01		1:43:29		1:43:52	1:44:04	1:44:17		1:44:41 …
athematic	ANAKIN AND PADMÉ								athematic
	A-section		B-section		A-section	B-section	A-section		
---	Dm	Dm	→V/Gm	→V/Cm	Cm	→V/Fm	Fm	→v/Fm	---
timp, vc	vn	ob	vc	vn	fl, hpsc	vn	tutti	tutti	marimba

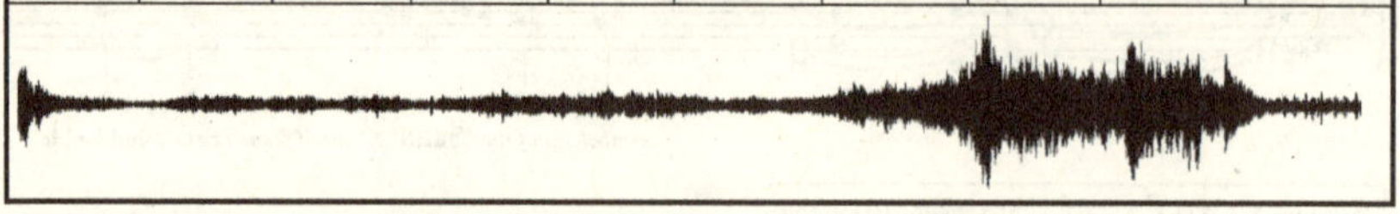

Figure 6.13 Form of love pledge from "Entrance of the Monsters" (AOTC, 6m2, 1:42:50–1:45:40)

tenderly by electric piano during Anakin and Padmé's fireside chat, is for once tonally closed; but Williams cadences only weakly on the tonic via a ♭II→i[6] modal progression. And here again, musical surroundings cloud the theme's prospects of happiness—a small component is detached and spun into unmarked underscore, suggestive of the Dies Irae.

The fullest statement of ANAKIN AND PADMÉ is the love pledge that immediately precedes the "Entrance of the Monsters," where it serves as overture to that cue's abandoned theme and variations set. In almost every respect, this is the score's climax—the moment of attainment for a theme that requires ample space to breathe, an opportunity for pure lyric flight heard few places else in the saga. Figure 6.13 offers a schematic representation of the sequence. A waveform is included to illustrate the enormous crescendo that powers this melodramatic cue.

As the lovers, soon to be carted off to their execution, confess their love, Williams begins unfurling their ill-destined *canzone d'amore*. ANAKIN AND PADMÉ begins meekly at first, with quiet strings followed by a vulnerable solo oboe. From there, we hear the first extended rendition of the theme's modulating B-section in cellos, and afterward another, more assured wind-and-strings paragraph. Everything builds to the full-orchestra pronouncement of the theme, which comes on the heels of a massively telegraphed half-cadence. The couple kisses, the camera moves from a dark interior space to the blinding orange light of the arena exterior, and their love theme cries out in full tragic grandeur. This is the longest paragraph of foursquare melody in the movie, and maybe the most purely hypotactic—hierarchical, cadence-driven, and (almost) entirely uninterrupted—in the whole saga besides Episode IV's THRONE ROOM.

Alas, *even this* statement in "Love Pledge" cannot be allowed to stand as a 100% realized thematic arrival. Like so many other efforts before, the theme collapses in its final bars, on a now accustomed rug-pull of a chord, an inverted minor dominant. Their romantic actualization stymied again, the lovers cede musical territory to the music of the enemy. We hear a passage of insectoid percussion and BRUTE tetrachords $[E_3\text{-}G_3\text{-}C_4\text{-}E\flat_4]$, the kind Williams favors for savage beasts and grim situations. Those scuttling sonorities lay sonic groundwork for the ARENA MARCH, and then the lovers are off to face their next trial.

Simultaneous rhetorical and structural closure for this luckless theme is achieved, at long last, in *Attack of the Clones*' final shot: Anakin and Padmé, just wed in secret, gazing off at the sun setting over an idyllic vista. The whole 126-measure finale that builds to this scene is among the series' best, its only competitor in terms of mythic splendor being *Empire*. Williams scores the pair's covert nuptials with a redo of sorts of the Love Pledge, presenting a non-modulating version of the love theme in full, A- and B-sections both. Unlike the prior closest attempt, this time ANAKIN AND PADMÉ does secure a resolution, unquestionably so, pictured in Figure 6.14.

The love theme's consequent phrase stretches to accommodate an extended cadential progression. Its final measure is swollen by six beats, allowing Williams to hammer home a protracted (and for once uninverted) dominant. This supercharged cadence discharges, and with it an entire film's worth of pent-up angst, onto the E♭ major that commences the End Credits. Closure for ANAKIN AND PADMÉ happens at a formal hinge, between the events of the movie and the extra-diegetic space of the credits; this makes for an uncommonly satisfying, indeed operatic, feeling of achievement. It

Figure 6.14 Final cadence in *Attack of the Clones* "Finale" (AOTC, 7m3, 2:15:38)

also bodes badly for the lovers, that their harmonic consummation did not happen *within* their story but in a sense was imposed by an outside force, the unbending need for textual closure. No subsequent iteration of "Across the Stars" is allowed to even hint at a happy ending. Not the conclusion of *Attack of the Clones*' End Credits, where the love theme yields, uncannily, to ANAKIN's and then VADER's theme. Nor *Revenge of the Sith*, where its every utterance is rhetorically bleak, structurally unresolved, or both. Nor any of its numerous concert arrangements, each one bleaker than the last. In this musical tale of woe, one single, fleeting perfect cadence is all the lovers will ever enjoy.

Teleological Genesis in *The Last Jedi*

Forced Nostalgia

No discussion of thematic arcs in *Star Wars* could leave out the remarkable journeys taken by a handful of leitmotifs in *The Last Jedi*. All the major ideas introduced in *The Force Awakens* (REY, KYLO, POE, RESISTANCE) undergo development, facing an assortment of musical conflicts and tough truths that, by film's end, leave them far from where they began. However, this evolutionary energy cannot be said to affect themes born *before* the Sequels, some of which sound more fixed than ever. *The Last Jedi* exemplifies both the best and most frustrating aspects of Williams's more self-referential idiom in the Sequel Trilogy. In terms of sheer density of thematic references, Episode VIII stands as the series' high-water mark. The score hosts twenty-nine independent leitmotifs, and over 250 leitmotivic instances, with some cues ("Revisiting Snoke," "Lesson Two") entering a Wagnerian state of endless melody, dense with meaning, memory, and psychological insight. Some of the athematic music is among the trilogy's most impressive too. Set pieces both big ("The Fathiers," "The Spark") and small ("Learning the Force," "The Mirror Scene") outdo analogous cues from *The Force Awakens* in terms of musical interest and show Williams swinging for the fences in terms of emotional impact and compositional audacity.

At the same time, many individual moments of melodic identification are rather *unsymphonic* by the series' standards, and Williams sounds much more hemmed in than before. Overzealous temp tracking is partially to blame. Director Rian Johnson was upfront about temping the movie entirely with other *Star Wars* music, maximizing a practice established in Episode VII.[32] The extent to which Williams felt obligated to this temp track is hard to prove in specific instances, but the original music he penned was clearly influenced by Johnson's attitude of extreme self-referentiality.[33] There are positive upshots to this approach: revisiting some long-neglected materials, for example, most notably the LUKE AND LEIA theme, heard during the siblings' reunion on Crait [2:07:37]. Episode VIII is as richly enmeshed within the Skywalker Saga's musical lore as possible, but the cost of such reflexivity is a kind of solipsism, weighted in favor of mention over use, too often insisting to the listener: "remember, this is *Star Wars*!" This is nostalgia for its own sake, and it quickly reaches a point of emotional diminishing returns. Ironically, *The Last Jedi* is both the most self-critically written screenplay of the Saga films and, at times, the most uncritical in its scoring.[34]

As noted in Chapter 4, the FORCE theme's treatment in Episode VIII is one reason that a *zero alteration* category of thematic transformation is warranted. Leaning on this leitmotif in *The Last Jedi* is justifiable on a purely narratival level: no Skywalker-saga film since *Empire* includes such a deep meditation on the nature of the Force. Yet the ubiquity of the melody ends up sapping the mythic potency of what ought to be the saga's most important musical icon. Williams deploys the FORCE theme liberally, always at the most semantically obvious of junctures, and with an uncharacteristic lack of substantive variation in many of the theme's thirty iterations. Granted, those few times where the theme is genuinely transfigured are some of the most arresting moments in the Sequel Trilogy: these include the uncommonly defeated statement at the end of the Battle of D'Qar [11:40]; the contrapuntal overlaying with KYLO REN in "Luke in the Falcon" [33:45]; the hair-raising chromatic sequence in "The Last Jedi" [2:16:10]. Yet the majority of instances are more forced, citations that end up turning what should be a leitmotivic special event into something perfunctory, or worse, irritating. We are a long way from the refreshing new angles on the theme in *Revenge of the Sith*, or the promises of reconfiguration in *The Force Awakens*—to say nothing of the surprising flux of form and meaning from the original *A New Hope* score!

There is, however, one boon that results from the overreliance on the FORCE in *The Last Jedi*: drawing attention to connections it has with *other* themes. In terms of macro-transformational techniques, *zero alteration* with one theme facilitates *family resemblance* when it comes to others. Consider the statement of "The March of the Resistance" that concludes "Admiral

Figure 6.15 Family resemblances between Force, Resistance, and Rose

Holdo" [36:32], a mournful cue that elegizes the fallen rebels and their incapacitated leader, General Leia Organa. Figure 6.15 compares both themes, along with Rose's motif, to be discussed shortly. The Resistance march's incipit shares with the Force its opening leap and initial stepwise ascent ($\hat{5}$-$\hat{1}$-$\hat{2}$-$\hat{3}$) exactly. The triplet turn that follows in each ($\hat{3}$-$\hat{2}$-$\hat{3}$ versus $\hat{3}$-$\hat{4}$-$\hat{3}$) is a structurally comparable, if mirror-inverted, neighbor figure.

Prior to "Admiral Holdo," Williams's arrangements of the Resistance March tended to obscure its latent equivalencies with the Force. Here, by contrast, the theme is presented in such a way that highlights the semblance. This is achieved by situating the leitmotif in a field of Force parameters: orchestration (French horn in its mellow middle register); tempo (a slow, flexible 60–75 bpm); rhythm (altering Resistance's usual sixteenths for triplets); and harmonization (a descending bass that facilitates the leitharmonic i→VI). The equivalence is not absolute, though, and one aspect that is pure Resistance shines through after a few bars—its tendency to modulate up a fifth, a surprisingly pervasive tonal schema in Episode VIII's score.[35]

All three new leitmotifs in *The Last Jedi*—Rose, Luke in Exile, and Desperation—resonate with the Force. Of them, the chilly and Sibelian theme for Luke in Exile is least directly affiliated with the Force, its melodic language sounding more immediately (and aptly) redolent of Jedi Steps and Rey's melodic identifications. Those leitmotifs do have explicitly rendered linkages with the Force theme, making Luke in Exile's connection strong but secondhand. Deeper, and perhaps more surprising, is a sympathetic vibration with Rose's theme. The most prominent and well-developed new idea in the *Last Jedi*, Rose begins with a note-for-note conversion of the Force's opening idea, $\hat{5}$-$\hat{1}$-$\hat{2}$-$\hat{3}$-$\hat{4}$-$\hat{3}$, into the major mode. Unlike the Resistance in "Admiral Holdo," there is never any mistaking this for anything other than an autonomous theme. The six-note succession is metrically displaced and modally flipped relative to the Force and is followed with a strongly individuating chromatic continuation. Nevertheless, it is a theme that seems like a natural extension of lydian-lightened variants of the Force in *Empire* and *The Force Awakens*. This musical linkage with Rose Tico—an unassuming but morally clear-sighted mechanic, *not* a Jedi—accords with the film's democratizing, egalitarian view of the Force.

Desperate Measures

The most dramatic point of contact with the Force in *The Last Jedi* is with the Desperation theme. But to appreciate this contribution, we must step back and consider first a far less prominent particle: the Tension pitch pattern. First heard in *The Force Awakens*, Tension spends its time in Episode VIII growing in both length and importance, culminating in the arrival of Desperation as a bona fide leitmotif. Both source and destination are shown in Figure 6.16. The former is depicted as an unmeasured five-note embryo, the latter a fully fledged adult. Between the two lies a true musical arc, of growth from humble beginnings, through intermediary stages of striving and conflict, and toward an apotheosis.

The impact of the fully assembled Desperation depends on the innocuous nature of its original germ. Prior to *The Last Jedi*, Tension could

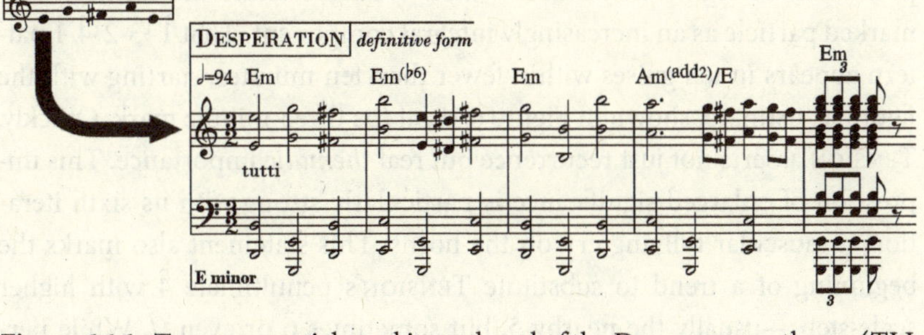

Figure 6.16 Tension particle and its end goal of the Desperation theme (TLJ, 7m67a, 1:51:36)

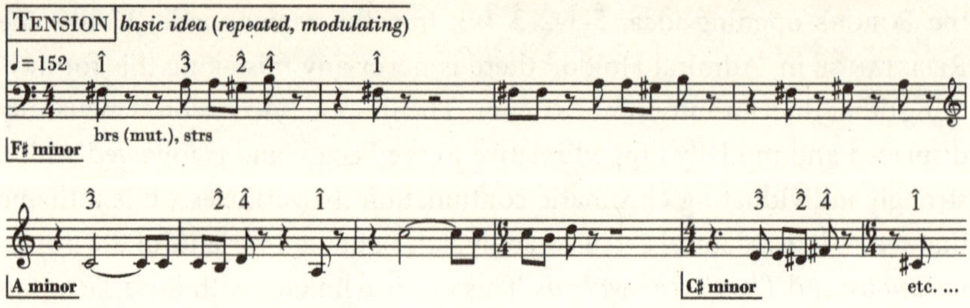

Figure 6.17 TENSION in "On The Inside" (TFA, 7m62A, 1:43:08)

hardly even be considered an incidental motif, appearing a half-dozen times in Episode VII's written score, and not once on the commercial soundtrack album. Granted, some themes with even fewer iterations cast a long leitmotivic shadow, LUKE AND LEIA in *Return of the Jedi* being a prime example. What TENSION lacks in *The Force Awakens* is melodic definiteness or semantic saliency. It is neither a memorable nor a characteristic musical idea, more a generic agitato based on a repeatable $\hat{1}$-$\flat\hat{3}$-$\hat{2}$-$\hat{4}$-$\hat{1}$ pattern—a favorite "meta-motif" in Williams's idiolect since the mid-1990s.[36] Figure 6.17 displays the clearest instance, from the cue "On the Inside." This statement is typical of the way TENSION is deployed in these early settings: syncopated, non-lyrical, basically a little minor-mode time-killer that phases imperceptibly in and out of other, more marked, material. One small feature that is noteworthy, though, is its tendency to modulate chromatically. As usual in *Star Wars*, the exact keys (here F#, A, and C# minor) matter less than the relationship between them: in this case a transposition up by minor and major third, respectively.

Immediately in the first scene in *The Last Jedi*, Williams aims a thematic spotlight on the TENSION motif. The opening Battle of D'Qar consists of a patchwork of eight cues, across which Williams treats the formerly unmarked particle as an increasingly integral component. That $\hat{1}$-$\flat\hat{3}$-$\hat{2}$-$\hat{4}$-$\hat{1}$ pattern appears in ten guises within fewer than ten minutes, starting with the figure-as-ostinato, shown in Figure 6.18, at the three-minute mark. Quickly, TENSION asserts not just recurrence but real *thematic* importance. This impression of enlarged significance is particularly strong with its sixth iteration, a muscular rallying cry on the horns. This statement also marks the beginning of a trend to substitute TENSION's penultimate $\hat{4}$ with higher scale-steps—usually the nearby $\hat{5}$, but sometimes $\hat{6}$ or even $\natural\hat{7}$. While perhaps an indication of the schema's ill-definedness, the widening of TENSION's

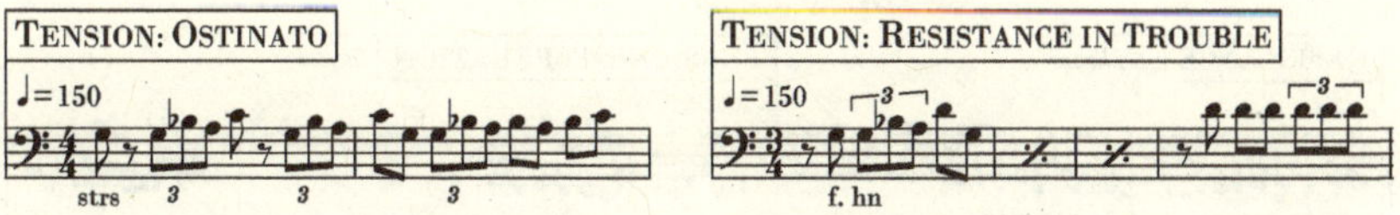

Figure 6.18 Two representative forms of TENSION (TLJ 1m3 and 1m6, 3:05, 8:36)

contour helps differentiate the new form from its cousins. Insofar as it recurs in this specific guise in two subsequent battles [28:30 and 2:02:05], the horn motif warrants a sub-thematic label, TENSION: RESISTANCE IN TROUBLE, also in Figure 6.18.

Over the course of *The Last Jedi*, the five-note idea becomes a veritable red thread, leading through multiple locations and side plots, now expanding, now shrinking back down, rarely absent from the soundtrack for more than a minute or two. Amazingly, the TENSION pattern is heard on forty occasions in Episode VIII, more often than any other thematic strand in the film—or any Saga film in general, excepting the forty-odd statements of "The Imperial March" in *Empire*.

What happens to TENSION has the hallmarks of Schoenbergian developing variation. The deeper into the score one listens, the more its variants sound goal-directed, until it becomes a soundtrack-defining powerhouse. In light of the cell's teleological quest, it may be more appropriate to designate the second motif in Figure 6.18 something like TENSION-EN-ROUTE-TO-DESPERATION. This pupating leitmotif does not attach right away to moments of heightened symbolic import like other well-known themes. Instead, it appears at first content to stay nestled in its cocoon, coloring the action without drawing too much attention to itself. Many of its statements arise as bridges between established themes, or as part of inconspicuous accompaniment that underscores them. The balance does change as the movie goes on, though. As pressure from dramatic circumstances ramps up—musically conveyed by interaction with other leitmotifs—DESPERATION is pushed closer and closer to its telic state.

One of the themes that TENSION-en-route-to-DESPERATION encounters, and in the process absorbs musical qualities from, is the RESISTANCE march. The thematic dialectic is on display in "We Need a New Base" and "Prep for Battle" (together folded into the track "The Supremacy" on the soundtrack album). These two cues are part of a complex that accompanies a devastating surprise attack on the Resistance fleet [26:43–29:14]. As the situation for the heroes goes from bad to worse, Williams starts spinning through a set of

Figure 6.19 Tension-en-route-to-Desperation in "Prep for Battle" (TLJ, 2m13, 28:14)

Tension variants—first *grave*, then *deciso*, and finally *martellato*. These figures trade off with the Resistance and, as the cue nears fever pitch, the Kylo Ren leitmotif.

Within this frenetic context, Tension starts taking on structural parameters of the Resistance theme. The busy passage in Figure 6.19, heard as Kylo Ren launches a surprise attack, highlights some of these cross-thematic resonances. Repeated upward neighbor figurations and space-filling scales, once the gestural domain of the Resistance, now mark Tension-en-route-to-Desperation. So too does the former's tendency reach for $\hat{5}$ (recall this change was already happening in the Battle of D'Qar), and to modulate continually up by fifth. Those iterated tonal vaults—B to F♯, then F to C to G to A—are unaccustomed for the third-favoring Tension but typical of the Resistance march. The score, like our heroes, feels caught off guard here, forced to devise a counterattack plan on the fly, and it is far from a perfect one. Like a two-voice fugal exposition that keeps forgetting to head back to its starting key, the passage gathers momentum without a tonal goal in sight, and scant hope of returning home.

What Themes Grow Beyond

The gestating Desperation theme assumes true *leitmotivic* weight in a cue called "Ladies Parting," reduced in its entirety in Figure 6.20. Williams

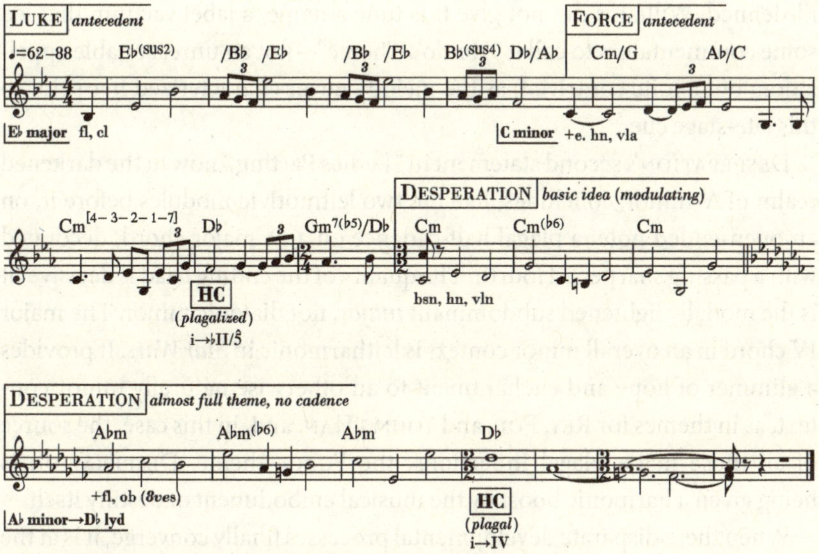

Figure 6.20 "Ladies Parting" (TLJ, 6m57, 1:36:15)

accompanies this sentimental scene through a simple chain of three themes with no interstitial material. First is a tentative statement of the LUKE theme in E♭, heard as Admiral Holdo informs Leia that she intends to go down with the Resistance ship. A graceful pivot-chord modulation (♭VII/E♭ = ♭II/Cm) ushers in a rendition of the FORCE, ending similarly on a modal half-cadence (♭II→$\text{v}^{\text{ø}4}_{3}$/Cm), now swelling in volume and poignancy. There can be no doubt: a big musical arrival is being telegraphed. But where might this cue be going, that the two most iconic themes of the saga seem to be serving as prefatory for something more momentous?

With a cut to resistance ships blasting off, Williams provides his musical answer. All that half-cadential anticipation discharges onto a twofold statement of the DESPERATION theme in its maturing—if not yet fully autonomous—form. Broad in outline and measured in pace where TENSION was clipped and syncopated, the melody has at last broken free from its intervallic predecessor. As in prior cases of emerging themes, its leitmotivic status is sanctioned by coming on the heels of one of the other "big" themes of the series, or in this case two of them. Still, DESPERATION has a bit more story to tell before achieving its true telos. The theme lingers still in another motif's shadow: not TENSION at this juncture, from which it is actively *dis*sociating itself, but the FORCE. And, perhaps as a result, its semantic target remains ill-defined. Williams did not give this tune a name, a label vacuum that led some commentators to call it "Holdo's Theme"—not an unreasonable appellation, but a mite contrived, as the melody never characterized her prior to this late-stage cue.[37]

DESPERATION's second statement in "Ladies Parting," now in the darkened realm of A♭ minor, concludes, like the two leitmotivic modules before it, on an open-ended note: a plagal half-cadence on a D♭ major chord, decorated with a passing sharpened fourth. The quality of the ending triad is decisive: it is the modally lightened subdominant *major*, not diatonic minor. The major IV chord in an overall minor context is leitharmonic in *Star Wars*. It provides a glimmer of hope and enchantment to an otherwise naturally minor context, as in themes for REY, POE, and YOUNG HAN, and, in this case, the source of all those major-plagal inflections: the FORCE theme. DESPERATION is being given a harmonic boost by the musical embodiment of destiny itself.

When these disparate developmental processes finally converge, it is at the moment of highest narrative urgency in the movie, with three intercut plot threads involving Rey/Ren, Finn/Rose, and Poe/Leia/Holdo all converging in climactic fashion. Williams dryly titled the cue "Important Scene." DESPERATION is the focal point throughout, standing now on its own—uninterrupted and unchallenged, grammatically coherent as a melody and no longer dependent on a semiotic assist from other themes.

Figure 6.21 charts the form of this very "Important Scene." Where prior statements of DESPERATION had a tendency to liquidate back into unmarked underscore, Williams now goes to pains to fortify the theme's long-telegraphed autonomy. Notable is the presence of a genuine melodic conclusion for the first time: an ear-catching hook in the theme's fourth measure. DESPERATION is given the breathing room needed to grow and change *within* its own musical span, sequencing and expanding in texture in such a way that maximizes its intensificatory potential. No longer proceeding by rote transposition, like in "Prep for Battle," there is now a microcosmic "theme-and-variations" script at play, and with it a mini-narrative of struggle and overcoming. After an annunciatory fanfare and roiling ostinato (based, tellingly, on the TENSION pattern), three modules based on DESPERATION are heard in succession, first in A, then C, and finally E minor. This constitutes a neat replication of the third-stacking sequence of its progenitor, way back in *The Force Awakens*. In addition to different tonal footing, each rendition has different orchestration, rhythmic support, and bass counterpoint.

1:51:00 1:51:11 1:51:14 1:51:22 1:51:26 1:51:36 1:51:43 1:51:50 1:52:00

1		2		3	4		--
TENSION		DESPERATION		DESPERATION	DESPERATION		SILENCE!!!
fanfare and buildup	vamp	theme	vamp	theme	theme	hammer-blows, horn rip	--
Am		Am		C♯m	Em		--
tpt → tbn		f. hn → tbn		tpt	tutti		--
Rebels race away, Poe gets Holdo's plan, she sets course		Holdo ship reverses, Hux gets her plan, orders fire		Rey and Ren vie for lightsaber, Holdo shows resolve	Rey+Ren struggle, Finn+ Rose on chopping block, Holdo cranks hyperdrive, lightsaber shatters		Hyperspace!! First Order obliterated!

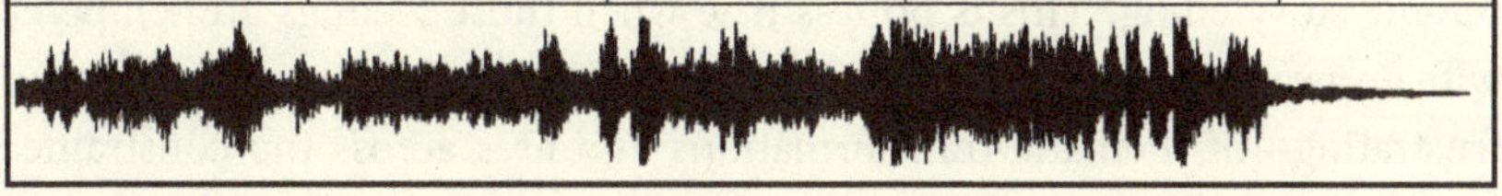

Figure 6.21 Form of "Important Scene" (TLJ, 7m67, 1:51:00–1:52:00)

Even the absence of music contributes to the impact of this leitmotivic apogee. The cue's final flourish is followed by near-total silence—not just in the score, but sound effects and dialogue too, all of which recede, save for a quiet bass rumble. Figure 6.21 retains a representation of this sonic negative space, to emphasize how silence serves a musical purpose in its own right. The auditory gambit here is as unprecedented in the saga as Holdo's hyperspace ramming maneuver. It is hard to imagine Williams's preceding music being set in higher relief.

It is in this way that "Important Scene" witnesses the apotheosis of a true, grammatically coherent theme, the endpoint of a score-spanning story of musical suggestion, differentiation, and eventual actualization. After its genesis, what future developments of the DESPERATION leitmotif are in store? Very little, it turns out. Like the wreckage left of First Order fleet, the theme fragments and recedes into the dark for the remaining thirty minutes of the film. The cue that follows the Holdo Maneuver, "After the Big Explosion" [1:52:13], offers a few echoes of declining distinctiveness of DESPERATION for Finn and Rose's travails on the now deteriorating Star Destroyer. But by the time its contours are heard last, in the guise of a faintly similar trumpet phrase [1:52:58], it is as a mere lead-in to a big statement of the REBEL FANFARE to match BB8's heroics. What was briefly a theme of unquestionable dramatic and musical salience has retreated back into the unmarked underscore whence it came. Or, as Yoda might say, the leitmotif's destiny has been fulfilled, and now it may rest.[38]

⁂

Thematic arcs of all sizes are present in *Star Wars*, even if they rarely follow the perfect, unimpeded trajectories available to absolute music or imagined by idealists like Arnold Schoenberg. The skill and creativity with which Williams develops his materials across the Saga are on abundant display in musical narratives such as traced in Episodes VI, II, and VIII. These macro-transformative feats offer a source of delight and even awe, and one need not be a deep textual diver to experience the emotional power of their symphonic storytelling. This is no less true when those feelings are tempered with an awareness of the limitations—sometimes productive, sometimes just frustrating—of thematic transformations and arcs across the constrained canvases of film.

We move now to musical storytelling in a different register. The kind where matters of great thematic significance transpire in the past tense. Where the score hovers between passive commentator and active agent in the plot. Where repetition and summation lead to profound change and new beginnings. It is time to consider musical narration.

7
Epic Storytelling

Keeping Mythic Distance

Like all good myths, the Skywalker Saga films begin with an invocation of distance: "A long time ago," the all-knowing expositor silently announces, "in a galaxy far, far away." These ten blue words conjure a past, one not just chronologically remote but fundamentally apart from our everyday experience. It is what the philosopher and literary theorist Mikhail Bakhtin calls the "absolute past"—"absolute" in the sense that it is a realm closed off to us.[1] Inaccessible. Frozen. Impossible. The yellow film title bursts out of this primeval state, and with it, a colossal major chord, as though the resonant frequency of the *Star Wars* cosmos has been struck. On its heels flows the scroll of expositional text, recounting those events that lead up to each installment, easing the filmgoer into a plot ever *in medias res*. And with this crawl, always, comes the "Main Theme." Whether its semantic association with Luke is yet to be made or firmly in mind or forgotten, the theme's expressive role is never less than clear: it is our musical invitation into the absolute past.

It is hard to defamiliarize such a cultural touchstone. Part of the impact of the opening of *Star Wars* stems from its very entrenchment. Even for those experiencing it for the first time, hearing the "Main Title" is a kind of rehearing, a sonic conjuration of an idealized, nostalgized, and even mythologized moviegoing experience. LUKE's brassy leitmotif is an avatar of a lost musical age, one of high romance and heroism. The iconicity of John Williams's music is a matter of obligation. What it is saying in particular is not as important as the fact that it is there, right on cue, to say it—just as it always has. In other words, the "Main Title" is a ritual.

There is a strangeness to this ritual, too. For the opening of each film to posit a world so discontinuous with our own—physically, temporally, emotionally—and to couch it in a musical idiom so long out of style; that is a deliberate and charged artistic decision. The strangeness can be difficult to resolve today, given how overexposed the title crawl and its heraldic music are to most audiences. But one need not have virgin ears to appreciate that LUKE's clarion call is in a specific sense *aloof*. Not aloof in expressive register, granted—the "Main Title" is as bombastic and extroverted as film music gets. Rather, the title cue seems designed to more than summon but to prolong that "far, far away" feeling, and to do so in a way the rest of the crawl text does not. Williams's theme is all optimism and victory, a stark affective contradiction of the ever-changing, ever-dire galactic crises being spelled out on screen. Once noticed, the emotional distancing effected by this music-versus-plot discrepancy might seem discordant with the easily digestible adventure that each *Star Wars* film enacts as soon as the opening crawl fades away. The logic behind this dissonance is counterintuitive but based on a venerable principle of storytelling: for audiences to feel properly invested in the fantastical yarn soon to be spun, the narrative should go out of its way to hold them at a remove. Sight and sound collaborate in these introductory sequences to produce the distinctive tenor of epic narration, a storytelling stance that is *distancing*, *ritualistic*, *cyclical*, and *self-reflexive*—four qualities with definite musical manifestations, both within and after the opening credits. Together, these narrational qualities allow the listener to tap into that mythic mindset where everything is significant and the unattainable absolute past can be accessed.[2]

For a franchise so front-loaded with narrational legwork, the Skywalker Saga is otherwise light on moments of literal diegetic narration—something that happens throughout the Ring Cycle, for example.[3] We rarely hear the dramatis personae of *Star Wars* report on events of the past at length, as they do incessantly in Wagner's spacious operas. Nor is there a true chorus figure, someone (or something) who provides detached insight or augury. There are no in-universe fate-spinners like the Norns, no fourth wall-breaking quipsters like Loge. Once the opening crawl has scrolled by, a given *Star Wars* film barrels forward, its dramatic action dictated by the maxim of "show, don't tell." The benefits of active, enactive storytelling are many, as any screenwriter will attest. But there are tradeoffs. When events are shown, rather than told, the audience is denied a chance to imagine and interpret the narrative on their own. And, significantly, the agenda and truthfulness of the narrator—whoever or whatever we construe that to be—is far harder to subject to any kind of inflection.

Since characters take little time expositing in this series, the mythic quality must be conveyed by other means. And so most of the duties performed by epic storytellers in other genres are entrusted to nonverbal cinematic parameters: hence the preference in *Star Wars* for an objective, god's-eye view camera over first-person POV shots; the reliably monumental production design; and the editing style that routinely hurls the viewer between the farthest-flung worlds. Above all, it is music that acts as the series' Greek chorus, its *epic narrator*. Williams's score furnishes those distancing, ritualistic, cyclical, and self-reflexive qualities, often in abundance. It provides a near-constant layer of commentary. And it ties together all the plot's complex incidents through a leitmotivic network with a deep sense of memory and internal history—and, as the previous analyses have demonstrated, an amazing capacity for transformation and prophecy.

How is it that Williams is able to construct this narrational mode? The epic nature of *Star Wars*' musical underscore is most clearly revealed in those rare scenes of explicitly verbalized storytelling, either in-universe monologues or texted diegetic score. Williams's *symphonic* conception of *Star Wars*—its scope, structure, and working symbolism together—enables that special combination of mythic distance plus emotional investment so basic to the success of the series.

We can begin to unpack Williams's approach to mythic storytelling by inspecting a pair of scenes in which an old Jedi Master relates a past tragedy to their young pupil. However, getting into deeper analysis will require venturing into some subtle hermeneutic territory. The study of narrative and narration is a discourse full of esoteric disagreements and heady ideas. But if concepts like rupture, metalepsis, and would-be-diegetic music seem forbidding, take heart: if anything can serve as an explanatory aid to musical narratology, it should be the most popular movie franchise of all time.

All that theoretical legwork prepares us for the heart of this chapter, a trio of case studies: "Duel of the Fates" in *The Phantom Menace*, "Threepio's Bedtime Story" in *Return of the Jedi*, and "Palpatine's Big Pitch" in *Revenge of the Sith*. In one way or another, these sequences all sit outside the narrational norms of *Star Wars*. But their very displacement is what allows them to shed so much light, not just on weird moments of heightened epic narration, but on the series' more customary forms of through-composed leitmotivic underscore. These are scenes in which *Star Wars* tells the story of itself.

Jedi Master Narratives

From the beginning, Williams understood his role in fulfilling George Lucas's vision as that of a musical mythmaker. Reflecting in 1999 on the franchise, he remarked:

> This sequence [of films] and this lure that [Lucas] created that taps into some collective memory that we all have—which I suppose is in itself a

> kind of definition of what myth is, as distinct from history—all adds up to the effectiveness of this experience. History is what *happened*, what we know about; we know where it happened and when it happened. But myth, we're not quite sure *if* it happened, but we all understand that it probably did, but we don't know where. And this is a *Star Wars*ian kind of element, that I think explains a big portion of the why it resonates beyond just a sort of space show for people.[4]

The paradoxical combination of factual haziness and universal comprehensibility expressed here could easily have come from Bakhtin. Or, perhaps more plausibly, from the popular comparative mythologist Joseph Campbell, whom Lucas claimed as a major influence on his conception of the Skywalker saga, and Williams a source of retroactive clarification.[5] Poetical as it may sound, Williams's belief in this Campbellian well of "collective memory and cross-cultural shared history," and his role as a musical conduit for it, is neither insincere nor irrelevant to a deeper analysis of the music of the Skywalker Saga.[6]

Later in the 1999 interview, Williams invokes one of his creative guiding metaphors: a great tree whose full extent we are only ever imperfectly aware of.

> It's a fascinating and unique thing to me, the way all of these branches of the *Star Wars* tree seem to keep growing out. . . . The whole project—all the films—takes on a kind of animate, organic quality that just adds to the interest I think for all of us fortunate enough to be working on it, and also for all of the audience taking part. It's almost like a certain kind of definition of the word "community"—I mean we're all taking part in something that's going along, that's bigger than any one of us.

Although he does not liken himself to a narrator per se, Williams's language does indicate he thinks of his task in terms of *narrational* responsibilities. The composer's role is a mediator between the underlying myth and the audience. He goes on to claim the score is an indispensable "part of the storytelling mechanism that the audience receives." Music is, in effect, a community-building endeavor. Symphonic underscore provides the *Star Wars* films a needed set of "aural beacons and reference points" to help navigate the intertwining branches and dense foliage of surface incident. These beacons, which for Williams include but are not limited to leitmotivic identifications, behave in a manner similar to tools an oral storyteller might employ—literary or rhetorical devices like rhyme, refrain, or analogy that serve a mnemonic and clarifying effect. If the Skywalker Saga is a sprawling tree, then Williams, from his nondiegetic perch, is the one casting down sturdy ladders with which to climb it.

Though certainly not its only function, music in *Star Wars* can serve a role analogous to a chorus in a stage play, offering information and commentary beyond what the characters are aware of. This is particularly true of extra-diegetic pieces and paratexts, whose disconnection from the action automatically imparts a wider, more independent musical point of view—these will be the subject of Chapter 8. But within many underscore cues, especially the more discursive and musical prose-like ones, there are moments in which Williams's music tells us something more than the screenplay.

Consider, for example, the moment in *The Rise of Skywalker* when KYLO REN's theme plays as Rey tells Finn "People keep telling me they know me. I'm afraid no one does" [1:07:02]. With such an incongruous placement, the leitmotif seems to intimate a truth Rey herself has yet to grasp. The exact nature of that truth is, however, not altogether obvious; as Buhler observes, music in *Star Wars* often "seems to intuit connections that are beyond immediate rational comprehension."[7] Perhaps the music in this means to foreshadow Rey's dark side heritage, her dreadful kinship with the fallen Ben Solo. Or maybe it is telling us that it is Ren alone who really knows Rey, feels what she is going through, understands her better than she does herself. We need not ascribe these meanings to Williams himself—given the editorial jumble that is Episode IX, the motivic citation might even have been tracked from elsewhere by the music editor. There are times when the "branches of the *Star Wars* tree" are too dense and tangled to trace an easy interpretive path. However intended, knots of ambiguity like KYLO's unbidden appearance are the bread and butter of mythical narration. They open up rich avenues for personal meaning to focused listeners and provide a satisfying affect of ill-defined meaningfulness for those who prefer their *Star Wars* immersive, not subversive.

It is unusual for Williams's role as musical narrator to overlap with an instance of diegetic storytelling; as noted earlier, the Skywalker Saga is un-Wagnerian in that respect. Nevertheless, each Saga film tends to have at least one sequence where a single character talks at length, relating an occurrence in the past to another interested party. No visual effects or text inserts or flashbacks are required—the latter being foreign to the Skywalker Saga until the Sequel Trilogy in any case. Indeed, without the crutch of visualization, scenes of diegetic storytelling invariably promote audio and music to a higher status than they already occupy in the series and its progressive self-mythologization.

The way Williams-as-narrator steers the series' mythic currents is felt palpably in a pair of monologues: Obi-Wan Kenobi's narration to Luke in *A New Hope* and Luke's "Lesson Two" to Rey in *The Last Jedi.* These sequences are rhymes in Lucas's sense: both involve an aged Jedi mentor offering to their current pupil an account—a pointedly incomplete one—of the training and downfall of their previous pupil. The scenes differ on some important axes, too, most obviously length (the cue for the former is less than a minute, the latter more than three), but also emotional weight (the former is understated, the latter full of naked pathos). The biggest discrepancy concerns how these scenes fit within the larger mythopoetic project of *Star Wars*. Kenobi's narration occurs when the series was only just establishing its own mythology and thus was not as invested in self-analysis or critique. Nor was the saga supplied at that point with a rich enough leitmotivic or topical lexicon with which to conduct such an analysis musically. By contrast, Luke's tale occurs eight movies deep into the franchise, with a robustly developed legendarium and rich musical tapestry to match. In *A New Hope*, everything is new, even the past. *The Last Jedi* is by contrast saddled by the weight of what came before, and the movie knows it; Rian Johnson's screenplay persistently thematizes the ambiguity, context-dependency, and fallibility of mythic narrative. That the film ultimately affirmed the necessity of heroic mythmaking was a point lost on some viewers, though Williams certainly picked up on that thread.

The cue for Obi-Wan's monologue, "The Force," avails itself of the limited library of thematic materials Williams had on hand in 1977. The entire scene is full of expository dialogue, but the relevant portion begins with Old Ben's description of the lightsaber as an "elegant weapon from a more civilized age." Music, described synoptically in Figure 7.1, enters as soon as Luke asks about his father. A double statement of the IMPERIALS motif, muttered by clarinet in its mellow chalumeau register, accompanies Kenobi's account of the unnamed pupil who "betrayed and murdered" Luke's father. Though the IMPERIALS motif proves irrelevant beyond *A New Hope*, after which point it is upstaged by the VADER's theme, its placement in "The Force" is important. Before, the short motif was connected to a somewhat diffuse antagonistic entity—the Empire, especially as represented by anonymous Stormtroopers—rather than a strongly individuated threat. With

33:55 34:05 34:16 34:25 34:32 34:54 35:00

0	1			2	
UNSCORED	IMPERIALS			FORCE	
--	motto	athematic connective	motto	antecedent only	fade out
--	Gm	⇝	Gm	C♯m	IV/C♯m
--	cl (solo)	fl	cl	f. hn (solo)	strs
"For over a thousand generations…	"How did my father die?"	"…the Empire…"	"…He betrayed and murdered your father."	"The Force?" / "Now, the Force is what gives a Jedi his power…"	R2 beeps

Figure 7.1 Form of Obi-Wan's narration to Luke (ANH, "The Force," 4m2)

Kenobi's narration to support it, the little melody's denotation is firmly established: not a generic bad guy, but *DARTH VADER'S THEME*™.

However small a role the IMPERIALS motif ends up playing in the wider Skywalker Saga, it does some heavy semiotic lifting in this cue, and not just by focusing *A New Hope*'s musical depiction of villainy. As we have seen in several earlier thematic analyses (REVELATION, DESPERATION), new or nascent themes tend to gain entry into the category of leitmotif by being presented in close proximity and sharp contrast with more established, semantically unambiguous leitmotifs. For Obi-Wan's narration, the straightforward IMPERIALS motif serves that purpose as a kind of leitmotivic guarantor.

Up to this point in *A New Hope*, it would have made little sense to lend the memorable melody heard during the "Binary Sunset" a specific label; it was semiotically untethered, a floating receptacle of vague pregnancy. Now, more than a half-hour into the film, its mystical signified is for the first time articulated with lexical specificity. One contributor to this moment of symbolization is the formal and denotative legitimacy vouchsafed by the preceding IMPERIALS motif. The second is what happens on screen. Kenobi, responding to Luke's inquisitiveness, identifies the "Force" by name, describing it as an energy field that "binds the galaxy together." This dialogue matches the first phrase of this properly *leading* leitmotif, stated again by solo French horn. Articulated in these ways—with firm formal footing and denotative specificity—the *FORCE THEME*™ binds to its referent and begins in earnest to participate in the score's wider Wagnerian web.

Kenobi's narration serves a simple though important task of sharpening known motifs and transforming unassigned ones into "aural beacons and reference points." Luke's narration to Rey in *The Last Jedi* is more complex in its structure and aims, and it shows what can be done when a series is not just rich but weighted down by epic expectations. The collision of mythic persona and brutal reality is summed up at the end of the narration: "I failed. Because I was Luke Skywalker, Jedi Master. A legend." Williams's music, while not as withering as Mark Hamill's performance, is nevertheless fully involved—and perhaps implicated—in rendering this critique.

Figure 7.2 summarizes the shape of Luke's lesson. The cue is emblematic of Williams's underscoring style for the Sequel Trilogy: lean in orchestration, efficient in harmony, elephantine in its memory of the musical past. Of particular note is the way keys and key changes are enlisted to guide the sequence—and the way orchestration makes these relationships highly audible. Over the course of the cue, something of a triple tonic complex emerges, a trio of important and mutually reinforcing keys (B♭, F♯/G♭, and D) connected by major thirds. This alone lends "Lesson Two" a sense of medium-range tonal consistency not always observed in *Star Wars*. The high B♭-minor string chords heard at the onset of the cue, for example, are firmly linked with the near-identically scored, voiced, and harmonized sonorities during the flashback to the burning Jedi academy two minutes later. The B♭-F♯/G♭-D complex also

59:06	59:14	59:21	59:31	59:42	59:55	1:00:09	1:00:15	1:00:30
1.		**2.**	**3.**	**4.**			**5.**	
JEDI STEPS		**FORCE**	**EMPEROR + VADER**	ATHEMATIC			**HAN & LEIA**	
--	basic idea	basic idea	basic ideas	--	--	**LUKE & LEIA** (?)	antecedent (dissolving)	--
B♭m	B♭m	B♭m	F♯m↔Dm	F♯m/C♯→ Gm/B♭	Gm(♭6)	Gma7(2)	C→B♭→ G♭/B♭→	F♯m/F
wws, vln	vc	wws	f. hn	fl , e. hn	vln	f. hn (solo)	vc, f. hn	fl, e.hn
--	"Lesson two…	"…But if you strip away the myth…	"…Darth Sideous to rise…	"And a Jedi who saved him."	"For many years, there was balance.	"…to pass on my strengths…	"…Leia… trusted me…	"…I took him…

1:00:40	1:00:49	1:00:55	1:01:25	1:01:35	1:01:50	1:02:00
6.				**7.**	**8.**	
ATHEMATIC				ATHEMATIC → **KYLO**	**REY**	
build-up	stinger	elegy (**PATHOS**?)	chorale	discursive, basic idea	antecedent + segue	
D7(♭6)	atonal	⟿B♭m$^{(5\text{–}\sharp 4)}$/F→ F♯m/C♯→B♭m(sus2)	B♭m(sus2)→ F♯m/C♯→Dm	Dm [i(sus2,4)→iv^{6}]	Dm [i→v^{6}→VI$^{(\sharp 4)}$]	
wws	tutti	strs	low wws, brs	fl (solo), cl (solo)	f. hn	
"I went to confront him."	"No!"	"He must have thought I was dead...	"…Jedi Master. A legend."	"The galaxy may need a legend...	…And you didn't fail Kylo Ren. Kylo Ren failed you."	

Figure 7.2 Form of Luke's narration to Rey (TLJ, "Lesson Two," 4m36)

undergirds some malignant local chord progressions. The most striking is a downward hexatonic chain (B♭m^{sus2}→F♯m/A→Dm) in low reeds and brass, heard when Luke bitterly refers to himself as a "legend"; this heart-sinking chord cycle is actually an iterated application of Vader's signature chord progression. Although the cue's conclusion does not break the dismal tonal cycle per se, there is a hint at the possibility of redemptive change. Rey's motif disperses some of the cue's overall bleakness in the shift to her own key of D natural minor, and the erstwhile inky darkness of B♭ minor is now integrated into a phrase-ending ♭VI$^{\sharp 4}$ chord. The effect is bittersweet, but bright-eyed.

Williams moves fluidly between athematic and leitmotivic modules in "Lesson Two," with the former taking on some of the heaviest dramatic beats in the scene. (We saw something similar with "Revisiting Snoke" in Chapter 3.) The midpoint of the cue corresponds to a flashback, when the audience witnesses how Luke remembers Ben Solo's betrayal. It is the first of three *Rashomon*-esque renderings of this incident from *Star Wars* past, and here it is set with an atonal stinger chord, raw and impersonal.[8] Meanwhile, those leitmotifs Williams does incorporate are treated in subtle and psychologically insightful ways—a far cry from the perfunctory citations audible elsewhere in *The Last Jedi*. Most narratively straightforward is the quiet rendition of Jedi Steps, which inaugurates the cue and serves as a summons to learn at the foot of a master. The motif also furnishes a pair of secondary parameters—the key of B♭ minor and a high string texture—that serve an associative function throughout.

The Force theme rendition that follows is standard issue at first, invoked with Luke's allusion to the Jedi Knights of old, just like it was for Kenobi in *A New Hope*. But it has the interesting property of being formally cut off—and quickly. Luke's description of the "romanticized, deified" Jedi Knights is laced with resentment. In his mind, their legacy was "one of failure," and their leitmotivic insignia itself fails to get past its initial two-bar basic idea. The Force, presumed to represent an unalloyed good in almost all other cases, cedes immediately to a weird amalgam of the Emperor and Vader motifs, combining the melodic contour of the former and chord progression of the latter. The thematic crossbreed sounds as Luke recounts the ease with which Darth Sidious undercut the vulnerable and hubristic Jedi; as with the Force, this hateful hybrid is as much a reflection of Skywalker's view of the purported heroes of the Old Republic as it is their nemeses, the Sith.

While the narrational perspective shifts throughout "Lesson Two," two modules within it specifically focalize Rey and Luke's subjectivities. The cue assumes the former's perspective is at its end, with REY's stoic leitmotif emerging from the foregoing musical ordeal as an expression of determination and moral surety. Luke's tormented psyche, on the other hand, is articulated musically when the subject of Ben Solo comes up, which occasions what might be the saddest variant of the HAN AND LEIA theme in the whole saga. The pain in Hamill's voice, the difficulty he even has in forming the words "but Leia . . . trusted me with her son," is mirrored in Williams's underscore. A love theme for a murdered best friend and estranged sister, once bursting with promise, now sags with pity and regret. The melody loses its grip on its C-major tonic almost immediately with an unprecedented shift to B♭, and from there, submits itself to a desperately alienated chord pair of G♭ and E♭m^{sus4}.

In addition to the more conspicuous references, "Luke and Rey" is also populated by more oblique thematic suggestions. One is purely backward looking. The string elegy heard when Luke relives his discovery of the burning Jedi temple recalls a twice-stated threnody from *The Force Awakens*: the PATHOS theme. In Episode VII, this material was deployed to mourn a pair of tragedies: the first on a galactic scale, the annihilation of the political seat of the Republic by Starkiller Base; the second more personal, Kylo Ren's murder of Han, and Leia's reaction thereupon. With the destruction of Luke's temple now recalled in *The Last Jedi*, those political/personal stakes are narratively fused. The exact notes of the PATHOS theme are not duplicated, though a linkage is nevertheless drawn through other parameters: distinctive high string homophony, several details of harmony and voicing, especially the B♭m$^{(5-\sharp4)}$/F sonority. Though it is easy to focus on the density of overt motivic invocations in Episode VIII, moments like this—suggestive and perhaps fortuitous *evocations*—are just as rife, and often more potent.

In keeping with the variably tensed quality of "Lesson Two," Williams's sidelong glance at the PATHOS theme is retrospective. Other indirect references during Luke's narration are proleptic, anticipating developments to come. For example, the French horn solo [A_3-E_4-A_4-G_4-$F\sharp_4$] that leads into HAN AND LEIA replicates the intervallic curve, and more unspecifiably the affective temperament, of the vanishingly scarce LUKE AND LEIA melody. That theme's explicit reintroduction is reserved for the siblings' reunion several acts later. In that context, it provides one of the emotional high points of the Sequel Trilogy. Meanwhile, at the end of 4m36, a figure for solo winds [F_5-E_5-A_4-C_5-$B\flat_4$] snakes about with the exact contour and rhythm of Kylo Ren's aggressive theme. Yet it lacks Ren's defining $\hat{5}\to\sharp\hat{4}$ snarl, or his accustomed brutal orchestration. This softened, diatonicized transformation of Ren's motif prefigures the systematic redemption of the theme in *Rise of Skywalker*—something not Luke, nor Rey, nor even Williams himself knew was coming. Even if a happy motivic accident, the coincidence of this reimagining of Ren's theme with Rey's line "I need someone to show me my place in all this" is eerily fitting, given its fate in Episode IX. Even more than Buhler's claim that music can "intuit connections," Williams's underscore when in this epic-narrational mode can retroactively make otherwise baffling narrative choices feel motivated and earned. In its uncanny ability to anticipate and reevaluate, sometimes it seems as if the musical narrator is smarter than the characters or even the filmmakers.[9]

Diegetic Disturbances

Diegetic narration can be an occasion for epiphany and self-overhearing, bonding and manipulation, foretelling the future and recontextualizing the past. As the monologues in Episodes IV and VII reveal, scenes of narrated exposition are crucial theaters for musical mythmaking. Yet spoken backstory also pauses the movie's plot in its tracks. In-universe narration such as provided by Obi-Wan and Luke is always disruptive to the forward flow of action, no matter how important the expository revelations bestowed or musical insights imparted. Such disturbance is often by design, however, and in the eyes of many theorists of narrative, it is a precondition for truly effective epic storytelling. Crucially, disturbance of plot is a key mechanism by which untexted music like Williams's symphonic underscore takes on the quality of an active and independent narrating voice.

In her influential study *Unsung Voices: Opera and Musical Narrative in the Nineteenth Century*, Carolyn Abbate elevates the concept of *disjunction* to a prime principle of musical storytelling. Abbate's theory, steeped in the philosophy of narrative and calibrated to address Late Romantic music (the vast monologues in Wagner especially), resists paraphrase. But her central insight is intuitive enough: when instrumental music breaks its expected flow or does something intensely unexpected, it opens up space for a new kind of narrating voice—a musical explainer or commentator or intervener. Rupture of musical expectations can be ear-catching to the point of illusion-breaking for listeners. And while such distanciation is a desirable trait for epic storytelling, it works better as a special effect than a ubiquitous mode of fictive address. Musical narration through disjunction is "a rare and peculiar act," as Abbate frames it, "a unique moment of performing narration within a surrounding music." Provocatively, she considers it the *only* sort of narrativity music is capable of; even the most programmatic music never acts like a chorus by default. But we need not adopt this more controversial stance to appreciate why Abbate's disjunction-based model of musical narration is useful for interpreting *Star Wars*.[10]

What counts as "unexpected" in a film score is established by generic and in-text regularities of musical structure, style, and audio-visual correspondence. Even at their most self-critical, all nine Skywalker Saga movies are at heart Classical in orientation, committed to unity and continuity, unwilling to let any parameter—musical or otherwise—overthrow basic filmic norms. For sure, surprises occur: a cue might shift idioms midstream, a sharp new timbre may pierce the audio track like a dagger. But rarely are expectancy violations permitted to take the listener out of the fictional world. No matter how locally disruptive a musical rupture might be in *Star Wars*, the effect is ultimately in service of fortifying the mythic integrity of the larger film.

One such hyper-salient but assimilable disruption can be heard during the final leg of "Battle of the Heroes" in *Revenge of the Sith*. Moments before the duel's climax, Obi-Wan shouts "I have failed you," which prompts an unprecedented Force variant to push away the cue's governing theme. The moment is depicted in Figure 7.3. Twisted in dissonant agony, cutting into an otherwise monothematic set piece, and orchestrated—uncharacteristically for the motif—with full chorus, this Force transformation lands as a shock. The thematic variant contravenes our expectations of the kind of cue "Battle of the Heroes" had been until this point—monothematic and enclosed, a

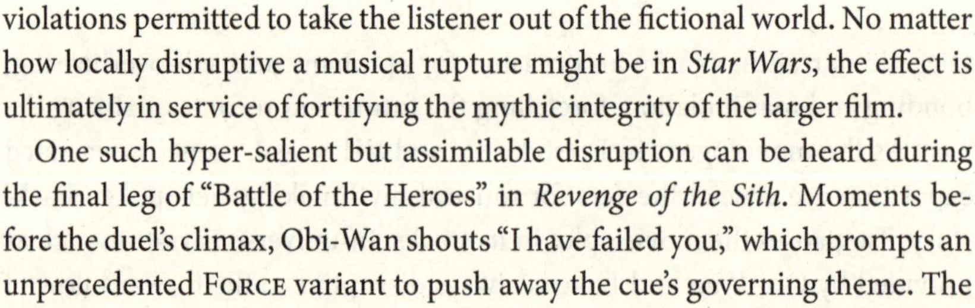

Figure 7.3 Dissonant version of Force in "Battle of the Heroes" (ROTS, 6m9, 1:58:28)

set piece sealed off from the rest of the series. More pointedly, the variant violates deep-rooted assumptions of how the FORCE theme ought to "go," its behavior as one of those "aural beacons" set up by Williams. The overlapping disjunctures make the leitmotif more heavily marked than usual, turning it into a musical question in need of explanation—or a wound in need of dressing. The sudden FORCE annunciation suggests the work of an amorphous but active musical storyteller, a power directing events from the shadows. "Listen!," the score seems to say, pointing to itself, "how the Dark Side can come to corrupt even the noblest of themes."

Among the strongest means for producing musical disjunction is the blurring of the diegetic/nondiegetic boundary. This subject has proven to be a productive site of interest for film musicologists, with a huge and often contentious literature to match, full of complex typologies and fine distinctions. But behind the sophisticated theorizing are issues that are easy to explain, if befuddling to resolve. Put simply, some movie music fails to fit into the clean categories of "source" and "underscore," to use the terms applied by filmmakers. In this zone—what Robynn Stilwell dubbed the "fantastical gap"—we find music that is neither part of the same world as the film's characters (a jizz-wailing standard from an on-screen Cantina Band, say), nor self-evidently outside it (an End Credits suite performed by the LSO, say).[11] The formal and expressive effects of such category-defying sound tend to produce an effect called *metalepsis*. Following Guido Heldt, who imports the term from the foremost theorist of diegesis Gérard Genette, metalepsis is "a short-circuiting of levels of narration." At stake is not simply *where* the music physically comes from—this may be deeply relevant to the interpretation of a scene, but it may just as easily be trivial. Rather, traversing the fantastical gap impacts *how* music tells a story, the way listeners understand, even if just implicitly, its influence on events—and themselves in relation to it.

Examples of fourth-wall-shattering metalepsis in mainline *Star Wars* films are nonexistent. Williams's nondiegetic underscore stays in its lane: we do not expect characters to whistle their leitmotifs as they work, nor armies to rally their troops to the strains of their namesake fanfares or marches. The same demarcation is true for source music, as amusing as it may be to imagine those catchy tunes from the Mos Eisley Cantina migrating into the symphonic underscore.[12] Nevertheless, there is something unsatisfying about insisting on the diegetic/nondiegetic distinction too forcefully. While overt breaches of the fantastical gap are prohibited, the films do sometimes tiptoe along its edges. What arises is a coy dance where the usually effaced machinery of Williams's score sneaks into actual diegetic spaces, or vice versa. Even when not skirting the source/underscore boundary, there is a sense that Williams's music is a living and integral part of the filmworld. Music is something just "in the air" that can never be described as incidental, no matter how scrupulously it adheres to textbook delineations of source/underscore. Sensing that *Star Wars* sets the terms of its musical primacy for itself, Ben Winters claims that the score "functions in much the same way as . . . the force," a field that surrounds and binds all, able to both "control your actions" and "obey your commands."[13] Whether this agency and pliability pertains to the characters, the narrator/narrative voice, or us in the audience, Winters leaves strategically unspecified.

Music in *Star Wars* is undeniably heightened and heightening, much more expressively responsive than the average movie score, imparting to the proceedings an aura of mythic import—enchantment even.[14] That said, some scholars of screen music balk at Winters's submission that nondiegetic music is part of the literal world depicted on screen, not just in *Star Wars* but in general. Yes, the distinction between the filmworld being depicted and the mechanisms doing that depicting is one that should be nuanced, but that does not mean the entire dichotomy must be collapsed.[15] However, just as we need not accept Abbate's most provocative claim (*only* disjunctive music conveys narrative) to see the truth of a less categorical framing (disjunctive music is *particularly* suggestive of narrative), we can treat Winters's position of film-musical realism as an available listening stance. It is one of many such standpoints, not a fundamental truth of cinematic perception. Instead of accepting the implausible notion that music in the series is audible to its characters and actively directs the plot, we may consider the music to be so indispensable and responsive that it is *as if* it is audible to characters, *as if* it directs the plot. This counterfactual clause is crucial. To keep the fictive integrity of *Star Wars* from completely dissolving, filmgoers must accept that nondiegetic score exists apart from the world depicted, that Williams's music is not constantly echoing across the wastes of Tatooine or between the supertowers of Coruscant, unacknowledged yet somehow sensed by Luke and company. Nevertheless, there are times that relaxing the conceptual immiscibility between source and underscore is not just warranted but demanded by the text, and these moments revolve around a kind of *as-if* hearing.[16]

One option for the Ben Winterian listener would be to simply ignore diegesis in the first place. Instead of seeking narrative immersion or investment, this listener would concentrate on the music as such, like one might do for an opera with an incomprehensible plot, or ballet whose choreographic stylization prevents the suspension of disbelief. The contested ontology of diegesis does not matter when there is no story to buy into in the first place. Admittedly, it is unlikely that any audience, even the most cinesymphonically inclined, would naturally arrive at so radical a stance. There is a good reason: film music's innate intermittency, subordination, and referentiality make it exceptionally difficult to bracket it off from the narrative apparatus.[17] Nevertheless, the implications of this extreme position are worth examining, and we will return to them in Chapter 8 when we discuss musical paratexts.

Another option for a Winterian listener is to focus on moments of potential metalepsis and not fall for the instinctive need to rationalize them according to the diegetic/nondiegetic binary. The main sites of metaleptic play in *Star Wars* are instances of what Heldt calls "would-be-diegetic music": music that "does not have a diegetic source, but that we can imagine *could* occur in the diegesis at this point."[18] Cues that accompany highly ritualized or communal activities often fit this category. The award ceremony at the end of Episode IV, with its trio of ceremonial topics—fanfare, march, procession—is a paradigm case. That sequence is noted by both Heldt and musicologist Anahid Kassabian as music that "occupies an ambiguous position within the narrative world of the film, while retaining a limited but clear relationship to the events of that world."[19] No, Williams's galactic spin on "Pomp and Circumstance" cannot be definitively attributed to an onscreen source. Nor is it disruptive stylistically; the THRONE ROOM theme's Edwardian idiom and thematic vocabulary are of a piece with the rest of the nondiegetic score. The ceremony has a metaleptic dimension because one imagines it is the kind of music that *would* be appropriate, in-universe, for this celebratory rite. Certainly, Williams's cue is not neutral background music; the tone is unambiguously triumphal, and the topics are formal to the point of stiltedness. Heldt would say the score "takes sides in a diegetic conflict" here, expressing a "fantasy collectivity" on behalf of the whole Rebel Alliance. So much for the impartial epic narrator!

The would-be-diegetic quality of the THRONE ROOM is a special effect, not a permanent feature of the Skywalker Saga scores. Yet we can also locate telltale signs of metaleptic slippage in certain scenes of internal storytelling. One elegant example comes at the conclusion of *The Last Jedi.* An entirely ancillary character, a slave boy barely glimpsed during an earlier scene on Canto Bight, is shown recounting Luke Skywalker's final deed. What was witnessed by the audience just moments earlier in the film is already galactic common knowledge. The tale of heroic self-sacrifice utterly captivates his small audience of fellow kids but is cruelly interrupted by an adult stable master. Even without sound—the tale is told in an untranslated alien tongue—the scene is easily intelligible, thanks to the way the boy stages Luke's apotheosis with ersatz action figures. Much of Episode VIII's underlying thesis is pinned on this scene. As news of the Jedi Master's martyrdom spreads even to the most downtrodden of the galaxy's inhabitants, an event in recent history—"what *happened*" in Williams's words—transforms into myth, and a flawed human becomes a symbol of heroic resistance.

Though brief, Williams's music for the Canto Bight narration, shown in Figure 7.4, does heavy narrational lifting. (Note: in the film, mm. 5–8 are cut and the remaining measures are pitch-shifted up a semitone.) Texturally, the cue is unusual for *Star Wars.* We hear arpeggiated figures in 6/8 time, plucked by harp and celesta, with gentle asides from flute and clarinet. This is a metrical/timbral combination unheard before in the series, strongly evocative of a music box or similar object of childhood music-making. The only comparable passage is from the cue that accompanies the birth of the twins in

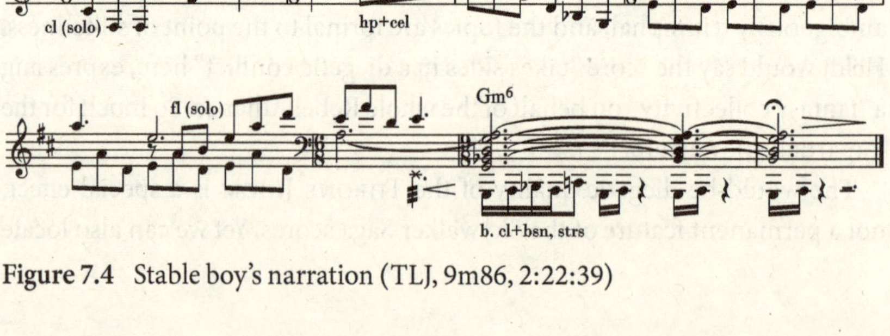

Figure 7.4 Stable boy's narration (TLJ, 9m86, 2:22:39)

Episode III, and that cue is considerably darker in affect.[20] The textural rupture in Canto Bight is compounded by the way this intimate scoring comes *after* the far more conventional end of the film: a scene of the heroic cadre blasting off into hyperspace, matched with a characteristic orchestral swell. The little berceuse that follows is not source music—how could it be?—but it is exactly the sort of music one imagines these kids would hear in staging this puppet show.

Once the lullaby-like texture is established, Williams briefly quotes LUKE's theme. The toy-like presentation of that leitmotif has just a single precedent in the series, "Threepio's Bedtime Story," to be detailed shortly. That it should be children who are accompanied by this would-be-diegetic music is significant; it is easier to conceive of a youth having access to an enchanted, superdiegetic musical realm than an adult. If music functions, as Winters proposes, like the force, then it is fitting that these younglings, yet to be schooled in the ways of the diegesis, should prompt a metaleptic transference. Indeed, one member of the puppet show audience, "Broom Boy," is shown to be able to wield that power a few moments later, bridging a fantastical gap in a cleverly dramatized way.

The tinkling treatment of LUKE's theme at the end of *The Last Jedi* is as indisputable an instance of musical mention as any in the series. Mention, as discussed back in Chapter 3, involves the score pointing back at itself in some way. But that thematic citation in the Canto Bight cue also opens up another, rarer type of musico-narrational play: *epic self-reflexivity*. Like motivic mention, this form of referentiality relies on the listener's ability to recognize a musical recurrence as such. But epic self-reflexivity goes beyond semantic recognition, requiring a temporary disinvestment in the narrative, an *un*-suspension of disbelief. On its face, this would seem to be the starkest achievable form of mythic distanciation—what strategy could be more estranging than pointing to such a normally effaced element of a text's construction? Here we are faced with an apparent paradox of epic storytelling: when used sparingly and shrewdly, self-reference reinforces rather than dissipates filmic cohesion.

To understand why a piece of pop entertainment would walk the self-reflexive tightrope, it is useful to turn to a genre one does not usually associate with *Star Wars*: the Hollywood musical. In her landmark 1977 study, "The Self-Reflexive Musical and the Myth of Entertainment," Jane Feuer considers the so-called backstage musical, in which the show is all about putting on another show. Classics like *42nd Street* and *Singin' in the Rain* can feel surprisingly unsettled, testing just how much of the artificiality of the narrative apparatus they can get away with revealing. At the same time, few genres are *more* invested in reinforcing the mystique of show business than backstage musicals. How is this balance struck, and what parallels can be drawn with Williams's space operas?

Feuer formulates three overarching "myths" that Hollywood musicals hold to firmly, ensuring that any indulgence in self-reflection ultimately serves to "perpetuate rather than deconstruct the codes of the genre."[21] First is the *myth of spontaneity*, through which "performance, which is actually part of culture, appear[s] to be part of nature." In other words, the audience is allowed to see how the product they consume is made, but that disclosure is worked into the narrative in a smooth and justifiable way. Second is the *myth of integration*, which regards reflexive art as ultimately being about community formation through performance, not winking self-indulgence. This integration takes place on the plot level—typically, loner characters are brought into a community, and lower or more vernacular cultural energies are channeled into expressions of high culture. And it is reflected back on the viewer: "By promoting audience identification with the collectively produced shows," Feuer writes, "the myth of integration seeks to give the audience a sense of participation in the creation of the film itself."[22] Last, there is the *myth of audience*. This is the idea that the inclusion of a diegetic spectator to an in-world diegetic performance, far from being alienating to the film-viewer, is a shortcut to identification and immersion. Of special relevance to *Star Wars* is Feuer's observation that backstage musicals frequently tap into repertoires the real audience already knows well, even if the diegetic audience does not—songs from earlier shows or films that had since become standards, for instance. Leveraging this kind of prior familiarity enables all sorts of play with filmgoer expectations and gives opportunities for pleasurable recognition and insider status that also reinforce the myth of integration.

There are many ways a text besides a film musical can demystify itself through epic self-reference. Space opera is particularly amenable to the strategy of comedic deflation, in which matters of dire import are taken a little less seriously. Again, *The Last Jedi* provides a clear example: the DEATH STAR motif, once intended for a weapon of planetary genocide, is assigned to a First Order ironing board (a harmless background prop!) [1:30:47]. The gag is affectionate, easily missable, and at most gently disruptive, a source of passing amusement for attentive listeners. By contrast, in more modernist works of art, self-reflexivity is enlisted to violently shatter immersion, often for the purposes of critiquing a text's ideological foundations from within. No mainline *Star Wars* film would ever overturn its diegesis so radically, nor purposefully alienate its audience for the sake of their critical edification. Still, there are moments where these films do more than just briefly wink back at us, as we will see. One places an actual chorus at the forefront of the audience's attention but occludes its words through layer upon layer of translational re-mystification and editorial manipulation. Another involves a character fluent in over 6 million forms of communication—6 million and 1 if you count quasi-diegetic musical scoring. And one last instance centers on the series' most skillful—and dishonest—storyteller.

Twisting Branches in *The Phantom Menace*

Singing in Tongues

John Williams is an avowed dendrophile—a lover of trees. Starting in 1995 with his bassoon concerto *The Five Sacred Trees*, many of his concert works would revolve around sylvan themes, including *Heartwood*, *TreeSong*, *Rosewood*, and the horn and harp concerti. As noted, Williams's formulation of the *Star Wars* myth in 1997 was that of a great tree, whose branches "seem to keep growing out," lending the whole saga an "animate, organic quality." It is fitting that the composer cultivated this arboreal metaphor while reflecting on *The Phantom Menace* specifically: the score's biggest barnburner was inspired by a medieval Welsh poem entitled "The Battle of the Trees." This new piece would become a musical emblem for the Prequel Trilogy as a whole, likely the most recognizable new outgrowth of the *Star Wars* tree since "The Imperial March" in 1980. And, for the first time, it was music that listeners could sing along to, at least in principle.

"Duel of the Fates," as both the set piece and its thematic constituents have come to be called, counts as one of those big, bold swings Williams took with the Prequels. The use of a written text for nondiegetic scoring was a real novelty in Episode I, and its presence in such a prominent context indicated a reinvestment in music's role as an active and assertive pseudo-narrator. The "fates" invoked in the title are no mere flourish: the piece involves a chorus in both form and function. Previously, voices were confined to producing indistinct vocables—namely, the "oohs" and "aahs" associated with the EMPEROR's leitmotif. But the climactic melee between Darth Maul and Qui-Gon and

Obi-Wan cried out for something more phonologically arresting. The scene struck Williams as having a ritualistic quality, akin to a "religious ceremony" that took place at "a great pagan altar" or "big temple." For these reasons, he felt it was suited to accompaniment by a large mixed choir.[23] The cue he wrote for the heart of the sequence (and subsequently expanded into the "Duel of the Fates" concert piece) would thus become the score's main showcase for the London Voices, eighty-eight lungs strong.

Williams did not ask the chorus to mimic the exact incidents on screen. There was plenty of hyper-synchronized action scoring already in the film, but this fight called for a less imitative, more commentative contribution. Instead, voices in "Duel of the Fates" would narrate the stakes of this clash between Jedi and Sith. Or, more accurately, the chorus would make it *seem* as though narration was taking place, that an epic gloss was being draped over the duel, albeit in a linguistic form that was cryptic and impossible to parse on a purely semantic level. Timbre, not timber, is the ultimate source of the set piece's expressive power.

For most of the fight sequence, the orchestra chugs along with an insistent Duel of the Fates ostinato and theme. A number of passages foreground the choir, including the music that accompanies the reveal of Darth Maul's double-bladed lightsaber, represented in Figure 7.5. Here, the choir chants a succession of sharply articulated but elusively signifying words: *Korah Matah Korah Rahtahmah…*

The provenance of these words and the others that join them is a story unto itself. It is a twisty journey, one that illustrates how Williams, seeking to conjure the absolute past, manufactured a sense of distance and obscurity. Williams's literary source, "The Battle of the Trees" ["Cad Goddeu"] first appears in a Middle Welsh manuscript, *The Book of Taliesin*, dating from the first half of the fifteenth century, alongside sixty other poems. Attributed to

Figure 7.5 Maul's twinblade ignition to Duel of the Fates (TPM, 7m3, 1:51:03 [tracked])

Taliesin, a pseudo-historical bardic figure from the sixth century, the text recounts (or prophesies) a strange battle of magically enchanted trees. The event is described in a dreamlike manner characteristic of its genre, blending references to medieval Welsh folk heroes, Christian theology, and military campaigns of uncertain historicity. Williams, no Celticist, discovered "The Battle" neither through the original manuscript nor a meticulously assembled scholarly edition, but as it appeared in translation in Robert Graves's *The White Goddess*. Written in 1948, the book blends poetic analysis and a highly speculative (and often flagrantly ahistorical) form of comparative mythology, similar in spirit to other midcentury manifestos like Campbell's *The Hero with a Thousand Faces*. The book includes two English versions of "Cad Goddeu," one by nineteenth-century writer D. W. Nash, and one by the author. Graves, who could not read Welsh, relied on Nash's translation as the springboard for his own, more poeticized and idiosyncratic treatment.[24]

Williams acquired a copy of *The White Goddess* in 1970 and was thoroughly captivated. As biographer Tim Greiving puts it, "The book lit up John's theories about a shared cultural memory and our mystical relationship with trees, and it would seed many song lyrics and concertos down the road."[25] From Graves's version of the poem, Williams chose one quatrain, which corresponds to lines 23–24 of the "Cad Goddeu" manuscript. Figure 7.6 includes the original Middle Welsh, Graves's translation, and a more modern literal translation from the respected Celticist Patrick Ford.[26]

The composer found the stanza to be "a good mystical, cryptic piece of business," and was stimulated by the notion of a war waged in the imagination.[27] Philologically speaking, this talk of a double battle, with one front on a material plane and the other on a psychological one, is entirely Graves's invention. But it fits easily into the mythopoetics of *Star Wars*, where lightsaber

Original Middle Welsh	Graves Translation	Ford Translation
Achat erdygnawt dan uon ytauawt. Achat arall yffyd ynywegilyd.	Under the tongue-root a fight most dread, and another raging behind in the head.	And a fierce host beneath the base of his tongue/ and another host is on his necks.

Figure 7.6 Words from "Cad Goddeu" inspiring "Duel of the Fates"

duels are as much battles for the souls of their combatants as they are contests between physical bodies. The implication of a second fight occurring "behind in the head" is especially apt for *The Phantom Menace*, with its shadow conflicts orchestrated by Palpatine—to say nothing of the internal war soon to play out in Anakin Skywalker's psyche.

After selecting his text, Williams claims he condensed Graves's stanza down to simpler phrases, one of which he noted was "most dread/inside the head."[28] He then embarked upon a process of lexical estrangement. Williams requested translations into several other languages from "some friends at Harvard," settling on Classical Sanskrit for two reasons. One is its musicality: almost all of the language's words end in vowels. The other is obscurity; Sanskrit is, per the composer, "less well-known" to Western audiences, and thus capable of serving as an aesthetic shortcut to a vague, esoteric effect. Williams's exoticism need not be excused or belabored here.[29] Suffice it to say, the appropriative usage of a (still living) language purely for its phonetic mystique is dissonant with *The Phantom Menace*'s outward themes of symbiosis and cross-cultural understanding.

Already, these textual manipulations of "Cad Goddeu" resembled a mythical version of the children's game of telephone, and the alterations continued into the choral writing itself. In setting the vocal parts, Williams further abstracted his transliterated words, modifying, combining, and reordering their syllables freely. At no moment does the ultimate "Duel of the Fates" set piece or its derived cues contain anything easily intelligible to someone versed in Sanskrit, and certainly not Medieval Welsh folklore.

Establishing exactly how the individual words in "Duel of the Fates" relate to specific Sanskrit models presents a difficult task. We can make some educated guesses, however.[30] The first word, "Korah," translates literally to the word for "movable joint" and "bud" in Sanskrit (*kora*), obviously not what Williams was going for. But the phonologically similar *ghora* (घोर) means "dreadful," which comes straight from the Graves text. The situation is similar with "Matah": its direct translation is *mata* (मत), which can mean "thought" or "intention." But close by is *mastaka* (मस्तक), meaning "head" or "skull."[31] "Rahtamah" corresponds to no word in Sanskrit, and the close by *ratha* (रथ), meaning "chariot," does not relate to the "Battle of the Trees" at all. There are three explanations for this odd word out. Most plausible is *ghoratama* (घोरतम), meaning "most dreadful." Second is *rasana* (रसना), meaning "tongue"—a happy coincidence, even if it was not Williams's intent. A third possibility is that "Rahtama" is not a translation at all but a shuffling of syllables from the previous two words. Without Williams's written notes or sketches, a definitive translation will probably never be possible.[32]

Not that translatability was ever really the point anyway. These vowel-rich utterances are pure musical matter, hewn from their literary source in a way untraceable to any listener without prior knowledge of the external texts or the conditions of their inclusion. As noted by A. E. Wagstaffe in her survey of changing interpretations of "The Battle of the Trees," simple lexical sense was never what Williams was after. "The resulting 'translation' is therefore meaningless in terms of the sung words," Wagstaffe argues, "but is loaded with meaning transferred from contemporary conceptualisations of 'Cad Goddeu' absorbed by the composer. Ideas about ancient power are," she continues, "expressed in a symbolic language that can never be completely translated or understood."[33] Or, as Williams himself describes it, the unplaceable text "gave ["Duel of the Fates"] an atmosphere that was at once mysterious and old and dramatic—[and], I hope, effective."

Fate of the Duels

The resulting music for Episode I's three-way fracas has all the traits we expect of epic musical storytelling. The "Duel" erects a great *distance* between itself and the listener through its antique subject matter. Like the practice of speaking in tongues found in some religious traditions, the piece's text is emptied of lexical content, giving an impression of oracular meaningfulness, not despite but by virtue of the fact that its actual words are nonsense. It is *repetitive* in the extreme. All of its motivic subcomponents embody ceaseless cyclicality: the OSTINATO figure is repeated 126 times in "The Great Duel" cue alone; the instrumental THEME is a perfect musical palindrome; and the choral CHANT constantly reiterates the same words, with a brusque declamatory rhythm often fixed on a single reciting tone. The cue bears trappings of *religious* or *ritual* music. Its sonic kin are movements of apocalyptic severity from liturgical and pseudo-liturgical works like Orff's *Carmina Burana* and the Requiem masses of Mozart and Verdi.[34] And "Duel of the Fates" is *self-reflexive*. At times, the score casts an inward gaze on itself—the CHANT's characteristic progression is the same i↔♭vi that undergirds Vader's leitmotif, and the concert arrangement even smuggles the head of his motif into the bass line at one moment (see mm. 66–72). But "Duel of the Fates" exudes a self-reflexive aura mostly thanks to its formative literary conceit, that idea of a battle fought across two metaphysical planes, mind and body. "Duel of the Fates" is Williams's poetic way of encapsulating what the Skywalker Saga myth, in all its spiritual and Manichean weight, is ultimately *about.* This is *Star Wars*, singing the story of itself.

It is safe to say the composer's hopes that the music was "effective" were fulfilled. The Episode I duel is commonly held up by fans and critics as one of the few inarguable artistic successes in an otherwise inconsistent film, its music being no small part of that verdict.[35] "It was bombastic, ominous, choral, and it would inspire the presence of apocalyptic choir in Hollywood soundtracks for years to come," writes Chris Taylor. "Williams's music, the oxygen of *Star Wars*, was still operating at peak flow."[36] Given the high esteem in which "Duel of the Fates" is held, listeners might be surprised to learn the extent to which the sequence's high-vaulted music is *not* what Williams intended. The original scoring for the Maul duel involved four cues: "The Fight Begins," "The Great Duel," "Qui-Gon's Noble End," and the second half of "Blowups and the Death of Darth Maul." However, the Battle of Naboo—which has three other fronts to follow besides the saber fight—proved a tough nut for Lucas and his editing team to crack. Every aspect of the climactic conflict of Episode I ended up heavily manipulated, motivated by concerns of pacing and intelligibility, and facilitated by a new nonlinear digital editing practice that allowed eleventh-hour tinkerings.[37] The epic battle Williams initially spotted, scored, and recorded no longer fit Lucas's recut version. And so it fell to Williams's long-time music editor Ken Wannberg to construct a new sonic scaffold for the duel, one made up of broken-down slabs of already completed music.

An overview of the portion of the Battle of Naboo occupied by the three-way melee is offered in Figure 7.7. (The other three fronts also partake of the Duel of the Fates leitmotivic complex; recall, for example, Chapter 5's analysis of "The Droid Battle.") The final cut bears little resemblance to what Williams initially scored, much of which is a riot of tracked, looped, and micro-edited snippets. Most of these bits are drawn not from "The Great Duel," Williams's extended set piece for the Maul fight, but rather a standalone concert arrangement he prepared for the film's credits, what today is simply called "Duel of the Fates." And while much of that piece is modeled on the first half of "The Great Duel," few of its 155 measures map directly to that unused cue. Indeed, so complete is the upstaging of "The Great Duel" by the "End Credits'" presentation of Duel of the Fates that one

Phase	Action	Originally Intended Cue(s) (speculative)	Actual Final Cue(s)
A 1:50:25–1:51:14	Maul reveal, Jedi approach, others disperse	6m4a: "The Fight Begins" and/or selections from 6ma: "The Big Army" (mm. 33–50?)	7m3 "End Credit" [orchestra-only] (mm. 1–4, 5, 80–81, 86–91, 112–113 [x2], 116–119)
	Jedi ignite, melee begins		7m3 "End Credit" [w/ chorus] mm. 120–123 (subtracted beats)
B 1:52:03–1:52:44	Fight moves from hangar to power generator	6m4a: "The Fight Begins," and/or selections from 6m7 "The Great Duel"	7m3 "End Credit" [with chorus] mm. 100–119, mm. 120–123 (subtracted beats)
C 1:55:24–1:56:47	Combat rages in power generator area…	6m7 "The Great Duel" (to mm. 53)	7m3 "End Credit" [with chorus] mm. 1–2, 122–131, 138–155
	Moves to hall with red energy barriers		Unscored (14 sec), 6m7 "The Great Duel" mm 48–52
D 1:59:13–2:00:11	Maul vs. Qui-Gon, Qui-Gon fatally wounded	6m8/9 "Qui-Gon's Noble End" (mm.3–23)	6m8/9 "Qui-Gon's Noble End" (mm. 3–23), overlain/looped with 6m7 "The Great Duel" mm. 76–78
E 2:01:20–2:02:22	Maul vs. Obi-Wan	6m8/9 "Qui-Gon's Noble End" (mm. 55–58)	6m10 "Qui-Gon's Noble End" (mm. 56–58)
	Obi-Wan disarmed and sent into pit	6m10 "Blowups and The Death of Darth Maul" (mm. 1–5)	
F 2:03:56-2:04:32	Obi-Wan recovers, bisects Maul, mourns Qui-Gon	6m10 "Blowups and The Death of Darth Maul" (mm. 55–73)	6m11 (new) "End of Maul" (mm. 8–82)

Figure 7.7 Phases of the Maul/Jedi melee in *The Phantom Menace*

suspects Wannberg, Lucas, perhaps even Williams himself may have felt that the concert arrangement was a more compelling, more *definitive* musical statement than the underscore that served as its genesis. Though necessary from an editorial point of view, the resultant chimera of cues is not nearly so architecturally sound musically. As music editor and musicologist Nicholas Kmet notes in a video essay on the sequence, "On a micro-level, it is clearly the film providing structure for the music. Removed from the picture, the [edited] score is extremely unfulfilling, because it in no way resembles the aesthetically pleasing cues from which it is drawn."[38] In place of the original, sturdy oak of a set piece, the theatrical version of "Duel of the Fates" is a hybrid creature, the product of editorial splicing and grafting, necessarily less stable than its contributing branches.

The strange treatment of these cues in-film adds another layer of mistranslation to the journey from "Cad Goddeu" to "Duel of the Fates"—one necessitated by film-editorial exigency more than a deliberate form of mythic distanciation. If Williams mistranslates Graves, and Graves mistranslates Taliesin, then the final cut of Episode I does the same to the score. Absent a carefully produced recording that restores the four initially intended cues, the originally envisioned musical experience of the Maul duel may never be realized. Thankfully, the "Duel of the Fates" concert arrangement is a splendid capstone in its own right. And the Battle of Naboo, despite its cobbled-together nature, works as an audiovisual totality well enough, thanks to Wannberg's keen musical instincts.[39]

Throughout *The Skywalker Symphonies*, I have stressed the symbiotic nature of leitmotivic writing: themes validate, respond to, and influence each other. Unlike other famous *Star Wars* themes, "Duel of the Fates" never truly became part of the series' verdant leitmotivic ecosystem. Despite being built up as a decisive musical agent in the Prequel trilogy, "Duel of the Fates" recedes in importance after *The Phantom Menace*. A segment recurs, basically unaltered, as the young Skywalker speeds to rescue his doomed mother in Episode II. In that context, it acts as a sonic signal that the moment represents a turning point in the Jedi Knight's fall, but it offers little new in terms of symphonic development or psychological shading. A large portion of the concert arrangement is later repurposed for the clash of titans in *Revenge of the Sith*—not, however, for the core agon between Anakin and Obi-Wan (which is fueled by the new BATTLE OF THE HEROES), but Yoda and Palpatine. The use of gnomic Sanskrit vocals also persists, in less pronounced form, in Episode III, in the guise of a choral obbligato in a few cues. One of these is based on the punny phrase (presumably also a fuzzy translation) of "grievous are the crimes of the Empire." For this lyric, Williams tellingly noted that "we will not know [those words' literal meaning], but we will understand what the message is."[40] By Episode III, Sanskrit vocals have transformed from an external poetic allusion to an internal topic.

Textural and timbral elements of "Duel of the Fates" would also be summoned, albeit sparingly, in the Sequels—namely, with Supreme Leader Snoke's quiet, lexically indecipherable choral leitmotif. The original set piece and its various CHANT subcomponents were also meant to play a significant role during the final climax of *The Rise of Skywalker*. Such a recall would have provided an elegant symmetry between first and final episodes in the Saga. Regrettably, those choral cues—many of which were would-be-diegetic—were cut from the final film. Ultimately, the rich storytelling potential of "Duel of the Fates" was only partially realized. Yet the theme's convoluted literary origin and layers upon layers of manipulation and occultation make for a striking—if at times frustratingly, ironically apt—illustration of self-mystification.

Bedtime Stories in *Return of the Jedi*

Aural History

Close to the midpoint of *Return of the Jedi*, high in the treetops of a forest moon, all narrative momentum grinds to a halt. On the eve of the Battle of Endor, Threepio—presumed to be a god by the impressionable Ewoks—regales his newfound congregation with an impromptu radio drama. Beginning with an Ewokese call to attention ("Moochana makawartas! Moochana makawartas!"), Threepio proceeds to recount, in sketchy detail and with lo-fi sound effects, the basic plot of the previous two films. The tightly packed Ewoks listen to his tale with rapt attention, responding viscerally with shocked squeals and approving oohs. The human audience members are less uniformly engrossed. Luke watches on with an enigmatic expression, betraying a trace of a smirk when his exploits on Hoth are recounted. Han plays along as best he can, but seems mildly exasperated that, instead of planning battles, he's subjected to yet another irritation from this insufferable droid. Leia, for her part, seems genuinely captivated. As Threepio wraps up his tale, the Ewok elders confer, and, to the sound of diegetic drums, a pronouncement is issued: "Wonderful! We are now part of the tribe."

Perhaps some viewers share Han's impatience at this point. Why arrest the plot for such a digression? And why turn everything over to Threepio—the trilogy's loquacious comic relief—when the fate of the galaxy is at stake? Music holds the key. But before considering the function of Williams's cue, "Bedtime Stories," we should grant that the droid's speechifying does end up serving a few pure plot points. For one, it informs the pre-industrial Ewoks of the ongoing galactic civil war and provides a conduit of empathy for the human protagonists, separated by the language barrier, to join the Endorian community. It also provides a modicum of character development for Threepio—recall that back in *A New Hope*, he claimed that "I'm not much more than an interpreter, and not very good at telling stories." Here, two movies later, he assumes, rather persuasively as far as the Ewoks are concerned, the role of the Rebellion's unofficial historian (or propagandist), enough to sway the species to lend their guerilla support in the coming battle.

Figure 7.8 offers a formal synopsis of the form of this unique cue. Threepio's tale, spoken in the Ewok tongue with supplementary sound effects and pantomime, helps familiarize the species with the saga according to parameters that are intelligible and impressive to them. Yet the way he tells the story is also a travesty: one need not speak Ewokese to notice how little sense could be made from the incidents he strings together with minimal causal logic. True—myth thrives in smoothing over messy contradictions of reality. It is at the level of particulars that the sequence is farcical; it comes across as how one imagines a young child with a short attention span might recount the

1:15:50 1:15:59 1:16:07 1:16:14 1:16:19 1:16:25 1:16:30 1:16:38 1:16:46 1:17:00

1	2	3	4	5	6	7	8	9
CALL 1	**LUKE**	**VADER**	CALL 2	**FORCE**	**R.F.** (?)	**LUKE**	CALL 3	**HAN & LEIA**
B♭5	E♭	Gm	Gdim7	Cm	Gdim7	A	B$_4$-F$_4$-B♭$_3$	D
bsn	recorder	cl	e. hn	f. hn	tbn	recorder	f. hn	recorder
C3P0's call to attention	Leia's hologram	Vader, Death Star	Obi-Wan's intro	Vader vs. Obi-Wan	AT-ATs on Hoth	Luke's heroics on Hoth	Falcon travels to Cloud City	Han Solo put into deep freeze, Sail Barge Battle

Figure 7.8 Form of "Bedtime Stories" (ROTJ, 8m5, 1:15:50–1:17:00)

Topic	Description	Ex.
Ewoks theme	Off-kilter march ala Prokofiev (esp. "March from *The Love of Three Oranges*"). A-section marked by staccato dotted rhythms, repeated $\hat{5}$-$\sharp\hat{4}$ descent, indecision as to whether in major or minor. Brassier B-section based on triadic planing, repeated notes, contrasting registers. Usually heard in woodwinds or trumpet(s), with support from pitched percussion and pizz strings.	1:28:52
Call motif	In simplest form just an ascending perfect fifth, like a hunting horn. Often spun out to a longer idea with repeated ascending fifths, and more rarely, a full grammatical theme. What might happen if the Ewoks got their paws on the Rebel Fanfare.	1:06:06
Tribal timbral palette	Tuned drums, rattles, shakers, recorders, xylophone, toy piano, shofar, assorted vocalizations (e.g. chirps, squeals, whoops, chants). Heard in a variety of source music and underscore contexts.	1:11:51
Incidental motifs	Host of subsidiary ideas, including Jawa-like ostinato figures, Casualties, Cancan, and the two different quasi-diegetic cues that conclude Episode VI.	1:03:40

Figure 7.9 The Ewok musical jamboree

plot of *Star Wars*. If there is an impression of being in the presence of a master storyteller here, an aura of mythic significance that enchants both diegetic and real-world audience alike, it is due to Williams's, rather than Threepio's, narration.

Much of the mythopoetic effect of "Bedtime Stories" resides in its assimilation of the idioms elsewhere in the film associated with the Ewoks, who are characterized with surprising richness for such minor characters. Figure 7.9 enumerates the thematic and timbral vocabulary with which Williams depicts the forest folk.

Elements of several of these thematic constituents, especially the Call and Tribal elements, are heard equally in diegetic and nondiegetic cues in Episode VI's Endor scenes. But it is only in "Threepio's Bedtime Story" that all aspects of the Ewoks' musical characterization converge. The cue is a toy model for Wagnerian musical prose, hitting on pertinent leitmotifs and style topics with each beat of Threepio's speech. The essential ploy here is apparent from the first bars, shown in Figure 7.10. The initial vocal

Figure 7.10 Call to attention and first thematic citations in "Bedtime Story" (ROTJ, 8m5, 1:15:50)

summons "Moochana makawartas" is echoed with a simple musical Call motif: a twice-repeated fifth (the Ewoks' characteristic interval) from a pair of bassoons, with faint rolling of a wood drum underneath (the Ewoks' characteristic timbre, along with recorder and hunting horn). As the narration begins, Williams places the Luke theme in a decidedly unaccustomed register and timbre: solo recorder, ranging from $E\flat_6$ to $E\flat_7$, supported by more open fifths, now on the harp. Everything is pint-sized here. The instrumental forces are microscopic compared to the Late Romantic grand orchestra that supports every other cue in the series. Also telescoped are the leitmotifs, with just two measures given to Luke before an analogously miniaturized module for Vader is heard, as soon as Threepio brings up "Oos batata rundi Darth Vader!" The theme, humbled in this manner, hardly sounds like a serious threat any longer, though apparently it is still enough to frighten the Ewoks.

The two-measure capsules continue coming after "The Imperial March" micro-module. These segments either contain a horn-call topic like that which opened the cue, or treat a familiar leitmotif to an Endorian twist, starting with the Force at m. 9, then Rebel Fanfare (or is it the Imperials motif?) at 1:16:25, and Luke five seconds later. The cue culminates, if that is the right word for such a meek span of underscore, with a rendition of Han and Leia on solo recorder. The loveliness of this music is enough to draw both Leia and Wicket the Ewok to snuggle in closer to poor Han. This closing

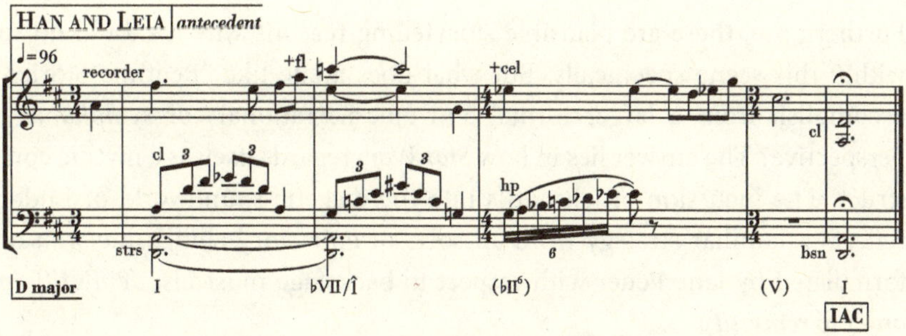

Figure 7.11 Concluding statement of Han and Leia in "Bedtime Story" (ROTJ, 8m5, 1:16:46)

module is rendered in Figure 7.11. Unlike almost all other instances of this and other love themes in the series, the leitmotif ends, and with it the cue, on a perfect authentic cadence. *Exeunt* Threepio, Bard of Endor.

Alert readers will have grown suspicious by some of the things claimed in this analysis of *Jedi*'s "Bedtime Story." Surely, the Ewoks are not being frightened by Vader's leitmotif? Nor could any on-screen personage, human or fur-ball, possibly be moved to acts of physical affection by the strains of Han and Leia. How could they? It is *nondiegetic* score. They cannot hear that—by definition!

But here lies the magic of this scene, why that mythic aura feels so strong: "Bedtime Stories" marks the first of very few occasions that the source/underscore boundary is skirted in the Skywalker Saga. That it does so timidly here—this is not fourth-wall-shattering by any stretch—is part of why Williams gets away with the trick. Specific instruments within the Timbral (recorder, drums, horn) category all have direct diegetic correlates in actual Ewok music-making, if not in this tableau specifically, then in sequences before and after. The precision and brevity of leitmotivic reference goes beyond any needle-drops heard earlier in traditional underscore, suggesting the musical citations are manifested directly through Threepio's speech acts. And the admixture of these recurrent themes with horn calls—the first of which is probably interpreted as off-screen source music—only further helps integrate these twenty-three measures of music into the fictional world depicted.

"Part of the Tribe"

Thus far, we have established that musical *metalepsis* in Heldt's sense ("the short-circuiting of narrative levels") is taking place in Threepio's tale.

Furthermore, there are plausible storytelling reasons why it should do so within this scene specifically. But what does a cue like "Bedtime Stories" accomplish from a larger formal and epic-narrational—or *symphonic*—perspective? The answer lies in how *Star Wars* regards itself as a mythic construct. The incursion of leitmotifs into the diegetic soundworld of Endor reflects a familiar strategy from all sorts of epic storytelling, one we saw formulated by Jane Feuer with respect to backstage musicals: *demystify in order to remystify*.

The demystification occurring in "Bedtime Stories" is achieved by puncturing the solemnity of the *Star Wars* musical lexicon. Themes most emblematic of the Saga's Wagnerian ambitions—the Force, Vader, etc.—get reduced to a parade of playful imitations, made to inform and entertain the cuddly and fairly ridiculous Ewoks. And it is not just the themes in themselves that are gently undercut here, but the way leitmotivic underscore is supposed to flow, normally in Williams as in Wagner spilling forth organically, with clever transitions and sequences blurring together individual units of musical time. Instead, "Bedtime Stories" presents a regular and literal-minded chaining of completely quantized thematic incipits, much cruder than how Williams constructs his musical prose elsewhere in the series.

That "Bedtime Stories" demystifies the score is obvious enough, but the ways in which it remystifies will require a little more unpacking, and it is here Feuer's three myths—spontaneity, integration, and audience—prove their usefulness.

Spontaneity: If there ever were a logical opportunity for Williams's leitmotifs to sneak into the fictive realm, it makes sense here. The Ewoks are shown to be an enthusiastically musical people, with performances enacted in every social context (hunt, feast, battle, celebration) they face. Their native timbres (tribal drums, shofars, pipes) have plausible analogs in the Western orchestra, and Williams can easily merge the harmonic and melodic vocabulary of their nondiegetic leitmotifs (Prokofievian wrong notes, chromatic and quartal harmonies, open fifths) with the idioms of preexisting themes.

Integration: The "Bedtime Story" sequence has an integrative function. It joins together an on-screen community of rebels and aliens. It offers a simplified digest of the original trilogy's plot and its musical materials. And although it lacks historical coherence (due to Threepio's dumbed-down account of events) or much musical continuity (due to Williams's atomized treatment of his themes), it is nevertheless musically *instructive*. The cue functions beautifully as a tutorial for leitmotivic neophytes, with many of the hallmarks of Wagnerian musical prose and none of the baggage.

Audience: By giving us versions of the series' leitmotifs that even Ewoks can comprehend, and making clear their symbolic power with a proxy of an appreciative on-screen audience, the scene invites us to buy into the universal intelligibility of these musical signs—and the pseudo-Romantic idiom they normally occupy. Even in a primitive form, Williams's leitmotifs are able to accurately and *persuasively* represent the stakes of the drama. Inter-species legibility within the film thus implies inter-audience legibility in the real world. Intelligibility is then magnified for *Star Wars* insiders, rewarding those with foreknowledge of the series' thematic catalog by presenting a cascade of (not too hidden) leitmotivic Easter eggs.

The real measure of success of a self-reflexive, narration-heavy scene is how smoothly it can transit back into the standard *plot* mode of the film. By the end of Threepio's story, when we see Han and Leia (and Wicket) embrace, the cue states their love theme with more sustained attention—five measures now, instead of two—and greater harmonic complexity than its surroundings. (Note the clarinet arpeggios in the penultimate measures, and the way they span a dissonant minor ninth/augmented octave.) These details, small though they may be, help Williams's music to be reintegrated into *Return of the Jedi*'s normative vein of nondiegetic underscore. The curtain was lifted, but only so that it could be drawn back, as if to say "yes, these motifs are cute gimmicks but *listen*, are they not still emotively and thematically resonant?"

Williams's irreverence helps make Threepio's scene a musical valediction. Remember that, at the time of its release, *Return of the Jedi* was the final entry in the Skywalker saga, and thus these and other self-mythologizing gestures were warranted. There is some irony to the fact that "Bedtime Stories," of all cues, should be the densest in terms of leitmotivic content per measure of the whole Original Trilogy. Dramaturgically, this might be the closest analog in *Star Wars* to one of those scenes of self-recapitulation that occupy huge swathes of the *Ring* cycle. There is, for instance, the Norns' prologue in *Götterdämmerung*, a seamlessly through-composed colossus of epic narration, and, at 304 measures, an effective, if not efficient, review session for Wagner's library of leitmotifs. At twenty-two bars, Williams's canvas is tiny, his themes infantilized and deflated, here more than ever calling cards rather than integral, dynamic materials prone to development or transformation. In this sense they are functionally equivalent to Threepio's sound effects, low-fidelity citations of the sonic icons of the series—Vader's breathing, the thud of an AT-AT, the clash of lightsabers.

"Bedtime Stories" may well be a parody of the leitmotif technique in *Star Wars*, but there is a sense in which it is also its apotheosis. For sure, the *musical* actualization of leitmotifs takes place in other contexts—the well-developed and autonomous forms the themes inhabit in, say, End Credits or concert arrangements—places where musical signs shed lexical specificity and revert to Abbate-esque "pure musical" flow. And yet, it is during Threepio's ambivalently diegetic performance that the semiotic nature of Williams's themes is at its most overt, when melodic identifiers are being offered in a purposefully underdeveloped way—as hooks, meant for the uninitiated to latch onto a complex and alien story. And for those who enter into this story via these simple symbols, a sense of community, and eventually insider-hood, is granted. Leitmotivic apotheosis à la Threepio thus resides in accessibility rather than autonomy. The cue is Williams's way of saying "you are now part of the tribe."

Insidious Influences in *The Revenge of the Sith*

Threepio's narration ends up being his most impactful character moment, and for the remainder of *Return of the Jedi* and all six subsequent entries, he lapses back into a state of befuddled uselessness. The loquacious droid might seem an odd bedfellow to be paired with Palpatine—first Senator, then Chancellor, Emperor, and eventually Lich. In a quite literal sense, Sheev Palpatine is the author of the entire saga, a mastermind whose malignant will is behind everything that happens from Episode I through Episode IX. Threepio, for the most part, is just along for the ride. And yet, the closest rhyme with the Endor oration, both in terms of plot ramifications and flirtation with musical metalepsis, is the Chancellor's opera house chat with Anakin in Episode III: the "Legend of Darth Plagueis the Wise" monologue.

Palpatine's telling of this "old Sith Legend" is the musical fulcrum around which *Revenge of the Sith* turns, with sonic ramifications that stretch even into the Sequel Trilogy. Anakin, not the saga's most discerning thinker, is played like a fiddle. The Chancellor stokes his mark's ego, reinforces his suspicions toward the Jedi, and discloses a forbidden tale about a mysterious master who could thwart death himself—precisely what Anakin most desperately desires, having been wracked with premonitions of his beloved Padmé's demise. Like Threepio's tale, the sequence's musical make-up is atypical, involving three parameters—timbral, harmonic, and topical—set in strong contrast with the rest of Williams's soundtrack, a throbbing disjunction that begs for interpretation. Even more than the Endor narration, the accompaniment goes beyond would-be-diegetic into a realm of real diegetic↔nondiegetic seepage. At the same time, few scenes reinforce the mythic aura of *Star Wars* more strongly than this one.

Palpatine's Musical Persona(s)

Properly interpreting this sequence will require a quick survey of the archvillain's thematic characterization across the whole Saga. Palpatine is a man of many faces, and accordingly, he commands a host of musical signifiers. As with the Ewoks, it is worthwhile to itemize these sonic markers, though given his overall importance to the series, more detail is warranted for a few aspects of the Emperor's mutable physiognomy. An antagonist of Palpatine's sort should be eclectic and changeable, always prepared with music calibrated to the response *he* wishes to elicit from others. His scoring is upfront and cackling in its villainy when his wish is to dominate or intimidate, and as honeyed or concealed (or simply absent) as it needs to be when his intent is cloaked. No fewer than ten overlapping musical topics follow Palpatine as his plots unspool, only one of which is strictly speaking a leitmotif. Figure 7.12 offers a catalog of the master-manipulator's musical make-up.

The Emperor leitmotif is only the tip of this topical iceberg, which includes leit-timbres, leit-textures, and a handful of one-cue wonders so definitional to his characterization they warrant recognition. Unsurprisingly for a man of many masks, Palpatine's music is eclectic in its influences. Male voices singing at the bottom of their range are the Sith's signature "instrument"—as they are for his puppet Snoke.[41] However, they become an element of the Saga's timbral palette only in *Return of the Jedi*. Palpatine's musical debut in *Empire*, during his communication with Vader via hologram, is voice free. The passage [53:03] is redolent of the so-called "Night Music" of Béla Bartók, its high string lines weaving in and out of dissonant trichords

Topic	Description	Ex.
Emperor Leitmotif	Grammatical theme. Low, slow, and oozing malignance. Melody given to male chorus, harmony w'wind block chords, portamento strs	ROTJ [1:32:36]
Basso Drone	Detachable leit-timbre, becomes a mark of his continuing, if implied, presence in Sequels in Snoke's infrasonic leitmotif	ROTJ [53:44]
Chants & Whispers	Additional vocal topics: Sanskrit chants, whispers, choral pads, Exegol outbursts, etc.	TPM [51:25]
Eerie Polyphony	High, quiet string textures, feat. dissonantly slithering counterpoint	ROTS [14:41]
Genial Politicking	Variably affable, stentorian, or noble melodies heard throughout the prequels, conveying little hint of menace	TPM [1:31:37]
Corruptions	Traces of Palpatine's musical parameters felt infecting others' themes, typically but not exclusively through harmony	AOTC [26:13]
Siren Song	Wordless soprano vocalise, giving impression of horrible temptation and/or tortured internal conflict; specifically female voice.	AOTC [2:12:20]
Necromantic Canon	Hollow-sounding, meandering canonic textures; anticipated in AOTC, solidified in ROTS, recalled/developed in TROS	TROS [1:44:37]
Fascistic Chorale	Fearsome music for brass scoring declaration of Galactic Empire in ROTS. Recalls *Nixon*'s "The Miami Convention"	ROTS [1:35:45]
Sith Psalmody	Pseudo-liturgical style with functional harmony & hymn-like texture; resurrected in hushed "Anthem of Evil" in TROS	ROTS [46:25]

Figure 7.12 Palpatine: A Musical Physiognomy

while figures for celesta float like will-o-the-wisps through the black mire.[42] (A decidedly un-Bartókian element of this cue is the squirming microtonal pedal produced by an ARP synthesizer.) The gestalt of the cue is of inscrutable activity, slow and strange, pitched at the extremes of hearing, the unpredictably overlapping string parts like whispered incantations above a fathomless void.

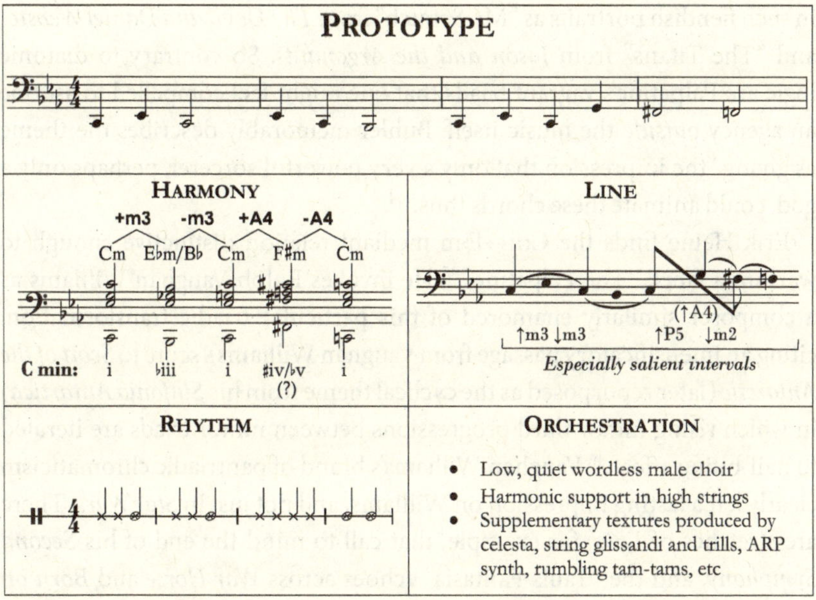

Figure 7.13 EMPEROR, prototype and parameters

The EMPEROR's leitmotif is dissected in terms of its prototypical shape and various structural parameters in Figure 7.13. Though hardly marked in rhythmic or linear profile, the theme is as vivid as they come harmonically. Palpatine's leitmotif draws primarily from a nineteenth-century well in its snaking progress through chromatically estranged triads. Such harmonic witchcraft became a tried-and-true shorthand for the uncanny and sublime in later film music. A more specific referent is what Stephen C. Meyer dubs "ominous priests music," a topos in Romantic opera (*Don Carlo, Les Huguenots*) that would be incorporated into Hollywood biblical epics. Meyer calls this idiom "not only menacing, but also transcendent," an affective blend that owes to the way it calls up genres associated with the holy (hymn, chorale, psalm) and darkens them through disquieting orchestrations and chord progressions.[43] This distancing of an antique idiom is perfect for evoking the darker side of the absolute past. Palpatine effectively takes one of the angelic choirs featured in a score like *The Robe* (Newman) or *Ben-Hur* (Rózsa) and gives it a satanic makeover. The EMPEROR's use of minor triads in minor third- and tritone-based transformations (e.g., Cm↔E♭m, Cm↔F♯m) as a harmonic proxy for diabolism dates back at least to Liszt (*Faust* and *Dante* symphonies), though a more proximal source might be Bernard Herrmann, in such fiendish portraits as "Mr. Scratch" from *The Devil and Daniel Webster* and "The Titans" from *Jason and the Argonauts*. So contrary to diatonic logic are Palpatine's vagrant triads that one might feel compelled to ascribe an agency *outside* the music itself. Buhler memorably describes the theme as giving "the impression that only a very powerful sorcerer, perhaps only a god, could animate these chords thus."[44]

Erik Heine finds the Cm↔E♭m mediant relation distinctive enough to warrant a label, "The Palpatine."[45] He invokes Ralph Vaughan Williams as a composer similarly enamored of this particular triadic transformation, citing an intensificatory passage from Vaughan Williams's score to *Scott of the Antarctic* (later repurposed as the cyclical theme from his *Sinfonia Antartica*) in which rising minor third progressions between minor triads are iterated to nail-biting effect.[46] Vaughan Williams's brand of pantriadic chromaticism clearly left a lasting impression on Williams, and not just in *Star Wars*. There are stretches of *Jaws*, for example, that call to mind the end of his *Second Symphony*, and the "Tallis Fantasia" echoes across *War Horse* and *Born on the Fourth of July*.[47] However, with respect to Palpatine's musical portraiture, the British symphonist's imprint is strongest not in the villain's leitmotif but in his auxiliary topics.

One Vaughan-Williamsism arises in the "Necromantic Canon" from *Revenge of the Sith* as the villain instructs his new apprentice [1:18:34], and Williams later deploys it in the PSALM OF THE SITH in *Rise of Skywalker* as Rey confronts Palpatine [1:44:37]. These moments resemble similar passages of ghostly chromatic counterpoint in several of Vaughan Williams's symphonies.[48] Meanwhile, the "Siren Song" topic that appears at the conclusion of *Attack of the Clones* [2:12:21] is a close cousin to the vocalise for female soloist that occurs at intervals in Vaughan Williams's *Sinfonia Antartica*.[49] Its descendant in Episode II is less florid but marginally more active harmonically, swathed in a succession of skin-crawling chords—F♯$^{+}$, C♯m|Dm, F♯|Gm. In Vaughan Williams's score, the vocalise is at once a representation of the desolation of the polar landscape and a siren call that lures men like Scott to their doom. In *Attack of the Clones* it has a comparable function, serving up chilly dread ("... Excellent, everything is going as planned.") while also feeling strangely alluring, in the way a hypnotist might beguile his victims. Williams referred to the passage's "ghostly ambiance that really only the human voice can do."[50] It is the most apt musical rendering of the appeal of the Dark Side in the series.

The seductiveness of the "Siren Song" topic points to another salient quality in the Emperor's music: its ability to charm and corrupt. Though not frequent, there are moments where Palpatine's influence can be heard warping music that might otherwise be heard as sitting on the "light side" of the leitmotivic ledger.[51] When the camera turns to Ian McDiarmid's face during Qui-Gon's funeral in Episode I, an A-minor chord starts writhing atop the provisional D♭-major tonic [2:08:17], answering Mace Windu's question of "who was destroyed, the master or the apprentice?" In the next and final scene [2:08:28], an on-screen band of Gungans plays a rollicking piece of diegetic celebration music, what Williams called "Augie's Municipal Band." The heroes beam and the mood is bright—the visual rhyme is with the victory ceremony at the end of Episode IV. But the real winner is Chancellor Palpatine, as it is his leitmotif, or rather a major/pentatonic reworking, that echoes across the Naboo parade grounds. The tune in this chipper state is sung by a wordless *children*'s choir. The dramatic irony is thick: here is the most innocent of timbres, unwittingly rendering the series' foulest theme.

The Timeless Art of Seduction

Like "Threepio's Bedtime Story" on Endor, "Augie's Municipal Band" manages the rare feat of migrating an element of symphonic underscore (the melodic contours of the EMPEROR motif) into the real universe of *Star Wars*. Unlike Threepio, Palpatine's manipulation of the fantastical gap is masked, giving him—and Williams—a measure of plausible deniability.[52] The metaleptic traversal at the end of Episode I is but a foretaste of the more profound disjuncture that occurs in *Revenge of the Sith*'s Plagueis tale. The venue for Anakin's temptation is noteworthy: the "Galaxies Opera House," Coruscant's luxurious temple to the arts. It is no coincidence that Palpatine's most effectively deceptive speech takes place within a diegetic performance space—in particular, an opera house—which comes loaded with cultural, economic, and intertextual connotations. For him to choose an elite fine-arts destination to be the site of seduction makes a cruel kind of sense: Palpatine is essentially an aristocrat, while Anakin comes from abject poverty and slavery. The choice of a palace of wealth and social power is the technique of a groomer, a way of unsettling his visibly uncomfortable and out-of-place mark.

The night's show is a weird, aqueous ballet called "Squid Lake." But we are witnessing two performances: one on stage and one in the Chancellor's private box. Palpatine is playing a part for Anakin, never outright lying but always exploiting the credulous Jedi's anxieties and suspicions. That the monologue should occur against the backdrop of another show—itself ominous and vague and only ever partially glimpsed by the audience—gives the set piece a distinct *mise-en-abyme* quality, of plots within plots, deceptions piling upon deceptions. Were Palpatine's true intentions not completely transparent to even the most naive viewer at this point in the series, the theatrical setting would give proof to his true nature, as a malign, rather than merely hammy, actor. For everyone else who watches Episode III knowing full well Palpatine is the big bad, the scene's recursive nature underlines the Chancellor's role as narrative manipulator extraordinaire.

The music Williams wrote for this sequence falls into two cues, "Palpatine's TV Set" and "Palpatine's Big Pitch." Figure 7.14 depicts the sequence's overall form. Unusually for *Star Wars*, the constituent cues overlap in places, with a few seconds of the former phasing in and out with the latter at times—likely as much a decision of the music and sound editing team as Williams himself. Though "TV Set" is the more radical of the two, it is worth considering first the more traditional underscore that makes up the "Big Pitch." This fifty-measure cue accompanies Palpatine's critique of the hypocrisy of the Jedi and his monologue about his heavily implied former master, Darth Plagueis "The Wise." In most respects, "Palpatine's Big Pitch" is conventional *Star Wars*ian musical prose, its most salient feature being its lack of leitmotifs—nary a note of VADER or the EMPEROR's themes in their definitive forms. In their place,

42:39	44:25	44:55	45:15	45:55	46:24	46:55	47:20 (–48:00)
3m2a **Palpatine's TV Set**	3m3 **Palpatine's Big Pitch** (with spans of 3m2a intermittently fading in)						
BASSO DRONE	skulking strings	grave brass 1, skulking strs	SEDUCTION + BASSO DRONE	skulking strs. + BASSO DRONE	PLAGUAL CADENCE **[IAC]**	tritone harmonics + BASSO DRONE	grave brass 2, transitional crescendo
B_1 pedal	⇝	Dm→C♯m	Bm→Dm	⇝	C♯m	C♯$_1$ pedal	C♯⇝Bm→Dm
Ani arrives, updates Palp, others leave, Palp describes Jedi plot	"They're planning to betray me…	"They asked you to do something…	"Remember back to your teachings…	"The Jedi are selfless."	"It's a Sith Legend…	"He could actually save people from death?"	"The only thing he was afraid of was losing his power…"

Figure 7.14 Form of the opera house scene, *Revenge of the Sith* (ROTS, 3m2A and 3m3, 42:39–48:00)

Figure 7.15 SEDUCTION motif in "Palpatine's Big Pitch" (ROTS, 3m3, 45:16)

Williams offers a fair amount of low, skulking string writing (see Chapter 3, Figure 3.7), as well as some leitmotivic premonitions and abstractions.

Midway through, "Palpatine's Big Pitch" introduces a descending clarinet figure, SEDUCTION. This motif lends an air of transgressive catechism to Palpatine's forbidden lesson to Anakin: "All who gain power are afraid to lose it. . . . Good is a point of view. . . . The Sith and the Jedi are similar in almost every way. . . . " Figure 7.15 displays this chilling passage. The stratified three-voice texture in which the SEDUCTION motif is embedded unrolls with dreadful purpose, like three devils, each whispering a different lie in Anakin's ear. The rhythmic gait and melodic turns of VADER's mature theme are withheld here, but a *harmonic* foreshadowing of that leitmotif is clear—the background hexatonicism, the $\flat\hat{1}/\sharp\hat{7}$ ambivalence, the implication of the i$\leftrightarrow$♭vi associative progression. All that's needed is a little push.

Williams pays off the SEDUCTION motif during a later scene in which Anakin is anointed as a Sith, in the cue "I Am the Senate."[53] As the fallen Jedi kneels and pledges himself to his dark mentor's teachings, a transposed and varied version of the seduction motif (Figure 7.16) issues from horns and is immediately imitated at the octave by tuba. Palpatine looks down approvingly, to the sound of a i$\leftrightarrow$♭vi progression for low brass, then dubs his new apprentice: "Henceforth, you will be known as Darth . . . Vader." With that line, a baptismal statement of VADER's true anthem—melody, rhythm, harmony all—is pronounced in full. Touches like these, prefiguring and then refiguring a theme, are among the best aspects of *Revenge of the Sith*'s score. They build to and compensate for the abrupt, even inexplicable, way Anakin turns to a murderous monster as the screenplay tells it.

When Vader's theme does emerge in its full form in "I Am the Senate," it is augmented with an overlay of vocal droning that, rather than being

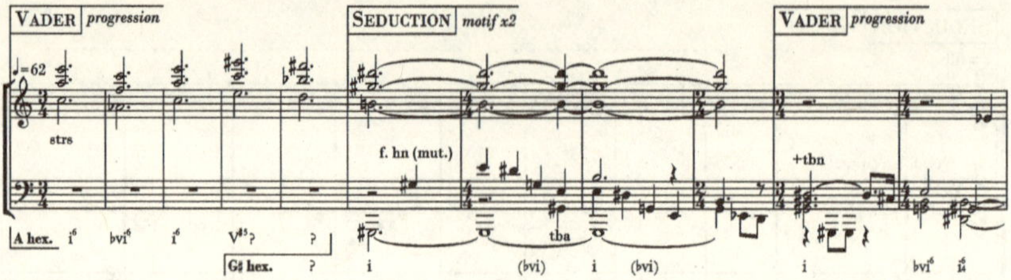

Figure 7.16 Recall of SEDUCTION Motif in "I Am the Senate" (ROTS, 4m6, 1:16:10)

written into the score, was spliced on top of Williams's music. The source of this sinister extra layer of music is the first part of the Opera House sequence, "Palpatine's TV Set", an oddly named cue that was, at its time, *sui generis* in the Skywalker Saga. Though lasting a minute and a half, the cue comprises just four measures of notated music and contains only two instrumental lines. One is for a gong, stroked ad lib with a superball mallet to create an unearthly sound heard occasionally in science-fiction scores. (This same timbre initiates Williams's score for *E.T.*, and is subtly present during Palpatine's holographic introduction in *Empire.*) The other is a glacial succession of four vowels, "oh," "ah," "eh," and "ee," rendered quietly by men's chorus, with instructions to sing "quasi Tibetan monk" style, on an abyssal pitch, the B below the bass clef staff, below the bottom of the male vocal register.[54] The timbre that results is as close as the series comes to treating sound design as score in the contemporary manner—hazy, spacious, rich in shifting overtones, and deeply unnerving. More than anything, it is the *stasis* of it all that makes "Palpatine's TV Set" a singularity in the *Star Wars* musical firmament: here is a cue based on the complete nullification of melody.

This wall of *basso profondo* fog makes for an oddly dark, decidedly unballetic kind of music to diegetically accompany the Mon Calamari swim routine. And yet, source music it is—at least at first—emanating from the vast concert hall and taking on its resonant acoustic properties. Though there are no on-screen singers, it is plausible that Anakin and Palpatine are hearing this music too, along with those dancers, wriggling about each other like sperm, in and out of an oversized, watery ovum. But "Palpatine's TV Set" is also *more* than source music: it rings too many affective and leit-timbral bells, bringing to mind patterns already well established in Williams's symphonic underscore for the series.

As we have seen, wordless vocals were established as the timbre of choice for the Emperor all the way back in *Return of the Jedi.* Palpatine's "instrument" has always pushed against typical associations of musical vocality. The voice in his control is obscure and mendacious rather than intelligible and direct, not a marker of living presence but of something inaccessible, unnatural, other. Wordless voices continue to function in this perverse fashion in the Prequel Trilogy, even as new choral cues *with* texts—most having dark and conflicted signifieds, if not the Emperor himself as subject—now enter the *Star Wars* lexicon for the first time. But here in the Opera scene, the Emperor's musical instrument undergoes a critical abstraction. Already stripped of words, it is now stripped of melody as well, becoming pure unnerving texture—a sign of the Dark Side's total sonic control over the soundtrack.

The way this vocal malignancy has seeped out of one narrative layer and spread to another is especially insidious at those junctures where the aforementioned blurring of "TV Set" and "Big Pitch" is most evident. The end of the passage bearing the SEDUCTION motif, for example, sees the droning vocals slither back to the fore of the mix, as if to serve as a closing stroke that ends Palpatine's first line of attack on Anakin's ethical foundation. This diegetic bleed-in has real musical consequences too: where Williams's cue as originally written shifts from a B-minor point of reference (mm. 13–19) to D minor (m. 20), that new tonal center is undercut by the imposed persistence of B_1 in the bass, supplied by those tenebrous choristers.

Soon after, Palpatine (and Williams) releases the rhetorical ace up his sleeve, a fable concerning a "Dark Lord of the Sith so powerful . . . he could even keep the ones he loved from dying." For four measures, all diegetic and pseudo-diegetic sounds besides Ian McDiarmid's voice vanish, and the score quietly introduces an idea of great significance. With a chamber texture unique to this passage (six violas and four cellos, faintly illumined with a synth pad halo), Williams rolls out a diatonic progression in C♯ minor. Reproduced in Figure 7.17, the PLAGUAL CADENCE—what else could this be called?—is a beacon of functional, tightly voice-led, resoundingly *tonal* harmony, cutting through a fog of impenetrable chromaticism. As soon as Palpatine delivers his clincher clause, "to create life," Williams closes the phrase with what William Caplin would call an *iconic cadence*: a trope of Romantic music in which a mannered and old-fashioned cadence stands out in a piece otherwise largely bereft of them.[55] Old-fashioned in this cue is an understatement: the passage sounds several hundred years earlier in style than the average *Star Wars* cue. The iv→V^4_2→ i progression and $\hat{1}$-$\hat{7}$-$\hat{1}$ melody that supports Palpatine's revelation has a distinctly scholastic quality, in both

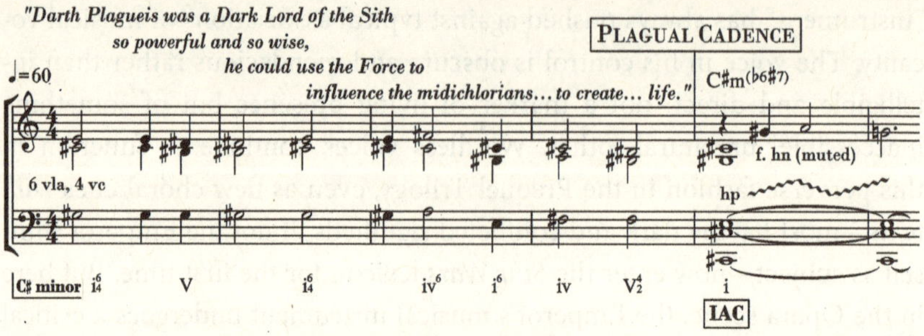

Figure 7.17 PLAGUAL CADENCE in "Palpatine's Big Pitch" (ROTS, 3m3, 46:24)

senses: in its by-the-book formality and the undertones of a sacred harmonic idiom, specifically Renaissance Christian in character. Indeed, the PLAGUAL CADENCE sounds archaic and reverent. Maybe even a little reassuring.

The tonal surety of Plagueis's progression sets it apart, not just within the 3m2A/3m3 complex but *Revenge of the Sith* as a whole, and affords one of only four authentic cadences in the score that are not connected to the FORCE theme. (Those others, in "Lament" and "Boys Continue/Battle of the Heroes," were inspected in Chapters 2 and 4.) Functional diatonicism is remarkably uncommon in the Prequel Trilogy, particularly in connection with the antagonists. Similarly rare is the emulation of sacred music—"liturgico" as noted in the conductor's score during the chorale. Indeed, the material this hymn most resembles is not from the Skywalker Saga, but another miraculous subject: the Holy Grail, as represented in Williams's score to *Indiana Jones and the Last Crusade* by a leitmotif comparably minor in mode and ecclesiastical in inflection. This PLAGUAL CADENCE stands as a startling contravention to the usually iron-clad harmonic dichotomy Buhler observes in *Star Wars*, wherein the Light Side is represented by functional, semiotically fluid tonal music, the Dark Side a perverse, nonfunctional pantriadic chromaticism. This inversion is exactly what makes the short passage effective. Its aim is to scramble the listener's well-calibrated ears, to use an insinuatingly beautiful type of music that can bypass suspicions and render the receiver susceptible to poisoned promises.[56]

The above description of the PLAGUAL CADENCE intentionally leaves vague *who* that receiver is. A conventional interpretation is that the passage is for the filmgoers; the mysterious hymn is meant to get the audience to, if not outright root for the bad guy, then at least become intrigued by whatever mythos-enriching information he has to offer. But a reading some might consider to be *unnatural* is also possible. Just as in Threepio's narration, it is useful to entertain the notion that putatively nondiegetic music, even though not heard by an on-screen character, might nevertheless be working toward the same rhetorical goal as the diegetic storyteller it accompanies. This musical ploy is *for* Anakin as much as for us; he is a man whose every choice is driven by a craving for control and a terror of loss. The charms of such rigorous and regulated harmony, bathed in a set of sanctified associations, might prove irresistible to a man who is desperate and rootless. If Darth Sidious can seem to manipulate the score itself at times, it stands to reason that his pupil can be manipulated *by* his dark diegetic enchantments too.

With "Duel of the Fates," "Threepio's Bedtime Story," and "Palpatine's Big Pitch," we see three sequences in which music ceases merely responding to the action and starts to evaluate, participate, even steer it. Though their effect is subtle at times, these cues expose the inadequacy of the term "underscore" to describe such active and assertive musical storytelling. The scenes they accompany do not provide much plot momentum, but Williams's cues make these *decisive* moments within their respective films and the *Star Wars* franchise as a whole. With their capacity for sonic self-reference and summation, these special episodes are overt turns to the epic-narrational mode—distancing, ritualistic, repetitive, reflexive—in a way only ever implicit during the majority of the saga.

Narratological analysis is often bound up with questions as to the nature and agenda of the implied storyteller, a tale's "organizing intelligence." In these cues, we find different avatars for the master storyteller of *Star Wars*. One is considered a literal god by the gullible Ewoks. Another is a sneakier but no less powerful creator of stories, insofar as Palpatine is the figurative author of everything that unfolds narratively in the series. And there is, of course, John Williams, whose music bubbles to the surface in unaccustomed ways in these rare scenes. Yet for all their peculiarities, these cues of epic narration merely foreground what music has been doing all along: steering with supreme forcefulness the story throughout, from the moment that B♭ major erupted with the first film's opening frame. When it comes to who is really orchestrating this generation-spanning myth, Palpatine has nothing on Williams.

8

Star Wars as Concert

"Hear It Again for the First Time"

"Own One of the Most Memorable Aspects of the Star Wars Trilogy Special Editions... The Music"

"Hear Star Wars the Way It Was Meant to Be Heard!"

The Work Concept Awakens

Advertisements can be sources of unexpected insight. The slogans quoted above could be found splashed across a set of print ads from 1997 for the *Star Wars: Special Edition* "Deluxe Edition" Soundtracks.[1] Timed to coincide with the theatrical re-release of the Original Trilogy (with Lucas-sanctioned "improvements"), these albums represented a milestone in the reception of Williams's music. Produced by Nicholas Redman and distributed by RCA Victor, they each boasted two holographically bedazzled CDs, neatly slipped inside a miniature hardcover book with probing liner notes written by Michael Matessino.[2] In an article in *Film Score Monthly* discussing the albums' genesis, Matessino expressed a feeling of deep responsibility and pride in the product: "All involved truly believe that the end result will please the entire spectrum of listeners from neophyte to veteran."[3] And indeed, these Special Editions albums were received like manna from soundtrack heaven.[4]

Of course, the Skywalker Saga did not lack a discographic legacy prior to the late 1990s. In addition to the single-disc original soundtracks, fans could avail themselves of compilations like *John Williams Conducts John Williams: The Star Wars Trilogy* (1990, Sony Classical). Or they could immerse themselves in a series of artfully produced "symphonic suites" on RCA Victor (1978 and 1983) and Varèse Sarabande (1980) labels, all under the baton of film-music evangelist Charles Gerhardt. Aficionados would also certainly have picked up *The Original Soundtrack Anthology*, a four-disc boxed set from the Arista label (1993), also produced by Redman. But the

Special Edition sets offered something genuinely new, much more than a luxury repackaging of the same numbers with some incremental sonic improvements.[5] Here, for the first time, was very nearly *all* the music, great swaths of which had never been available on record, especially from Episode VI.[6] And there was more: each CD also contained a trove of cut passages, alternates, source cues, and, in the case of *A New Hope*'s "Main Title," a fascinating series of additional takes smuggled into a secret track. Around the world, the cups of soundtrack completionists ran over.

The *Star Wars* Special Edition sets were comprehensive, systematic, and polished. Everything about the albums, from the metallic seals embossed on their covers to Matessino's track-by-track exegeses, seemed to trumpet their status as standalone texts—artifacts of cultural significance and compositional integrity, worthy of preservation. No longer just movie scores, these were proper musical *works*. And proper musical works deserve to be heard in full: hence the meticulous inclusion of virtually every note Williams wrote for the series in film-chronological order. The Special Editions represent a turning point in the formation of the *Star Wars* musical "work-concept."[7]

Far from being an innate status, the idea of a musical object being a "work" is always acquired and historically contingent. We see this consolidation of *Star Wars*' work-concept in high gear in those remarkable promotional slogans quoted above. According to the ads, Williams's music is a detachable "aspect" of special memorability that can now be "owned" as a product and an infinitely repeatable experience. One's cherished memory of this franchise is paradoxically something that can be heard *again* but also "for the first time." For sure, a good digital remastering can make old music sound as if brand new. But the promise of an *originary* reencounter with Williams's scores suggests a deeper prize: an authentic symphonic experience. It is as though what one might have previously heard in the context of the film itself was incomplete or unrepresentative.

This sentiment is also embedded in the most remarkable of the slogans, where the listener is enjoined to "Hear Star Wars the Way It Was Meant to Be Heard." Here too, this could be read as simply a reference to the album's superior sonic quality. But the deeper implication is about textual autonomy: John Williams's music, presented in full and on its own, is *more* aesthetically fulfilling than the obvious alternative, in the film, with all that pesky dialogue and distracting imagery. Imagine *Star Wars* not as a movie but as a concert, heard in the privacy of one's home. Is this not the logical endpoint of George Lucas's frequent claim that his films are, at heart, silent movies? Of course, no sane advertising executive would have approved a message that overtly disassociated a musical score from its blockbuster source franchise. But we can hypothesize that subtext literalized: "*The Best Way to Hear Star Wars Music! Without the Star Wars*."[8]

To approach *Star Wars* as these advertisements endorse, as works of art separable—and preferably separated—from their multimedia containers, is to take cine-symphonic listening to its counterintuitive extreme. We need not go nearly so far. But it is important to recognize that John Williams's contribution to the saga has always had a second existence, one outside the bounds of the movies themselves. How could the scores not, with a franchise as obsessed with transmedial saturation as *Star Wars*? Consciously steering your attention to the score, whether as it occurs inside the film or in one of these freestanding forms, does not detract from the enjoyment or integrity of the filmworld. The 1997 Special Edition albums, like all *Star Wars* music on disc, constitute what literary theorists call a *paratext*: a creative product that sits outside the frame of some larger artwork, but which is still relevant, maybe even essential, to its functioning. Strictly speaking, paratexts are auxiliary objects, but their role in shaping interpretation and the parent text can be decisive. With a book, paratexts may be confined to the material object—aspects like front matter, footnotes, cover art, and so on. But just as easily, these outside elements can surround the text, in forms as diverse as author interviews, bookstore stands, and written analyses. These same paratextual manifestations exist for film music.

A movie soundtrack is an archetypal cinematic paratext, capable of more than just hype. The OST can enrich, clarify, or even substitute for the main text for a sufficiently invested listener. And unlike other cinematic paratexts—trailers, DVD extras, branded merchandise—musical supplements have a way of taking on a life of their own. Perhaps this is because of music's tendency to float away from signification, even in the most vivid and referential cases (recall our discussion of semantic drift in Chapter 3). Maybe it is music's seeming direct line to our emotions, its propensity to cause our bodies to respond in physical sympathy, or its sheer impressiveness as a product of human technical skill and labor. Or it could just be the case that, with a body of music as rich and satisfyingly presented as the Skywalker Saga (in the *Special Edition* albums, at least), we really have a paratext that has ascended—or, rather, we have caused to ascend—to unqualified *text* status.

There are many musical traces from *Star Wars* that straddle the text/paratext boundary, of which recordings (soundtracks, singles, expanded reissues, and so on) are only the most obvious examples. Over the course of this chapter, we will dive into this musical world with one foot inside the Skywalker Saga films and one foot out. As will become evident, each musical paratext, whether a night at the symphony or a compact disc, involves three recurrent issues: how to achieve formal coherence for music written to be subordinated to film; how to produce a sense of satisfying closure; and how to strike a balance of musical novelty and repetition. The way Williams addresses these challenges makes for a most fascinating subject for deep musical analysis, and in the pages that follow, we will see just how much the musical afterlife of *Star Wars* survives—and thrives—in forms fully detached from the movie theater.

A full account of every musical paratext spawned from *Star Wars* could easily fill a book. There are folios of sheet music, MIDI files, jazz covers, disco remixes, TV commercials, video games, theme parks, and, yes, analytical texts like this one. Without discounting their significance, the focus of this chapter will be on the paratextual forms that are directly the product of Williams's labor: authorized albums, orchestral performances, and multimedia screenings. Not accidentally, these are also the paratexts that are either heard in concert venues or aspire to the condition of concert programs. Although some taxonomic bookkeeping is in order—in as diverse a textual universe as this, categories are important—the overriding concern will be formal and interpretive. At the end, we will apply these tools and categories to a culminating case study, "The Forest Battle" from *Return of the Jedi*. A closing section will reflect on the psychology of listening and relistening, and in doing so set up the following, final chapter.

Original Soundtrack Albums

Complete and chronological, the *Star Wars* "Special Edition" albums may claim with some justification to represent Williams's music "the way it was meant to be heard." But they were specialty items, aimed at collectors and connoisseurs. Most listeners encounter Williams's music in a different format, one whose significance is revealed by the fact that its name is used for both the musical score itself and its paratextual presentation: the soundtrack. More accurately described as the *original soundtrack album* (OST), the soundtrack may be aimed at a more casual consumer base, but it is a work of no lesser artistic merit or analytical fascination. After the concert arrangements, these are the musical paratexts most directly bearing the composer's imprimatur, and most likely to be held up as *the text* for those who wish to hear Williams's efforts in a standalone form.

Soundtrack albums, limited by disc capacity and listener attention, are prime sites for negotiating those challenges brought up at the head of the chapter, especially selectivity and ordering. Williams always takes care to present a satisfying album experience, with judiciously chosen score highlights arranged into a coherent package. Completionists may grumble at seemingly inexplicable omissions and duplications and bristle at tracks presented in anything other than strict film chronology. On the flip side, some *Star Wars* OSTs contain music *not* heard in the film—sometimes highly salient music like the "Speeder Chase" and "Anthem of Evil" tracks on *The Rise of Skywalker*. The aim of a good OST is not to simply reproduce what the composer wrote down or what filmgoers heard, but rather to *represent* it.[9] Doing so necessarily involves aesthetic compromises, but it also provides opportunities for reframing and refinement.

In discussing *The Phantom Menace*, Williams offered some insight into this seldom discussed side of his creative process.

> The first thing we need to do is to hone down the score from 120 minutes to approximately 80 or 75 minutes that a CD will hold. And what I do in that process is to continue to file the music down so that it makes a musical program, in the same way that I would build a concert program with an orchestra that would have a beginning, a middle, and an end, with a set of varying dynamics, the way you'd plan a menu almost. That speed is varied and dynamics are varied so that you have aural interest. You don't want to put all the loud music together and all the soft music together, any more than you would in a concert program. . . . And so this [album] becomes solely the aural representation of the soundtrack, and so I work out a musical program that I think is most listenable and most engaging in terms of the musical sounds themselves.[10]

The composer's vision of a successful soundtrack album is *explicitly* the same as for a concert program.[11] It must be varied and well paced, with care given to the distribution of pieces of differing tempi and dynamic levels. One would not want to attend a concert where all the most exciting, fast-paced music happened within the first fifteen minutes; the same is true for a movie score album. To craft a convincing beginning, middle, and end for a soundtrack-as-concert is to dole out cues in such a way that small climaxes build to large ones, thematic promises posed early are paid off later, and a broad arc of rising and falling action is conveyed purely in *musical* terms, not the presence of literal plot points.

Williams adheres to no simple formula in constructing his OSTs; each sets its own musical priorities, invents its own version of what the ideal seventy-five to eighty minutes of *Star Wars* score should be. While it contains its own peculiarities and compromises, the official album for *Revenge of the Sith* is representative enough to stand as a case study. Figure 8.1 summarizes the relationship of the *Revenge* soundtrack to the score "as written." Much material is missing, including any sign of YODA's leitmotif and arguably the turning-point cue of the Prequel Trilogy, Anakin's official christening as "Darth Vader." The disc's order is loosely chronological but punctuated by discontinuities. "Battle of the Heroes" is the music for the final leg of Anakin and Obi-Wan's climactic duel, but it appears as the album's third track. This is not so strange, as Williams often frontloads his soundtrack albums with notable set pieces and concert arrangements. Only four of the disc's fifteen tracks correspond to a single cue from the nearly sixty that Williams penned for the episode. Many tracks contain passages from two or more cues, sometimes from widely separated scenes. This too is typical: the Original Soundtrack (OST) for *Star Wars* included tracks that were composites of two or more cues, and this practice persisted through all subsequent episodes. Reconstructing Williams's thought process behind these "programming" choices has never been straightforward. Complicating matters is the fact that these albums' constitution is not univocal in terms of authorship. In the case of Episode III, the film's music editors Kenneth Wannberg and Ramiro Belgardt were heavily involved in the disc's presentation as well. Nevertheless, despite its seemingly anarchic sequencing and authorial fuzziness, the *Revenge of the Sith* OST represents the score well and coheres as a musical argument—so long as one is not fixated on what is missing or misplaced.

Many of these peculiarities of album programming are embodied in Track 13, "Grievous Speaks to Lord Sidious." A little under three minutes long, this track grafts a full-throated proclamation of the cyborg General's leitmotif from the end of Act 1 [27:35] onto a depressive recollection of ANAKIN AND PADMÉ located well into the film's final act [1:41:39]. The result sounds incongruous if one expects the album to simply retell the story of the movie.

Track Title	Time	Cue [* indicates presence of cuts]	Leitmotifs	Dynamic/Tempo
1. "Star Wars *and* The Revenge of the Sith"	0:00–1:17 1:16–3:15 3:15–4:45 4:46–7:31	1m2 "Main Title" 1m3 "Boys into Battle" 1m4 "They're Coming Around" 1m5 "The Elevator Scene"*	Luke Force -- Grievous	Loud & Fast
2. "Anakin's Dream"	0:00–4:46	2m6 "Scenes and Dreams"*	Anakin & Padmé, Force	Quiet & Slow
3. "Battle of the Heroes"	0:00–3:44	6m9 "Revenge of the Sith DVD Version"	B.O.T.H., Force	Loud & Fast
4. "Anakin's Betrayal"	0:00–4:04	5m3 "Lament"*	Lament	Moderate & Slow
5. "General Grievous"	0:00–1:23 1:24–2:20 2:20–3:34 3:35–4:07	3m7 "Riding the Lizard" 4m4 "Rolling With Grievous" 4m4a "Fighting With Grievous"* 4m4 "Rolling With Grievous" (ending)	Force -- -- --	Loud & Fast
6. "Palpatine's Teachings"	0:00–1:37 1:38–2:27 2:28–5:27	3m2a "Palpatine's TV Set 4m3 "Palpatine's Seduction* 3m1 "Council Meeting*	-- Shmi (?) Vader, Force	Quiet & Slow
7. "Grievous and the Droids"	0:00–2:38	2m1 [Untitled]	Luke, Force	Loud & Fast
8. "Padmé's Ruminations"	0:00–1:36 1:36–3:17	4m5a "Padme's Ruminations" 5m1 "Palpatine Instructs Anakin"*	Anakin & Padmé --	Quiet & Slow
9. "Anakin vs. Obi-Wan"	0:00–3:57	6m4 "Heroes Collide"*	B.O.T.H., Vader, Force	Loud & Fast
10. "Anakin's Dark Deeds"	0:00–2:14 2:15–4:06	5m7 "Anakin's Dark Deeds" 6m1 "It Can't Be"*	-- --	Loud & Moderate Quiet→Loud & Slow
11. "Enter Lord Vader"	0:00–4:16	5m6 "Moving Things Along"	Vader, Emperor	Loud & Moderate
12. "The Immolation Scene"	0:00–2:42	7m1 "The Immolation Scene"	--	Moderate & Slow
13. "Grievous Speaks to Lord Sidious"	0:00–1:50 1:50–2:50	2m5 "Grievous Travels to Palpatine" 6m2 "A Moody Trip"	Grievous Anakin & Padmé	Loud & Moderate Quiet & Slow
14. "The Birth of the Twins *and* Padmé's Destiny"	0:00–1:26 1:26–3:37	7m3 "The Birth of the Twins"* 7m4 "The Death of Padme"	Funeral, Force	Quiet & Slow
15. "A New Hope *and* End Credits"	0:00–1:22 1:22–4:00 4:00–6:43 6:44–13:05	7m7 "A Home for the Twins"* 7m8a "End Credits" (from *ANH*) 7m8b [Battle of the Heroes + transitions] 7m8c "Throne Room & Finale"* (from *ANH*)	Leia, Luke, Force, Luke, Rebel Fanfare, Leia B.O.T.H., Force, T.R., Force, Luke, R.F.	Moderate & Slow Fast & Loud (credits)

Figure 8.1 Structure of *Revenge of the Sith* OST

But it works quite well musically. The transition [1:20] is seamless, with the source cue of the former ("Grievous Travels to Palpatine") ending in the same E-minor tonality that begins the latter ("A Moody Trip"). There is also a nice motivic echo: the trumpet figure that closes 2m5 is corroborated intervallically with a descending three-note motif—the MISERY TRICHORD—that saturates 6m2 and much else besides. At a higher level, the ANAKIN AND PADMÉ quote allows the love theme one last gasp—a crucial ingredient in the score's tragic arc but conspicuously absent in the penultimate OST track, "The Birth of the Twins and Padmé's Destiny."

Even where ostensibly contiguous cues share the same track, important music may still be missing. For example, the film's opening Battle of Coruscant is represented on Track 1 ("Main Title and Revenge of the Sith") and appears to run through three cues, 1m2 through 1m5, in correct film order. However, the sequence's musical climax, a short but eventful cue entitled "Get 'Em, R2" (1m4a) is omitted on disc; lost, in the process, is a catchy one-cue-wonder for the buzz droids and, more pertinently, the Prequel Trilogy's sole iteration of the REBEL FANFARE [6:59]. This may be a throwaway moment in the score's overarching narrative, but other excisions are not so incidental. Indeed, the OST seems almost to go out of its way to omit music for several key sequences, including some passages treated elsewhere in this book: chunks of the end of both "Anakin's Betrayal" and "Anakin's Dark Deeds" and the whole of "Palpatine's Big Pitch."

Listeners vexed by the absence of important musical moments on the official soundtrack do have one ironic consolation: that same album just as often contains fine music that, by accident of mixing or editing, was *not* audible in the film. The fifth track on the *Revenge* OST, "General Grievous," offers exactly this, containing four minutes of the wildest action music Williams penned for the Saga. The whole track is an object lesson in how disconnected cues can be linked and recombined to form a satisfying entrée on the soundtrack's menu. "General Grievous" may not fit most listeners' prior conception of an iconic *Star Wars* composition. Yet it is a fitting example of how elements of an inherently subordinated film score may be reworked for a compelling independent listen, an experience of hearing again "for the first time."

Despite its title, "General Grievous" is not a character piece in the mold of "Princess Leia's Theme" or "The Imperial March." In fact, the villain's strutting leitmotif is not heard within the track—not so much as an allusive intervallic or rhythmic hint. Rather, the track is a compilation of three cues involving the general's discovery and defeat midway through the movie. The first portion, "Riding the Lizard," follows Obi-Wan as he tracks Grievous down while mounted on an alien sauropod. The track's other two components derive from "Rolling with Grievous" and "Fighting with Grievous," corresponding to the chase sequence and ensuing melee that results in the General's smoldering end. Figure 8.2 depicts its overall make-up, with information about the sources of its various sections as well as descriptive language about relevant motivic and expressive features.

Between "Riding the Lizard" and "Fighting with Grievous" lie three cues and one insert that are absent from this track but heard in various states of completion in the film. One set (3m8, 4mX, 4m1A) accompanies Obi-Wan's initial standoff with the robotic general, before the chase ensues. In the movie, much of this sequence, including the quadruple saber duel, is tracked with GRIEVOUS's leitmotif from a much earlier cue, "Grievous Travels to Palpatine." After this cyborg-centered fracas, the scene cuts to Coruscant, where the Chancellor finally drops his mask to Anakin, all accompanied by 4m3 "Palpatine's Seduction." Unlike other instances of missing or out-of-sequence material, the omission of these cues from the track "General Grievous" is a boon to the piece's formal and emotional coherence. Excluding them allows the track to build and sustain momentum, free from lulls or disruptions, with nary an extraneous theme. In fact, the constituent cues that are heard on "General Grievous" are motivically interlinked, although not in a leitmotivic

A-SECTION			**B-SECTION**		
A1	A2	A3	B1	B2	B1'
Source Cue: 3m7 "Riding The Lizard"			4m4 "Rolling w/Grievous"	4m4a "Fighting w/ Grievous"	4m4 "Rolling…"
In Score: mm. 1–63 (full)			mm. 1–50 (full)	mm. 1–47 (1, 48–56 cut)	mm. 26–50
In Film: 56:02–57:31			1:05:25–1:05:55 (cut), 1:05:56–1:06:12	1:06:12–1:07:27 (many micro-edits)	*OST only, not in film*
Tonal Center (all minor-ish): G→…			B♭→B→A♭→C	F⇝B⇝C⇝B⇝A⇝B♭	B→A♭→C
Active but furtive music (A1), sowing seeds of whole track, esp. ASYMMETRICAL OSTINATO and HUNT motifs. Brief nod to **FORCE** (A2), then module of quiet and mounting tension (A3)			Rampaging chase music. Same motivic materials to A1 but intensified, unrelenting. Shrieks for winds, more percussion, expanded tonal range.	Wild fight music. Erratic structure; small cells driven by mimetic scoring. OSTINATO gone, HUNT persists. Ends on throbbing dissonance [B♭-D♭-G♭-A-C]	"Resolves" dissonant chord. OSTINATO, wind shrieks back. Ends with bang.

Figure 8.2 Form of "General Grievous" (*Revenge of the Sith* OST, track 5)

Figure 8.3 "General Grievous" track opening

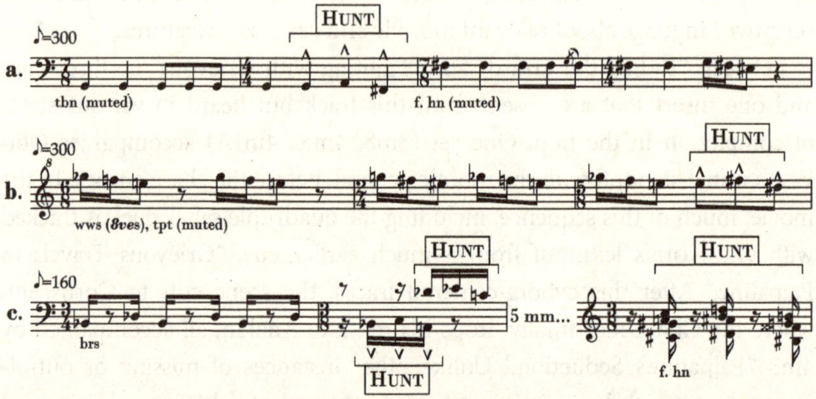

Figure 8.4 Various presentations of the HUNT motif in "General Grievous" track. **a.** 0:27, from "Riding the Lizard"; **b.** 1:40, from "Rolling with Grievous"; **c1., c2.** 2:33, 2:45, from "Fighting with Grievous"

sense—the only important recurring theme is an understated growl of the FORCE early on. Rather, the track is united through a consistent set of rhythmic and melodic cells. Right at the onset, "General Grievous" announces that it is going to be concerned with metrical unpredictability. The track begins with a riot of mixed meters, bestial percussion, and punchy dissonances—music Obi-Wan might describe as "uncivilized." The first few measures of "Riding the Lizard," shown in Figure 8.3, expose most of the track's recurrent features, including an ASYMMETRICAL OSTINATO bass and a pervasive $\hat{1}$-$\hat{2}$-$\hat{7}$ HUNT figure that is typically heard in heavily accented notes of equal duration.

The three-note HUNT motif rears up in all three component cues of "General Grievous." The idea is subject to a process of, if not developing variation (there is no goal or culmination), then consistent and kaleidoscopic reinvention. A sampling of these trichordal particles is given in Figure 8.4. The first (8.4a) incorporates the pattern into the closest thing the set piece has to a grammatical theme; the four-measure excerpt is akin to an antecedent, with a nearly identical consequent directly thereafter. This "tune" underscores the General's orders to the Separatist leaders to evacuate to Mustafar. The second passage (8.4b) is a spiraling line for high woodwinds heard throughout the set piece as an upper voice counterpart to the asymmetrical ostinato rampaging below. The final example hails from the man-versus-droid brawl, much of which is inaudible or cut from the film. Among the new tricks Williams teaches the trichord are a call-and-response routine within another quasi-period melody (8.4c) and a few measures later, a dissonant harmonization in which each pitch crowns a chord built from a perfect fifth, minor second, and minor third. While hard, maybe impossible to hear in the movie's presentation, with the OST's rendering, these motivic splinters jut out in aural prominence, helping to form an economical—if affectively chaotic—piece.

The most significant "arrangement" decision in the General Grievous track is the wholesale repetition of the last twenty-five seconds of "Rolling with Grievous" after "Fighting with Grievous." In another context, this out-of-sequence splice might be taken as crude, but here it is well-calculated for both formal and expressive reasons. The film-chronological ending, corresponding to Obi-Wan's narrow victory, is notably anti-climactic—Grievous, like many secondary baddies in *Star Wars*, dies a bit of a chump, and his music fizzles out with little fanfare. The protracted crescendo constructed in "Rolling," however, presents a satisfyingly intense and well-telegraphed way to conclude. It dovetails well with the perfunctory ending of "Fighting," installing at the cues' hinge a stepwise boost of key (A→B♭→B♮), typical of Williams's approach to tonal intensification. The new transition also helps "resolve" the throbbingly dissonant sonority that caps the General's demise.

Most important from the standpoint of overall listening coherence, the repetition of such a large passage has the effect of bringing back the Asymmetrical Ostinato, thereby lending the track a sense of unity to balance out its feral constituents. While not everything on the *Revenge of the Sith* album is as thoughtfully constructed, "General Grievous" stands as a successful musical digest of a non-continuous set piece, uniting scattered and refractory bits of a score into a genuine *piece*.

Titles and Credits

Not everyone who enjoys *Star Wars* ends up purchasing the soundtrack album or attending a concert dedicated to its music, of course. But anyone who has ever seen a Skywalker Saga film will have heard at least one musical paratext: the Main Title sequence. This cue serves a function not unlike an overture for an opera or musical—indispensable, certainly, but also perched on a different storytelling plane from the main musical action to come. (As discussed at points in Chapters 2 and 5, the Main Title functions at once as a referential beacon and means of imposing mythic distance.) This extra-diegetic level is also occupied by what comes *after* the action. Less obligatory for audiences to sit through, but just as substantive as the Main Titles, the End Credits are big canvases, ideal for thematic summation. These paratextual postludes tend to follow the logic of the suite: a succession of strongly contrasting and clearly demarcated musical ideas, where developmental rigor and tonal coherence are of secondary concern to melodic and emotional variety.

Figure 8.5 shows which leitmotifs can be heard in each entry's End Credits. For simplicity's sake, the table does not convey sub-themes, incidental motifs, or recurrences of melodic idea.[12] After the customary statement of LUKE's theme and the REBEL FANFARE (after *Empire*, always in E♭ and C major, respectively), Williams proceeds to spotlight each movie's new leitmotifs in these suites. Without exception, these themes are given more breathing room than typically afforded in nondiegetic underscore. Accordingly, the End Credits are where one is most likely to hear a leitmotif's bridge or B-section at length, as with YODA, ANAKIN AND PADMÉ, and PSALM OF THE SITH in

Film	Leitmotifs featured in order of introduction
IV	LUKE, R.F., LEIA
V	LUKE, R.F., YODA, VADER, HAN AND LEIA
VI	LUKE, R.F., EWOKS, LUKE AND LEIA, T.R.
I	LUKE, R.F., D.O.T.F., ANAKIN
II*	LUKE, R.F., ANAKIN AND PADMÉ, GLOOM, ANAKIN, VADER
III	LUKE, R.F., LEIA, B.O.T.H., FORCE, THRONE ROOM
VII	LUKE, R.F., REY, KYLO A, FINN, POE, RESISTANCE, FORCE
VIII**	LUKE, R.F., ROSE, LEIA, LUKE IN EXILE, RESISTANCE, TENSION, YODA, DESPERATION
IX	LUKE, R.F., FRIENDSHIP, P.O.T.S., VADER, REY, VICTORY, T.R.
*Differs in the film from album; see discussion of "Across the Stars" **Several alternate versions, one including KYLO A and an alternate bridge for ROSE.	

Figure 8.5 Leitmotifs in each film's end credits

Episodes V, II, and IX, respectively.[13] Williams is economical in the construction of the suites. Small transitions are sometimes written to join discrete thematic modules, though just as often the sections abut directly. In the final member of each trilogy (VI, III, IX), music is drawn wholesale from preexisting extra-diegetic pieces. Meanwhile, Episodes VI and especially VII feature sizable spans drawn from underscore set pieces. Regardless of their level of novelty or through-composition, the End Credits are places where music can be heard and enjoyed *on its own terms.* Williams's suites provide a form of catharsis that is important to the functioning of the overall film—essential, even, as we shall see is the case with Episode II. Indispensable or not, credits in *Star Wars* are special; filmgoers who leave before they finish rolling effectively cut their aesthetic experience short.

Many of the End Credits suites are based on—or provide the essential material for— Williams's concert arrangements. The most significant standalone piece from the saga, whose name tellingly vacillates between "Star Wars—Main Theme" and "Star Wars (Main Title)," is itself a merger of Episode IV's opening and closing cues. Williams described this amalgamation as having "the feeling of an overture," and accordingly placed it as the first track on the OST album.[14] The formal structure of this overture is summarized in Figure 8.6. Like several other Original Trilogy concert arrangements, "Star Wars—Main Theme" has a simple shape, essentially an ABACA plan, where a unifying Main Theme (M.T.) alternates with episodes of contrasting material. The first two large-scale sections (A and B) comprise the entirety of the "Main Title," beginning with LUKE's theme

m. 1 62 98 126 148 190

Source Cue: 1m2 "Main Title"		Source Cue: 12m2 "End Title"		
A: Main Theme (Heroic) Statement + Crisis		**B:** M.T. Restatement + Second Theme (Lyrical)		**C:** M.T. Restatement 2 + Coda
opening fanfare, **LUKE** (A + B + A-phrases)	STARRY NIGHT, PLANETS CHORDS, **R.F.**	**LUKE** (A + B + A-phrases)	STARRY NIGHT → **LEIA + R.F.**	trans. → **LUKE** (A+B-phrases) + aspects of **LEIA**, **R.F.** (augmentation), **T.R.**
B♭	⇝ (C)	C	⇝E→V/E=I/B	C → G

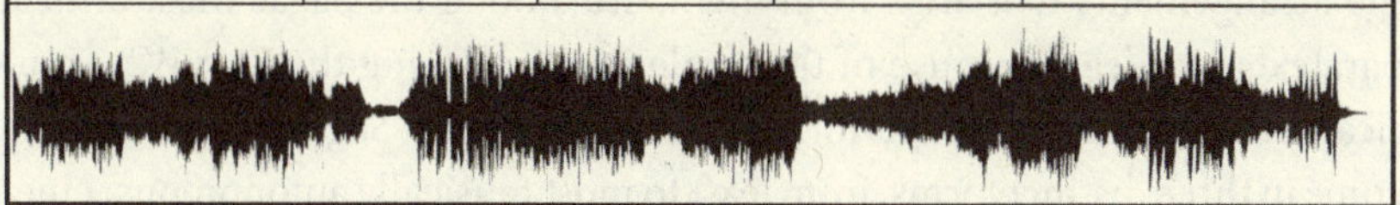

Figure 8.6 Form of "Star Wars—Main Theme"

in B♭ major, passing through the harmonically ambiguous "Starry Night" material, and reaching the cue-closing blasts of the "Planets Chords" and REBEL FANFARE tag, both set in the key of C. In the film, this tense music accompanies the sight of Vader's Star Destroyer assailing the Rebel ship, after which it segues without incident into similarly anxious music for "The War." In a concert arrangement, however, the jarring material up to measure 97 presents a compositional conundrum: here is a moment of maximum strain and tonal tension set in opposition to the heroic security of the opening subject. It will need to be resolved somehow if the piece is going to end happily.

That resolution comes, *deus ex machina*-like, in the form of a restatement of LUKE's theme. The closing module from 1m2 serves as an efficient means of segueing into the *New Hope* "End Titles." This new formal section does not start with its first measure in D♭ major, but seventeen bars in, once C has been established as the new key. The arrangement then follows 12m2 exactly. We hear another rotation of LUKE, a rendition of LEIA's theme counterpointed with the REBEL FANFARE, and a final section in G major that recalls the THRONE ROOM and ties everything together elegantly.[15] Despite the perfunctory connection between 1m2 and 12m2—the seam sounds less convincing the more one attends to it—"Star Wars—Main Theme" is well-proportioned and satisfying as an expression of *A New Hope*'s core themes. It has motivic and topical variety without sounding diffuse, and a modicum of thematic development without sounding academic. Most important, the piece finishes strongly, with the hallmarks of a romantic overture, down to the requisite minor plagal cadence and big timpani-accented final chord.

Live Performances

Unsurprisingly, the "Star Wars—Main Theme" is the paratext most commonly heard outside the context of a traditional movie screening and most frequently performed in live orchestral settings.[16] Concerts, and the arrangements that arise from them, are among the Saga's most critical paratexts, not least because of their role in establishing the *Star Wars* musical work-concept. The performance of Skywalker Saga music tends to come in three distinct forms, from least to most musically autonomous: cine-concerts, music-driven montages, and traditional concerts.

The least filmically separable manifestation of *Star Wars* music is the live-to-picture exhibition, or "*cine-concert*" in Brooke McCorkle Okazaki's more evocative nomenclature.[17] In a cine-concert, a professional orchestra plays a full score in exact synchrony with a projected version of the movie, its music track extracted but otherwise identical to a theatrical release. Cine-concerts surged in popularity in the first decades of the twenty-first century, with Williams's filmography—and the Original Trilogy in particular—assuming a central position in the growing live-to-picture canon.[18] A cine-concert is a marvelous way of hearing something "again, for the first time," bringing as it does an energy and virtuosity that only a living ensemble can supply. The undertaking is especially impressive for the brass, who are asked to play opera-length durations of difficult music without breaks. Film music is written to be recorded in short bursts, not all in one go. Audiences at a live-to-picture performance behold something intended as a staggered relay race transformed into a marathon.

Cine-concerts are not just feats of endurance; they also represent impressive deeds of textual reconstruction. As we have seen, the music track in every *Star Wars* film is an editorially constructed amalgam, not something that can be reproduced directly from Williams's conductor's score. And this is one reason that cine-concerts are not necessarily the *ideal* means of celebrating a film's music. When an orchestra is asked to play an incoherent hodgepodge like the film version of "Scherzo for X-Wings," what the audience hears is nowhere close to the composer's original intentions. But even if a film were re-cut to fit Williams's cues-as-composed, music's apparent prioritization in cine-concerts can prove illusory. An orchestra of the Boston Symphony's caliber could be chugging along with a magnificent rendering of, say, *Return of the Jedi*'s "Sail Barge Battle." But it is human nature to focus on what is happening on screen and what is spoken out loud. In the battle for audience attention, ocularcentrism (the tendency to privilege the eye) and vococentrism (the tendency to privilege the voice) create something of a perceptual Sarlacc pit: easy to be sucked in, nigh impossible to escape.

An alternative to a live-to-picture performance that preserves a degree of visual attraction is the *music-driven montage*. Here, an orchestra performs excerpts or arrangements while an assemblage of clips is projected overhead. Speech may be present, but intermittently so, and in a poetic or iconic register, rather than a purely expositional one.[19] Williams conducted one such montage in 1997 with the Boston Pops (May 23/24 and July 12), in which three minutes of its seven-minute runtime was based on unaltered film underscore, and four from extra-diegetic and concert arrangement sources. More elaborate was *Star Wars: A Musical Journey*, a touring concert that ran in 2009 with Dirk Brossé conducting and Anthony Daniels providing narration. The program incorporated around twenty musical selections from the then-six episodes, performed against a (mostly) silent series of projected montages. These montages were generally abstract, revolving around characters or loosely defined plot points or scene archetypes. The "Asteroid Field," for example, was matched with clips of chases and races from across Episodes I through VI—not just the eponymous sequence from V, but the podrace in I, the sonic charge chase in Episode II, and so on. Like a maximized version of Williams's montage from the previous decade, the orchestral selections included some unaltered film cues but spent proportionally more time with standalone arrangements. Per its press release, the show gave "audiences a chance to see, hear, and experience Star Wars from a new and unique perspective."[20] Though, as with cine-concerts, this perspective was still invested heavily in optical spectacle, with its huge LED screens, augmented by a rock concert-style laser show.[21]

On the other side of the integration-versus-independence spectrum from cine-concerts is the live performance of film music without any additional visual or sonic reference to their textual sources: that is, *traditional orchestral concerts*. Williams himself deserves some credit for making this as robust a category as it is today. Granted, concert performances of film music were hardly unheard of prior to *Star Wars*. The practice extends back to the early years of sound cinema—Dmitri Tiomkin was conducting his own film music with the Hollywood Bowl back in 1938.[22] And by the 1960s, hearing film music at the symphony was, if not yet commonplace, then neither all that novel or remarkable an experience, either.[23] But the craftsmanship and crowd-pleasing nature of Williams's music proved a significant contributor to hard-won legitimation of the genre within the jealously guarded temples of classical music. Another factor was Williams's historic tenure with the Boston Pops, both as conductor and conductor laureate, where, for decades he programmed film music, which could be heard by this splendid ensemble not just inside Symphony Hall but on radio broadcasts, "Evening at Pops" TV episodes, and across dozens of albums on the RCA and Sony Classical labels. In so persistently advocating film music in these venues, Williams raised the profile of the artform as a whole.

Concert Arrangements

As with his approach to the original soundtrack albums, Williams's presentation of music from the *Star Wars* films in concert has always been an act of careful curation. While the sounds of the Skywalker Saga are to this day a fixed presence at "Film Night" with the Boston Pops, entrées from the series are rarely the only thing on the musical menu. Boston audiences have not been treated to a complete "unstaged" performance of a *Star Wars* score front to back, as is sometimes done with ballets and operas of compelling intrinsic musical interest.[24] Nor has Williams devised any large-scale concert piece that incorporated *Star Wars* thematic materials, though ample models exist for such a work—Korngold's Symphony in F♯ and Violin Concerto, Vaughan Williams's *Sinfonia Antartica*, Prokofiev's Op. 78 "Nevsky" Cantata, to name a few. Rather, the composer has ensured the afterlife of *Star Wars* in performance through his *concert arrangements*. These are short pieces, usually between three and five minutes long, revolving around a single theme or set piece, generally designated by their titles. The complete corpus is listed in Appendix 2. Among these are warhorses like "The Imperial March" and the aforementioned "Star Wars—Main Theme," as well as some relative esoterica like "The Adventures of Jar Jar" from *The Phantom Menace* and "Adagio" from *The Force Awakens*. Williams created three dozen of these pieces, several existing in multiple versions, most being available for purchase and study in the "Signature Edition" scores published by Hal Leonard. That the composer has invested so much time and energy in these pieces over the years is no surprise: more than any other *Star Wars* musical paratext, they conform to the stable and traditionally *classical* definition of work-concept.

As with the soundtrack albums, the ways in which Williams constructs these arrangements vary a great deal with musical and dramatic subject matter. Instead of a comprehensive overview, it will serve to highlight a handful of issues that recur in these pieces—their developmental procedures; their large-scale formal arcs; and their expressive transformations in cases where the composer revisited and reimagined his earlier work.

Developmental Procedures

Few of the concert arrangements are drawn directly from nondiegetic underscore, and fewer still from scenes involving what we have characterized as

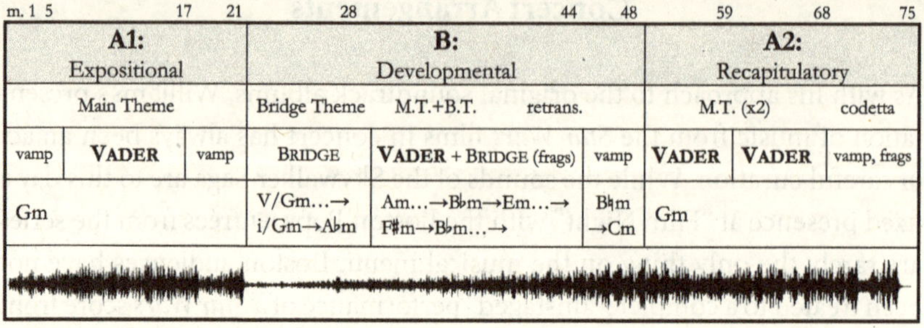

Figure 8.7 Form of "The Imperial March"

musical prose—that is music that is multi-thematic, through-composed, and paratactic rather than hypotactic in character. Though these pieces thus do not represent Williams's approach to *scoring* these films, the disinclination toward prose in concert arrangements is understandable—these works tend toward full and formally bounded statements of single themes after all. This is not to say that aspects of that musical prose style are altogether absent in these pieces. Developmental procedures are at work in most of them, generally comparable to the varieties of micro-transformations we have observed throughout the Saga's underscoring. "The Imperial March" is typical in this regard. Summarized formally in Figure 8.7, the piece sneaks a pseudo-developmental section betwixt its mighty annunciations of the Dark Lord's sentential Main Theme. Procedures quite familiar from musical prose—and Classical development sections, for that matter—are readily audible in this turbulent area from measure 21 to measure 47. Within this span, we hear motivic fragmentation and composing-out of the Vader idea, as well as the new Bridge motif that stems from it. Other paradigmatic developmental strategies include faster and more wide-ranging shifts of tonality; looser thematic forms; a nervous, motoric texture; more variegated orchestration than the flanking sections; an initial pulling back of intensity at the start of the movement; and a powerfully telegraphed retransition on the other end. And though "The Imperial March" is most definitely *not* in, say, sonata allegro form, there nevertheless is an undeniably *classical* logic to its large-scale form.[25] We hear it in the way Williams initially presents the piece's main Vader subject. We hear it in how he then works it out motivically in a development full of storm and stress. And we hear it finally in how he restates the theme in a tonally and melodically fortified manner at the end—Vader not just repeated, but in a sense *achieved* following a tempestuous ordeal.

Medial sections dedicated to the development of material become increasingly common in Williams's arrangements after the Original Trilogy. Though worlds away from "The Imperial March" in affect, "Across the Stars," a concert piece on Episode II's love theme for ANAKIN AND PADMÉ, rhymes with that concert arrangement in its unsettled central segment. The form of the piece is depicted in Figure 8.8. Like the concert presentation of VADER's leitmotif, Williams's treatment includes a contrasting B-section, though this one is tri-thematic. Initiated by the soupy GLOOM theme, this pseudo-development slices ANAKIN AND PADMÉ's ill-fated melody into pieces, all churning over a THREAT ostinato, resulting in a modulatory, proto-Imperial stew. Unlike in "The Imperial March," the medial passage recurs too. It does so after the climactic recapitulation of the ANAKIN AND PADMÉ theme, now in the piece's closing key of E minor, serving in this post-climactic setting a hybrid function: recapping a pair of secondary thematic ideas and preparing the way for the sullen codetta to come.

Of all the concert arrangements, "The Rise of Skywalker" from Episode IX is the most redolent of a traditional sonata movement. To be clear, it does *not* adhere to sonata structure in its tonal organization. The concert arrangement thoroughly contradicts the form's deeply ingrained primary expectations for monotonality (the piece should begin and close in the same key) and thematic normalization (the second subject needs to be restated and confirmed in that home key). However, the arrangement *does* channel

m. 1	5	14	22	26	35	43	52	60
A1: Expositional							**B1:** Bridge / Developmental	
ANAKIN & PADMÉ (1st pass: tentative form)			**ANAKIN & PADMÉ** (2nd pass: full 32-bar form)				**GLOOM**	THREAT + **ANAKIN & PADMÉ**
vamp	A-phrase	B-phrase	vamp	A-phrase	B-phrase	A-phrase	period	ostinato + A-phrase (frags)
Dm		→V/Gm, →V/Cm	Cm		→V/Cm, →V/F	Fm→ V/Fm	⇝V/G♯(?), ⇝V/Fm	Fm→D♭m→A/C♯→iv/F♯m

75	84	92	101	109	113	122
A': Recap pt. 1/Climax			**B2:** Recap pt. 2/Coda pt. 1		**A3:** Coda pt. 2	
ANAKIN & PADMÉ (3rd pass: full 32-bar form)			**GLOOM**	THREAT	**ANAKIN & PADMÉ** (4th pass: dissolving form)	
A + B + A-phrases			period	ostinato	A-phrase	vamp + A (frags)
F♯m	→V/Bm, →V/Em	Em→V/Em	⇝V/Fm(?), ⇝V/Em	Em	Em	

(final measure: 128)

Figure 8.8 Form of "Across the Stars"

m. 1	18	37	52	56	75	95 (–99)
A: Expositional		**B**: Developmental			**C**: Recapitulatory/Coda	
Victory Main Theme	**Friendship** Second Theme	*Part 1* S.T.	*Part 2* M.T.	*Part 3* retrans., M.T.	M.T. (breakthrough & apotheosis)	S.T. (frags)
compound period	compound period	fragmentation, reharmonization, sequencing of **Friendship**, **Victory**, free fanfaric material			compound period + cadential extension	free, (**R.F.**?), **Fr'ship**
D♭ → E → D♭ …	D♯ → F♯ …	⇝(A)⇝(C)⇝(E)⇝B^{sus}→D^{sus}⇝V/B♭			B♭→D♭→B♭→V/B♭	⇝ B♭

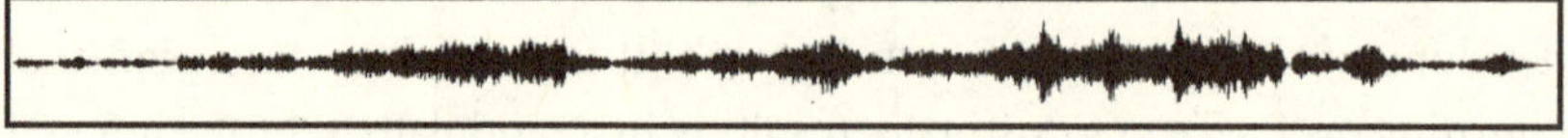

Figure 8.9 Form of "Rise of Skywalker"

many of the genre's defining secondary features, via its rotation through and synthesis of contrasting thematic and tonal blocks, its persistently developmental character, and its crystal-clear ternary organization.

The intriguingly referential shape of "The Rise of Skywalker" is summarized in Figure 8.9. Williams's arrangement has a summational quality; it stands as one of many musical expressions of the sentiment "let us finally say goodbye" that he wrote for the series and is surely the warmest and most humane in spirit. The mood of leave-taking arises from a number of factors, foremost being the sentimental tone of both of its themes, a Victory chorale and a Friendship cantilena. Presented in isolation, both thematic subjects could sound maudlin. But being ensconced within a large-scale ternary structure mitigates some of their saccharine aspects, putting them instead through something of a "through struggle, victory" expressive arc. A symphonic metanarrative could scarcely be more Beethovenian.

The opening Expositional zone in "The Rise of Skywalker" offers the Victory and Friendship subjects in leisurely succession. A substantial Developmental zone follows with a more angst-ridden tenor, the two themes reordered and refracted in numerous ways. A protracted and strenuous build-up passage follows, finally breaking into a Recapitulatory zone in which the Victory theme is transfigured into a tutti hymn of praise and cadential extension in the form of a brass chorale. After that, a short codetta ties it all up in a bow with some free material that alludes to the Rebel Fanfare and a closing gesture drawn from the songful Friendship theme. Remarkably, the bulk of the Developmental and Recapitulatory zones of "The Rise of Skywalker" were adapted from a film cue—the end of the Battle of Exegol. This repurposing of material is no slight, nor evidence of artistic laziness. Rather, it indicates just how much Williams had, by this, his last entry in the saga, come to reconcile developmental rigor with concert-ready coherence—not just in his arrangements, but in dramatic underscoring itself.

Large-Scale Arcs

Toward the end of "Rise of Skywalker," Williams includes a cadential phrase for brass meant to echo a similar passage in "Rey's Theme." His treatment of the Sequel Trilogy's chief protagonist is a portrait of a character in the process of discovering her identity. Athletic but uncertain, heroic but cautious, doughty but introverted, her theme is animated by productive contradictions. The ambivalence is tonally represented in Rey's harmonic disposition, modally minor and yet prone to infusions from the major, much like the Force, with which her theme is affined. A summary of this idiosyncratic piece is offered in Figure 8.10, with additional layers of information meant to give a sense of the piece's expressive arc, including the placement of form-determinative cadences and a set of impressionistic emotional descriptors.

"Rey's Theme" begins in a tentative way, lonely and withdrawn like the scavenger herself at the start of her journey. But as the arrangement progresses, her leitmotif (or, rather, trifecta of motivic materials: Gallop, Chimes, and Theme proper) takes on ever-greater assuredness and thematic definition. The piece is timbrally wide ranging and prone to modulatory

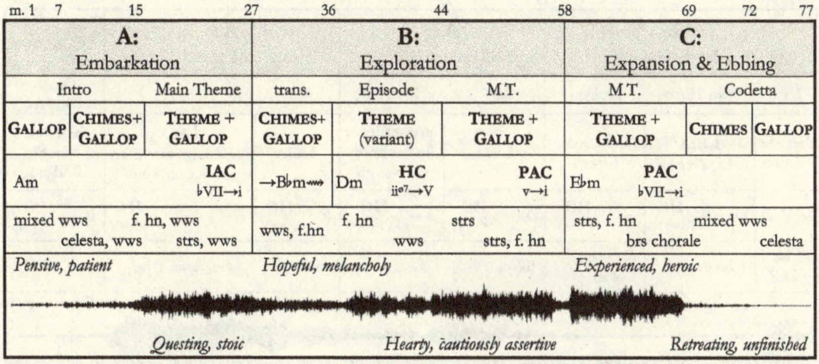

Figure 8.10 Form of "Rey's Theme"

wanderlust. Yet changes of orchestration and key are never used for their own sake, but instead as a means of discovering new capacities of Rey's musical character. The vault from D to E♭ minor at measure 58 is especially powerful, a shift of perspective akin to scaling one last summit, from which one gains a maximally expansive vista over the whole musical landscape. By the climax of "Rey's Theme," her theme conveys genuine heroism, exemplified by the aforementioned brass chorale. Yet Williams concludes not with a big bang but a recession—back into quietude and uncertainty where we started. Rey's story is, after all, unfinished. Not just unfinished, in fact, but in 2015 *unknown* to everyone listening, Williams included.

Rey's concert arrangement stands in revealing counterpoint with the other major heroine theme from the series. As already noted with respect to the "Star Wars—Main Theme," many of the most iconic pieces have simple structures based on alternation of the main theme with contrasting episodes. "Princess Leia's Theme" is the quintessential example here, with two short bridges breaking up four increasingly ardent passes through the plucky senator's leitmotif. Figure 8.11 offers a synopsis of the arrangement's form. As was the case with "Rey's Theme," the analysis lends special emphasis to cadences and lead melodic instruments, both of which are form-determinative.

Williams breathes life into the highly sectional and repetitive structure of "Princess Leia's Theme" through a variety of means. Timbral interest is kept high through vivid orchestration, with the perfumed second bridge (mm. 29–33) being especially striking. The piece's single authentic cadence is reserved for the final moment; every other harmonic hinge is an unresolved

m. 1	5	15	19	29	34	44	59 … 65
A1: Statement			**A2:** Restatement		**A3:** Restatement & Climax		Codetta
Intro	Main Theme	Bridge 1	M.T.	Bridge 2	M.T.	M.T.	Quasi-Cadenza
thematic intro	**LEIA** (*a*+*d*, *d''*+*b*+*b''*)	spun from *b*-motif	**LEIA**	quasi-cadenza based freely on *b*-motif	**LEIA**	**LEIA** (*a*+*d*, huge extension +cadence on *b*-motif)	based on *b*-motif, Bridge 1
→V/D	D **HC** iv→V	⇝ **HC** Fr^{+6}→V	D **HC** $ii^{ø7}$→V	D⇝ **HC** ♭VI→$ii^{ø7}$	E **HC** $ii^{ø9}$→V	E **HC** $ii^{ø9}$→V	E **PC** $ii^{ø7}$→I
fl, ob (solos)	f. hn (solo)	ob, e. hn (solos)	fl (solo)		strs	strs, wws, f. hn	fl, vn (solos)
	Envisioning		*Enticing*		*Exalting*		*Evanescing*

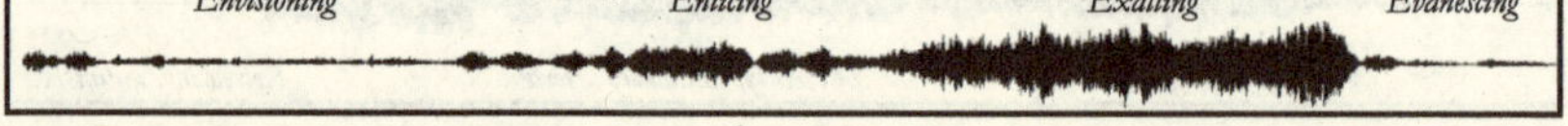

Figure 8.11 Form of "Princess Leia's Theme"

half-cadence of one sort or another. Sections are increasingly loud and texturally dense, with a keening countermelody in the horns emerging during the third pass through the Main Theme. And the melody inexorably climbs in register over the course of the arrangement, reaching $D\flat_5$ (m. 10), F_6 (m. 27), G_6 (m. 42), C_7 (m. 56), and eventually E_7 (m. 63). "Princess Leia's Theme" feels like one gigantic crescendo, straining for ever-higher peaks of intensity. There is a clear eroticism underlying the arrangement that is unique in the *Star Wars* concert corpus—even the explicit love themes for Han and Leia and Anakin and Padmé do not engage in such passionate climax-building, formally speaking. While a tad perverse in retrospect, such a hearing is in keeping with how Williams understood the leitmotif in 1977: as an eventual *love* theme for Luke and Leia. The words given to the four large-scale sections in Figure 8.11 (*Envisioning, Enticing, Exalting, Evanescing*) are meant to capture this suggestive aspect without veering too close to crass literalism.

Transformative Revisions

Given the composer's penchant for tinkering with his own works, it is no surprise that several of Williams's concert arrangements come in multiple versions. What is startling is how profound some of these revisions are, with a few constituting wholly different interpretations of the musical material and mythic topics they represent. Take, for instance, the love theme from Episode V, "Han Solo and the Princess." Williams's initial arrangement, part of a suite prepared for the release of *Empire*, initially hews to the contours of the "interrupted kiss" cue from that film. At the moment where Threepio spoils the mood, Williams continues ramping things up, eventually attaining a passionate and consummated climax. As depicted in Figure 8.12a, this "1.0" iteration of the theme has one of the simpler formal

m. 1 5 13 21 25 33 37 45 58 66

A1: Statement			A2: Restatement & Intensification			A3: Restatement & Climax/Codetta	
HAN & LEIA			HAN & LEIA		LEIA (frag)	HAN & LEIA	
intro	A-phrase	B-phrase	vamp	A-phrase	B-phrase + sequential detour	A-phrase	B-phrase + cadential extension
D♭...	Fm=iii/D♭ ⇝ V/D♭		D♭...	Fm=iii/D♭ ⇝ V/B♭		B♭... V→I/B♭	III♯→I/B♭

Figure 8.12a Form of "Han Solo and the Princess" (1980 version)

plans: three passes through the A- and B-sections of the HAN AND LEIA melody, with no thematic contrast besides a slight developmental window during the second B-phrase; the greatest musical interest here is how LEIA's motif peeks in and then facilitates a large-scale modulation from D♭ to B♭ major.

Williams's return to the franchise in the mid-2010s prompted a wholly new vision of the theme. His 2018 revision of "Han Solo and the Princess" differs radically from its predecessor in both structural and affective terms. Figure 8.12b shows just how distinct a work it is. The original B-phrase is largely dispensed with in favor of a new, more motivically economical line. Once heard, the new material seems to rub off on the A-phrase too, absorbing its intervallic and harmonic turns into its own profile. The overall formal structure is more intricate—matured, perhaps—with a new episode that houses a heart-on-sleeve string passage and a more stoic brass chorale. After the big climactic tutti, a closing flute quasi-cadenza at the end is nakedly sad. The whole piece feels at once more expansive than its predecessor and much less sunny in outlook. The 2018 revision alters the basic affective character of the theme, shifting it from an expression of youthful ardor to something still deeply loving but decidedly more melancholic, regretful even. This change of outlook reflects the in-text narrative, as Episode VII reveals the scoundrel and the senator do not enjoy a storybook ending after *Return of the Jedi.* It also bears the emotional wounds of a real-world tragedy: Carrie Fisher's untimely death in 2016, a loss Williams, who knew Fisher even when she was a baby, felt acutely.[26] With thirty-eight years of baggage and nostalgia, "Han Solo and the Princess 2.0" is weighted down by the past in a way more raw and honest than the average piece of music from this series.[27]

0:00 0:15 0:40 1:05 1:10 1:51 2:31 2:56 3:16 3:41 4:18 5:00

<table>
<tr><td colspan="3">A1:
Statement</td><td colspan="2">A2:
Restatement & Developmental</td><td colspan="2">B:
Developmental & Intensification</td><td colspan="3">A3:
Restatement & Climax</td><td>A4:
Cadenza/ Coda</td></tr>
<tr><td colspan="3">HAN & LEIA</td><td colspan="2">HAN & LEIA</td><td colspan="2">strongly contrasting episodes, retransition</td><td colspan="3">HAN & LEIA
(full 32 bars + PAC)</td><td>HAN & LEIA
(codetta)</td></tr>
<tr><td>intro (new)</td><td>A-phr. (orig.)</td><td>B-phr. (new)</td><td>intro (new)</td><td>A-phr. (new) + ext. & trans.</td><td>STRING ELEGY</td><td>BRASS CHORALE</td><td>A (orig.)</td><td>B (orig.)</td><td>A (new)</td><td>A (new) frags, cadence</td></tr>
<tr><td colspan="3">F→V/A→A(Am)↝V/A</td><td colspan="2">V/A → V/D♭</td><td colspan="2">D♭→D♭m→A→A♭m→ B♭m7♭5/F♭=VI/A♭m, A♭m→A♭↝V/E♭</td><td colspan="3">E♭…Fm↝V→I/E♭(x2)</td><td>E♭(E♭m)→E♭</td></tr>
</table>

Figure 8.12b Form of "Han Solo and the Princess" (2018 version)

Anakin's Turn(s)

While not nearly as structurally sweeping as those made from Han and Leia 1980 to 2018, the changes undergone by Anakin's motif across its multiple arrangements are if anything more mythopoetically consequential. Collectively, the concert treatments of "Anakin's Theme" represent a sort of redemption for an idea whose thematic-transformational potential was never properly achieved in-film. The leitmotif, which as we have seen presages elements of "The Imperial March," was built up in Episode I as a major player in the tragic musical narrative to come—"a thought," as Williams suggested at the time, "that is probably going to emerge as a more important thought as we move on to the next couple of episodes." This promise was left largely unfulfilled, however, as the cannily constructed theme underwent only two new statements in the Prequel trilogy after *The Phantom Menace*: a basically unaltered version in Episode II [8:16] and a near-atonal wisp in Episode III [31:26]. Williams's *paratextual* treatments of the theme thus assume a heightened significance, as they become spaces where the storytelling power of Anakin's theme might be realized.

In its original 1999 form, "Anakin's Theme" is among the most through-composed of Williams's arrangements. Once the main melodic period is presented, the piece spins out as one continuous thought, gradually moving from subtle to overt Vader allusions. Though Figure 8.13 breaks the arrangement into discrete episodes and thematic restatements, the seams are artfully concealed. The "Imperial" taint is particularly evident in the climactic

	m. 1	5		15	25	39	49
	A0 Intro	**A1** Statement		**B** Developmental	**A2** Restatement & Climax	**A3** Coda	
	Anakin	**Anakin**		spun from **Anakin**	**Anakin**	**Anakin** (cons.) →**Vader** (frags)	
	cons. (no ant.)	vamp	period	discursive, chained 2-mm. phrases [x5]	extended period + new consequent & chromatic cadence [x2]	vamp	period with modified & extended cons.
	E	A		Am⇝(D, C, F, Am)→	A→C→A ♭vi→I/A [x2]	A	→♭vi→I/A(x3), A5
Vader nods:			*hidden* *subtle*	*very subtle*	*less subtle* *unsubtle*		*obvious* *almost overt*
2023a changes				+vamp			+written out diminuendo
2023b changes			+vn solo throughout, orchestration rebalanced accordingly	+vamp	+new *3rd* cons. +cadence [x2]	+vamp (rev.)	+huge expansion: cadenza, codetta, overt **Vader**

Figure 8.13 Form of "Anakin's Theme" (1999 version) and revisions

section, with the telltale minor submediant ($\flat$vi) appearing with each $\hat{1}$-$\flat\hat{6}$-$\hat{3}$-$\hat{1}$ cadential turn. The topic of Skywalker's musical fate thus broached, a short codetta presents shards of Vader's leitmotif in near-explicit terms, clouding the lydian glow of the rest of the piece. Williams ends on an A open-fifth chord—neither major nor minor, modally noncommittal but hardly an auspicious sign for the Jedi prodigy.

Slouching Towards "The Imperial March"

Two updates to this arrangement arrived in 2023—over twenty years since Williams had last worked with the theme. The alterations relative to the original are summarized at the bottom of Figure 8.13. The first revision (2023a) gives the arrangement additional heft by interpolating into its core a vamp that had previously occurred only at the piece's periphery. This is a small change in terms of added measures but a pronounced one in formal implications, making "Anakin's Theme" clearly ternary in organization, at the expense perhaps of its former fluidity.

An additional change to the first 2023 revision is a written-out ritardando within the original's codetta, turning what initially took fourteen beats to complete into twenty-five. This stretching effect takes place during the portion of the arrangement that was closest to a direct quotation of "The Imperial March." The end of "Anakin's Theme" in 1999 was already foreboding, but efficiently so, a whisper of warning that was over before one could fully register it. However, with those four measures in the 2023 version stretched out on the post-cadential rack, the listener is forced to dwell on what will become of the once innocent, now estranged melody.

These changes in emphasis are taken one step further in the version of "Anakin's Theme" Williams prepared later in 2023, as the last of seven solo-violin showcases on *Star Wars* themes offered to Anne-Sophie Mutter. Naturally, the most salient change is the addition of a violin obbligato to what was originally a decidedly non-soloistic piece. For the first third of the piece, Mutter simply carries the melodic line, though starting in the second rotation—here also set off by that newly interpolated vamp—her part alternates between main voice and countermelodic embellishment. The climactic passage is enlarged with an extra *third* pass through the theme's

Vader-esque cadential progression, this time more delicately scored, with the orchestra's bass entirely dropping out. The theme sounds positively angelic here—angelic, that is, until the low strings return, and with them the baleful F-minor chords that, harmonically speaking, are the root of the theme's eventual turn to the dark side.

The final minute and twenty seconds of the Mutter revision are where the most profound formal and affective transformations on "Anakin's Theme" take place. After yet another slight alteration to the lydian vamp, the whole conclusion settles on an A_2 pedal. Above this immovable tonal object, Mutter enters a quasi-cadenzic reverie, florid but also strangely enervated. The exposed solo passage is based on the same phrase that was rhythmically augmented in "Anakin 2.0," its F-minor malignancy now fully metastasized. The quasi-cadenza section makes text what in prior versions was subtext: this is fully Darth Vader's territory now.

The final two phrases in the Mutter arrangement, given to solo harp and violin respectively, are unprecedentedly overt. The choice of harp alone for Vader's theme reverberates with proleptic dread: this was the instrument that provided the final word on Anakin's thematic material in Episode VI upon his death. (The same cue was reused, or more accurately *recompiled*, to interesting effect in Episode IX for Rey's traversal of the ruined Death Star.) Williams's arrangement for Mutter then fades off into infinity, in the manner that many of the composer's more contemplative concertos do. While a drawn-out *morendo* such as closes this "Anakin 2.5" is unlikely to bring the concert house down for its virtuosity, it is a marvelously apt ending, and a chillingly effective way to lay Anakin to rest—again.

Anakin's youthful leitmotif appears in one other paratextual context, and it is arguably the most essential to his thematic arc. The "End Credits" for *Attack of the Clones* conclude with a thematic succession that encapsulates the character's journey from slave boy to lovelorn teen to Sith Lord. The suite is mostly based on the Anakin and Padmé love theme—indeed, the credits are identical with the first "Across the Stars" concert arrangement up to this coda. Williams initiates the closing paragraph [OST Track 13, 9:38] with a recollection of Anakin's tune, now in E-minor and carried by forlorn French horn. Only the antecedent phrase is completed, with the music immediately turning back to the tragic love theme. That melody is itself unsettled, its bass slouching toward "The Imperial March." A micro-cadenza for flute follows. It too is based on the contours of ANAKIN AND PADMÉ, now undergirded by an undisguised VADER's theme in the double basses. And then the music stops: not in some ambivalent half-major, half-minor realm, but in the pure blackness of E minor.

Incredibly, this inspired coda—the only place where all leitmotivic constituents of Anakin's fall from grace converge—was cut from the film.[28] In its place was inserted a straight repetition of what is now known as the "Across the Stars" concert arrangement, which does not end in such a darkly prophetic way.[29] Only those who heard the soundtrack album will ever have accessed this essential part of the telling of *Star Wars*' musical myth.

Action Showcases

Whether involving themes or cues, commercial albums or concert programs, the process of converting film music into a form that can stand on its own is a complex challenge. Each paratext examined thus far is an answer to a set of artistic puzzles described at the beginning of this chapter. How to achieve self-sufficiency for music designed to serve a story, with all the constraints and peculiarities of musical logic that dramatic subordination entails? How to provide satisfying closure for a composition meant to be left open-ended? And how to strike a balance of representativeness—narrative, thematic, emotional—and inherent musical interest? Over the whole run of the Skywalker Saga, Williams took great care in curating his soundtracks and fabricating his arrangements. Clearly, he relished the task of cracking these puzzles—and indeed solving them anew in some cases, as with "Han Solo and the Princess" and "Anakin's Theme." This paratextual menagerie represents the composer's own preferred method of independent musical appreciation—as well as the preservation, and implicitly canonization, of his *Star Wars* scores.

The puzzle of wresting autonomy from inherently subordinated forms is especially difficult—and, one can surmise, compositionally enticing for Williams—when it comes to action music. Notable arrangements in this vein include "Here They Come," "The Asteroid Field," "Duel of the Fates," and "Scherzo for X-Wings." With musical paratexts based on action set pieces, the composer has often described their presentation outside the film as an act of recuperation. Whether drowned out by sound effects, cut up beyond recognition, or simply unused, action cues are paradoxically the saga's most technically complex and least consciously heard music. Cues for fights, battles, and chases are beholden to dramatic, editorial, and visual imperatives, tasked with responding to the film at a pace that sometimes—but not always—militates against traditional "piece-like" listening. Attending to action music through a paratextual presentation is thus another way to experience hearing it "for the first time."

Before conducting the "Scherzo for X-Wings" at one of the Boston Pops' annual Film Night concerts, Williams described his motivation for its performance with unusual candor:

> [The scene from Episode VII] is very loud . . . as the X-Wings go through the trench. But you didn't hear too much of it, since the sound effects were a little loud. So I always think it's fun—I guess for me to brag a bit, in a funny way—when we go to the movies, we hear an orchestra like this [the Boston Pops], an absolute virtuoso orchestra, you hear what they do, which is quite incredible. We go to the movies all this [orchestral] virtuosity happens, and we really don't hear it most of the time. But if you take it away from the film, it loses so much energy. In any case, here's what you *might* have heard as the X-Wings fly through the trenches.[30]

As is his wont, Williams tempers even the slightest suggestion of self-aggrandizement by redirecting praise onto the musicians who realize his music. He further undercuts what seems like a nascent grievance about how his hard work was drowned out and battered on film by claiming that, divorced from its parent film, his music "loses so much energy." Maybe so, though that set piece gains *new* energy once heard clearly and performed by live musicians.[31] Particularly with the quicksilver "Scherzo for X-Wings," describing what the orchestra is asked to do as "quite incredible" is an understatement!

Hedges and displacements of responsibility aside, the profusion of action set pieces among Williams's catalog of *Star Wars* paratexts attests to his true feelings on the matter: these are pieces worth trumpeting. Doing justice to this segment of the Skywalker soundscape will take more than just this section—Chapter 9 is dedicated to treating an entire battle sequence as a cine-symphonic encounter. But we can begin to understand what is at stake when action cues are recast into self-standing "pieces" with another expedition to Endor.

The Ewoks Go to War

"The Forest Battle" from *Return of the Jedi* has a peculiar distinction: it is the only music in the *Star Wars* canon to include the performance instruction "Can-Can-ish." The passage that receives this designation contains a rendition of one of the piece's two main thematic ideas, an off-kilter melody here high-kicked off by trumpets, cheered on by chuckling woodwinds and a jungle's worth of odd percussion. Figure 8.14 displays the theme; only the main melodic line is shown, with the complex texture and even more complex harmonization reduced for clarity.

One of *Return of the Jedi*'s one-cue-wonders, this CANCAN is set in a burlesque chromatic idiom favored by Williams for moments of broad comedy. The mode is a lydian that veers toward the octatonic. The key is basically D♭ major but pestered with dissonant irritants. And while the melody frolics along in the first two measures of Figure 8.14, a cluster ($D♭_4$-$D♮_4$-$E♭_4$-F_4) chugs away in the trombones, with upper strings smuggling in an additional $F♭_5$. The CANCAN's characteristic progression is a transposition up by whole step, in this instance from D♭ to E♭ major, a harmonic smile that promises a functional I→V/V→V progression—or, more *Star Wars*ian, a lydian I→II♯→I loop. But the melody comes back down in the wrong place—D♮, not D♭ major—which then initiates its own capriciously modulating restatement on a new tonal plane.

The Ewoks' CANCAN carouses in this way through much of the "The Forest Battle." Upon its introduction rather deep into the piece (mm. 51–53), the theme's nonchalance stands in exaggerated, almost ludicrous contrast with the piece's dead-serious opening SHAMBLE motif. This inaugurating idea (Figure 8.15) is a typical Williams action motif, set atop a lumbering ostinato, its staccato minor thirds tiptoeing across an octatonic minefield. With

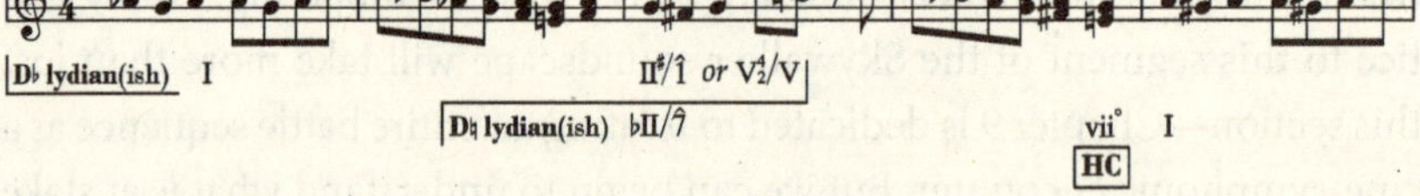

Figure 8.14 CANCAN theme from "The Forest Battle" (m. 63; compare ROTJ, 11m5, 1:47:06)

Figure 8.15 SHAMBLE theme from "The Forest Battle" (m. 1; compare ROTJ, 11m5, 1:45:26)

each successive iteration, the CANCAN punctures the threat of the SHAMBLE a bit more, until, by the piece's climax, a carnivalesque atmosphere dominates and any trace of musical menace has been thoroughly routed. This is most true for the CANCAN's definitive statement at mm. 125–128. Launched by four percussion slams, belted by unison trombones, and enlivened by off-beat trumpet quavers, it is hard not to hear Offenbach's famous dance from *Orpheus in the Underworld* peeking through. The notion of a race of teddy bears being the ultimate saviors of the galaxy in Episode VI is already ridiculous. Is it any more outlandish, "The Forest Battle" asks, to imagine the occasion culminating in a chorus line of Ewoks, kicking up their tribal skirts at an Endorian cabaret?

"The Forest Battle" ranks among the more successful of Williams's action-cues-turned-concert-scherzi. It is also one of the most heavily changed from its filmic predecessor, although those changes are not evenly distributed across the arrangement's 159 measures. The piece's source cue, "The Ewok Battle," accompanies the phase of the ground battle when the Endorian natives, with some help from Chewbacca, turn the tide in the Rebels' favor. Though the passage excerpted in Figure 8.14 hails from "The Ewok Battle" (mm. 70–73), it is not marked in that source cue "Can-Can-ish." Which is not to say that the overall effect is any less amusing—the added presence of boobams, a bizarre drum capable of doubling the melody, ensures as much. Williams's hectic scoring follows the pint-sized warriors as they employ a variety of guerilla tactics to pelt, smash, and trip up an entire legion of the Emperor's "best" troops. The Ewoks' indigenous ingenuity appears to be the symbolic target of the CANCAN motif, while the Stormtroopers and their surprisingly vulnerable Walkers are assigned a SHAMBLE motif, itself a relative of the IT'S A TRAP theme that kicked off the fray in the first place. The ostinato underneath the SHAMBLE (shown in m. 1 of Figure 8.15) is in the same family as the AT-AT music from *Empire*; this one is a little more limber, as befits the marginally more maneuverable AT-ST. The figure embeds a BRUTE tetrachord, a pitch collection we have seen is common across the trilogies, composed of a minor third, perfect fourth, and minor third.

Aspects of this mordant sonority—expressed first as D_2-F_2-$B\flat_2$-$C\sharp_3$—are worked out across the film cue and concert arrangement alike. Additional thematic reinforcements arrive in the form of the Ewoks leitmotif, whose subcomponents (Horn Call, Bridge, and Theme) populate the set piece's penultimate section. Moments of flamboyant Mickey Mousing punctuate the cue. Williams catches the death spiral of a speeder bike and the wobbling of a walker with great specificity and humor. Generally, though, "The Ewok Battle" is more melodically driven and quadratic in phrase rhythm than previous legs of the Battle of Endor. Indeed, it already works quite well as a standalone piece of music. Quite well, except that the cue lacks a real ending—a significant issue, and one to which we will return shortly.

Figure 8.16 provides a breakdown of "The Ewok Battle" side by side with its concert arrangement. Differences are indicated in the middle column, though these pertain solely to the melodic/formal layout of the piece, not to orchestration, which is subtly altered across the arrangement. The chart is based on the recorded versions of these pieces as presented on the official soundtrack album. In principle, an additional column could be added for the version *as heard* in the movie; however, as a practical matter, a listing of every discrepancy would be too tortuous to describe or interpret easily. As is almost always the case with *Star Wars* action cues, what is heard in the movie is already heavily modified relative to the cue as originally recorded, and the "Ewok Battle" is one of the most micro-edited in the original trilogy. Numerous measures are cut, rearranged, or looped, and the last two bars—a giddy restatement of the Cancan—are omitted in favor of segueing directly into the next cue, "Leia Is Wounded." "The Ewok Battle" scene also includes an insert [1:46:32–1:46:37], heard during the first instance of friendly AT-ST fire. This tiny cue is the sole moment of underscore heard in *Jedi* that is unavailable on the 1997 Special Edition soundtrack release. It also happens to host the inaugural statement of the Cancan theme, though even *it* is editorially manipulated, with only two of this cue's six measures retained.

Given the disarray with which it is heard in film and the congenial tone of its themes, "The Ewok Battle" would have struck Williams as an obvious subject for standalone rearrangement. "The Forest Battle" was offered as the opening number on the B-side of the Original *Return of the Jedi* LP album. It premiered in concert, retitled as "The Forest Victory," at a Boston Pops performance on May 8, 1983, a few weeks before the film itself was released.

MATERIAL	EWOK BATTLE	CHANGE?	FOREST BATTLE
SHAMBLE A, B-submotifs	mm. 1–18	Essentially same	1–18
Variation of SHAMBLE A	--	Interpolation	19–23
SHAMBLE B, A	19–34	Essentially same	24–39
AT-ST motif	35–46	Excision	--
Fanfare	47–49	Essentially same	40–42
Fanfare tag + CANCAN insert [11m5x]	50 (+2)	Excision	--
CANCAN	51–65	Essentially same	43–57
SHAMBLE A	66–69	Essentially same	58–61
SHAMBLE tag	--	Interpolation	62
CANCAN	70–73	Essentially same	63–66½
CANCAN (2nd phrase)	--	Interpolation	66¾–70
Spinning speeder	74–79	Excision	--
EWOKS (Horn call)	80–87	Essentially same	71–78
EWOKS (Bridge motif)	88–94a	Essentially same	79—85
EWOKS (Bridge motif tag)	94b	Excision	--
EWOKS (Main theme 1st phrase)	95–98	Essentially same	86–89
EWOKS (Main theme 2nd phrase)	--	Interpolation	90–93
CANCAN	99–101	Essentially same	94–97
Tripping walker, CANCAN tag	102–112	Original ending	--
All new, spun from CANCAN	--	New ending	97–159

Figure 8.16 Relationship between "Ewok Battle" cue and "Forest Battle" concert arrangement

As detailed in Figure 8.16, most measures that did not make it into this arrangement come from short modules of Mickey Mousing without a thematic connection to the SHAMBLE or CANCAN. The biggest such span is an eleven-measure hunk of heaving AT-ST material—actually an incidental motif-to-be, as it recurs in the next cue [1:48:21] when the commandeered walker approaches Han and Leia. Up until around 60% of the way through "The Forest Battle," the passages new to the concert arrangement are similarly small. In two spots, Williams expands a brief thematic citation by including a second melodic phrase, providing either a functional consequent to the film cue's antecedent (EWOK Main Theme at m. 95) or a modulating restatement (the CANCAN in D major at m. 66¾). These extensions may make the concert arrangement less action-oriented, but the benefit of having complete presentations of melodic structures—especially the EWOK THEME, which otherwise would sound like a formal non sequitur—is well-motivated.

The most impressive difference between film and concert form is the arrangement's enormous expansion at the point where the cue concludes.

m.1	43	71	80	88	95	103	118	138	160
A: Subject	**B:** Countersubject	**C:** Ewokese Episodes					**D:** Climax & Coda		
SHAMBLE	CANCAN alternating with SHAMBLE	**EWOKS** HORN CALL	**EWOKS** BRIDGE	**EWOKS** MAIN THEME	CAN-CAN	ODDITY	CANCAN intensification and apotheosis	false ending pile-up	
Dm⇝	A⇝A→Dm→ D♭→D→…	F	C⇝B♭	C	B⇝ V/B→	Bm→ Cm→	B♭⇝C… **PAC** V→I	C (*and bow!*)	

Figure 8.17 Form of "The Forest Battle"

Williams offers sixty-two straight measures of material unheard in "The Ewok Battle," allowing him to develop the CANCAN considerably and send it off with a hefty climax and coda. This new section replaces the slight and necessarily indecisive conclusion of the original cue. That lack of closure is, of course, fully warranted given the cue's dramatic function: "The Ewok Battle" falls two-thirds of the way through the movie's wall-to-wall-scored final act, at a stage where the victory is not yet assured.[32] But Williams treats "The Forest Battle" as a way to summarize the whole conflict, and this means building up to and then hammering home a maximally happy ending.

A high-level synopsis of "The Forest Battle" is given in Figure 8.17. The piece is cast in four broad sections determined by tone, thematic material, and formal function. The first two sections serve a loosely defined expositional role. The initial "Subject" section is dominated by the SHAMBLE motif (which itself comprises two submotifs, not indicated); this large-scale A-section presents the musical threat that the piece eventually overcomes. The following "Subject vs. Countersubject" B-section pits the SHAMBLE against three progressively more assertive takes on the CANCAN.

The following C-section, "Ewok Episodes," is where cue and arrangement truly diverge. The thematic material is more discretized than the heated but continuous exchanges from the piece's first half, passing through five distinct themes. All but one fall into neat eight-bar periods. The first four are associated clearly with the Endorians: HORN CALL, BRIDGE, and THEME from the Ewoks' motley leitmotivic complex, followed by another extended rendition of the CANCAN. The fifth episodic module, an "ODDITY" theme, is puckish and angular. Shown in Figure 8.18, it too is a kind of half-major/half-minor scale—call it the Endorian mode—and sounds even more Prokofievian than the citrusy EWOK leitmotif. Despite a rhythmic affinity with those earlier-introduced motifs, this oddball melody does not stem from the "Ewok Battle"

Figure 8.18 Oddity theme with two continuations

at all; it is repurposed from an unused version of a much earlier cue from *Jedi*—"Jabba's End" (4m4). In that context, it appears to have been meant to accompany the antics of R2 and 3PO as they flee from the crime-lord's capsizing pleasure barge. The only substantial difference between source and arrangement is again one of turning a formerly asymmetrical phrase into a neat quadratic one. A canon on the Oddity theme (mm. 109–112) was cut off unceremoniously by a stinger after only three measures in the original "Jabba's End"; in the arrangement, Williams adds one extra measure to let this imitative episode to complete itself.

The fourth and final section of "The Forest Battle" commences after the Oddity interlude with a series of increasingly fervent statements of the Cancan. And so begins one of the most emphatically end-weighted of all Williams's concert arrangements. The paragraph begins with a thickset dominant prolongation of the piece's definitive—and almost completely unprepared—key of C-major. (In a neat, emergent example of motivic economy, the rising scale-fragments that urge this dominant forward derive from the Cancan's last measure and Oddity's second.) After discharging onto the tonic at measure 137, the music proceeds to feint repeatedly at concluding. In all, there are a half-dozen places where Williams could have closed the piece but instead carries on with ever more absurd determination. The false endings are powered by a variety of closure-producing gestures: dominant-to-tonic motions, leading-note resolutions, upward sweeping chromatic lines, emphatically repeated bass notes and tutti chords. It is as though the piece has too much momentum to just stop.[33]

The absurd profusion of endings in "The Forest Battle" stands in ironic contrast with the utter lack of closure of the film cue. It smacks of hypercorrection, an overcompensation for the inherent open-endedness of "The

Ewok Battle"—and perhaps, more provocatively, the nature of nondiegetic underscore in general. Recall Buhler's objection that *Star Wars* music rarely earns its thematic victories. There is a sizable portion of both cue (mm. 51–73) and standalone arrangement (mm. 31–73) where the two contrasting themes are in active opposition to one another. And the SHAMBLE makes one final, formally futile play for supremacy in the coda at measure 145, technically *after* the last statement of the CANCAN. But the maniacally triumphal ending is disproportionate to any of the foregoing motivic strife. This piece seems to celebrate, in the most self-consciously exaggerated way possible, precisely the weakness Buhler critiques—and in doing so defuses it.

This brand of irony has a distinctively Ewokian accent. The Ewoks are a comical species, and their improbable combat prowess undermines the seriousness of the Empire's threat. It thus makes a perverse sort of sense that the paratext devoted to their heroic exploits should start with a terrible ostinato and defeat it through a delirious, interminable cabaret dance. There may be a personal rationale for the fixation on endings as well. As far as Williams knew in 1983, *Return of the Jedi* was the final entry in the *Star Wars* saga, and "The Forest Battle" therefore stood as its last concert showpiece. The inflated coda's role is meant not only to close off an incomplete nondiegetic cue but also to serve as a cap to the series that catapulted Williams to global recognition. This idea, of eternal ending, is one to which we will return at the close of this book.

The Joys of Rehearing

Although the formats examined in this chapter ranged across several categories—live versus recorded, cue versus arrangement, original versus revised—one thing they have in common is *rehearing*. The ability to hear something more than once is a profound ingredient of what makes music of any genre meaningful, and it is of special importance to symphonic film scoring. Knowing a movie in advance helps a listener understand and appreciate its music when it is presented in a paratextual format. But so does the less-common inverse: paratext then text, music then film.

Consider once more "Across the Stars," now from the perspective of a *re*listener. Suppose you get to know the ANAKIN AND PADMÉ theme very well by exposure to the concert arrangement—any version will do—but have *not* yet seen *Attack of the Clones*. Or, more plausibly, have not seen it in a while.

Now imagine watching the film. How might your experience of Episode II differ, and what features might leap to your attention, now that you are equipped with musical foreknowledge? Maybe you feel more carried away by the Anakin and Padmé theme when it is granted an extended statement. Or more caught off guard when, for example, it fails to cadence during the infamous interrupted kiss. What is happening in your mind's ear during the "Finale," where for the first time the concert version and film cue align? Does knowing the sad fate of the characters (or their theme) in *Revenge of the Sith*—and its grim presentation in Williams's updated arrangements—shade your perception of its more unbridled and romantic guises in *Attack of the Clones*?

This inversion of the normal order of listening to film music has some important implications. For one, musical foreknowledge can alter your relationship with a film. It is hard to imagine internalizing "Across the Stars" and then approaching Episode II without being more vividly attuned to the leitmotif's presence in the film, more primed to its interactions and transformations. Granted, the freshness of first encountering the theme as an audience member in 2002 cannot be recaptured. And perhaps cinematic immersion of a more general sort is broken, if by immersion we mean a passive state of being carried away by the plot, unconcerned with filmic construction or interpretation. But puncturing one form of immersion—in this case, the one where music remains a layer of unconsciously apprehended affective wallpaper—in no way precludes other sorts of captivation. Heightened attentiveness to the music-as-such is permitted in other forms of narrative multimedia such as ballet, opera, and musical theater. Even when the hall is darkened and the orchestra hidden away, an active awareness of the score hardly seems to violate the aesthetic integrity of the larger text. So why not a film score?

Knowing how the soundtrack "goes" ahead of time, even if only for one theme, is a pathway to an enriched experience, one that is not one iota less emotionally involving than the standard practice in which the film and its score are encountered simultaneously. There is a joy in humming (internally, or perhaps not!) in concert with a film, in participating through your musical imagination in its narration, in "scoring along."

Musical pleasure is a complex and personal thing, but there are cross-cultural commonalities. The ability to participate in music-making is one surefire source of delight. Importantly for us filmgoers, one need not be actively performing or moving for this highly engaged state to arise. "Virtual participation," as the leading theorist of musical repetition Elizabeth Margulis calls it, is a significant source of enjoyment, and is liable to arise in contexts featuring heavy repetition.[34] This can be structured internally, in "the music itself," as through earworm-worthy ostinati or leitmotifs. But pleasurable repetition—and the agreeably participative stance it engenders—can just as easily be an external matter, the product of relistening. Some forms of participation are tied to the listener's body and can range in physicality from outright dancing to quiet toe-tapping to fully unconscious beat-entrainment. Margulis notes that "listeners often have some sense of executing the sounds [of music themselves], whether by semi-realistic imagined guitar strumming or piano playing or some more metaphoric, less literal sense of embodying the sound," in which case enjoyment stems from a feeling of being "physically *played by the piece*."[35]

Other participatory pathways are more cerebral, though they need not be as intellectual as reading a book by a music theorist! Dreaming up imagery to match the music's progress, or even just noticing how music makes you feel as it happens—these are no less edifying, no less active modes of appreciation. Communal experience is one vector of virtual participation, and a relevant one in cases where a film score is presented to a wide audience, as in a cine-concert. The thrill of liveness breeds entirely new forms of listener investment. But we should not discount how intensely participative listening in solitude can be. Something about the intimacy of listening through headphones in particular seems able to make the music feel as though it is meant just for you, maybe even brought into existence by you, a private soundtrack for your life. As Margulis frames it, the more you relisten, "the more the music seems to dissolve boundaries, occupy your subjectivity, and connect your inner sensibilities with the outer world."[36]

Whether embodied or intellectual, public or private, musical participation also involves one other big principle of musical enjoyment: anticipation. Psychological research confirms what most listeners implicitly understand: we enjoy having our musical foreknowledge rewarded and predictions confirmed. Or, alternatively, *subverted*, though the best musical surprises are presented in emotionally legible and stylistically sanctioned ways. Anticipatory pleasure is intense and continuous if you know a piece ahead of time, and it is thus closely affiliated with the cognitive boons of processing fluency (broached in Chapter 2) and aesthetic rewards of thematic recognition and labeling (described in Chapter 3). But you need not be a soundtrack aficionado or Easter egg hunter for your experience of a film score to be enlivened by the vicissitudes of musical expectancy. David Huron's model of anticipation in music reveals how each stage of sonic expectation is filled with emotional potency, from the rousing formation of musical predictions to the delicious tension of awaiting their corroboration, and the sweet release upon confirmation—or piquant jolt in the case of an unforeseen surprise.[37] The force of "sweet anticipation" is no less potent when hearing something new, provided you are attentive and sensitive to the general "rules" of a musical idiom. Like a kiss, a long-telegraphed cadence works as well—maybe even better—when you know exactly where it is headed.

The combination of sympathetic participation and the thrill of anticipation is a large part of what makes temporally bound art forms like film and music so gratifying. Participation and anticipation are the reasons we rewatch movies and relisten to symphonies, seek out paratexts and attend concerts; together they offer more than enough delight to justify the cinesymphonic appreciation of film music. The consistency of style and the recurrence of themes in the Skywalker Saga make possible an especially rich expectancy structure, one in effect even for—or as Williams justifies it, *especially* for—first-time listeners. By the time *Attack of the Clones* ends, you'll know full well how the ANAKIN AND PADMÉ leitmotif ought to go, regardless of prior exposure or musical expertise. So, when the couple's theme starts one last time at the close of the film, you will have been well prepared to project a conclusion—melodic completion and a full cadence. And when that ending does arrive, sweeping and definitive, what a payoff it is!

Relistening is a proven pathway to an intensified musical experience, as it widens what Margulis calls "the horizon of involvement." Repetition helps shift your attention from the surface and onto more global musical structures, often where Williams's most advanced compositional wizardry is realized. But, again, it is not a prerequisite—what matters is Margulis's aesthetic orientation, "a perceptual openness, a willingness to notice and believe in connections and meaning that may not be instantly apparent."[38] Luckily for listeners open to such music-centric experiences and re-experiences, the Skywalker Saga is rich in such connections and meanings. And no installment repays rehearing more than *The Empire Strikes Back*.

9

The Battle Symphony of Hoth

We've only just begun to understand the audio-visual process, the very subtle and complex affair that is seeing/hearing. How much do we hear when we see? How much do we see when we hear? How do these relationships change? How can we manipulate them?

—John Williams

The Case for *Empire*

John Williams claimed that we have "only just begun to understand the audio-visual process" nearly five decades ago.[1] The use of pre-recorded music in film is now over a century old. The formal study of screen composition is an established academic discipline with a rich literature and no shortage of theories concerning that "subtle and complex affair that is seeing/hearing." Our understanding of how musical multimedia is structured and perceived is immeasurably more sophisticated today than when *The Empire Strikes Back* premiered. Yet the puzzles and prospects of the audio-visual process are as excitingly open today as they were in 1980. For all their insight, musicologists will never settle the question of "how much we [hear/see] when we [see/hear]." Nor will filmmakers, despite theirs being an art of audience manipulation. The nature of the seeing/hearing relationship is, as Williams implies, dynamic and personal, explored anew by the individual listener/viewer each time they experience a movie.

In Chapter 1, I introduced the idea of cine-symphonic listening, a mode of film appreciation where orchestral underscore is a significant and sustained subject of one's attention. Here, we will see how far that concept can go. This final chapter puts forward an approach to the audio-visual relationship that may seem counterintuitive at best, a violation of the way film is supposed to work at worst. The goal is to hear a fifteen-minute segment of *Empire*'s score with fresh ears—neither a subordinated component of a larger film, nor a paratext ripe for extraction and arrangement, but rather *a large-scale, multi-movement symphonic work, a genuine piece that calls for multiple hearings, both in and out of film, to fully appreciate.* That segment? The Battle of Hoth.

Arriving at this novel way of hearing a film score will take a few steps. First, we will consider the score for Episode V as a totality, as an uncommonly gratifying feat of (mostly) unified musical storytelling. Because the sequence in question is a huge action set piece, the next section is a survey of how Williams scores large battles in *Star Wars*, and how these sequences fall into a tradition of the orchestral aestheticization of warfare more generally. After these preliminaries comes the payoff: a musical analysis of the Battle of Hoth as a kind of modern-day *Schlacht Sinfonie*, or "Battle Symphony." The analysis unfolds across three sections. The first lays out the compositional techniques deployed across the set piece that make it so continuously compelling as a sonic whole. The second section zeroes in on one of its constituent cues, "Luke's First Crash." The final section takes the multi-movement symphonic analogy to its limit, presenting a case that the whole fifteen-minute span is a true *piece* of music, a subtle and complex affair that can stand alongside the great program works and tone poems of the orchestral repertoire.

Of the nine Skywalker Saga scores, *The Empire Strikes Back* presents the easiest case for music-centric appreciation.[2] As mentioned in the first chapter, Williams's contribution to Episode V is more original and more deeply felt than its predecessor. *Empire* represents a high-water mark for the franchise in musical integrity; it is a score that stands equally well on its own as it does implanted within its film. Williams's orchestration is nowhere more masterly, particularly when tasked with painting alien locales like the frigid wastes of Hoth and sludgy mires of Dagobah. The orchestra expands relative to *A New Hope*, both in instrumentalists (from 97 to 104) and timbral variety.[3] The synthesizer, here an ARP 2600, makes its first nondiegetic appearance in a handful of cues; so does a chorus in one, isolated passage during "City in the Clouds." Auxiliary instruments barely heard in *A New Hope*—celesta, piano, and mallet percussion—now play a large and consistent role. And contributing to the sonic assault of the Battle of Hoth are series-unique E♭ clarinets, Wagner tubas, and anvils. They join an already enlarged orchestra with "five piccolos, five oboes, a battery of eight percussion, two grand pianos, [and] three harps," all of which the composer deemed necessary "to achieve a bizarre, mechanical, brutal sound for the sequence showing

Imperial Walkers."[4] With all these new timbres, Episode V's underscore moves in ways unique to the Skywalker Saga; the soundtrack stampedes, slithers, and scintillates.

As Williams's ensemble widened, so did the potential for unusual timbral combinations and extended techniques. The London Symphony Orchestra's woodwinds are lavished with attention especially, on display in almost every cue, often through brief but flavorful solos. And while not necessarily the most diverse *Star Wars* score in terms of sheer instrumental variety—that honor goes to *Attack of the Clones*—Episode V possesses the Saga's most vividly *differentiated* tone colors. Never mind the splashy new themes: ample delight may be derived just from enjoying the brilliant colors that Williams draws from his players. Much of this coloristic vitality occurs during unmarked athematic passages, potential throwaway material for a lesser score. But in *Empire*, even the longueurs are not devoid of musical interest.

A good example of this painterly approach is found in the cue "Yoda Appears." It is one of a handful of dissonant swamp-music passages, spans vibrant in tone painting but with little thematic definition. The cue's first thirteen measures are given in Figure 9.1. The approach here is characteristic of

Figure 9.1 Painterly orchestration in "Yoda Appears" (ESB, 5m2, 46:06)

Williams's moody underscoring in *Empire*, with daubs of color traded between wind instruments. The lead voice passes from bass clarinet to flutes, and then to English horn, piccolo doubled with bassoon, and so on. Here is a clear example of an idea broached in Chapter 1, that harmony can be a function of orchestration in *Star Wars*. Which pitches sound at any time in this cue supervene on more foundational decisions of timbre: accustomed versus extreme tessitura; spectral smoothness versus roughness; spectral density versus clarity. The short module for English horn is particularly evocative, with its Impressionistic melodic profile and harmonic pigmentations—note the non-orientable $B^{7(\sharp 11)}$ chord and gnomic triplet responses in muted trombones and basses below. All this time, nothing much is happening on screen; Luke retrieves some parts from his sunken X-Wing and goes on to offer R2 a recharge. But the accompanying music is a veritable tone-poem of bizarre—and bizarrely beautiful—timbral effects.

Empire is not just a colorful score; it is a virtuosic one. Williams's orchestration, especially in the soundtrack's intricate action set pieces, is technically demanding to a degree rare in Hollywood. The whiplashing melodies in "The Asteroid Field," the devilishly hard brass licks in "This Is Not A Cave" and "Attacking a Star Destroyer," the *perpetuum mobiles* in "Hyperspace": these sequences rank among the most difficult to play—and thus thrilling to hear—in the *Star Wars* oeuvre. But virtuosity in *Empire* is never for its own sake. More so than anything in Episode IV besides "TIE Fighter Attack," the film's action cues are motivically distinctive and formally tight, to the benefit of listeners who hear them in an extracted state. This technical brilliance is appreciable, for the most part, within the movie itself, too. The audio mix keeps music mostly unobscured, excepting the loudest exchanges of blaster fire during the shootout on Bespin ("Luke Pursues the Captives") and a few legs of the Battle of Hoth.

As with his orchestration, Williams's harmonic palette in Episode V is enriched relative to *A New Hope*. Several pitch configurations rise to, if not a motivic level, then certainly that of score-spanning *tinta*. One is what we have been calling the "Brute" tetrachord, a fusion of minor thirds separated by perfect fourth (e.g., E-G-C-E♭) that fits into both hexatonic and octatonic scales. While it appears throughout the score, that sonority receives a sustained workout during the Battle of Hoth. Another unifying device is the use of falling figures that are dissonantly harmonized by parallel interval-classes 1 or 2—that is, seconds, sevenths, ninths, and their ilk. This is an intervallic/

Figure 9.2 Dissonant falling figures across *Empire*. **a.** "Luke's Escape" (1m3, 9:08); **b.** "Crash Landing" (5m1, 42:00); **c.** "This Is Not A Cave" (6m3, 58:53); **d.** "The Magic Cave" (6m5/7m1, 1:03:22); **e.** "Attack Position" (7m2, 1:08:10); **f.** "Chewie Chokes Lando" (1:42:16)

textural idea with a palpable sense of "wrongness," owing to those linear and horizontal dissonances, and the particle is, among *Star Wars* scores, almost unique to *Empire*.[5] Dissonant falling figures shade a diverse set of otherwise unrelated cues, the flute line in bar three of "Yoda Appears" being one instance. Figure 9.2 exhibits a gallery of further instances.

Another recurrent tonal device is the aforementioned hexatonic collection, a six-note pitch resource that can be derived in three ways: juxtaposition of two augmented triads a half-step apart (e.g., B^+ and C^+); a cycle of triads related by the interval of a major third (e.g., C→Cm→A♭→G♯m→E→Em→C); and a scale of alternating semitones and minor thirds (e.g., C-E♭-E♮-G-A♭-B). Many passages in *Empire* arise from one or more of these patterns, and most tap into the collection's historical connotations of matters cosmic and uncanny.[6] The hexatonic scale provides harmonic support for two very differently valenced new leitmotifs—Vader and the Droids—but also appears throughout the film in thematically unmarked underscore. The score's very first cue, "Imperial Probe," revolves around varied presentations of this otherworldly scale. The opening four measures are shown in Figure 9.3; the gyrating flute and string trills make for a smooth continuation with the already spacey texture that concludes the "Main Title." The modules that follow in "Imperial Probe" similarly dwell in hexatonic or near-hexatonic spaces, notably in the polychordal iteration of Vader's leitmotif on piccolo—the series' first. Williams's writing here draws associative power not just from the intrinsic weirdness of the collection, but specific intertextual references

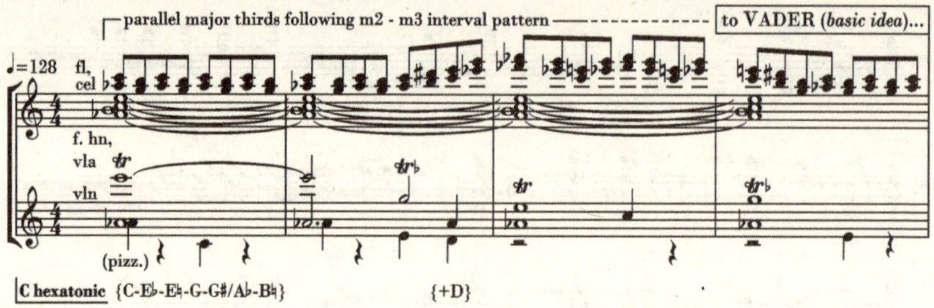

Figure 9.3 Establishment of a hexatonic tint in "The Imperial Probe" (ESB, 1m2, 1:56)

to both Vaughan Williams's *Scott of the Antarctic* and Bartók's "Elegia" from the *Concerto for Orchestra*.[7] However, unlike the analogous post-"Main Title" passage in *A New Hope* which invoked Holst's "Mars" with little adjustment, the referentiality here is better assimilated into Williams's evolving *Star Wars*ian sound. The upshot is an introductory cue that is disorienting yet resonant, a clear signal to listeners that the unqualified (musical) victory of the previous entry is a thing of the past.

Picking out unifying harmonic devices like *Empire*'s falling figures and hexatonic collections is not intrinsically difficult, but it does help to know what to listen for. With more esoteric details like these, a Margulis-style rehearing, as discussed in Chapter 8, is especially useful. Once the score's broader strokes are internalized, it becomes easier to "hear through" the eventful musical surface, to notice those features that subtly penetrate and bind disparate cues. There are also the decidedly *un*subtle unifying devices in Episode V: the themes, which can be grasped right away. Much of the score's memorability owes to the introduction and working-out of new leitmotifs for Yoda, Vader, and Han and Leia. Highly contrasting in affect but comparable in terms of weight and formal scope, these "big three" are afforded many opportunities for symphonic treatment. They are joined by four sharply defined subsidiary motifs (Droids, Boba Fett, Cloud City, Dark Side) and the banner melodies of the original film (Luke, Leia, Force, Rebel Fanfare). New and returning, these themes are all spotlit at moments, subject to understated development at others. Equipped with a thicker thematic catalog, Williams's approach to Wagnerian musical prose, tentatively explored in *A New Hope*'s "The Force" and "The Princess Reappears," is now more confidently realized in cues like "Yoda's Entrance" and "Luke's Departure." The wealth of new thematic material helped address a compositional challenge that did not exist in the mostly linear narrative of Episode IV: how to maintain continuity of musical thought within the frame of a complexly edited film, with two parallel plots for much of the runtime.

Starting in Episode VI, Williams's underscore often flips on a dime as demanded by profuse changes of scene, incident, and editing. But in *Empire*, the composer struck a balance between close musical coordination and what theorists have called *la grande ligne*, or "the long line." Though more intuitive than rigorously defined, the long line is a handy way of describing how composers can sustain musical logic and flow over large durations, with a clear forward drive, unimpeded by inessential or redundant ideas.[8] Cohesion in this lofty sense is obviously in the ear of the beholder and rarely the main priority of any film composer. Nevertheless, careful attention can do wonders for scores where, despite all the subordination to which music is subject, a long line (or bundle of lines) does run through a passage, cue, or indeed whole score. In practice, the construction of such symphonic continuity requires canvases sufficiently broad for the expression of long-breathed themes, as well as an artful treatment of transition and the concerted development of important motivic cells. We encountered one manifestation of the latter in Chapter 5's examination of motivic seeding in Episode V.

Climax building is also crucially important to the long line, and in *Empire*, Williams is methodical in the way he builds up and releases tension. He accomplishes it locally with a handful of tried-and-true techniques like drawn-out pedal points, deceptive resolution pileups, and intensificatory chromatic sequences—the bread and butter of late Romantic composers. But Williams also fashions emotional apexes on a more holistic level. The movie's dénouement on Cloud City is organized around a succession of crescendos and thematic payoffs, of which the midpoint of "Carbon Freeze" and the conclusions of "Through the Window" and "Losing a Hand" are among the most grandiose—and all explored in Chapter 5. (The final climax, the ending of "To Hyperspace," will be discussed shortly.)

Irvin Kershner singled out Williams's skill for through-composition, noting "he's very good . . . at maintaining a long piece of music and getting all the variations without making it what we call 'Mickey Mouse,' where you accent every little bump, every little crash."[9] In fairness, Williams's music is as fastidiously synchronized in *Empire* as ever—one need only inspect "The Asteroid Field" with an ear to where image and score align to appreciate this. But where mimetic scoring does occur, it is generally executed in a refined way. Williams structures the busiest cues such that musical accents align with the unfurling of traditionally structured and often lengthy grammatical themes, rather than interrupting them, as would increasingly be the case in subsequent entries. The upshot is a score of grand sweep in its prosodic spans and positively balletic during tightly spotted sequences. Again, the two principal melodies in "The Asteroid Field" (both examined in Chapter 5) are demonstrative, catching the frenetic action without ever bending to it. Indeed, music in this iconic set piece almost transcends synchronization and approaches choreography.

Like its predecessor, the *Empire Strikes Back* divides into a three-act structure, neatly organized around changes of setting and character groupings. The film's geographies are appropriately matched with distinguishing musical idioms—brittle Bartókian expanses for Hoth, murky dissonances for Dagobah and the asteroid cave, and disarming Waltonian cheer for Bespin. The tripartite dramatic frame also aligns beautifully with different stages of musical development, facilitating the impression of a film-spanning thematic arc, such as those discussed in Chapter 6 but now distributed across a trio of equally important leitmotifs. The "big three" all have their own journeys from adumbration to apotheosis, though these arcs occur at different phases of the drama. Although many bold statements of VADER's march pepper the score, it is the gleefully malicious and phrase-structurally complete iteration during Act I's Battle of Hoth [33:05] that marks its highest point of melodic attainment. YODA's leitmotif, meanwhile, reaches its expressive summit during the X-Wing lifting scene in Act II [1:12:17]. And HAN AND LEIA's love theme, denied closure much as ANAKIN AND PADMÉ's would be in Episode II, takes lyric flight in three progressively fuller forms during Act III [1:35:49, 1:48:21, 2:01:09]—four, if we count the aforementioned cadence at the end of the cine-symphonically essential credits [2:05:39].

All these factors—orchestrational brilliance, harmonic and thematic depth, striving for that mythical "long line"—make *Empire* a singularly gratifying film score for devoted ears. However, while treating it as a concert-by-other-means can free us to appreciate its musical power and inventiveness, the score still insists on its origin as a dramatically contingent and sometimes *dis*-integrated work. Episode V is rife with "anti-symphonic" elements too, and not just the intermittency and tonal free-for-all that marks all Williams's *Star Wars* scores. For example, with forty-four renditions, "The Imperial March" is ubiquitous, well past the point needed for thematic consistency. Though this prevalence fits the drama like a glove—the Empire is supposed to be implacable and omnipresent, after all—the leitmotif's relentlessness, especially during the film's second act, would seem overkill were one presented with the soundtrack as a purely musical expression. And if such music's doggedness can sometimes sound non-symphonic, so too can its absence. There are stretches of fine music in *Empire*, available for any listener's delectation on the expanded soundtrack release, that were cut or replaced in the final film. Usually this was done for good reason. Luke's encounter with Vader in the carbonite chamber is a prime example. The original underscore, with its rousing spins on the Yoda and Force themes, is undoubtedly stirring. But pregnant silence, mixed with Vader's taunts and the weird ambience of the sepulchral space, fills the confrontation with far more dread than the London Symphony Orchestra would have.

One especially notable "anti-symphonic" feature of the score is also one of the most narratively consequential. The end of the final action cue, "To Hyperspace," amounts to a musical *deus ex machina*. When Artoo suddenly fixes the Millennium Falcon's hyper-drive, and the heroes escape Vader's clutches one last time, Williams tosses aside the cue's driving ostinato in favor of a glittery block-chord progression, loosely affiliated with the Rebel Fanfare. This phrase, depicted in Figure 9.4, dispels almost an entire soundtrack's worth of tension—not through an earned thematic transformation or telegraphed cadence, but rather a bolt out of the blue. Williams snaps the long line here, to great effect.

Arguably, the need for an earned musical payoff at this dramatic juncture is moot: the movie had already passed through several awe-inspiring climaxes in the immediately preceding scenes. And the subsequent finale cue, with its sweeping and apotheotic statement of the Han and Leia theme, is hardly wanting for the impression of musical closure. The *deus ex mechanical*

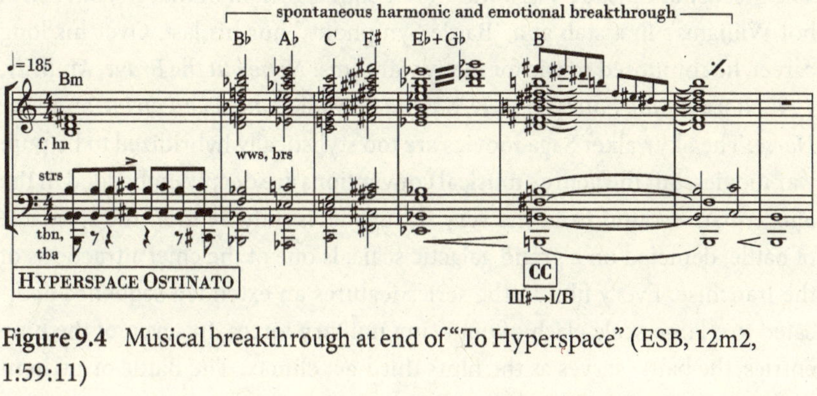

Figure 9.4 Musical breakthrough at end of "To Hyperspace" (ESB, 12m2, 1:59:11)

resolution of "To Hyperspace" is not even all that anti-symphonic—from a certain point of view. In the post-Wagnerian symphonic milieu, the idea of the formal *Durchbruch*, or "breakthrough," was a recognized device in its own, highly dramatic way.[10] A breakthrough could be any unanticipated musical event that arrives and instantly reorients the score around itself, such as the chorale that bursts forth in the Finale of Mahler's First Symphony. The chromatic progression that draws "Hyperspace" to a close may well leave a symphonically oriented listener wondering "*wait, that was it?!*" Few standalone works of art music, post-Wagnerian or not, would snatch tonal victory from the jaws of defeat so summarily. But, as always, dramatic context is key: as the middle chapter of an ongoing trilogy, maximally earned resolution is understandably something Williams would defer. (And *Return of the Jedi* has those properly big payoffs in spades at the end of the Battle of Endor.)

Together, the disunifying aspects of Episode V's score serve a useful function, reminding us of the knotty and contingent nature of even the most integrated-seeming of film soundtracks. Indeed, for highly attuned listeners, part of the enjoyment comes from discerning all the score's quirks, alternatives, discrepancies. To know all the ways a work of art *could* have gone is a powerful aesthetic pleasure in its own right. That said, when the overall quality of the score is so high, little wrinkles like the contrived close of "To Hyperspace" do not detract much from its ability to satisfy as a purely musical experience.

Scoring War

The first act of Episode V is a war movie soundtrack in miniature, but it was not Williams's first stab at a "Battle Symphony," nor his last. Over his long career, he composed music for many war films: *None but the Brave*, *Midway*, *1941*, *Born on the Fourth of July*, *Saving Private Ryan*, *The Patriot*, and *War Horse*. The Skywalker Saga movies are too stylistically hybridized to be pure war movies, but the genre's musical conventions are deeply embedded in the *Star Wars*ian sound from the very start. This is only natural: the spectacle of battle, depicted on a grand galactic scale, is one of the chief attractions of the franchise. Every film in the series features an extended sequence dedicated to a large-scale clash of opposing military forces. In seven of the nine entries, the battle serves as the film's third-act climax. The Battle of Yavin in

Episode IV established many of the series' dramatic conventions for such set pieces: ticking countdowns, heavily guarded targets, and a daunting asymmetry between the outgunned good guys and overconfident bad guys. In keeping with the movie's referential ethos, the visual and sonic grammar of *A New Hope*'s climax was plucked from movies like *The Dambusters* and *The Guns of Navarone*, often with minimal adjustment.

Williams's music for the assault on the Death Star is similarly precedent setting—and intertextually allusive. Musical topics one would expect in a symphonic rendering of warfare such as snare tattoos and zippy fanfares are prevalent, though not always easily audible against the whir of X-Wings and racket of futuristic artillery. As with much else in *A New Hope*, the imprint of external models is strong. The primary source here is the "Battle in the Air" from William Walton's otherwise unused score to *The Battle of Britain*—a rip-roaring cue that must have left an impression on Williams when he attended the recording sessions in 1969.[11] But the Battle of Yavin sequence also introduces a suite of more idiosyncratically *Star Wars*ian devices, like quartal canons in brass and octatonic agitatos in the strings, which would come to pervade subsequent galactic set pieces. Perhaps the most striking of these tropes-to-be is the last minute statement of the FORCE theme [1:55:38] that punctures through the frenzy, its then-unprecedented lydian refiguration harmonizing with Obi-Wan's words "use the Force, Luke."[12]

For all its codification of *Star Wars*ian musical warfare, the Battle of Yavin is also uncharacteristic in telling ways. For one, a substantial portion of the set piece [1:39:34–1:53:23] bears no music. Subsequent battles unvaryingly feature wall-to-wall scoring, raising the risk of musical oversaturation. This threat is addressed—if not always prevented—by a greater reliance on contrastingly low-intensity, unmarked, or non-mimetic scoring than present in *A New Hope*'s more jam-packed cues. The sequence is further atypical in featuring only one battlefront and one focalized character: the Death Star and Luke Skywalker. Appropriately, its music is relatively simple in form and concentrated in effect. It is the only major battle in the entire Saga with no significant musical edits to speak of—none of the tracked passages, inserts, and alternates that later become rife. *Empire* is mostly spared editorial complications, but *Jedi*'s Battle of Endor comprises sixteen cues, with numerous small-scale edits and one large instance of tracking: the DEFEAT theme from Episode V replaces newly written score as the Rebels arrive at the Death Star II core. By contrast, the three cues that make up *A New Hope*'s final sequence—"Standby," "Approaching the Target," and "The Last Battle"—form a straightforward and, at just over nine minutes, smartly paced musical piece. (It can be heard as such on the 1997 Special Edition album, where the three cues are nicely edited into a single continuous track, "The Battle of Yavin.") In Chapter 4, we saw how LUKE's theme contributes to the anxiety ramp that is "The Last Battle," but the design of the cue as a *whole* is the real feat of musical nail-biting. From the aforementioned beatific statement of the FORCE theme to the polytonal afterglow of the REBEL FANFARE, its final two minutes build an almost unbearable degree of tension, until all is released by a simple C-major chord, fired with the precision of a proton torpedo.

Figure 9.5 summarizes all the saga's battles, breaking down their subsidiary skirmishes and the leitmotifs enlisted in them. The number of discrete cues for each sequence is also specified, though cue count alone is an imperfect indicator of a sequence's complexity, as it ignores duration, revisions, inserts, and tracked measures. Scenes of pitched combat increase in both length and musical intricacy as the franchise progresses, reaching a peak of activity in the four simultaneous fronts in Episode I. The compositional challenges for such sequences are enormous, and the rewards of careful planning are not guaranteed due to editorial meddling and sound-effect submersion. Williams's strategy for the Battle of Naboo was to supply the entire conflict with a bespoke leitmotivic complex, in the form of DUEL OF THE FATES. As discussed in Chapter 7, this thematic through-line was subjected to enormous retroactive manipulation. Yet even in its editorially compromised state, Williams's music helps keep the four plates Lucas set spinning from flying off into total narrative disarray.

To craft a coherent musical argument amid the fog of an action sequence is a tall order for any film composer. And to *follow* that argument without getting caught up in its moment-to-moment pyrotechnics is no small feat for a cine-symphonic listener. Within their cinematic contexts, the battles of *Star Wars* tend to feature the most virtuosic and elaborately constructed music of any particular episode. Yet these are the same sequences that are most prone to effacement—not just by the vagaries of editing and sound design, but the overall intensity of spectacle and narrative tension, which naturally consume the filmgoer's attention. Despite being the film musical idiom most firmly wedded to filmic image and incident, battle music—this least autonomous of genres—benefits the most from attentive listening, especially in live performance. Nothing beats the thrill of witnessing actual human beings pull off incredible feats in playing such challenging cues. Given the way that

Battle	Cues	Front	Featured leitmotifs in order of appearance
IV. Yavin	3	Aerial	Luke, Rebel Fanfare, Death Star, Imperials, Force
V. Hoth	5	Ground	Luke, Rebel Fanfare, Vader, Force
		Base	Droids, Leia, Han & Leia, Vader
VI. Endor	16	Aerial	Throne Room, It's a Trap, Vader, Rebel Fanfare, Luke, Death Star, Victory
		Ground	Vader, Ewoks, Leia, Han & Leia
		Throne	Vader, Luke, Emperor, Force
I. Naboo	10	Aerial	Duel of the Fates, Anakin, Force
		Ground	Duel of the Fates, Droid Army, [Anakin – tracked]
		Palace	Duel of the Fates
		Catwalk	Duel of the Fates, Force, Qui-Gon
II. Geonosis	2	Ground	Anakin and Padmé, [Duel of the Fates, Luke, Conspiracy, Mystery – tracked], Force, Yoda
III. Coruscant	8	Aerial	Force, Rebel Fanfare, Grievous, [Duel of the Fates, Force -- tracked], Happy Landings
VII. S.K. Base	11	Aerial	Rebel Fanfare, Luke, Kylo C
		Forest	Force, Rey A, Kylo A/B/C, Han & Leia, Pathos
VIII. D'Qar	8	Aerial	Tension, Rebel Fanfare, Poe, Kylo A/C, Resistance, Finn/Pursuit, Leia, Luke, Battle of the Heroes, Force
VIII. Krait	10	Ground 1	Force, Resistance, Rose, Kylo A, Tension
		Aerial	Rey A/B, Rebel Fanfare
		Ground 2	Rey A, Luke and Leia, Han and Leia, Force, Kylo A/B
IX. Exegol	21 (est.)	Aerial/Ground	Emperor, Resistance, Kylo A, Luke, Rebel Fanfare, Poe, Force, Victory, Tension, Fr'dship
		Throne	Rey A, Emperor, Psalm of the Sith, Sith Artifacts, [Duel of the Fates – cut], Knights of Ren, Rey B, Kylo A, Force, Mystery, Pathos

Figure 9.5 Overview of battle sequences in the Skywalker Saga

battle music in *Star Wars* is often subordinated in situ, a score-first venue may well be the only situation in which Williams's highest-octane music is even audible.

While showcasing live performers and eliminating competing stimuli may remove some obstacles to cine-symphonic appreciation, doing so introduces at least as many contradictions. The enjoyment of battle music in a standalone setting depends on a sometimes impossible task: cobbling together a coherent "piece" when no stable text exists in the first place, to the consternation of many an album producer, concert programmer, and playlist curator. But the deepest tension of all for action cues is that of subject matter. Battle music wears its extramusical origins on its sleeve more brazenly than any other type of cue. For this reason alone, sequences like the Battle of Yavin or Naboo are hard to square with any traditionalist view of symphonic music. Exciting and vivid compositions like these are no objects of detached contemplation!

The martial subject matter of these pieces also confronts listeners with a moral issue. That violence might inspire rousing, interesting, or just plain *fun* music is a paradox at the base of a great deal of art. Expressions of true horror and pathos are rare and brief in the Skywalker Saga, with its sanitized and mythically distanced battles.[13] But the *molto tragico* idiom employed for events like the galactic massacre in Episode III [1:23:34] or the Hosnian Cataclysm in Episode VII [1:09:34] is comparable to the composer's treatment of non-fictional tragedies in other contexts. Williams never condescends to these stories, no matter how campy or absurd. When a lament marks the death of an unnamed Ewok in *Return of the Jedi* [1:40:01, 1:43:20], the seriousness of musical tone might be blunted by the obvious fantasticality of its context. When listened to on its own, such detachment may not be so easy.

The enjoyment of *Star Wars*' battle music is thus a complicated prospect, but it is hardly without precedent. The history of Western music is full of bloody conflicts represented through sound. One format in particular provides a neat stylistic model: the Battle Symphony. Critically denigrated but ever popular with audiences, pieces in this combative vein began as a variant of the "characteristic symphony," an umbrella genre that developed in the late 1700s for works of more audacious programmaticism than the standard instrumental fare. In Europe, battle symphonies had their heyday between the 1780s and 1810s, experiencing a second surge of popularity in the United States during the Civil War.[14] The genre was largely initiated by the enormously popular *Battle of Prague* (c. 1785–1788) by the Czech composer František Kočvara. This piece established many of the formal expectations of militarily themed characteristic works: vividly contrasting themes for the opposing armies; mimetic renderings of sounds such as cannons and horse gallops; and a normative order of sections—preparation music for the lead-up, fighting music for the heat of combat, lamentation music for casualties, and celebratory music for the victorious outcome. Most of Kočvara's successors are now forgotten figures like Druschetzky, Reichardt, and Wranitzky. But the genre remains in the popular imagination today because of a singular figure: Beethoven. His Op. 91 *Wellingtons Sieg* (Wellington's Victory) was the apogee of the form, an orchestral barnburner from 1813 with antiphonally opposed percussion contingents, warring French and English national tunes, a glorious and briefly fugal finale. While hardly tasteful by the composer's standards—or ours, in truth—the piece is tremendous fun and more than a little nascently cinematic.

Beethoven's model proved hard to top, though a few successors to his potboiler have found a place in the standard repertoire. These include figures who influenced Williams like Liszt (*Hunnenschlacht*), Tchaikovsky (*1812 Overture*), and Strauss (*Ein Heldenleben*). However, at the level of technique, the typical *Star Wars* battle sequence owes more to twentieth-century composers than Romantic-era ones. Of those from the more modern era, "Mars" from *The Planets* is an oft-cited and obvious source of inspiration. Less frequently noted, but arguably more deeply integrated into Williams's war-idiom, is the style of Shostakovich—perhaps the most unflinching portraitist of military carnage in music. Among the more bloodthirsty of Shostakovich's symphonic movements, 7/i, 10/ii, 11/ii, and 12/i resonate powerfully with Williams's *Star Wars* style, especially in material from the Original Trilogy.[15]

While the sounds and sensibilities of the Battle Symphony lived on in the work of modern concert composers, the genre's strongest legacy would be at the movies. And here Williams had his pick of antecedents. In Korngold, we hear a model for the heroic gestures and quicksilver shifts of *Star Wars'* tonal idiom, with the opening clash in *The Sea Hawk* and concluding swordfight in *The Adventures of Robin Hood* being especially prototypical. The war music of Miklós Rózsa for films like *Ben Hur* and *El Cid* offered Williams a study in sustaining tension over a long span, through the careful juggling of leitmotifs and the generative potential of ostinato. And in Alex North's scores—especially the climactic set piece from *Spartacus*—we hear an arsenal of strange instruments and timbral effects that would later be arrayed in the Battle of Hoth.[16]

Two of the strongest models for *Star Wars*' martial idiom come from outside the Hollywood system, and interestingly, both made a leap from film *to* concert hall. One is Sergei Prokofiev's "Battle on the Ice," the centerpiece of his *Alexander Nevsky* cantata, drawn from the film score of 1938. The other is William Walton's "Charge and Battle" from the 1944 adaptation of *Henry V* and later included in the best-known suite extracted from that score. Both Prokofiev's and Walton's battles follow the general formal trajectory enshrined 150 years before by Kočvara. And both exist as concert pieces, arranged for standalone performance from their filmic sources—notably without any profound changes to structure or scoring. Perhaps this lack of re-working is a testament to Prokofiev's and Walton's instincts for crafting satisfying forms within the constraints of cinematic underscore. But their ready acceptance into the concert repertoire implies an existing acceptance of "battle musical logic" from listeners trained on not just film scores, but several centuries' worth of similar illustrative works.

By pointing to the existence of a long-standing concert genre, I do not mean to sneak Williams's war music through a back door into the symphonic canon. Even if such validation were necessary, comparisons with "characteristic" works are unlikely to win *Star Wars* any converts among traditionalists. For all their popularity, battle symphonies have always been targets of vituperation from critics, and to say a work like "Wellington's Victory" has a fraught relationship with the classical canon is to put things mildly.[17] What matters is the fact that there is a long-standing *listening culture* for instrumental renderings of warfare, and a substantial repertoire to support it, from Beethoven to Shostakovich to Williams.

Within that listening culture, the appeal of battle pieces is manifold, though the core elements of their allure remain durable whether listeners find themselves in 1813 Vienna hearing Beethoven's crowd-pleaser or at their home in 2026 listening to the "Battle of Hoth" on their headphones. The genre's enduring appeal rests on several pillars:

- **Listening in the moment**: Battle sequences, wedded as they are to programmatic scaffolding, are often simple and loose in structure, allowing one to remain in the musical present, without conscious concern for formal hierarchy, tonal closure, or thematic corroboration. That such high-level processes still operate in the finest instances of battle music (as they certainly do in *Empire*) makes the genre a best-of-both-worlds proposition: gripping for newcomers and rewarding for deeper or repeat listeners.

- **Listening to extremes**: In few other genres do composers engage in sonic experimentation, excess, and extremity as unabashedly as in battle pieces. Works in this vein offer a place to hear otherwise novel and radical compositional techniques, especially timbral ones, in a comfortable setting.[18]
- **Listening with topical clarity**: Although battle pieces tend to present a veritable onslaught of sonic stimuli, they are among the most topically dense in instrumental music, making them highly intelligible from an emotional and associative perspective. Add to that an emphasis on repetitive textures and rhythms (marches, ostinati) and it becomes easy to be "physically played by the piece" in Margulis's sense.
- **Listening with moral clarity**: Musical renderings of war, especially in nationalistic and/or mass-appeal contexts, feature extreme and morally simplifying contrasts. Battle lines are drawn between good and evil through themes, tonalities, idioms, etc. An escape from the ambivalences of the real world can be gratifying, if only ever temporary.[19]
- **Listening for thrills**: Battle music fulfills a similar psychological need as a horror novel or rollercoaster: a means of experiencing and processing negative emotions (anxiety, fear, grief, helplessness) in a safe way. In the case of *Star Wars*, those negative emotions are leavened with positive ones—excitement, familiarity, triumph, and so on.
- **Listening imaginatively**: The vividness of battle pieces makes them easy sites of personal narrative construction in one's mind's eye—or self-insertion if one craves an especially engrossing experience.

To hear *Star Wars* cine-symphonically—or rather *battle-symphonically*—is to open ourselves to the multiple forms of appreciation and engagement described above. This does not mean we must ignore the extramusical circumstances in which action scoring was forged, or somehow treat a given "Battle of X" set piece like some forgotten masterpiece of absolute music. But neither must we feel anxious about the music's contingency, its directness, its "popcorn" appeal. As we turn our sights onto the Battle of Hoth and train some heavy analytical artillery on its formal edifices, it is worth remembering a simple, childlike truth: for all its complexities, this kind of music, like the movies it accompanies, is meant to be fun to hear.

Drawing Battle Lines

To claim that Battle of Hoth represents a musical pinnacle in the series is not to slight the other set pieces listed in Figure 9.5. But over the course of fifteen and a half minutes, the assault on Echo Base in *The Empire Strikes Back* achieves a rare trifecta: impeccable coordination of music with on-screen action and emotion, a persistently high level of compositional invention from measure to measure, and a sense of balance and unity across the whole. These three qualities—aptness, interest, and cohesion—are by no means mutually implicative, certainly not for a set piece this lengthy. The maintenance of musical interest is especially remarkable; no other battle in the series is as rich with individually compelling new materials nor as imaginative in its development of old ones. That this trifecta was attainable in the first place is a testament to the unified vision of Episode V's filmmaking team. Much credit is owed to the editorial department led by Paul Hirsch in constructing the taut and thrilling sequence. And Williams's intricate scoring could never have been realized were it not for the orchestrators—Herbert Spencer, Angela Morley, Al Woodbury, and Fred Steiner—who translated the composer's dense sketches into performable music.

Before diving into the nuances of this cine-symphonic conflagration, a brief but necessary side note on orchestration and authorial autonomy. Kathryn Kalinak rightly notes that the number of orchestrators for *Empire* is extraordinary.[20] What Kalinak omits, however, is an acknowledgment that Williams's sketches for Episode V are, like those for all his other scores, essentially fully orchestrated already, requiring the orchestrating team to interpret and transcribe his shorthand and not much else.[21] Williams explains—and demonstrates—his process clearly in a BBC documentary made during the scoring of the film:

> I, at the piano, sketch on a 10, or 8 line sketch pad. So on 6, 8, or 10 lines of sketch, I can indicate very precisely what the orchestration ought to be. But if I then had to put that on 32 lines, or 50 lines in the orchestra, I would be slowed up by about a hundred percent. So I can do approximately 2 minutes of score [a day] with Herb [Spencer's] help.[22]

The composer goes into considerable detail regarding his collaborative process in other interviews, always stressing that the orchestration is entirely his invention, while orchestrators help translate his shorthand and transfer it to fair copy score ready for typesetting.[23] (One must remember Williams cut his teeth in Hollywood as an arranger-orchestrator and learned to write for this "instrument" with great fluency.) The workflow Williams describes is not self-aggrandizement, being consistently corroborated by his orchestrators, including Herbert Spencer and Conrad Pope.[24] Examination of the composer's sketches definitively confirms his attested practice, though as of the time of this book, they are not easily available for study.[25]

Returning to the set piece at hand—as a series of musical events, the Battle of Hoth is immediately and irresistibly powerful. Like any good action set piece (or battle symphony), its emotional impact is direct, its basic structure easy to follow. Within its 528 bars, the music hits hard and hits often. But the visceral simplicity of effect is the product of some of the saga's most sophisticated music in terms of motivic density, harmonic complexity, and orchestrational nuance. Providing a full accounting of the intricacies of this "*Battle Symphony of Hoth*" is beyond the scope of this, or any, analysis. But even if fully plumbing the sequence's depths exceeds what this study can accomplish, the effort is still endlessly compelling.[26] Here, we will focus on three pertinent aspects: tonal quilting, melodic concatenation, and intensificatory sequencing.

Tonal Quilting

As with all *Star Wars* battles, the conflict on Hoth is scored in chunks rather than in one grand sweep. The storytelling progression is strikingly close to the Kočvara model. Five discrete cues cover different phases of the skirmish, with the stage-setting "Drawing the Battle Lines" and big finish "The Rebels Escape Again" neatly framing three cues that accompany scenes of active combat and casualties: "Leia's Instructions," "The Snow Battle," and "Luke's First Crash." Figure 9.6 offers a bird's-eye view, noting the extent of these cues and the broad narrative beats they hit. Unusually, the music Williams initially composed and recorded is retained in the final film with very little editorial adjustment. Micro-edits are apparent in just two spots in "Luke's First Crash": a measure and a half of looped athematic material [30:01–30:02]; and an awkward repetition of the first two measures of the Vader leitmotif

21:52–23:57	23:58–25:49	26:12–29:28	29:29–33:36	33:37–36:26
3m1	**3m2**	**3m3**	**3m4/4m1**	**4m2**
"Drawing the Battle Lines"	**"Leia's Instructions"**	**"The Snow Battle"**	**"Luke's First Crash"**	**"The Rebels Escape Again"**
48 mm.	63 mm.	143 mm.	150 mm.	125 mm.
Fond farewells and anxiety on Echo Base; Imperials arrive; Vader revises command structure.	Leia commands; Imperials approach, Rebel transport escapes; Luke & Dak take off.	Ground battle commences; speeders launch and attack walkers; Dak dies; Rebels trip walker.	Echo Base in chaos; Rebels retreat; Luke crashes, destroys walker; Empire destroys shield.	More Echo Base chaos; Han, Leia & co. evade and escape Vader in Falcon; Luke escapes.

Figure 9.6 High level overview of the Battle of Hoth

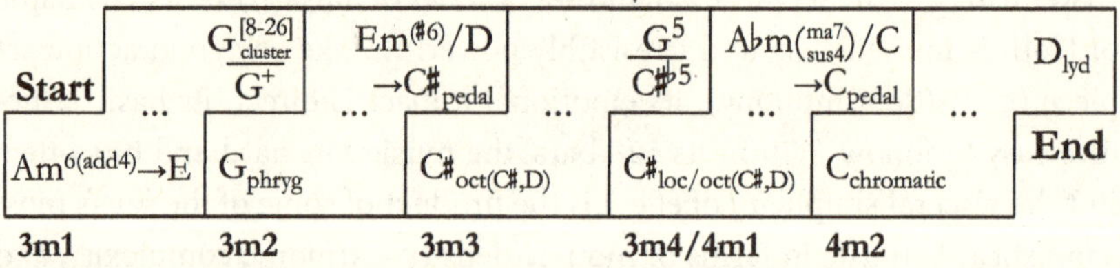

Figure 9.7 Tonal quilting between cues in the Battle of Hoth

[33:12–33:18]. The only drastic alteration of the score is the stretch of musical silence [25:49–26:13] that follows "Leia's Instructions." This segment was originally meant to be accompanied by the first fifteen and a half measures of "The Snow Battle," which comprise a lumbering vamp over a C♯-octatonic tonal field. But the omission of this material in the final film is no huge loss. The window of musical silence focuses sonic attention where it belongs—on the dreadful diegetic tramp of the distant walkers. Williams's music reasserts itself at 26:13 and carries through without further interruption until Luke zooms away from Hoth on his X-Wing at the end of "The Rebels Escape Again." The battle is lost, but the heroes live to fight another day.

The editorially imposed gap between "Leia's Instructions" and "The Snow Battle" notwithstanding, all five cues were composed so as to proceed to one another without pause, *attacca*. Each new musical stage begins on the same tonal tuft as its predecessor, guaranteeing a degree of local harmonic cohesion. This alone is not so remarkable. Overlapping cues often share the same chord at their point of contact to minimize tonal disruption. What is especially artful here is the sense of inexorable *progression* through which one harmonic patch leads into the next. This is not mere continuity, but setup and resolution across cue boundaries, what could be called tonal quilting. The stitches Williams uses for each transition are represented schematically in Figure 9.7.

Figure 9.8 Hopeful Rebels theme (ESB, 3m1, 25:40)

The effectiveness of tonal quilting is well-illustrated by the way Williams concludes the buoyant Hopeful Rebels theme on the trailing edge of the second cue, "Leia's Instructions." In any other musical genre, a tune like this, shown in Figure 9.8, would land and remain on a satisfying D-major triad, embodying in a way the callow optimism of Luke's copilot Dak, he of the ironic line "right now, I feel like I can take on the whole Empire myself!"[27] Certainly, this is how Hopeful Rebels would end had it occurred in the context of a Waltonian ceremonial march, on which the tune and its harmonization are clearly modeled. Our ears are not destined for this naïve closure, however.

Anticipating the hellacious battle in store, Williams seizes on a latently tense aspect of the Hopeful Rebels theme—its repeated Em^7/D chords—and insists upon it past the point of comfort. With growing volume and a sudden ritardando, the dissonant sonority appears to be snagged in the cue's penultimate measure. The addition of a C♯ makes matters worse, its sting against the D-bass sounding like a tonal problem rather than an easily resolved leading-tone. Sure enough, with one fell stroke, the cadential chord discharges, *wrongly*, down to C♯. This will be the tonal center of the first thirty-five bars of "The Snow Battle," and its unwelcome arrival signals the first of several harmonic and formal catastrophes to come. (It is during this cue that poor Dak meets his end.) The aforementioned excision of the first twenty-four seconds of "The Snow Battle" diminishes this effect only slightly: C♯ is still fresh enough in the ear after "Leia's Instructions" for one to register tonal follow-through once that key resumes at 26:13.

Melodic Concatenation

Tonal quilting grants the Battle of Hoth both continuity and driving momentum. However, given the sheer profusion of often only briefly maintained keys, these stitches do not constitute an especially high-level unifying device. As usual, Williams relies on modulation as a locally expressive device, not a vehicle for deep tonal planning. More significant from a global vantage than harmonic entwining is the *thematic* interconnectedness of the battle. The Battle of Hoth is, bar for bar, one of the richest sequences in the series in terms of density of incidental motifs and set piece themes. The entirely non-leitmotivic 3m3 "The Snow Battle" alone boasts a dozen distinctive musical ideas, none with direct repetitions in any other *Star Wars* cue. Absence of literal recurrence does not entail lack of motivic preparation or corroboration, though. Much of the ear-catching melodic material builds upon ideas heard before in preceding passages or cues, while simultaneously serving as developmental grist for what follows—the macro-thematic transformation we have called "melodic concatenation." The result is the opposite of a parade of one-cue wonders: the Battle of Hoth is a showcase for almost all the thematic transformational devices introduced in Chapter 4, macro and micro, including a surprisingly vigorous helping of developing variation for such a chaotic set piece.

The two major themes from "The Snow Battle," for example, are related via this concatenative technique. Figure 9.9 illustrates the key points of derivation from the ponderous and discursive AT-AT Assault theme and

Figure 9.9 Melodic concatenation of Heroes Under Fire from AT-AT Assault motifs

its sprightly successor, the Heroes Under Fire melody. The most direct linkage is an accented lower-neighbor figure, heard at various junctures and pitch levels throughout the AT-AT Assault melody. Another motivic seed sprouts from the irregular and dissonantly harmonized woodwind stabs that punctuate the AT-AT Assault module, often mimicking the neighbor figure of the main tune. Last, at the theme's midpoint, the staccato syncopations, accompaniment at first, become incorporated into the melody itself. The onset of the next module introduces the Heroes Under Fire theme, a catchy and four-square tune, unlikely to be confused with its lumbering motivic predecessor. But it will not sound like a stranger either: its staccato syncopations and lower-neighbor figures, secondary aspects of the AT-AT Assault, form the basis of the new theme's opening melodic hook.

Figure 9.10 arrays a handful of melodically concatenated segments from the Battle of Hoth, organized in reverse chronological order. The Sawing Strings ostinato that initiates and persists through much of the final cue "The Rebels Escape Again" spills directly out of the countermelody atop Vader's leitmotif in the closing bars of "Luke's First Crash." Before that, an Under-siege Agitato owes its contour and modal orientation to the concluding bars of the expansive Rebel Logistics theme stated twice in

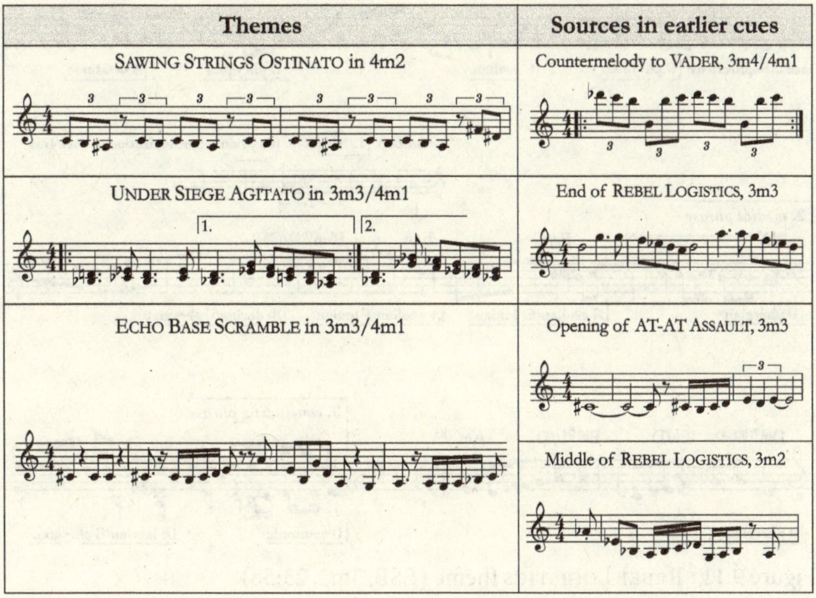

Figure 9.10 Melodic concatenation throughout the Battle of Hoth

"Leia's Instructions," first monophonically, then with contrapuntal elaboration. (A frantic counterfigure to the AGITATO in high winds is itself an instance of the descending second score-spanning motif mentioned earlier.) The ECHO BASE SCRAMBLE that begins "Luke's First Crash" further adapts a motivic seed—double descending fourths—from the REBEL LOGISTICS melody in its second measure. At the same time, the SCRAMBLE draws its melodic incipit almost note for note from the one-cue wonder AT-AT ASSAULT that dominates "The Snow Battle."

The REBEL LOGISTICS theme, already a fount for much of the set piece's melodic material, itself has a complex structure and set of associative resonances, including intratextual rhymes. The theme in all its militant severity is depicted in Figure 9.11. Steely in tone and discursive in shape, the melody accompanies Leia's issuing battle commands to the rebel soldiers. While strictly non-leitmotivic, REBEL LOGISTICS belongs to the same family as Episode VI's similar *unisoni* BATTLE PREP theme and anticipates the RESISTANCE MARCH from the Sequel Trilogy. Introduced in the first measure

Figure 9.11 REBEL LOGISTICS theme (ESB, 3m2, 23:58)

of "Leia's Instructions" and revisited at its conclusion in a contrapuntally elaborated guise, the melody is a quintessential set piece theme: memorable in its own right and formally crucial to boot, but restricted to a single cue. It is also yet another product of melodic concatenation. The opening phrase, with its dotted rhythm and sixteenth-neighbor figure in G phrygian, stems from a rising chromatic sequence in its predecessor cue, "Drawing the Battle Lines." And that chromatic figure is *itself* derived from "The Imperial March" vamp that immediately precedes it—such is the motivic economy of this sequence!

Though its nineteen measures do not divide into neat foursquare phrases, the REBEL LOGISTICS melody does follow a loosely Classical sentence structure in its delineation of initial, medial, and concluding segments. The first two measures lay out the theme's basic ideas—dotted repeated note, neighbor figure, leaping fourths, and a scale fragment in sixteenths—and immediately vary them in measures 3 and 4. The succeeding ten measures are effectively one big middle phrase, with a more striving, hopeful tenor. It is during this wide-ranging continuation that the theme's leaping fourths begin morphing into a LUKE-allusive submotif, noted in the second system of the diagram. (As mentioned, this cell will later serve as the basis of the UNDER SIEGE AGITATO.) The medial section of REBEL LOGISTICS builds to a cadence, with a very *Star-Wars*ian plagalized dominant-to-tonic progression ushering in the concluding three measures, right when Leia says "Understand? Good luck!" This parting encouragement prompts a compressed tutti restatement of the opening motif, mutated midstream by a snap modulation that draws us into the next scene and corresponding musical module.

Tonally, REBEL LOGISTICS is far from straightforward. The theme's scalar implications shift dynamically and unpredictably as the theme moves on, and it only settles on a D tonic toward the end. The modes indicated below the staff in Figure 9.11 should be interpreted as approximate and fluid, not rigid descriptions. What begins as a G phrygian-sounding melody progressively orients itself around C in the lead-up to measure 3. This tonal field is short-lived, however, as C blends into D phrygian (or perhaps A locrian) between measures 3 and 4. The middle section is even less well-defined, with an increased rate of harmonic change that obscures, in a patently Williamsesque manner, the scale/chord/key trichotomy. It's hard to know where we are musically, and that's the point.

Intensificatory Sequencing

Rather than fretting about momentary tonal classifications, it is better to view the Rebel Logistics module as housing one of several expertly constructed intensificatory sequences that pervade the Battle of Hoth and grant the set piece much of its nail-biting urgency.[28] No two are the same, though there are some commonalities: a gradually rising melodic line, chromatic and nonfunctional harmonic support, and a discharge with cadential (or quasi-cadential) character onto an emphatically underlined new key. Quite a few have the outline of a chromatic wedge, in which outer voices diverge by step away from their starting point; this, like the hexatonic scale and diminished third, is another Episode V specialty.[29] Figure 9.12 enumerates the most salient of these intensifying passages.

Cue, Time	Action	Musical Material
3m1, 22:13–22:45	Goodbyes, Rebel General discovers arrival of Empire	Bass descent by semitone from C♯ to G. (See **Fig. 9.14**)
3m2, 24:04–24:26	Leia instruct troops	Middle section of Rebel Logistics (See **Fig. 9.11**)
3m3, 27:44–27:53	Build-up to Luke's discovery of Dak's death	Rising triads, tetrachords over dissonant G-C-D-G bass.
3m3, 28:20–28:35	Build-up to speeder attack on walkers	Rising hexachordal clusters, atonal melody. Oboe battery.
3m4/4m1 30:41–31:06	Luke under fire, crashes	Rising brass line over D, followed by wedge figure.
3m4/4m1, 32:52–33:01	AT-AT explodes, collapses	Rising triads over dissonant pedals, cadencing in G.
4m2, 34:51–35:05	Han struggles to fix Falcon	Stepwise ascent, leading to Han and Leia. (See **Fig. 9.13**)
4m2 35:20–35:26	Snowtroopers under fire, Falcon roars to life	Compressed resumption of stepwise ascent.

Figure 9.12 Intensificatory sequences in the Battle of Hoth

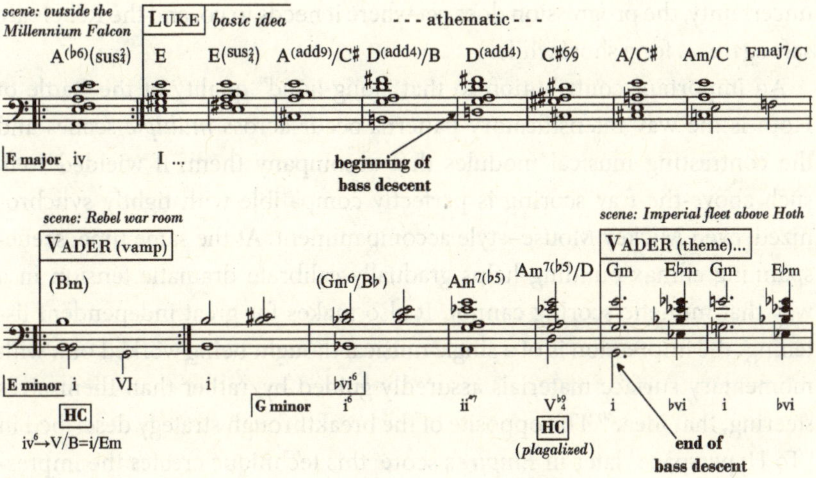

Figure 9.13 Single-scene intensificatory sequence in "Rebels Escape Again" (ESB, 4m2, 34:51)

Williams deploys these intensificatory sequences both within scenes and across them, as a means of drawing multiple battlefronts together. A neat example of the former occurs in "The Rebels Escape Again," shown in harmonic reduction in Figure 9.13. The heroes have made it onto the Millennium Falcon, but the temperamental ship refuses to start. With Imperial forces closing in, Han Solo needs a good idea. "Would it help if I got out and pushed," snipes Leia. "It might," Han snaps back. Williams paints the harried atmosphere with a modulatory progression that chugs away in the strings for twelve measures. The trajectory is from lightly prolonged minor keys to more extensive and functionally reinforced major ones: first B♭, then C, B♮, and A♭, and finally B again—the key that houses the Han and Leia leitmotif when Han instructs Threepio to shut up. Though not powered by a traditionally structured melody, the passage is steered by a simple melodic process, inching upward from the starting pitch of B♭$_3$ and eventually making it up to B♮$_4$. Each individual step feels uncertain and risky, largely due to the pervasive tonal ambivalence of the sequential chain. The second chord within each measure always falls on the third beat, but it might lead either up or down. That chord also always back-relates as an auxiliary harmony to the one that preceded it, but it might do so either as a diatonically simple function or some strange hybrid sonority. And yet, despite the instant-to-instant uncertainty, the progression does get where it needs to go, and the Rebels are safe again . . . for a short while.

An important contribution to that "long-lined" quality of the Battle of Hoth is the way intensificatory patterns occur across *multiple* scenes and the contrasting musical modules that accompany them. If wielded well, such above-the-fray scoring is perfectly compatible with tightly synchronized, even Mickey Mouse–style accompaniment. At the same time, scene-spanning climax-building helps gradually calibrate dramatic tension in a way that mimetic scoring cannot. It also makes for great independent listening: the impression is of a single musical thought being worked out, with momentary surface materials assuredly guided by, rather than themselves steering, that idea.[30] The opposite of the breakthrough strategy described in "To Hyperspace" later in *Empire*'s score, this technique creates the impression of musical inevitability.

For a fine example of intensificatory sequencing used in service of the long line, one need look no further than the Battle of Hoth's first twenty measures, given in reduction in Figure 9.14. "Drawing the Battle Lines" begins with a retroactively functional iv♭6→I motion into E major, setting up a warm zone for Luke's theme as he bids farewell to Han and Chewie. However, the passage loosens E major's grip quickly, with a set of extended diatonic sonorities perched over D, C♯, and C♮ bass notes, and the Luke-based module concludes as it began, with an uncommitted chord. That slip downward from C♯ to C♮ provides a bridge into the next scene, in which a Vader-suggestive

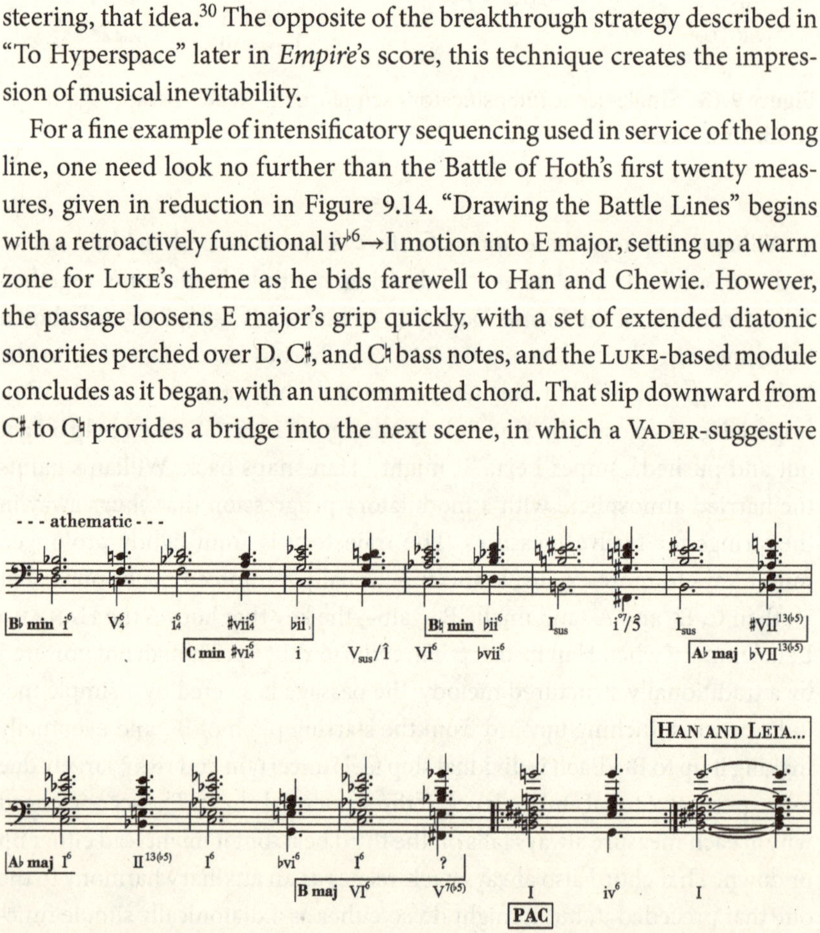

Figure 9.14 Scene-spanning intensificatory sequence in "Drawing the Battle Lines" (ESB, 3m1, 22:13)

oscillation between tonic B minor and its submediant G accompanies talk of incoming Star Destroyers. With General Rieekan's line "prepare for ground assault," the holding pattern between B and G concludes, and a new wedge draws the bass B_2 down to $B\flat_2$ and A_2, and the top voice up from B_3 to $C\sharp_4$, D_4, and E_4. With a concomitant swell in volume, the final step in the harmonic vice is an Am7(♭5)/D sonority. This chord is enlisted to serve as a dissonant but functional dominant, exploding onto G minor as the scene transitions to the Imperial Fleet above Hoth, a ringing statement of VADER's march in tow. The whole twenty-measure passage thus bridges, invisibly but inexorably, the space between an optimistic E major and malign G minor, and does so through a heart-sinking semitonal descent spanning three distinct scenes. It is a cunning opening salvo from Williams, the first of many.

The Resistance Movement

Rather than poring over each of the five segments of the Battle of Hoth in equal detail, it will pay to inspect one, "Luke's First Crash," as though it were an individual movement within a larger symphonic work. This 150-measure cue exemplifies the marvelous balance Williams strikes in *Empire*: precision-targeted accompaniment of complex action that nonetheless gratifies on its own, as pure music. What precedes it, "The Snow Battle," is an athematic hellstorm, as bleak a rendering of violence as the composer would ever pen for the series. By contrast, "Luke's First Crash" is fun and accessible, with an emphasis on the heroic efforts of the rebel resistance. The cue includes the three major protagonist leitmotifs carried over from Episode IV—LUKE, FORCE, and REBEL FANFARE—as well as the sole iteration of the DROIDS theme contained within the larger set piece. The resumption of thematic articulation lends "Luke's First Crash" more points of emotional identification than the impersonal hostilities of "The Snow Battle." But the tone is hardly uniformly genial, as anxious or villainous music is still "in control" over most of the cue's course, not least with the triumphal statement of VADER's march that ends it. "Luke's First Crash" also features two set piece themes, ECHO BASE SCRAMBLE and UNDER-SIEGE AGITATO, which as shown in the previous section both exhibit close ties with motifs established in the prior three cues. And though hardly tuneful, the remaining underscore is as full of character as anything else during the battle. A particularly ingenious module is shown in Figure 9.15, music that

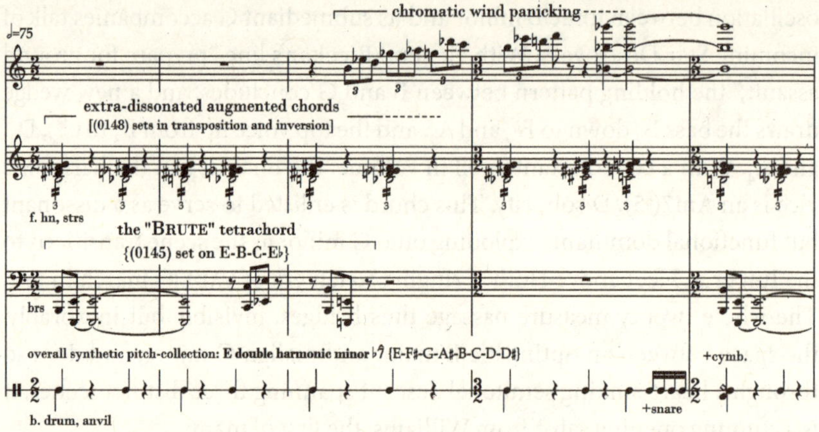

Figure 9.15 Crushing AT-AT music from "Luke's First Crash" (ESB, 3m4/4m1, 31:11)

nearly crushes Luke underfoot. Between the dissonantly pounding (0148) horn chords, the wide-striding and syncopated ostinato on a BRUTE tetrachord [E-B-C-E♭], and the anvilicious percussion writing, battle-symphonic listeners will find plenty to be (over)stimulated by.

The overall form of "Luke's First Crash" is shown in Figure 9.16. The sequence intercuts two arenas. The first is Echo Base, where one group of protagonists (Han, Leia, Chewie, the droids) face worsening peril. The second is the battlefield outside, where the other heroes (Luke and his squadron) suffer a crashing setback—and explosive victory—in their defensive charge against the Imperial Walkers. A four-part division of the cue results, with a pair of relatively low-intensity A-sections for the distress inside the base, and a pair of loud and strident B-sections for the tumult outside. Together, the A1 and B1 paragraphs constitute a large-scale unit. Both showcase the ECHO BASE SCRAMBLE theme, and the end of the latter [31:28, the rough midpoint of the cue] acts as a convenient moment of formal reorientation. At this musical hinge, the calamity incurred during B1 is left dangling, while the resumption of less cacophonous music with the A2-section lends an impression of restarting—and the prospect of a better outcome than the cue's first half. Success is indeed attained, midway through B2, with a blaze of major-mode glory to match Luke's ingenious destruction of one AT-AT. Narratively and musically, it is a short-lived victory, and the cue concludes with a hefty module dedicated to "The Imperial March" in its blackest regalia.

29:28	29:52	30:00	30:07	30:20	30:24
A1. Echo Base Interior		**B2.** Hoth Battlefield Exterior			
ECHO BASE SCRAMBLE	**DROIDS**	largely athematic AT-AT music			**VADER**
C♯m→(Bm)→(F♯m) …	D^{aug}	Em-ish	Cm→(Dm)	(B♭m)	Cm
Preliminary, urgent. Revolves around militaristic, discursive ECHO BASE SCRAMBLE. DROIDS serves as transition to...		High intensity, loud. Angular, shrill figures vaulting across 8ves, above tramp of percussive bass. VADER serves as transition to...			

30:29	30:41	31:05	31:11	31:28	31:36	31:46	32:03
B2 cont. Hoth Battlefield Exterior				**A2.** Echo Base Interior			
SCRAMBLE	intensificatory sequence and crisis	**LUKE**	AT-AT music	AGITATO	**LUKE** + AGITATO	AGITATO	**LUKE**
Cm→Dm/C	C→…G♭(♯9♯11)/D♭	Gm	(Em)	Gm/D	Gm→Gm/F5	F♯m→Gm	B♭
Intensificatory. SCRAMBLE reprise leads to chromatic sequences, culminating in **crisis chord**.		Inhuman, brutal; harsh chromaticism syncopated bass.		Anxious and embattled, like an interlude. UNDER-SIEGE AGITATO treated as ostinato, overlays LUKE, serves as transition to…			

32:12	32:29	32:51	32:55		33:06	33:36
B2. Hoth Battlefield Exterior						
FORCE + weepy countermelody	**REBEL FANFARE** and motives derived therefrom	pitch plateau	intensificatory sequence, fanfare		**VADER**	
Am→Gm	E♭⇝D⇝A…⇝C/G	high D_6	…⇝G	**HC**: G becomes **HC**: C	Cm	**CC** $V^{\flat 9(\flat 5)}/\hat{1}$→i
High intensity, melodramatic. Moves from tragic FORCE to ecstatic breakthrough built from pantriadic harmony. Suspenseful pitch plateau leads to blazing G-major glory, but also cadential backdoor into VADER.					Cruel reversal; triumph undone by gleefully nasty VADER theme in complete statement.	

Figure 9.16 Form of "Luke's First Crash"

A little over a minute and a half of "Luke's First Crash" is taken up by the aforementioned leitmotifs. However, the way those themes are deployed changes markedly—and in a form-defining way—over the course of the cue. The first few leitmotivic citations are brief, non-developmental, and literal in their relation to their signifieds. But in the A2 and B2 sections, Williams's themes start assuming more musical autonomy and expressive breathing room, and by the end, he delivers one of the most purely *musical* utterances in the whole film, a complete rendition of the VADER leitmotif—the high point of its melodic arc in the *Empire* score. The leitmotivic trajectory in "Luke's First Crash" revolves around the same use/mention axis described in Chapter 3 and typified in "The Falcon Still Flies" from *The*

Force Awakens. But where thematic integration in Episode VII's action cue was flighty and non-chronological, here the use/mention distinction plays out in a linear and concerted fashion. This evolutionary process is one of several sources of the unusually *purposeful* feeling in this cue, an impression that it sounds more like absolute music, less like a sonic accessory, as it goes.

The first two citations in "Luke's First Crash," of the DROIDS and VADER leitmotifs respectively, are succinct and hew to the mention paradigm. They attach literally to their semantic targets: the sight of R2 and C-3PO fretting in the former, and the onslaught of the Empire war machine with the latter. Literality does not mean an absence of larger formal or expressive implications, however. The DROIDS motif has an important bookending function, for example, closing the A1 section and telegraphing the arrival of B1. Williams maximizes the idea's innate harmonic ambiguity, situating it in a disoriented augmented-scale space that shuts down the rambling but locally diatonic SCRAMBLE motif. That unmoored augmented sonority also prepares the way for the next module, behaving as a kind of exquisitely dissonant triple-leading tone chord for the upper pitches of the $\mathrm{Em}^{\mathrm{ma7}}$-based clangor starting at 30:30. A dozen bars later, the VADER quotation similarly draws its form-functional meaning from the SCRAMBLE melody. In this case, the snippet of the Dark Lord's theme supplies stability after a spate of athematic and atonal chaos, and in so doing elegantly steers the music back *into* the SCRAMBLE theme, now brassy and brazen.

Three non-consecutive statements of the LUKE theme are next to appear in this cue, each a little longer and less semantically dictated by on-screen events than the last. After his speeder crashes, Skywalker's leitmotif is lent a quick, calling card–style mention in the horns. Notable here is the phrygian inflection; this darkening of mode was previewed in *A New Hope* but is pervasive in *Empire*. In this weakened state, the theme does not manage to progress far before being crushed underfoot by the AT-AT's thundering bass tread. The next crack at LUKE's theme [31:36] is not much more auspicious. Similarly cast in G-phrygian, the leitmotif now provides a canonic countermelody to the UNDER SIEGE AGITATO and does so while following the exploits of Han and Leia. This is among the first of many semantically generalized usages of this theme, less a direct motto for Luke Skywalker, more a floating signifier. A few measures later, a longer statement of the melody reclaims a measure of resolve—it appears now in B♭ major, its tonal home base—just as Leia accepts that fleeing is her only option.

Figure 9.17 FORCE and weeping countermelody in "Luke's First Crash" (ESB, 3m4/4m1, 32:12)

The sight of heavy rebel casualties prompts a similarly non-literal statement of the FORCE theme (Figure 9.17) in A minor, a whole step lower than the previous module. Though capable of conveying misfortune by dint of its minor tonality, Williams wrings extraordinary pathos from the theme here. He offers it to trumpets and trombones in octaves, pitting that line against a syncopated series of sighs in the strings. (Even those sighs have motivic bona fides, deriving locally from the similar wind slips in the previous measures and more remotely from the UNDER SIEGE AGITATO.) Self-harmonized in weepy parallel thirds, rising in register and desperation, the string countermelody has a distinct vocal quality, like an expression of ever-increasing concern: "oh no, *oh no*, ***oh no***!" The FORCE is further treated to an unusual harmonic darkening, exchanging the accustomed major subdominant with a phrygian Gm/B♭ [♭vii^6] at its midpoint.[31] The leitmotif then fully transposes itself to G-minor for its consequent phrase, and leads down by step to E♭ major—not an unexpected chord were the theme to progress normally. But the E♭ that sounds at 32:28 does not "belong" to the FORCE any longer; it announces the beginning of a new module, one that sweeps aside the dismal tone and replaces it with a feeling of unalloyed triumph.

More than most leitmotifs, the brief and infinitely iterable REBEL FANFARE is prone to "composing out." This developmental tendency is borne out in the module devoted to the theme in "Luke's First Crash," beginning immediately with that surprise veer into E♭ major. It is during this paragraph that Skywalker takes down the Imperial goliath with a cleverly placed explosive. With the tragic FORCE theme brushed aside, the LSO brass spend the next fourteen measures jubilating, with not a trace of darkness to curb their hyper-major enthusiasm. This is the first positive music since the HOPEFUL REBELS incidental theme two cues ago, and Williams pulls no punches. The passage is not merely lively; it is hyperactive, gleefully coruscating across keys as fast as the ♩=150 metronome allows. Each individual move is based on the harmonic parameters of the Rebel Fanfare: triadic planing and minor-third root progressions. But registering individual, discrete chord progressions is beside the point here: more important is the gestalt, an outburst of pantriadic euphoria.

Just as the trumpets seem to have exhausted their fanfaric fusillade, the passage regathers energy during a D_6 pitch plateau, a moment of suspense as the AT-AT begins to teeter. And with the walker's eventual detonation, the brass launches another volley of major-mode merriment, centering now over G major, cadentially secured and everything! But in Williams's harmonic syntax, what behaves as a firm authentic cadence in one key can be just as easily reinterpreted as an open-ended *half* cadence in another. And so that bright and enriched G-chord does not really mark a happy ending; it clears the runway for a big, perverse resolution into *C minor*. It is there that the cue's true champion, "The Imperial March," enjoys its uninterrupted thirteen-measure victory lap. Success in "Luke's First Crash" is easy come, easy go, leitmotivically speaking. And just as the Rebel Fanfare constituted musical "use" in one sense—extensive thematic transformation—this brandishing of Vader's theme amounts to another mode of integration: the kind that results from just letting a theme run its course, as pure, loud, unapologetic *music*.

John Williams's *Eroica*

We have seen the overall craft that went into Williams's score to *The Empire Strikes Back* and the ways he turned the Battle of Hoth specifically into a cinematic and orchestral showstopper. A closer look at a segment of that tapestry, "Luke's First Crash," revealed a cue that proved a compelling "piece" in its own right, exhilarating to hear once and rewarding to revisit. Perhaps at this point, the case for cine-symphonic appreciation of *Empire*'s score has been made. To press the comparison with concert music risks saddling Williams's compositions with listening values and expectations that they simply cannot support.

When musical winners and losers trade places as spontaneously as they do in "Luke's First Crash," it may seem odd to insist on the "symphonic" descriptor. Absolute music is not supposed to take unforeseeable detours in form and affect. Nor should it possess such unbalanced thematic proportions. The Droids and Force leitmotifs are granted but a single iteration, while the cue-defining SCRAMBLE theme is present only for the first A- and B-sections and uncorroborated during the cue's climax or denouement. And this is to say nothing of tonal organization, whether at the level of the individual cue or the set piece as a whole. Only the most motivated listener could discern an inexorable plan from the tonal meanderings of this fifteen-minute span. However, these are shortcomings only from the perspective of pure symphonic listening; they are not problems at all for *battle* symphonic listening. If that genre teaches us anything, it is that audiences are willing to sacrifice a little in the way of formal and thematic coherency if it means gaining a lot in terms of thrills.

Another lesson may be taken from the symphonic repertoire more broadly: great works of instrumental music are cumulative, their individual parts serving as stages within a more globally conceived experience. Remember Peter Franklin's characterization of the post-Wagnerian symphony: "a cumulatively cogent structure of action, anticipation, and reminiscence." The dramatic reversals and abandoned themes in "Luke's First Crash" turn out not so problematic when heard as waypoints within a longer span of musical time. In well-crafted film music, just as in concert music, the "long line" can carry across discretely written cues. Taken on its own, "Luke's First Crash" satisfies as an exciting if imbalanced tone poem. But when presented in sequence within the rest of the set piece, suddenly its formal idiosyncrasies sound less like liabilities, its role within a larger musical argument more persuasive. One would not extract a single movement from a late-Romantic symphony and claim that the ideal experience was to hear it in isolation. The same can be said for any of the individual components of this extraordinary sweep of cine-symphonic storytelling from Episode V.[32]

What happens then, when we treat the five cues that make *The Empire Strikes Back*'s musical centerpiece as a symphonic unity? Most works with the generic label "symphony" are composed out of bounded but cyclically interdependent sections—movements. Figure 9.18 offers a listening guide to *The Battle Symphony of Hoth*, treating it as an amalgamated suite in four movements of comparable length, placed in a specific order. The first and second film cues, "Drawing the Battle Lines" and "Leia's Instructions," are a bonded pair, united in thematic substance and contiguous in film. Their fusion into a "Movement I" requires no special justification, and indeed that is exactly how 3m1 and 3m2 are treated in the 1993 Star Wars Trilogy OST Anthology boxed set produced by Nicholas Redman—as a single four-minute track. Movement II is given to "The Snow Battle," while "Luke's

‘Movement’	I. “Drawing the Battle Lines” / “Leia’s Instructions”	II. “The Snow Battle”	III. “Luke’s First Crash”	IV. “The Rebels Escape Again”
Leitmotifs	**Luke, Vader, Rebel Fanfare**	–	**Droids, Vader, Luke, Force, Rebel Fanfare**	**Leia, Vader, Han and Leia**
Set Piece Themes	Rebel Logistics, Hopeful Rebels	AT-AT Assault, Heroes Under Fire	Echo Base Scramble, Under-Siege Agitato	Sawing Strings Ostinato
BPM Range	80–100 / 120–170	160–180	140–155	145–155
Dynamic Level	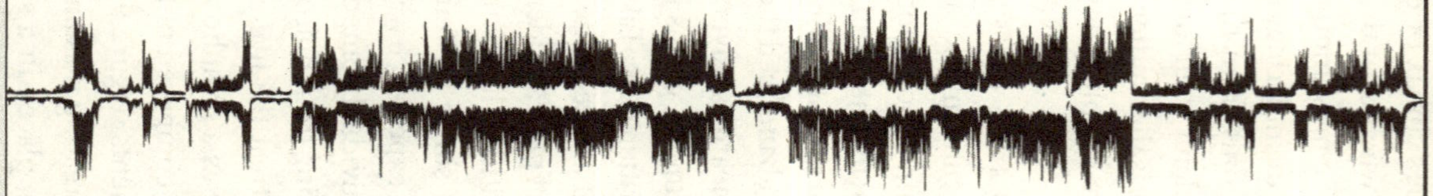			
Symphonic Aspects	• Sectional, preludial, discursive • Stalwart, expectant, cautiously optimistic in tone • Mostly tonal and functional • Establishes basic musical parameters for the whole—topics, themes, tempi • Supplies motives for rest of sequence, as well as a one-cue-wonder at its end to provide false hope	• Continuous, unrelenting, developmental • Horrific, hopeless in tone • Entirely atonal, chromatic, esp. octatonic materials • Estranged from rest of score leitmotivically, but *not* motivically • Fastest, most virtuosic • Showcases percussion, low brass in brutish, patterns and mechanical rhythms	• Sectional, developmental • Melodramatic, gleeful in tone • Mix of atonality, functional tonality, triadic chromaticism • Many leitmotifs, but also suffused with incidental motifs and set piece themes • Full of musical crises, breakthroughs, and reversals • Prominent intensificatory passages; reaches highest climaxes of the whole	• Continuous in texture; sectional in themes • Hurry-like tone, constant triplet ostinati • Mostly tonal; atonal in bridge passages • Sense of two themes clashing and alternating; more lyrical theme wins out at end. Very strong feeling of tonal closure and thematic payoff

Figure 9.18 A Cine-Symphonic Listening Guide for “The Battle Symphony of Hoth”

First Crash" and "The Rebels Escape Again" stand as Movements III and IV, respectively. For each of the movements, Figure 9.18 indicates thematic content, tempo range, and dynamic level. The bottom row is devoted to miscellaneous symphonic attributes, a broad umbrella that encompasses continuity versus sectional organization, general affect and intensity level, tonal idiom, and density of thematic material.

More than formal diagrams presented earlier, Figure 9.18 represents a listening perspective as much as an objective encapsulation of the music itself. Even if Williams had presented this material with an explicit label of *The Battle Symphony of Hoth*, it would be regarded as a curious entry in the genre, and for a simple reason: the component movements simply lack the vivid contrasts of volume and tempo characteristic of the form since its inception in the eighteenth century. Certainly, there is no lyrical adagio movement here. But other contrasts between the four movements are razor sharp, including tonal language, motivic content, affect, and dramatic incident. And above all, there is a proper symphonic *arc* here. That arc exists not just in the program handed down from the *Schlacht-Sinfonien* of old—sections for preparation, confrontation, lamentation, and celebration—but in the deeper, more dialectical working-out of themes, both musical and poetic.

For a *Star Wars* set piece, what happens on the snowfields of Hoth is atypically ambivalent in tone. The protagonists experience a mix of defeat (Echo Base is destroyed, the Rebels completely routed) and success (the protagonists narrowly escape, and Luke manages a minor if symbolically weighty victory against the Imperials). This commingling of distress and triumph maps exceptionally well onto a prototypically symphonic plot: *per aspera ad astra*, "through struggle to the stars." Beethoven's most iconic instrumental compositions often chart this expressive arc. The paradigm case is the vast first movement of his Third "Eroica" Symphony, particularly its heaven-storming development section. A similar musical narrative is enacted across the whole of his Fifth and Ninth symphonies. These are pieces where musical obstacles are not easily brushed aside, but grappled with mightily, continuously, and with no guarantee of success. To compare these most vaunted monuments of Western culture to an action sequence from a model of twentieth-century popcorn entertainment may seem perverse. On first inspection, the Battle (Symphony) of Hoth does not project the seriousness of purpose, nor does it exhibit the formal rigor of Beethoven's monuments. Yet Williams's own "Eroica" nevertheless draws a great deal from the striving rhetoric established in those epochal works.[33] As more time passes between Episode V's premiere and today's listeners, the composition's own seriousness and rigor become more evident. And conversely, its crowd-pleasing and programmatically contingent elements become less cause for embarrassment.[34]

If we listen to this set piece with an ear for the "through struggle to the stars" archetype, the first order of business is to identify what, musically, is doing the struggling. Helpfully, the basic terms of musical conflict are laid out in the Battle Symphony's Movement I ("Drawing the Battle Lines/ Leia's Instructions"), with central thematic players placed in stark opposition within the first two dozen measures. The piece's chief motivic processes are also initiated—namely, the spinning-out of new incidental themes via melodic concatenation, as epitomized in the thematic nexus that is the Rebel Logistics theme. An early success arrives via the Hopeful Rebels anthem, with an assist from the Rebel Fanfare. But, as with many symphonic openers, there are issues left unaddressed that a single movement cannot solve.

The second movement, "The Snow Battle," functions as the cycle's scherzo. The cue is paced at a higher clip than its surroundings, and its prime musical attractions are rhythmic and timbral rather than melodic. And while awash with motivic connections and concatenations, the set piece is the only member of the suite that lacks citations of the *Star Wars* leitmotivic lexicon; this grants it a self-sufficiency that is also typical of symphonic scherzi. "The Snow Battle" is also the darkest phase of the cycle, described aptly as a "brutal, bellicose piece" in the liner notes to the original *Empire* album.[35] The closest kindred in the symphonic repertoire are the savage (and patently cinematic) scherzi from Shostakovich's 10th through 12th symphonies. There is no reprieve in "The Snow Battle": no tuneful depictions of heroic pluck, no ennobling chorales or hymns to the fallen—just unremitting sonic violence.

Relief does arrive, partially, in Movement III, but not before much storm and stress. As we have seen, "Luke's First Crash" witnesses many turns of musical fortune, both good and ill alike. Not unrelatedly, the cue also contains the most active leitmotivic development within any movement. Less musically abstract or abrasive than "The Snow Battle," and less formally single-minded than its successor "The Rebels Escape Again," "Luke's First Crash" makes for an excellent emotional and dramatic climax to *The Battle Symphony of Hoth*. Here is where all the biggest breakthroughs and payoffs take place, including the bombastic apotheosis of the REBEL FANFARE and the coda, that steamroller of a rendition of "The Imperial March." As a movement in a multi-part whole, "Luke's First Crash" has it all: trials, tribulations, and triumphs—the latter for both sides!

The Finale of this *Battle Symphony of Hoth* is given to "The Rebels Escape Again," and by most criteria it makes for a fine finish to a sci-fi *Schlacht Sinfonie*. Williams introduces little new by way of thematic material or orchestrational effects, but if the pace of invention slackens a bit, dramatic tension remains as high as ever. A constant stream of string triplets produces a perpetuum mobile effect specific to Movement IV, while a focus on long statements of recognizable melodies lends "The Rebels Escape Again" an ersatz recapitulatory function. Also distinctive is the feeling of pitched battle between opposed thematic forces. On one side, there is the implacable "Imperial March," and on the other, a leitmotif that to this point was absent from the set piece: HAN AND LEIA. No, the contest is not truly *dialectical* in the sense that theorists of symphonism require: the themes do abut one another, but they do not interact, and certainly do not reconcile their differences! Nevertheless, the overriding impression during "Rebels Escape Again" is one of dynamic opposition and hard-won triumph—rhetorically quite unlike the summary victory and collapse heard in Movement III.

VADER has the upper hand at first in "Rebels Escape Again," presiding over the movement's stormy first minute with an iron fist. But once *Empire*'s love theme pushes through, the motivic balance of power shifts. On the heels of the chromatic sequence discussed earlier (Fig. 9.13), HAN AND LEIA's material makes a doughty attempt to turn the musical tide, but VADER's theme barges in once more. This makes for a terrifying leitmotivic jump-scare, but it also represents the Dark Lord's last musical intrusion. Another intensificatory passage follows, briefer and less patient than before, as if sensing victory is within grasp. This leads to a considerably longer-breathed iteration of *Empire*'s love theme, one that rebels against its phrasal confines and builds to a mammoth cadential discharge from $G\flat^7/C$ onto F major. On film, this harmonic resolution corresponds to a shot of the Millennium Falcon bursting off Hoth; in *The Battle Symphony of Hoth*, it fits what a music theorist might dub "Essential Structural Closure." The HAN AND LEIA leitmotif continues to spin with unfettered exuberance. The theme shuttles from F to D major and, after another massively telegraphed cadence, clinches that key—with giddy lydian inflections, naturally—for the sight of Luke zooming away from the forsaken icy planet. On a narrative level, this victory is qualified: the Rebels are routed and Vader is in hot pursuit of half of the named protagonists. Yet there is another filmic contingent to root for, one enlisted to supply adrenaline, emotion, and gravitas. For the forces of music—Williams, the LSO, we the listening audience—*The Battle Symphony of Hoth* has been a pure triumph.

***

Musically speaking, Act 1 of *The Empire Strikes Back* does something any standalone work of music must: it ends well. Williams closes his galactic "Eroica" with a great crescendo, surging toward a cathartic release in the form of Han and Leia's theme, which takes well-earned lyric flight at the movement's end. "The Rebels Escape Again" provides a fine finale for the full cycle too, counterbalancing the epic urgency of earlier material and paying off thematic and emotional promises made hundreds of measures before. As a work in the thrilling tradition of Beethoven's *Wellingtons Sieg*, Williams's *Battle Symphony of Hoth* has it all: lots of big hero moments, catchy and long-breathed themes, amazing orchestral effects, and a large-scale arc that satisfies on dramatic terms. Moreover, as a participant in the stream of serious and sophisticatedly crafted music in that other plane of Beethovenian rhetoric, this work is equally impressive. The set piece is host to cunning motivic development, meticulously laid long lines, and more measure-to-measure ingenuity than any other span in the Skywalker saga.

There are plentiful anti-symphonic aspects here too, to be sure. Listening to the Battle of Hoth with attentive ears does not mean ignoring all the thematic non-sequiturs, the static and coloristic episodes, the cues with minimal contrast of volume or tempo. These are not liabilities to cine-symphonic listening, but assets, ways of keeping the proceedings exciting and unpredictable. Cinematic musical quirks are gifts to the imaginative listener and the participative listener—those who, like Peter Franklin's post-Wagnerian concertgoers, use music to light up their personal prosceniums of the mind. The remarkable symphonic integration of the Battle of Hoth, a trait that it shares with *The Empire Strikes Back* as a whole, makes it a tour de force of long-lined scoring. The anti-symphonic contingency and caprice, intrinsic to the medium, make it something even rarer—music that sounds new each time it is heard, whether for the second time or the hundredth. Perhaps it is unreasonable to expect a symphony orchestra to perform the entirety of Episode V's score on its own, "unstaged" as it were. But one could certainly do worse than programming the fifteen-minute *Battle Symphony of Hoth* as a standalone piece. With or without images, this is dazzling, sophisticated, symphonically conceived music, a feast for attentive and returning listeners. And it happens to be a nonstop orchestral thrill ride, the Skywalker Saga's best.

Afterword: Endless Endings

Running like a leitmotif through commentary on the symphony is the notion of "the finale problem." This refers to the distinct challenge of writing a last movement that adequately matches the rhetorical and formal weight of what came before, particularly the kinds of riveting and eventful first movements characteristic of composers from Beethoven onward.[1] It's a problem that affects the Skywalker Saga, too; the last entries of the trilogies are considered their least satisfying installments, Episode III being a partial exception. While the issues taken with these closing entries primarily revolve around matters of narratival coherence and originality, the soundtrack too faces its own suite of finale problems. For one, there is the need to offer music in a cycle-concluding entry commensurate with the gravitas of preceding episodes. *Revenge of the Sith* fulfills this imperative; the degree to which *Return of the Jedi* and *Rise of Skywalker* do is debatable. Related but not equivalent is a peculiarly *leitmotivic* finale problem—that is, the expectation to deliver on the thematic promises of prior scores. By that measure, Episode IX is actually an unequivocal success, VI generally successful (save for devotees of the abandoned Droids motif), and III decidedly mixed, given the failure to make good on the abundantly telegraphed promises of Duel of the Fates and Anakin's theme.

Another finale problem beset the *Star Wars* musical universe, though it is one with less of an analogue in the symphonic genre: the fact that the story never seems to stop ending. The epigraph at the top of this page comes from *The Rise of Skywalker*, one minute before the credits roll [2:11:30]. It represents the final measure of the final newly composed cue of the final score in the saga, what Williams entitled "Return to Tatooine." The figure is not especially sophisticated in itself, just a broken minor triad in a rocking 6/8 meter, played quietly by celesta and harp. Yet it is dense with memory, being a direct echo of another motif, one examined on the first page of this book: the lead-in to *A New Hope*'s "Binary Sunset." In both, a patiently unfolded triad prepares for a statement of the FORCE theme in G minor, presented with that special combination of vulnerability and gravitas that only a solo French horn can impart. In both, the simplicity and sparseness of musical material belies an immense amount of meaning. The vamp in *A New Hope* holds in it the undisclosed promise of a myth being constructed for the first time before our very ears—and with it, an awesomely powerful *musical* moment in the form of the iconic leitmotif it clears space for. In *The Rise of Skywalker*, the chord signals potential of another sort: potential for listeners to make an almost unlimited number of backward musical associations. That unbending chord is repeated far more times in "Return to Tatooine" than its rhyme in "Binary Sunset," ringing out for twenty-five of cue's twenty-six measures (the piece runs at just 1:47). The triad's repetition endows "Return to Tatooine" with a feeling of fathomless pastness, a sense that this particular configuration of an E♭-minor triad is somehow reverberating with everything that came before it. At the same time, it refuses to be pinned to any one leitmotivic origin or singular emotional prompt. It is an attempt to end a story that has ended many times already, a narrative process that, by definition, cannot stop.

No theme is ever really gone.

Depending on how you calculate it, John Williams has scored the conclusion of *Star Wars* between three and a dozen times. Back before anyone knew the 1977 movie would be anything more than a standalone popcorn affair, he supplied what we now call Episode IV with two symphonic endings. The first is the "Throne Room" sequence, an orchestral payoff wherein music, no longer subordinated to dialogue or dramatic incident, can complete multiple themes in their grammatical entirety. The second is the extra-diegetic credits sequence that follows. This suite, later enfolded into the "Star Wars—Main Theme" concert piece, treats listeners to a curtain call of the score's big themes (and big intertextual influences), wrapping them all up with an archetypal "Hollywood" cadence.[2] Together, the "Throne Room" and "End Credits" cues create the musical model for all subsequent finales, not just in terms of symphonic recapitulation and coda-crafting, but a clear set of narrational and affective expectations that are squarely in line with the mythopoetic aims detailed in previous chapters: cyclicality, rituality, and distance. All that is missing from the epic inventory is self-reflexivity. But as soon as more entries in the saga begin piling up, and the final musical word kept being overwritten, internal references would start reverberating loudly.

Skipping over *The Empire Strikes Back*, which all involved understood to be a middle chapter, *Return of the Jedi* has five candidates for the series' "ultimate" measure. The first three could be heard in 1983. As in Episode IV, there is an in-film ending: the quasi-diegetic song "Yub Nub" that accompanies the final shots on Endor. Unlike *A New Hope*, a more traditional underscore cue, "Light of the Force," marks the conclusion of the trilogy's underlying leitmotivic process, with another solemn intonation of the FORCE in G minor for Vader's funeral pyre; this particular iteration of that theme takes an unexpectedly beatific turn toward A dorian after its normally final cadence. Also analogous to *A New Hope* are the "End Credits," identical with Episode IV's but for a slight alteration to the last musical paragraph, with a formerly generic triumphal chord progression now overlain with the THRONE ROOM theme, the first of an unending chain of reflexive glances backward that will increasingly define the saga. A fourth ending to *Jedi* is strictly extra-textual: "The Forest Battle," that impertinent concert piece, itself obsessed with the idea of concluding over and over (and over) again. And then, in 1997, when Williams was invited to supply a new cue for *Jedi*'s Special Edition, audiences received a fifth conclusion: the "Victory Celebration," which, depending on one's point of view, is either a finale with gravitas commensurate to the occasion, or a needless substitute for the endearingly campy original.

The Prequels yielded another trio of musical endings. First, there is the in-film epilogue to *Revenge of the Sith*, aptly entitled "A New Hope." A wordless sequence just like the "Throne Room," the cue presents LEIA and LUKE's themes before shifting to an ineluctable standard: the FORCE theme, set in—where else?—G minor, intoned by—what else?—a solo French horn. As the Lars family stares off at the binary sunset, Williams's music gazes in two directions, just as it did in Episode IV, yearning for the past but looking toward the future—which, as far as *Star Wars* viewers are concerned, already happened 28 years prior. Episode III keeps the cycle spinning, concluding with the same credits music as *Jedi*'s. The film's single, summative concert arrangement, "Battle of the Heroes," is unlike "The Forest Battle" in nearly every other way. Yet the piece does have a sly false ending before its final spasm in D minor, as though the music is teasing us. "We're done now. Oh, not quite. Really, this time. Ah, we're still not there. Here it comes . . ."

Where the Prequels posed an opportunity to end in a way that led seamlessly into the (old) beginning of the story, Episodes VII–IX presented Williams with a different finale problem: how to write music for a story after it had already been satisfyingly and definitively finished. Of course, opinions vary on the success of the Sequels, whether in sum they constitute a coherent or necessary addition to the franchise. But as an extended meditation on that quality of *afterness*, they are remarkable and compelling musical texts. Unlike with previous trilogies, Williams was unsure if he would return for successive entries, meaning that each of the Sequels was at one time conceivably his musical last word. In light of this uncertainty, it is understandable that the symphonic endings become more uniform. Where it was a potent leitmotivic choice in Episode III, the FORCE now becomes obligatory music heard right before the credits roll. What was at first a meaning-saturated rhyme stiffens into a ritual, a formal device as invariant as Luke's theme is during the Main Titles. As if to compensate for the perfunctory nature of this FORCE frame, the End Credits in *The Force Awakens* and *The Last Jedi* are full of invention and novelty. The former quietly closes with LUKE's theme on celesta following a contrapuntal blend of REY and FORCE themes; the latter a codetta on REY's theme and CHIMES motif, likewise scored for celesta.[3] Both convey an affective mixture of childlike innocence and wizened, contemplative detachment—a mood also cultivated at the conclusion of many of Williams's more personal concert works.

In its credits sequence, *The Rise of Skywalker* returns to the model for final entries in the series, replicating the concluding bars of *A New Hope*-by-way-of-*Return of the Jedi*. This is hardly surprising: of the nine Skywalker symphonies, *The Rise of Skywalker* is the most *about* the idea of *Star Wars*. Nowhere is this autopoetic quality more apparent than the movie's cavalcade of musical endings, which number five—six if you include the eponymous concert arrangement. (That piece, with its bittersweet but gracious final bars, feels more than any others concerned with offering genuine, non-ironized or overly referential finality.) All Williams's Episode IX endings serve a different narrative and musical function. The movie's essential plot—defeating Palpatine and the First Order once and for all—is only the first matter that needs closing. A personal ending for the Sequel Trilogy's cast of characters is also demanded. That is delivered through the reunion scene that hosts that leitmotivic pageant, "Bows," we examined back in Chapter 3.

Episode IX then refers to the model of *Revenge of the Sith*, returning to that location about which Luke once said, wrongly, it turns out: "If there's a bright center to the universe, you're on the planet that it's farthest from." This rather poetic third ending sees Rey visit her spiritual homeland, stopping at the Lars homestead to figuratively bury Anakin's children. When asked by a wandering nomad, she assumes for herself the mantle of that storied family name. This initiates the fourth and final in-narrative ending. To few listeners' surprise, the utterance of the name "Rey Skywalker" occasions the requisite FORCE frame, again complementing a parting shot of the hero, silhouetted against the Tatooinian sky.

Satisfyingly inevitable is one way to describe this FORCE-filled bookend; formulaic and perfunctory another. However, the aforementioned third ending, a cue entitled "Return to Tatooine," is at once similar to and distinct from everything else in the saga. And within it, Williams does a far better job in conveying that mythic fullness of meaning and memory crucial to the series' core aesthetic. But for a brief citation of Rey's CHIMES—accompanying a shot of her sliding down a sand hill [2:10:20], much as she did in Episode VII—the cue is seemingly athematic. Quiet and desolate, the little cue is simple on its surface, even for the composer's leaner Sequel Trilogy style. But within its austere bars, Williams plumbs some of the score's deepest wells of memory and feeling. "Return to Tatooine" is a quiet finale, but one of truly symphonic heft, closing not just a single film, nor trilogy, nor even the nine-score generational saga per se, but the whole idea of *Star Wars*.

The cue's unifying thread is the six-note motif included as this Afterword's epigraph. Little more than a minor triad, the figure sounds in every measure, save the two CHIMES bearers. Constant, cyclical, always ending and then restarting, this motif becomes so ingrained during the cue that slight alterations bear momentous symbolic weight. Overall, "Return to Tatooine" divides into two broad paragraphs, the first overall quiet and in D minor, the second surging then subsiding and perched a semitone higher in E♭ minor. That tonal relationship is in fact leit-harmonic, affiliated closely with Rey, as we have seen. The singing string line beneath the harp and celesta arpeggios replicates no one theme exactly but in its intervallic silhouette resembles JEDI STEPS, the leitmotif introduced in *The Force Awakens* for Rey's first encounter with Luke. The modulation into E♭ occurs as Rey buries the Skywalker twins' lightsabers together [2:10:50], symbolically laying to rest their legacies at the site of mythic (and franchise) origin. For the briefest of moments [2:11:05], the unbending arpeggios, now swelling across the whole orchestra, are modified by one pitch, C♭ instead of B♭. The difference is a single eighth note, but the change could not be more pregnant: the arpeggio, for that instant, bears the outline of the theme of the father. Nine movies of hearing $\hat{6}$-$\hat{3}$-$\hat{1}$ in minor as a sign of Vader make this hard to unhear.

And it is not just the father that is recalled in this cue, but the grandmother also. The wistful horn line that initiates the cue's recession [2:11:12] has to it the rhythm and melodic profile of a one-cue-wonder from *Attack of the Clones*: the minor-sixth spanning horn theme played when teenage Anakin buries his mother Shmi, in essentially the same spot Rey is symbolically interring her spiritual ancestors. Unlike the VADER, REY, and JEDI STEPS allusions, this one is unlikely to be intentional on Williams's part—the callback is too obscure, and the Sequel Trilogy's avoidance of Prequel references too thorough. But it is a meaningful rhyme, one enabled by the consistency of Williams's compositional vocabulary and the density of connections afforded by his symphonic approach to the series. In this one, sparse piece, "Return to Tatooine" elegantly ties all three trilogies together. Finale problem: solved. And solved on precisely the musical terms the Skywalker Saga—the *whole* Saga—set for itself.

After Rey completes her funeral rite for Luke and Leia, a stranger enters the frame, offering the most on-the-nose query possible to our protagonist: "There's been no one for so long. Who are you?" After a beat, Rey responds with the series' controversial final line: "Rey . . .Rey Skywalker." This line triggers the aforementioned re-re-revisiting of the FORCE theme, and with it, the movie's final image. Luke and Leia look on as approving ghosts, and Rey and BB-8 gaze off at the binary sunrise. One may quibble with the logic or narrative merit of Rey's assumption of the Skywalker nominal mantle. But the line's greater mythic significance was grasped, clearly and sagely, by the composer. The musical close of Episode IX is an ending for something perpetually re-beginning, a finale problem that is its own solution. In Williams's own words:

> I just think the last couple words of the film are so completely magical. We have to have forty years of preparation for that, to get the full feeling of what that [passing of the Skywalker baton] means. I felt so satisfied, so complete in a way. Nine episodes in a great tale, beautifully done over many many years. And that means that it's not an ending. It's here with us, and it will stay there. It makes *our* lives part of that story.[4]

Appendix 1

Label	First Heard	Appears In	Incipit (Transposed into C)
1 LUKE	IV [0:00:28]	I, II, III, IV, V, VI, VII, VIII, IX	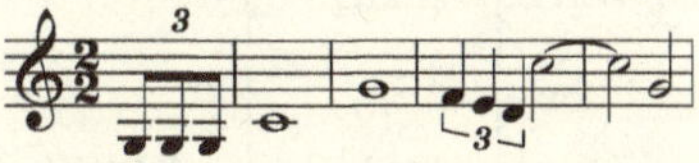
2. REBEL FANFARE	IV [0:02:06]	III, IV, V, VI, VII, VIII, IX	
3. FORCE	IV [0:04:53]	I, II, III, IV, V, VI, VII, VIII, IX	
4. LEIA	IV [0:05:07]	III, IV, V, VI, VII, VIII, IX	
5. IMPERIALS	IV [0:05:42]	IV (OSTINATO in III, IX)	
6. DEATH STAR	IV [0:08:48]	IV, VI, VIII	
7. JAWAS	IV [0:12:58]	I	
8. THRONE ROOM	IV [1:59:24]	IV, VI	
9. VADER	V [0:01:55]	I, II, III, V, VI, VII, VIII, IX	
10. HAN AND LEIA	V [0:03:32]	V, VI, VII, VIII, IX	
11. DROIDS	V [0:06:44]	V	
12. DARK SIDE	V [0:15:20]	V (soundalikes in III, IX)	
13. YODA	V [0:49:43]	I, II, III, V, VI, VIII, IX	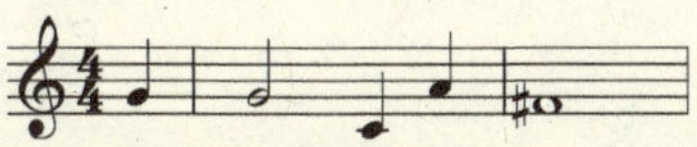

Label	First Heard	Appears In	Incipit (Transposed into C)
14. **Boba Fett**	V [1:06:13]	V	
15. **Cloud City**	V [1:21:31]	V	
16. **Jabba**	IV [0:52:44] (tracked)	I, IV, VI	
17. **Victory Fanfare**	VI [0:35:39]	VI	
18. **Emperor**	VI [0:38:17]	I, II, III, VI, VIII, IX	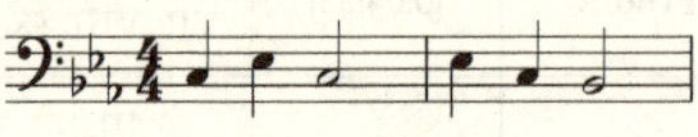
19. **Revelation**	VI [0:43:22]	VI (anticipated in V)	
20. **It's a Trap!**	V [0:56:20]	VI	
21. **Ewoks**	VI [1:28:54]	VI	
22. **Luke and Leia**	VI [1:20:24]	VI, VIII, IX	
23. **Droid March**	I [0:10:11]	I, II, III	
24. **Darth Maul**	I [0:27:43]	I	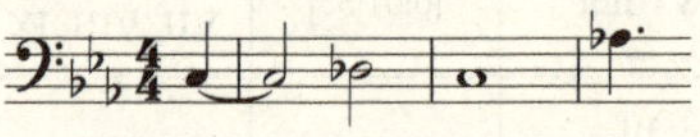
25. **Jar Jar**	I [0:28:55]	I	
26. **Anakin**	I [0:32:41]	I, II, III	

Label	First Heard	Appears In	Incipit (Transposed into C)
27. Qui-Gon	I [1:11:08]	I	
28. Shmi	I [1:15:00]	I, II, III	
29a. Duel of the Fates (Chant)	I [1:50:25]	I, II, III, IX (cut)	
29b. Duel of the Fates (Ostinato)	I [1:47:59]	I, II, III	
29c. Duel of the Fates (Theme)	I [1:46:40]	I, II, III	
30. Funeral	I [2:07:17]	I, III	
31. Conspiracy	II [0:04:21]	II	
32. Gloom	II [0:09:50]	II, II	
33. Anakin and Padmé	II [0:29:06]	II, III	
34. Mystery	II [0:34:59]	II, IX (soundalike in VIII)	
35. Pastorale	II [0:47:48]	II	
36. Descent	II [0:54:22]	II, III (c.f. *Dies Irae*, used in I–IX)	
37. Grievous	III [0:08:18]	III	

Label	First Heard	Appears In	Incipit (Transposed into C)
38. Happy Landings	III [0:23:40]	III	
39. Lament	III [1:01:05]	III	
40. Battle of the Heroes	III [1:47:53]	III, VIII	
41. Map	VII [0:02:40]	VII, VIII	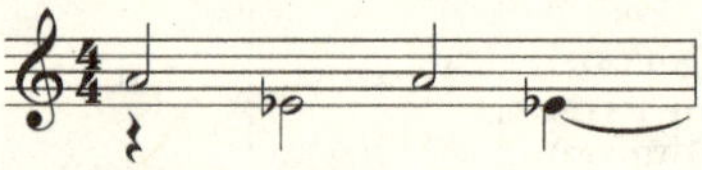
42a. Kylo Ren (aggressive)	VII [0:06:11]	VII, VIII, IX	
42b. Kylo Ren (hesitant)	VII [0:28:25]	VII, VIII, IX	
42c. Kylo Ren (menacing)/ First Order	VII [0:09:32]	VII, VIII	
43a. Rey (Galop)	VII [0:11:38]	VII, VIII, IX	
43b. Rey (Chimes)	VII [0:11:48]	VII, VIII, IX	
43c. Rey (Theme)	VII [0:12:16]	VII, VIII, IX	
44. Poe	VII [0:21:53]	VII, VIII, IX	
45. Finn/ Pursuit	VII [0:30:00]	VII, VIII	
46. Snoke	VII [0:51:50]	VII, VIII, IX (unused)	

Label	First Heard	Appears In	Incipit (Transposed into C)
47. RESISTANCE	VII [0:58:27]	VII, VIII, IX	
48. PATHOS	VII [1:10:15]	VII, VIII, IX	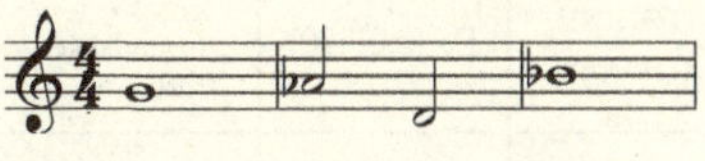
49. TENSION	VII [1:43:50]	VII, VIII, IX	
50. JEDI STEPS	VII [2:05:10]	VII, VIII, IX (?)	
51. LUKE IN EXILE	VIII [0:20:20]	VIII	
52. ROSE	VII [0:38:28]	VIII	
53. DESPERATION	VII [1:37:35]	VII	
54. SITH ARTIFACTS	IX [0:02:22]	IX	
55. PSALM OF THE SITH	IX [0:02:50]	IX	
56. KNIGHTS OF REN	IX [0:03:07]	IX	
57. HEROICS	IX [0:08:49]	IX	
58. FRIENDSHIP	IX [0:17:19]	IX	
59. VICTORY	IX [1:37:00]	IX	

Additional Noteworthy Themes from the Original Trilogy			
STARRY NIGHT	IV [0:01:52]	IV, VIII	
TATOOINE TRITONES	IV [0:07:20]	IV (soundalikes throughout)	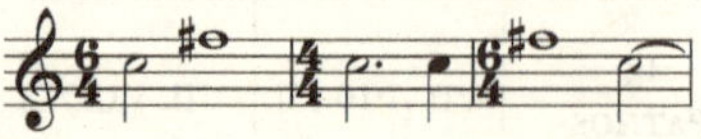
CANTINA BAND 1	IV [0:44:51]	IV	
TIE FIGHTER ATTACK	IV [1:34:32]	IV, VI, VIII	
HEROIC RESOLVE	IV [1:46:33]	IV, VI, IX	
OCTATONIC CORKSCREWS	IV [1:48:15]	IV, VI	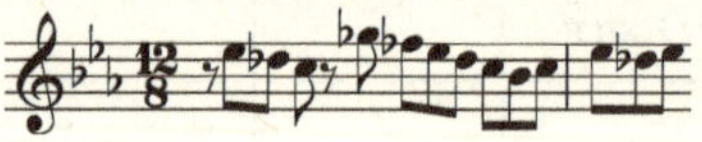
MYNOCKS!	V [1:00:03]	V	
ATTACKING A STAR DESTROYER	V [1:06:30]	V	
IT'S A TRAP! B-THEME	VI [1:34:15]	VI	
EWOK CASUALTIES	VI [1:40:03]	VI	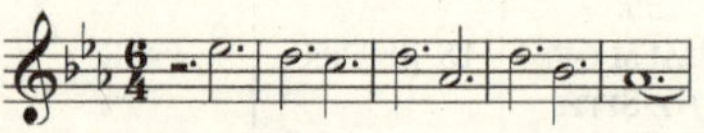

Non-Skywalker Saga Themes		
Themes from *SOLO*		
Themes from *OBI-WAN KENOBI*		
Themes from *GALAXY'S EDGE*		

Appendix 2

NAME	YEAR ARRANGED	PRODUCT CODE
1. "Star Wars – Main Title"	1977	073999971583
2. "The Battle"	1977	--
3. "The Little People"	1977	--
4. "Throne Room and Finale"	1977	073999971583
5. "Princess Leia's Theme"	1977 (rev. 2018)	073999971583
6. "Here They Come"	1978	884088585068
7. "The Cantina Band"	1978 (rev. 1990?)	884088585068
8. "Finale" (from Episode V)	1980	--
9. "Han Solo and The Princess"	1980; 2018 (rev. 2019, '21)	888680746414 (2018 v. only)
10. "The Asteroid Field"	1980	--
11. "The Imperial March"	1980	073999971583
12. "Yoda's Theme"	1980 (rev. 2018)	073999971583
13. "Jabba The Hutt"	1983	--
14. "Luke and Leia"	1983 (rev. 2018)	884088585068 (1983 v. only)
15. "Parade of the Ewoks"	1983	884088585068
16. "The Forest Battle"	1983	884088585068
17. "Montage" (from Episodes IV–VI)	1997	--
18. "Anakin's Theme"	1999 (rev. 2023a, '23b)	073999453034 (1999 v. only)
19. "Duel of the Fates"	1999	073999453034
20. "The Adventures of Jar Jar"	1999	073999453034
21. "The Flag Parade"	1999	073999453034
22. "Across the Stars"	2002; 2018 (rev. 2019, '21)	073999967913 (2002 v. only)
23. "Battle of the Heroes"	2005	073999860368
24. "March of the Resistance"	2015	888680608422
25. "Rey's Theme"	2015 (rev. 2018)	888680608422 (2015 v. only)
26. "Scherzo for X-Wings"	2015	888680608422
27. "The Jedi Steps"	2015	888680608422
28. "The Jedi Steps and Finale"	2015	888680608422
29. "The Resistance is Reborn"	2017	888680733896
30. "Adagio" (from Episode VII)	2018	--
31. "The Adventures of Han"	2018	888680793739
32. "Galaxy's Edge Symphonic Suite"	2018	--
33. "Psalm of the Sith"	2019	840126915495
34. "Rey and Ben"	2019	840126915495
35. "The Rise of Skywalker"	2019	840126915495
36. "The Speeder Chase"	2019	840126915495
37. "Obi-Wan"	2022	196288093381

Notes

Introduction

1. On the subject of peak musical experiences, including their sociological and psychological basis and importance in identity formation, see Green (2022).
2. Admittedly, a preadolescent's creaky voice is a poor substitute for the real article. However, to this day, I recommend my students preparing for musical recognition exams that if they wish to really memorize a tune, there is no better way than producing it with their own vocal cords. This intuition is backed by empirical studies that show listeners are considerably better at remembering vocal melodies over purely instrumental ones. See Weiss, Trehub, and Schellenberg (2012).
3. The phrase "cinematic listening" has recently received substantial attention from scholars of multimedia. Though used in many senses by different commentators, the basic idea is how the movies shape our experience of sound, both while we are attending to a film and (more provocatively) in any and all other contexts. See Cenciarelli (2021) for an introduction.
4. Not that acceptance among Classical music criticism is needed for something to be worthy of study, but it is telling that several prominent critics have written sympathetic evaluations—and in some cases, reevaluations—of Williams's *Star Wars* scores in recent years. See for example Ross (2016), Swed (2016), Midgette (2019), von Rhein (2019), and Hurwitz (2024).
5. The podcast and the video-essay have proven especially effective formats for *Star Wars* musical analysis. Standouts include "Art of the Score" (Pogson, Golding, and Buc); "Dominic Sewell Music" (Sewell); "Star Wars Music Minute" (Tan); and "What the Force?" (Gould).
6. Among the few studies that critically consider diegetic music in *Star Wars* are Mulliken (2010), Rutledge (2016), and Gresko (2019).
7. Rinzler's *The Sounds of Star Wars* (2010) is an invaluable resource regarding all things audio-related in the first two trilogies. One of the few studies to consider Williams's music in its broader audio ecosystem is Minnick (2022). See also Whittington (2007, 93–113).
8. The musical gender politics of the Saga have been explored in Lerner (2005), Graber (2018), and McTavish (2023). While mostly covering films other than the Skywalker Saga, studies by Fülöp (2012) and Edgar (forthcoming) provide important context on how Classic Hollywood composers established sexual and gender codes in music.
9. On *Star Wars*'s afterlife in other musical genres and styles, see Zlabinger (2016). On the contributions of composers other than Williams to the franchise, see Greenfield-Casas and McGlynn (2023), Crosby (2025), and Lawson (2025).
10. For the purposes of this study, ancillary themes Williams wrote outside the nine Saga films are not discussed. This includes his trailer music for Episode VII, themes and cues for *Solo* (2017), title theme for *Obi-Wan Kenobi* (2022), and symphonic suite for *Galaxy's Edge* (2019).
11. Among the many occasions Lucas described the *Star Wars* scores, or saga itself, in explicitly symphonic terms, see Scanlon (1977), Lucas (1990), Moyers (1999), Rinzler (2005a, 221), and Polo (2015).
12. See Caplin (2024) for a panoramic treatment of his theory and typology of cadences, and Lehman (2013) and Richards (2016) for modifications of the Caplinian approach to suit film music.
13. It is safe to point to Williams as being the sole composer. This extends to the task of orchestration, for which the role of the orchestrator, while considerable—these are dense scores in terms of instrumental detail—is essentially a stenographic task. This is rather uncharacteristic of Hollywood, but is true of Williams in general. For more on this point, see Chapter 9. For such a huge amount of music, it is remarkable how few authorial "problem patches" there are—only a dozen or so minutes overall. These include the revised Sail Barge Battle sequence from Episode VI and a handful of revised and unused cues from the Sequels, ostensibly prepared by William Ross but manifestly spun from Williams's original materials.

Chapter 1

1. Lucas (1990) and Svejda (2020).
2. Whether Lucas intended to retain the classical temp track is a matter of some dispute. In his notes to the original soundtrack album, Williams recalled that "at one point, George talked of integrating selections from the classical repertoire with the score" in the manner of the successful—if not uncontroversial—music track for Kubrick's *2001: A Space Odyssey*. But, after meeting with Williams, Lucas was persuaded to include an original score, particularly in its capacity for thematic identification and development, something impossible with a collage of disassociated excerpts (Williams 1977). This accords with Lucas's initial description of the decision. (Scanlon 1977, 48). However, on the account given by film historian J. W. Rinzler, the temp track was never meant to be permanent (2007, p. 242–247, 265). This view was reaffirmed by Lucas himself in later conversations (Maltin 1995). A plausible middle ground is that in his early meetings with the director, Williams *affirmed* for Lucas the rightness of including freshly written music, regardless of whether Lucas genuinely needed convincing. Whatever the case, the narrative that *Star Wars* could have been another *2001* were it not for the intercession of Williams has become one of its foundational musical myths, along with the score's role as reviver of the dead symphonic idiom.
3. Burlingame (2019).
4. Arnold (1980b, 263).
5. For a sampling of versions this claim with varying degrees of rigor and qualification, see Anderson-Bazzoli (2020), Audissino (2014a), Brown, J. (1999), Brown, R. (1994, 118), Burkholder et al. (2019, 968–969), Cooke (2010, 234), Debruge (2024), Dyer (1999, N13), Hubbert (2011, 396), Lack (1997, 330), Larson (1998, C10), Mangan (2002), Meyer, N. (1993), and Palmer (1986, 531–532). Helen Mitchell (2010) offers an excellent critical overview of this narrative, one of the most resilient in film music historiography.
6. Spielberg (1975).
7. For historical context on *Star Wars*' billboard-ascending, platinum certification-attaining success, see Jeff Smith (1998, 216–217) and (2014, 281).
8. Rózsa was still actively working in Hollywood at the time of the premiere of *Star Wars*. Though he bemoaned what he saw as the death of the symphonic score that made him so successful in the 1940s and '50s, in Williams Rózsa saw a worthy successor, someone who, along with Goldsmith, was restoring the moribund orchestral tradition. (Kraft 1982).
9. Fred Karlin (1994, 130) is one of the few writers on film music history to acknowledge Goldsmith's role in sustaining the symphonic tradition in Hollywood.
10. Dyer (1980, 22). Dyer further notes that "Williams downgrades all of the compliments on how he has restored the prestige of the symphonic movie score" (1980, 22).
11. Byrd (1997, 19).
12. Williams may veer a little close to historical determinism for music historians' liking here, but he stops short of making an essentialist claim about musical style. He says music is "indispensable" for film, not specifically "symphonic music," even though in practice big Romantic orchestral idiom has been used as a shorthand for emotional universalism throughout Hollywood's history. The historical contingency of this supposed universalism is pressured by Flinn (1992) and Slobin (2008).
13. See Audissino (2014, 119–133). Audissino regards Williams as a neoclassical composer in the sense that, in *Star Wars* and other scores, he recalled the compositional techniques and ethos of the Classic Hollywood period (c. late 1920s–1960s). This is distinct from the other musicological sense of "neoclassical," being a twentieth-century rechanneling of the style and aesthetics of Viennese Classical era (e.g., Haydn, Mozart). In terms of idiom, the Skywalker scores are still better captured by "Romanticism," allowing for possible modifiers of late-, neo-, or post-.
14. Ibid. (2014, 82).
15. The classic formulation of music's function in mainstream film can be found in Claudia Gorbman's *Unheard Melodies* (1987, esp. 70–98).
16. McBride (1997, 222). Ironically, *The Sugarland Express* would be the least symphonic, most idiosyncratic soundtrack of the pair's astonishing thirty feature film collaborations.
17. Lucas (1990, 5).
18. For quotes from Lucas about this silent film analogy, see Burlingame (2012) and 20th Century Fox and Lucasfilm [Star Wars Episode I EPK] (1999). The latter includes a revealing line about music's formal role in *Star Wars* being akin to how movies were accompanied before the sound era.

19. Larue (2001).
20. The discourse surrounding the symphony and symphonism is too vast to attribute each one of these qualities to a single thinker, but a few texts are worth singling out, including Adorno (2002 [1941]), Bonds (1997), Dahlhaus (1989), Elphick (2021b), Fanning (2013), and Haas, D. (1992). The survey of Russian and Polish symphonic thought offered by Beata Bolesławska is especially instructive (2019, 1–13). With respect to film musical symphonism specifically, this book also incorporates ideas from Cooke (2018), Cooper (2010), Flinn (1992), Franklin (2011), Lerner (2004), and Schneller (2014).
21. Lippincott (1977).
22. In the Original Trilogy, synthesizers are clearly audible in ESB [9:13, 53:03, and 1:04:35] and ROTJ [22:03, 27:59, 1:31:45, and 1:55:59]. The Prequels are more rife with such moments, but also tend to subtly blend synth with acoustic instruments to a greater degree. Examples include TPM [2:09, 4:04, 45:35, 1:24:22, and 1:56:19], AOTC [5:10, 10:48, 51:05, 1:10:36, 2:08:20, and 2:13:13], and ROTS [30:42, 34:03, 39:58, 55:08, 1:09:06, 1:25:15, 1:34:26, and 1:37:23].
23. Subsequent *Star Wars* scores would almost monotonically increase these performance forces, both within and across trilogies. For example, the first of the sequels, Episode VII, involved eighty-five instrumental players plus two dozen voices used to an extremely limited extent (the SNOKE theme). Episode VIII boasted 101 instruments and a far more active role for the sixty-four voices of the Los Angeles Chorale. Episode IX featured a 102-piece orchestra and 100 voices from that same chorus. See Niles (2015) and Burlingame (2018, 2019).
24. Godsil (2021, 24). Godsil's analysis of the development of LUKE's theme across Episode IV is a model for timbrally-informed analysis, truer to the real narrative effect of the soundtrack than a purely thematic approach could be.
25. Tellingly, when Joel McNeely composed a symphonic soundtrack for the *Star Wars* novel *Shadows of the Empire* (1995), his clearest referents were not to Williams's then-three *Star Wars* scores per se but rather to Ravel's *Daphnis*—plus some nods to Walton's *The Quest* and *Belshazzar's Feast*, Martin's *In Terra Pax*, Hindemith's *Symphonic Metamorphosis*, Corigliano's Symphony No. 1, and several pieces from Prokofiev (*Cinderella*, *Alexander Nevsky*, *Romeo and Juliet*). For his part, William Walton was also taken with Ravel's rapidly planing trumpet chords (cf. his score to *Major Barbara*).
26. McClary (2002, 21).
27. Cooke (2008, 456).
28. The idea of "symphonic aspirations" stems from the work of Karen Painter (2007).
29. The term "symphonism" is attributed to the Soviet composer and musicologist Boris Asaf'yev. Asaf'yev's conception of symphonism is wide-ranging and philosophically—and politically—charged. A work that exemplified symphonism would be fully integrated on both a motivic and a conceptual level, necessarily greater than the sum of its parts. "Not all symphonies are symphonic"—and, inversely, a work need not be labeled a "symphony" to fulfill the qualities of symphonism" (Haas 1992, 412–419). A film score could conceivably fulfill Asaf'yev's criteria, provided any internal discontinuities were minimized. Williams could not have known of Asaf'yev's theories directly. But the musicologist's influence in post-Revolutionary Russian musical aesthetics was considerable, and he molded the thinking and compositional rhetoric of a generation of Soviet symphonists, among whose ranks were Prokofiev and Shostakovich, figures of admiration and emulation for Williams.
30. Fanning (2013, 97).
31. Sibelian influences can be heard in distinct and isolated passages. The melodic turn that opens the "City in the Clouds" from *Empire* [1:18:15] resembles that of the primary subject from Sibelius's Violin Concerto's first movement. The LUKE IN EXILE theme from *Last Jedi* [21:12, 46:45] seems to be channeling the chilly air of the secondary subject from Sibelius 2/iv. Mahler's influence is contrastingly diffuse, less detectable in individual themes or melodic routines, more in a general approach to building climaxes, juxtaposing thematic topics, deploying the brass, and so on. The DEATH STAR motif does have a cognate in the creepy trumpet fanfare in the first movement of Mahler's Third (mm. 31–33), though in its polychordal disposition bears a likely more direct lineage from Bernard Herrmann. One could also impute a likeness between certain of Williams's menacing marches with those from a variety Mahler symphonic movements (cf. the Imperial and Resistance Marches with principle subjects of Mahler 2/ii, 6/i and 6/iv, and 9/iii). However, any resemblance there is likely the result of a more mediated influence via Williams's acknowledged model of Shostakovich (cf. those same leitmotifs with Shostakovich 1/i and 1/ii, 5/iv, and 10/ii, and 11/ii).

32. Ekman (1938, 191).
33. Quoted on Star Wars Official YouTube Page (2013).
34. Quoted from 20th Century Fox and Lucasfilm [Star Wars Episode II EPK] (2002).
35. Adorno, for whatever it is worth, thought little of Sibelius as a composer ([1934] 2001, 331–337).
36. Adorno ([1941] 2002, 257).
37. Franklin (2011, 94).
38. Ibid. (86).
39. Ibid. (97). Franklin's argument that listening to film may draw from symphonic attitudes has a fascinating converse: listening to concert music as mediated through, or predicated on, *cinematic* forms of attention. I suspect the latter is widespread. Michael Long characterized cinematic listening as an act of "simultaneous audiation and envisioning . . . of some accompanying diegesis or . . . series of images" (2008, 7). Ben Winters offers a serious and sustained exploration of this stance with respect to the genre of the late-Romantic symphony (2014, 119–148).
40. Franklin (2007, 14).
41. See Bonds (2014).
42. Indeed, it takes just a little simplification to describe the underlying meta-myth in both The Ring Cycle and Skywalker Saga with the same words. "The desire for power and the mishandling of affection leads to a broken world at large, one whose redemption can only come from a younger generation capable of pure love—and often revealed to include some uncomfortable familial twists!"
43. There exists a sizable literature on the Wagnerian nature of cinema, and the proto-cinematic nature of Wagner. Good resources on this topic include Paulin (2000), Ross (2020b), and the whole of the edited volume *Wagner and Cinema* (eds. Joe and Gilman, 2010). Surprisingly, little writing exists that sustainedly and with music-analytical rigor examines *Star Wars* through a Wagnerian lens. James Buhler's (2000) essay "Star Wars, Music and Myth" is a major exception here, as is the work of Matthew Bribitzer-Stull, the sixth and ninth chapters of his monograph *Understanding the Leitmotif* (2015) in particular. More delimited treatments of *Star Wars*' Wagnerian inclinations include Gonin (2011), Guido (2006), Paulus (2000), and Wolkenfeld (2007).
44. Defining leitmotif and distinguishing it from similar procedures has been a favored activity for Wagnerians since *Das Rheingold* premiered in 1869. Rather than enumerate the library's worth of books and articles that go into this issue, a single source is recommended to curious readers: Bribitzer-Stull's (2015) monograph, which gives a comprehensive and rigorous overview of the subject. An interesting recent development in leitmotif studies has been the examination of the technique vis-à-vis video game music analysis; Anatone (2023) provides several categories of game music motivicism that could back-apply to *Star Wars*.
45. Dahlhaus (1989, 196–197). The symphonism of Wagnerian music drama should not be taken as an immutable fact. As Carolyn Abbate points out, the "continuous network of interrelated thematic ideas" that results from leitmotivicism was perhaps the *only* consistent sense of "symphonic" that Wagner himself ever held in his own mind (1989b, 93). Abbate's attitude is essentially one of skepticism toward the notion that Wagner's music is in any way essentially symphonic in conception or effect. Indeed, many of her critiques of the opera-as-symphonic discourse could be profitably translated to the present film-music-as-symphonic one.
46. Adorno and Eisler ([1952] 2005, 33–50).
47. Buhler (2000, 53).
48. Though Wagner sketches the concept of musical prose in places within *Oper und Drama*, Schoenberg's 1947 essay "Brahms the Progressive" contains the classic formulation. Additional exegeses may be found in various of Dahlhaus's writings (1987; 1989a; 1989b, 195–206), as well as Auner (1991) and Liu (2022).
49. Schoenberg ([1947] 1975, 415). That this concept was formalized with respect to Johannes Brahms's music—the compositional antithesis of Wagner in the eyes of contemporaries and many subsequent critics—is not at all irrelevant, though it is left curiously unstressed by most musicologists following Schoenberg. Thomas Grey (1995, 283) is one of the few to draw a sharp distinction between Brahmsian and Wagnerian musical prose.
50. Musical temporality is an exuberantly well-theorized topic. Readers curious about the ability for narrative-driven Romantic-era instrumental music to project a feeling of tense should turn to Abbate (1996), Almén (2008), Taylor (2016). For a case for the innate tensedness of film musical underscore, see Franklin (2011, 87–101).

51. Johnson (1990). Long-range tonal organization is unfortunately beyond the scope of this book, but the author has covered it in other sources; see Lehman (2018b, 46–47, 80–82) and (2018c).
52. Wagner ([1859] 1987, 303).
53. Another poignant echo: the Force theme as it appears at the end of this cue rhymes with a comparable mid-trilogy decision made by Anakin in Episode II [1:14:23], when he decides to strike out in search of his mother—a choice that ends up having disastrous ramifications. A parallel scene in Episode VIII, when Rey decides to leave Luke mid-training [1:20:19], does not quote the Force directly but does feature a deconstructed variant of its consequent phrase.
54. Greiving (2025, 510).
55. One need only note the existence of many post-*Star Wars* fantasy/sci-fi scores that did not adopt an old-school symphonic approach to see that Williams's neoclassical approach was never monolithically adopted: *Blade Runner, Dune, Excalibur,* and the replacement score for *Legend,* for example.
56. For an excellent overview of the aesthetically divergent scoring idioms associated with (but not limited to, nor defining aspects of) Newman and Zimmer in post-Millennial scoring, see Reyland (2015). Both composers have routinely expressed deep and obviously genuine admiration of Williams. Newman, whom Williams has known since he was born and calls "Tommy," has a *Star Wars* connection—he orchestrated several cues from *Return of the Jedi,* most notably 13m2, "Darth Vader's Death." Greiving (2025, 513).
57. Quoted in 20th Century Fox and Lucasfilm [Star Wars Episode II EPK] (2002). The composer used virtually the same language twenty years prior, in describing his work on *Empire* thusly: "I wanted to try to develop material that would wed with the original and sound like part of an organic whole; something different, something new but an extension of what already existed" (Arnold 1980a). And those same sentiments run through Williams's commentary on the Sequel trilogy a decade later, as when he spoke of the need for Episode VII to "feel friendly and interrelated to the other scores . . . and at the same time be new and original" (Greiving 2015).
58. Greiving (2025, 531–532). Greiving notes the kiss between Rey and Ren as a particularly important scene that was not settled on until very shortly before Episode IX's premiere. In the end, the filmmakers opted to use Williams's original, old-fashionedly expressive cue for the scene. In public, Williams conveyed the same level of gratitude toward working on *Rise of Skywalker* as he did every other score, though he later confided that composing for a film as editorially unsettled as Episode IX "would drive you crazy if you let it." According to Greiving, the hectic pattern of rewrites and re-edits was stressful enough for producer Kathleen Kennedy to step in at one point to tell director J. J. Abrams that he was overwhelming his composer, instructing him that "you can't keep doing this" (530).
59. Highlights include Kylo's confrontation with Rey [1:03:36], Rey and Luke's reunion [1:30:21], Rey's approach of the throne [1:43:01], and Rey's resurrection followed by the kiss and Kylo's expiation [2:02:10].
60. Huvet (2020, 190; author's translation).
61. Huvet's analysis of Williams's music for the Prequels under the new digital editing regime is penetrating and authoritative, informed by interviews with Conrad Pope and Kenneth Wannberg and supported by fine-grained analyses of complex sequences like the Battle of Naboo, Conveyor Belt Scene, and Arena Battle.
62. Nicholas Kmet (2018, 211–212) describes Wannberg's critical role thusly: "Wannberg . . . first worked with Williams on *Valley of the Dolls* (Mark Robson, 1967), consistently serving as Williams's primary music editor until his retirement in 2005. In that rôle, Wannberg would have been responsible for helping facilitate communication between Williams and directors, spotting films and calculating timings for the music, overseeing the technical aspects of recording sessions, making necessary post-recording edits to the music, and representing Williams and the music during the final mix."
63. White (2024, 5).
64. Taruskin (2005, 568–569).

Chapter 2

1. The *Encyclopedia Britannica* entries on "John Williams" and "Star Wars film score" are demonstrative, being full of superlatives—"most enduring," "most iconic," "most influential," and "most memorable"—though these are couched with some strategic "some of" or "arguably" modifiers. See Eldridge (2025) and Schwarm (2014). Pop culture historian Richard Hall offers no such qualifications, stating that *Star Wars* is "the most iconic film score of all time" (2019, 236).

2. Townson (1980). Townson, who did more than almost any other single person to promote film music on record, was certainly familiar enough with the repertoire to make such a sweeping assertion with some authority.
3. The OST for *Star Wars* peaked at #2 on the Billboard Top 100 on 9/17/1977 and stayed in that spot for three weeks (1977, 82). It lasted on the charts for a total of eighteen weeks and became the best-selling non-pop album ever at the time. The radio success of the "Star Wars (Main Title)" single is equally unparalleled for an instrumental composition, remaining on the charts for seventeen weeks between July and November 1977, peaking at #10, again during the week of 9/17/1977.
4. The American Film Institute's "100 Years of Film Scores" from 2005 deemed *Star Wars* the "greatest American score of all time." *The Guardian* (2007) ranked it as the third greatest film soundtrack of all time, ABC Classic FM the second (2020), and the crowd-sourced Ranker.com the fourth, and *The Empire Strikes Back* at the top spot (2025). Turner Classic Movies' "Fifteen Most Influential Film Soundtracks" from 2010 lists the 1977 soundtrack as its most recent honoree. For a more objective historical contextualization on *Star Wars*' chart-ascending, platinum certification-attaining success, see Smith (1998, 216–217).
5. Lawson and MacDonald (2018, 261).
6. Belfi and Kacirek's (2020) study found themes from *Jeopardy* and *The Pink Panther* to be slightly more familiar, but less placeable by name by subjects. The LUKE theme was the most highly ranked of the *entire data set* (not just Movie/TV melodies), tied along with Scott Joplin's "The Entertainer," in terms of valence—that is, how emotionally positive or negative it struck listeners. The corpus is admittedly not huge, nor genuinely global in its range of melodic stimuli, though the fact alone that the *Star Wars* theme was included speaks to a perception of its potential for universal recognizability. Other empirical studies involving melodic familiarity that included *Star Wars*-sourced stimuli include De Barros Freitas (2020), Juslin et al. (2013), Korenman and Peynircioğlu (2004), Robbin (2007), Schaerlaeken et al. (2019), and Sikka et al. (2015).
7. Livingstone (1980, 75).
8. Data obtained via the Boston Symphony Orchestra Performance History Search (accessed 10/27/2024). Most performances occurred during the Boston Pops and Tanglewood seasons.
9. An informed and impartial assessment of *Star Wars*' impact is offered in Cooke (2008, 462–465).
10. Burlingame (2016).
11. Byrd (1997, 20).
12. I remember dreaming up scenarios similar to the one Peter Franklin describes with the child on the train; one was envisioning "The Asteroid Field" as accompaniment not to Han Solo's daring steering through an interplanetary minefield, but winding through a hectic overcrowded elementary school hallway, dodging other kids. Another is humming through the entirety of "Parade of the Ewoks" with my brother on the bus back from summer camp.
13. We need not give air to bad-faith hearings, though for reference, Audissino (2014b, 134–144) has offered a useful survey and critique of such perspectives.
14. Among the interviews in which Williams expresses admiration for Haydn are Sullivan (2007) and McKinley (2011).
15. Hubbert (2011, 387).
16. Page (1985).
17. Stock (2006).
18. Ibid.
19. Indeed, centering music at the exclusion of drama is a practice with ample precedents in Wagnerian reception. Take, for example, the existence of albums with names like *Wagner Without Words* and *Symphonic Synthesis from Parsifal*, to say nothing of the long-lasting appeal of "bleeding chunks" from his operas like "Ride of the Valkyries" and "The Wedding March" from *Lohengrin*. See Tovey (1935, 71) and Aaron (1993) for discussion of the bleeding-chunk aesthetic. It should be added that even in staged productions, a drama-bracketing experience is not uncommon. No less a Wagnerian than Bruckner was supposedly so enraptured by his idol's music, at the expense of paying attention to plot, that at the end of a performance of *Götterdämmerung* he had to ask why poor Brünnhilde was being burned (Haas, R. 1934, 23). We will grapple with these issues of textual autonomy in Chapters 8 and 9.
20. "In diesen Grundmotiven, die eben nicht Sentenzen, sondern plastische Gefühlsmomente, wird die Absicht des Dichters . . . am Verständlichsten" Wagner (1852, 194).
21. Quoted from 20th Century Fox and Lucasfilm [Star Wars Episode I EPK] (1999).

22. In his book, *Film Music: Cognition to Interpretation*, Juan Chattah offers a cognitively informed exploration of these various leitmotivic boons, drawing on the psychological concept of an "affordance." Affordances are tools lent to the listener that give them some ability, like remembering a plot-relevant detail more easily. Of special importance to Chattah is how leitmotif affords an *embodied* kind of empathy; well-crafted film music "connects us to the characters' bodies and minds and makes us participants in their actions" (2024, 65 and 85–99).
23. Byrd (1997, 18).
24. An interview with Williams by Grace Edgar (2018) revealed a similar reluctance on the composer's part to make material comparisons between his music and Wagner's. Williams seems too tactful to express annoyance at the question, though his routine disavowals do put in mind J.R.R. Tolkien's droll retort concerning perfunctory comparisons between his cycle and Wagner's: "both rings are round, and there the resemblance ceased" (1981 [1961], 306).
25. Chute (2011).
26. Ross (2020a).
27. For an extensive treatment of Korngold's thematic technique within his film scores, see Winters (2025, 133–158).
28. One commentator has also noted a similarity between VADER's theme and the leitmotif of the brutish Hunding in *Die Walküre* (Evensen 2004). While there are clear if limited rhythmic and intervallic similarities, the HUNDING motif is far less famous than SIEGFRIED's, and it seems unlikely Williams could have directly channeled it given his professed ignorance of the Ring. More likely, Hunding and Vader both draw from a larger topical cluster: the minor-mode antagonist march.
29. Richards (2016) defines grammatical themes as those that "fall into two halves which correspond to a kind of statement and its response, or a beginning and end, in that order." See Richards (2016, [3]).
30. In Richards's fine-grained system, the FORCE leitmotif is what he calls a "developing clause," a thematic archetype with a more intrinsically dynamic and cumulative shape than the period (2016, [29–34]). See also Richards (2013 and 2020a).
31. In Wagner's musical prose, SIEGFRIED, like all his leitmotifs, typically sounds for longer than a mere four measures. Sometimes the theme is drawn out in non-grammatical fashion, as through chromatic sequences; in other cases, it is lengthened—"grammaticized"—into traditional periods, as during "Siegfried's Funeral March." Conversely, the FORCE comes in all sorts of altered and clipped versions, esp. in *A New Hope*. In some cases, when the second of its four subphrases is omitted, the FORCE theme sounds vividly like SIEGFRIED's—for instance, the galloping variant during the Battle of the Resistance in *Rise of Skywalker* [1:42:43].
32. Ross (2018).
33. The FORCE theme is notably prone to semantic drift in *Revenge of the Sith*, partly as a function of its greater than usual exposure to interesting variation techniques, partly in its usage during scenes not plainly involving the Force.
34. The Brucknophilic resonances are clearer in the theme Williams composed on short notice for the *Obi-Wan Kenobi* Disney+ show. Besides the French horn solo that's close to a minor-mode paraphrase of Bruckner's Fourth (Mvt. 1, Main Theme), the dotted rhythmic figure in the piece's midsection suggests any number of Brucknerian chugging string ostinati.
35. Rinzler (2007, 246).
36. A few months later, in a discarded cue for *Superman*, Williams was still playing with the basic building blocks of the FORCE theme. This alternate version of "Fortress of Solitude" heard on the 40th Anniversary Remastered Soundtrack includes an uncanny soundalike to the FORCE at 1:00, 1:23, and 2:00. The *Superman* cue is like an inverse of the unused first draft of the "Binary Sunset" sequence from *A New Hope*, which completely *lacks* what would, in its revision, come to be the defining statement of that leitmotif.
37. Many other composers waded into the sirens' waters, including Boulanger ("Les Sirènes"); Dupont (*Antar*); Roussel (*Évocations*); Saariaho (*Oltra Mar*); Schmitt (*La Tragédie de Salomé*); Schoeck (*Venus*); Schreker (*Der Ferne Klang*); and Szymanowski (Symphony No. 3). As with so many other things, Wagner provides a decisive precedent, in the chorus of nymphs and naiads in Act 1 of *Tannhäuser*. For additional examples of sirenic choirs in Western art music, see Jumeau-Lafond (1997).
38. I am indebted to an anonymous reviewer for alerting me to this similarity.
39. A similar issue arises with claims of Gustav Holst–derived material in Episode IV. While a few cues are undeniably and directly channeling "Mars" from *The Planets* suite, others are likely

citing that famous piece secondhand or even thirdhand. One likely Holstian intermediary is Leighton Lucas's score for the 1958 film *Ice Cold in Alex* (cf. the movie's "Prelude" with Episode IV's "It's a Bird"); another Walton's unused score for 1969's *The Battle of Britain* (cf. the "Battle in the Air" with both "Mars and "The Battle of Yavin"). Commentators often underestimate the indebtedness of *Star Wars* music to such British war films. Case in point: another precedent for "The March of the Resistance" is the fugal exposition in Ron Goodwin's "Main Title" for *Where Eagles Dare* (1968).

40. On the subject of the constellation of influences surrounding "The Imperial March," see Tripp and Lehman (2022) and Tripp (2025). Among the most plausible sources for this iconic theme are Shostakovich (Symphony No. 1, Mvts. 1 and 2), Prokofiev (*Romeo and Juliet*, "Dance of the Knights"), and Elgar (Symphony 1, Movement 2). Fainter points in this musical constellation include Tchaikovsky (*Swan Lake*, "Finale"), Wagner (the "Tarnhlem" motif from the *Ring*), and a precursor motif that occurs in *A New Hope* (e.g., 7m3). At the fringes of the Imperial asterism are a huge number of sound-alikes and models-for-the-models-for-the-models: works like Bax (Symphony No. 1, Movement 1), Casella (Symphony No. 2, Mvt 3), Chopin (*Piano Sonata No. 2*, Mvt 1), Dvořák (*Noonday Witch*, RH 8), Holst ("Uranus" and "Neptune" from *The Planets*), Huppertz (*Metropolis* score, leitmotifs for Fredersen, Maschinenmensch), Ireland (*Epic March*), Mahler (Symphony No. 6, Movement 1), and Shostakovich (*The Gadfly* Overture).
41. Bourne (2024, 87). See also Chattah (2024, 201–211) for a lucid overview of topical analysis for screen media.
42. Danuta Mirka, a leading topic theorist, defines them as "musical styles and genres taken out of their proper context and used in another one" (2014, 2). A hunt topic, for example, fits this definition insofar as its use in a piece of instrumental music no longer signals an actual hunt, with riders, blood hounds, and so on. The insistence on decontextualization involves topic theory's formulation as a means of interpreting eighteenth-century instrumental music. Film musicologists tend to be far looser with that "taken out of their proper context" condition, and so shall we. In addition to the aforementioned work by Bourne and Chattah, see Neumeyer and Buhler (2001, 23–26), Lehman (2017, 502), and Buhler (2019, 189–198).
43. In the *Star Wars* title, this progression is A♭→F. Themes from *The Big Country* (Moross, 1958), *The Magnificent Seven* (Bernstein, 1960) and Williams's own *The Plainsman* (1966), *The Rare Breed* (1966), and *The Cowboys* (1972) are important reference points with respect to this Western topic. See Tagg and Clarida (2003, 357–362), Lehman (2013, [4.1–4.14]), and Barham (2014, 224–238.) For more on Williams's usage of this cadential trope, see Schneller (2013, 53–56).
44. In fairness, Bruckner would channel exactly that *Tristan*-esque texture in the revised Scherzo of his Fourth Symphony, and again, more abstractedly, in the Adagio of his Ninth.
45. Rinzler (2007, 243).
46. Quartally inclined fanfares are fairly easy to locate in film music. Miklós Rózsa's output contains many beyond *Ivanhoe*, and more than a few moments where Williams channels them, most sustainedly in Episode I's *Ben Hur*-inspired "Flag Parade." Another, less savory comparison may be made with the flag-raising cue in Herbert Windt's music for Riefenstahl's Nazi documentary *Olympia*—certainly coincidental, but striking nonetheless. Cooke (2008, 282–283) makes note of this specific moment, while Buhler (2000) and Ross (2020) comment on the Riefenstahl-esque (and ultimately Wagnerian) aesthetics in Episode IV's "Throne Room" sequence.
47. Rózsa assuredly knew his Wagner, but before claiming the *Ivanhoe* fanfare was itself modeled on *Tristan*, it behooves us to trace those mediating figures who might have come between them, like Rózsa's composition teacher Herrmann Grabner and *his* predecessor Max Reger, as well as his compatriots Bartók and Kodály, who were similarly disposed to quartal configurations. The quartally edged fanfare shows up with some regularity in post-Wagnerian Russian music of Borodin and Glazunov (cf. *Prince Igor* Overture, *The Kremlin* "Popular Festival" respectively). Nor must we stop at Wagner; there are plenty of composers contemporary with or predating him who wrote comparably stirring fanfares in major orchestral works—Raff, Weber, Mendelssohn, and countless other employers of the "fanfare" and "hunt" topoi.
48. Rinzler (2007, 246).
49. The Suk passage is obscure, even for someone as studied as Williams. Yet it is of interest as an accidental amalgam of LUKE and VADER leitmotifs—note the chromatic slippage between major-third related minor chords centers.
50. Compare also with Walton's *A Wartime Sketchbook* "Prologue" and "Epilogue" (from *The Foreman Went to France, The Next of Kin* and *Went the Day Well), Battle of Britain* March, *Crown*

Imperial, Granada Prelude, *Major Barbara* End Title, *March for A History of English Speaking Peoples, Orb and Sceptre, Richard III* Prelude, *Spitfire Prelude*, and *Symphony No. 1*, Movement IV. See Craggs (2015).

51. Three other film-based Luke-alikes are worth mentioning. John Barry's eponymous hit song for *Born Free* begins with a partially inverted doppelganger of the *Star Wars* theme. And Williams himself would repeat himself in *Heartbeeps* with a theme for the robot child Phil, and later in *Harry Potter and the Philosopher's Stone* with a brief fanfare during the train station sequence.
52. Ironically, this theme from the symphony was itself adapted from an unused cue from Korngold's score to *Juarez*. See Winters (2025, 230).
53. For nuanced examinations of *Kings Row*, both in connection to Williams and as a profound musical text in its own right, see Cooke (2018, 8–12), Lerner (2019, 132), and Winter (2025, 198–204).
54. Maltin (1995).
55. The enshrinement of Korngold as the quintessential composer of glittery adventure music was aided by a momentous series of film music albums on the RCA label in the 1970s. Conducted by Charles Gerhardt and produced by George Korngold (the composer's son), several of these recordings focused solely on Korngold's scores, and undoubtedly aided a resurgence of interest in Classic Hollywood compositional practices.
56. Another correspondence, not of theme but counterpoint, begins with the consequent phrase of the Luke theme, whose descending bass lines up with that of *Kings Row*. As a matter of topical reference, however, the steady tread of a descending bass is more allusive to the "Pomp and Circumstance" topos reproduced in innumerable pieces by Elgar and Walton.
57. Closer still is Korngold's theme for *The Prince and the Pauper* (1937), which shares with *Star Wars* what Richards (2016) calls a developing periodic structure, in which a small element of variation is built into the unfolding of the theme itself. As for *Kings Row*—the theme arguably has more in common on a large-scale structural basis with Korngold's own title for *The Private Lives of Elizabeth and Essex* (1939) than it does with *Star Wars*. On the structural makeup of these, and Korngold's melodies in general, see Lehman (2020).
58. Ross (2016).
59. In his nuanced and sympathetic consideration of John Williams's referentiality, Jeremy Orosz considers the *Star Wars* series at length. He argues that, compared to Episodes IV–VI, the Prequels host "passages that owe more plainly a debt to other sources" (2015, 316). To the author's ears, this debt is not as plain as Orosz casts it. The linkages he asserts between Duel of the Fates and Battle of the Heroes and parts of Dvořák's Ninth Symphony are structurally shallower and less audibly manifest than those derivations from Holst and Stravinsky he discusses in the Original Trilogy.
60. Compare "Chase Through Coruscant" with "Night Fight" from *Crouching Tiger, Hidden Dragon*; "Padmé's Ruminations" with "The Wheat" from *Gladiator* and "Gloradin" from *Heat*; and "Anakin's Dark Deeds" with *The Fellowship of the Ring*, "Three Is Company."
61. The Imperial Ostinato owes some of its strident character to the B-theme in the "Mars" movement from Holst's *The Planets*. The resemblance is most apparent after Rehearsal Number 4, when the horn motif emerges—a loose melodic model for the properly leitmotivic Imperial Motif. Other aspects of the ostinato have precedents in scores Williams worked on right before *Star Wars*. The "Augurs" chord is a considerably more literal aspect of the Shark theme from *Jaws*—compare Stravinsky's $E\flat^{7}|F\flat$ polychord with *Jaws*' characteristic $E\flat^{7}|E \leftrightarrow E^{7}|F$ oscillation. Though less specifically allusive, *Black Sunday* is profuse with a kind of pan-Stravinskian, jerkily octatonic writing that the composer would also integrate into *Close Encounters*; see especially the cues "The Blimp and the Bomb" and "The Explosion." To a degree, Stravinskian octatonicism was in the air in Hollywood at this time; several roughly contemporaneous scores by Jerry Goldsmith have comparably *Rite*-aided passages—*Beneath the Planet of the Apes, Capricorn One*, and *The Omen*, for instance.
62. Rinzler (2007, 246).
63. See also the cue "The Desert," which is a close paraphrase of the introduction to *The Rite*'s second half.
64. Orosz notes that this obstreperous ostinato is "unmistakably based on *The Rite*" and cites a number of subsequent manifestations in Episode IV's score (2015, 315).
65. Examples as they appear on OSTs include ESB, "Luke's Escape" [3:00] and "Luke's First Crash" [8:10]; ROTJ, "Fight with TIE Fighters" [8:00]; and AOTC, "Jango's Escape" [0:43] and "Entrance of the Monsters" [5:46].

66. Interestingly, this musical plot and the dramatic arc of the scene it follows are not in a one-to-one relationship. The objective peril Anakin and Obi-Wan face has *not* decreased by the sequence's end; the brightening of harmony after the 6:07 mark in "They're Coming Around" seems to signal Anakin's arrival to save the day, not a resolution of their predicament. It will be up to the next cue, 1m4 "Get 'Em R2," for the issue of the buzz droids to be resolved, handily, with the first new statement of the Rebel Fanfare [7:02] in twenty-three years
67. It helps that there is a terrific leitmotivic payoff to this cue: a galloping statement of the Force at the set piece's climax [1:42:33].
68. Lucas (2001).
69. Rinzler (2005a, 221).
70. James Clarke describes this rhyming tendency in explicitly symphonic terms: "Lucas often uses the [serialized structure of the franchise] like a symphony by repeating and reconfiguring moments from one episode in other episodes" (2002, 62).
71. Like the Stravinsky-sourced Imperial Ostinato, the sonorities that Williams has called his "Planets chords" stem from a specific and memorable section of the work, in this case the volcanic C-A♭-D♭-G tetrachords that end the "Mars" movement. Williams's are similarly voiced D♭|G simultaneities. The 1983 interview with Bob Grace in the *Houston Chronicle* in which Williams mentions those chords is useful in showing the composer clearing up quite definitively—and perhaps self-defensively—that this reference was intentional.
72. Quoted from 20th Century Fox and Lucasfilm [Star Wars Episode I EPK] (1999).
73. For a richly detailed examination of Anakin's theme, see Eschenfelder (2019, 104–124).
74. Conor Power (2025) notes that "nostalgia is selective" in the Sequels, and that "it was only the sounds of the esteemed and increasingly idealized original trilogy that were [deemed by Abrams and co.] worth reviving."
75. Dan Golding offers an account of the need to balance residual nostalgia for the Original Trilogy against what he calls the "Prequel Problem," noting that "the vehement rejection of the prequels across large sections of the moviegoing public mean that selling *Star Wars* in 2015 meant weaponizing nostalgia," which involved not only the use of an "idealized love of the original *Star Wars* films . . . [but also] subtly pointing to the shortcomings of the prequel trilogy" (2019, 50–62).
76. One especially apt rhyme is the music for Kylo Ren's reaction after realizing he fell for Luke's ploy in *The Last Jedi* [2:18:30]. This passage, stuttering with rage and regret, clearly echoes the brass explosion that characterizes Anakin's state of mind in *Revenge of the Sith* after his massacre of the Separatists [1:41:13]. That passage in turn is one of several in Episode III whose hammering minor triads evoke Tchaikovsky, in particular *Romeo and Juliet* and the *Manfred Symphony*. Caschetto (2018) also notes this connection.
77. On the "Dies Irae" in *Star Wars*, see Ludwig (2025, 211–224) and Carberry (2024, 72).
78. Quoted in "Endlessly Compelling" (20th Century Fox and Lucasfilm [Star Wars Episode I EPK], (1999).
79. Rinzler (2005b, 16).
80. On the plangent associations of the $\sharp\hat{4}$–$\hat{3}$ motion in screen music, see Osborn (2021).
81. Technically this is the second time the Force theme overpowered Palpatine, as a comparable juxtaposition occurs at the climax of *Return of the Jedi*. Although the Episode IX leitmotivic clash is certainly rousing, "The Emperor's Death" from Episode VI is more artfully integrated into the musical prose of the cue.

Chapter 3

1. Godsall (2019, 66). Although Godsall's discussion centers on Michael Giacchino, a composer who relishes a good Easter egg, he also touches on Williams's auto-allusions, including the scene in question from *E.T.: The Extra-Terrestrial.*
2. Another musical Easter egg in *The Last Jedi*—a diegetic snatch of Williams's theme from Robert Altman's *The Long Goodbye* on an out-of-frame piano [1:07:42]—only raises further questions!
3. An example in Wagner's own output is his self-citation of *Tristan und Isolde* when that tragic tale is mentioned in *Die Meistersinger*. Many other composers in Wagner's wake quoted his music, both to affectionate and derisive effect. Debussy, for example, mocked *Tristan* in the middle of his "Golliwog's Cakewalk." Nowhere was Wagner quotation done to more incisive effect than in travesties like Fauré's "Souvenirs de Bayreuth," a set of piano miniatures that ironed out the *Ring*'s musical prose into foursquare dance tunes, and in doing so drained Wagner's revolutionary idiom

of no small amount of mythic pomposity. Though less sardonic, the translation of Williams's *Star Wars* themes into disco tracks by Meco (1977) effects a similar de-mythification.

4. See Bribitzer-Stull (2015, 1–30) for an overview.
5. As with all the concepts in this chapter drawn from the study of language, there is an enormous philosophical discourse surrounding use and mention. For a summary of the subject and its relation to quotation more generally, see Cappelen, Lepore, and McKeever (2023). See also Christensen (1967) and Saka (1998).
6. Grey (1996, 95).
7. See, for example, Washington (1998) and Devitt and Sterelny (1999, 39–41).
8. Justin London's (2000) essay "Leitmotifs and Musical Reference in the Classical Film Score" stands as one of the few studies of leitmotif from the perspective of the philosophy of language. London considers these musical entities in terms of Saul Kripke's notion of the *rigid designator*—in essence, a theory of proper names. More useful than the rigid designator concept, which fits uncomfortably with the mutable and expressive materials of a film soundtrack, is London's discussion of the conditions under which leitmotifs come to designate anything at all, rigidly or not.
9. Interestingly, the *Star Wars* cue that this sprightly variant of Yoda's theme most resembles, "Training a Jedi" [ESB, 6m4], was unused. The *E.T.* reference could thus be read as a second opportunity for Williams to "Prokofify" the theme. This repurposing of cut material from one score into a subsequent one has many precedents in Hollywood, including Steiner and Korngold (Winters 2025, 102–103). While repurposing via tracking abounds in the Skywalker Saga, the only apparent instance of *composed* reintegration is the recovery of some strident measures from an alternate of Episode VII's "Torn Apart" into Episode IX's "Rey's Incredible Hand" [39:52–40:09].
10. In linguistics, the dichotomy is strictly analytical and value-free, though it is notable that mention is often demonstrated with reference to taboo words and phrases.
11. DeVoto (2004, 12).
12. Adorno and Eisler's broadside against Hollywood leitmotif reads like a simplification of the more nuanced—and ultimately far more damning—critique Adorno would level against leitmotif in the pages of *In Search of Wagner* (1952). There, Adorno claims Wagner's "supposed psychological variations [of leitmotifs] involve only a change of lighting," stymied by a developmental "inflexibility that sets limits to and even negates [their supposed] psychological dynamism," and bound to a necessity of external commentary (e.g., thematic catalogs) that belies the ultimate "bankruptcy of Wagner's own aesthetics of immediate unity" (35–36).
13. Adorno and Eisler (2007 [1947], 3).
14. From time to time, whiffs of this elitism still manifest in modern scholarship, as in Abbate's otherwise penetrating treatment of Wagner's early use of recurrent themes in *Der fliegende Holländer*, in which she describes leitmotif as "music's most familiar and least interesting narrative competence" (1996, 86).
15. Today's film musicologists are unlikely to defer to Adorno and Eisler's pronouncements. James Buhler's essay "Star Wars, Music, and Myth" is a partial exception. Though it bears no trace of the Frankfurt school's resentment of popular culture, in other respects Buhler's assessment is thoroughly and explicitly Adornian, deeming Williams's treatment of leitmotif as inorganic, nondevelopmental, and ideologically suspect. However, by positioning Wagnerian leitmotivicism as an ideal that Williams's regressive scores fail to attain, Buhler elides how all those critiques were lobbed with even more ferocity by Adorno against Wagner himself. Franklin (2017, 27–30) also detects and carefully unpacks this tension.
16. Abbate takes an especially strong version of this counterintuitive position, arguing that "Wagner's motifs have no referential meaning; they may, and of course do, absorb meaning at exceptional and solemn moments . . . but unless purposely maintained in this *artificial state* [italics added], they shed their specific poetic meaning and revert to their natural state as musical thoughts" (1989c, 45). Abbate's reasoning here and in other publications (1989a, 1989b, 1996) is more subtle than can be adequately summarized here. But it is worth noting that her skeptical position is *not* aligned with formalist or Adornian "symphonic" listening values. Quite the opposite—she holds that the notion of Wagnerian symphonism and the values it entails (organicism, autonomy, unity) is an agenda-driven fantasy, one "at best naïve, at worst dishonest" (1989b, 104).
17. The use/mention distinction is helpful in articulating the long-discussed (and often very fuzzy) opposition of Wagnerian "true" leitmotif with the "reminiscence motif" (*Erinnerungsmotiv*) and affiliated para-leitmotivic categories. With respect to the music of Williams, these issues

of lexical precision/mutability and developmental depth/superficiality have been broached by Anatone (2023, 259–262) and Power (2025).

18. Saka (1998, 113).
19. Thorau (2009, 114).
20. Dahlhaus and Deathridge (1984, 114).
21. Lippincott (1977).
22. The principal leitmotifs are LUKE, REBEL FANFARE, FORCE, LEIA, VADER, HAN AND LEIA, YODA, EMPEROR, ANAKIN, DUEL OF THE FATES, ANAKIN AND PADMÉ, KYLO REN (A, B), REY (A, B, C), RESISTANCE, POE, TENSION, FRIENDSHIP, VICTORY, and PSALM OF THE SITH.
23. The chromatic undulations in "Map Scene" are followed by the famous FORCE leitmotif; quite often, new ideas are granted leitmotivic legitimacy by coming into contact with other, more established themes, an idea examined more closely in Chapter 6.
24. Fittingly, these issues of identification and categorization of leitmotifs seem endemic to themes for navigational MacGuffins in this series. In *The Rise of Skywalker*, for example, the heroes pursue *two* objects—a WAYFINDER that points to the Sith home-world of Exegol and the magical DAGGER that in turn points to *it*. These receive a pair of incidental motifs that, by themselves, are inconspicuous in presentation and infrequent in occurrence. But while too paltry to be treated as leitmotifs individually, together the two ideas share symbolic and harmonic features, sufficiently so to warrant a kind of *meta*-leitmotivic category: SITH ARTIFACTS. The collapsing of these related ideas into a broader leitmotivic species concept is not so unlike the "lumping" that taxonomists engage when assigning morphologically unlike organisms to the same species based on a deeper genetic identity.
25. "Rey Awakens" (3m28) is in fact a rewrite of an earlier cue for the sequence, "Rey + Luke" (0m4), which begins with a much more direct restatement of music from Episode VII's "The Map Scene."
26. A classic example is the shift in English of the meaning of "awful" from awe-inspiring to intensely bad. For an accessible introduction to this subject in linguistics, see McWhorter (2016).
27. Buhler (2000, 44).
28. Ibid., 47.
29. Lippincott (1977).
30. No matter how rigorously applied, leitmotivic labeling has *always* produced ambiguities and mismatches. The literature on the *Ring* is filled with feverish hemming and hawing about certain motivic renditions—ask a Wagnerian about the "Renunciation of Love" theme in Act I of *Die Walküre* and expect an impressive display of hermeneutic contortionism. The words of the eminent British writer on Wagner, Ernest Newman, are worth remembering: "For the composer [of leitmotivic music], the range of psychological reference of a motive was far wider, and the terms of reference far subtler, than our ready-made tickets can provide for" (1991 [1949], 508–509).
31. Sideways (2020).
32. A coda that encapsulates all major leitmotifs is, unsurprisingly, an echt-Wagnerian touch. No film to date can quite match the thematic abundance of the finale to *Götterdämmerung*, whose world-ending cataclysm lasts eighty-one measures and features at least sixteen distinct leitmotifs.
33. Lippincott (1977).
34. It is with some irony that in 2022, Williams wrote a new leitmotif for the character, for the Disney+ series *Obi-Wan Kenobi*. He is reported to have claimed "I just want to write Benny a theme," implying the old knight lacked one before (Breznican 2022). Whether this was an acknowledgment of the semiotic evasiveness of the FORCE theme, or a case of leitmotivic retconning (or amnesia), the result is functionally irrelevant. The 2022 OBI-WAN theme is a pale reflection of its inspired predecessor.
35. Willman (2024).
36. Charlie Brigden says of the theme that it "acts as a subterfuge of sorts, overtly creating the image of the beautiful fairy tale princess who must be rescued and hiding the fact that while Leia is a beautiful princess, she is far, far away from a damsel in distress" (2020).
37. Bribitzer-Stull (2015, 64–65).
38. Speaking on Wagner's leitmotifs, Carl Dahlhaus and John Deathridge observe that "it is seldom wise to take the earliest form in which a theme or motif appears as necessarily its primary form, from which all subsequent forms derive as secondary variations. Rather, they are all different impressions of the same material, and all principally equal in status; but each impression throws

one particular feature of a situation, one trait of a character or one element of an idea into musical relief" (1984, 112).

39. Link (2009a, 185).
40. Neo-Riemannian theorists would analyze this as an instance of an **RP** transformation, which is analytical shorthand for "go to triad's Relative major/minor twin, then shift to triad of Parallel mode. For a detailed explanation of pantriadic chromaticism and neo-Riemannian theory in the context of film music, see Lehman (2018b, Ch. 3).
41. The transformed version of the SPEAR motif into WOTAN's LOVE motif in the third act of *Die Walküre* is the Wagnerian epitome of this technique.
42. These uses of the DEATH STAR motif in *A New Hope* occur at 8:44, 36:50, 40:56, and 56:58.
43. These two Dark Side cave sequences are musically affiliated in a whole host of ways. The most apparent connections are timbral: for example, they both showcase abyssal clarinet gurgles and muted trombone portamenti, and both feature the most conspicuous usage of synthesizer in their respective scores. Harmonically, the linkage also extends immediately *prior* to the entry into the caves: a sustained and tonally unmoored half-diminished chord (based on F in ESB, E in TLJ) induces an appropriately woozy state for both. The differences are marked too, particularly in the much leaner and motivically less-involved scoring of *The Last Jedi*'s cue.
44. Particularly illustrative is the trajectory of motifs for REY and KYLO REN across their various melees. Compare motivic interactions in their first duel in Episode VII [1:55:19] to the side-by-side fight in VIII [1:45:47] and full-fledged team-up in IX [1:51:30].
45. One rule-proving exception is the "Falcon Flight" [7:51] from *Rise of Skywalker*—clearly more of a fun-filled romp than an emotional journey told through action, Williams nevertheless constructs the short sequence as a delirious medley of rapid-fire leitmotifs—EMPEROR, RESISTANCE, HEROICS, REBEL FANFARE, and more.
46. In order to determine the prevalence of leitmotifs, I tracked thematic usage with a stopwatch while screening the most recent digital release of each film. Timing percentages refer only to dramatic action, beginning after the Main Title and concluding before the End Credits. Number of leitmotif statements composed refers to *all* music written by Williams, including cut and revised cues. Runtime reflects music *only* as heard in the final cut of the movie; artificially tracked, repeated, and edited cues are therefore included, while cut or rewritten ones are excluded. Totals are rounded to the nearest minute or percentage point.
47. The huge number of leitmotivic instances in *The Last Jedi* comes in no small part from the heavy repetition of the FORCE theme (30 iterations) and even more so the ubiquitous TENSION motif (at least 40 iterations).
48. See Huvet (2020, 113–114) for an alternative tallying of themes.
49. Precedents for this lugubrious topic are numerous. Low, chromatic, non-periodic string writing is of course associated with recitative since the Baroque era. Vocally unaccompanied versions of the trope become a mainstay of German Romantic opera, with such sinister scene-setting music as can be found in *Der Freischütz* and Wagner's *Lohengrin* and *Siegfried*. These latter depictions of the grotesque and dreadful arguably partake of the larger "ombra" topic, a kind of blanket category for all manner of spooky, sublime, and sickening instrumental writing from the eighteenth century onward. See McClellan (2014) on the ombra topic more generally, and Rosar (2010) for importation into Hollywood.
50. See Goldmark (2005) for historical and aesthetic background and Audissino (2020) for a rehabilitation of the term.
51. See Lehman (2018b, 27–28, 246n32).
52. This BRUTE tetrachord has a number of interesting properties. It has the set-class 4-19 (0347) and belongs to both the octatonic and hexatonic collections. In one inversion, it can sound like a triad with both a major and minor third. In another, a minor triad with a dissonant $\flat\hat{6}$ and $\sharp\hat{7}$—this gives it the useful ability to suggest a dissonant juxtaposition of i and ♭vi chords. It is also a key constituent of the so-called "alpha-chord," a Bartókian configuration of the octatonic scale generated from two stacked diminished seventh chords. See Lendvai (1971, 40–50). The alpha-chord has been used as a basis for describing much of Williams's action harmony; see, for example Richards (2021) and Sewell (2022).
53. Heine (2018, 121–122). The progression, which often but not always bears a i↔♭vi harmonic function, has a rich pedigree in Hollywood in connoting evil, an association that traces back to Wagner's *Ring* with its TARNHELM motif. The progression's usage in screen music has been scrutinized by Bribitzer-Stull (2015, 131–155) and Murphy (2023).
54. Lehman (2018b, 46–47, 81–83).

55. The passage also quickly alternates between instrumental groupings and choirs every few measures—a modular approach to orchestration that Nicholas Kmet has noted is characteristic of the Prequel trilogy (2018, 218–226). Writing about another representative cue in Episode I ("Talk of Podracing"), Kmet notes that "no instrument gets a complete statement of any melody; instead, the melodies are fragmented as they are passed throughout the orchestra. The accompaniment is similarly fragmented, as no single texture is utilized for more than three bars at a time. The result is a highly cellularized cue, constantly evolving as it weaves around the dialogue heavy sequence" (219).
56. See, for example, triplet trumpet cascades in Giacchino (*Rogue One*, "Scrambling the Rebel Fleet," 1:25), Powell (*Solo*, "Reminiscence Therapy," 4:42), and Haab (*Battlefront II*, "The Battle Unfolds," 4:22).
57. For background on these individual topoi, see Rosand (2001), Monelle (2000, 66–76; 2006, 129–130) and Murphy (2014a).
58. On occasion, however, an incidental motif might be "promoted" to leitmotif status, provided it is repeated in another film with sufficient verve and differentiation from its originary source. This happens, for example, with the DESCENT motif in *Attack of the Clones*, which graduates from an unassuming detail in two cues in Episode II to a film-defining theme in the already discussed "Lament" from Episode III.
59. Scanlon (1983).
60. Ben Burtt noted the singularity of this sequence too: "When it comes to this hypercritical moment in the duel between father and son, the music was more important in delivering the emotional satisfaction of the moment than the sound effects." See Rinzler (2013, 282).
61. The use of homophonic slabs of pantriadic chromaticism as a marker of the numinous has ample precedents in cinema; this sequence in *Jedi* suggests in particular the CRUCIFIXION theme from Alfred Newman's *The Robe.*
62. See Richards (2016).
63. For further exploration of Williams's techniques of thematic construction, see Zacharopoulos (2017).
64. See Richards (2024).
65. Ibid. (83).
66. This is in fact the case with "It Can't Be" from *Revenge of the Sith.* The sharply etched passacaglia portion is preceded by forty measures of more amorphous and unpredictable (though still carefully shaped) mood-setting music.
67. Dahlhaus (1989, 200).
68. Thomas Grey (1996) offers a useful reading of Wagnerian form through the metaphor of the maze and guiding thread, a conceit around which much leitmotivic reception was oriented historically. To approach a *Musikdrama*, one might try to view the whole musical text (maze) as if from above—a "tectonic" perspective that the formally irregular and non-hierarchical organization of Wagner's music dramas make difficult to sustain. Alternatively, one might concentrate "on the immediate experience of threading one's way through [the chain of musical events] as they occur," as though there were a single, necessary route through the piece. This accords with the hypotactic mode of listening, which also encounters difficulties in Wagner's (and Williams's) music. Last, one might adopt a paratactic ("associative") stance, where the musical maze might lead one down untold possible paths and into all sorts of loops and dead ends. Listening in this way is nonprescriptive, even nonlinear: "the experience of such form or process is determined more than ever by choices and interpretations made by the listener" (208–209).
69. Interestingly, the KYLO REN C motif was originally the sonic insignia of the FIRST ORDER in *The Force Awakens*, but in *Last Jedi* drifts away from its initial significatory task, becoming another component of Kylo Ren's musical personality.
70. The Episode VII End Credits were themselves adapted from a combination of two cues, 6m54B ("Remove these Restraints") and 7m67 "Rey vs. Ren," plus the concert arrangements for REY and RESISTANCE themes. This derivational chain explains why "Revisiting Snoke" ends where it does, in C♯ minor.
71. Franklin (2007, 97).

Chapter 4

1. See Rinzler (2007, 246) and Lippincott (1977).
2. Buhler (2000, 53).

3. Buhler finds in the THRONE ROOM theme a Mahlerian urge "to evolve and expose different facets of its character" over the course of its two dozen measures (2000, 52). As we have seen, this is typical of Williams's melodies for the series—they are motivically economical, non-repetitive, a model of "composing out" of an initial idea in an inventive and unpredictable way.
4. That conception is the Adornian one introduced in Chapter 1. Buhler's essay is patently Adornian, both in its social-ideological critique of *Star Wars* and the kinds of musical details he chooses to emphasize or exclude from analysis.
5. Buhler (2000, 52–53).
6. This tendency is as much the upshot of the scarcity of studiable scores as it is any principled aversion to music analysis. Until recently, high-quality analysis generally followed from meticulous consultation with archival and manuscript sources; this is the model behind the excellent single-score monographs published by the Scarecrow Press, for instance. Today, however, many notable film scores are garnering professionally edited and commercially available print editions, such as those prepared by Omni Music Publishing and Chris Siddal Publishing, making deep musicological dives possible for a much wider audience. Sadly, no such study scores exist, or appear forthcoming, for *Star Wars*.
7. A third, more extended treatment of this proto-THRONE ROOM motif can be heard in the original version of the Binary Sunset cue, appearing on the 1997 ANH Special Edition, Track 13 [1:20 and 1:37]
8. The THRONE ROOM has a contrasting middle section that corresponds exactly to the B-section of the main LUKE theme, as heard in the "Main Title." Williams would later claim that this section was actually written before the "Main Title," itself purportedly among the last pieces he composed for the score (Pacific Symphony 2020). This story of retroactive assimilation contradicts the composer's attested workflow: themes-first, underscore-second. It is also difficult to square with the fact that this particular melody's B-section occurs as an appendage to LUKE leitmotif in the action cue "The Swashbucklers" [1:28:23]. Williams offers an alternative account of the genesis of the LUKE theme in Elley (1978, 21–23).
9. Strictly speaking, Williams does develop the THRONE ROOM once more in *A New Hope*, though not in the score itself but in his concert arrangement, "The Throne Room and Finale." This piece includes an entire new rotation through the theme in G and E♭ major, as well as a small developmental section in which the melody is fragmented, sequenced, and allowed to interact with the PLANETARY DESCENT motif from the end of "Imperial Attack." (Notably, that development transforms the THRONE ROOM into something very similar to the octave-leaping WOTAN'S LOVE motif from *Die Walküre*—perhaps the only literal quotation of Wagner in the whole series.)
10. A similar line of reasoning can be applied to virtually every musical idea in the series, to limited profit. For example, what if the THRONE ROOM had served as the basis for one of those numerous fanfares for the Republic's capital in *The Phantom Menace*; would this not have nicely set up that political and moral "fallen" state that the Alliance in Episode IV sought to restore? Or alternatively, Williams could have seeded some of its elements into *Revenge of the Sith*, a hint at the first embers of the Rebel Alliance. The leitmotivic technique is uniquely susceptible to such retroactive "what if" scenarios; if taken as anything other than an idle thought experiment, such counterfactuals lead to interpretive paralysis.
11. The melodic routine of perfect fourths coming in quick succession at different transposition levels constitutes something of a minor motif (a "leit-intervallic" pattern, perhaps) in the Original Trilogy, always connected with scenes of battle and likely derived from the very first, quartally oriented measures of the Main Title. Other notable examples can be found in Episode IV [1:46:17, 1:48:04], Episode V [24:25, 29:28, 1:48:03], and Episode VI [33:36, 1:34:10]. It is hard to pinpoint just one source of this technique: quartal/quintal stacks occur in almost every one of Williams's stylistic touchstones—Korngold, Walton, Hindemith, Vaughan Williams, and Bartók especially.
12. I borrow the phrase "melodic concatenation" from Jack Gottlieb, who used it to describe a process in Leonard Bernstein's music in which a new theme "indirectly links back to a primary source through a series of evolved steps" (1964, 3).
13. Williams was not quite done with the THRONE ROOM after the Battle of Endor. When he prepared a concert version of *A New Hope*'s "Throne Room and Finale" in 1978, he replaced the generically Waltonian final cadence of the End Credits with an explicit citation of the THRONE ROOM melody (cf. "Spitfire Prelude and Fugue"). That revised ending was then adapted for Episode VI's End Credits. In this way, the THRONE ROOM is the last leitmotif to be heard during the Original Trilogy. Hardly a one-cue wonder any longer!

14. Macdonald (2001).
15. The sense that film musical themes can have a will of their own is an understudied topic. Ongoing work by Laine Gruver aims to bring established theories of musical agency into contact with the study of leitmotif.
16. Thomas (1991). Lurking in the background of Williams's invocation of *2001* is his awareness of—and likely sympathetic frustration regarding—Kubrick's infamous discarding of Alex North's original score.
17. Several promising approaches to analyzing thematic transformation, which for reasons of space or obscurity are not emphasized in this chapter, nevertheless deserve mention. *Contour theory* is the study of melodic shape, irrespective of specific tonal context or intervallic quantity. Preliminary findings within the *Star Wars* corpus appear in Hartsough (2023). *Pitch-class set theory* flattens horizontal melodic content and vertical harmonies alike into abstract collections, again without any assumption of tonal function. Set theory has not been applied consistently to this series, though the richly complex scales and chords that Williams employs do have referential and indeed developmental propensities; the in-depth analyses by Sewell of individual cues reveal many such complex procedures. Similarly interested in stripping away surface features to reveal deep connections, but now with respect to harmony rather than melody, is a system called *neo-Riemannian theory*—sometimes called transformation theory or pan-triadic theory. The methodology can characterize, for instance, a harmonic equivalence between the harmonic progression of the Rebel Fanfare and Imperial Motif, both effecting **RP/PR** loops (a specific type of chord-to-chord transformation). Another implement of potential use is *Schenkerian theory*, specifically its notion of "concealed repetition"—that is, the replication of pitch or contrapuntal patterns at various levels of linear-prolongational structure. This approach, though well tested on the Classical repertoire, has not seen any application to Williams's film music.
18. Heard no more, that is, in *A New Hope*. Recall the lesson of the Throne Room: even throwaway themes may be resurrected. In this case, That's no moon turns up in *Return of the Jedi* as the harmonic basis of "Battle Plans" [49:47], a cue whose theme bears the same planing chords, the same harmonization of an octatonic melodic skeleton, and the same layering of melody over a sharply dissonating bass. To the extent that any such resemblance could be accidental, it must be the result either of temp tracking (always a possibility after ANH) or a common musical ancestor. That ancestor could plausibly be either the Imperial Motif or Rebel Fanfare, both of which are based on parallel voice-leading between m3-related triads, and both of which are heard in proximity to That's No Moon in its original context. Another reference may be Leighton Lucas's score for the British war film *Ice Cold in Alex*—itself manifestly influenced by the ur-source of Holst's "Mars."
19. For an analysis of "Jango's Escape" as an exemplar of Williams's post-millennial style of action scoring, see Lehman (2021, 140–143).
20. Cadences of mixed authentic/plagal functionality in the Classical repertoire have been theorized by Swinden (2005), Rodgers (2021), and Caplin (2024, 528).
21. This contrapuntal section is audible on Episode II OST track 12, between 3:46–4:05.
22. A full sense of the editorial farrago that is Episode II's score requires more space than can be provided here. Happily, Huvet (2020, esp. 211–215 and 240–245) provides a comprehensive and deeply researched treatment of the confounding intersection of music and editing in this film. Huvet dedicates much attention to the impact of digital editing and the important role of the music editor Ken Wannberg in effectively "creating" film music. Huvet arrives at a similar conclusion regarding the semantic incoherence but *topical* appropriateness of the Arena March's placement in Episode III: "Le caractère martial et décidé de la fanfare s'accorde particulièrement avec la marche implacable de l'armée de Dark Vador et avec l'attitude résolue du personnage. Le rythme des pas des clones, calqué sur le tempo musical et marquant chaque temps de la mesure, suggère l'idée d'une avancée inexorable et sinistre."
23. Of the various ways Williams's music might be manipulated in editing, none is more injurious to developmental logic than excision. The most flagrant example is the treatment of large swathes of the Episode IX score. An entire new Heroics leitmotif is practically eradicated, and not one of the many choral cues channeling the Duel of the Fates (Chant) made it into the final cut.
24. Bond (2003, 11).
25. Byrd (1997, 18).
26. There are roughly a dozen cases of contrapuntal combination of prominent leitmotifs in the series: Leia + Rebel Fanfare (ANH, End Credits); Yoda + Rebel Fanfare (ESB, End Credits);

Luke + Vader (ROTJ, "Through The Flames"); Duel of the Fates + Vader (TPM, "The Great Dual[sic]"); Duel of the Fates + Force (TPM, "Blowups"); Anakin and Padmé + Vader (AOTC, End Credits); Anakin and Padmé + Force (ROTS, "I Am The Senate"); Vader + Funeral (ROTS, "Padmé's Funeral"); Rey + Force (TFA, End Credits); Finn + Poe (TFA, End Credits); and Rey + Force (TLJ, "Old Friends"). There are likely further instances of Rey, Ren, and Emperor motifs in juxtaposition in *The Rise of Skywalker*, given cues like 7m3 "More Fight," 7m24 "Hero Fight," and 8m5a "Mixing Themes" that we can hear, if imperfectly, in the final film.

27. In her analysis of thematic family relationships in the Original Trilogy, Irena Paulus makes a dubious claim that "Leia's theme is a backward form of Ben's [the Force] theme" (2000, 168). This would indeed be an elegant connection were Paulus's evidence for retrogradation stronger. As it stands, to make one theme behave like a reversal of the other, she ignores rhythm, mode, interval quality, and scale-degree identity—not to mention the not-irrelevant first downbeat pitch of the Force theme.
28. Richards (2020b).
29. A strain of overeager hermeneutics was especially detectable after the release of *The Force Awakens*, with many fan communities drawing conclusions as to Rey's parentage by selective analysis of the structure of her theme. Considering that Rey's Palpatinian lineage was an eleventh-hour decision during the making of *The Rise of Skywalker*, any attestations to Williams's intentional planting of thematic secrets prior to 2019 are untenable. But they do bespeak an intense and often ingenious mode of engagement among a community of passionate listeners. YouTube provides a repository of such at-the-time captivating analyses. See, for example, Slattery (2015), Disinterested (2016), Sideways (2017), The Filmmaking and Fandom Station (2017), and RedCaio (2019).
30. Hepokoski (2010, 26).
31. Schneller (2014). See also Lofthouse (2024) for a recent application of teleological genesis to film music, John Williams included.

Chapter 5

1. Compare the melodic and modal progression in the chorus of "Victory Celebration" [$\hat{1}$-$\hat{7}$-$\hat{5}$ over VI-v-III chords] with the high point of "It's Working" from *The Phantom Menace* [$\hat{1}$-$\hat{7}$-$\hat{5}$, VI-VII-III] and the end of the antecedent phrase of "Across the Stars" from *Attack of the Clones* [$\hat{1}$-$\hat{7}$-$\hat{5}$, VI-v-III].
2. Williams's self-described "Planets Chords"—repeated tutti sonorities of the type $D\flat^{(sus\sharp4)}$/G or $A\flat^{(sus\sharp4)}$/C) plainly modeled on Holst's "Mars"—are a good example. These almost always cadentially functioning harmonies appear throughout the movie, including early on (the end of the "Main Title"), midway through (the ends of "Burning Homestead" and "The Destruction of Alderaan"), and at its climax (the lead-up and explosive conclusion of the "Battle of Yavin"). See Grace (1983) for the composer's use of the phrase "Planets Chords."
3. The material associated with this race of diminutive scavengers is certainly distinctive: a long-breathed melody for solo English horn perched over an oompah-bass will tend to be. But the ideas that populate *A New Hope*'s Jawa-centric cues (2m2 and 2m3, "The Little People" and "More Little People") are leitmotivic in only a weak sense: they occur in a circumscribed portion of the film and are little disposed to variation of either structure or symbolism. It is more apt to see the Jawa music as a convergence of even smaller ideas—certain melodic turns, rhythmic gaits, and textural patterns that are more generally associated with the idea of "the Alien" in *A New Hope*.
4. While both extracts are demonstrably linked to the Jawas' music, neither so plainly spawned from the Strange germ as the serpentine tune from "The Water Snake." In this way, they are more representative of the technique of motivic seeding, pulling out a musical parameter or two without involving direct thematic replication or transformation.
5. This climax, with its staggered bass notes and tolling chordal slabs, makes quite explicit what had previously been a latent allusion to the theme to Holst's "Saturn" from his *Planets* suite.
6. Buckton (1980).
7. On Williams's use of modally inflected supertonics, both of which figure into Han and Leia's theme, see Schneller (2013, 64–68).
8. Readers unfamiliar with linear-reductive analysis might be befuddled by the Line diagram for this theme, as it encodes more information than necessary to appreciate just the motivic seed

under discussion and does so through the elegant but idiosyncratic stem-and-slur notational system of Schenkerian theory. For the curious, the seed constitutes a melodic "unfolding," a technique of melodically expanding an important harmonic interval—in this case the diminished third between A♭$_4$ and F♯$_4$—across two distinct linear streams of a compound melody.

9. When played against a tonic pedal, all three notes can occur simultaneously—a brief but sharply dissonant cluster of semitones, each with a unique scalar function.
10. See Kimmel (1980) and Kamien (1990).
11. The first notable purely harmonic motif in *Star Wars* is the B↔F oscillation at the end of Episode IV's "Imperial Attack" [7:20]. On the subject of this ear-catching tritone progression and its usage in scores for science fiction films, see Murphy (2006).
12. On the topic of absolute progressions in film generally, see Murphy (2014b, esp. 483–486) and Lehman (2018b, 75–76).
13. In the strictest terms, the arrival on the D chord behaves as an HC within the context of HAN AND LEIA's B-section, since it serves as the goal and form-functional conclusion of a discrete musical phrase. This is not to deny the rhetorical and structural might of V's resolution to I of G major, which is overwhelming—a PAC in effect if not morphology. (It is also short-lived, as the cue modulates to the End Credits' E♭ major via a plagal close a mere three measures later.) The boundary between 1) a half cadence whose ultimate dominant immediately and powerfully resolves to a tonic in the next phrase, and 2) an authentic cadence whose V→I progression elides two phrases, is a subtle and contentious one. See Burstein (2014) and Caplin (2024, 50–54 and *passim*).
14. Not pictured in Ex. 5.11 are the swirling figures occurring throughout the sequence, which elaborate—what else?—a diminished-third scale fragment. This idea, which suggests Mussorgsky's *Night on Bald Mountain*, constitutes a score-spanning mini-motif in its own right, occurring, among other places, right after VADER's theme in the "Carbon Freezing" sequence [1:36:44].
15. Another unambiguous statement of the VADER theme was cut from the film and possibly never recorded: the series' only true *major mode* rendition, played by celesta, at the conclusion of the Battle of Naboo (6m10, "Death of Darth Maul").
16. Though not mentioned in Joakim Tillman's (2018) essay on "The Villain's March Topic in John Williams's Film Music," the JAR JAR leitmotif shares a number of musical traits with his "Comic Villain" musical trope, in the same company as such shambolic tunes as the "March of the Villains" from *Superman* and Harry and Marv's theme from *Home Alone*. It is possible that those implausible resemblances between the "Imperial March" and Williams's music for the Gungan stem from an intermediary piece: Morton Gould's arrangement of Leon Jessel's "Parade of the Tin Soldiers." Williams knew this slice of light orchestral fare well, recording it for a Boston Pops album in 1992, *Joy to the World*; and several details beyond Gould's VADER-esque triadic outlines near the onset of the arrangement strongly evoke both Jar Jar's and Vader's materials. A second mediating reference (and possible source in turn for Gould) might be "The Battle and Defeat of Napoleon" from Zoltán Kodály's *Háry János*, another work Williams has channeled in the past (cf. certain set pieces from *Home Alone 2*). Mercifully, the Gungan's leitmotif exits the stage after Episode I, exchanged in Episode II by a few scattered passages of indistinct orchestral bumbling.
17. Listen closely to the bass line at 1:13:27 and the timpani solo at 1:56:28 of Episode IV, for example. Comparably allusive passages *post*-Vader occur throughout the Sequels too: notable sequences include "Jedi Steps," "The Spark," "Journey to Exegol" from Episodes VII, VIII, and IX, respectively. One could also point to Imperial sound-alikes in other Williams scores—the most suggestive being the main theme from *Nixon* (1996).
18. The name of this motif comes from Paul Dukas himself (Caballero 2004, 171–173). The *motif d'évocation* shares with the REBEL FANFARE its contour, rhythmic profile, and brassy orchestration. But, heeding the principle from Chapter 2, influence is always plural. In this case, there is also the aforementioned harmonic and intervallic derivation from the half-cadence in LUKE's theme, as well as a Holst-inspired fanfare from Leighton Lucas' score to *Ice Cold in Alex*, heard prominently in that film's Main Titles among other places. Many other such "resemblant FANFARES" may be found in assorted passages from William Schuman's Symphony No. 3; Hanson's Symphony No. 2 "Romantic" (noted by Orosz 2015, 305–306); Korngold's scores for *The Private Lives of Elizabeth and Essex* and *The Sea Hawk* (noted by Winters 2025, 120); most of Rózsa's scores for historical epics (*Ivanhoe*, *Ben Hur*, *El Cid*); and "The Hero at Battle" from Strauss's *Ein Heldenleben*.

Chapter 6

1. The study of narrative archetypes in instrumental music has enjoyed a resurgence thanks to work from scholars including Byron Almén and Michael Klein, with much of their conceptual apparatus being inspired by influential literary and semiotic theorists like Joseph Campbell and Northrop Frye. See, for example, Almén (2008) and Klein (2009). For an excellent overview of the application of narratology to screen music, see Reyland (2015).
2. Most notably, VADER's bridge motif is the basis of the "IT'S A TRAP!" theme heard at the commencement of the Battle of Endor [1:34:15].
3. Smiley (2015). Williams describes a similar workflow, with a few more musical specifics, in discussing the genesis of much of *Revenge of the Sith* backward from its big set pieces: "Lament," "Revenge of the Sith," and "The Immolation Scene." See Rinzler (2005b, 11–13).
4. Smiley (2015).
5. Almost every cue in Episode VII also has revisions, inserts, or alternates, sometimes as many as a half-dozen. When all these more textually tentative compositions are taken into account, *The Force Awakens* includes well over 150 cues.
6. For an analytical overview of these pieces, see Hull (2000), Bailey (1985), and Hepokoski (2010), respectively. Many of the macro-transformational categories introduced in Chapter 5 were devised specifically for late Romantic composers and have been applied to only a small corner of the repertoire as a result, one in which Liszt, Strauss, Bruckner, Mahler, and the Franck-school symphonists (d'Indy, Dukas, Chausson, etc.) also feature heavily.
7. See Adorno and Eisler (2007, 62–65).
8. Schoenberg (1975, 397). See Frisch (1990, 1–18) for a thorough examination of the concept, both in Schoenberg and later commentators and theorists like Adorno, Ratz, and Dahlhaus.
9. Developing variation is similar to the idea of *Fortspinnung* ("spinning out") used to characterize the motoric, motivically parsimonious impulse in the music of High Baroque composers. In both Fortspinnung and developing variation, there is a de-emphasis of symmetrical phrase structures in favor of spontaneity and continuity. Fortspinnung tends more toward affective and rhythmic uniformity than the Romantic idea of developing variation. As such, its best application in *Star Wars* is for spans of deliberately neo-Baroque music, the kinds Williams is fond of for battle-preparing scenes—"Leia's Instructions" in ESB [23:58], the aforementioned PREPARING TO JUMP in VI, and numerous cues in the Sequel Trilogy derived from the RESISTANCE march (e.g., TFA [1:33:06], TLJ [27:59], TROS [1:36:30]). Of course, in film, something is always ordained—timing and drama—making it rare that any motif is "taken for a spin" for very long. For a comparison of theoretical attitudes toward Fortspinnung versus development, see Mutch (2018).
10. Schoenberg does not mince his words: "Why there is lesser merit in such a [Wagnerian sequence-based] procedure than in variation is obvious, because variation requires a new and special effort. But the damage of this inferior method of construction to the art of composing was considerable. With very few exceptions, all followers and even opponents of Wagner became addicts of this more primitive technique: Bruckner, Hugo Wolf, Richard Strauss, and even Debussy and Puccini" (1975, 129).
11. Richards (2016, [6], [45–52]). Developing themes often progress in a more formally fluid manner than their non-developing counterparts, even in their most definitive and closed forms. As noted in Chapter 3, Richards distinguishes developing forms with other, more well-theorized melodic paradigms, which, rather than composing out an initial basic idea, involve strong contrasts against it (as in a period) or repetitions thereof (as in a sentence). This aligns closely with Schoenberg's own conception of intra-thematic development (Frisch 1990, 9).
12. Even more systematic in its motivic manipulations than "Approaching the Death Star" is *Jedi*'s "Faking the Code" [53:10]. With its cascade of FORCE and VADER variants, this suspenseful cue finds not only its melodic content but also its tonal design based on those themes, changing keys according to the chromatic logic of "The Imperial March."
13. Parker (2011).
14. Collins (2022).
15. There is a less common variant of the theme, heard most clearly during YODA's thematic apotheosis in *Empire* [1:12:18]. This version of the consequent phrase makes essentially the same climb but with a more sequential and tonal forward drive, produced through the inclusion of pattern-filling melodic $\hat{8}$-$\hat{7}$ motion and a ii-V-I cadential progression. In both versions of the consequent phrase, the lydian $II^{\sharp}$ chord is neutralized toward the end, reverting to the diatonic supertonic chord.

16. For more detail into the construction of this theme, see Zacharopoulos (2017, 246).
17. Wise (1983, 20) uses this motif to illustrate how "Williams' thematic material is very carefully worked out," but somewhat implausibly derives it from a mis-transcribed countermelody to LEIA's theme in *A New Hope*. Adams refers to it as the "Brother and Sister motif" and correctly describes it as an outgrowth of Yoda's theme (1999, 47). Like Adams, Huvet dubs it the "motif de l'autre Skywalker" (2020, 72–74). And while not explicitly associating the idea with YODA, she, like Wise, treats the "Yoda's Scene" cue as an exemplar of Williams's approach to continuous transformation, and the way the composer elegantly "braids and superimposes" his themes.
18. A comparable arpeggio figure occurred previously within "Yoda Raises the Ship" in Episode V, there as a diminuted backdrop to YODA's leitmotif, similarly spun out of the mode-mixed buildup on the a3 cell of Figure 6.2.
19. The only other places this connection between YODA and VADER themes is drawn are *unused*: first at the end of the pizzicato portion of Episode V's "Training a Jedi"; and (more interestingly, if briefly) in an unused portion of 10m3 "Chewie Chokes Lando." See also the lead-in to VADER's theme at the end of Episode I discussed in Chapter 5.
20. The harmonic language of the "Brother and Sister" cue alone is worth careful study, especially the exquisite string modules at 1:19:28 and 1:21:31, which have motivic connections to both REVELATION and LUKE AND LEIA themes. Curious readers should consult Dominic Sewell's (2021) sensitive treatment of the cue.
21. The rule-proving exceptions are sparse but significant—the full FORCE theme for the Binary Sunset scene [25:30] in Episode IV; the VADER theme for the first sight of the Imperial fleet [0:19:45] in Episode V, and REN and REY's respective motifs immediately upon their introductions [6:11 and 12:16] in Episode VII. The quick disclosure of these four critically important themes is a special effect, justified for specific dramatic and formal reasons. In the case of FORCE, the theme is the musical hinge of the whole film. The stirring rendition it receives in the Binary Sunset sequence establishes the mythic stakes better than Williams's gothic, athematic original version of the cue. With "The Imperial March," the early version heard in its full glory is tracked from the cue's concert arrangement, replacing less definitive presentation in an unused cue. KYLO REN's primary theme arrives like a sledgehammer, establishing early on his indomitability—and more shrewdly, the fact that his persona is based on the projection of over-the-top power and malevolence, rooted in insecurity. REY's leitmotif carries a sweeping, dialogue-free traveling montage that can sustain her questing melody. It also effects a neat formal symmetry with its extended and tonally analogous (A minor) iteration at the film's close, there used for another scene of geographic traversal.
22. Audissino (2017, 207).
23. Bouzereau (2004).
24. Bond (2003, p. 11).
25. A handful of themes never witness their rhetorical or structural payoff in the film's action. It is left to listeners who stay through the End Credits to grasp the complete melodic dimensions of the leitmotifs for LEIA, ANAKIN, ROSE, and PSALM OF THE SITH.
26. Huron (2006, 333–339). Huron's characterization of Wagner's music is based on his model of musical expectation, supported by empirical research and fine-grained analysis. But, in describing the contra-cadential style, he—like so many commentators on the composer—is moved to prose every bit as evocative and insistent as the music it describes: "Wagner's music 'yearns.' It is the music of hunger, rather than of fulfillment. It is music that leans and points, portends and implies, urges and compels. . . . It is music that tempts and titillates, denies and frustrates, deceives and thwarts" (2006, 339).
27. Williams (2013, 2).
28. Williams's music is a deliberate throwback to the love music of Hays Code-era Hollywood movies, where music could supply a libidinal energy otherwise strictly proscribed in other filmic parameters. Williams notes: "In earlier film at least, love stories may have been more idealistic. We can now have passionate scenes that are very explicit physically. But in earlier decades, all that had to be imagined. So I think the task and opportunity for the musician might have been to provide the erotic aspects that couldn't be shown. I think George [Lucas] had that in mind when he described to me the need for a love theme that was like the great love stories of the films of earlier times." Quoted from 20th Century Fox and Lucasfilm (2002) [EPK].
29. This being *Star Wars*, there are always more influences if one wishes to dig. Within Williams's output, comparisons may be drawn between the ANAKIN AND PADMÉ and the FLIGHT theme from *Hook* and the main theme from *Nixon*—an odd pairing! The A-theme also recalls the

strident opening theme from Lalo's *Symphonie espagnole*, the first fugal climax of Shostakovich's Symphony No. 11/ii, and one of the romantic motifs from Prokofiev's *Romeo and Juliet* (cf. the horn melody at m. 5 of "Love Dance"). The modulating B-theme suggests, at least in its initial measures, the saxophone melody of the first movement from Rachmaninoffs "Symphonic Dances" (cf. the melody three measures after RH12). Russian touches abound in Williams's love themes, though their lineage sometimes passes through other film music first. For example, a resemblance of the Han and Leia theme to the main subject from Tchaikovsky's Violin Concerto (cf. the main theme in Mvt. I) is likely mediated by a host of subsequent reworkings: Glière's Symphony No. 2 (cf. the first theme in Mvt. III); Rachmaninoffs "Rhapsody on a Theme by Paganini" (cf. variation 18); and Rózsa's *Spellbound* (cf. the theme heard at 21:05, 23:45, etc.).

30. Anakin and Padmé has some very deep melodic and rhythmic similarities to Luke's leitmotif, and possibly Shmi's as well; the reader is encouraged to entertain these—and perhaps other—resonances in this dense theme.
31. For a sustained examination of Williams's portrayal of romantic love in this series, see McTavish (2023, esp. 28–30 and 51–55).
32. See Bowman (2017) and Desowitz (2015).
33. For a perceptive critique of *The Last Jedi*'s temp-track-itis, and Williams's resultant overdependence on the Force theme, see Power (2025).
34. Alex Ross (2018) offers a contrary view, seeing the score as a playground of "intricate, ambiguous variations on his canon of themes."
35. Lehman (2018c).
36. The $\hat{1}$-$\flat\hat{3}$-$\hat{2}$-$\hat{4}$-$\hat{1}$ schema starts being a prominent stock phrase for Williams in his 1997 score for *The Lost World: Jurassic Park* (Lehman 2020, 126–127).
37. The crowd-sourced Wookieepedia, which typically reflects (or imposes) the consensus view of *Star Wars* fandom, labels this "Holdo's Theme." See www.starwars.fandom.com/wiki/Musical_score (2025).
38. Two more Desperation usages are notable. One is in the end credits, which includes a basically unaltered repetition of "Important Scene." The other is in an unused alternate cue for Luke's death (9m85b), where a brief nod to the motif in the woodwinds would have been heard after Skywalker became one with the Force.

Chapter 7

1. For applications of the Bakhtinian mode of literary timelessness—what he calls the "epic chronotope"—to screen music, see Buhler (2017) and Stokes (2017).
2. One form of self-reflexivity is to point to a text's status as an object of commerce. Guido Heldt interprets the *Star Wars* title sequence as performing a celebration of a heroic entertainment industry. The sequence "attests to the hope the film was made to fulfill: that it would be possible, well after the end of the studio system and the emergence of New Hollywood, to make a 1930s Errol Flynn pirate movie pastiche not in the spirit of parody, but of homage, and to lead a modern audience back to the pleasures of the golden age" (2013, 28). See also Biancorosso (2019) for treatment of the ritualistic aspects of opening and closing credits sequences.
3. Taruskin holds *The Ring* as the "supreme modern embodiment" of Bakhtin's epic time mode, particularly in those alternatively celebrated and derided stretches of extended narration and re-narration like Wotan's Act II monologue in *Die Walküre* or the Norns' entire prologue in *Götterdämmerung*, where "primeval origins and eventual destiny" are commingled with the dramaturgical present (2005, 251).
4. de Ven (1999).
5. Williams saw Joseph Campbell in person at a lecture at Skywalker Ranch in 1984. He reflected in 1997 that Campbell "taught me more about the film [*Star Wars*] than I ever realized while I was working on it, why it had such resonance. It was a new experience for me to hear a major intellectual telling me the meaning of my work." Dyer (1997, F8).
6. Shone (2004, 47).
7. Buhler (2000, 44).
8. Later revisitations of the flashback in Episode VIII will be met with greater thematic definition, culminating in the pronouncement of Kylo's motto [1:19:38] when we see the most objective perspective of the fateful encounter. Previously, our ears have been trained to hear that leitmotif as an expression of ultimate, intrinsic malice; here, for the first time, it sounds pathetic, a plea from someone tragically misunderstood.

9. A neat example is the placement of KYLO's theme into the ending of the "Adagio" concert arrangement from Episode VII. There, it seems to occupy a midpoint between the PATHOS-laden treatment in "Lesson Two" and the more definitive transformation the theme undergoes in Episode IX.
10. Another word for disjunction is "markedness," a concept from linguistics introduced to music theory and narratology by Robert Hatten (1994).
11. Stilwell (2007).
12. Williams's cameo as barkeeper "Oma Tres" (an anagram for "Maestro") in Episode IX is the nearest the films come to that, and it is a purely visual Easter egg.
13. Winters (2010, 233).
14. Howard Shore's *Lord of the Rings* scores offer instructive comparisons with *Star Wars* regarding the construction—and as importantly withholding—of this epic aura. See Buhler (2006) and Barker (2021, 341–345).
15. For variations of this critique, see Heldt (2013, 61) and Smith (2020).
16. This speculative stance is in fact precisely what Winters recommends to those skeptical of his film musical realism. Consider it a "thought experiment, asking: what would it be like *if* characters could hear the music that surrounds them, even though we might maintain that they cannot" (2014, 182).
17. Scholars increasingly acknowledge that immersion is not the be-all and end-all of aesthetic engagement in popular media. Katie Salen and Eric Zimmerman coined the phrase "immersive fallacy" to describe the prevalent but wrongheaded assumption that the "pleasure of a media experience lies in its ability to sensually transport the participant into an illusory, simulated reality" (2004, 450–451). While formulated with respect to digital games, their critique could be applied to film musicology and the presumption of "inaudibility" at the basis of most treatments of Classical Hollywood scoring practices.
18. Heldt (ibid., 68–69).
19. Heldt (2013, 59) and Kassabian (1993, 75–76).
20. On the associations of music boxes and similar instruments with childhood and nostalgia in screen music, see Link (2009b) and Good (2024, 51–76).
21. Feuer (1986 [1977], 454).
22. Feuer (1986, 449).
23. Quoted from 20th Century Fox and Lucasfilm (1999) [EPK].
24. Graves (1997 [1948], 23–43). A. E. Wagstaffe contends that Graves essentially "composed a new poem . . . by discussing, rearranging, amending, supplementing, and rewriting an earlier translation" (2021, 7–8).
25. Greiving (2025, 138).
26. "Book of Taliesin," NLW Peniarth MS 2, fol. 11R. Transcr. Kassandra Conley; Graves (1980, 42); Ford (2008 [1977], 184). Graves's version leaves out the context given by the sentences before and after "Achat erdygnawt . . . " in "Cad Goddeu." As a result, his image completely diverges from the actual meaning of the text—it is not a tree being described, but a monstrous beast. Patrick Ford's scholarly translation gives a more accurate picture: "I wounded a great scaly animal: a hundred heads on him and a fierce host beneath the base of his tongue, and another host is on his necks" (2008 [1977], 184).
27. Quoted from 20th Century Fox and Lucasfilm (1999) [EPK].
28. Dyer (1999, N14).
29. Williams employed Sanskrit in his score for *Indiana Jones and the Temple of Doom* as well, there as quasi-source music chanted by the movie's villainous Thuggee cult. Anahid Kassabian (2001, 104–107) reads the chanting as functioning primarily as exotic sonic threat—"words without melody to speak of"—positioning it as the undifferentiated Other against which Williams's heroic Western themes are valorized. Tellingly, Kassabian makes no note of the basis for the chant in an actual language, being either unaware of its Sanskrit origin or taking for granted that the intelligibility of those words is beside the point. "Duel of the Fates" operates through a superficially similar logic of semantic opacity, but Williams's deliberate estrangement process—translating, retranslating, and scrambling a specific literary source—suggests a more self-conscious aesthetic strategy than mere exoticizing. Whether that self-consciousness constitutes a meaningful ethical distinction is a question I leave open.
30. These translations are drawn by referencing both the most recent editions of Monier-Williams (2011 [1899]) and Cappeller (2009 [1891]).
31. Confusingly, a similar word, *mula* (मूल), means "root," also of importance to Graves's quatrain.

32. Of the remaining words in "Duel of the Fates," only one—"yoodha"—has an obvious and fitting translation in Sanskrit, *yuddha*, meaning battle. Easier to derive is the text Williams gave for Qui-Gon's funeral (7m1A). The reference phrase is "Death's long, sweet sleep." The cue's first word "Madhura" means sweet in Sanskrit (*madhura*); "swehpna" probably comes from *svapna*, meaning sleep; "go radomah" is ambiguous—it may stem from a combination of *ghora* ("dreadful") and *doman* (an antiquated word for "pain"). The final word, "mooritoo," is assuredly derived from *mrtyu*, meaning "death."
33. Wagstaffe (2021, 29–30).
34. James Deaville includes "Duel of the Fates" as a recent offshoot of the long-limbed "evil medieval" topic in Western music (2020, 722–23). Although Deaville finds Latin (or rather "nonsense Latin") rather than Sanskrit to be the go-to tongue for such gothic affects in film, the effectiveness of the topic is likewise a function of its textual unintelligibility. Karen Cook (2018) makes a similar point with respect to the use of choral chant in video games; fittingly, the trope can be heard in operation in Joel McNeeley's splendid score to *Shadows of the Empire*, a *Star Wars* novel/video game crossover.
35. For a sampling of reviews from various times and outlets, see Dreher (1999), Scheck (1999), Wilmington (1999), Berardinelli (2015), Kennedy (2000), and Lowry (2024). Tim Greiving (2017) even dedicated an entire article on *Slate* to a retrospective on how the piece "transcends the *Star Wars* Prequels."
36. Taylor (2014, 329).
37. Bouzereau and Duncan (1999, 135–136) and Dyer (1999, N12).
38. Kmet (2017, 7:03). See also Kmet (2018, 210–214).
39. Wannberg speaks candidly on the difficulties of cutting and mixing Williams's music in highly changeable films like *Star Wars*: "It's a real challenge to make these changes and keep the integrity of the music" (Jaquet-Francillon 1993, 6).
40. Quoted from bonus interview included with Williams (2005). The Sanskrit treatment of these words occurs in "Anakin's Dark Deeds" [1:35:00]. As elsewhere, the text is difficult to back translate. The only word easy to make out is "Rashtra" meaning "empire."
41. The Snoke leitmotif in the Sequel Trilogy is inspired by the quasi-Tibetan drones of *ROTS* 3m2A, now furnished with a Sanskrit text of unknown provenance, projected even less intelligibly than the text in "Duel of the Fates." The similarity of the music for this cipher of a character fueled speculation that the Supreme Leader was somehow connected with Palpatine and/or Plagueis—theories that turned out to be correct. See, for example, Trumbore (2015). Whether the Snoke = Palpatine thesis counted as genuine musical knowledge is a question for epistemologists. On the general importance of speculation to this franchise, and the way "fans back up their interpretations with expert reference to the smallest details of *Star Wars* texts," see Brooker (2002, xvii and 115–128).
42. One can rarely say for sure what a given scene was temp tracked with, but in this case we have an exact answer: the "Elegia" from Bartók's *Concerto for Orchestra*. Personal correspondence with Paul Hirsch, 1/7/2023.
43. Meyer (2015, 100–102).
44. Buhler (2000, 54).
45. Heine (2018, 122–123). In neo-Riemannian terms, the "Palpatine" progression is a PR/RL loop on a minor triad.
46. For a full analysis of this passage, see Lehman (2018b, 118–124).
47. In an interview with Williams, Jon Caps notes a harmonic similarity between a passage in the *Sinfonia Antartica* and the soundtrack for *The Poseidon Adventure*. Williams responds that the comparison "flatters me greatly," demonstrating that he knows the score well and that his "admiration and affinity for the music of Vaughan Williams is great" (1982, 4). The segment Caps is referring to is presumably the progression that occurs immediately before the End Credits, which is comparable to several intensificatory pantriadic sequences in Vaughan Williams's score.
48. Compare Symphony 6/ii and iv, and 7/iii. Vaughan Williams in turn was likely inspired by Bartók (cf. the opening fugue from *Music for Strings, Percussion and Celesta*).
49. Compare Symphony 7/i (RH7), and 7/iv (RH18).
50. Robb (2002, 30).
51. The embedding of aspects of the Emperor's theme in both Kylo Ren's and Rey's motifs occasioned much speculation in the early days of the Sequel Trilogy. Given the revelation of Rey's grandparentage in *Rise of Skywalker*, it is fitting that some iterations of her theme take on Palpatine-esque qualities, though the theme is surprisingly resistant to the Sith Lord's

debasements. Only when he refers to her as "Empress" does her theme truly mutate into something horrific, albeit briefly, with a Bm→E♭m^{ma7}|Am progression, which encodes aspects of the EMPEROR leitmotif as well as the new SITH ARTIFACTS motivic cluster from Episode IX.

52. As Abbate notes: "human narrators may . . . be revealed as immoral by giving tongue to lies, by speaking themselves buffoons, unreliable, or dubious. Then their stories will *ring false*, for while we may not *know* that the story is a lie, something about its presentation betrays the teller" (1996, 157).
53. Cut parts of the cue include further citations of the SEDUCTION motif, along with a statement of ANAKIN AND PADMÉ.
54. Williams first employed the distinctive overtone singing style in his score for *Seven Years in Tibet* (1997).
55. Caplin (2024, 544–550).
56. Williams wrote a follow-up to this ecclesiastical modality in *The Rise of Skywalker*: an a cappella choral rendition of the new PSALM OF THE SITH leitmotif, itself an agglomeration of the whole series' worth of musical signifiers for the Dark Side. Unfortunately, as with much else for the score to Episode IX, the composer's ultimate intentions for this hushed hymn are unknown; the cue was left unused, along with much of the score's choral writing, in the final cut. One can nevertheless hear this "Anthem of Evil" on its own on the OST's track 7.

Chapter 8

1. The sources of these slogans include one-sheet posters, online promotional language, and ads in magazines from 1997, for example, *The Guardian* (Mar 21, 1997, Screen Section, p. 9), *Hi Fi/Stereo Review* (Issue 62, p. 81); *Film Score Monthly* (Issue 2.1, p. 32); and *Star Wars Insider* (Issues 32, p. 86; 33, p. 78; and 36, p. 2).
2. The albums sold exceptionally well. All three topped the Billboard Charts for "Classical Cross-Over Album" for many weeks and hit the second through fourth spot for that category for the year 1997. (The OST for *Shine* was number one.) See *Billboard* (Dec 27, 1997–Jan 3, 1998, p. 64).
3. Matessino (1997a, 9).
4. A reviewer in *The Michigan Daily* said, "The new soundtrack is great. The music sounds spectacular remastered onto CD and the packaging is impressive too. The album was fine the first time around, but even more impressive 20 years later" (Gnatt 1997, 4B). For a window into film score collectors' euphoric reactions, see fan reviews by Clemmensen (1997), Daish (1997), Holm (1997), Lace (2004), Poblete (1997), and Southall (2003).
5. The digital remastering was not uniformly successful; for much of the ROTJ Special Edition release, the sonic quality is noticeably inferior to previous releases. See Malone (2012, 24–28) for a detailed breakdown of these albums.
6. Only three passages of underscore were missing, all minor: a brief alternative ending to ESB 5m3; a short insert for ROTJ 11m5 (discussed later in this chapter); an alternative version of ROTJ 14m3 (hearable on the Arista set). Additionally, and seemingly irretrievably missing, are a few funky source music cues from Max Rebo's Band. See Matessino (1997b).
7. The classic formulation of the musical work concept comes from Lydia Goehr, *The Imaginary Museum of Musical Works* (1992). While she focuses on Western art music, Goehr briefly reflects film music's relation to the work concept: "We usually speak of film music in terms of musical or film *scores.* But we could call these scores *worked*, if they were marketed and evaluated independent of the films (recall Prokofiev's *Alexander Nevsky*)" (244). For an informal and accessible introduction, see also Elphick (2021a).
8. This attitude is explicitly encapsulated in a 1997 article by Lukas Kendall on the Special Edition albums. Kendall attests that with these discs, "Williams takes us on a tour of a galaxy with the narrative as merely a guide. . . . [F]ans can sit back and purely enjoy the music—because there's no need to keep a mental check-list of what's missing and what goes where. That's all been done. Instead, enjoy having the music track virtually pried off the film so that you can venture within, hearing what may have been buried under sound effects, or clipped by a film edit or cross fade" (23).
9. Yet another form is the "For Your Consideration" (FYC) album offered to Academy Award voters. Such proprietary media are generally irrelevant to most listeners, though the FYC for Episode IX is notable for having leaked before the film itself, and for including a very different representation of the score than the OST.
10. Quoted from 20th Century Fox and Lucasfilm (1999) [EPK].

11. In another interview, Williams states he creates soundtracks as one "would make a concert piece," forgetting "how it was used in the movie" while focusing on "how would it make . . . the most compelling thing to hear" (Merluzeau 1993, 9).
12. A more detailed analysis of all the End Credits sequences can be found in Lehman (2025).
13. Rose's leitmotif is an extreme example: her bridge is only *ever* heard in Episode VIII's end credits, and a *second* B-theme exists in an earlier draft of the cue.
14. Lippincott (1977). Nielsen (2019) offers a comprehensive account of this overture-like piece's origins and structure, as well as the twisty journey it has taken on disc since 1977.
15. Worth keeping in mind is the existence of two endings for this piece. See Chapter 4, note 9.
16. The piece has been performed 166 times by the Boston Pops alone.
17. McCorkle Okazaki (2020, 3).
18. McCorkle Okazaki (ibid.) stresses the importance of Williams's scores—which are both popular with audiences and uncommonly gratifying for performers—in making cine-concerts an important part of the life of many of today's orchestras. Williams himself has not been involved with cine-concert treatments of any *Star Wars* films, or much else from his own pen for that matter. That said, his performance of *E.T.* live-to-picture in 2002 with the Los Angeles Philharmonic for its twentieth anniversary was a watershed in the popularization of the format (Audissino 2021a, 56–57).
19. Audiovisual montages also appear in pre-recorded formats, such as the 1999 Duel of the Fates music video and the 2005 Star Wars: A Musical Journey DVD. Most interesting are the "tone poems" released with the marketing campaign for Episode I: character-focused ads featuring poetic narration over film clips. The "One Truth" poem, for example, featured Darth Maul (Peter Serafinowicz) ominously speaking of the power of fear, underscored with bits of melodic identification, including a spark of the Emperor's theme, and a scrap of the Death Star motif. Although not leitmotivic primers, the "One" ads proved a nice showcase for Williams's scoring, their visual and sonic abstraction lending the ads a real musical quality, worthy of their musico-poetical labels.
20. Quoted from StarWarsMusicalJourney.com (2009).
21. This kind of spectacle was part of the series' concert experience from its inception: in November 1977, Zubin Mehta led the Hollywood Bowl in "The Star Wars Concert," which featured a dazzling and carefully integrated laser show. The performance—*Star Wars*' first in concert—yielded a twenty-two-minute standing ovation. Greiving (2025, 220) and Flannery (2025).
22. Tiomkin conducted a suite from *Lost Horizon* with the Bowl on August 16, 1938. Two weeks earlier, conductor Boris Moros conducted the orchestra's real first film music event, which included music from Tiomkin's *Spawn of the North* and Richard Hageman's *If I Were King*. Lichtenwanger (1938, 26).
23. Much of the growing popularity of film music in concert was due to the efforts of evangelizing figures like Elmer Bernstein and Henry Mancini. See Audissino (2021a, 14).
24. As of this writing, the closest a concert has come to this is the Williams-approved program conducted by Keith Lockhart and the Boston Pops, "Star Wars: The Story in Music," starting in 2023. The concert consisted mostly of concert arrangements and a smattering of action cues, accompanied by narration but not visuals.
25. Sonata form adheres to highly regulated norms of thematic contrast, cadential distribution, tonal teleology, and much else besides. Although no piece in *Star Wars* is structured this way, Schneller (2023) has persuasively argued sonata allegro form is channeled in the finale to Williams's score for *Story of a Woman* (1968).
26. Greiving (2025, 204).
27. Williams took this "Han Solo and the Princess 2.0" as his template when he created a *third* version for his ongoing collaboration with violinist Anne-Sophie Mutter. Besides turning the piece's melodic line into a vehicle for Mutter, Williams formally augmented the piece, lending it a new intro and outro, a different midsection, and many shifts of orchestration to accommodate the violin. Though less emotionally restrained due to the violin solo's extroversion, the affective tenor is still as bitter as it is sweet.
28. Critical reaction to this inexplicable change was fiercely negative. In his overview of the Episode II score, John Takis inveighed against Lucas's musically destructive choice, regarding it as an "insult on top of injury" of the overall "slaughter" done to the score in film (2002, 23). For even more vitriol spewed at this edit, see Kaplan and Kaplan (2002).
29. The textual stability of the Episode II credits-as-scored is even more complex. Four separate written versions exist, all close to "Across the Stars" but none exactly corresponding to what is

heard in either the film or soundtrack album. It is unknown whether the more substantially different versions were recorded, one of which includes a ten-measure opening passage based on the GLOOM theme.

30. Spoken at Boston Pops Film Night Concert, 5/12/2016. For an analysis of the "Scherzo for X-Wings" and its relationship to the film cue it was derived from, see Lehman (2018a, 24–25).
31. Williams has also bemoaned the gulf in audio fidelity between what is expertly prepared on a dubbing stage and what is then heard across a suboptimal stereo system in an individual movie theater Livingstone (1980, 76).
32. Interestingly, a "concert ending" to the "The Ewok Battle" exists on the RCA *Return of the Jedi* album conducted by Charles Gerhardt for RCA and released the same year as the movie. This amounts to a rather perfunctory two-measure bookend, though at the least it permits the set piece to conclude on the B-major tonic in root position. There is no indication that Williams himself crafted this adjusted ending. The Gerhardt album also includes the proper concert arrangement, here with yet another name, "Battle in the Forest."
33. Williams is fond of this technique, using it to puckish effect in "Hedwig's Theme" from *Harry Potter*, "Duel of the Fates" from *The Phantom Menace*, "The Duel" from *The Adventures of Tintin*, "The Adventures of Han" from *Solo*, as well as at the end of a number of his concert works (Tuba Concerto, "For Seiji," "Scherzo for Piano and Orchestra," and the first version of the Cello Concerto).
34. Margulis (2014, 111).
35. Ibid. (100).
36. Ibid. (112). Margulis's claims harmonize strongly with the work of theorists of musical embodiment, notably Arnie Cox (2016). Cox argues that musical understanding involves a sympathetic mimetic participation, a kind of embodied imitation of the act of performing which is implicit within the act of listening. Winters (2014) explores the implications of this participative model to cinematic sequences of screened performance, and to film music more broadly, both diegetic and putatively nondiegetic.
37. Huron (2006, 8–18).
38. Margulis (2014, 13).

Chapter 9

1. Arnold (1980a).
2. *Empire* is also a great score for teachers of film music history with which to demonstrate the rebirth of the symphonic idiom, perhaps a better vehicle for analysis than the idiosyncratic *Jaws* and *Star Wars*. In her influential book *Settling the Score*, Kathryn Kalinak devotes the last chapter to a treatment of this entry—and the Battle of Hoth especially—as a "master example of the continued strength of the structural model which underlies the classical score and the force of the late-romantic idiom which drives it" (1992, 188–189).
3. Rinzler (2010, 278).
4. Arnold (1980a).
5. Bartók offers a probable model for these dissonant seconds. Compare with the "Adagio" (esp. RH20) from *Music for Strings, Percussion and Celesta*.
6. Richard Cohn (1996) established the name for this collection and has theorized it extensively.
7. Rinzler (2010, 264) and Hirsch, Personal Correspondence, 7/1/23. The early cues in Episode V at times also appear to channel Walton; in particular Symphony No. 1/ii and Symphony No. 2/i.
8. The concept of "la grande ligne" stems from the immeasurably influential teacher and composer Nadia Boulanger. Copland, one of her most famous pupils, was a firm proponent of the idea, describing it as "the sense of forward motion, of flow and continuity . . . the feeling for inevitability, for the creating of an entire piece that could be thought of as a functioning entity" (1960, 50). For an application to film music analysis, see Cochran (1990).
9. Quoted from Buckton (1980).
10. This concept appears in the reception of Mahler's symphonies, first used by Paul Bekker and later refined by Theodor Adorno. Buhler, paraphrasing Adorno, defines the Mahlerian breakthrough as "a moment of structural reorientation, a deflection or 'turning aside' . . . from the expected formal course of the piece. It differs from simple interruption in having not just local, but also large-scale formal consequences" (1996, 129).
11. Greiving (2025, 128). Walton's "Battle in the Air" is itself patently influenced by Stravinsky's *Rite of Spring*, as well as by sections of his own score to *Major Barbara* (1941). We thus have yet

another case of palimpsestic musical referentiality in this series. For what it is worth, the "Battle of Yavin" is a more dramatically compelling and complexly structured piece than Walton's.

12. Comparable arrivals of the leitmotivic cavalry may be found in *The Phantom Menace* (FORCE in "Blowups"), *Revenge of the Sith* (REBEL FANFARE, "Get 'Em R2"), *Return of the Jedi* (REBEL FANFARE in "The Explosion"), *The Last Jedi* (REY and REBEL FANFARE in "Mechanical Trouble"), and *The Rise of Skywalker* (LUKE, "Dunkirk"), the latter being the series' most unabashed usage of the trope, both as a plot beat and a musical gambit.
13. Some of the few unromanticized depictions of violence in the franchise can be found in the TV series *Andor*. Sequences such as the Ferrix riot and Ghorman massacre are scored with a combination of diegetic protest music and unnerving, pointedly non-melodic underscore.
14. Richard Will (2002) identifies more than 150 military-inspired characteristic works composed after 1789, the turning point of the French Revolution. The tradition continued unabated in the young United States, where, as Elizabeth Morgan demonstrated, it was strongly associated with women pianists and, during the Civil War, women composers (2016).
15. Cooke (2018, 17) arrives at a similar conclusion and likewise identifies the "hard-driving," "dance-of-death scherzo" of Shostakovich's Tenth Symphony as a strong model for The Battle of Hoth.
16. Williams refers to *Spartacus* as North's masterpiece and cites its "bizarre and very difficult" and "exaggerated" instrumentation as key to its effectiveness. Quote from Bouzereau and Townson (2010).
17. Although beloved by contemporary audiences, *Wellingtons Sieg* would become an object of derision in the decades following its premiere. For critics, the piece represented—and continues to represent—an embarrassing lapse of taste from a composer for whom only humanity's loftiest ideals were to be ascribed. On the critical responses to Beethoven's potboiler, see Mathew (2006).
18. The battle symphonies of the late eighteenth century similarly placed value on what Will calls "the embodiment of extreme effort" that real-world warfare forces upon its combatants. "Performers of orchestral battles have to negotiate difficult passages at high speed and to play loudly for extended periods, often in extreme registers. . . . [A]n orchestra's *fortissimos* signify the noise of war but also the ensemble's own sweat, the triumph of will over matter that it, like an army, must achieve in order to 'win' the 'engagement.' In the roaring violence is heard also the pounding of hearts, the gasping of lungs, the straining of bodies under duress" (Will 2002, 199–200).
19. Will notes that this tendency toward historical and moral simplification had been a feature of the Battle symphony genre since the eighteenth century (2002, 191–193).
20. Kalinak (1992, 191).
21. International Musician (2015).
22. Quote from Buckton (1980). Williams's sketches for the *Star Wars* prequels and sequels would be written out on a sixteen-line score.
23. See for example Elley (1978) and Lurtsema (1983).
24. Johnson (1990) and Caschetto (2019).
25. For an overview of Williams's sketches for *The Empire Strikes Back*, and "The Snow Battle" specifically, see McCaulley (2020).
26. One aspect worth noting is the assortment of Hoth rhymes in subsequent Skywalker Saga scores. Among the clearest recollections are a passage in "The Falcon" from Episode VII [34:50] that echoes the climax of "The Snow Battle" [28:55], and the CATASTROPHE motif of Episode VIII [9:06, 2:10:19], which emulates the brass counterpoint from moments before [28:47] in that same cue.
27. Readers interested in hearing such a hypothetical ending can turn to the End Title/End Credits from *Jaws 2* (1978), whose final bars are virtually a dry run for Dak's little anthem—but with a successful, heartwarming cadence into D major.
28. "Sequence" is used here in the music-theoretical sense: a short melodic or harmonic unit repeated at different pitch levels.
29. Wedges do figure into Episode IV's Battle of Yavin [1:48:01, 1:48:28, 1:53:44], though overall Episode V hosts many more [24:31, 38:37, 58:52, 1:00:51, and 1:48:15].
30. More responsive, less patient styles have their place too, as a way of suggesting chaos and the fog of war; ironically, the best instance might be the Battle of Geonosis, which is an illogical hodgepodge as far as musical arguments go, but in its film achieves an apt sense of all hell breaking loose.

31. This use of the flattened supertonic degree ($\flat\hat{2}$) in the bass at the end of the FORCE's antecedent is the first instance of what would become an increasingly frequent alternative harmonization of the theme, reaching an almost default status in *Revenge of the Sith*. (One instance was described in Chapter 7, Figure 7.3.)
32. Granted, there is precedent for performing individual symphonic movements when they are particular audience pleasers, such as the Andante from Haydn's 96th and, most famously, the Allegretto from Beethoven's Seventh. (Other sometimes excerpted movements include Beethoven 5/i, Dvořák 9/ii, Tchaikovsky 6/ii, and Mahler 5/iv.) However well a piece like the Allegretto works in isolation, it nevertheless makes an even greater impact when heard as part of the whole.
33. In a backhanded compliment characteristic of negative appraisals of Williams's work from classical critics, a reviewer in 1980 says of a Boston Pops recording of *Star Wars* that the "orchestra, rising to the occasion, plays all of it as seriously as if it were the *Eroica*" (Simeis 1980, 77). If this book has one argument, it is that this is in fact the highest, most warranted praise.
34. Not for nothing, the most noble and esteemed of Beethoven's works have also always been tremendous crowd pleasers.
35. An even more fitting descriptor might be "presto con malizia," used by William Walton for the scherzo of his First Symphony.

Afterword

1. The idea of the "finale problem" predates any specific music theorist, but it receives its definitive expression in Bekker (1921) in his writing on Mahler. See also Brinkmann (1995, 203–226) and Talbot (2001).
2. That cadence is unabashedly Waltonian, practically a paraphrase of the first few measures of his "Spitfire Prelude." Williams also wrote an alternate two-measure ending tag for the original End Credit cue, though whether this was recorded is unknown.
3. The Signature Edition for *The Force Awakens* suite includes two different "concert" options for the finale, one quiet, the other bombastic.
4. Quote from "The Maestro's Finale" (2020).

Glossary

absolute past Storytelling milieu in a past chronologically remote and fundamentally apart from and unlike everyday experience. (see also **epic storytelling, musical mythopoetics**)

adumbration Technique of thematic development in which melodic aspects of a well-defined theme are subtly hinted at in earlier, otherwise unrelated musical passages.

alpha-chord Sonority drawn from octatonic collection, typically a four-note set constructed from a minor third, minor second, and minor third (e.g., C-E♭-E♮-G). In *Star Wars*, generally treated either as a mixed major/minor chord or as a dissonant blend of tonic and minor-submediant pitches, as in voicing C-E♭-A♭-B♭, referred to as the "Brute tetrachord."

alternate In film composition, a revised version of a cue, rewritten either in part or entirety.

"Augurs" chord Sonority inspired by the second tableau of Stravinsky's *Rite of Spring*, generally a thickly voiced dissonant polychord, loudly and quickly repeated, with unpredictable accents.

authentic Pertaining to a cadence that proceeds from a chord with dominant function (typically V) to the tonic. (compare **plagal, plagalized**)

Battle symphony (***Schlacht Sinfonie***) Genre of multi-movement instrumental music from the eighteenth century with passages or movements associated with and programmatically depicting armed warfare.

breakthrough (***Durchbruch***) Sudden, formally unanticipatable event that completely changes music's previous tone and direction, often summarily resolving preceding tensions and problems.

Brute tetrachord See **alpha-chord.**

cadence Fundamental element of syntax in tonal music. A conventionalized harmonic and melodic routine at the end of a musical phrase that clearly articulates one of the main harmonic functions in the phrase's key, normally the tonic (for authentic cadences) or dominant (for half cadences). Signals various levels of thematic closure and provides formal and affective punctuation. Cadences are uncommon but always of decisive dramatic importance in *Star Wars* underscore.

cadence cancellation Denial of cadential closure as method of thematic **deferred consummation.**

chorale A slowly paced homophonic musical texture with a homogeneous and often richly-scored timbre; hymn-like in form and associations.

chromatic Referring to any pitch collection or progression that includes notes outside a single seven-pitch diatonic scale; in tonal music, indicated by presence of accidentals not native to a given key signature. (compare **diatonic**)

cine-concert A performance format in which a film is screened with its music performed live by a full orchestra.

cine-symphonic listening A way of listening to film music when orchestral underscore is a significant and sustained subject of attention or imaginative engagement, either inside or outside the movie itself.

cue A single piece of film underscore that is composed, recorded, and edited as a continuous whole. May be as brief as a few seconds or as long as many hundreds of measures; may be bounded by silence or segued smoothly into a subsequent cue.

cyclicality Feature of epic storytelling in which narrative elements (incidents, motifs, character archetypes) regularly recur across different situations or installments.

deferred consummation Technique of thematic development in which a theme's full form is not presented or allowed satisfying closure until a critical or climactic moment.

developing variation Technique of thematic development in which motivic ideas are continuously varied instead of being literally repeated.

diatonic Referring to the seven-note pitch collection or progression drawn therefrom with the interval structure whole-whole-half-whole-whole-whole-half. Encompasses the basic major and minor scales as well as the diatonic modes (e.g., dorian, phrygian, etc.). Compare chromatic.

diegetic Describes music that originates in the narrative world of the film itself, can in principle be heard by characters, as in, for example "The Cantina Band" cue. Alternatively called **source music.**

discursive theme A melody that is lengthy and accumulative, built from smaller motifs but that cannot be neatly split into symmetrical halves.

distanciation Feature of epic storytelling that intentionally creates a disconnect (temporal, emotional, cultural) between the audience and text.

epic storytelling Mode of relaying narrative that is cyclical, distancing, ritualistic, and self-reflexive; closely tied to the impression of mythic significance and affect. (see also **absolute past, musical mythopoetics**)

extra-diegetic Describes music that is formally part of the film but does not accompany events depicted within it; in *Star Wars*, comprised of Main Titles and End Credits cues.

finale problem Challenge of writing a conclusion to a work (especially a multi-movement cycle like a symphony) that adequately matches the rhetorical and formal weight of what came before.

grammatical theme A melody, usually eight or sixteen measures, built from smaller motifs and that divides clearly into a beginning half and an ending half. Includes familiar thematic archetypes like the period and the sentence.

hexatonic A symmetrical six-note scale constructed from alternating minor thirds and half steps (e.g., C-E♭-E♮-G-A♭-B). Common subsets include major and minor triads, augmented triads, split-third chords, add-♭6 chords, major seventh chords, and alpha-chords. Supports progressions between major-third related triads, including the "Vader" progression. (see also **alpha-chord, octatonic, "Vader" progression**)

hypotaxis Mode of musical organization based on balanced and hierarchically connected sections and subsections, in which musical elements relate and coordinate with each other through musical dependency relationships such as cadences, hypermetrical patterns, and directed motivic development.

incidental motif Recurrent musical idea that lacks the melodic definition or symbolic consistency of a leitmotif.

insert In film composition, a brief musical passage added to an already composed cue or edited scene.

intensificatory sequencing Repetition of a musical idea (model) at differing pitch levels in a way that continually builds tension, as through higher register, tonal distance, instrumental density, dissonance level.

leit-harmony A harmonic object or relationship that recurs and bears consistent symbolism apart from its presence in a specific theme.

leitmotif A musical idea within a larger work that is melodically distinctive, associated with a symbolic target, prone to variation, and noticeably recurring. (see also **melodic identification, musical prose, principal leitmotif**)

leitmotivic drift Tendency of a leitmotif's meaning to shift over the course of a score, shedding original denotations and potentially absorbing new ones.

long line (*la grande ligne*) Sense that music retains continuity across long and potentially contrasting sections, with successive musical ideas related in a logical and inevitable way.

melodic concatenation Technique of thematic development in which motifs from one module provide the basis for new motifs in successive modules.

melodic identification John Williams's preferred term for the recurring themes in *Star Wars* that attach to and develop alongside characters, settings, and ideas. (compare **leitmotif**)

metalepsis A crossing or blending of narrative levels, as when music from the nondiegetic score is unexpectedly suggested in a film's diegetic soundscape.

micro-editing Practice of manipulating already composed and recorded cue(s) through cutting, looping, splicing, or reordering of material; generally needed when film undergoes continual edits during post-production after the composition phase.

mimetic scoring Music that precisely catches physical on-screen action with synchronized, often sonically imitative musical gestures. Alternatively called Mickey Mousing, scoring the action.

mode A scale with a distinct interval structure and characteristic sound. The **diatonic modes** are based on the interval structure present in the major scale and natural minor scale, rotated to different starting pitches. Examples common in *Star Wars* include *lydian* (major with $\sharp\hat{4}$), *mixolydian* (major with $\flat\hat{7}$), and *dorian* (minor with $\sharp\hat{6}$). Composite or synthetic modes are also heard frequently in the series.

module A discrete segment of a larger cue, possessing a defining theme, texture, key, or other unifying musical characteristic, rarely more than a few dozen seconds.

motivic seeding Technique of thematic development in which a parameter of a leitmotif is extracted and worked into many cues, without explicitly recalling or building to its source theme.

motto theme A melody that is brief and self-standing, which cannot be broken down into smaller motifs.

musical mythopoetics Creation of grand narratives (historical, moral, spiritual) through the resources of music.

musical prose Style of composition marked by continuous flow of ideas, flexibility of phrase lengths, radical tonal mutability, pervasive thematic variation and development, and suitability for dramatic underscoring. Ascribed variously to Brahms's instrumental music and Wagner's operatic music.

musical tense Capacity for music to suggest different temporal frames, through, for example, foreshadowing or reminiscence.

nondiegetic Describes music that is part of the film's storytelling apparatus without being part of the film's narrative world itself—for example, the "Binary Sunset" cue.

octatonic A symmetrical eight-note scale constructed from alternating half and whole steps (e.g., C-D♭-E♭-E♮-F♯-G-A-B♭). Common subsets include major and minor triads, diminished triads, split-third chords, minor seventh chords, alpha-chords, and "Planets-chords." Supports progressions between minor-third and tritone related triads. (see also **alpha-chord, hexatonic, "Planets"-chord)**

OST (*Original Soundtrack Album*), the official commercially released album associated with a film. Contrasted with albums not meant for wide dissemination (i.e., "For Your Consideration" recordings for awards voters) and expanded or archival re-releases of film scores.

ostinato A short and rhythmically well-defined musical figure repeated persistently, often in the same voice and at the same pitch level. Among the most-deployed compositional devices in action and suspense cues.

pantriadic chromaticism Harmonic idiom marked by use of consonant triads (major, minor) without reference to a single tonic, diatonic collection, or key-defining set of functional patterns.

parataxis Mode of musical organization based on succession and contrast, in which musical elements are placed one after the other without explicit hierarchical connection.

paratext Media that exist outside the formal boundaries of a text while being drawn from, relating to, or enriching the experience of that text.

pitch plateau A sustained pitch in a high register, with little to no additional music underneath, often conveying suspense or ambiguity.

plagal Pertaining to a progression or cadence that proceeds from a chord with subdominant function (typically IV) to the tonic. (compare **authentic**)

plagalized Pertaining to a progression with a hybrid function in which an authentic motion—especially a $\natural\hat{5}$ to $\natural\hat{1}$ bass progression—is inflected by, or combined with, elements of a plagal progression, often through pitches associated with ii°, ♭II, or iv.

"Planets" chord Sonority inspired by the concluding chords of Holst's *Mars*, generally a widely spaced D♭ (♯4)/G or D♭ (♯4)/C-type chord, often with a loosely dominant function.

planing Technique of accompanying a melodic line with rhythmic and intervallic duplicates of itself at lower pitch levels; also called parallel voice leading. Ubiquitous in *Star Wars*, especially in upper brass writing.

principal leitmotif A leitmotif of high salience in a score, marked by abundance rather than simple recurrence and transformation rather than simple variation.

psychological scoring Music that paints a character's internal state or perspective. (compare **mimetic scoring**)

rituality Feature of epic storytelling that gives the impression of, or even directly enacts, an obligatory and closely orchestrated communal experience.

self-reflexivity Feature of epic storytelling in which narrative refers back to itself and/or refers to itself *as* a text.

set piece theme (alternatively **one-cue wonder**) A highly distinctive and sequence-defining theme that occurs only in one cue.

spotting Pre-compositional process in which director and composer (plus, potentially, editors and orchestrators) screen a rough cut of a film to determine placement and character of desired music.

stinger A short, emphatic musical gesture closely synchronized with a visual event, used for punctuation or surprise. (see also **mimetic scoring**)

teleological genesis Technique of thematic development in which the full form of leitmotif (telos) is attained gradually and in goal-directed fashion through assembly of initially unremarkable motivic materials.

temp tracking Practice of assembling and placing preexisting music over a rough cut of a film as a temporary guide for the composer.

thematic arc A coherent, incremental process of musical change in which the development of a leitmotif mirrors a dramatic trajectory or plot thread.

thematic development The manipulation of one or more parameters of a thematic prototype, as through techniques like fragmentation, sequencing, reharmonization; typically results in less stable, more processual and dynamic musical spans.

thematic parameter One of a set of essential structural features of a theme, such as intervallic structure and rhythmic profile, that may be independently adjusted or detached in the course of a score.

thematic prototype An idealized version of a theme against which variations and transformations are judged.

thematic transformation The process of taking one distinctive musical idea and altering its structure deeply enough to result in a new and independently distinctive musical idea. Generally goal-directed and always dramatically significant. (compare **thematic development**)

through-composition Style of musical construction that proceeds continuously without literal repetition of sections. In film scoring, implies sustained large-scale musical logic and emphasis on smooth transitions within and across cues. (see also **long line**, **musical prose**)

timbral palette The overall set of orchestrational colors, textures, and playing techniques that define a module, cue, or score.

tint (*tinta*) A distinguishing and recurrent element of a whole film score that is *not* primarily melodic in character.

tonal quilting Method of smoothly transitioning between adjacent cues where the final harmony of the first cue sets up and resolves into the initiating harmony of the second cue.

topic (alternatively style topic, topos) Widely employed and understood musical figures with strong and stable extramusical associations, such as the fanfare, march, lament bass, sirens, music box.

tracking Practice of taking a cue written for one scene and using a part or whole in a different scene—and, in *Star Wars*, sometimes a different film.

underscore General term for film music that accompanies on-screen action, especially scenes of sustained dialogue; has many functions, including providing commentary, establishing mood and setting, generating formal cohesion. (compare **diegetic music**, **musical prose**)

use/mention (musical) A distinction between a musical idea that functions integrally within a cue and communicates its meaning directly (use) and a musical idea that functions by pointing to itself self-consciously as a unit of discourse (mention).

"Vader" progression Harmonic relationship embedded within "The Imperial March" of two minor triads separated by a major third. Strongly associated with evil in *Star Wars* and in Williams's music more generally. Often, but not exclusively, suggestive of minor tonic (i) to minor flat submediant (♭vi) progression.

work concept Idea of a musical composition as a unified, autonomous artistic whole.

wrong-note bass Placement of a pitch in the bass that is noticeably outside the harmony implied by the main melodic line, often a chromatic step away from a chord tone (ex., C/D♭, C/E♭, C/F♯...). In *Star Wars*, often part of a wrong-note bass *line* that moves independently and dissonantly under a theme.

Bibliography

"John Williams: Back Again to a Galaxy." 2015. *International Musician*, June 15. http://www.internationalmusician.org/john-williams.

"The Maestro's Finale." 2020. [Blu-Ray Digital Exclusive Featurette for *Star Wars Episode IX: The Rise of Skywalker*, dir. J. J. Abrams]. Lucasfilm Ltd. and Walt Disney.

20th Century Fox Home Entertainment and Lucasfilm. 1999. "Star Wars: Episode 1 'The Phantom Menace' Music EPK" [Electronic Press Kit].

20th Century Fox Home Entertainment and Lucasfilm. 2002. "Star Wars: Episode 2 'Attack of the Clones' Music EPK" [Electronic Press Kit].

20th Century Fox Home Entertainment and Lucasfilm. 2005. "Endlessly Compelling: The Music of Episode III" [Webisode]. http://www.starwars.com/video/endlessly-compelling-the-music-of-episode-iii.

Abbate, Carolyn and Parker, Roger. 1989a. "Introduction: On Analyzing Opera." In *Analyzing Opera: Verdi and Wagner*, edited by Carolyn Abbate and Roger Parker, pp. 1–26. Berkeley: University of California Press.

Abbate, Carolyn. 1989b. "Opera as Symphony, a Wagnerian Myth." In *Analyzing Opera: Verdi and Wagner*, edited by Carolyn Abbate and Roger Parker, pp. 92–124. Berkeley: University of California Press.

Abbate, Carolyn. 1989c. "Wagner, 'On Modulation,' and *Tristan*." *Cambridge Opera Journal* 1.1, pp. 33–58.

Abbate, Carolyn. 1996. *Unsung Voices: Opera and Musical Narrative in the Nineteenth Century*. Princeton, NJ: Princeton University Press.

ABC Classic. 2020. "What We Learned – Classic 100: Music in the Movies." *Listen*. http://www.abc.net.au/listen/classic/read-and-watch/news/classic-100-music-in-the-movies-voting-analysis/11894016.

Adams, Doug. 1999. "Sounds of the Empire." *Film Score Monthly* 4.5, pp. 22–25, 47.

Adorno, Theodor and Eisler, Hanns. (1947) 2007. *Composing for the Films*. London: Continuum.

Adorno, Theodor, translated by Rodney Livingstone. (1952) 2005. *In Search of Wagner*. London: Verso.

Adorno, Theodor, translated by Susan H. Gillespie. (1934) 2001. "Gloss on Sibelius." Reprinted in *Jean Sibelius and His World*, edited by Daniel Grimley, pp. 331–337. New Jersey: Princeton University Press.

Adorno, Theodor. (1941) 2002. "The Radio Symphony." In *Essays on Music*, edited by Richard Leppert, pp. 251–270. Berkeley: University of California Press.

Almén, Byron. 2008. *A Theory of Musical Narrative*. Bloomington: Indiana University Press.

American Film Institute. 2005. "AFI's 100 Years of Film Scores." AFI Website. http://prdaficalmjediwestussa.blob.core.windows.net/images/2019/08/scores25.pdf.

Anatone, Richard. 2023. "Leitmotivic Strategies in Nobuo Uematsu's *Final Fantasy* Soundtracks." *Music Theory Spectrum* 45.2, pp. 257–283.

Anderson-Bazzoli, Christopher. 2020. "Summon the Heroes." LA Phil Website. http://www.laphil.com/musicdb/pieces/3851/summon-the-heroes.

Anon. Fourteenth century. "Book of Taliesin," National Library of Wales, Peniarth MS 2, fol. 11R.

Arnold, Alan. 1980a. Liner note in *The Empire Strikes Back Original Soundtrack*. Composed and Conducted by John Williams. RSO Records.

Arnold, Alan. 1980b. *Once Upon a Galaxy: A Journal of the Making of Star Wars, The Empire Strikes Back*. New York: Ballantine Books.

Audissino, Emilio. 2014a. "Golden Age 2.0: John Williams and the Revival of the Symphonic Film Score." In *Film Scores and Their Relation to Classical Concert Music*, edited by Sebastian Stoppe, pp. 109–123. Glückstadt: VWH Verlag.

Audissino, Emilio. 2014b. *John Williams's Film Music: Jaws, Star Wars, Raiders of the Lost Ark, and the Return of the Classical Hollywood Music Style*. Madison: University of Wisconsin Press.

Audissino, Emilio. 2017. *Film/Music Analysis: A Film Studies Approach*. Cham: Springer International Publishing.

Audissino, Emilio. 2020. "The Function of Mickey-Mousing: A Re-Assessment." In *Sound & Image: Aesthetics and Practices*, edited by Andrew Knight-Hill, pp. 145–160. Oxford: Routledge.

Audissino, Emilio. 2021a. *Film Music in Concert: The Pioneering Role of the Boston Pops Orchestra*. Cambridge: Cambridge University Press.

Audissino, Emilio. 2021b. *The Film Music of John Williams: Reviving Hollywood's Classical Style*. Madison: University of Wisconsin Press.

Auner, Joseph. 1991. "Review of Carl Dahlhaus, 'Schoenberg and the New Music.'" *Music Theory Spectrum* 13.1, pp. 106–111.

Bailey, Robert. 1985. *Wagner: Prelude and Transfiguration from Tristan und Isolde (Norton Critical Scores)*. New York: Norton.

Barham, Jeremy. 2014. "Music and the Moving Image." In *Aesthetics of Music: Musicological Perspectives*, edited by Stephen Downes, pp. 224–238. New York: Routledge.

Barker, Martin. 2021. "'You Sorta Listen with Your Eyes': How Audiences Talk About Film Music." In *The Oxford Handbook of Cinematic Listening*, edited by Carlo Cenciarelli, pp. 336–351. New York: Oxford University Press.

Bekker, Paul. 1921. *Gustav Mahlers Sinfonien*. Berlin: Schuster and Loeffler.

Belfi, Amy and Kacirek, Kaelyn. 2020. "The Famous Melodies Stimulus Set." *Behavior Research Methods* 53, pp. 34–48.

Berardinelli, James. 2015. "Star Wars: The Phantom Menace (United States, 1999). *ReelViews*. http://www.reelviews.net/reelviews/star-wars-the-phantom-menace.

Biancorosso, Giorgio. 2019. "Beginning Credits and Beyond: Music and the Cinematic Imagination." *Echo* 3.1. http://www.echo.ucla.edu/article-beginning-credits-and-beyond-music-and-the-cinematic-imagination-author.

Billboard. 1977. "Billboard Top LPs & Tape." *Billboard* Magazine, September 17, 1977. http://www.worldradiohistory.com/Archive-All-Music/Billboard/70s/1977/Billboard 1977-09-17.pdf.

Billboard. 1997. "The Year in Music." *Billboard* Magazine, December 27–January 3. http://www.worldradiohistory.com/Archive-All-Music/Billboard/90s/1997/Billboard-1997-12-27.pdf.

Bolesławska, Beata. 2019. *The Symphony and Symphonic Thinking in Polish Music Since 1956*. New York: Routledge.

Bond, Jeff. 2003. "God Almighty! FSM Finally Talks to John Williams." *Film Score Monthly* 8.1, pp. 10–13.

Bonds, Mark Evans. 1997. *After Beethoven: The Imperative of Originality in the Symphony*. Cambridge: Harvard University Press.

Bonds, Mark Evans. 2014. *Absolute Music: The History of an Idea*. New York: Oxford University Press.

Boston Symphony Orchestra. 2025. "Performance History Search" [Online Archive]. http://www.archives.bso.org/ (Accessed 5/4/2025).

Bourne, Janet. 2024. "Topic Theory and Film: Coming of Age in 1994's and 2019's *Little Women*." In *Film Music Analysis, Studying the Score*, edited by Frank Lehman, pp. 88–109.

Bouzereau, Laurent and Duncan, Jody. 1999. *Star Wars: The Making of Episode I, The Phantom Menace*. New York: Ballantine.

Bouzereau, Laurent and Townson, Robert, directors. 2010. *Conversations on Alex North's Spartacus: The Celebration of a Masterpiece* [Documentary]. Varèse Sarabande.

Bouzereau, Laurent. 2004. "Music and Sound" [DVD Featurette for *Saving Private Ryan*, dir. Steven Spielberg]. DreamWorks Home Entertainment.

Bowman, Edith. 2017. "Episode 69: Rian Johnson on the Music of Star Wars & Other Movies." *Soundtracking with Edith Bowman*, December 18 [Podcast]. http://audioboom.com/posts/6557819-episode-69-rian-johnson-on-the-music-of-star-wars-other-movies.

Breznican, Anthony. 2022. "*Obi-Wan Kenobi* Composer Natalie Holt Reveals 'Haunting' Approach." *Vanity Fair*, April 22. http://www.vanityfair.com/hollywood/2022/04/obi-wan-kenobi-composer-natalie-holt-john-williams.

Bribitzer-Stull, Matthew. 2015.*Understanding the Leitmotif: From Wagner to Hollywood Film Music.* Cambridge: Cambridge University Press.

Brigden, Charlie. 2020. "What Makes the 'Star Wars' Score Timeless." *Film School Rejects*, May 4. http://www.filmschoolrejects.com/star-wars-score-timeless.

Brinkmann, Reinhold, trans. Peter Palmer. 1995. *Late Idyll: The Second Symphony of Johannes Brahms.* Cambridge: Cambridge University Press.

Brooker, Will. 2002. *Using the Force: Creativity, Community and Star Wars Fans.* New York: Continuum.

Brooks, Harper. 2025. "The Best Movie Scores of All Time, Ranked." *Ranker.* http://www.ranker.com/list/best-motion-picture-scores/harper-brooks (Accessed 3/17/2025).

Brown, Jim. 1999. Interview with John Williams on "Our Man in Hollywood." *NBC Today Show.* http://www.youtube.com/watch?v=ncpyS_qr0zA.

Brown, Royal S. 1994. *Overtones and Undertones: Reading Film Music.* Berkeley: University of California Press.

Buckton, David, director. 1980. *Star Wars: Music by John Williams* [Documentary]. Aired May 18, BBC Television.

Buhler, James. 1996. "'Breakthrough' as Critique of Form: The Finale of Mahler's First Symphony." *19th-Century Music* 20.2, pp. 125–143.

Buhler, James. 2000. "Star Wars, Music, and Myth." In *Music and Cinema*, edited by James Buhler, Caryl Flinn, and David Neumeyer, pp. 33–57. Hanover: Wesleyan University Press.

Buhler, James. 2001. "Analytical and Interpretive Approaches to Film Music (II): Analysing Interactions of Music and Film." In *Film Music: Critical Approaches*, edited by K. J. Donnelly, pp. 39–61. Edinburgh: Edinburgh University Press.

Buhler, James. 2006. "Enchantments of *Lord of the Rings*: Soundtrack, Myth, Language, and Modernity." In *From Hobbits to Hollywood: Essays on Peter Jackson's Lord of the Rings*, edited by Ernest Mathijs and Murray Pomerance, pp. 231–248. Amsterdam: Brill.

Buhler, James. 2017. "Branding the Franchise: Music, Opening Credits, and the (Corporate) Myth of Origin." In *Music in Epic Film: Listening to Spectacle*, edited by Stephen C. Meyer, pp. 3–26. New York: Routledge.

Buhler, James. 2019. *Theories of the Soundtrack.* New York: Oxford University Press.

Burkholder, J. Peter et al. 2019. *A History of Western Music*, 10th ed. London: W. W. Norton.

Burlingame, Jon. 2012. "Spielberg and Lucas on Williams." *Film Music Society*, February 8. http://www.filmmusicsociety.org/news_events/features/2012/020812.html.

Burlingame, Jon. 2016. "AFI Honoree John Williams Looks Back on Six Decades of Iconic Themes." *Variety*, June 9. variety.com/2016/film/spotlight/john-williams-afi-1201792072-1201792072.

Burlingame, Jon. 2018. "John Williams Is on Target to Set Yet Another Oscar Record." *Variety*, January 10. http://www.variety.com/2018/film/awards/john-williams-could-set-oscar-record-1202658996/.

Burlingame, Jon. 2019. "With 'Rise of Skywalker,' Composer John Williams Puts His Coda on 'Star Wars.' *Variety*, December 18. http://www.variety.com/2019/music/production/john-williams-star-wars-rise-of-skywalker-1203446034/.

Burstein, L. Poundie. 2014. "The Half-Cadence and Other Such Slippery Events." *Music Theory Spectrum* 36.2, pp. 203–227.

Byrd, Craig L. 1997. "Interview with John Williams." *Film Score Monthly* 2.1, pp. 18–21.

Caballero, Carlo. 2004. "Silence, Echo: A Response to "What the Sorcerer Said." *19th-Century Music* 28.2, pp. 160–182.

Caplin, William. 2024. *Cadence*. New York: Oxford University Press.

Cappelen, Herman, Lepore, Ernest, and McKeever, Matthew. 2023. "Quotation." In *The Stanford Encyclopedia of Philosophy*. http://plato.stanford.edu/entries/quotation/.

Cappeller, Carl. (1891) 2009. *A Sanskrit-English Dictionary: Based Upon the St Petersburg Lexicons*. Cambridge: Cambridge University Press.

Caps, John. 1982. "Keeping in Touch with John Williams." *Soundtrack! The Collector's Quarterly* March, pp. 3–7.

Carberry, Chris. 2024. *The Music of Space: Scoring the Cosmos in Film and Television*. Jefferson: McFarland.

Caschetto, Maurizio. 2018. "John Williams and the Music of Star Wars–A Further Step into a Larger Musical World." *John Williams Fan Network*, April 28. http://www.jwfan.com/?p=10681.

Caschetto, Maurizio. 2019. "Legacy Conversations: Conrad Pope." *The Legacy of John Williams*, April 26. http://www.thelegacyofjohnwilliams.com/2019/04/26/conrad-pope-interview.

Cenciarelli, Carlo. 2021. "The Possibilities of Cinematic Listening: An Introduction." In *The Oxford Handbook of Cinematic Listening*, edited by Carlo Cenciarelli, pp. 1–24. New York: Oxford University Press.

Chafe, Eric. 2005. *The Tragic and the Ecstatic: The Musical Revolution of Wagner's Tristan und Isolde*. New York: Oxford University Press.

Chattah, Juan. 2024. *Film Music: Cognition to Interpretation*. New York: Routledge.

Christensen, Niels Egmont. 1967. "The Alleged Distinction Between Use and Mention." *Philosophical Review* 76.3, pp. 358–367.

Chute, James. 2011. "John Williams to Premiere Work at SummerFest." *San Diego Union Tribune*, August 13. http://web.archive.org/web/20211202165450/http:/www.sandiegouniontribune.com/entertainment/classical-music/sdut-la-jolla-music-society-summerfest-john-williams-2011aug13-htmlstory.html.

Clarke, James. 2002. *George Lucas*. England: Old Castle Books.

Clemmensen, Christian. 1997. "Film Tracks Theme of the Month: Star Wars Special Edition Trilogy." *Filmtracks*. http://web.archive.org/web/19980114142514/http:/www.filmtracks.com/special/starwars.

Cochran, Alfred W. 1990. "The Spear of Cephalus: Observations on Film Music Analysis." *Indiana Theory Review* 11, pp. 65–80.

Cohn, Richard. 1996. "Maximally Smooth Cycles, Hexatonic Systems, and the Analysis of Late-Romantic Triadic Progressions." *Music Analysis* 15.1, pp. 9–40.

Collins, Andrew. 2022. "John Williams at 90: A Classic FM Exclusive." *Saturday Night at the Movies* Radio Program, August 28. http://www.classicfm.com/composers/williams/john-90th-birthday-exclusive-interview.

Cook, Karen. 2018. "Beyond (the) Halo: Chant in Video Games." In *Studies in Medievalism XXVII: Authenticity, Medievalism, Music*, edited by Karl Fugelso, pp. 183–200. Woodbridge: D. S. Brewer.

Cooke, Mervyn. 2008. *A History of Film Music*. Cambridge: Cambridge University Press.

Cooke, Mervyn. 2010. *The Hollywood Film Music Reader*. New York: Oxford University Press.

Cooke, Mervyn. 2018. "A New Symphonism for a New Hollywood: The Musical Language of John Williams's Film Scores." In *John Williams: Music for Films, Television, and the Concert Stage*, edited by Emilio Audissino, pp. 3–26. Turnhout: Brepols Publishers.

Cooper, David. 2010. "Film Form and Musical Form in Bernard Herrmann's Score to *Vertigo*." *Journal of Film Music* 1.2–3, pp. 239–248.

Copland, Aaron. 1960. "Nadia Boulanger: An Affectionate Portrait." *Harper's Magazine* 221.1325, p. 49.

Cox, Arnie. 2016. *Music & Embodied Cognition: Listening, Moving, Feeling, & Thinking.* Bloomington: Indiana University Press.

Craggs, Stewart. 2015. *William Walton: A Catalogue.* Oxford: Oxford University Press.

Crosby, Lauren. 2025. "The Sound of Boba Fett: *Star Wars* Leitmotifs in Streaming Television." *Émergences* 1(1). http://publications-prairial.fr/emergences/index.php?id=181.

Dahlhaus, Carl and Deathridge, John. 1984. *The New Grove Wagner.* New York: W. W. Norton.

Dahlhaus, Carl, translated by Derrick Puffett and Alfred Clayton. 1987. "Musical Prose." In *Schoenberg and the New Music,* pp. 105–119. Cambridge: Cambridge University Press.

Dahlhaus, Carl, translated by J. Bradford Robinson. (1980) 1989. *Nineteenth-Century Music.* Berkeley: University of California Press.

Dahlhaus, Carl, translated by Mary Whittall. (1974) 1989. *Between Romanticism and Modernism.* Berkeley: University of California Press.

Dahlhaus, Carl, translated by Roger Lustig. (1978) 1989. *The Idea of Absolute Music.* Chicago: University of Chicago Press.

Dahlhaus, Carl. 1987. "Symphonie und symphonischer Stil um 1850." In *Jahrbuch des Staatlichen Instituts für Musikforschung Preußischer Kulturbesitz,* edited by Dagmar Droysen-Reber and Günther Wagner. pp. 34–58. Berlin: Kassel.

Daish, Tom. 1997. "Star Wars: Special Edition." *SoundTrack Express.* http://web.archive.org/web/19970812010249/http://www.bath.ac.uk/~ns6tod/osts/starwars.htm.

De Barros Freitas, Carina Patricia. 2020. "Neuroimaging Studies on Familiarity of Music in Children with Autism Spectrum Disorder." PhD Dissertation, University of Toronto.

de Ven, Luc Van. 1999. "An Interview with John Williams." *Soundtrack!* 18.70.

Deaville, James. 2020. "Evil Medieval: Chant and the New Dark Spirituality of Vietnam-Era Film in America." In *The Oxford Handbook of Music and Medievalism,* edited by Stephen C. Meyer and Kirsten Yri, pp. 709–728. New York: Oxford University Press.

Debruge, Peter. 2024. "'Music by John Williams' Review: Steven Spielberg and Friends Pay Rapturous Tribute to the Master Composer." *Variety,* October 23. http://www.variety.com/2024/film/reviews/music-by-john-williams-review-steven-spielberg-1236189330.

Desowitz, Bill. 2015. "May the Score Be with You: Music Editor Ramiro Belgardt Returns for 'Star Wars' Reboot." *Cinemontage,* December 1. http://cinemontage.org/may-score-music-editor-ramiro-belgardt-returns-star-wars-reboot.

Devitt, Michael and Sterelny, Kim. 1999. *Language and Reality.* Cambridge: MIT Press.

DeVoto, Mark. 2004. *Debussy and the Veil of Tonality: Essays on His Music.* Hillsdale: Pendragon Press.

Disinterested. 2016. "Rey's Theme Is Derived from Ben Kenobi" [Video Essay]. YouTube. http://www.youtube.com/watch?v=_2UXz01kv8Q.

Dreher, Rod. 1999. "Tiresome, Says Rod Dreher." *New York Post,* May 18, 1999.

Dyer, Richard. 1980. "Where Is John Williams Coming From?" *Boston Globe Magazine,* June 29, 14ff.

Dyer, Richard. 1997. "John Williams: New Horizons, Familiar Galaxies." *Boston Globe,* June 4, F8ff.

Dyer, Richard. 1999. "Making Star Wars Sing Again." *Boston Globe,* March 28, pp. N2, N12–N14.

Edgar, Grace 2018. "Building a Sound World for Star Wars." Presentation Delivered at *Music and the Moving Image* Annual Conference, May 26.

Edgar, Grace. Forthcoming. *Atomic Measures: Scoring Women in Cold-War Action Cinema.* New York: Oxford University Press.

Ekman, Karl, translated by Edward Birse. 1938. *Jean Sibelius: The Life and Personality of an Artist.* Helsinki: Holger Schildts Förlag.

Eldridge, Alison. 2025. "John Williams: American Composer and Conductor." *Encyclopedia Britannica.* http://www.britannica.com/biography/John-Williams-American-composer-and-conductor.

Elley, Derek. 1978. "An Interview with John Williams," Part I. *Films and Filming*, July/August: pp. 20–24.

Elphick, Daniel. 2021a. "The Work Concept" [Video Essay]. *The Cult of Musicology*, February 16. YouTube. http://www.youtube.com/watch?v=Ub9Zn9YduD4.

Elphick, Daniel. 2021b. "Boris Asafiev and Soviet Musical Thought: Reputation and Influence." *Muzikologija* 30: pp. 57–74.

Eschenfelder, Melinda. 2019. "Musical Narratives: Thematic Combination and Alignment in Fantasy & Superhero Films." Master's Thesis, University of Oregon.

Evensen, Kristian. 2004. "The *Star Wars* Series and Wagner's Ring: Structural, Thematic and Musical Connections." Web Essay. http://web.archive.org/web/20071231053542/http://www.trell.org/wagner/starwars.html.

Fanning, David. 2013. "The Symphony Since Mahler: National and International Trends." In *The Cambridge Companion to the Symphony*, edited by Julian Horton, pp. 96–129. Cambridge: Cambridge University Press.

Feuer, Jane. (1977) 1986. "The Self-Reflexive Musical and the Myth of Entertainment." In *Film Genre Reader*, edited by Barry Grant, pp. 454–467. Austin: University of Texas Press.

Flannery, Daniel. 2025. "Star Wars Concert" [Webpage and Video]. http://dflannery.com/star-wars-concert.

Flinn, Caryl. 1992. *Strains of Utopia: Gender, Nostalgia, and Hollywood Film Music.* Princeton: Princeton University Press.

Ford, Patrick. (1977) 2008. *The Mabinogi and Other Medieval Welsh Tales.* Berkeley: University of California Press.

Franklin, Peter. 2007. "The Boy on the Train, or Bad Symphonies and Good Movies." In *Beyond the Soundtrack: Representing Music in Cinema*, edited by Daniel Goldmark, Lawrence Kramer, and Richard Leppert, pp. 13–26. Berkeley: University of California Press.

Franklin, Peter. 2011. *Seeing Through Music: Gender and Modernism in Classic Hollywood Film Scores.* New York: Oxford University Press.

Franklin, Peter. 2017. "Mystical Intimations, the Scenic Sublime, and the Opening of the Vault: De-classicizing the Late-romantic Revival in the Scoring of 'New Hollywood' Blockbusters c. 1977–1993." In *The Routledge Companion to Screen Music and Sound*, edited by Miguel Mera, Ron Sadoff, and Ben Winters, pp. 26–37. New York: Routledge.

Frisch, Walter. 1990. *Brahms and the Principle of Developing Variation.* Berkeley: University of California Press.

Fülop, Rebecca. 2012. "Heroes, Dames, and Damsels in Distress: Constructing Gender Types in Classical Hollywood Film Music." PhD Dissertation, University of Michigan.

Gnatt, Brian A. 1997. "Williams' Re-release of 'Star Wars' Soundtrack Is out of This World." *Michigan Daily* (Weekend Magazine), January 30, 1997, p. 4B.

Godsall, Jonathan. 2019. *Reeled In: Pre-Existing Music in Narrative Film.* New York: Routledge.

Godsil, Daniel. 2021. "Building Worlds: Timbre in Music For Cinema and Tonbilder: Suite for Instrumental Ensembles & Amp." PhD Dissertation, University of California Davis.

Goehr, Lydia. 1992. *The Imaginary Museum of Musical Works; An Essay in the Philosophy of Music.* Oxford: Clarendon, New York: Oxford University Press.

Golding, Dan. 2019. *Star Wars After Lucas: A Critical Guide to the Future of the Galaxy.* Minneapolis: University of Minnesota Press.

Goldmark, Daniel. 2005. *Tunes for Toons: Music and the Hollywood Cartoon.* London: Oxford University Press.

Gonin, Philippe. 2011. "L'héritage Wagnérien dans la musique de John Williams." In *John Williams: Un alchimiste musical à Hollywood*, edited by Alexandre Tylski, pp. 95–112. Paris: L'Harmattan.

Good, Jordan. 2024. "Taking Play Seriously." Master's Thesis, Tufts University.

Gorbman, Claudia. 1987. *Unheard Melodies: Narrative Film Music.* Bloomington: Indiana University Press.

Gottlieb, Jack. 1964. "The Music of Leonard Bernstein: A Study of Melodic Manipulations." PhD Dissertation, University of Illinois.

Gould, Marie-Claire. 2018. "What The Force" [Podcast]. http://whattheforce.ca/category/articles/page/5.

Graber, Naomi. 2018. "A Rose by Any Other Theme." *Musicology Now*, February 16. http://www.musicologynow.org/quick-take-a-rose-by-any-other-theme/.

Grace, Bob. 1983. "'John Williams': Scoring Big in the Movies." *Houston Chronicle*, November 13.

Graves, Robert. (1948) 1997. *The White Goddess: A Historical Grammar of Poetic Myth.* New York: Farrar, Straus and Giroux.

Green, Bem. 2022. *Peak Music Experiences: A New Perspective on Popular music, Identity and Scenes.* Oxford: Routledge.

Greenfield-Casas, Stefan and McGlynn, James Denis. 2023. "'We Are What They Grow Beyond': Visions (and Sounds) of a Transnational *Star Wars.*" *Musicology Now*, December 18. http://www.musicologynow.org/we-are-what-they-grow-beyond-visions-and-sounds-of-a-transnational-star-wars.

Greiving, Tim. 2015. "John Williams on 'Force Awakens' Score: 'I Felt a Renewed Energy, and a Vitality.'" *LA Times*, December 18. http://web.archive.org/web/20160302035330/http:/www.latimes.com/entertainment/arts/culture/la-et-cm-star-wars-force-awakens-music-score-john-williams-20151217-story.html

Greiving, Tim. 2017. "Here's Why 'Duel of the Fates' Transcends the *Star Wars* Prequels." *Slate*, December 17. http://www.slate.com/culture/2017/12/duel-of-the-fates-transcends-the-star-wars-prequels.html

Greiving, Tim. 2025. *John Williams: A Composer's Life.* New York: Oxford University Press.

Gresko, Andrew. 2019. "Sound, Spectator, and Psychoanalysis in Star Wars: Episode IV: A New Hope." Master's Thesis, Tufts University.

Grey, Thomas. 1995. *Wagner's Musical Prose: Texts and Contexts.* Cambridge: Cambridge University Press.

Grey, Thomas. 1996. ". . . *wie ein rother Faden*: On the Origins of "Leitmotif" as Critical Construct and Musical Practice." In *Music Theory in the Age of Romanticism*, edited by Ian Bent, pp. 187–210. Cambridge: Cambridge University Press.

Guido, Laurent. 2006. "Entre opéra wagnérien et culture de masse: l'univers musical de Star Wars." *Décadrages* 8-5, pp. 52–75.

Haas, David. 1992. "Boris Asaf'yev and Soviet Symphonic Theory." *Music Quarterly* 76.3: 410–432.

Haas, Robert. 1934. *Anton Bruckner.* Potsdam: Atheneum Verlag.

Hall, Richard A. 2019. *Pop Goes the Decade: The Seventies.* Bloomsbury: London.

Hartsough, Adrian. 2023. "'These Aren't the Contours You're Looking For . . . Or Are They?': A Pitch Contour Analysis of Leitmotifs from Star Wars Episodes I–IX." Presentation at *Colloque international John Williams, dernier des symphonistes?*, December 22.

Hatten, Robert. 1994. *Musical Meaning in Beethoven.* Bloomington: University of Indiana Press.

Heine, Erik. 2018. "Chromatic Mediants and Narrative Context in Film." *Music Analysis* 37.1, pp. 103–132.

Heldt, Guido. 2013. *Music and Levels of Narration in Film: Steps Across the Border.* Minneapolis: University of Minnesota Press.

Hepokoski, James. 2010. *Sibelius: Symphony No. 5.* Cambridge: Cambridge University Press.

Hirsch, Paul. 2023. Personal Correspondence. January 8, 2023.

Holm, Peter. 1997. "Music from the Movies CD Review: Star Wars." *Music For The Movies.* http://web.archive.org/web/20030425192457/http:/musicfromthemovies.com/pages/reviews/star_wars.html.

Hubbert, Julie. 2011. *Celluloid Symphonies: Text and Context in Film Music History.* Berkeley: University of California Press.

Hull, Kenneth, editor. 2000. *Johannes Brahms: Symphony No. 4 in E Minor, Op. 98 (Norton Critical Scores)*. New York: Norton.

Huron, David. 2006. *Sweet Anticipation: Music and the Psychology of Expectation*. Cambridge: MIT Press.

Hurwitz, Dave. 2024. "The Greatest Recordings EVER! Star Wars (Original Soundtrack)" [Video Review]. *The Ultimate Classical Music Guide by Dave Hurwitz*, November 22. YouTube. http://www.youtube.com/watch?v=zlt18cd5e0U.

Huvet, Chloé. 2020. *Composer Pour L'Image À L'ère Numérique: Star Wars, D'une Trilogie, À L'autre*. France: Vrin.

Jacquet-Francillon, Vincent. 1993. "A Conversation with Kenneth Wannberg." *Cantina Band*, pp. 4–10.

Joe, Jeongwon and Gilman, Sander L., eds. 2010. *Wagner & Cinema*. Bloomington: Indiana University Press.

Johnson, Carl. 1990. "Interview with Herbert Spencer." *Cue Sheet* 7.3.

Jumeau-Lafond, Jean-David. 1997. "Le chœur sans paroles ou les voix du sublime." *Revue de Musicologie* 83.2: pp. 263–279.

Juslin, Patrik et al. 2013. "What Makes Music Emotionally Significant? Exploring the Underlying Mechanisms." *Psychology of Music* 42.4. doi.org/10.1177/0305735613484548.

Kalinak, Kathryn. 1992. *Settling the Score: Music and the Classical Hollywood Film*. Madison: University of Wisconsin Press.

Kamien, Roger. 1990. "Aspects of the Neapolitan Sixth Chord in Mozart's Music." In *Schenker Studies*, edited by Hedi Siegel, pp. 94–106. Cambridge: Cambridge University Press.

Kaplan, Jon and Kaplan, Al. 2002. "Star Wars Episode 2 1/2: Attack of the Kaplans." *Film Score Monthly* Daily, May 12. http://www.filmscoremonthly.com/daily/article.cfm/articleID/3766/Star-Wars-Episode-2-12-Attack-of-the-Kaplans.

Karlin, Fred. 1994. *Listening to Movies*. New York: Schirmer Books.

Kassabian, Anahid. 1993. "Songs of Subjectivities: Theorizing Hollywood Film Music of the 80s and 90s." PhD Dissertation, Stanford University.

Kassabian, Anahid. 2001. *Hearing Film: Tracking Identifications in Contemporary Hollywood Film Music*. New York: Routledge.

Kelly, Ray. 2016. "Review: John Williams, Boston Pops Bring 'Star Wars' Universe to Stormy Tanglewood." *Mass Live* August 14. http://www.masslive.com/entertainment/2016/08/john_williams_brings_star_wars.html.

Kendall, Lukas. 1997. "Did You Know There's No Theme for Han?" *Film Score Monthly* 2.1, pp. 22–26.

Kennedy, Colin. 2000. "Star Wars Episode I: The Phantom Menace Review." *Empire*, January 1, 2000.

Kimmel, William. 1980. "The Phrygian Inflection and the Appearances of Death in Music." *College Music Symposium* 20.2, pp. 42–76.

Klein, Michael L. 2009. "Ironic Narrative, Ironic Reading." *Journal of Music Theory* 53.1, pp. 95–136.

Kmet, Nicholas. 2017. "Structure in Film & Film Music: A Video Essay" [Video Essay]. YouTube. http://www.youtube.com/watch?v=LJvaSUH4Usw.

Kmet, Nicholas. 2018. "Orchestration Transformation: Examining Differences in the Instrumental and Thematic Colour Palettes of the Star Wars Trilogies." In *John Williams: Music for Films, Television, and the Concert Stage*, edited by Emilio Audissino, pp. 209–228. Turnhout: Brepols Publishers.

Korenman, Lisa and Peynircioğlu, Zehra. 2004. "The Role of Familiarity in Episodic Memory and Metamemory for Music." *Journal of Experimental Psychology: Learning, Memory, and Cognition* 30.4, pp. 917–922.

Kraft, David and Kraft, Richard. 1982. "An Interview with Miklós Rózsa." *Soundrack, The Collector's Quarterly* 1.3/4.

Lace, Ian. 2004. "September 2004 Film Music CD Reviews: Star Wars/ The Empire Strikes Back/Return of the Jedi." *Musicweb-international.com.* http://www.musicweb-international.com/film/2004/Sep04/star_wars.html.

Lack, Russel. 1997. *Twenty Four Frames Under: A Buried History of Film Music.* London: Quartet Books.

Larson, Susan. 1998. "John Williams' 'Many Facets.'" *Boston Globe,* July 27, p. C10.

Larue, Jan et al. 2001. "Symphony." *Grove Music Online.* doi.org/10.1093/gmo/9781561592630.article.27254.

Lawson, Matt and MacDonald, Laurence. 2018. *100 Greatest Film Scores.* Lanham: Rowman and Littlefield.

Lawson, Matt. 2025. "Star Wars After Williams: New Sounds of a Galaxy Far, Far Away." *Émergences* 1(1). http://publications-prairial.fr/emergences/index.php?id=193.

Lehman, Frank and Tripp, Samantha. 2022. "Recursive References and In-Universe Instances of the Imperial March" [Video Essay]. YouTube. http://www.youtube.com/watch?v=lYV7O3uSZn0&.

Lehman, Frank. 2013. "Hollywood Cadences: Music and the Structure of Cinematic Expectation." *Music Theory Online* 19.4. http://www.mtosmt.org/issues/mto.13.19.4/mto.13.19.4.lehman.html.

Lehman, Frank. 2017. "Methods and Challenges of Analyzing Screen Media." In *The Routledge Companion to Screen Music and Sound,* edited by Miguel Mera, Ron Sadoff, and Ben Winters, pp. 497–516. New York: Routledge.

Lehman, Frank. 2018a. "Film-as-Concert Music and the Formal Implications of 'Cinematic Listening.'" *Music Analysis* 37.1, 7–46.

Lehman, Frank. 2018b. *Hollywood Harmony: Musical Wonder and the Sound of Cinema.* New York: Oxford University Press.

Lehman, Frank. 2018c. "Motives, Modulations, and 'The March of the Resistance' in *The Last Jedi. Musicology Now* February 18. http://musicologynow.org/quick-take-motives-modulations-and-the-march-of-the-resistance-in-the-last-jedi.

Lehman, Frank. 2020. "Form und thematische structur in Vorspann musik von Erich Wolfgang Korngolds." In *FilmMusik – Musik im Vorspann,* edited by Guido Heldt, Tarek Krohn, Peter Moormann, and Willem Strank, pp. 9–50. Munich: Richard Boorberg Verlag.

Lehman, Frank. 2021. "John Williams's Action Music in the Twenty-First Century." In *Music in Action Film: Sounds Like Action,* edited by James Buhler and Mark Durrand, pp. 116–148. New York: Routledge.

Lehman, Frank. 2025. "Complete Catalogue of the Musical Themes of Star Wars" [Online Thematic Catalogue]. http://www.franklehman.com/StarWars.

Lendvai, Ernő. 1971. *Béla Bartók An Analysis of His Music.* London: Kahn and Averill.

Lerner, Neil. 2004. "Nostalgia, Masculinist Discourse and Authoritarianism in John Williams' Scores for *Star Wars* and *Close Encounters of the Third Kind.*" In *Off the Planet: Music, Sound and Science Fiction Cinema,* edited by Philip Hayward, pp. 96–108. Bloomington: Indiana University Press.

Lerner, Neil. 2019. "'The Caverns of the Human Mind Are Full of Strange Shadows': Disability Representation, Henry Bellamann, and Korngold's Musical Subtexts in the Score for *Kings Row.*" In *Korngold and His World,* edited by Daniel Goldmark and Kevin C. Karnes, pp. 131–166. New Jersey: Princeton University Press.

Lichtenwanger, William J. 1938. "Hollywood Bowl Ends Seventeenth Season." *Musical America* 58.14, pp. 26–29.

Link, Stan. 2009a. "Leitmotif: Persuasive Musical Narration." In *Sound and Music in Film and Visual Media: A Critical Overview,* edited by Graem Harper, Ruth Doughty, and Jochen Eisentraut, pp. 180–193. New York: Continuum.

Link, Stan. 2009b. "The Monster and the Music Box: Children and the Soundtrack of Horror." In *Music in the Horror Film,* edited by Neil Lerner, 38–54. New York: Routledge.

Lippincott, Charles. 1977. Liner note in *Star Wars Original Soundtrack.* Composed and Conducted by John Williams. 20th Century Records.

Liu, Lucy Y. 2022. "Brahms's 'Musical Prose' Reconsidered." *Music Analysis* 41.1, pp. 50–93.

Livingstone, William. 1980. "John Williams and the Boston Pops: An American Institution Enters a New Era." *Stereo Review*, December, pp. 74–77.

Lofthouse, Charity. 2024. "Film Music and Dialogic Form." In *Film Music Analysis: Studying the Score*, edited by Frank Lehman, pp. 134–155. New York: Routledge.

London, Justin. 2000. "Leitmotifs and Musical Reference in the Classical Film Score." In *Music and Cinema*, edited by James Buhler, Caryl Flinn, and David Neumeyer, pp. 85–98. Hanover: Wesleyan University Press.

Lowry, Brian. 2024. "As 'The Phantom Menace' Turns 25, Six (non-Jar Jar) Things the 'Star Wars' Prequel Got Right." *CNN Entertainment*, May 3. http://www.cnn.com/2024/05/03/entertainment/star-wars-phantom-menace-turns-25/index.html

Lucas, George, director. 2001. *Star Wars Episode I: The Phantom Menace* [DVD and DVD Extras]. Twentieth Century Fox Home Entertainment.

Lucas, George, director. 2002. *Star Wars Episode II: Attack of the Clones* [DVD and DVD Extras]. Twentieth Century Fox Home Entertainment.

Lucas, George. 1990. Liner notes in *John Williams Conducts John Williams: The Star Wars Trilogy.* Composed and Conducted by John Williams. Sony Classical.

Ludwig, Alex. 2025. *Hearing Death at the Movies: Film Music and the Long History of the Dies Irae.* Switzerland: Palgrave Macmillan.

Lurtsema, Robert. 1983. Interview with John Williams on *Morning Pro Musica.* WGBH, June 23 [Radio Program].

Macdonald, Hugh. 2001. "Transformation, thematic." In *Grove Music Online.* http://www.oxfordmusiconline.com/grovemusic/view/10.1093/gmo/9781561592630.001.0001/omo-9781561592630-e-0000028269.

Malone, Chris. 2012. "Recording the Star Wars Saga." http://www.malonedigital.com/starwars.pdf.

Maltin, Leonard. 1995. Interview with George Lucas on *Star Wars Trilogy* [VHS Box Set]. Twentieth Century Fox Home Entertainment.

Mangan, Timothy. 2002. "John Williams: A Lifetime of Noteworthy Achievement." *Orange County Register*, July 28. http://archive.seattletimes.com/archive/20020728/wjohnwilliams28/john-williams-a-lifetime-of-noteworthy-achievement.

Margulis, Elizabeth Helmuth. 2014. *On Repeat: How Music Plays the Mind.* New York: Oxford University Press.

Matessino, Michael. 1997a. "Return of the Trilogy: This Time, the Force Is with Us." *Film Score Monthly* 2.1, 9–12.

Matessino, Michael. 1997b. "Original Soundtrack Recordings from *STAR WARS TRILOGY SPECIAL EDITION*" [FAQ]. RCA Victor Website. http://web.archive.org/web/19980121151320/http://www.rcavictor.com/starwars/faqs.html.

Mathew, Nicholas. 2006. "History Under Erasure: "Wellingtons Sieg", the Congress of Vienna, and the Ruination of Beethoven's Heroic Style." *Music Quarterly* 89.1, 17–61.

McBride, Joseph. 1997. *Steven Spielberg: A Biography.* New York: Simon and Schuster.

McCaulley, David. 2020. "How John Williams Writes a Sketch | Composer Toolbox: Episode 6" [Video Essay]. *David McCaulley: Film Scoring, Analyses, Video Essays.* January 15. YouTube. http://www.youtube.com/watch?v=smnuXlDg5-s.

McClary, Susan. (1991) 2002. *Feminine Endings: Music, Gender, and Sexuality.* Minneapolis: University of Minnesota Press.

McClellan, Clive. 2014. "*Ombra* and *Tempesta*." In *The Oxford Handbook of Topic Theory*, edited by Danuta Mirka, pp. 279–300. Oxford: Oxford University Press.

McCorkle Okazaki, Brooke. 2020. "Liveness, Music, Media: The Case of the Cine-Concert." *Music and the Moving Image* 13.2, 3–24.

McKinley Jr., James C. 2011. "John Williams Lets His Muses Carry Him Along." *New York Times: Arts Beat*, August 19. archive.nytimes.com/artsbeat.blogs.nytimes.com/2011/08/19/john-williams-lets-his-muses-carry-him-along.

McTavish, Laura. 2023. "John Williams's Musical Treatment of Cinematic Heroines: Romance and Heroism in Star Wars, the Skywalker Saga." MA Thesis, University of Kansas.

McWhorter, John. 2016. *Words on the Move: Why English Won't—and Can't—Sit Still (Like, Literally)*. New York: Henry Holt.

Merluzeau, Yann. 1993. "A Conversation with John Williams." *Cantina Band Newsletter* 4.16, pp. 3–15.

Meyer, Nicholas. 1993. "Star Wars & Music," Liner Notes Essay in *Star Wars Trilogy: The Original Soundtrack Anthology*, pp. 11–15. Arista Records and Twentieth Century Fox Film Scores.

Meyer, Stephen C. 2015. *Epic Sound: Music in Postwar Hollywood Biblical Films*. Bloomington: Indiana University Press.

Midgette, Anne. 2019. "As a Classical Music Critic, I Used to Think the 'Star Wars' Score Was Beneath Me. I Was Wrong." *Washington Post*, January 18. http://www.washingtonpost.com/entertainment/music/as-a-classical-music-critic-i-used-to-think-the-star-wars-score-was-beneath-me-i-was-wrong/2019/01/17/80fe0744-18f0-11e9-88fe-f9f77a3bcb6c_story.html.

Minnick, Jonathan. 2022. "Distant Ecologies: Sci-Fi Film Scores and the Music of the Final Frontier." PhD Dissertation, University of California, Davis.

Mirka, Danuta. 2014. "Introduction" to *The Oxford Handbook of Topic Theory*, edited by Danuta Mirka, pp. 1–57. New York: Oxford University Press.

Mitchell, Helen. 2010. "Against All Odds: The Decline and Resurgence of the Symphonic Film Score in Hollywood." *Journal of Film Music* 2:2–4. doi.org/10.1558/jfm.v2i2-4.175.

Monelle, Raymond. 2000. *The Sense of Music: Semiotic Essays*. Princeton: Princeton University Press.

Monelle, Raymond. 2006. *The Musical Topic: Hunt, Military and Pastoral*. Bloomington: Indiana University Press.

Monier-Williams, M. (1899) 2011. *A Sanskrit English Dictionary: Etymologically and Philologically Arranged with Special Reference to Cognate Indo-European Languages*. New Delhi: Motilal Banarsidass.

Morgan, Elizabeth. 2016. "Combat at the Keys: Women and Battle Pieces for the Piano During the American Civil War." *19th-Century Music* 40.1, pp. 7–19.

Moyers, Bill. 1999. "The Mythology of 'Star Wars' with George Lucas." *Billmoyers.com*. http://billmoyers.com/content/mythology-of-star-wars-george-lucas/.

Mulliken, Seth. 2010. "Ambient Reverberations: Diegetic Music, Science Fiction, and Otherness." In *Sounds of the Future: Essays on Music in Science Fiction Film*, edited by Mathew J. Bartowiak, pp. 88–99. Jefferson: McFarland.

Murphy, Scott. 2006. "The Major Tritone Progression in Recent Hollywood Science Fiction Films." *Music Theory Online* 12.2. http://mtosmt.org/issues/mto.06.12.2/mto.06.12.2.murphy.html.

Murphy, Scott. 2014a. "Scoring Loss in Some Recent Popular Film and Television. *Music Theory Spectrum* 36.2, pp. 295–314.

Murphy, Scott. 2014b. "Transformational Theory and the Analysis of Film Music." In *The Oxford Handbook of Film Music Studies*, edited by David Neumeyer, pp. 471–499. New York: Oxford University Press.

Murphy, Scott. 2023. "An Eightfold Taxonomy of Harmonic Progressions, and Its Application to Triads Related by Major Third and Their Significance in Recent Screen Music." *Journal of Music Theory* 67.1, pp. 141–169.

Mutch, Caleb. 2018. "The Formal Function of *Fortspinnung*." *Theory and Practice* 43, pp. 1–32.

Neumeyer, David and Buhler, James. 2001. "Analytical and Interpretive Approaches (I)." In *Film Music: Critical Approaches*, edited by K. J. Donnelly, pp. 16–38. Edinburgh: Edinburgh University Press.

Newman, Ernest. (1949) 1991. *The Wagner Operas.* Princeton: Princeton University Press.

Nielsen, Steen Kaargaard. 2019. "The Saga of the Star Wars Soundtrack Album Overture: On Forty Years of Reconception, Deconstruction, Suppression and Restoration." *16:9*, Spring. http://www.16-9.dk/2019/01/star-wars-soundtrack.

Niles, Laurie. 2015. "The Orchestra Awakens: Inside the 'Star Wars' Recording Sessions." On *Violinist.com*, December 15. http://www.violinist.com/blog/laurie/201512/17235/.

Orosz, Jeremy. 2015. "John Williams: Paraphraser or Plagiarist?" *Journal of Musicological Research* 34.4: 299–319.

Osborn, Brad. 2021. "The Subdominant Tritone in Film and Television Music." *Current Musicology* 107, pp. 62–92.

Pacific Symphony. 2020. "Virtual Family Concert—John Williams: Maestro of the Movies (Ask the Composer Featuring John Williams" [Virtual Concert Segment]. http://web.archive.org/web/20200616032344/http://www.pacificsymphony.org/VirtualConcert.

Page, Tim. 1985. Interview with John Williams on "Meet the Composer." Radio Show, WYNC, August 28. http://www.wnyc.org/story/john-williams/

Painter, Karen. 2007. *Symphonic Aspirations: German Music and Politics, 1900–1945.* Cambridge: Harvard University Press.

Palmer, Christopher. 1986. "Williams, John." In *The New Grove Dictionary of American Music* Vol. 4, edited by H. Wiley Hitchcock and Stanley Sadie. London: Macmillan Press Limited.

Parker, Kevin, ed. 2011. *A Conversation with the Masters: The Empire Strikes Back 30 Years Later* [Documentary]. 20th Century Fox Home Entertainment.

Paulin, Scott. 2000. "Richard Wagner and the Fantasy of Cinematic Unity: The Idea of the *Gesamtkunstwerk* in the History and Theory of Film Music." In *Music and Cinema*, edited by James Buhler, Caryl Flinn, and David Neumeyer, pp. 58–84. Hanover: Wesleyan University Press.

Paulus, Irena. 2000. "Williams Versus Wagner or an Attempt at Linking Musical Epics." *International Review of the Aesthetics and Sociology of Music* 31.2, pp. 153–184.

Poblete, Randall. 1997. "Star Wars: Special Edition Soundtrack." *MovieTunes.* http://web.archive.org/web/19980125183243/http:/www.movietunes.com/soundtracks/1977/starwars/review1.html.

Pogson, Andrew, Golding, Dan, and Buc, Nicholas. 2017–2024. "Art of the Score" [Podcast]. http://www.artofthescore.com.au.

Polo, Susana. 2015. "Stephen Colbert and George Lucas Talk Star Wars, Wooden Dialogue and Howard the Duck." *Polygon.* http://www.polygon.com/2015/4/18/8448685/stephen-colbert-george-lucas-tribeca-talk?ref=birchtree.me.

Power, Conor. 2025. "'Reminiscence Therapy': Musical Nostalgia in the *Star Wars* Sequel Trilogy (2015–2019)." *Émergences: Perspectives Nouvelles sur John Williams* (1) 1. http://www.publications-prairial.fr/emergences/index.php?id=171.

PR Newswire. 2010. "Turner Classic Movies Announces the Network's Choices for 15 Most Influential Film Soundtracks." http://www.prnewswire.com/news-releases/turner-classic-movies-announces-the-networks-choices-for-15-most-influential-film-soundtracks-82794362.html.

RedCaio. 2019. "Hidden Connection Between Palpatine, Rey, and Kylo Ren Themes (Star Wars: The Rise of Skywalker)" [Video Essay]. YouTube. http://www.youtube.com/watch?v=8uvEtIWpLYI.

Reyland, Nicholas. 2012. "The Beginnings of a Beautiful Friendship? Music Narratology and Screen Music Studies." *Music, Sound, and the Moving Image* 6.1, 55–71.

Reyland, Nicholas. 2015. "Corporate Classicism and the Metaphysical Style: Affects, Effects, and Contexts of Two Recent Trends in Screen Scoring." *Music, Sound, and the Moving Image* 9.2, pp. 115–130.

Richards, Mark. 2013. "John Williams Themes, Part 1 of 6: The Force Theme." Web Essay. *Film Music Notes.* http://filmmusicnotes.com/john-williams-themes-part-1-the-force-theme/.

Richards, Mark. 2016. "Film Music Themes: Analysis and Corpus Study." *Music Theory Online* 22.1. http://www.mtosmt.org/issues/mto.16.22.1/mto.16.22.1.richards.html.

Richards, Mark. 2020a. "John Williams—Star Wars, the Force Theme—Analysis." Video Essay. *Film Music Notes*. http://www.youtube.com/watch?v=RF8LZaM-u80.

Richards, Mark. 2020b. "New Themes and Their Meaning in The Rise of Skywalker" [Web Essay]. *Film Music Notes*. http://www.filmmusicnotes.com/new-themes-and-their-meaning-in-the-rise-of-skywalker.

Richards, Mark. 2021. "Action-Music Harmony" [Online Course]. http://www.filmmusicnotes.com/action-music-harmony-1-3.

Richards, Mark. 2024. "John Williams's *Star Wars* Themes: Good vs. Evil Conflicts as a Structural Principle for Leitmotifs." In *Film Music Analysis: Studying the Score*, edited by Frank Lehman, pp. 63–86. New York: Routledge.

Ridley, Aaron. 1993. "Bleeding Chunks: Some Remarks About Musical Understanding." *Journal of Aesthetics and Art Criticism* 51.4, pp. 589–596.

Rinzler, J. W. 2005a. *The Making of Star Wars: Revenge of the Sith*. New York: Del Rey Books.

Rinzler, J. W. 2005b. *The Making of Star Wars: Revenge of the Sith—The Final Chapter* [eBook]. New York: Del Rey Books. http://www.jwrinzler.com/uploads/3/4/4/6/3446315/the_final_chapter.pdf.

Rinzler, J. W. 2007. *The Making of Star Wars: The Definitive Story Behind the Original Film*. New York: Ballantine Books.

Rinzler, J. W. 2010. *The Making of The Empire Strikes Back*. New York: Ballantine Books.

Rinzler, J. W. 2010. *The Sounds of Star Wars*. California: Chronicle Books.

Rinzler, J. W. 2013. *The Making of Return of the Jedi*. New York: Del Ray.

Robb, Brian. 2002. "Across the Stars." *Star Wars Insider* 61, pp. 22–32.

Robbin, Miranda. 2007. "Double Dissociation Between Rules and Memory in the Neurocognition of Music." PhD Dissertation, Georgetown University.

Rodgers, Stephen. 2021. "Plagal Cadences In Fanny Hensel's Songs." In *The Songs of Fanny Hensel*, edited by Stephen Rodgers, pp. 129–145. New York: Oxford University Press.

Rosand, Ellen. 2001. "Lamento." In *Grove Music Online*. http://www.oxfordmusiconline.com/grovemusic/view/10.1093/gmo/9781561592630.001.0001/omo-9781561592630-e-0000015904.

Rosar, William. 2010. "The Penumbra of Wagner's *Ombra*." In *Wagner and Cinema*, edited by Jeongwon Joe, pp. 152–164. Bloomington: Indiana University Press.

Ross, Alex. 2016. "Listening to Star Wars." *New Yorker* Cultural Comment, January 1. http://www.newyorker.com/culture/cultural-comment/listening-to-star-wars.

Ross, Alex. 2018. "A Field Guide to the Musical Leitmotifs of 'Star Wars.'" *New Yorker* Culture Desk, January 3. http://www.newyorker.com/culture/culture-desk/a-field-guide-to-the-musical-leitmotifs-of-star-wars.

Ross, Alex. 2020a. "The Force Is Still Strong with John Williams." *New Yorker* Persons of Interest, July 21. http://www.newyorker.com/culture/persons-of-interest/the-force-is-still-strong-with-john-williams.

Ross, Alex. 2020b. *Wagnerism: Art and Politics in the Shadow of Music*. New York: Farrar, Straus and Giroux.

Rutledge, Gregory E. 2016. "Jedi Knights and Epic Performance: Is the Force a Form of Western-African Epic Mimicry?" In *A Galaxy Here and Now: Historical and Cultural Readings of Star Wars*, edited by Peter W. Lee, pp. 106–137. Jefferson: McFarland.

Saka, Paul. 1998. "Quotation and the Use-Mention Distinction." *Mind* 107.425, pp. 113–135.

Salen, Katie and Zimmerman, Eric. 2004. *Rules of Play: Game Design Fundamentals*. Cambridge: MIT Press.

Scanlon, Paul. 1977. "George Lucas: The Wizard of 'Star Wars.'" *Rolling Stone Magazine*, August 25. http://www.rollingstone.com/feature/george-lucas-the-wizard-of-star-wars-2-232011/.

Scanlon, Paul. 1983. "George Lucas Wants to Play Guitar as 'Star Wars' Takes a Vacation." *Rolling Stone*, July 21. http://www.rollingstone.com/tv-movies/tv-movie-news/george-lucas-wants-to-play-guitar-as-star-wars-takes-a-vacation-51960/.

Schaerlaeken, Simon, et al. 2019. "'Hearing Music as . . .': Metaphors Evoked by the Sound of Classical Music." *Psychomusicology: Music, Mind and Brain* 29.2–3.

Scheck, Frank. 1999. "'Star Wars: The Phantom Menace': THR's 1999 Review." *Hollywood Reporter*. http://www.hollywoodreporter.com/movies/movie-news/star-wars-phantom-menace-review-752675/.

Schneller, Tom. 2013. "Modal Interchange and Semantic Resonance in Themes by John Williams." *Journal of Film Music* 6.1, pp. 49–71.

Schneller, Tom. 2014. "Sweet Fulfillment: Allusion and Teleological Genesis in John Williams's 'Close Encounters of the Third Kind.'" *Music Quarterly* 97.1, pp. 98–131.

Schneller, Tom. 2023. "Between Liberation and Domesticity: John Williams's Score for *Story of a Woman*." Paper presented at *Music and Moving Image Conference*, May 28.

Schoenberg, Arnold. (1947) 1975. "Brahms the Progressive." Reprinted in *Style and Idea*, edited by Leonard Stein, pp. 398–441. New York: St. Martin's Press.

Schroeder, David. 2002. *Cinema's Illusions, Opera's Allure: The Operatic Impulse in Film*. New York: Continuum International Publishing Group.

Schwam, Betsy. 2014. "Star Wars: Film Score by Williams." *Encyclopedia Britannica*. http://www.britannica.com/topic/Star-Wars-film-score-by-Williams.

Schwerdtfeger, Conor. 2016. "Star Wars: Will John Williams Score Episode 8? Here's What We Know." *Cinamablend*, May 7. http://www.cinemablend.com/new/Star-Wars-John-Williams-Score-Episode-8-Here-What-We-Know-129577.html.

Sewell, Dominic. 2007–. "Dominic Sewell Music" [YouTube Channel]. YouTube. http://www.youtube.com/@DominicSewellMusic.

Sewell, Dominic. 2021. "Brother and Sister—from Return of the Jedi—Orchestration and Short Score with Analysis" [Video Essay]. YouTube. http://www.youtube.com/watch?v=yGydYlrJPZU&.

Sewell, Dominic. 2022. "Star Wars—The Empire Strikes Back 3M3 The Snow Battle" [Video Essay]. YouTube. http://www.youtube.com/watch?v=fIHn1e521DY.

Shone, Tom. 2004. *Blockbuster: How Hollywood Learned to Stop Worrying and Love the Summer*. New York: Free Press.

Sideways. 2017. "The Hidden Secret Message Behind Rey's Theme (Spoilers!)" [Video Essay]. YouTube. http://www.youtube.com/watch?v=FstNC8T4LjA.

Sideways. 2020. "Why the Music in The Rise of Skywalker Felt Misleading" [Video Essay]. YouTube. http://www.youtube.com/watch?v=L_8-dWSLDWI.

Sikka, Ritu et al. 2015. "An fMRI Comparison of Neural Activity Associated with Recognition of Familiar Melodies in Younger and Older Adults." *Frontiers in Neuroscience* 9. DOI = 10.3389/fnins.2015.00356.

Simeis, Steve. 1980. "High-brow (Digital) Popcorn." *Stereo Review*, December, p. 77.

Slattery, Damian. 2015. "Rey's Theme—Clue?—Star Wars: The Force Awakens" [Video Essay]. http://www.youtube.com/watch?v=8vtYQrNugfI.

Slobin, Mark. 2008. "The Steiner Superculture" and "The Superculture Beyond Steiner." In *Global Soundtracks: Worlds of Film Music* edited by Mark Slobin, pp. 3–62. Middletown: Wesleyan University Press.

Smiley, Tavis. 2015. Interview with John Williams on *Tavis Smiley Show*. PBS, December 15, 2015.

Smith, Jeff. 1998. *The Sounds of Commerce: Marketing Popular Film Music*. New York: Columbia University Press.

Smith, Jeff. 2014. "'The Tunes They Are A-changing': Moments of Historical Rupture and Reconfiguration in the Production and Commerce of Music in Film." In *The Oxford Handbook of Film Music Studies*, edited by David Neumeyer, pp. 270–290. New York: Oxford University Press.

Smith, Jeff. 2015. "The Auteur Renaissance, 1968–1980." In *Sound: Dialogue, Music, and Effects*, edited by Kathryn Kalinak, pp. 83–106. New Brunswick: Rutgers University Press.

Smith, Jeff. 2020. "Once More into the Breach: Interrogating Ben Winters's Nondiegetic Fallacy." In *Voicing the Cinema: Film Music and the Integrated Soundtrack*, edited by James Buhler and Hannah Lewis, pp. 260–277. Urbana: University of Illinois Press.

Southall, James. 2003. "Star Wars: Routine Score for Three Banjos and a Kazoo." *Movie Wave*. http://www.movie-wave.net/titles/star_wars.html?mobile-app=true&theme=falseCampfire.

Spielberg, Steven. 1975. Liner note in *Jaws: Music from the Original Motion Picture Soundtrack*. Composed and Conducted by John Williams. MCA Records.

Sponheuer, Bernd. 1980. "Der Durchbruch als primäre Formkategorie Gustav Mahlers." In *Form und Idee in Gustav Mahlers Instrumental Musik*, edited by Klaus Hinrich Stahmer, pp. 117–164. Wilhemshaven: Heinrichshofen.

Star Wars Official YouTube Page. 2013. "Interview: John Williams on Scoring Star Wars: Episode VII." Video Interview. http://www.youtube.com/watch?v=kQ4jZr1w0AI.

StarWarsMusicalJourney.com. 2009. "Star Wars: A Musical Journey—Performed Live!" [Promotional Website]. http://web.archive.org/web/20090727063827/http:/www.starwarsamusicaljourney.com.

Stilwell, Robynn. 2007. "The Fantastical Gap Between Diegetic and Nondiegetic." In *Beyond the Soundtrack: Representing Music in Cinema*, edited by Daniel Goldmark, Lawrence Kramer, and Richard Leppert, pp. 184–204. Berkeley: University of California Press.

Stock, Francine. 2006. Interview with John Williams on "The Film Programme." Radio Show, BBC Radio 4, Friday 14. http://www.bbc.co.uk/radio4/arts/filmprogramme/filmprogramme_20060414.shtml.

Stokes, Jordan Carmalt. 2017. "The Western as National Epic: Musical Persona and Narrative Distance in *High Noon*." In *Music in Epic Film: Listening to Spectacle*, edited by Stephen C. Meyer, pp. 210–235. New York: Routledge.

Sullivan, Jack. 2007. "Conversations with John Williams." *Chronicle of Higher Education* 53.19, January 12. http://www.chronicle.com/article/conversations-with-john-williams.

Svejda, Jim. 2020. Interview with John Williams on "KUSC at the Movies!" http://www.kusc.org/articles/evening-program-movies-week-interviews-on-demand.

Swed, Mark. 2016. "Why It's Good AFI Is Honoring 'Star Wars' and 'Jaws' Composer John Williams. *Los Angeles Times* June 9. http://www.web.archive.org/web/20160609125816/http://www.latimes.com/entertainment/arts/la-et-cm-john-williams-afi-20160607-snap-story.html.

Swinden, Kevin J. 2005. "When Functions Collide: Aspects of Plural Function in Chromatic Music." *Music Theory Spectrum* 27.2, pp. 249–282.

Tagg, Philip and Clarida, Robert. 2003. *Ten Little Tunes: Towards a Musicology of the Mass Media*. New York: Mass Media Musicologists' Press.

Takis, John. 2002. "Star Wars Episode Tunes: Attack on the Score." *Film Score Monthly* 7.4, pp. 10–23.

Talbot, Michael. 2001. *The Finale in Western Instrumental Music*. New York: Oxford University Press.

Tan, Chrysanthe. 2021. "Star Wars Music Minute" [Video/Podcast]. http://www.starwarsmusicminute.com.

Taruskin, Richard. 2005. *The Oxford History of Western Music*. New York: Oxford University Press.

Taylor, Benedict. 2016. *The Melody of Time: Music and Temporality in the Romantic Era*. New York: Oxford University Press.

Taylor, Chris. 2014. *How Star Wars Conquered the Universe: The Past, Present, and Future of a Multibillion Dollar Franchise*. New York: Basic Books.

The Filmmaking and Fandom Station. 2017. "Rey's Mysterious Origins Revealed by the Genius of John Williams" [Video Essay]. YouTube. http://www.youtube.com/watch?v=iopYTbJKClE.

The Guardian. 2007. "The Fifty Greatest Film Soundtracks." *The Guardian.* http://www.theguardian.com/music/2007/mar/18/features.musicmonthly14.

Thomas, Tony. 1991. "A Conversation with John Williams." *Cue Sheet* 8.1, pp. 6–15.

Thorau, Christian. 2009. "Guides for Wagnerites: Leitmotifs and Wagnerian Listening." In *Richard Wagner and His World*, edited by Thomas S. Grey, pp. 133–150. Princeton: Princeton University Press.

Tillman, Joakim. 2018. "The Villain's March Topic in John Williams's Film Music." In *John Williams: Music for Films, Television, and the Concert Stage*, edited by Emilio Audissino, pp. 229–251. Turnhout: Brepols.

Tolkien, J. R. R., edited by Humphrey Carpenter. 1981. *The Letters of J. R. R. Tolkien.* United Kingdom: George Allen and Unwin.

Tomlinson, Gary. 2014. *Metaphysical Song: An Essay on Opera.* Princeton: Princeton University Press.

Tovey, Donald Francis. 1935. *Essays in Music Analysis*, Vol. 2. Oxford: Oxford University Press.

Townson, Robert. 1980. *The Empire Strikes Back: Symphonic Suite from the Original Motion Picture Score* [Album Liner Notes]. Composed by John Williams, Conducted by Charles Gerhardt. Varèse Sarabande.

Tripp, Samantha. 2023. "Villainy with a British Accent: The 'Imperial March' as Imperial(ist) March." Master's Thesis, Tufts University.

Tripp, Samantha. 2025. "The British Invasion: The Anglophile Influence in 'The Imperial March.'" *Émergences: Perspectives Nouvelles sur John Williams* (1) 1. https://publications-prairial.fr/emergences/index.php?id=128.

Trumbore, Dave. 2015. "Star Wars: The Force Awakens': Theories on Supreme Leader Snoke." *Collider*, December 21. http://collider.com/star-wars-the-force-awakens-supreme-leader-snoke-theories-andy-serkis/.

von Rhein, John. 2019. "John Williams Explores Galaxies Far and Near in Enjoyable CSO Program of His Film Music." *Chicago Tribune*, May 13. http://www.chicagotribune.com/2018/04/27/john-williams-explores-galaxies-far-and-near-in-enjoyable-cso-program-of-his-film-music/.

Wagner, Richard. (1813–1883) 1987. *Selected Letters of Richard Wagner*, translated and edited by Stewart Spencer and Barry Millington. London: J. M. Dent.

Wagner, Richard. 1852. *Oper und Drama: Dritte Theil – Dichtkunst und Tonkunst im Drama der Zukunft.* Leipzig: Verlagsbuchhandlung von J. J. Weber.

Wagstaffe, Anne Elizabeth. 2021. "'Cad Goddeu', The Battle of the Trees': Texts and Interpretations." Master's Thesis, University of Wales Trinity St David.

Washington, Corey. 1998. "Use/mention Distinction and Quotation." In *Routledge Encyclopedia of Philosophy.* Taylor and Francis. doi:10.4324/9780415249126-X039-1.

Weiss, Michael W., Trehub, Sandra E., and Schellenberg, E. Glenn. 2012. "Something in the Way She Sings: Enhanced Memory for Vocal Melodies." *Psychological Science* 23.10. doi:10.1177/0956797612442552.

White, Daniel. 2024. *The Music of Harry Potter and the Lord of the Rings: Sounds of Home in the Fantasy Franchise.* New York: Routledge.

Whittington, William. 2007. *Sound Design and Science Fiction.* Austin: University of Texas Press.

Will, Richard. 2002. *The Characteristic Symphony in the Age of Haydn and Beethoven.* Cambridge: Cambridge University Press.

Williams, John. 2013. *Across the Stars (Love Theme from Star Wars Episode II) Signature Edition.* Milwaukee: Hal Leonard.

Williams, John. 2016. *Star Wars: The Force Awakens (Suite for Orchestra).* Milwaukee: Hal Leonard.

Willman, Chris. 2024. "John Williams Faces His Legacy: 54 Oscar Noms, 'Star Wars' Mistakes and Changing the Movies Forever." *Variety*, March 6. http://www.variety.com/2024/film/news/john-williams-oscars-star-wars-steven-spielberg-collaborations-1235929403/.

Wilmington, Michael. 1999. "Star Wars: Episode I—The Phantom Menace." *Chicago Tribune*.

Winters, Ben. 2010. "The Non-Diegetic Fallacy: Film, Music, and Narrative Space." *Music & Letters* 91.2, pp. 224–244.

Winters, Ben. 2014. *Music, Performance, and the Realities of Film: Shared Concert Experiences in Screen Fiction*. New York: Routledge.

Winters, Ben. 2025. *Korngold in America: Music, Myth, and Hollywood*. New York: Oxford University Press.

Wise, Peter J. 1983. "Star War—Return of the Jedi: The Score." *CinemaScore: The Film Music Journal* 11/12, pp. 17–20.

Wolkenfeld, Stefan. 2007. "George Lucas' Space Opera Star Wars und ihre Bezüge zu Musikdrama und Orchestersprache des 19. und frühen 20." *European Journal of Musicology* 10.

Zacharopoulos, Konstantinos. 2017. "Musical Syntax in John Williams's Film Music Themes." In *Contemporary Film Music: Investigating Cinema Narratives and Composition*, edited by Lindsay Coleman and Joakim Tillman, pp. 237–262. London: Palgrave Macmillan.

Zlabinger, Tom. 2016. "Hearing the Force: Manifestations and Transformations of Music from Far, Far Away." In *A Galaxy Here and Now: Historical and Cultural Readings of Star Wars*, edited by Peter W. Lee, pp. 7–32. Jefferson: McFarland.

Discography

McNeely, Joel, composer and conductor. 1996. *Star Wars: Shadows of the Empire*. Varèse Sarabande.

Meco. 1977. *Star Wars and Other Galactic Funk*. RCA Victor. DXLI-3043.

Williams, John, composer and conductor. 1977. *Star Wars Original Soundtrack*. 20th Century Records.

Williams, John, composer and conductor. 1980. *The Empire Strikes Back Original Soundtrack*. RSO Records.

Williams, John, composer and conductor. 1990. *John Williams Conducts John Williams: The Star Wars Trilogy*. Sony Classical.

Williams, John, composer and conductor. 1992. *Kid Stuff: An Afternoon at the Movies*. Philips.

Williams, John, composer and conductor. 1993. *Star Wars Trilogy: The Original Soundtrack Anthology*. Arista Records and Twentieth Century Fox Film Scores.

Williams, John, composer and conductor. 1997. *Star Wars: A New Hope—The Original Motion Picture Soundtrack* (Special Edition). RCA Victor.

Williams, John, composer and conductor. 1997. *The Empire Strikes Back—The Original Motion Picture Soundtrack* (Special Edition). RCA Victor.

Williams, John, composer and conductor. 1997. *Return of the Jedi—The Original Motion Picture Soundtrack* (Special Edition). RCA Victor.

Williams, John, composer and conductor. 1999. *The Phantom Menace Original Motion Picture Soundtrack*. Sony Classical.

Williams, John, composer and conductor. 1999. *The Phantom Menace Original Motion Picture Soundtrack—Ultimate Edition* [Deluxe Album]. Sony Classical.

Williams, John, composer and conductor. 2002. *Attack of the Clones Original Motion Picture Soundtrack*. Sony Classical.

Williams, John, composer and conductor. 2005. *Revenge of the Sith Original Soundtrack Album* [Album, special Walmart Exclusive Edition]. Sony Classical.

Williams, John, composer and conductor. 2015. *The Force Awakens—Original Motion Picture Soundtrack*. Walt Disney Records and Lucasfilm Ltd.

Williams, John, composer and conductor. 2017. *The Last Jedi—Original Motion Picture Soundtrack*. Walt Disney Records and Lucasfilm Ltd.

Williams, John, composer and conductor. 2019. *The Rise of Skywalker—Original Motion Picture Soundtrack.* Walt Disney Records.

Williams, John, composer and conductor. 2019. *Across the Stars: Anne-Sophie Mutter, John Williams Deluxe Edition* [Blu-Ray]. Deutsche Grammophon.

Williams, John, composer and conductor. 2022. *Williams: Violin Concerto No. 2 & Selected Film Themes.* Deutsche Grammophon.

Williams, John, composer; Gerhardt, Charles, conductor. 1978. *Music from John Williams's Close Encounters of the Third Kind / Star Wars.* RCA Victor.

Williams, John, composer; Gerhardt, Charles, conductor. 1980. *The Empire Strikes Back: Symphonic Suite from the Original Motion Picture Score.* Varèse Sarabande.

Williams, John, composer; Gerhardt, Charles, conductor. 1983. *Music from the John Williams Score Star Wars: Return of the Jedi.* RCA Victor.

Williams, John, composer; Lockhart, Keith, conductor. 2017. *Lights, Camera . . . Music! Six Decades of John Williams.* BSO Classics.

Williams, John, composer; Mehta, Zubin, conductor. 1978. *Cinema Gala: Star Wars, Close Encounters of the Third Kind.* London Records.

Williams, John, composer; Kojian, Varujan, conductor. 1983. *John Williams: The Star Wars Trilogy.* Varèse Sarabande.

General Index

For the benefit of digital users, indexed terms that span two pages (e.g., 52–53) may, on occasion, appear on only one of those pages.

Musical Index

For the benefit of digital users, indexed terms that span two pages (e.g., 52–53) may, on occasion, appear on only one of those pages.

Terms in small caps refer to themes and motifs. Figures are indicated by an italic *f*. Cues are in quotation marks followed by the abbreviation for the film.